Rules for the Use of Quantifiers

Quantifier-negation (QN): A negation sign may be moved across a quantifier in accordance with the following equivalences:

$$(x) \sim (\ldots x \ldots) \equiv \sim (\exists x)(\ldots x \ldots)$$
$$\sim (x) (\ldots x \ldots) \equiv (\exists x) \sim (\ldots x \ldots)$$
$$\sim (x) \sim (\ldots x \ldots) \equiv (\exists x)(\ldots x \ldots)$$
$$(x)(\ldots x \ldots) \equiv \sim (\exists x) \sim (\ldots x \ldots)$$

Instantiation and Generalization Rules
General restrictions:

1) The same variable must replace all occurrences of the same name (for universal but not existential generalization), and vice versa (for both types of instantiation).

2) The quantifier that is added (in the case of generalization) or dropped (in the case of instantiation) must include the entire line within its scope.

Universal instantiation (UI):
$$\frac{(x)(\ldots x \ldots)}{\ldots a \ldots}$$

Existential generalization (EG):
$$\frac{\ldots a \ldots}{(\exists x)(\ldots x \ldots)}$$

Existential instantiation (EI):
$$\frac{(\exists x)(\ldots x \ldots)}{\ldots a \ldots}$$

Restriction: *a* must not have occurred previously in the proof, or in the conclusion.

Universal generalization (UG):
$$\frac{\ldots a \ldots}{(x)(\ldots x \ldots)}$$

Restrictions:

1. *a* was introduced by UI or in the assumption of a conditional or *reductio* proof (not in a premise or by EI);
2. the inference does not occur within a conditional or *reductio* proof whose assumption contains *a*; and
3. the statement . . . *a* . . . does not contain any other name introduced by EI on a line containing *a*.

The Art of Reasoning

Expanded Edition
(with Symbolic Logic)

The Art of
Reasoning
Expanded Edition
(with Symbolic Logic)

David Kelley

W · W · Norton & Company   New York London

Copyright © 1990, 1988 by David Kelley

PRINTED IN THE UNITED STATES OF AMERICA.

The text of this book is composed in Caledonia, with display type set in Optima. Composition by New England Typographic Service, Inc. Manufacturing by Arcata Graphics/Haliday. Book design by Margaret Wagner.

ISBN 0-393-95913-9

W. W. Norton & Company, Inc., 500 Fifth Avenue, New York, N.Y. 1010

W. W. Norton & company Ltd., 37 Great Russell Street, London WC1B 3NU

1 2 3 4 5 6 7 8 9 0

To Susan

Contents

Preface

The Art of Reasoning is a text on thinking skills, designed for courses in informal logic and critical thinking. It covers a fairly traditional range of topics: classification and definition, argument analysis, fallacies, the syllogism, inductive generalization, argument by analogy, statistical reasoning, explanation. In selecting and presenting the material, however, I have put more emphasis than is customary on assimilating the principles of logic in the form of skills. The canons of reasoning are applied to a wide range of examples from everyday experience, political debate, and material discussed in courses across the curriculum. And about a third of the book consists of exercises. Each section of a chapter is followed by a practice quiz, with answers in the back of the book so that students can test their understanding of the material. Each chapter ends with a variety of exercises that have been designed to test reasoning skills in many different combinations and on a wide range of tasks.

Though the principles and techniques of reasoning I have covered are fairly standard, I am indebted to certain writers for insights that affected my formulations and my choices about what to include. My treatment of definitions owes a great deal to Ayn Rand, especially for her view of concepts as file folders. H. W. B. Joseph was an invaluable guide to the cognitive aspects of categorical syllogisms. Chapter 14, which presents Fred Sommers's version of term logic in textbook form for the first time, would not have been possible without the generous help of Professor Sommers. Needless to say, these writers are not responsible for the use I have made of their work.

My pedagogical approach to logic emerged from a course on critical thinking that I taught at Vassar College for seven years. I am indebted to the students who took the course for their help, wittingly or otherwise, in shaping the material to their needs; and to my former colleagues in the philosophy department at Vassar—especially Jesse Kalin, Audrey McKinney, and Anthony Weston—for many valuable discussions about teaching logic. I am grateful as well to Gwen Broude, Carol Christensen, and Kenneth Livingston for advice and comments on statistics and scientific method; and to Michael Berliner, Roger Donway, Allan Gotthelf, James Grant, and Julian Simon for the ideas and exercise materials they provided over the years.

A preliminary version of *The Art of Reasoning* was used by instructors at seven colleges and universities during the spring of 1987: Wojciech Chojna, Temple University; Gerard Downey, LaSalle College; Kenneth P. Freeman, Colorado State University; Richard Hensen, Rutgers University; Robert Kirkpatrick, University of Southwestern Louisiana; Peter Lipton, Williams College; and Audrey McKinney, Vassar College. Their detailed comments, criticism, and reports on classroom experience with the book were enormously helpful. I am indebted as well to those who reviewed earlier versions of the manuscript: Gary Atkinson, College of St. Thomas; J. Anthony Blair, University of Windsor; Charles Kielkopf, Ohio State University; Robert Kirkpatrick, University of Southwestern Louisiana; Susan Lowndes, Rockland County Community College; Jon Moline, St. Olaf College; Eric Snider, University of Toledo; Thomas D. Sullivan, College of St. Thomas; and Anthony Weston, SUNY—Stony Brook. Though I am entirely responsible for the contents of the work, their influence can be found in every chapter.

Any book is a collaboration between author and publisher, and I have been particularly fortunate in that regard. The catalyst for this project was Diane Odom, a former sales representative for W. W. Norton; without her energy and initiative the project would never have been undertaken. It would not have been carried to completion without the enthusiasm and meticulous standards of quality of the Norton staff. I am especially grateful to Allen Clawson, John Darger, and Nancy Palmquist; and to my editor Roby Harrington, who oversaw the entire project with exceptional care and finesse.

The book is dedicated, finally, to my wife, Susan McCloskey, for her unfailing support, as well as for the many hours she took from her own work to read the manuscript and test the exercises.

The Art of
Reasoning

1

Introduction

This is a book about thinking. It's a book about *how* to think.

In a broad sense, the word "thinking" refers to anything that goes on in our minds. When I say "a penny for your thoughts," I want to know what's on your mind—whether it's a sensory experience, an image, a feeling, a memory, a question, an anxiety, a problem you're trying to solve, or simply a daydream. As long as you are conscious, there is always something going on up there; in this sense, you can't help thinking. You don't need this book, you don't need to take a course. You just have to stay awake. In a narrower sense, however, thinking is a particular *kind* of mental activity, the kind involved in solving a problem, planning an action, studying for a test, defending your position on a controversial issue. This is still a pretty broad concept, but we have excluded some things.

In the first place, we can distinguish thinking from feeling. Thinking is a cognitive process we use in the attempt to gain knowledge or to understand something, as distinct from our emotional responses to things. This distinction does not mean, as people too often assume, that someone with strong emotions is necessarily illogical, or that a logical person must be unemotional. On the contrary, there is no reason we cannot have both: clear, logical minds, and passionate feelings. But thinking and feeling do have different roles to play, different jobs to do, in our mental lives.

Secondly, thinking is purposive. It differs from activities such as daydreaming and fantasizing, in which we simply let our minds wander where they will. Thinking is something we have to *do*, usually with some degree of effort. And because it aims at a goal, it is something that can be done with varying degrees of success. You may or may not succeed in solving the problem, forming a plan, grasping the material, proving your case. In this way, too, it differs from daydreaming, where the concepts of success and failure don't really apply. Thinking is a skill. It's a skill that everyone has in some degree, but it's also a skill that everyone can improve.

Philosophers have sometimes debated whether logic is a science or an art. By "science" they mean a body of knowledge to be learned, like physics or history. By "art" they mean a skill or craft to be mastered, like carpentry or playing the piano. We are going to approach logic primarily as an art. Of course, we can't separate the art from the science completely. A carpenter must know something about the properties of wood, a piano player something about musical theory. In the same way, we'll have to learn some of the principles that make up the science of logic. But not all of them—only those necessary for developing the skill of thinking. From time to time I will point out some of the theoretical questions that arise in the course of our discussions, for those who may wish to pursue them, but this is not a text in logical theory.

Even so, there is a great deal of ground to cover. There are many principles to be learned, and a good deal of practice will be necessary to incorporate them into your thinking skills, your habits of thought. Before we begin, let's look a little more closely at the kind of skill that thinking is, and get an overview of the material to come.

Thinking Skills

When we engage in thought, our goal is normally to find out something. We are trying to answer a question, solve a problem, prove a conclusion, learn a body of material. We want to know what caused the Civil War, or which of the candidates to vote for, or how to get home for the holidays without it costing an arm and a leg, or what the man or woman of our dreams really feels about us. In all these cases, we could say that we are trying to acquire knowledge that we didn't have before. And in most cases we can't acquire that knowledge by direct observation. We have to do some reasoning, putting two and two together, making **inferences,** drawing conclusions from the information we already have.

The core of logic has always been the study of inference, and most of this book is devoted to that subject. We will be talking about different kinds of inferences, and about which ones to use in which sorts of situations. We will study rules for evaluating inferences, and learn to distinguish the good ones from the bad ones. As a preview, let's look at a particular case.

Some states have passed laws requiring that seat belts be used in cars. Supporters of the law say that those who wear seat belts have a better chance, statistically, of surviving an accident than those who don't. Opponents often point to particular cases in which someone survived because he was *not* wearing a seat belt. Which is the better sort of evidence? Are the opponents making too much of the exceptions? Are the supporters making proper use of the statistics? Let's assume, just for the sake of discussion, that wearing seat belts really is safer. Is that enough to justify the law? No—not by itself. The greater safety of seat belts would justify the law only if we take the position that the government should require us to do what is safe. Some people would defend that position. Others say we should be free to decide these things for ourselves. So there are really two issues here: the safety of seat belts, and the proper role of government. Can the second one be settled by statistical evidence? If not, then what sort of evidence *is* relevant?

The purpose of logic is to answer the questions I raised in the last paragraph. Logic alone won't tell you whether to support mandatory seat belt laws. It *will* give you a method to follow in making that decision and backing it up. It will show you how to break an issue down into subissues, so that you can be sure to consider all the relevant points. It will give you principles for deciding what sort of evidence is appropriate to a particular issue. And it will give you principles for determining how much weight to put on a given piece of evidence.

The value of these logical skills is not limited to political arguments. In many college courses, students are presented with competing ideas or theories and asked to discuss them critically. In a philosophy class, the issue might be free will versus determinism; in literature, it might be different interpretations of *Hamlet*. Discussing these ideas critically means presenting reasons for or against them. To understand a scientific theory, such as the theory of evolution, you need to understand something about the evidence for it. In our own personal lives, finally, we all have choices to make, major ones or minor, and here too we need to weigh the reasons on each side and try to consider all the relevant issues.

Logic can also help us develop other, more subtle skills. Most of us have been in discussions that were frustrating because they kept going around in circles. That often happens when people "talk past each other"—when they are not really addressing the same issue. Suppose someone argues that it's wrong to treat abortion merely as a medical procedure, like removing an appendix, because the fetus is a potential person. Someone else might argue that a woman should have the right to make decisions concerning her own body. These two people are both dealing with the topic of abortion, but they may not be addressing quite the same issue. The first person may be trying to show that abortion is morally wrong, while the second is denying that it should be made illegal. Whether abortion is right or wrong in moral terms, and whether it should be legal or illegal, are different issues. They are related (which is why they are easily confused), but not identical.

If the two people could identify the difference, they might find that they don't disagree after all. The one who says that abortion should be legal might be willing to agree that abortion is nevertheless a serious action that would be wrong to take without an equally serious reason. And the one who says that abortion is morally wrong might be willing to agree that it's still a decision that a woman should be legally free to make on her own. Of course, the argument might not work out so neatly. But we'll never know until we try, and we can't try until we know how to distinguish one issue from another. That's a skill that logic can help you develop.

In this particular case, the problem of talking past each other would be fairly easy to fix, because the two different issues are signaled by two different words: "immoral" versus "illegal." A more difficult problem occurs when two people are using the same word, but with two different meanings. Suppose there is an argument over whether student work should be graded. If one person is referring specifically to letter grades, while the other is referring to *any* form of evaluation, they are probably going to talk past each other. If we take the different meanings of the word into account, we would have to say that here again the people are not debating the same issue. But the problem is harder to fix because the difference in meaning lies below the surface of the language. And "grade" is a fairly concrete word. Think of the possibilities for miscommunication in words like "democracy," "freedom," "love," or "art."

This brings us to another area of logic: concepts and definitions. Whenever we reason, we make use of abstract words. In the abortion debate, for example, the key issues are whether the fetus is *alive,* whether it is a human *person,* whether it has *rights.* The italicized words are abstract concepts, and the debate often turns on how to define them. People often talk past each other when they use words with different meanings. Even when that is not a problem, it is always valuable to make the meaning of our words as clear and explicit as possible. Some concepts, such as "democracy," are extremely hard to define, and great minds have spent lifetimes in the effort. Logic won't guarantee success, but it can give us a method to follow, and the method will pay immediate dividends in terms of the clarity and precision of our thinking. It will also make it easier to master new concepts and words that are introduced in most courses at school.

So far we have talked about skills involved in taking ideas apart: breaking an issue down into its components, distinguishing between closely related ideas, analyzing the meaning of a word. But we also need to put them together again. Thinking involves integrating ideas as well as differentiating them. To understand a line of reasoning, we need to break it down into its parts, but we also need to put it in its wider context. In working on a problem, the most creative solutions often come when we notice similarities to problems in other areas. In a college course, it's important to understand each component part of the material, but it's equally important to organize the material as a whole into a coherent framework.

Indeed, we can often integrate ideas from different courses. In a religion or ethics class, for example, you might have discussed the idea that money is the root of all evil. How does that relate to the economist's description of money as a medium of exchange? In a political science class on democracy, you might discuss the idea that people are capable of governing themselves. Is that supported or contradicted by what you've learned in psychology, history, and philosophy? As these examples illustrate, integration means the awareness of logical relations on a larger scale. An idea in one area may provide evidence for an idea in another, quite different area. Or the two ideas may contradict each other—in which case they cannot both be right. Reasoning skills will help you spot these logical relations.

Objectivity

An understanding of logic may help you win arguments and persuade other people. But that is not the only value of logic. It is not even, in my view, the main value. The goal is to acquire knowledge, to find out what's true. Winning an argument doesn't necessarily mean that your position is the right one, nor does losing necessarily mean you're wrong. Whether an opinion is true or false depends on the facts, and the main value of logic is that it helps us stay in touch with the facts. Its value is to teach what I like to call the *art of objectivity*.

In the context of discussions with other people, objectivity means not only presenting your own ideas logically, but also listening to what others say. Objectivity does not require that you be neutral, nonpartisan, or indifferent to the issue. It does require that you try to look at the matter from the other person's perspective. Even if your view is right, it is rare that any single perspective reveals the *whole* truth. It requires that you give a fair hearing to the evidence and arguments for the other side. Even if you reject them in the end, knowing *why* you reject them will give you a better understanding of your own position. To a certain extent, objectivity is an attitude that you have to choose, and logic won't make the choice for you. But objectivity also involves a skill. Even with the best will in the world, we can't really be objective unless we know how to follow and evaluate the arguments we hear, how to isolate the relevant issues clearly, how to avoid ambiguity and vagueness in the words we use.

Another aspect of objectivity is especially important in communicating with others. In order to get our ideas across successfully, we have to take account of the other person's context. A point so obvious to me that it hardly seems worth mentioning may *not* be obvious to someone else, and if I fail to mention it, he may not understand what I am saying. Objectivity is the ability to step back from our own thinking, so that we can see it critically, through the eyes of someone who does not share our outlook, our preferences, our idiosyncrasies. All that we can reasonably ask of our audience is the ability to follow logical connections. In this respect, logic, like language, is a shared framework without which we could not communicate.

This sort of objectivity is especially important in writing, where the reader is not present to ask questions if the message isn't getting through. If I fail to make clear what issue I am addressing, or if I use terms in new or ill-defined ways, the reader can't interrupt to ask what I am talking about. He's stuck with what I've put down on paper. If my presentation is vague, or fails to consider a relevant alternative, or makes a questionable assumption, the reader can't stop me to ask for an elaboration. In writing, therefore, we have to be on our best behavior, logically speaking. Many writing problems are really problems in logical thinking. Conversely, writing exercises are one of the best ways to practice the techniques of logic, and you will find many such exercises in this book.

But objectivity is not just a social virtue. It goes beyond open-mindedness to opposing views, and it goes beyond sensitivity to the cognitive needs of others. The ability to step back from our train of thought and examine it critically is a virtue even if we are not interested in communicating it. It is a virtue because it is the only way to check the results of our thinking, the only way to avoid jumping to conclusions, the only way to stay in touch with the facts. The results of our thinking cannot be any better than the processes by which we arrive at them. There is no Book of Life with answers in the back where we can see whether we got it right. Good thinking is a self-directed, self-correcting process, alert to the dangers of hasty judgment, and never afraid to ask—or answer—the question "Why?" Once again, this is partly a matter of attitude, a matter of choice, and logic won't make the choice for you. But it will give you the tools you need. It will give you a compass to steer by.

PART ONE

Concepts and Propositions

Language is our basic tool of thought and speech. We could not get very far in our thinking without the use of words, and we certainly could not communicate our thoughts. Words expand the range of our senses, bring order to our experiences, allow us to learn from the experiences of others, and preserve the thoughts of preceding generations. In learning to speak, each of us has acquired an amazingly powerful and versatile set of tools. But the tools will not do what we want unless we know how to use them properly.

One of the major functions of language is to divide the world up into categories. Except for proper names, most words stand for *groups* of things: tigers, tables, tests, and so forth. Organizing a set of things into groups is called *classification*, and a word that stands for such a group expresses a *concept*. Chapter 2 is concerned with concepts and classification. We will learn the rules for classifying things in the most effective way, and we'll see how concepts can be arranged in hierarchies of *species* and *genus*.

In order to use concepts with precision, and to understand the relationships among different concepts, we need to *define* them. In Chapter 3, we

9

will learn a set of rules for evaluating definitions, and some techniques for constructing good ones.

Finally, we use concepts to make statements about things. In logic, we analyze statements in terms of the *propositions* they assert. In Chapter 4, we'll see how to identify propositions, and how to tell whether two statements assert the same or different propositions.

2

Classification

Suppose that I asked you to classify the courses you've taken in college. You might classify them by subject matter: art, biology, history, etc. Or you might classify them by level: introductory, intermediate, advanced. You can probably think of other ways to classify them. Whichever way you choose, you are grouping together courses that have something in common, and distinguishing them from other courses. In effect, you are creating a set of file folders in your mind, and then putting each course into the proper folder.

Classifying things together into groups is something we do all the time, and it isn't hard to see why. Imagine trying to shop in a supermarket where the food was arranged in random order on the shelves: tomato soup next to the white bread in one aisle, chicken soup in the back next to the 60-watt light bulbs, one brand of cream cheese in front and another in aisle 8 near the Oreos. Or imagine trying to research a term paper in a library that had no card catalog, no Dewey decimal or Library of Congress numbers, just shelf after shelf of books in random order. In either case, the task of finding what you want would be extremely difficult and time-consuming, if not impossible.

In the case of a supermarket or a library, someone had to design the system of classification, just as I asked you a moment ago to design a way of classifying your courses. But there is also a ready-made system of classification embodied in our language. The word "dog," for example, groups together a certain class of animals and distinguishes them from other animals. This may seem too obvious a grouping to be called a classification. Well, it is obvious—because you have mastered the word. But as a child learning to speak, you had to work hard to learn the system of classification your parents were trying to teach you. Before you got the hang of it, you probably made mistakes, like calling the cat a dog, or failing to realize that trees are plants. And if you hadn't learned to speak, the whole world would seem like the unorganized library; you would be in the position of an infant, for whom every object is new and unfamiliar.

Concepts and Referents

Classification is one of our basic cognitive tools, and there are rules that will help us classify in the most effective way. Before we turn to those rules, however, we need to learn some new terminology. Whenever we classify, we make use of **concepts.** A concept is an idea that represents a class of things we have grouped together; it functions as a mental file folder. In classifying your courses, you used concepts such as ART, HISTORY, and INTRODUCTORY. (We will use capital letters to indicate a concept.) In order to learn the word "dog," you had to acquire the concept DOG. A scientist who discovers a new phenomenon forms a concept for that class of thing, and expresses the concept in a new word (e.g., "quark"). As the examples illustrate, concepts and words are intimately related. A concept is an idea; a word is the linguistic vehicle we use to express the idea. Later, we will look at some of the properties of those vehicles. But for now let's concentrate on the concepts themselves.

Referents

If a concept is a mental file folder, what about the things that are put in the folder? These are called the **referents** of the concept. Thus the referents of DOG are all the individual dogs in the world, the referents of CHAIR are all the individual chairs, and so on. We can diagram the relation between a concept and its referents as follows:

The asterisks stand for individual objects. The slanting lines indicate that certain objects (Lassie, the hound of the Baskervilles, etc.) are included within the concept, while other things are excluded

(Morris the cat, the Taj Mahal, and everything else in the world that is not a dog).

Genus and Species

Now let's consider the concept ANIMAL. We could diagram this separately, and the diagram would look like the one we just did for DOG. But these concepts are obviously related: dogs are a type of animal. That means we can represent both concepts in the same diagram:

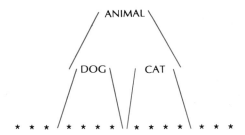

Notice that all the referents included in DOG are also included in ANIMAL, but ANIMAL includes many other things as well—cats (as the diagram indicates), squirrels, fish, and all the other types of animals. ANIMAL is a broader concept because it includes more; DOG is a narrower concept. Whenever we encounter this relationship, we use the term **genus** for the broader concept, and the term **species** for the narrower one. Thus DOG and CAT are both species within the genus ANIMAL; and of course there are many other species that could go in the diagram.

You may be familiar with the idea of genus and species from biology. In logic, these terms have a slightly different meaning. For one thing, biologists have a much more elaborate system, with many levels of classification: species, genus, family, order, class, phylum, kingdom. But we don't need all these levels; genus and species are enough for our purposes. In biology, moreover, "genus" and "species" refer to specific levels of classification, but in logic we use the terms in a more flexible way. A genus can be any wider group to which a given species belongs. That's why I said ANIMAL is a genus; in biology, it is a kingdom. And a species can be any subclass within a given genus. "Genus" and "species" are relative terms, like "mother" and "daughter." Your mother is also a daughter—in relation to *her* parents. In the same way, a given concept can be either a genus or a species, depending on our perspective. DOG is a species in relation to ANIMAL, but it is a genus in relation to the narrower concept BEAGLE.

By using the genus–species relationship, we can create very complex systems of classification. Biology provides the clearest examples. Individual animals are classified as dogs, cats, etc.; these species are then classified into genuses: mammals, birds, fish, insects, etc.; these are themselves species of higher genuses, such as vertebrates and invertebrates; and so on. But we can organize concepts of other kinds into similar hierarchies. The items in your house can be classified as tables, chairs, etc.; these are species of the genus FURNITURE, which in turn is a species of the genus MAN-MADE OBJECTS (or ARTIFACTS), and so on. If you classified your courses by subject matter—art, history, economics, physics—you might go on to classify these disciplines into wider groups, such as humanities, social sciences, and physical sciences. Indeed, *every* concept can be placed within some hierarchy of genus and species (and, as we will see, most concepts can be placed within many different hierarchies).

Abstract and Concrete

There is one final point we need to understand before we turn to the rules of classification: the distinction between *abstract* and *concrete*. The referents of our concepts are concrete; each is a single, individual object. If we had separate names for each referent (as we do in the case of people, or cities), the names would also be concrete. But a concept (such as PEOPLE or CITY) is abstract. The word "abstract" here means two things. It means first that a concept refers to a group of objects, not just to a single thing (as a name does). The concept PEOPLE includes all human beings, CITY includes all cities. Secondly, a concept is abstract because it groups together things that differ from one another. There are many differences among people, among cities, among the referents of any concept. We group them together, not because they are identical, but because they are *similar*.

Abstractness is a relative property. Any concept is abstract to some degree. But a species is less abstract than the genus to which it belongs. The genus is a larger and broader group; it has more referents than the species does. And the referents of the genus are less similar than are the referents of the species. There are many more differences among animals, taken as a group, than there are among dogs. Thus, as we move up a species-genus hierarchy, we are moving in the direction of increasing abstractness. As we move down the hierarchy, we are moving in the direction of greater concreteness.

It's important to stress that the term "concrete" is not limited to physical, tangible things, nor does the term "abstract" mean "intangible." The feelings we have at a given moment, for example, are not tangible, but they are concrete: each is an individual, particular occurrence. And the concepts we use to classify feelings are measured in the same way as other concepts. The concept LOVE is more abstract than its species, such as ROMANTIC LOVE, but less abstract than its genus, EMOTION.

The distinction between abstract and concrete allows us to extend our notion of classification. So far, we have been classifying objects: animals, furniture, cities, etc. But we also have concepts for qualities, like colors; for actions, such as running; and for relationships, such as marriage. These concepts can also be placed in species-genus hierarchies on the basis of their degree of abstractness. RED, BLUE, and GREEN are species of the genus COLOR, which might in turn be classified as a species of the genus PHYSICAL QUALITY (as distinct from nonphysical qualities such as intelligence). RUNNING, WALKING, and SWIMMING are species of the genus LOCOMOTION. MARRIAGE and FRIENDSHIP are species of the genus PERSONAL RELATIONSHIP. (In our society, marriage is also a legal relationship; this is an example of the way hierarchies of classification can overlap.)

You can see that in all these cases, the genus is the more abstract concept, the species the more concrete. *Every* concept, not just those for objects or entities, has some particular degree of abstractness, and every concept fits into some species-genus relationship. This fact is the basis for the technique of defining concepts that we will study in the next chapter. It is also a useful point to keep in mind for writing. Suppose, for example, that you wrote a story about someone named Joan, and you said "Joan moved to the other side of the room." If your teacher asked you to use a more concrete verb, you might rewrite the sentence: "Joan walked to the other side of the room." (Can you think of a verb that would be even *more* concrete?)

We need to be careful, though, in comparing two concepts on the basis of their relative abstractness. The comparison really makes sense only when the concepts have some genus-species relationship. Then we can say: concept X includes concept Y and more besides; therefore X is more abstract. But if the concepts are not related in this way, how could we compare them? If the concepts are TREE and MONEY, how could we tell which is more abstract? Sometimes we can make intuitively plausible judgments even when the concepts are unrelated—intuitively, GOVERNMENT seems more abstract than OWL—but it is usually safer to make such comparisons only within a particular genus-species hierarchy.

Practice Quiz

A. For each of the following pairs of concepts, a) determine which is the genus, which the species; and b) name two other species of the same genus.

1. MAN, ANIMAL
2. GARMENT, COAT
3. VEHICLE, CAR
4. ANGER, EMOTION
5. MATERIAL SUBSTANCE, SOLID

B. Arrange the following lists of terms in order of increasing abstractness.

1. Performer, Elton John, singer, human
2. Cattle, organism, mammal, steer, animal
3. Quadrilateral, square, figure, rectangle
4. Alloy, steel, mineral, metal
5. Exxon, corporation, multinational company, institution

Rules of Classification

Classification is the process of sorting things into categories. The set of things to be classified—animals, college courses, or whatever—constitutes a genus, and the task is to subdivide the genus into species so that each item can be assigned its place. There is usually more than one way to do this, as we noticed earlier in regard to college courses, depending on our needs, our purposes, and the kind of information we have available. But even if there is no single best way of subdividing a genus, some ways are better than others, and there are guidelines for selecting the better ones. The two basic rules of classification are stated in the box below.

1. A single principle or set of principles should be used consistently so that the categories (species) are mutually exclusive and jointly exhaustive.
2. The principles used should be essential ones.

Mutually Exclusive, Jointly Exhaustive

The terms "mutually exclusive" and "jointly exhaustive" may not be familiar to you, but their meaning is implicit in the old saying "a place for everything and everything in its place." Let's start with the second half of the saying. The goal of classification is to put each item in its place—to assign each member of the genus to a species. But we cannot assign an item to one particular species if it belongs to more than one. Suppose you tried to classify your courses into the following categories: art, biology, history, economics, and introductory. Where would you put "Introduction to Art"? Because your categories overlap, we don't know whether to classify this as an introductory or an art course. The first rule of classification, then, is that the species must not overlap. We express this in logic by saying the species must be **mutually exclusive:** each species must exclude all the members of every other species.

The first part of the old saying—"a place for everything"—means that a good classification divides up the genus completely, allowing us to assign every member of the genus to a species. We express this in logic by saying that the classification must be **jointly exhaustive:** the species taken together (jointly) must cover (exhaust) all the objects in the genus. If you had taken a philosophy course, the classification of courses I gave in the last paragraph would not be jointly exhaustive. The only birds I can recognize by sight are owls, robins, and seagulls, but these species obviously don't exhaust the genus BIRD.

A classification cannot be expected to exhaust a genus in the sense of including every member, known and unknown. Biologists are sure that many species of plants and animals have not yet been discovered, but it would be unreasonable to fault their classification system for being incomplete. The jointly exhaustive rule is relative to our present knowledge of the domain we are trying to organize, with the understanding that we will create new categories, if necessary, as our knowledge expands. Even for the things we already know about, it can happen that the only way to achieve a jointly exhaustive division of a genus is to have a "miscellaneous" category for items left over when we've set up our species. But it's desirable to avoid this if possible, since MISCELLANEOUS is not a real species. It says, in effect, "These things do not necessarily have anything in common, but I don't know where else to put them." So before you give up and settle for miscellany, it's usually worth seeing whether a different subdivision of the genus would work better.

Consistent Principle

A good classification should divide the genus into species that are mutually exclusive and jointly exhaustive. How do we go about creating such a division? Let's consider first an example of how *not* to do it. In one of his stories, J. L. Borges describes a mythical book called *The Chinese Emporium of Benevolent Knowledge.*

> On those remote pages it is written that animals are divided into (a) those that belong to the Emperor, (b) embalmed ones, (c) those that are trained, (d) suckling pigs, (e) mermaids, (f) fabulous ones, (g) stray dogs, (h) those that are included in this classification, (i) those that tremble as if they were mad, (j) innumerable ones, (k) those drawn with a very fine camel's hair brush, (l) others, (m) those that have just broken a flower vase, (n) those that resemble flies from a distance. [Jorge Luis Borges, *Other Inquisitions 1937–52*]

These categories are obviously not mutually exclusive. A stray dog (g) might well resemble a fly from a distance (n); an animal belonging to the Emperor (a) might also be drawn with a very fine camel's hair brush (k). The categories overlap in countless ways. Strictly speaking, the classification *is* jointly exhaustive, because of "others" (1). But that's cheating: (1) is a "miscellaneous" category. Without it, the classification would leave out many animals.

It's not hard to see why the classification is inadequate. It does not follow any *consistent principle* for dividing up the genus. It jumps from the question of ownership (a), to condition after death (b), to training (c), and so on. Since there is no necessary relationship among these various principles, the classification is bound to be chaotic. In classifying, we should try to follow a consistent principle. If we classify college courses by subject matter, we should stick to that principle throughout, and not include species like INTRODUCTORY that involve a different principle. Similarly, there are various ways to classify furniture: by function (tables, chairs, etc.), by style of design (Danish, colonial, Louis XIV, etc.), by material (wood, plastic, chrome, etc.). But whichever principle we choose, we should follow it consistently.

When we diagram a classification, we can represent the principle we're following by enclosing it within brackets under the name of the genus. For example:

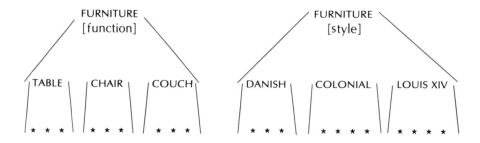

As the diagram illustrates, the principle is an attribute that all members of the genus possess, and the species are defined by the way they differ in regard to that attribute. Thus, in the diagram on the left, the concept **TABLE** groups together things that have the same *function,* and distinguishes them from chairs, couches, etc., which have different functions. In the diagram on the right, the concept **DANISH** groups together articles of furniture that have the same *style,* and distinguishes them from furniture designed in other styles. We can find this same structure in any system of classification, though it may not always be so easy to name the principle explicitly.

The need for a consistent principle does not require a *single* principle. Animal species, for example, differ from each other in many ways: shape, color, and other external properties; internal anatomy and physiology; behavior; method of bearing young; and so on. Biologists use all these properties in classifying animals. It is appropriate to use multiple principles of classification whenever we are dealing with complex phenomena; in such cases, a single principle would often be artificial and not very useful.

When we use more than one principle, however, we should take extra care to make sure that the resulting categories are mutually exclusive. Suppose we try to classify people on the basis of personality into two categories: extroverts and introverts. Extroverts are outgoing, adventurous, frank, open; introverts are reclusive, cautious, reserved. Where would we put someone who is adventurous, but reserved in the presence of other people? What about someone who is outgoing and frank with people, but timid about physical danger? The problem here is that the various attributes don't always fit together according to our stereotypes of extroverts and introverts; so these categories are not mutually exclusive. We should either pick one of the attributes—e.g., outgoing vs. reserved—so that everyone would fit into one or the other category, or create more categories to handle the variety of personality types.

The first rule for classifying, then, is to use a single principle or set of principles consistently so that the resulting categories are mutually exclusive and jointly exhaustive. In many cases, however, this will leave more than one possible way to divide the genus. A second rule will help us select among those alternatives.

Essential Attributes

The rule is to classify according to the *essential attributes* of the things we are sorting. An essential attribute is a fundamental one. If we divide a genus according to an essential attribute, we are grouping together things that are fundamentally similar, and separating things that are fundamentally different. And because a fundamental attribute underlies and explains many of a thing's superficial attributes, things that are fundamentally similar will probably have many attributes in common; things that share a superficial, nonessential attribute may well have nothing else in common.

Let's consider the animal kingdom once again. Biologists classify animals into the categories MAMMAL, REPTILE, AMPHIBIAN, BIRD, INSECT, etc. The principles they use include mode of reproduction (does the animal lay eggs or bear its young alive?), internal physiology (vertebrate versus invertebrate, warm-blooded versus cold-blooded), and means of locomotion (swimming, flying, crawling). These principles are aspects of two fundamental attributes essential to all forms of life: an organism must maintain itself by acting on the environment, and it must reproduce itself. This classification of animals, then, is based on essential principles, and the advantages of the classification are obvious. Animals that survive and reproduce in similar ways are likely to have a great deal in common, and can naturally be studied as a group.

By contrast, suppose that we classify animals according to a nonessential attribute:

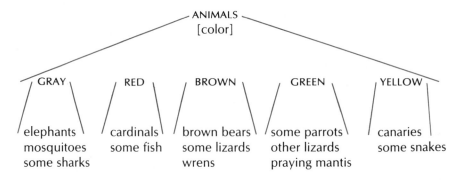

Of course this is not a complete classification of animals, but it is enough to see what's wrong with classifying them by color. The items that are grouped together in each category have nothing else in common. The differences among elephants, mosquitoes, and sharks are much more fundamental than the superficial similarity in color. And the items in each category often have more in common with items in other categories. The similarities between green and brown lizards are much more fundamental than the superficial difference in color. As a result, this classification is useless. Knowing that a certain animal belongs to one of these categories tells you almost nothing about it. Imagine having to act on the information that a gray animal was approaching, without knowing anything else about it.

How does the distinction between essential and nonessential attributes apply to other areas? Let's look at a few examples.

The essential attribute of a man-made object is usually its function. Such objects are created to serve a purpose, and the purpose explains why they are designed the way they are. If you came across an unfamiliar tool in a museum, your first question would probably be: What's it for? If you knew the answer to that question, then you would understand why the tool has a certain shape and internal structure, why it is made of the material it is, and so on. The same is true for human institutions. Thus, if you were studying corporations, it would be natural to classify each according to its function: does the corporation produce goods or services? is it a nonprofit or for-profit organization?

In the physical sciences, essential attributes are those that underlie and explain the surface properties we can observe directly, and scientists have pushed deeper and deeper into the structure of matter in the search for these underlying causes. Ancient Greek philosophers, for example, divided matter into four elements: earth, air, water, and fire. This was a reasonable classification, given what they knew, since it implicitly recognizes the three states of matter—solids (earth), gases (air), and liquids (water)—as well as a type of energy (fire). But modern chemists have replaced that early system with the table of elements, classifying matter according to the kinds of atoms that make it up. The properties of the atoms explain many of the observable features of matter: they explain why some elements are gases at room temperature, why metals conduct electricity, and so on. The table of elements is therefore a classification by essential attributes.

In dealing with other people, our standards for what is essential are too complex even to summarize here, but let's look at a case in which one of these standards is applied: the issue of discrimination. In the abstract, discrimination means noticing differences among people and classifying them into groups on the basis of those differences. We do this all the time. Teachers discriminate among students in assigning grades; employers discriminate among job applicants; everyone discriminates among people in choosing friends. What most of us object to is not discrimination (or classification) per se, but discrimination on the basis of attributes, such as race or sex, that are not *essentially* related to the treatment a person deserves. Thus an employer who adopts an equal opportunity policy is choosing to classify job applicants by ability, training, and character rather than by race or sex—on the ground that ability, training, and character are essentially related to job performance, whereas race and sex are not.

The word "essential" always has the sense of "fundamental" or "important." But as the examples illustrate, standards for what is fundamental or important vary from case to case. Identifying essential attributes may take years of research (as in science), and it always takes a good deal of thought. Moreover, people with different purposes may regard different attributes as essential. For most of us, the essential attribute of a piece of furniture is its function; but an interior decorator, who is likely to be more concerned with aesthetic issues, might find it more useful to classify furniture by style. There is no simple, mechanical rule we can follow in distinguishing essential from nonessential principles of classification. You will have to use your judgment, and you will have to accept the possibility that reasonable people may disagree. Nevertheless, the examples also indicate the value of looking for essential attributes: they bring clarity and coherence to the organization of our knowledge.

A good classification thus divides a genus into species according to a single essential principle or set of principles. Contained within that summary statement are two basic rules:

1. A single principle or set of principles should be used consistently so that the categories (species) are mutually exclusive and jointly exhaustive.
2. The principles used should be essential ones.

Practice Quiz

Evaluate each of the following classifications. First determine whether it employs a consistent principle, and is mutually exclusive and jointly exhaustive. If it passes that test, then determine whether the principle is an essential one. If it is not, try to think of a specialized purpose for which the principle might be an essential one.

1. Books: paperbacks, hardbacks, first editions
2. Records: 33, 45, 78
3. Foods: meats, vegetables, junk food, fruits, breads
4. Movies: thrillers, Westerns, pornographic, foreign
5. Students: under 5 feet tall, 5 to 6 feet tall, 6 feet tall and over
6. Sports: team, aquatic, individual, noncompetitive

7. Jobs: clerical, sales, managerial, service, manual
8. People: those who would rather be hosts, those who would rather be guests

---

Levels of Organization

So far we have treated classification as if it were always a matter of sorting things into categories or dividing a genus into species (two ways of describing the same operation). And this is indeed the task we face when we start from scratch. But we do not always start from scratch. We often deal with concepts that reflect preexisting classifications, and the task we face is to locate the concepts at the right level of a species-genus hierarchy.

Suppose you were studying religious affiliations. People describe themselves as Baptists, Methodists, Catholics, Unitarians, Jews, etc. These are indeed different religions, but they do not all belong on the same level of classification; they are not all species of a single genus. Jews, for example, should not be compared directly to Methodists. They should be compared to Christians—a category that I did not include on the list. And Catholics should be compared to Protestants, another term missing from the list. Thus the classification might look like this:

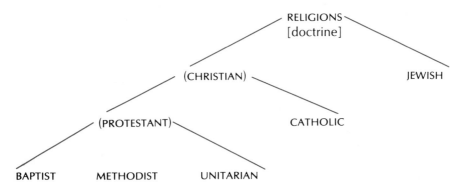

This diagram illustrates several points. First, concepts on the same level of organization should have roughly the same degree of abstractness. It is clear in this case that CATHOLIC and PROTESTANT belong on the same level and that BAPTIST, METHODIST, and UNITARIAN are narrower (less abstract) subdivisions within the category PROTESTANT. Secondly, when it is necessary to separate levels in this way, we must often add concepts that were not given to us originally. The new concepts in this case are **PROTES-TANT** and **CHRISTIAN**, and we indicate that they were not on the original list by putting them in parentheses. Finally, the diagram gives us ideas about ways in which we might want to flesh out the classification: are there other religions besides Christianity and Judaism? Are there other branches of Protestantism? Are there categories within Catholicism and Judaism?

This sort of analysis is often required when you are learning a new subject, and have to learn a new set of concepts. Separating the different levels of organization will help you understand the concepts much more clearly than if you try to master each concept as an individual, isolated unit. In a course in legal theory, for example, you might encounter concepts like **FELONY, TRESPASS, MISDE-MEANOR, HOMICIDE, TORT.** In order to grasp these concepts, you would need to understand that felonies and misdemeanors are the two species of crimes, regarded as offenses against public order and prosecuted by the state; and that a tort (such as trespass) is considered a civil wrong, an offense for which a private individual must bring suit. A diagram would help you keep these relationships in mind:

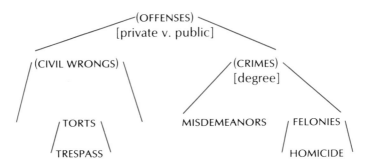

In addition to clarifying the new concepts, this diagram would provide a skeleton or outline for organizing all the other crimes and offenses you learn about.

Notice that one of the concepts we had to fill in here was the genus, **OFFENSES.** This is the first case we've seen in which the genus was not given at the outset, but it is not an uncommon case. When you are learning a new set of concepts, or organizing an old set, you will often have to find an overarching concept for the entire domain. Such generic concepts will of course be more abstract than concepts for the corresponding species, and it may help to be familiar with some of the highest level abstractions we use to organize our knowledge of the world. One fundamental distinction is between living and nonliving (animate versus inanimate) objects.

Another distinction is between natural objects (living or nonliving) and man-made ones. Yet another basic division is between physical and mental phenomena: the external world of material things versus the internal world of thoughts and feelings. (Mental phenomena in turn are often divided into cognitive and motivational states— thinking versus feeling.) Perhaps the most abstract set of generic concepts is one devised by the ancient Greek philosopher Aristotle. He divided the world into things (in the sense of whole objects), actions, relations, quantities, times, and places. When you are looking for a genus, it may help to remember these fundamental concepts. You may not need anything so abstract, but if you are stuck, they may help you get oriented.

One final word of warning. Classification is the process of dividing a genus into its species. This is not the same as breaking an object down into its parts or elements. Engines and driveshafts are parts of cars, but they are not themselves types or species of cars. In this case, the point is pretty obvious, but it's easy to get confused when we are learning new concepts. Suppose you have just learned in biology that an enzyme is a type of protein, and that a protein is a large organic molecule made up of a sequence of amino acids. Since enzymes are a species of protein, you could use the diagram on the left to capture the relationship:

But the diagram on the right is fundamentally incorrect. An amino acid is *not* a species of protein. It is a component of a protein. Both the species-genus and the part-whole relations are important for our understanding of the world, but they should not be confused.

Practice Quiz

A. Fill in the blanks in the classification diagram below.

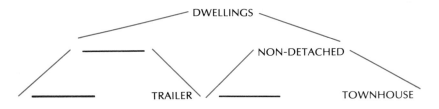

B. Arrange the following concepts in a classification diagram, making sure that each concept is on the appropriate level of abstractness, and adding concepts where necessary to complete the diagram.

MUSIC, LITERATURE, PAINTING, POETRY, VISUAL ARTS, STILL LIFE

C. The classification diagram below violates several of the principles discussed in this section. Identify the errors, and fix the diagram.

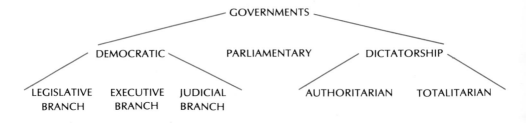

Classification and Outlining

Before we leave the subject of classification, it is worth noting one practical application of the skills you have been learning. When you set out to write an essay, you should usually begin by making an outline. An outline is, in effect, a classification of the material you want to include in the essay. An outline typically has the structure:

    I. First main topic
       A. First subtopic
       B. Second subtopic
       C. Third subtopic
    II. Second main topic
       A. First subtopic
       B. Second subtopic

If you turned this structure ninety degrees clockwise, and made a few adjustments, it would look very much like our classification diagrams:

If an outline is a type of classification, then the rules of classification apply. Let's see how. A frequent problem in writing is redundancy: the same point is repeated at different places in the essay. When this happens, it is probably because the divisions in the outline are not mutually exclusive, leading you to feel that the same point was equally relevant to two different topics. Another frequent problem is the dangling point: a fact or idea doesn't fit into the flow of the essay, but appears to have been inserted more or less randomly. The problem here is usually that the outline is not jointly exhaustive; it doesn't really cover all the material you want to include.

We have seen that the way to achieve a mutually exclusive and jointly exhaustive classification is to follow a single principle or set of principles consistently. The same is true in writing: an outline should follow a single basic thread of argument, or pattern of analysis, or narrative line. And since there is usually more than one such principle you could follow, choose the one that is most essential, given your purposes. If you are writing about the American Revolution, for example, you might organize the material in chronological order. If your basic goal is to tell the story of the Revolution, this would be a good principle to follow. But if your goal is to discuss the role of ideas versus the role of economic interests as causes of the Revolution, then it might be better to organize the material under those headings.

Finally, it is always a good idea in writing, as in classifying, to keep track of the levels of organization. If you have made a certain point a subtopic in your outline, you are treating it as less important than a main topic—just as a species is less abstract than a genus. But you might find, in writing the essay, that you have a great deal to say about that point, and are giving it more emphasis than the main point. In that case, you should revise the outline to reflect this change in emphasis.

SUMMARY

Classification is the process of putting things together into groups on the basis of similarities. A concept is an idea that represents such a group. The concepts involved in a system of classification are organized into hierarchies of species and genuses. Every concept is abstract to some degree; a genus is more abstract than its species.

When we subdivide a genus into species, we should use a consistent principle, so that the species are mutually exclusive and jointly exhaustive. We should also use essential attributes, so that the members of each species are fundamentally alike, and fundamentally different from members of other species.

When we learn a new set of concepts, we need to identify the genus-species relationships among the concepts. Concepts at the same level of abstractness should be placed at the same level in the hierarchy.

Exercises

A. In each of the following sentences, replace any **boldfaced** words with more abstract ones, and any *italicized* words with more concrete ones.

1. Joan *walked* across the room.
2. The tall stranger **whirled** around and dashed his *drinking implement* against the fireplace.
3. Our daughter is going out with a *nice* young man.
4. My **kingdom** for a **horse!**
5. Mary expressed herself *with feeling.*
6. Life is but a *nonobjective sensory experience.*
7. **A government** cannot exist without popular support.
8. The only problem with Jeff is that he has this *thing* about math.
9. Around the bend lay a set of *dangerous* rapids.
10. In the years ahead, our country will face *many* problems.

B. Classify the objects in each of the following genuses, in accordance with the rules of classification. Make sure that your classification is mutually exclusive and jointly exhaustive, that you use a single principle or set of principles, and that the principle is an essential one. For extra credit, you might also classify the objects in each domain in accordance with a nonessential principle.

1. Clothing
2. Household appliances
3. Publications
4. Countries
5. Jobs

C. Diagram each of the following sets of concepts. (Some are at the same level of abstraction, and some are not.) Be sure to fill in concepts where necessary.

1. WATER, SOLID, OXYGEN, GASOLINE, CARBON DIOXIDE, IRON

2. FRIEND, CLIENT, RELATIVE, COLLEAGUE, AUNT, HUMAN RELATIONSHIPS
3. HORIZONTAL, RECTANGULAR, LARGE, ROUND, INFINI-TESIMAL, VERTICAL
4. DECIDUOUS TREES, LETTUCE, PINE, DANDELION, CAR-ROT, OAK
5. HONESTY, VICE, LAZINESS, INTEGRITY
6. ANGER, WISH, MEMORY, LOVE, COGNITION

D. Each of the following passages proposes a system of classification for some domain. Identify the concepts the author is using, diagram the genus-species relationships among them, and note any points at which the passages fail to make these relationships clear.

1. "The human species, according to the best theory I can form of it, is composed of two distinct races, *the men who borrow*, and *the men who lend*." [Charles Lamb, *Essays of Elia*]
2. ". . . digital computers operate by carrying out a number of discrete steps, each of which involves the change of one or more basic engineering components from one physical state to another. (Usually, only two states are possible.) Analog computers are not like this, because the physical parameters used to represent information are continuously variable—like voltage levels, for instance." [Margaret Boden, *Artificial Intelligence and Natural Man*]
3. "Q. What is the difference between turtles, tortoises, and terrapins?
   "A. Turtles, tortoises, and terrapins all belong to a group of four-legged reptiles that have hard outer shells, scaly skins, and horny beaks. They are in the order Chelonia or Testudinata. Generally, turtles live in salt water; those that live on land are called tortoises. A few edible fresh-water turtles are called terrapins." [*New York Times*, January 6, 1987]
4. "The first link between an organism's present and its past is forged by its *sensory registers*. These hold incoming sensory information for fractions of a second after the stimulus is withdrawn. Such registers probably exist for all the senses. . . .
   "When we call on memory in ordinary life, we require much more than the sensory registers can possibly give us. . . . Remembering things like telephone numbers or people's names or where we parked the car are all cases that involve a level of processing vastly beyond anything that the sensory registers can hold. We clearly have to assume an additional memory system. But is one more enough?

"Many psychologists have argued for the existence of at least two further systems beyond the sensory registers. One is *short-term memory*, which holds information for fairly short intervals, say, up to a minute. The other is *long-term memory*, in which materials are stored for much longer periods, perhaps for a lifetime." [Henry Gleitman, *Psychology*, 2d ed.]

5. "Racketeering includes two kinds of business, both based on intimidation. One is criminal monopoly, the other extortion.

"'Criminal monopoly' means the use of criminal means to destroy competition. . . .

"We can distinguish altogether three kinds of 'monopoly': those achieved through legal means; those achieved through means that are illegal only because of antitrust and other laws intended to make monopoly difficult; and monopolies achieved through means that are criminal by any standards—means that would be criminal whether or not they were aimed at monopolizing business." [Thomas C. Schelling, *Choice and Consequence*]

6. "From the standpoint of the individual all contributions to government are either gratuitous, contractual or compulsory. Every governmental revenue must fall within one of these three great classes. Individuals may make the government a free gift, they may agree or contract to pay, or they may be compelled to pay. . . .

"The taxing power may manifest itself in three different forms, known respectively as special assessments, fees and taxes. These three forms are all species of taxation in the wider sense, so far as they differ on the one hand from contractual revenue. . ., and on the other hand from the remaining divisions of compulsory revenue, like expropriation and fines. What is common to all three is that they are compulsory contributions levied for the support of government or to defray the expenses incurred for public purposes. That is the essence of the taxing power. But, although they are all forms of taxation in this wider sense, the differences between fees and special assessments on the one hand, and taxes in the narrower sense on the other, are so marked that they must be put into separate categories." [Edwin R. A. Seligman, *Essays in Taxation*, 10th ed.]

E. Many colleges have a distribution requirement; students must take some courses in each area of the curriculum. In order to have such a requirement, the college must divide the curriculum into various categories. Evaluate the following system—which is actually used at a well-known college—according to the principles of classification. (Or substitute the system your college uses.)

Arts	*Foreign languages and literatures*
Art	Chinese
Drama	French
English	German
Music	Greek
Physical education	Hispanic studies
	Italian
	Latin
	Russian

Social sciences	*Natural sciences*
Anthropology	Astronomy
Economics	Biology
Education	Chemistry
Geography	Computer science
History	Geology
Philosophy	Mathematics
Political science	Physics
Religion	Psychology
Sociology	

F. Choose some domain of study that you are familiar with (or would like to be), and make a classification diagram for some of the basic concepts in that domain. Here are some ideas for possible areas:

1. Psychological disorders
2. Investments
3. A specific region of the plant or animal kingdom
4. Crimes
5. Communications media
6. Subatomic particles
7. Literary genres

3

Definitions

A **definition** is a statement that gives the meaning of a concept. As we saw in the last chapter, concepts serve as mental file folders we use to organize our knowledge about classes of similar things. Definitions tell us what is in the folders. In the case of simple, relatively concrete concepts—such as TABLE or RUNNING—we can get along pretty well without definitions. You can tell just by sight whether something is a table, whether someone is running. But most of the concepts we use are more abstract and more complex. By telling us what they stand for, and how they relate to other concepts, definitions are an important tool of knowledge. To see more clearly *why* definitions are so valuable, let's look at some of the problems they help us to solve.

The Functions of a Definition

First, a definition can clarify the *boundaries* of a concept. A child who has just learned the concept PLANT can point to some obvious and clear-cut examples, such as houseplants or outdoor shrubs. But it will take a while before the child understands the full range of the concept—including trees, moss, and so on. At a more advanced level, a person might know that sociology and economics are social sciences, but not be sure about less clear-cut examples like geography or psychology.

We can represent this situation on our standard diagram:

In the diagram on the left, the boundaries of the concept are fuzzy. The person knows that *c* is included, but isn't sure about *a* or *b*; this would represent the child's understanding of PLANT. In the diagram on the right, the boundaries are sharp and precise. The person not only knows that *c* is included in the concept, but also knows that *b* is included while *a* is not. Clear-cut cases like *c* are called "paradigm" or "prototypical" examples, and we usually learn them first. Indeed, when we are asked to define a term, we often begin by thinking of typical examples—hence the popularity of sayings like "happiness is a warm puppy." But such "definitions" will not help us with more difficult cases like *a* or *b*, which lie near the border of the concept. To decide whether they are included in the concept, we need some criterion we can use; we need an explicit test for membership in the class. A definition gives us such a test.

Some people would argue that a concept cannot ever have completely sharp borders. On the color spectrum, for example, orange lies on the border between red and yellow, and it isn't clear which way to classify it. Nor can we solve the problem by treating orange as a separate category between red and yellow, because then there would be colors on the borderline between red and orange. In biology, the one-celled organism *Euglena* sits on the border between plants and animals: it has chorophyll and engages in photosynthesis, like a plant; but it also has flagellae for swimming, like an animal. Fortunately, we do not have to settle the theoretical issue of whether concepts can—or should—have completely sharp borders. The important point is that there are *degrees* of precision in understanding a concept's boundaries, and definitions help us become *more* precise.

A second function of a definition is to clarify the relationships among concepts. Concepts are not isolated, self-contained units; they form networks of interrelated ideas. We have already seen that they fit together into genus-species hierarchies. But there is more to it than that. The function of a concept is to group things together into classes on the basis of similarities. In some cases, like TABLE or

RED, the objects and their similarities are perceptible. You can literally see the similarity among tables, or among red objects. More often, however, the referents of a concept and the attributes they have in common are not directly observable, and we have to learn about them by means of other concepts that we already understand.

Consider the concept GOVERNMENT. If you were trying to explain this concept to someone, what concrete objects could you point to? A police officer? The flag? The White House? These are merely symbols or instruments of government, and would convey only a child's understanding of the concept. Actual examples, such as the United States government, are not things you can literally point to. You would have to explain in abstract language that the concept GOVERNMENT refers to an *institution* with the *authority* to make *laws* for a *society*, to *enforce* those laws, and to protect its *citizens* against foreign powers. Each of the italicized words expresses a concept necessary for understanding what governments have in common; each is a link in a long chain that connects the concept GOVERNMENT to its referents in reality. If the chain is weak—if the person didn't understand the intervening concepts—then he wouldn't really understand the concept GOVERNMENT either. He might learn to use the *word* more or less appropriately, but he would have only a hazy notion of what he was talking about. And if the person does understand the intervening concepts, your definition allows him to grasp the meaning of the new concept.

Our ability to acquire new concepts on the basis of old ones is enormously valuable. It allows us to expand the range of our knowledge, and to profit from discoveries that other people have made. But it poses the danger that we will acquire a concept only as a vague idea, without any clear understanding of the class of things it actually stands for. It also poses the danger that different people using the concept will have radically different ideas of what the concept includes. Definitions help us ward off these dangers. They keep a concept tied to its referents by relating it clearly to other concepts that serve as links in the chain.

Suppose that an artist puts an egg on top of a brick, and exhibits the arrangement as his latest sculpture. Would this be a case of art? Some people would doubtless argue that it is; others would argue with equal vehemence that it is not. This is a disagreement about whether something is to be included in the concept ART. And it is not just a borderline case problem. The supporters would claim that the exhibit is a clear and unambiguous example of art, and the critics would claim that it clearly and unambiguously is *not* art. The only way to settle the issue would be to find a definition of ART that both sides could agree to. In general, the more abstract a concept is, and the longer the chain of other concepts that link it to its referents, the more important a definition is. It won't always be easy to find a definition—in the case of ART, people have been trying for a long time—but even the effort to find one can clarify our understanding of a concept.

A third function of a definition is to provide a summary statement about the referents of our concepts. If we think of a concept as a file folder where we put all the information we have about a certain class of things, then we have to realize that these folders may contain enormous amounts of information. In one way or another, for example, virtually all knowledge in the humanities and social sciences is relevant to the concept MAN. Definitions help us keep our filing system in order by giving us summary statements about what is in each folder. A good definition *condenses* the knowledge we have about the referents of a concept, giving us just the highlights, the key points, the essence. Because it performs this service, a definition is valuable even in cases, such as MAN, where we already know what class of things the concept stands for.

In summary, the main functions of a definition are: 1) to sharpen the boundaries of a concept by stating criteria for membership in the class of referents; 2) to indicate the relations between a concept and other concepts; and 3) to condense the knowledge we have about the referents of a concept. In the next section, we'll examine the structure of definitions, and the rules they must satisfy in order to fulfill those functions.

Rules for Definitions

If we're looking for a definition, why not just use the dictionary? Isn't that what dictionaries are for? Well, yes and no. A dictionary is a good place to begin our search for a definition. But dictionaries are concerned with *words*. They often give nothing more than synonyms, and rarely provide the full context we need to understand the *concept* which a word expresses. To define a concept, we usually have to go beyond the dictionary.

Different types of definition are appropriate for different tasks, and particular disciplines such as mathematics or biology often have specialized techniques for defining their terms. But logicians have identified six rules for constructing a type of definition that is suitable for general purposes. The rules are stated in the box below.

Rules for Definitions

1. A definition should include a genus and a differentia.
2. A definition should not be too broad or too narrow.
3. A definition should state the essential attributes of the concept's referents.
4. A definition should not be circular.
5. A definition should not use negative terms unnecessarily.
6. A definition should not use vague, obscure, or metaphorical language.

Include Genus and Differentia

1) *A definition should include a genus and a differentia.* To understand what this means, consider the classic definition of MAN: "Man is a rational animal." Notice that the definition has two parts. The term "animal" names the wider class to which MAN belongs; it classifies MAN as a species of the *genus* ANIMAL. The term "rational" specifies an attribute that distinguishes MAN from other species of the same genus. This part of the definition is called the *differentia*—it differentiates MAN from other animals. A differentia can rarely be expressed in a single word, like "rational," but it always serves the same function of differentiating a concept from other species. Thus the genus is like your last name, which indicates the family you belong to; the differentia is like your first name, which distinguishes you from other members of your family. A definition that has this structure is called a definition by genus and differentia.

The most common way to violate this rule is to leave out the genus. And the usual sign of this omission is the use of the word "when," as in "fear is when you think you're in danger." What's missing in this definition is the genus: fear is the *emotion* one feels in response to the awareness of danger. The word "where" is sometimes used in the same way, as in "a denouement is where the conflict is resolved and the story ends." Here again, the genus is missing. This definition does not tell us what *kind* of thing a denouement is—namely, an element or stage in the plot of a literary work.

Like the differentia, the genus need not be specified by a single word. If we define an automobile as a motor vehicle intended for personal transportation, the genus is contained in the phrase "motor vehicle." A definition of MARRIAGE might start out, "A man and a woman are married when. . . ." This definition does include a genus, even though it uses the word "when," because it says that marriage is a type of relationship between a man and a woman. When we define a concept that designates an action, we often use a verb phrase, as in "to practice is to perform an activity for the sake of improving one's skill." The English language gives us many ways to specify a genus. To identify the genus, we need to look for the element in a defining statement that refers to a wider class.

Why is it so important to specify a genus? The primary reason is that knowing the genus helps us identify the referents of a concept, and the genus conveys a great deal of information about them. If you don't know what a *florin* is, for example, the most useful thing I can tell you is that it's a type of Italian coin. In the same way, the statement that man is an animal locates our species within the biological order, and conveys a vast amount of information in summary form—that we are living beings, that we are mortal, that we have specific needs for survival and reproduction, and so on. Suppose we are trying to define HONESTY. What is its genus? Is it an action: telling the truth? Or is it a character trait: a *commitment* to telling the truth? It makes a difference which genus we choose. Consider a person who never lies, but only because he never has any reason to; if he stood to gain from lying, he wouldn't hesitate to do so. If we define honesty in terms of actions, then we would have to consider this person honest; if we define honesty as a kind of commitment, we would consider him dishonest.

Not Too Broad or Too Narrow

2) *A definition should not be too broad or too narrow.* A definition is too broad if it includes things that are not referents of the concept. For example, the definition "Man is a two-legged animal" is too broad because the defining phrase "two-legged animal" includes birds as well as humans. We can represent this problem in a diagram:

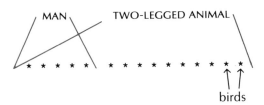

A definition is too narrow if it fails to include things that *are* referents of the concept. An example would be "Man is a religious animal." This definition is too narrow because, no matter how widespread religious belief may be, some people are atheists. We can see this by drawing a diagram:

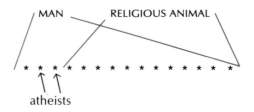

Being too narrow and being too broad are opposite flaws in a definition. But both have to do with the relation between the concept and its referents. The point of a definition is to identify the referents of a concept. A definition that does not pick out the right referents—a definition that includes too much or too little—is not doing its job properly. It is like an incompetent doorkeeper at a party, letting in people who weren't invited, or turning away people who were invited.

We can tell whether a definition is too broad or too narrow by looking for *counterexamples.* A counterexample is a specific instance that proves a definition wrong. If a definition is too narrow, a counterexample is something that belongs in the concept, but is excluded by the definition. Atheists are counterexamples to the definition of man as a religious animal. On the other hand, if a definition is too broad, a counterexample is something that does not belong in the concept but is included in the definition. Birds are counterexamples to the definition of man as a two-legged animal. Let's look at a few other cases. "A college is a degree-granting educational institution." A counterexample would be a high school. High schools are degree-granting educational institutions, but they are not colleges. So this definition includes too much; it's too broad. "A cigarette is a sheaf of chopped tobacco rolled in white paper." What about the brands that are rolled in brown paper? They are counterexamples proving that the definition does not include enough; it's too narrow.

We should notice, finally, that a definition can be both too broad and too narrow. Suppose we define murder as the act of killing another person outside a military context. By this definition, killing someone in self-defense would be an act of murder, but it isn't. So this definition is too broad. But it is also too narrow. Suppose a soldier kills another member of his own regiment in cold blood. This would be murder, but the definition would exclude it because it occurred in a military context. So the same definition can violate the rule in both ways; it can simultaneously be too broad and too narrow. We can represent this possibility on a diagram:

Before we turn to the other rules, let's pause here for some practice.

Practice Quiz

Identify the genus and the differentia in each of the following definitions. Then determine whether the definition is too broad or too narrow (each definition is one or the other or both), and find a counterexample.

1. A *pleat* is a fold in the fabric of a skirt.
2. A *salad* is a food dish containing lettuce.
3. An *antidote* is a substance that counteracts snakebite.
4. A *pen* is a writing implement that can be clipped to a pocket.
5. To *nod* is to move one's head forward and down, indicating assent.

State the Essential Attributes

3) *A definition should state the essential attributes of the concept's referents.* The referents of a concept often have many attributes in common. Some are relatively superficial, some are essential. As we saw in discussing the rules of classification, the term "essential" means *fundamental:* an essential attribute causes or explains the existence of other attributes. For example, the heart makes a certain thumping noise, so we might try to define it as "the organ that goes lub-dub, lub-dub." But the "lub-dub" sound is a superficial trait; it is merely a by-product of the heart's essential function, which is to circulate the blood. This essential function explains many of the heart's other properties: the way it beats, the way it is hooked up to the veins and arteries, even the sound it makes. But explanation is a one-way street. The "lub-dub" sound does *not* explain the heart's function. Remember that one purpose of a definition is to condense the knowledge we have about the referents of a concept. Defining by essential attributes is the best way to achieve

this purpose, because then you convey not only those particular attributes, but also the ones they underlie and explain.

The rule of essentiality applies to the genus as well as the differentia. Dogs, for example, belong to various wider groups: they are animals, they are playmates, they are a means of self-defense. But ANIMAL would be the best genus to use for general purposes in defining DOG, because a dog's animal nature is more fundamental and explains more about it than does the fact that it can play with human beings or defend them.

In regard to the differentia, the rule of essentiality will help us choose among attributes when there is more than one that would differentiate a concept from other species of the same genus. Consider the concept MAN. Many attributes, in addition to the faculty of reason, are common and distinctive to humans: technology, language, social institutions, the accumulation of knowledge from one generation to the next, laws, moral codes, certain complex emotions such as reverence or moral outrage, a sense of humor, a brain of a certain size and complexity, a certain physical shape and posture. But reason is the common element, the underlying cause, for many of these attributes. Not for all of them—reason doesn't seem to have much connection with our physical shape and posture. But it is reason that allowed us to develop abstract language and technology, to create social institutions based on general rules and laws, to pass along knowledge to the next generation, and so forth. Reason gives us a differentia that condenses the greatest amount of knowledge about MAN.

As we saw in the chapter on classification, there is no hard and fast rule for determining which attributes are essential. Our view of what is essential to a class of objects may change as we acquire more knowledge about them, and it may involve controversial issues on which people disagree. The rule of essentiality means: pick the most essential attribute you can, given everything you know, using your best judgment. And the guidelines to follow are the ones discussed in the previous chapter: look for the attribute that explains the most. For man-made objects, actions, and institutions, look for the basic function. For objects in nature, such as biological species or physical substances, look for underlying traits that cause and explain the more superficial attributes.

Avoid Circular Definitions

4) *A definition should not be circular.* Suppose we define *ownership* as the legal relation between a person and something that he owns. Because this definition uses the word "owns," it defines the concept OWNERSHIP in terms of itself. Instead of explaining what it

means to own something, it assumes that we know this already. It tells us how the concept relates to itself, but not how it relates to other concepts or to reality. This definition doesn't go anywhere; it just moves in a circle.

The same problem arises if we use synonyms in a definition. Suppose we define ownership as the legal relation between a person and something that he *possesses.* "Owns" and "possesses" are synonyms, different words that express the same concept. In terms of concepts, therefore, the definition is still circular: the concept **OWNERSHIP** is still being used to define itself. The same objection would apply if we define *man* as the *human* animal, *large* as the attribute possessed by something that is *big,* or *folly* as a *foolish* act. In each case, the italicized words are synonyms.

Circularity can take an even subtler form when two different concepts are used to define each other. Suppose that we define a husband as a man who has a wife. So far, so good: **HUSBAND** and **WIFE** are distinct concepts. But if we now define a wife as a woman who has a husband, then we have a circular *pair* of definitions. A better approach would be to define the relationship of marriage first; then we could define both **HUSBAND** and **WIFE** in terms of that relationship. Or consider the more difficult concept of **ART**. Some people have tried to define a work of art in terms of the response it is intended to evoke in the audience: they define **ART** in terms of **AESTHETIC EXPERIENCE**. That may or may not be the best approach. But if you take that approach, you have to be careful not to define **AESTHETIC EXPERIENCE** as the response an audience has to art.

Avoid Negative Terms

5) *A definition should not use negative terms unnecessarily.* At the turn of the century, the automobile was described as a "horseless carriage." That phrase certainly does describe the automobile, but it would not be a good definition. The differentia "horseless" tells us about one source of power that automobiles do *not* use. But there are many sources of power automobiles do not use; what we want to know is the source they *do* use. As another example, suppose that when I introduced the term "differentia," I defined it as the part of the definition that is not the genus. That would not have been much help to you in understanding what a differentia is. In general, negative definitions should be avoided because knowing what a thing is not doesn't tell us much about what it is. For that reason, a negative definition usually violates the rule of essentiality as well.

Some concepts, however, are inherently negative, and thus require negative terms in their definitions. A *bachelor* is a man who is not married, *failing* means not succeeding, an *empty* space is one with nothing in it. How do we know whether a concept is negative? In some cases, a suffix or prefix gives us a linguistic clue: *im*mortal, worth*less*, *a*symmetric. In the absence of such clues, you will have to use your judgment; there are no hard and fast rules. But it's a good idea to start by looking for some positive attribute and falling back on a negative one only if the search fails.

Avoid Vague, Obscure, or Metaphorical Language

6) *A definition should not use vague, obscure, or metaphorical language.* We might think of this as the "clarity" rule. The purpose of a definition is to clarify our understanding of a concept. At the very least, therefore, the language we use in a definition should not be *less* clear than the concept being defined. Unfortunately, there are too many ways of being unclear to list them all in this rule. But vagueness, obscurity, and metaphor are the three most common problems.

A *vague* definition is unclear because it does not give any precise criterion for membership in the concept. Suppose we define *maturity* as the stage of psychological development in which a person becomes well-adjusted. How do we tell whether a person is well-adjusted? Does adjustment mean passive acceptance of the social environment, or can it include a critical outlook? Is it primarily a set of cognitive skills, or an emotional state, or both? As these questions indicate, the term "well-adjusted" is vague. It isn't clear who belongs in the class of well-adjusted people, and who does not; the class has fuzzy boundaries. Of course, the concept MATURITY has fuzzy boundaries. But a definition should not make the problem worse. It should not have borders that are even fuzzier than those of the concept being defined.

An *obscure* definition is unclear because it uses abstract or technical language that is more difficult to understand than the concept itself. An example would be a definition of *death* as the cessation of one's participation in finitude. The problem here is not necessarily one of vagueness. In the appropriate context of a philosophical theory about human life and afterlife, this definition might have a perfectly clear and definite meaning. But that's the problem: it has a clear meaning only in a specialized context. For general purposes, the defining terms are too obscure to be useful. The same would be true of technical definitions in law, science, or other specialized areas. Such definitions may be perfectly clear to specialists, but if the concept is employed outside the specialty, then we also need a general purpose definition that is intelligible to laymen.

A *metaphorical* definition is unclear because it doesn't give us the literal meaning of the concept, but only an analogy that we have to interpret. A famous Broadway musical maintained that "Life is a cabaret." Like any good metaphor, this one uses a simple image to convey a complex thought that would take many paragraphs to explain in literal terms. But for a definition, we need the literal terms. A metaphor leaves too many questions unanswered. In exactly what ways is life like a cabaret? How far does the analogy extend? Is this the essential truth about life, or just one perspective? Metaphors are valuable tools of thought and communication, but they can't do the work of definitions.

Altogether, then, there are six rules of definition:

1. A definition should include a genus and a differentia.
2. A definition should not be too broad or too narrow.
3. A definition should state the essential attributes of the concept's referents.
4. A definition should not be circular.
5. A definition should not use negative terms unnecessarily.
6. A definition should not use vague, obscure, or metaphorical language.

These rules give us standards for evaluating definitions proposed by other people. They also give us guidelines for creating definitions—as we will see in the next section.

Practice Quiz

For each of the following definitions, identify the genus (if it has one) and the differentia. Then identify which rule it violates (it may violate more than one rule).

1. A *necklace* is a jewel worn on a pendant around the neck.
2. A *squirrel* is a rat in a fur coat.
3. *Liberty* is a political condition in which people are free.
4. An *orphan* is a person who does not have a living parent.
5. *Garbage* is what's left when you finish eating.
6. A *conservative* is a person who opposes legalized abortion.
7. A *drunk* is a person who is not sober.
8. *Education* is when someone learns something.
9. A *conspiracy* is a collusion in machination.
10. *Eloquence* is the ability to arouse emotions by means of words.

Constructing Definitions

Definitions do not appear out of thin air. Nor is there a big book somewhere with all the right definitions in it. We have to construct our own. To find definitions that satisfy the rules we've learned, we need procedures we can follow—a technique for constructing definitions.

Of the six rules of definition, the first three are the most important. If you can find a genus and differentia which, together, are neither too broad nor too narrow, and which state the essential attributes of the referents of the concept, you can be pretty sure that your definition will satisfy the remaining three rules. We can think of those other rules as backup tests. To define a concept, therefore, the first step is to find the genus. Then look for a differentia that states the essential attributes of the referents and distinguishes them from other species of the same genus. Finally, double-check your definition by looking for counterexamples, and by making sure that your definition is not circular, negative, or unclear. Let's look a little more closely at each step. Then we'll apply our techniques to a particular case.

Choosing the Genus

When we form a concept, we do it by grouping together certain things (the referents of the concept), and contrasting them with other things. Comparing and contrasting are essential to conceptual thought. Whenever you are dealing with a concept X, it is always appropriate to ask, "X—as opposed to what?" In a definition, it is the differentia that answers this question. The differentia distinguishes the concept from other species of the same genus. But until we have the genus, we don't know what distinctions to draw. Suppose we want to define CUP. We would use what we know about classification to locate the concept in a genus-species hierarchy:

Now we know that our definition will have the form, "A cup is a drinking vessel that_____." And we're in a good position to fill in the blank—to find the differentia. We know we have to distinguish cups from mugs and glasses, so we'll look for properties, such as shape or function, that will best do the job.

In choosing a genus, remember that we are defining concepts, not words per se. Sometimes a single word expresses two different concepts, located in different genuses. So we would need separate definitions for the two concepts. The word "alienation," for example, can refer to an emotion: the feeling of an unbridgeable gulf between oneself and something else—another person, society, the world. Or it can refer to an economic condition, as when Karl Marx claimed that under capitalism the workers are alienated from the products of their labor. If we are concerned with alienation in the first sense, then it belongs in the genus EMOTION, and should be contrasted with other emotions. If we're concerned with the other sense of the term, then the genus might be ECONOMIC CONDITIONS, and alienation would have to be differentiated from other such conditions.

The same point applies when a word is used metaphorically. A metaphor typically applies a concept from one genus to things in some other genus. An army, for example, is a military organization, but the term "army" is used metaphorically to describe nonmilitary groups that are similar in one way or another: an army of ants, "Arnie's army" (the fans of Arnold Palmer), and so on. If we tried to define ARMY in such a way as to include these metaphors, we couldn't use MILITARY ORGANIZATION as the genus. Indeed, there is no genus we could use, because we could not possibly anticipate every metaphorical use of the term. But we don't need to include the metaphorical uses. The purpose of a definition is to give the *literal* meaning of a concept.

When we choose a genus, we need to consider the appropriate level of abstraction. As noted, the genus of CUP would be DRINKING VESSEL. But a drinking vessel is a kind of *utensil*, which is a kind of *tool*, which is a kind of *man-made object*. Each of these terms is more abstract than the one before, and covers a wider range of things. Any of them could serve as the genus. Why choose the narrowest one, DRINKING VESSEL? On the other hand, we used ANIMAL as the genus in defining MAN, but this is *not* the narrowest genus. Man is also a vertebrate, a mammal, and a primate. Why choose the wider genus, ANIMAL? The answer in both cases lies in the rule that a definition should state essential attributes. If we chose UTENSIL as the genus for CUP, then our differentia would have to include the information that a cup is a utensil used for drinking. That's an essential attribute, so we might as well include it in the genus. On the other hand, man's similarities to other primates, mammals, or vertebrates are not as essential as our similarity to all animals. So unless we have a specialized purpose, as biologists do, there is no need to mention these other similarities. Remember

that a definition is selective. Its purpose is to condense the information we have about a concept by stating only the fundamental facts.

Choosing the Differentia

The main thing to keep in mind when you look for a differentia is
that it should distinguish the referents of the concept from other
species in the same genus. It should name an attribute possessed by
all the referents of the concept, and not possessed by members of
the other species; this will ensure that the definition is neither too
broad nor too narrow (rule 2). And the attribute should be an essential one. You may be able to find many attributes shared by all the
referents, but you should not include them all unless they are all
necessary to distinguish the concept from other species in the
genus. Once again, a definition should be selective, so look for the
essential attribute (rule 3).

When we apply rule 2, we should keep in mind the possibility of
borderline cases. Suppose we're defining CITY. Cities are distinguished from other municipalities mainly on the basis of population.
Our definition should thus include any place large enough to be
considered a city, and exclude any place too small. A place with
1000 residents is obviously a village or town, while a metropolis of
2 million is clearly a city. But there is no sharp line between a large
town and a small city. So if we are not sure exactly what to include
in the concept CITY, how can we tell how broad or narrow our definition should be? The answer is two-fold. If we need a concept with
a precise borderline, as we may if we are taking a census, or doing
economic research, then we will have to stipulate a precise criterion
of population size, and turn the concept into a technical one. If we
do not have this specialized need for precision, then we should
define a city simply as a *large* municipality. The term "large" would
clearly include the metropolis of 2 million, it would clearly exclude
the village of 1000, and it would leave the borderline area unclear.
Thus it would match the content of the ordinary concept, including
the vague areas around the borders. In general, we can expect a definition to help clarify the borderlines of a concept, but we can't
expect it to eliminate vagueness that is inherent in the concept.

When we apply rule 3, there's another qualification to keep in
mind. As we have seen, an essential attribute is one that underlies
and explains other attributes of the referents. One of the goals of
science is to identify such attributes. But it is not always appropriate
to incorporate scientific theories when we define a concept for ordinary use. We can define water as the substance with the chemical
structure H_2O, because that chemical structure, which explains

many of the other properties of water, is so well established that it has become common knowledge. But it would *not* be appropriate to define man as the animal with the largest and most complex brain— even though it was the evolution of the brain that gave us our capacity for reason. The problem here is that the relationships between the brain and reason are not very well known yet; the available theories are speculative and incomplete, and it wouldn't serve our purpose to incorporate them into a definition. So the rule of essentiality must be qualified: the differentia should name the most essential attributes that are fairly well understood.

For the same reason, it is not a good idea to include controversial information in a definition. Our concepts, and the definitions we give them, provide the framework for thought and discussion. Ideally, the framework should be a neutral one, so that people on opposite sides of an issue can make use of the same concepts in presenting their arguments—and thus understand each other. We can't always achieve such neutrality, but it's a goal to aim at. I may be convinced, for example, that psychological depression results from repressed anxiety, but this theory about the unconscious cause of depression is still controversial. If I'm going to discuss the matter with a psychologist who rejects that theory, we should define depression in terms of properties we can agree on, such as the conscious feelings involved.

Double-checking the Results

Once we have found the genus and differentia, the final step is to test our definition. We should make sure that it is not circular, that it is not negative (unless the concept itself is a negative one), and that it does not use vague, obscure, or metaphorical language. And we should make an effort to find counter-examples. That is, we should look for things that are included in the concept but would be excluded by the definition: they would prove that the definition is too narrow. And we should look for things that are *not* included in the concept, but *would* be included by the definition; in that case, our definition is too broad. If we have looked for counterexamples and haven't found any, then we can be more confident that our definition is correct.

Applying the Technique

Now that we've reviewed the general procedure to follow in constructing a definition, let's see how it works in practice by trying to define the concept GAME. This is not an easy concept to define. Indeed, the philosopher Ludwig Wittgenstein argued, in a famous book, that GAME could not be defined because the many varieties of games do not share any one property that would distinguish them from everything else.

> Consider for example the proceedings that we call "games." I mean board-games, card-games, ball-games, Olympic games, and so on. What is common to them all? . . . [I]f you look at them you will not see something that is common to *all*, but similarities, relationships, and a whole series of them at that. . . . Are they all 'amusing'? Compare chess with noughts and crosses [tic-tac-toe]. Or is there always winning and losing, or competition between players? Think of patience [solitaire]. In ball-games there is winning and losing; but when a child throws his ball at the wall and catches it again, this feature has disappeared. Look at the parts played by skill and luck; and at the difference between skill in chess and skill in tennis. . . . And we can go through the many, many other groups of games in the same way; can see how similarities crop up and disappear. [Ludwig Wittgenstein, *Philosophical Investigations*]

Wittgenstein is certainly right that there are many different kinds of games, and that there are many differences among them. This shows that the concept GAME is fairly abstract. But does it show that the concept is indefinable? Let's take his argument as a challenge, and see whether we can come up with a definition.

As usual, we should start by looking for the genus. A game is a kind of human activity, so we need to contrast it with other human activities. The first thing that should occur to us is that games can be contrasted with work. There's a basic difference between working and playing; games belong in the second category. Of course, people sometimes describe their jobs as games, as in "I'm in the real estate game." But this is clearly a metaphor; it's intended to startle the listener precisely because a job is *not* literally a game. So games belong in the genus we've described as "play." To make it clear that we are talking about the leisure activities of adults as well as children, let's use the term *recreation*. What else does this genus include? In addition to games, RECREATION includes activities such as hobbies and pastimes, vacation traveling, and dancing. Our classification now looks like this:

This is probably not an exhaustive list of recreational activities (can you think of any others?). And of course recreation and work are not the only human activities. Among other things, we have left out family and social life. But this classification is enough for our purposes.

Before we turn to the differentia, let's pause to consider the nature of the genus we have isolated. Recreation is an activity, and so is work. Physiologically, both involve the expenditure of energy. The difference clearly has something to do with goals and rewards. It will help us to understand games if we explore this difference a little further. What goal does one pursue in work? Take a doctor as an example. In one respect, a doctor's goal is restoring people to health: that is the function of medicine. In another respect, a doctor's goal may be to make money, or to help people or to use his mind in solving problems. Notice that the first goal is common to all doctors: restoring health is a goal intrinsic to medicine, it is the *function* of medicine. On the other hand, the personal goals that doctors have are not intrinsic to medicine as a profession. They vary from one doctor to another; they're a matter of the individual's *motivation*. We could draw this same distinction between function and motivation in any line of work.

Now let's consider recreation. Here, too, personal motivation differs from one individual to another. Some people play to relax, some play to prove themselves; professional athletes and gamblers play for money. The common element in a given type of recreation, therefore, will have to be a goal intrinsic to the activity itself—analogous to the function of a given line of work. This is where the essential difference lies between work and recreation. In any type of work, the function is producing a good or service that has value in its own right, apart from the activity of producing it. In recreation, the intrinsic goal is not productive in that sense. The activity is an end in itself, something we do merely for the sake of doing it. This would be true even for a professional athlete. He is being paid to play the game, to create an exciting spectacle that other people want to see. In that sense he is working, not playing. But the game itself (football, golf, or whatever) is still a form of recreation because the goals internal to the game (getting a touchdown, sinking the putt) are not valuable in and of themselves. They have value only as elements in an activity that people value for its own sake.

Keeping all this in mind, let's try to find a differentia that will distinguish games from other types of recreation. In the passage quoted above, Wittgenstein emphasized the ways in which games differ from one another: some are played with cards, others with balls, others with boards; some are physical, some are mental; some involve mostly skill, others mostly luck. So none of these properties can serve as our differentia, which has to be a property common to all the referents. What about competition between players? Most games do have a competitive element, but this definition would still be too narrow, because some games do not involve competition. In the passage quoted above, Wittgenstein mentioned solitaire as a counterexample; jacks would be another. Couldn't we say, though, that in these cases we are competing against ourselves? We often do describe solitary games this way. The problem is that this description is metaphorical. If we took it literally, it would mean that you are your own opponent. If you are competing against yourself, and you win, who loses?

But let's not give up yet. When you play solitaire, you may not literally be competing, but it's still true that you can win or lose. That's because the rules of the game set a certain goal, such as turning up all the cards; if you achieve the goal, you win. Here we have something that looks like a universal property, and an essential one. What would a game be without *rules?* In every game, there is a set of rules that says what the goal is (the object of the game), and also says what means you can use to achieve the goal. This is what creates the challenge of a game, and leads us to use the metaphor of competing with ourselves. Even in competitive games, the existence of rules is a more essential attribute than competition, because the rules create the competition: they specify the number of players and the terms on which they will compete.

Our definition, then, might be stated as follows: *a game is a form of recreation constituted by a set of rules that specify an object to be attained and the permissible means of attaining it.* Notice the word "constituted" here. It was carefully chosen to convey the idea that the very structure of the game depends on the rules. Notice also that the differentia fits in well with our analysis of the genus. We saw that recreation should not be distinguished from work in terms of personal goals. Either activity can be done for fun or profit. They should be distinguished rather in terms of the goals intrinsic to the activities. And our differentia tells us where a game's internal goal comes from.

Let's test the definition by looking for counterexamples. Is it too broad? Would it include anything that is not a game? It's certainly true that other recreational activities are governed by rules. In skiing, there are traffic rules—you shouldn't bump into other people. In stamp collecting, there's a legal rule against stealing the stamps you want. But each of these rules is superimposed on an activity that could be done without them. They do not give the activity its goal; they merely impose external constraints on the means one can use. So these activities are not constituted by rules in the way our definition requires.

Is the definition too narrow? Would it exclude any games? What about Wittgenstein's example of the child throwing a ball against the wall and catching it? Well, in a sense, there is a rule here that specifies a goal and the permissible means: "Throw the ball against the wall and catch it before it bounces." That isn't much of a rule. But then, this isn't much of a game. It is not clear whether the child's activity satisfies our definition, but it's equally unclear whether the activity should be considered a game. What we have here is a borderline case, and as we have seen, we cannot demand that a definition have sharper boundaries than the concept it defines (unless we need to turn the concept into a technical one). All we can ask is that the definition include everything that is clearly a member of the concept, exclude everything that is clearly not a member, and leave the same set of borderline cases uncertain.

So far as I can see, therefore, our definition is a good one. You'll have to decide for yourself whether you agree—perhaps there is something I've overlooked. But regardless of whether we agree on the outcome, the process of reasoning behind it illustrates the technique to follow in defining a concept.

Practice Quiz

Define one of the following concepts: NEWSPAPER, FLATTERY, APART-MENT. Locate the concept in a genus-species hierarchy, find an essential attribute that distinguishes the concept from other species in the genus, and look for counterexamples. When you are satisfied that you have found the right genus and differentia, formulate your definition as concisely as possible in a sentence.

SUMMARY

A definition is a statement telling us what a concept means. Its function is to identify the referents of the concept, condense the knowledge we have about the referents, and relate the concept to other concepts.

A definition should mention the genus to which the concept belongs, and the essential attributes (the differentia) distinguishing the referents of the concept from those of other species in the same genus. A definition should be neither too broad nor too narrow. It should not be circular, or use negative terms unnecessarily, or use language that is unclear.

In constructing a definition, we should find the genus first, then look for a differentia that isolates the right class of referents and names their essential attributes, and finally double-check the result by looking for counterexamples and checking against the other rules.

Exercises

A. a) State which rule (or rules) is violated by each of the following definitions; and b) reformulate it so that it is a good definition of the italicized term.

1. An *army* is the branch of a country's military that uses tanks.
2. A *lamp* is a movable light source intended for indoor use and resting on the floor.
3. A *handshake* is when two people clasp each other's right hand.
4. A *genus* is the generic class to which the referents of a given concept belong.
5. A *disease* is a condition of an organism requiring medical attention.
6. A *craftsman* is someone who makes what he does look easy.
7. A *gullible* person is a person who can be fooled. (Note: this is not circular merely because "person" is repeated; we are trying to define GULLIBLE, not PERSON.)
8. *Thinking* is purposeful mental activity whose goal is to avoid error.
9. *Psychology* is the science that studies human behavior.
10. A *condominium* is a nonrented unit in a multi-unit residential building.
11. To *reform* is to improve an organization by changing its policy.
12. An *executive* is a person responsible for executing a policy.

B. The verbal form of a definition is often used for jokes, witty observations, or insights. Ten examples are given below. If these were intended as serious definitions, what rules would they violate?

1. "A gentleman is a person who never insults another person unintentionally." [Anonymous]
2. "Happiness is having a large, loving, caring, close-knit family in another city." [George Burns]
3. "Propaganda is the art of persuading others of what you don't believe yourself." [Abba Eban]
4. "Hypocrisy is the tribute that vice pays to virtue." [La Rochefoucauld]

5. "Old age is when the liver spots show through your gloves." [Phyllis Diller]
6. "Home is the place where, when you have to go there, they have to take you in." [Robert Frost]
7. "Conservative, n. A statesman who is enamored of existing evils, as distinguished from the Liberal, who wants to replace them with others." [Ambrose Bierce]
8. "What is a cynic? A man who knows the price of everything, and the value of nothing." [Oscar Wilde]
9. "A definition is the enclosing a wilderness of ideas within a wall of words." [Samuel Butler]
10. "Love means never having to say you're sorry." [Erich Segal]

C. Evaluate each of the following definitions. If you think it is faulty—in some cases, this will be a difficult and controversial decision—state what rule or rules you think it violates.

1. "A human being is an organism that can survive outside its mother's uterus." [Letter to the editor, *New York Times*, May 12, 1981]
2. "It is high time to expose this bandying of words to obfuscate the issues and to proclaim the basic meaning of 'liberal' in our political history. In simple terms, a 'liberal' is one who accepts the inevitability of change in government to best serve a dynamic society forever on the move." [Letter to the editor, *New York Times*, July 27, 1976]
3. "Poverty can be defined objectively and applied consistently only in terms of the concept of relative deprivation. . . . Individuals, families and groups in the population can be said to be in poverty when they lack the resources to obtain the types of diet, participate in the activities and have the living conditions and amenities which are customary, or are at least widely encouraged or approved, in the societies to which they belong." [Peter Townsend, *Poverty in the United Kingdom*]
4. "PROPEL: means 'apply a force to'; its object must be under a certain size and weight, but for our purposes we will say that any object is acceptable." [Roger Schank, "Representation and Understanding of Text," in *Machine Intelligence 8*]
5. "A crime is an act committed in violation of a law that prohibits it and authorizes punishment for its commission." [James Q. Wilson and Richard Herrnstein, *Crime and Human Nature*]
6. "Frankness is saying whatever is in our minds." [Richard C. Cabot, *The Meaning of Right and Good*]
7. "I define a free press as one that protects and, if need be, strengthens government of the people, by the people, and for

the people." [Walter Karp, "Forum: Can the Press Tell the Truth?" *Harpers Magazine*, January 1985]

8. "A democratic government has always meant one in which the citizens, or a sufficient number of them to represent more or less effectively the common will, freely act from time to time, and according to established forms, to appoint or recall the magistrates and to enact or revoke the laws by which the community is governed." [Carl Becker, *Modern Democracy*]

9. "Literature is the effort of man to indemnify himself for the wrongs of his condition." [Ralph Waldo Emerson, "Walter Savage Landor"]

10. "In fact, one can define an organization as a purposive structure of authority relations." [Charles E. Lindbloom, *Politics and Markets*]

11. "Thinking is a momentary dismissal of irrelevancies." [Buckminster Fuller, *Utopia or Oblivion*]

12. "I define science as the organization of our knowledge in such a way that it commands more of the hidden potential in nature." [Jacob Bronowski, *Science and Human Values*]

13. "Regulation [in the sense of government regulation of the economy] is simply the delegation, by the legislative branch, of law-making authority to an executive department." [Letter to the editor, *Reason*, January 1985]

14. "[An experiment is] an operation carried out under controlled conditions in order to discover an unknown effect or law, to test or establish a hypothesis, or to illustrate a known law." [*Webster's New Collegiate Dictionary*]

15. "A *tax* is a compulsory contribution from the person to the government to defray the expenses incurred in the common interest of all, without reference to special benefits conferred." [Edwin R. A. Seligman, *Essays in Taxation*]

D. In each set of sentences below, the italicized word is used in each sentence. Does it express the same concept in each sentence? Within each set, compare each sentence with every other sentence, and consider the following possibilities: the word expresses the same concept, the word expresses two different concepts, or the word in one sentence involves a metaphorical extension of the concept it expresses in the other.

1. a) Cotton clothes will *shrink* if put in the dryer.
   b) My *shrink* says I worry too much about being perfect.
2. a) It's my *party*, and I'll cry if I want to.
   b) Will the Wilson *party* please come forward—your table is ready.

3. a) I think I failed the trigonometry *test* today.
   b) I took my car in to have the battery *tested.*
   c) At a certain age, children misbehave to *test* their parents.
4. a) My history teachers always *stress* the importance of using primary sources.
   b) Between her job and her marital problems, Beth is subject to a lot of *stress.*
   c) Cast iron will break under *stress,* while wrought iron will bend.
5. a) The earth completes one *revolution* around the sun in 365 and ¼ days.
   b) The philosophy of natural rights played an important role in the *revolution* of the American colonies.
   c) "Glisten" is a *revolutionary* new hair care product.

E. Arrange the concepts below in a classification diagram, showing the species-genus relationships. Then define each concept.

TABLE, BED, FURNITURE, DESK, CHAIR

F. Define each of the following concepts.

1. BACHELOR
2. DIFFERENTIA
3. BORROW
4. COMPUTER
5. OBEY
6. JOURNALISM
7. NOVICE
8. JEALOUSY

G. Examine the following definitions of TERRORISM. Identify the similarities and differences among them, and decide which one you think is the best.

1. "Terrorism is the use of violence for political ends [including] any use of violence for the purpose of putting the public or any section of the public in fear." [British Government Terrorist Order]
2. "Terrorism is the deliberate and systematic murder, maiming, and menacing of the innocent to inspire fear for political ends." [Jonathan Institute]
3. "Terrorism is violence deliberately directed against civilians as the primary target for the purpose of demoralizing or extorting concessions from an enemy or attracting attention to a cause." [Letter to the editor, *New York Times*, April 6, 1986]

4. "Terrorism is defined as the unlawful use of force or violence against persons or property to intimidate or coerce a government, the civilian population or any segment thereof, in furtherance of political or social objectives." [FBI official definition]

5. "Terrorism has come to denote only one kind of violence— perpetuated sporadically by organizations and individuals who believe in coercive intimidation to further political or religious goals." [Letter to the editor, *New York Times*, July 8, 1985]

H. For each of the following sets of words, use what you know about definitions to explain the relationships among them. Decide which members of each set are synonymous, and explain the difference in meaning between nonsynonymous words.

1. Game, sport
2. Brave, bold, courageous
3. Hurt, offend, insult
4. Sincere, honest, frank
5. Educate, instruct, train
6. Idealist, crusader, zealot
7. Adorn, decorate, garnish
8. Seductive, tempting, attractive

I. Learning to distinguish what's essential from what is not essential will help make your writing more concise; and conversely, trying to write more concisely will help focus your mind on essentials. Here are two exercises to try:

1. Explain how to play a game such as tic-tac-toe or hearts to someone who has never heard of it, in the fewest possible words.
2. Write a letter to your parents or a friend, asking for money and explaining why you need it. Then rewrite the letter as a telegram that will cost you a dollar a word to send.

4

Propositions

In the last two chapters we studied concepts. In the rest of the book, we'll be concerned primarily with **propositions.** A proposition is a statement, an assertion. For example:

> A Buick is a car.
> Cars are vehicles.
> Most cars have four wheels.

You can see that these propositions all involve the concept CAR. The concept identifies a certain class of things; the propositions assert something about that class. Concepts give us an indispensable tool for thought and speech by grouping together similar objects, actions, properties, and relationships. But a concept by itself is not a complete thought, and a word by itself doesn't say anything. Concepts provide a framework, but the actual units of thought and speech are propositions.

An understanding of propositions is a vital skill in reasoning. When we take a position on an issue, we are asserting that a certain proposition is true. If we can't distinguish between propositions that are similar but not identical, then we don't really know what we believe, and we can't tell whether someone else's position contradicts our own. When we weigh the evidence for and against some conclusion, we need to use the principles of logic, and the principles of logic identify certain relations among propositions. In this chapter, we will study propositions—what they are, and how to tell them apart.

Propositions and Sentences

One essential feature of a proposition is that it is either true or false. If I utter the phrase, "The Empire State Building," I have named a certain structure in New York City. But the phrase is neither true nor false. It doesn't say anything; it's just a name. If I utter a sentence, however, like "The Empire State Building is over 1000 feet tall," then I *have* made a definite assertion. And even if you don't happen to know whether it is true or false, you know that it must be one or the other.

As this example illustrates, a proposition is normally expressed in a sentence. But not all sentences serve the purpose of making assertions. Interrogative sentences ask a question: "Have you finished your term paper yet?" Imperative sentences issue commands: "Finish your term paper!" The role of making an assertion is normally reserved for *declarative* sentences, the kind that end in a period. Declarative sentences assert (declare) that something is a fact. To assert a proposition, then, we need a declarative sentence, and that's the kind we'll be studying.

Each of the following is a declarative sentence:

Jack is a Baptist.
Some birds fly south for the winter.
I would like a Jaguar XJ-S for Christmas.

These three sentences make very different assertions, but they have the same basic structure. Each one has a *subject:* "Jack," "Some birds," and "I." And each one has a verb phrase ("is a Baptist," "fly south for the winter," and "would like . . . ") that tells us what the subject is or does. In grammar and logic, the verb phrase is usually called the *predicate.* A sentence must have this basic structure—subject and predicate—in order to be complete. A sentence may be *more* complex than this, as we will see, but it cannot be *less* complex. A subject without a predicate, or a predicate without a subject, is an incomplete sentence; it is a sentence *fragment.* Thus the following are all fragments:

Game.
The Pillsbury Dough Boy.
ran too fast for me to catch him.
was two blocks south of the library.

The first two examples might serve as subjects, the second two as predicates, but none of them, by itself, makes a statement.

To assert a proposition, therefore, we need a complete declarative sentence, with a subject and a predicate. But we can't equate propositions and sentences. A proposition is a thought, a sentence is the linguistic vehicle we use to express the thought—just as an individual word is the linguistic vehicle we use to express a concept. Two different sentences may express the same proposition, just as two different words may express the same concept. And a single sentence may express more than one proposition. We need to understand how this works.

Our goal is not to study language for its own sake, but to understand how it can be used to formulate and convey our thoughts. Our goal is to look past the surface complexities of language, in order to see what is really being said. We need to learn how to identify the propositions asserted by a given sentence, and how to tell when two sentences express the same proposition. In the next section, we'll see how individual words contribute to the meaning of a sentence, and how variations in the words it uses can affect the proposition it asserts. Then we'll turn to the grammatical structure of the sentence, and see how the rules of grammar allow us to formulate more and more complex sorts of thoughts.

Propositions and Word Meaning

Suppose we have two sentences that differ only in one word: "Jack is an *X*" and "Jack is a *Y*." If "*X*" and "*Y*" express the same concept, then these two sentences assert the same proposition; if the words express different concepts, then the sentences assert different propositions. That's the general rule, and it's often easy to apply. If the two words are synonyms, the resulting sentences make the same statement: Jack is a lawyer, Jack is an attorney. If the words are unrelated, the sentences obviously make different statements: Jack is *tall*, Jack is *married*. But there are other possibilities in between these extremes.

For example, the words might be related in a genus-species hierarchy. The three sentences

Jack is a Christian,
Jack is a Protestant, and
Jack is a Baptist.

express different propositions because the terms in the predicate—*Christian, Protestant,* and *Baptist*—are at different levels of abstraction. Each is a genus of the one below it, and a species of the one above it. The three statements do not place Jack in the same class of people: the class gets narrower and narrower as we go down the list.

Our study of definitions has shown us other, more subtle ways in which concepts can differ even though they are related. Consider the sentences

Basketball is a game, and
Basketball is a sport.

We know from our definition of GAME that it is not quite the same concept as SPORT, though the two are closely related. It's not that one is more abstract than the other; neither includes the other as a species. But they do not cover exactly the same class of activities. Some games are not sports (tic-tac-toe), and some sports are not games (hiking). The difference lies in the differentia we use to define the two concepts. Games are characterized by rules; we are contrasting games with less structured types of recreation. Sports are distinguished by their physical character; we are contrasting them with less strenuous types of recreation. Thus the test for whether two words express the same concept is: Do they pick out the same class of things? Do they isolate those things on the basis of the same distinguishing properties? To apply this test, we use the techniques of classification and definition.

Connotations

Two words that express the same concept are usually considered to be synonyms: "couch" and "sofa," "car" and "automobile," "own" and "possess," and so on. But sometimes words that express the same concept have different *connotations*. They convey different images or feelings, they elicit different associations in our minds, they express different attitudes. For example, in a letter of recommendation for a student, I could make the same point with either of two sentences:

Mary has a *firm command* of the subject matter.
Mary has a *good comprehension* of the subject matter.

These sentences assert the same proposition, because the italicized phrases express the same concept. But the first conveys the image of power and control over the material, whereas the second is more bland; it doesn't really convey any image at all. A good writer makes use of such differences in connotation to achieve a desired effect. But we shouldn't be misled by different connotations into thinking that different propositions have been asserted. This is especially important when the connotations involve strong positive or negative attitudes.

On the negative side, we have derogatory slang terms for racial and ethnic groups, or for professions. To pick two of the less offensive ones: "cop" used to be a derogatory term for a policeman; "shrink" is an impolite term for a psychotherapist. In each case, the slang term stands for exactly the same class of people as the more polite term, and expresses the same concept. The *only* difference is in connotation. On the positive side, the clearest examples are euphemisms. "Sanitary engineer" describes the same occupation as "garbage collector," but has a more dignified sound. In an earlier age, when people were more delicate in discussing bodily functions, it used to be said that animals *sweat*, men *perspire*, ladies *glisten.*

We need to be careful, though. Words that differ in connotation may also differ in literal meaning; they may not express the same concept. An unmarried couple who share the same address are sometimes described as *living together*, sometimes as *living in sin.* There's an obvious difference in meaning here: one phrase classifies the couple with sinners, the other does not. Again, the word "underprivileged" is often used to refer to the poor. And the two terms do pick out the same class of people: those who lack material wealth. But the word "poor" carries no implication about *why* they lack material wealth—it might be their own fault, society's fault, or bad luck—whereas "underprivileged" specifically implies that it is society's fault. So the two sentences

The Smiths are poor, and
The Smiths are underprivileged

assert slightly different propositions. Before we decide that two words differ merely in connotation, therefore, we should make sure that they do not also differ in literal meaning. We should ask whether they attribute different properties to their referents, or classify them in different ways.

Metaphors

A special problem arises in the case of metaphors. We have seen that a metaphor, such as "Life is a cabaret," is not appropriate in a definition. But metaphors are extremely valuable in other contexts, and we use them all the time. They allow us to make our language more colorful and interesting; they convey similarities and shades of meaning that would otherwise be difficult to express. For that very reason, however, it is often difficult to interpret a metaphorical sentence: to formulate in literal terms the proposition it asserts.

For example, when the poet says "My love is like a red, red rose," he is making a comparison. But in what respects? He is not making a biological comparison: he doesn't mean that he is dating a form of plant life. Presumably he means his love is beautiful—that is the literal meaning of the metaphor. Yet the two statements

My love is like a red, red rose, and
My love is beautiful

do not express quite the same proposition. "Beautiful" is a very abstract word. The point of this metaphor is to convey the particular *kind* of beauty she has: the dark and delicate, regal beauty of a red rose, not the more exotic beauty of an orchid, or the sturdier, sunnier beauty of a daffodil. And roses have thorns. So perhaps the poet also means to say that his love is prickly and temperamental. You can see that it would be extremely hard to find a literal statement that asserts exactly the same proposition.

Why do we have to find a literal translation? Why can't we just say that the poet is expressing the proposition: my love is like a red rose? Well, sometimes we *can* let it go at that. We can savor the metaphor without analyzing it. In the context of reasoning, however, where we are concerned with the logical relationships among propositions, a literal translation is usually necessary. To know how a given proposition is logically related to others, we have to know exactly what the proposition does and doesn't say. If two people are using metaphorical terms in an argument, we won't know whether they are really talking about the same issue until we formulate their positions in literal terms. In these situations, we have to interpret metaphors, and the only rule we have is a fairly vague one: we should give as full, sensitive, and reasonable an interpretation as we can.

Usually it is not difficult to find a reasonable interpretation. Few of the metaphors we encounter are as rich in meaning as the ones we find in poetry. For example, to describe something as a "Band-Aid solution" is to say that it doesn't solve the underlying problem, but is only a short-term or superficial cure. This is a one-dimensional metaphor, and is easily put into literal terms. Our language is also filled with "dead" metaphors: words so often used to express an idea metaphorically that they now contain that idea as part of their literal meaning. Thus we often speak of *grasping* a fact: "grasp" is a physical metaphor for the mental act of understanding, but it has been used so often that *understanding* is now considered one of the literal meanings of the word. In the same way, we often describe pains as *sharp*, people as *dense*, spicy food as *hot*, relationships as *stormy*, and so on. If you think about it, you can see that each of the italicized terms is based on a metaphor that is now incorporated into its literal meaning. In such cases, there is no need for interpretation at all.

In summary, the meaning of a sentence—the proposition it expresses—depends partly on the meanings of the words it contains. To identify word meanings, and to decide whether two words or phrases have the same meaning, we use the techniques of classification and definition to identify the concepts they express, and we ignore any further differences in connotation. And if a word or phrase is being used metaphorically, we will normally have to find a literal interpretation.

Practice Quiz

For each pair of sentences below, determine whether they express the same proposition.

   1. a) You have a lovely view from your window.
      b) You have a beautiful view from your window.

   2. a) Stealing is a sin.
      b) Stealing is a crime.

   3. a) Kim is not very bright.
      b) Kim is not dealing from a full deck.

   4. a) The elderly person ahead of me was doing about 25 mph.
      b) The geezer ahead of me was doing about 25 mph.

   5. a) Wendy is a journalist.
      b) Wendy works for a newspaper.

   6. a) George is a mellow individual.
      b) George is an unmotivated slob.

   7. a) The adversary's intelligence operative was terminated with extreme prejudice.
      b) The enemy spy was killed.

   8. a) Henry proposed to her.
      b) Henry asked her to marry him.

   9. a) It was a tense moment.
      b) It was an anxious moment.

  10. a) She is very nice.
      b) She is a breath of fresh air.

11. a) That remark was offensive.
    b) That remark was insulting.

12. a) I am angry at him.
    b) I'm so mad I could push a bead up his nose.

Propositions and Grammar

A sentence is made up of words, but if it is to have any meaning, the words cannot be put together randomly. They must be structured in a certain way, just as building materials—bricks, beams, pipes, and shingles—must be put together in a certain way to make a house. The rules of grammar tell us how to put words together, as a blueprint tells us how to assemble a building. A mastery of grammar allows us to formulate a thought clearly, no matter how complex or subtle it is, and to express the thought in a way that allows other people to share and appreciate it. In this section, we'll look at some of the ways in which the grammatical structure of a sentence affects the propositions it can express.

We've seen that it is possible to change the words in a sentence without changing the proposition it asserts. We can also change the grammatical structure without changing the proposition. For example:

Jane did better than Tom on the test.
Tom did worse than Jane on the test.

"Jane" is the subject of the first sentence, while "Tom" is the subject of the second. But the sentences obviously describe the same relationship between them. Logically, they are equivalent; they assert the same proposition. In the same way, the two sentences

The Mets beat the Red Sox, and
The Red Sox were beaten by the Mets

are logically equivalent. The first is in the active voice, the second in the passive; but they describe the same action.

For our purposes, the more important fact about grammar is that it allows us to assert more than one proposition in a single sentence. This is true even of the simplest type of sentence, which contains a single subject and predicate, because we can use adjectives and other modifiers to incorporate additional information. Suppose someone says, "We live in a red house near the lake." The statement contains the following information:

1) We live in a house.
2) The house is red.
3) The house is near the lake.

Each of these is a proposition asserted by the sentence, and the speaker is saying that each proposition is true.

It is possible to construct much more complex sentences, using conjunctions (and, or, but), relative clauses (which, who), and other grammatical devices. Here is a sentence along with its breakdown into constituent propositions:

> The Democratic Party, which lost control of the Senate in 1980, regained control six years later in a surprising victory, winning seats in areas that normally vote conservative, such as the West and Midwest.

1) The Democratic Party lost control of the Senate in 1980.
2) The Democratic Party gained control of the Senate in 1986.
3) The victory in 1986 was surprising.
4) Democrats won seats in areas that normally vote conservative.
5) The West normally votes conservative.
6) The Democrats won seats in the West.
7) The Midwest normally votes conservative.
8) The Democrats won seats in the Midwest.

Once again, the sentence asserts each of these propositions. If the sentence is true, then (1)-(8) must be true as well, and vice versa. The original sentence is a much more economical way of presenting the information, but it is logically equivalent to the constituent propositions, taken as a set.

When we encounter a complex sentence like the one above, how do we identify the constituent propositions? The best approach is to imagine that we are the ones making the statement, and to ask: what are we committing ourselves to? What has to be true for the statement as a whole to be true? How many distinct facts are involved? Or we can imagine that someone else has made the statement, and think of all the possible ways of challenging it. Think of all the propositions which, if they were false, would undercut the statement as a whole. Either way, you will need to use your understanding of grammar to apply the technique. It would take a separate book to describe all the grammatical devices we can use, and all the rules for using them properly. But we should consider three points that are especially important for logic.

Restrictive and Nonrestrictive Clauses

A clause is a grammatical unit containing a subject and predicate. Every sentence, therefore, contains at least one clause. But a sentence may also contain one or more subordinate clauses that modify words in the main clause. For example, in the sentence

1) The Japanese, who eat lots of fish, have fewer heart attacks,

the subject of the main clause ("The Japanese") is modified by the clause "who eat lots of fish." A subordinate clause normally asserts a proposition in addition to the one asserted by the main clause. But this is not always true, as we can see by comparing (1) with

2) The Japanese who eat lots of fish have fewer heart attacks.

What is the difference between these sentences? Well, in (2), the subordinate clause restricts the reference of the term "Japanese" to a certain subclass of the Japanese people: those who eat lots of fish. As a result, we are making a single statement about that subclass, and we are not making any statement about the Japanese people as a whole. We could diagram the statement as follows:

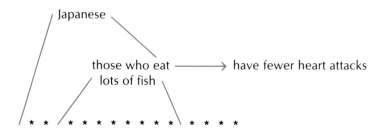

In (1), on the other hand, the commas tell us that the clause introduces a separate point, and does *not* restrict the reference of the subject term. So (1) makes two statements: that the Japanese (all of them) have fewer heart attacks, and that the Japanese (all of them, again) eat lots of fish. Thus:

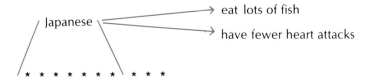

It's clear that the presence or absence of the commas makes a big difference to the meaning of the sentence, even though all the words are the same. A clause like (2) is called a *restrictive* clause, because it restricts the reference of the term it modifies; (1) is called a *nonrestrictive* clause. This distinction applies primarily to clauses introduced by "who" and "which," so when we encounter them, we need to ask whether the clauses are restrictive or nonrestrictive.

Conjunctions

The easiest way of combining propositions within a single sentence is to use a conjunction. In the sentence "Jack and Jill went up the hill," the conjunction "and" joins two subjects to make two statements: that Jack went up the hill, and that Jill went up the hill. We can do the same thing with predicates, as in "Jack fell down, and broke his crown," or with two complete sentences:

[Jack fell down and broke his crown] *and* [Jill came tumbling after].

When we join two complete sentences, the result is a compound sentence which we can represent symbolically as "*p and q*," where the letters *p* and *q* stand for the separate components. Thus each of the following sentences is an example of the structure *p and q*:

[Roses are red] and [violets are blue].
[Nothing works any more] and [nobody cares].
[I'm okay] and [you're okay].
[I'm okay] and [you're a cockroach].

In all these cases we have two propositions asserted in a single compound sentence. In logic, *p and q* is treated as a distinct proposition, above and beyond *p* and *q*—even though the compound proposition is nothing more than the sum of its parts. The reason is that with other conjunctions, the resulting compound proposition *does* say something more than the sum of its parts. Consider the sentence

[I went to the kitchen] because [I was hungry].
p because *q*.

This statement asserts that I went to the kitchen, it asserts that I was hungry, *and* it asserts that there is a certain relationship between these facts: my hunger was the cause or reason for going to the kitchen. Thus the conjunction "because" gives us additional information, over and above the sum of the components. As a result, we are really asserting three propositions: *p*, *q*, and *p because q*.

Here are some other examples of the same thing:

1) *p*, but *q*.
2) Although *p*, *q*.
3) *p* before *q*.
4) *p* after *q*.
5) *p* while *q*.

In each case, the sentence asserts *p*, it asserts *q*, and it asserts that there is a certain relationship between *p* and *q*. In (1) and (2), the relationship is one of contrast or seeming conflict. These sentences say that *p* and *q* are both true even though they may seem incompatible. In (3), (4), and (5), the compound proposition asserts that there is a *time* relationship between *p* and *q*.

Let's consider, finally, two other conjunctions that are extremely important in logic.

6) If *p*, then *q*.
7) *p* or *q*.

Like the previous conjunctions, *if* and *or* assert that a certain relationship exists between the component propositions. Unlike the previous ones, however, these sentences do *not* assert that the component propositions are true. The sentence "If my cat could talk, I'd be ruined" does not assert that my cat can talk, nor does it assert that I am ruined; all it says is that *if* the first were true, the second would be true as well. Similarly, the sentence "Either my cat is talking, or I am hearing things" does not assert that my cat is talking, nor does it assert that I am hearing things; all it says is that one or the other of these propositions must be true. In both (6) and (7), therefore, only one proposition, the compound one, is actually being asserted.

The conjunctions *if* and *or* reveal something important about the way language functions. When we make a statement, we are asserting something. But if the statement is a complex one, involving more than a single proposition, we may not actually be asserting *all* the propositions. A complex sentence may *express* a proposition without *asserting* it. So we have to modify our rule for breaking a sentence down into its constituent propositions. In addition to the propositions it asserts to be true, we need to consider the propositions it expresses but does not assert—like *p* and *q* in a sentence of the form *if p, then q*. Let's turn now to another example of the same distinction.

Noun Clauses

Suppose you are discussing a candidate for public office, and someone mentions the candidate's unusual religious affiliation. You
might find yourself saying:

The fact [that Johnson is a Druid] is irrelevant.

The phrase within the brackets is called a noun clause. Like any
clause, it contains a subject ("Johnson") and a predicate ("is a
Druid"). Unlike the clauses we considered earlier, however, it
doesn't modify the subject of the main clause. It *is* the subject. The
noun clause turns the sentence "Johnson is a Druid" into the subject of a longer, more complex sentence. As a result, you have
asserted two propositions. You have asserted that Johnson is a
Druid (if you're saying this is a fact, then you're saying that it is
true). And you have asserted that this fact is irrelevant. On the
other hand, suppose you had said:

It is irrelevant [whether Johnson is a Druid].

Once again, the bracketed words are a noun clause. You are still
expressing two propositions, and still asserting that Johnson's religion is irrelevant. But this time you are *not* asserting that Johnson is
a Druid. The word "whether" implies that you are leaving this as an
open question.

A noun clause can also occur in the predicate of a sentence. It
will still express a proposition, but once again the proposition may
or may not be asserted. Compare these two sentences:

1) The president knows that war is imminent, and
2) The president believes that war is imminent.

In both cases we are making an assertion about the president. In
both cases we use a noun clause, "that war is imminent," to convey
what it is that the president knows or believes. And in both cases
the noun clause expresses a proposition. The difference is that (1)
asserts the proposition, while (2) does not.

If we say the president *knows* that war is imminent, we imply that
the imminence of war is a fact. You can't know what isn't so. In sentence (1), therefore, we are not only attributing a certain view to
the president, we are also endorsing his view as correct. So we are
making two assertions; one about the president, the other about
war. In (2), on the other hand, we are *not* endorsing the president's
view. The word "believes" does not carry this implication. Even if

we happen to agree with him, we are not committing ourselves. So in this case we are not asserting the proposition expressed by the noun clause. The only thing we're asserting is the proposition that the president does have this belief.

Notice that the difference between (1) and (2) results from the verbs we used: "knows" versus "believes." The English language contains a large class of verbs that we use to describe what people say and think. We can classify these verbs on the basis of whether or not they imply the endorsement of what is said or thought. Thus:

$$X \begin{cases} \text{believes} \\ \text{said} \\ \text{argued} \\ \text{is convinced} \\ \text{suspected} \end{cases} \text{that } p. \quad X \begin{cases} \text{knows} \\ \text{acknowledged} \\ \text{proved} \\ \text{is aware} \\ \text{realized} \end{cases} \text{that } p.$$

In the column on the left, we are making an assertion about X, but we are not asserting p. We mention p only to describe X's thought or statement. In the column on the right, however, we *are* asserting p. In addition to the statement about X, we are committing ourselves to the truth of p.

In the study of grammar, the distinction we have just drawn between these two classes of verbs would be a fairly minor one, hardly worth belaboring. In the study of *argument*, however, it is crucial to know whether a speaker is endorsing a given proposition as one of his own premises, or merely reporting that someone else accepts that proposition. We will begin our analysis of arguments in the next chapter. Meanwhile, we can summarize the material we have studied in this section in the form of two basic points. First, a single sentence may contain more than one proposition, so we need to break complex sentences down into their constituent propositions. Second, when we do so, we need to distinguish between the propositions that are asserted and those that are expressed but not asserted.

Practice Quiz

For each of the following sentences, identify the propositions it expresses; then determine which of them are asserted.

1. John acknowledged that he had made a mistake.
2. I would like a Jaguar XJ-S for Christmas, but I haven't been good this year.

3. If Deborah takes the new job, she will make more money.
4. I met a man who had only one shoe.
5. I met George McGovern, who ran for president in 1972.
6. The Greek philosopher Democritus believed that all objects are made of atoms.
7. Many insects communicate by means of chemical substances, known as pheromones.
8. Although Miss Devon, the district attorney, did not have enough evidence to convict the thief, she knew that he was guilty.
9. After a harsh editorial appeared in the student newspaper, the president of the college said that students should be seen but not heard.
10. Because he is a living organism, man is mortal; because he is rational, he is aware of his mortality.

SUMMARY

The units of thought are propositions. A proposition is a statement; it makes an assertion that is either true or false. A proposition is normally expressed in a declarative sentence containing a subject and a predicate, but two different sentences may assert the same proposition, and a single sentence may assert more than one proposition.

To identify the proposition or propositions asserted by a sentence, we must consider both the meanings of the words composing the sentence, and the grammatical structure of the sentence. In this context, two words have the same meaning if they express the same concept, even if they differ in connotation. If a word or phrase is being used metaphorically, we must find a literal interpretation in order to determine what proposition is being asserted.

It is possible to vary the grammatical structure of a sentence without changing the proposition it asserts. Grammatical devices such as conjunctions, restrictive and nonrestrictive clauses, and noun clauses also allow us to combine more than one proposition into a single complex sentence. To break a complex sentence down into its components, we identify the propositions which the sentence asserts to be true as well as the propositions it expresses without asserting.

Exercises

A. For each of the following sentences, find another sentence that will express the same proposition (or propositions). You may change the words, or the grammatical structure, or both, so long as the meaning is preserved.

1. Joanne and Bob met for lunch.
2. The dog fell asleep on the couch.
3. It probably won't rain today.
4. John bought his stereo at a 50% discount.
5. Shakespeare was both a poet and a playwright.
6. *Out of Africa* was a good movie, but the pace was too slow.
7. Since Wednesday is a holiday, the mail will not be delivered.
8. All men are created equal.
9. If I move to Chicago, where my family lives, I will be able to see them more often.
10. John Calvin said that people are innately evil, but I don't believe him.

B. The following statements are from accident reports that people have filed with insurance companies. Identify the propositions asserted in each one.

1. "A pedestrian hit me and went under my car."
2. "I collided with a stationary truck coming the other way."
3. "I pulled away from the side of the road, glanced at my mother-in-law, and headed over the embankment."
4. "The pedestrian had no idea which direction to go, so I ran over him."
5. "As I approached the intersection, a stop sign suddenly appeared in a place where no stop sign had ever appeared before."
6. "I told the police that I was not injured but on removing my hat, I found that I had a fractured skull."
7. "An invisible car came out of nowhere, struck my vehicle, and vanished."
8. "Coming home, I drove into the wrong house and collided with a tree I don't have."
9. "The indirect cause of this accident was a little guy in a small car with a big mouth."
10. "The accident happened when the right front door of a car came around the corner without giving a signal."

C. For each word below, find two other words that express the same concept, one with a more positive connotation, the other with a more negative connotation. If you were given "elderly person," for example, you might complete the series as follows:

| *Positive* | *Neutral* | *Negative* |
| senior citizen | elderly person | geezer |

You may use metaphors as well as literal terms.

1. Government official
2. Communist country
3. Deceased person
4. Overeating
5. Dirty
6. Prostitute
7. Elated
8. Businessman
9. Married
10. Mentally retarded

D. For each of the following sets of propositions, write a single sentence in which all the propositions are asserted. You may reword them so long as you do not change the meaning.

1. John ran seven miles yesterday. John has been practicing for the marathon. John did not find the run very strenuous.
2. Professor Nash holds that Tupperware was invented by Neanderthal man. The view that Tupperware was invented by Neanderthal man is not widely accepted by anthropologists. Professor Nash is an anthropologist at Ellipse University.
3. Opposites are usually not attracted to each other. Lauren loves opera. George hates opera. Lauren and George have been happily married for ten years.
4. Freedom of speech is a necessary component of a democracy. Ruritania censors newspapers. If freedom of speech is a necessary component of a democracy, then a country that censors newspapers is not a democracy.
5. The law generally holds a manufacturer responsible for harm caused by its product. If the manufacturer warns a buyer that a product is dangerous, the law will not hold the manufacturer responsible for harm. If a buyer is harmed by a product through the buyer's own negligence, the law will not hold the manufacturer responsible for the harm.

E. The following passages are very repetitive. Determine how many distinct propositions each one asserts; then rewrite it so that each proposition is asserted only once.

1. The problem with Hamlet is that he is very indecisive. He can't seem to make up his mind about anything. He's always thinking

about what he should do, but he never does it. He seems unwilling to make a decision, to take a stand. He wanders around pulling his hair out, and nothing ever comes of it.

2. The soul is immortal. It does not die, but lives forever. It existed before birth, and will continue to exist after death. It is completely indestructible. There is nothing that can make it go out of existence. The soul exists forever, and cannot be destroyed. It is therefore separate from the body. The soul is one thing, the body another. The body dies; the soul lives forever. They are utterly distinct.

3. "The object of this Essay is to assert one very simple principle, as entitled to govern absolutely the dealings of society with the individual in the way of compulsion and control, whether the means used be physical force in the form of legal penalties, or the moral coercion of public opinion. That principle is, that the sole end for which mankind are warranted, individually or collectively, in interfering with the liberty of action of any of their number, is self-protection. That the only purpose for which power can be rightfully exercised over any member of a civilized community, against his will, is to prevent harm to others. . . . The only part of the conduct of any one, for which he is amenable to society, is that which concerns others. In the part which merely concerns himself, his independence is, of right, absolute. Over himself, over his own body and mind, the individual is sovereign." [John Stuart Mill, *On Liberty*]

F. For each of the following passages, list all the propositions it expresses; then indicate which are asserted by the speaker, and which are not.

1. "Man is born free, and everywhere he is in chains." [Jean-Jacques Rousseau, *The Social Contract*]
2. "Last night I dreamt I went to Manderley again." [Daphne du Maurier, *Rebecca*]
3. "Happy families are all alike; every unhappy family is unhappy in its own way." [Leo Tolstoy, *Anna Karenina*]
4. "Blessed are the poor in spirit: for theirs is the kingdom of heaven.
   Blessed are they that mourn: for they shall be comforted.
   Blessed are the meek: for they shall inherit the earth." [*Gospel According to St. Matthew*]
5. "It is a truth universally acknowledged, that a single man in possession of a good fortune, must be in want of a wife." [Jane Austen, *Pride and Prejudice*]

6. "I come to bury Caesar, not to praise him.
   . . . The noble Brutus
   Hath told you Caesar was ambitious;
   If it were so, it was a grievous fault,
   And grievously hath Caesar answer'd it."
   [William Shakespeare, *Julius Caesar*]
7. "But not only has the bourgeoisie forged the weapons that bring death to itself; it has also called into existence the men who are to wield those weapons—the modern working class— the proletarians." [Karl Marx and Friedrich Engels, *Manifesto of the Communist Party*]
8. "Men fear Death, as children fear to go in the dark; and as that natural fear in children is increased with tales, so is the other." [Francis Bacon, "Of Death," *Essays*]
9. "I went to the woods because I wished to live deliberately, to front only the essential facts of life, and see if I could not learn what it had to teach. . . ." [Henry Thoreau, *Walden*]
10. "We hold these truths to be self-evident: that all men are created equal; that they are endowed by their Creator with certain inalienable rights; that among these rights are life, liberty, and the pursuit of happiness; that to secure these rights, governments are instituted among men, deriving their just powers from the consent of the governed. . . ." [*Declaration of Independence*]

G. People who conduct opinion polls try to word their questions as neutrally as possible, so that positive or negative connotations won't bias the response. The three questions below were used during 1979 to measure opinions about the energy shortages that occurred at that time. Which do you think is the most neutral?

1. "Do you think the shortage of oil we hear about is real or are we just being told there are shortages so oil companies can charge higher prices?" (CBS/*New York Times*)
2. "President Carter has told us that we are running out of oil. Do you think things are as bad as the president said, or do you think things are not as bad as all that?" (CBS/*New York Times*)
3. "Some people say there is a real shortage of gasoline and fuel oil because demand has outrun the supply. Others say there really isn't a shortage of gasoline and fuel oil and the big companies are holding it back for their own advantage. What do you think—that there is or is not a real shortage of gasoline and oil?" (Roper)

H. Suppose that you are an attorney representing someone (X) who is suing someone else (Y) for fraud, and suppose that the legal definition of fraud is as follows:

> Fraud consists of a misrepresentation of existing fact upon which the defendent [Y] intends that the plaintiff [X] will rely, and upon which the plaintiff justifiably relies to his detriment.

How many distinct propositions would you have to prove in order to win your case?

PART TWO

Arguments

In this part, we begin our study of reasoning. Reasoning is concerned with the *truth* of propositions; its goal may be to *discover* whether a given proposition is true, or to *justify* one's belief that it is true, or to *explain* why it is true, or to *persuade* someone else of its truth. In all of these cases, reasoning makes use of logical relationships among propositions, and we analyze and evaluate reasoning by identifying those relationships.

Chapter 5 will cover the basic unit of reasoning, which in logic is called an argument. We'll learn how to identify the premises and the conclusion of an argument, how to analyze its logical structure, and how to evaluate it. Chapter 6 is concerned with fallacies—spurious arguments in which the premises do not really provide evidence for the conclusion, although they may appear to do so. We are going to review some of the more common fallacies, and learn how to spot them in everyday thought and speech. In Chapter 7 we will look at more complex arguments, and study some of the finer points of analyzing and evaluating them.

5

Basic Argument Analysis

Here is a miscellaneous list of propositions:

1) It is raining outside.
2) It is not raining outside.
3) I was born in the year____. [Fill in the blank]
4) Thomas Jefferson was the first president of the United States.
5) Rivers in Taiwan flow uphill.
6) A person who is extremely sarcastic probably feels inadequate.
7) The government should restrict ownership of handguns.

By the criteria that we studied in the last chapter, each of these is a proposition in good standing: it expresses a complete thought, in a complete sentence. But they are not all true. Thomas Jefferson was *not* the first president, rivers in Taiwan do *not* flow uphill—(4) and (5) are both false. How do we tell whether a proposition is true? In many cases, we have to rely on *reasoning*. We have to look for evidence, pro and con.

Reasoning

To understand the need for reasoning, let's go down the list, starting with proposition (1).

Obviously I can't know whether it's raining where you are, now, as you read this. But you can tell by direct *observation*, the evidence of your own senses. We rely on observation for much of our knowledge about the places we live, the people we know, the events we take part in. But this category, however broad, represents only a fraction of what we know. Think of your experience as a window on the world. No matter how much you've seen and done, only a small portion of the world has passed before your window. For every fact you've observed directly, you know a great many things that you haven't observed. How?

Consider proposition (3). How do you know what year you were born? Obviously you did not witness your own birth. You know what year it was because your parents told you. They *did* have direct experience of the event, and you trust what they told you. Proposition (4) is a more complex example of the same thing. Since you were not alive during Jefferson's presidency, how do you know that he was not the first president? You learned from a history teacher or a textbook or a reference work that Washington was the first president, Jefferson the third. Of course, neither your teacher nor the authors of those books witnessed Jefferson's presidency, any more than you did. But they learned about it from other people, who learned about it from still other people, extending back in a chain to people who were alive in 1800 and kept records of events at that time. A great deal of our knowledge comes from other people in this way. Because we can communicate what we experience, human beings can merge their separate windows into one giant window.

Still, much of the world lies beyond even that window. We have knowledge that transcends the collective experience of human beings in general. We know things about the origins of our planet, the reaches of outer space, the inner life of atoms—none of which has been directly observed by anyone. We know these things by *reasoning.* When we reason, we are using relationships among propositions to push our knowledge beyond the limits of what we can experience directly.

In some cases, two propositions are related in such a way that if one is true, the other must be false; they are incompatible. Look at (1) and (2) again. I don't know which of these propositions is true, in your locality, at the moment you are reading this. But I do know that (1) and (2) cannot both be true; it can't be raining and not raining at the same time, in the same place. The two propositions *contradict* each other. Propositions may also have the opposite relationship: if one is true, the other must be true as well. In that case, one proposition supports the other and provides evidence for it. As examples of this relationship, consider the last three propositions on the list.

We all know that rivers in Taiwan do not flow uphill; proposition (5) is false. But few of us have actually been to Taiwan and observed the rivers there, or even talked to people who have seen them. That doesn't matter. We know from experience that the fluid character of water makes it flow in the direction of the forces acting on it, and we know that the primary force is gravity, which pulls water downward. These are general principles that apply everywhere, and they imply that rivers in Taiwan must behave like rivers in our own environment. We know that (5) is false, even though we've never observed Taiwanese rivers, because it contradicts general principles that *are* based on experience.

What about proposition (6)? Is it true or false that extremely sarcastic people usually feel inadequate? This is more speculative than the previous example; most of us would have to stop and think about it. We might sort through the people we know, picking out the ones who are highly sarcastic, and asking whether they strike us as people who feel inadequate. Or we might go to the library and see whether psychologists have done any studies on the question. Or it might occur to us that sarcasm often expresses hostility, and that unprovoked hostility often stems from feelings of inadequacy. But no matter which line of thought we pursue—and ideally we should weigh *all* the evidence—we would decide whether (6) is true or false by relating it logically to knowledge we already have.

Proposition (7), finally, is one side of a controversial political issue. In this case, unlike the previous two examples, people tend to have strong opinions for or against the proposition, and they often argue about it. For that very reason, questions of truth and falsity may seem inappropriate here. But they *are* appropriate. When people argue about gun control, they are not merely voicing personal preferences. They are trying to show that their position is true. An advocate of gun control will try to show that there's no other way to achieve some value such as reducing crime. An opponent of gun control will try to show that it contradicts some principle such as the right of self-defense. Either way, the goal is to support one's position by citing reasons.

Premise, Conclusion, and Argument

These examples involve different types of reasoning, but they also illustrate a common pattern. In each case we are trying to establish the truth of some proposition: that water runs downhill in Taiwan, that extremely sarcastic people feel inadequate, that the government should (or should not) restrict ownership of handguns. In logic, this proposition is called the **conclusion**. And in each case we support the conclusion by appealing to other propositions that we take as given. These are called **premises**. In the first example, the premises were the law of gravity and the fluid character of water. In the last example, the premise used by advocates of gun control was the proposition that restricting gun ownership would reduce crime, and the premise used by opponents was the proposition that people have a right to self-defense. Considered by itself, a proposition is neither a premise nor a conclusion. Just as a concept is a genus or a species only in relation to other concepts, a proposition is a premise or a conclusion only in relation to other propositions.

A set of premises together with a conclusion is called an **argument.** In everyday speech, this term is often used to mean a quarrel between two people. But it is also used to mean an appeal to evidence in support of a conclusion, as when we say "John argued that charging admission for the concert would exclude too many people." In logic, we use the term *argument* in the latter sense. It means a set of propositions in which some (the premises) are asserted as support or evidence for another (the conclusion). In this chapter, we will study the basic techniques for analyzing and evaluating arguments. Before we turn to analysis and evaluation, however, let's consider how we can *recognize* an argument when we encounter it.

Recognizing Arguments

When we listen to someone speak, or read a written text, we take in a sequence of statements. And we expect there to be some relationship among the statements, some organizing principle or structure. The relation of premise and conclusion is only one such principle. In a narrative passage, there is usually no argument; the author is describing a sequence of events, and the organizing principle is the order of their occurrence. In a descriptive passage, the author states a series of facts about something; the series may be organized in various ways, but again there is usually no argument. What distinguishes an argument from these other patterns is the effort to back up a statement logically. The author is not just telling us something that he takes to be true; he also presents *reasons* to convince us that it *is* true, or to explain *why* it is true. This intention is usually signaled by certain verbal clues. For example, the word "therefore" indicates that a statement is intended as a conclusion. The word "because" usually indicates a premise.

There are many such *indicator* words in English. Here is a list of the more common ones:

Premise indicators	*Conclusion indicators*
Since	Therefore
Because	Thus
As	So

For	Consequently
Given that	As a result
Assuming that	It follows that
Inasmuch as	Hence
The reason is that	Which means that
In view of the fact that	Which implies that

When you encounter such words, it is a good sign that you are in the presence of an argument, and you can use the indicators to distinguish the premises from the conclusion.

But you cannot use them mechanically. Some of the words are used in contexts other than argument. In the statement "Since I arrived in Dry Gulch, I haven't seen a single green thing," the word "since" indicates a temporal relation, not a logical one. On the other hand, the absence of indicator words does not necessarily mean the absence of an argument. If I say "Dry Gulch is an arid place—I haven't seen a single green thing," I am offering evidence in support of a conclusion, even though I used no indicator words. Remember that we are not interested in language per se. An argument is a relationship among propositions, and we are interested in that relationship, regardless of whether it is made explicit by means of indicator words. So the fundamental technique for recognizing arguments is to read carefully, asking what point the author is trying to make, isolating the propositions asserted, and identifying the relationships among them. Let's go over a few examples.

Here is a passage from a newspaper account of a speech President Reagan made in 1984: "'The truth is,' Mr. Reagan said, 'politics and morality are inseparable, and as morality's foundation is religion, religion and politics are necessarily related. We need religion as a guide.'" [*New York Times*, August 24, 1984] There are three propositions here: (1) politics and morality are inseparable; (2) morality's foundation is religion; and (3) religion and politics are necessarily related. The final sentence is essentially a restatement of (3). Do we have an argument? Well, the word "as" indicates that (2) is intended as a premise. The word "necessarily" suggests that (3) is a conclusion. It means: if you accept (1) and (2), you *have* to accept (3). So in essence the president is saying: politics depends on morality, morality depends on religion, therefore politics depends on religion. That's an argument.

Let's try a more difficult example. The following passages are from Alexis de Tocqueville's classic work, *Democracy in America*:

[1] In America the principle of the sovereignty of the people is neither barren nor concealed, as it is with some other nations; it is recog-

nized by the customs and proclaimed by the laws; it spreads freely, and arrives without impediment at its most remote consequences.

[2] In America the people appoint the legislative and the executive power and furnish the jurors who punish all infractions of the laws. The institutions are democratic, not only in their principle, but in all their consequences. . . . The people are therefore the real directing power.

Both passages express the same basic idea: that America is a democratic country. And both are concerned with the same aspect of democracy: the principle that the people are sovereign, that government is by consent of the governed. The first passage asserts this idea without argument. The three propositions separated by semicolons are not related as premises and conclusion; they are three different aspects of the same point, three ways of saying how pervasive the democratic principle is. In the second passage, however, we do find an argument. The word "therefore" in the last sentence indicates that the author is trying to establish a conclusion: the people are the real directing power. And he states several premises to support that conclusion. The people elect the legislative branch (Congress) and the executive (the president), and they serve as jurors in criminal trials. These premises are not introduced by indicator words, but the author is clearly citing them as evidence for his thesis.

So far I have asked you to distinguish arguments from nonarguments in a basically intuitive way, with some help from indicator words. The distinction will become easier to draw as you learn more about the inner workings of arguments—a topic we will turn to next.

Practice Quiz

For each of the following paragraphs, determine whether it contains an argument. If so, identify the premises and the conclusion.

1. Cable television can provide the viewer with more channels than broadcast television, and it usually delivers a higher quality picture. For these reasons, the number of cable subscribers will probably continue to grow rapidly.
2. The first cable companies served remote rural communities. These communities were too far from any broadcast station to receive a clear signal over the air. Tall towers, usually located on hills, picked up the signals and distributed them to individual homes.
3. Since the first cable companies increased the TV stations' audience

and their advertising revenues, broadcasters doubtless welcomed the growth of the new industry.

4. Now that cable companies are serving the suburbs and cities, they pose a competitive challenge to broadcast television.

5. Nearly half the homes in the country subscribe to cable television. Basic cable service usually includes local TV channels, such as the three networks, and one or more news channels. For an additional fee, subscribers can also receive movie channels and other specialized programs.

6. It is rarely economical for two companies to lay cables in the same area and compete directly. This suggests that cable television is a natural monopoly, and should be regulated by the government.

7. On the other hand, cable competes with broadcast TV, satellite TV, and other media. And as a medium of communication, it is protected by the First Amendment. So perhaps it should not be regulated.

Diagramming Arguments

We could think of the premises as the raw materials for an argument, and the conclusion as the final product. To understand an argument, we need to know what happens in between—on the factory floor, so to speak. We need to understand the inner workings of the argument, the individual steps that lead from premises to conclusion. To isolate these individual steps, we use a diagramming method that employs just two symbols, but is flexible enough to handle arguments of any complexity.

The Diagramming Method

One symbol is an arrow pointing from premise to conclusion. This represents a single step in reasoning; it represents the relationship between a premise and the conclusion that is inferred from it directly. Suppose you argued against gun control on the ground that it would violate the right of self-defense. Then your reasoning could be diagrammed as follows:

Restricting handgun ownership would violate the right of self-defense.

$$\downarrow$$

The government should not restrict handgun ownership.

This is an extremely simple argument. It has a single premise, and there is a single step in the reasoning. So the structure of the argument is fully represented by a single arrow.

But what if there is more than one premise? Then we have a decision to make. In some cases, two or more premises work together to make a single argument for a conclusion. In other cases, the premises do not work together; each one offers a separate line of support for the conclusion. These two patterns are diagrammed in different ways, so we have to decide which pattern is present in a given argument. To illustrate the distinction, let's reexamine two arguments that we have already discussed.

The first is President Reagan's argument about politics and religion. In essence, he said: (1) politics depends on morality, and (2) morality depends on religion, therefore (3) politics depends on religion. This argument illustrates the first pattern. Premises (1) and (2) must be combined in order to have an argument for (3). The conclusion here is like a horizontal beam, supported at each end by one of the premises; take away either premise and the beam will fall. The premise that politics depends on morality, taken by itself, does not tell us anything about religion, so it doesn't give us any reason to think that politics depends on religion. In the same way, the premise that morality depends on religion, taken by itself, does not tell us anything about politics, so again we would have no reason to think politics depends on religion. It is only when we put the premises together that we have an argument. We represent this fact by using a second symbol, the plus (+) sign, to join the premises. Using the numbers to stand for the individual propositions, we would diagram the argument like this:

We use a single arrow, drawn from the line joining the premises, to represent the fact that the premises together make up a single argument.

By contrast, consider de Tocqueville's comments on democracy. The argument could be stated as follows. (1) The people choose the legislature and the president, and (2) the people serve as jurors to decide whether someone may be punished for a crime. Therefore (3) the people control the actions of the government. Premises (1) and (2) *independently* support the conclusion. If we think of the conclusion once again as a horizontal beam, then the premises in this case are like vertical posts placed in the middle, not at the ends. The more posts there are, the more support there is for the beam, but taking away one post will not necessarily cause the beam to collapse. Thus the fact that we elect our government officials, taken by itself, does provide some evidence that the people control the government, regardless of whether we also use juries in criminal law. And the existence of the jury system, taken by itself, does provide some evidence for popular control (though admittedly not much), regardless of whether we elect our representatives. So in diagramming this argument, we don't use the plus sign. We use two arrows to join each premise to the conclusion separately:

A set of premises, then, can support a conclusion in two distinct ways. We can refer to the first pattern as an argument with *additive* premises (because of the plus sign), and to the second pattern as an argument with *nonadditive* premises. In either case, there can be any number of premises. In order to tell whether a set of premises is additive or not, we look at each premise separately, and ask whether it would support the conclusion by itself, without the other premises. The other side of the coin is to ask what would happen if one of the premises were false. Would that destroy the whole argument? Then the premises are additive; they depend on each other to support the conclusion. Or would part of the argument remain standing? Then the premises are nonadditive; each supports the conclusion independently. If you apply these tests and still aren't sure, it would be a good idea for now to treat them as additive; that is the more cautious approach. As we learn more about specific types of argument, we'll learn more detailed rules about when two premises must be combined to support a conclusion.

In an argument with nonadditive premises, there are two (or more) arrows converging on the conclusion. What about the opposite situation? Can we have arrows *diverging* from a single premise to two or more different conclusions? That is, can a single proposition serve as evidence for more than one conclusion? Certainly. As we noticed earlier, the law of gravity implies that rivers in Taiwan flow downhill. That same premise would tell us that rivers flow downhill in Nepal, or Nebraska, or anywhere else. So we could formulate a large number of propositions, one for each locale, and each would be supported by the law of gravity. If we numbered all the propositions, the diagram would look like this:

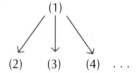

In all the arguments we have examined so far, a given proposition served either as a premise or a conclusion, but not as both. But that's only because we have been dealing with very simple arguments. In everyday thinking, as well as in science and other academic subjects, we often find chains of inferences: a premise gives us evidence for a certain conclusion, which in turn supports a further conclusion, and so on. Or conversely, we look for a premise to back up our position, and then look for a further premise to back up the first premise, and so on. For example, if someone opposes gun control on the ground that it violates the right of self-defense, we might ask: why assume that people have such a right? The person might answer: because people have a right to life, and therefore have a right to defend themselves. So we have four propositions to deal with:

1) People have a right to life.
2) People have a right to self-defense.
3) Gun control violates the right of self-defense.
4) The government should not restrict gun ownership.

And the argument would be diagrammed:

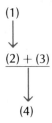

This argument has two steps, and proposition (2) serves both as the conclusion of the first step and as a premise of the second. An argument can have any number of steps.

Let's summarize and review what we've learned so far. We have established four points about the structure of arguments, and for each point there is a diagramming rule.

1. An argument must have at least one premise and one conclusion; use an arrow to represent the link between them.
2. An argument may have more than one step, so that a given proposition can be both a conclusion (of one step) and a premise (of another step); use separate arrows to represent each step, with the final conclusion on the bottom line.
3. A single premise may support more than one conclusion; draw divergent arrows.
4. A single conclusion may be supported by more than one premise, either additively or nonadditively; use a plus sign and a single arrow for additive premises, convergent arrows for nonadditive ones.

Point 1 is true of all arguments; indeed, it is true by the very definition of an argument. Points 2–4 describe the various ways in which arguments can differ in structure, and for each one we have a way of representing it in a diagram. So no matter how complex an argument is—no matter how many steps it has, or how many conclusions each premise supports, or how many premises support each conclusion—we should now be able to diagram the argument.

Applying the Method

To apply this method, the first step is to identify the conclusion and the premises, and to give them numbers. The numbers are merely a convenience, so that we don't have to keep writing out the propositions, and it doesn't matter which numbers you use. When you diagram an argument from a written text, however, it does matter that you assign numbers to *all* the propositions that play a role. If the text contains a complex sentence, you may have to break it down into its constituents. Moreover, we assign numbers *only* to the propositions that are being asserted. If an argument contains a statement of the form *if p, then q*, the entire statement gets a single number; don't number *p* and *q* separately. Once we have isolated and numbered the premises and the conclusion, we can diagram the structure of the argument. Let's try it on a few examples.

The first is an argument by the biologist Richard Lewontin, in support of the theory of evolution.

It is an empirical claim, I think, [1] that all living organisms have living organisms as parents. The second empirical claim is [2] that there was a time on earth when there were no mammals. Now, if you allow me those two claims as empirical, then the claim [3] that mammals arose from non-mammals is simply a conclusion. [Quoted by Tom Bethell, "Agnostic Evolutionists," *Harpers Magazine,* January 1985]

This is a fairly easy argument to analyze, because the author leads us through it by the hand. He tells us that proposition (3) is the conclusion, and he identifies (1) and (2) as his premises. The premises are clearly additive. If we accepted premise (1) but rejected (2), the argument would collapse. The fact that living organisms have living organisms as parents proves nothing about mammals unless we also know that there was a time when mammals didn't exist. For the same reason, the argument would collapse if we accepted (2) but rejected (1). So the diagram is simple:

$$\underline{(1) + (2)}$$
$$\downarrow$$
$$(3)$$

Notice that in the text of the argument, I put the numbers in the middle of the sentences, not at the beginning. The reason is that the words at the beginning of the sentences are there to introduce each proposition and explain its role in the argument. Those words serve as a kind of verbal scaffolding Lewontin uses to build his argument. But our diagram allows us to replace the scaffolding with arrows and plus signs. In each sentence, the relevant proposition is contained in a noun clause beginning with "that"—so that's where we put the number. (For the same reason, if you were to write out each proposition instead of just numbering them in the text, you would not need to include indicator words. They too are verbal scaffolding that is replaced by diagram signs.) Notice, finally, the author's insistence that (1) and (2) are empirical claims. His point is that they are not mere assumptions; they are based on scientific evidence. If he had actually stated the evidence, then his argument would have more than one step, and (1) and (2) would be conclusions drawn from the evidence as well as being premises for (3).

For our second example, let's try to construct an argument of our own. Remember the proposition that extremely sarcastic people feel inadequate? Let's see whether we can find an argument to support the claim. Following one line of evidence I suggested earlier, we might notice that chronic sarcasm, especially when it is not provoked, seems to express hostility. And why would someone express unprovoked hostility all the time? Isn't it usually because the person feels inadequate in some way? Let's write these ideas down in a list. And since the order in which we number the propositions in an argument is arbitrary, we'll start with the conclusion this time:

1) Extremely sarcastic people feel inadequate.
2) Extreme sarcasm is a form of unprovoked hostility.
3) Unprovoked hostility results from feelings of inadequacy.

Sentences (2) and (3) are clearly additive premises; neither one alone supports the conclusion. So if we pause to diagram the argument, we would have:

Now suppose someone challenged us on premise (2)—or suppose we ourselves wondered why it strikes us as true. Can we offer any further argument for it? After all, sarcasm can be playful and witty. It can be an indirect way of expressing fondness, or any number of other feelings. Yes, we might answer, that's true in small doses. But chronic and extreme sarcasm always seems to have the goal of undercutting or belittling another person. And the desire to undercut someone, when it isn't provoked, is a kind of hostility. So now we have two further premises:

4) Extreme sarcasm is an effort to undercut someone.
5) The desire to undercut someone is a kind of hostility.

Like (2) and (3), these are additive premises, and we can expand the diagram:

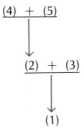

Now we have an argument in two steps. If we wanted to discuss the issue thoroughly, we would have to look for reasons to support premise (3) as well, and we would want to consider other lines of evidence in addition. The diagram would get more and more complex. But we would proceed in the same fashion, listing premises and adding them to the diagram as we go.

Let's try one more example, this one from a newspaper commentary on the farm problem. In addition to illustrating the diagramming technique, this example will bring out an important point about isolating the propositions involved in an argument. Read it through once for content, then again to notice the numbers I've inserted.

> The most important question is whether or not good farming can be understood as an industry. The answer is [1] that it cannot be so understood. The reasons are complicated but they may be summed up in two facts: first, [2] farming depends upon living creatures and biological processes, whereas [3] the materials of industry are not alive and the processes are mechanical; and, second, [4] a factory is, and is expected to be, temporary, whereas [5] a farm, if well farmed, will last forever—and, if poorly farmed, will be destroyed forever. [Wendell Berry, "Stockman and the Plowman," *New York Times*, Op-ed, February 26, 1985]

Notice first that I numbered the second sentence but not the first. The first sentence poses a question about farming without making a definite assertion; the assertion comes in the second sentence. So proposition (1) is: farming is not (cannot be understood as) an industry. This in fact is the conclusion, as the author indicates by calling it "the answer," and by following it with a list of reasons. The reasons are given in a very long sentence in which I have isolated four propositions.

You can see that I have not given a number to each and every separate proposition. What I have labeled (2), for example, actually contains two distinct assertions: (2a) Farming depends upon living creatures, and (2b) Farming depends upon biological processes. The other premises could also be broken down further; (5) is especially complex. Why not number all these component statements separately? Because they don't play separate roles in the argument. The author says explicitly that his reasoning "can be summed up in two facts," suggesting that he is giving two distinct lines of argument. And when we examine his reasoning, we find that he differentiates farming from industry along two lines: biological versus nonbiological materials and processes; and long versus short time frames. So we don't need to break down his statements any further. We can treat what he says about farming and industry, on each dimension, as a single proposition.

Since the author tells us that there are two lines of argument, we should expect that the diagram will contain two arrows converging on the conclusion (1). But we have four premises. How can this be? Notice that (2) and (3) are additive premises. The premise that farming depends on biological materials and processes doesn't prove anything about whether farming is an industry—until we add the premise that industry does *not* use such materials and processes. So (2) and (3) are joined by a plus sign, and connected to the conclusion by a single arrow. The same analysis would apply to (4) and (5), and the diagram as a whole is as follows:

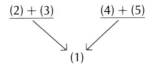

Notice that (2) and (3) are *not* combined in an additive way with (4) and (5). That's because these are separate, nonadditive lines of argument. Suppose, for example, that we rejected premise (3) on the ground that biogenetic industries do use biological materials and processes. In that case, the argument represented by the left-hand arrow would collapse. But this would not affect the argument represented by the right-hand arrow. The author could still argue that there is a difference in time frame between farming and industry.

As these examples illustrate, the diagramming technique gives us a single method for analyzing arguments that differ in subject matter and in structure. But we have only begun to exploit this tool. In the next section, we will see how it helps us to *evaluate* arguments.

Practice Quiz

Diagram each of the following arguments. (For further practice, diagram the arguments in the previous Practice Quiz, page 84.)

1. Annette must come from a wealthy family. Last week she bought a diamond choker for her ocelot.
2. I don't think it would be a good idea to take the American Revolution course this term, because it conflicts with a course I need for my major, and my schedule would have more balance if I took a science course instead.
3. Key West, the southernmost city in the continental United States, is located at the tip of the Florida peninsula. This means not only that it enjoys year-round warm weather, but also that it is vulnerable to Caribbean hurricanes.

4. Tax reform involves two different measures: it reduces tax rates, and it closes tax loopholes. It seems to me that tax reform is politically possible only if the reduction in rates comes first, and the loopholes are closed later. The reason is this. Until rates are reduced, the loopholes are valuable to interest groups, and many of these groups are powerful enough to block reform.

5. An encyclopedia is a valuable possession for a family to have, and well worth the money. For adults, it is a quick reference tool. For children, it provides a form of learning that complements what they get in school. Why? Because in school they have to follow a structured program, whereas an encyclopedia lets them go from topic to topic following their own curiosity.

Evaluating Arguments

A diagram is a valuable tool of analysis. It is like an X-ray picture of an argument, revealing its internal structure. But analyzing an argument is not an end in itself. The real goal is to *evaluate* the argument, and analysis is only a means to this end. How do we evaluate arguments? What standard shall we use? Remember that the whole point of reasoning is to determine the truth or falsity of propositions that we are not in a position to verify directly by sense perception. So a good argument is one that establishes the *truth* of its conclusion.

Logical Strength

To prove a conclusion, an argument must have two essential features that we do not always distinguish very clearly in everyday thought and language. First, its premises must be true. An argument is a method of establishing the truth of a proposition by relating it to facts we already know. So we have to start from facts; false premises don't prove anything. Secondly, the premises must be logically related to the conclusion in such a way that if the premises *are* true, the conclusion is likely to be true as well. In other words, it is not enough that the premises be true; they must also be *relevant* to the conclusion. Their truth must give us a reason for thinking the conclusion is true.

The first feature of a good argument—the truth of the premises —pertains to the external relationship between the argument and reality. The second feature—the relevance of the premises—is a matter of the internal coherence of the argument. In keeping with our analogy of vertical posts supporting a horizontal beam, we will refer to this second feature as the logical *strength* of the argument: the capacity of the premises to support the conclusion.

The two features are related, but distinct. The truth of the premises does not guarantee that the argument is strong, nor does the logical strength of an argument require that the premises are true. These are two separate issues. To see why, consider an analogy. If you had to know how many square feet there are in a floor, you would measure the length and the width, and then multiply them. To get the right answer, you would have to measure accurately *and* multiply correctly. So there are two kinds of error you could make. You could start with the right measurements but do the multiplication wrong; that would be like using an argument whose premises are true but provide no support for the conclusion. Or you could make a mistake in measuring, but still multiply correctly; that would be like a strong argument whose premises are false. Just as we can multiply any two numbers, regardless of whether the numbers accurately represent the object we measured, so we can derive logical implications from any set of premises, regardless of whether the premises are true.

Let's look at an example. Suppose I'm trying to persuade you that Harry is a lousy driver, and my argument is that he got a parking ticket ten years ago. Assuming he did get the ticket, my premise is true, but my argument is very weak. One parking ticket doesn't prove anything about his driving skills. The conclusion simply does not follow from the premise. But now suppose my argument is that Harry is a philosophy major, and all philosophy majors are lousy drivers. This time one of the premises (the second one) is clearly false, so the argument can't even get off the ground. But you can see that if it *were* true, then the conclusion would have to be true as well. The argument is logically very strong, because the proposition that Harry is a lousy driver follows from the two premises. In everyday discussion, we would not usually consider an argument strong unless the premises were true—that is, unless the argument had factual strength as well as logical strength. In logic, however, STRENGTH is a semi-technical concept that pertains solely to the internal relation between premises and conclusion, not to the relation between the premises and reality. An argument can have the most preposterous or outrageous premises and still be logically strong.

Of course, such an argument would not prove its conclusion. Proof requires true premises as well as logical strength. So why do we have to draw such a sharp distinction between the two features? The reason lies in a kind of division of mental labor. To decide whether the premises are true, we usually need information from other sources, such as science, or history, or our own observations. Once we have that information, logic can then tell us how to derive conclusions that are well supported by it. Logic is in the business of providing standards for measuring the internal strength of arguments. And these standards are extremely valuable, even when we aren't sure whether the premises are true. When we encounter an argument that strikes us as wrong, the standards will help us locate the problem and state our objections precisely. When we hear a conclusion that we're inclined to agree with, the standards will help us resist the temptation to accept a weak argument for it. And if we're not sure whether a proposition is true or false, the standards will tell us what sort of evidence would be relevant.

Assessing Logical Strength

Logical strength is a matter of degree. It means the degree of support that the premises confer on a conclusion—the degree to which the premises, if true, would make it likely that the conclusion is true as well. The stronger an argument is, the tighter the relationship between premises and conclusion; the weaker it is, the looser the relationship. To illustrate the different degrees of support along the continuum, let's use the example of Harry's driving skills. At the bottom end of the continuum is the argument that he got a parking ticket. As we noted, this premise gives no support whatever to the claim that he's a lousy driver. Now suppose we knew that he once dinged his door in a parking lot. That is not much evidence—one ding does not a lousy driver make—but it's something. It's enough to raise a question in our minds. If we acquired the further information that he had failed Drivers' Ed three times, and had been involved in a major accident, we would have a much higher degree of support for the conclusion; the evidence makes it probable that he is not a good driver. If we knew in addition, finally, that his vision was 20-200, and that he had trouble telling the brake pedal from the accelerator, our premises would make the conclusion virtually certain; the argument would be extremely strong.

As we study the different types of argument in later chapters, we will learn the standards for evaluating strength that are appropriate to each type. But for now, all that matters is the general principle illustrated by the preceding example: we assess strength by seeing how much free play there is between premises and conclusion. The technique is to assume that the premises are true, and then ask whether there could still be a reasonable doubt as to whether the conclusion is true. Assuming that the premises are true, is the stated conclusion the only one consistent with the evidence they provide?

In that case the argument is strong. Or are there other conclusions that would be equally consistent with the evidence? In that case the argument is weaker.

In the diagram of an argument, each arrow stands for a logical relationship between premise and conclusion. So for each arrow, we have to make a judgment about strength, and the strength of the argument as a whole is a function of the strength of its components. When you "add up" the components, there are two principles to follow. First, an argument with more than one step can be no stronger than its *weakest* step. Secondly, when there are nonadditive premises within a single step—that is, when two or more arrows converge on the same conclusion—the argument is at least as strong as the *strongest* component. Let's examine each of these principles.

Researchers who study intelligence have found that identical twins are more alike in intelligence than are fraternal twins. They infer that intelligence is genetically determined to some extent, because identical twins are genetically identical, whereas fraternal twins are not. Some people have made the further inference that one's level of intelligence cannot be increased by training or education. Here we have four propositions:

1) Identical twins are more alike in intelligence than fraternal twins.
2) Identical twins are genetically identical, whereas fraternal twins are not.
3) Intelligence is genetically determined to some extent.
4) Intelligence cannot be increased by training or education.

The structure of this argument is:

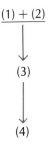

(1) + (2)

(3)

(4)

(Actually, the argument is much more complex because the first step, from (1) + (2) to (3), involves sophisticated statistical methods. But we can work with what we have here.)

In the first step, the premises offer fairly strong evidence for the conclusion. To be sure, there is a *little* free play, a little slippage between premises and conclusion. Perhaps the greater similarity of identical twins is the result of being treated more alike by their parents and teachers—an environmental, not a genetic, explanation. But that hypothesis seems like grasping at a straw. In the absence of further evidence, (3) would be the more reasonable conclusion to draw from the twin studies. But the second step, from (3) to (4), is much weaker. The fact that a trait has a genetic basis doesn't mean that it is unaffected by the environment. Nearsightedness has a genetic basis, but it can usually be corrected by eyeglasses, contact lenses, or surgery. Some genetically-based diseases can be countered by diet or exercise. So it may be that intelligence can be improved by training or education. The argument as a whole, therefore, is a chain with one weak link, and we have to give the argument a low score for logical strength. A chain can't be stronger than its weakest link.

Let's turn now to the second principle. In one of his essays, Carl Sagan made the following argument (as usual, I have inserted the numbers): "[1] Science is based on experiment, [2] on a willingness to challenge old dogma, [3] on an openness to see the universe as it really is. Accordingly, [4] science sometimes requires courage. . . ." [*Broca's Brain*] The conclusion here is obviously (4), and (1)–(3) appear to be nonadditive premises for it. So the diagram would be:

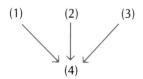

The arrow on the left represents the subargument: science is based on experiment, therefore it requires courage. But what is the connection between courage and doing experiments? Experiments might require intelligence, or curiosity, but why courage? Unless Sagan is thinking of experiments involving dangerous substances, this argument seems extremely weak. What about the next arrow, from (2) to (4)? Here we are on firmer ground. Challenging old dogma exposes one to ridicule and hostility, so it *does* take courage. The subargument on the right, finally, seems as weak as the one on the left. An "openness to see the universe as it really is" may call for curiosity again, or a sense of objectivity, but once again the link with courage is a weak one. (We might help Sagan out here by arguing that such openness involves the willingness to challenge old dogma—but then this is not a separate subargument, but a restatement of the middle one.) So we have a convergent argument with two very weak links, and one fairly strong one. How should we evaluate the argument as a whole? It is at least as strong as the middle link. That subargument does not depend on the other premises, so it is not weakened by them. On the contrary, if they contribute anything at all, they increase the strength of the argument as a whole. A convergent argument is more like a web than a chain, and a web may be stronger than any one of its individual strands.

Thus the strength of an argument is a function of the subarguments that make it up. So far, we have assessed the strength of those subarguments intuitively, by trying to estimate the size of the gap between premises and conclusion. But there's another method we can use, based on a refinement of the diagramming technique.

Assumed Premises

An argument is a relationship between a set of premises and a conclusion. But people rarely express in words all the premises they are using. In most arguments, some premises are assumed but not stated; they are implicit, not explicit. The argument in favor of gun control, for example, was that restricting ownership of guns would reduce the level of crime. The argument clearly assumes, without actually saying it, that a reduction in crime would be desirable. Very often, as in this case, a premise is left implicit because it is obvious and noncontroversial. Everyday speech would be horribly stilted and tedious if we tried to put every single one of our premises into language. It makes sense to state only the new, the substantive, the controversial premises of an argument. But sometimes it is the substantive and controversial premise that is left unspoken, making an argument seem more plausible than it really is.

When we analyze an argument, it is important to identify the implicit premises. They can then be labeled—using letters instead of numbers, to distinguish them from the explicit premises—and included in the diagram. The gun control argument, for example, would be diagrammed as follows:

1) Restricting gun ownership will reduce crime.
a) Reducing crime is desirable.
2) The government should restrict gun ownership.

Notice, by the way, that (1) and (a) are additive premises. This will always be the case when we fill in implicit premises. Our justification for reading an assumed premise into an argument is that the assumption is necessary in order to link a stated premise with the conclusion. By the very nature of the case, the implicit premise has to work together with some explicit premise. If we introduce a new *nonadditive* premise, we are adding a new line of argument and not merely analyzing the argument which the speaker actually gave.

We will return to the subject of implicit premises in Chapter 7. The important thing for now is to see how they can help us measure logical strength. Strength is a function of the gap between premises and conclusion: the larger the gap, the weaker the argument. Now it is always possible to narrow the gap by introducing a new premise. For example, we saw that the argument "Harry got a parking ticket ten years ago; therefore he's a lousy driver" is hopelessly weak. But we could make it stronger by adding the premise "Anyone who gets a parking ticket is a lousy driver." This may seem like cheating, but it isn't. We are not getting something for nothing here. We are buying a greater degree of strength, but we are paying for it by committing ourselves to a new premise, whose truth we would now have to defend. There is a tradeoff between the strength of an argument and the premises it assumes. A strong argument has a small gap between the stated premises and the conclusion, and the gap can be filled by a fairly innocuous premise that would be easy to defend. A weaker argument has a larger gap, which could be filled only by a more substantial premise that would be harder to defend. A thoroughly weak argument has a huge gap, which could be filled only by a premise that is obviously false, like the one above. So we can measure the gap, and thus determine the argument's strength, by seeing what sort of premise it would take to fill the gap.

Let's try this out on another example that we're already familiar with. We have analyzed de Tocqueville's argument about democracy as a case of nonadditive premises:

1) The people elect their representatives.
2) The people serve on juries.
3) The people control the government.

And we observed parenthetically that the subargument on the right seems much weaker than the one on the left. We can back up this judgment by identifying the premise that would be necessary to make the argument stronger. To say that the people control the government is to say that they control the government's *actions.* When they serve on juries, the action they control is the action of punishing criminals. So to make the inference from (2) to (3) a strong one, we need the premise that punishing criminals is the *only* action government takes, or at least the main one. This is a major assumption, to say the least. We would be going way out on a limb. After all, governments wage war, impose taxes, regulate the economy, and do many other things in addition to punishing criminals. The need to make such a dubious assumption confirms our sense that the argument is very weak.

Let's apply the same technique to a new argument. A newspaper columnist writes that the Cold War "is not really even an ideological dispute since, as China proves, a communist government alone is not enough for us to grant a nation enemy status." [Richard Cohen, "Reagan, Gorbachev Gave World a Lift," *Poughkeepsie Journal,* November 27, 1985] The conclusion is (1) that the Cold War is not an ideological dispute. What is the argument? The author mentions China, but doesn't actually assert any proposition about it. Let's put China on hold and come back to it. The proposition that *is* asserted as a premise is (2) that we do not regard every communist country as an enemy. Now we know what to do with China: it's intended as an example of that proposition. So the author is assuming, as common knowledge, the premises (a) that China has a communist government, and (b) that China is not regarded as an enemy. (a) and (b) are the evidence for (2), which in turn is the reason for (1). Thus:

In the first step of this argument, the author gives a single example to support a general proposition. That would normally be a rather weak argument, but not in this case. The author is not claiming that we *never* regard communist countries as enemies. He is simply denying that we *always* consider them enemies. This is a more limited claim, and a single example is sufficient to prove it. So the first step of the argument is quite strong. What about the second step? This, too, seems reasonable, but there *is* a certain gap here, so let's look for a proposition that would fill it. The obvious candidate is: (c) If the Cold War were an ideological dispute, then we would regard any communist country as our enemy.

If we add this premise to the argument, the second step would be:

$$\frac{(2) + (c)}{}$$
$$\downarrow$$
$$(1)$$

which is certainly strong. The question now becomes: is (c) a major assumption or a minor one? Is it virtually self-evident, or could it be challenged? Well, someone might argue as follows: the Cold War is indeed an ideological dispute in which China is our *opponent;* but whether or not we consider a nation an *enemy* is a strategic issue, at least in the short run, and there are short-run strategic advantages in playing China off against Russia. We may or may not find this argument persuasive. But it does reveal that premise (c) is not self-evident. To make that assumption, we have to go some distance out on a limb. And since the author does make that assumption, by inferring (1) from (2), his argument is weaker than it seemed at first.

We have seen, then, that evaluating an argument is largely a matter of assessing its logical strength. An argument may have false premises and still be strong, and it may have true premises but be weak; the truth of the premises and the strength of the argument are separate issues. A good argument must have both features, but logic is concerned primarily with the latter. We evaluate logical strength by the size of the gap between premises and conclusion, and we measure the gap by finding the assumed premise that would be necessary to bridge it. The strength of an argument as a whole, finally, is a function of its components. If an argument has more than one step, it can be no stronger than its weakest step. But if a given step involves converging lines of support, then the argument is at least as strong as the strongest line.

Practice Quiz

Analyze each of the following arguments, and then evaluate it for strength. Remember that your judgment about strength should be based on the connection between premises and conclusion, not on whether you think the conclusion or the premises are true. Identify implicit premises where necessary.

1. I'm sure now that Richard and Lisa are in love. They both have that dreamy look, and besides, I just saw them talking together.
2. Without this welfare program, some poor people would have no means of support, so we simply must not eliminate it. For the government has an absolute duty to provide everyone with at least the bare essentials of life.
3. A welfare program is a type of expropriation: it takes money out of one person's pocket and puts it in someone else's. Since the function of government is to protect individual rights, including property rights, it should not be engaged in welfare.
4. The Soviet Union wants to advance its interests in southern Africa, and the media have been agitating about apartheid in South Africa. The Soviet Union wants to prevent the Strategic Defense Initiative, and the media have run lots of hostile stories about "Star Wars." What other conclusion can we draw but that the media are dupes of the Soviets?
5. People are allowed to vote when they're 18, and males have to register for the draft. Since 18-year-olds are considered old enough to have these responsibilities, surely they are old enough to decide whether to drink alcohol. Therefore the drinking age should not be raised to 21.

SUMMARY

Reasoning is the process of providing evidence for the truth or falsity of a proposition by relating it logically to other propositions. The unit of reasoning is an argument: a set of propositions in which some (the premises) are asserted as support or evidence for another (the conclusion). Arguments are usually, though not always, signaled verbally by indicator words.

To analyze an argument is to identify its logical structure: the logical relationships between premises and conclusion. The various possible relationships can be diagrammed using arrows and plus signs. This technique allows us to distinguish between additive and nonadditive premises, and to identify the individual steps in an argument.

To evaluate an argument, we must determine whether the premises are true, and we must assess the logical strength of the argument: the degree to which the premises, if true, support the conclusion. To determine the truth of the premises, we normally depend on our own experience or on information provided by other disciplines; logic is primarily concerned with methods of assessing strength. The primary method is to estimate the size of the gap between premises and conclusion. Another method is to find the assumed premise that would close the gap, and estimate its plausibility. In either case, the strength of an argument containing more than one step is a function of the strengths of the component steps.

Exercises

A. Each pair of arguments below has the same conclusion. Determine which one has the greater logical *strength*. Your assessment of strength should not depend on whether you agree with the premises or the conclusion.

1. a) Cross-country skiing is one of the best forms of exercise: my cousin is a cross-country skier and she's in great shape.
   b) Cross-country skiing uses all the major muscle groups, and gives the cardiovascular system a good workout, so it is an ideal form of exercise.
2. a) The fact that average wages of manufacturing workers increased by a factor of five between 1900 and 1975 indicates that the standard of living has improved a great deal during this century.
   b) In 1900 there were no VCRs, no TV dinners, no Disneyland. Our standard of living certainly has improved since then.
3. a) Marriage is a good institution because it creates jobs for people in the bridal business.
   b) Marriage is a good institution because all married people are happy.
4. a) The U.S. government should not aid UNITA, the rebel group in Angola. To do so would be to side with South Africa, which also provides aid to UNITA, and thus to discredit ourselves in the eyes of other African nations.
   b) We should not aid UNITA because the inconsistent words and deeds of its leader, Jonas Savimbi, make it impossible to tell whether he wants freedom for his country or power for himself.
5. a) Affirmative action programs should be abolished because they are too expensive to enforce.
   b) Affirmative action programs violate the principle of equal treatment regardless of race or sex, and should therefore be abolished.

B. Diagram each of the following arguments. Then choose one of its premises, and find some further argument to support it.

1. If you want to see deer in the woods, you have to be quiet. Deer tend to run when they hear noise.
2. It is extremely dangerous to carry a can of gasoline in the trunk of your car. Gasoline is highly flammable, and a gallon has enough explosive power to propel two tons of metal for twenty miles or more.
3. We shouldn't give in to the demands of terrorists when they take hostages. That will only convince them that their tactic works, and thus encourage them to use it again.
4. There is a significant difference between totalitarian governments on the left and authoritarian governments on the right. Authoritarian governments sometimes give way to democratic ones, but no totalitarian government has ever done so.
5. Religious cults typically demand that followers regard the leader's life as more valuable, and his judgment more reliable, than their own. A self-confident person would not find either demand acceptable, so you won't find many such people attracted to cults.

C. Determine whether each of the following passages contains an argument. If it does, diagram the argument.

1. "We should frankly recognize that there is no side of a man's life which is unimportant to society, for whatever he is, does, or thinks may affect his own well-being, which is and ought to be a matter of common concern, and may also directly or indirectly affect the thought, action, and character of those with whom he comes in contact." [L. T. Hobhouse, *Liberalism*]
2. "There are three possible parts to a date, at least two of which must be offered: entertainment, food, and affection. It is customary to begin a series of dates with a great deal of entertainment, a moderate amount of food, and the merest suggestion of affection. As the amount of affection increases, the entertainment can be reduced proportionately. When the affection *is* the entertainment, we no longer call it dating. Under no circumstances can the food be omitted." [Judith Martin, *Miss Manners' Guide to Excruciatingly Correct Behavior*]
3. "The existence of biological predispositions [toward crime] means that circumstances that activate criminal behavior in one person will not do so in another, that social forces cannot deter criminal behavior in 100 percent of a population, and that the distributions of crime within and across societies may, to some

extent, reflect underlying distributions of constitutional factors." [James Q. Wilson and Richard Herrnstein, *Crime and
Human Nature*]

4. "Since all psychotherapies, including placebos, apparently
   'work' to some extent, and since the nonplacebos propose
   divergent explanations of their effects, those nonplacebos all
   probably work by means other than the ones specified in their
   accompanying theories." [Frederick Crewes, "The Future of
   an Illusion," *New Republic*, January 21, 1985]

5. "I'm a sick man . . . a mean man. There's nothing attractive
   about me. I think there's something wrong with my liver. . . .

   "I've been living like this for a long time, twenty years or so.
   I'm forty now. I used to be in government service, but I'm not
   any more. I was a nasty official. I was rude and enjoyed being
   rude. . . .

   "When petitioners came up to my desk for information, I
   snarled at them and felt indescribably happy whenever I managed to make one of them feel miserable." [Fyodor Dos-
   toyevsky, *Notes from Underground*]

6. "The Soviet Union, for all its military power, is not a great commercial power. Aside from certain raw materials, it does not
   produce much Americans would want to buy. Oil and gas are its
   main hard-currency exports, but it is having production problems in those businesses and is faced with falling world market
   prices to boot." [*Wall Street Journal* editorial, December 12,
   1985]

7. "To a plant, breathing involves a built-in cost-benefit analysis.
   The wider the gas-exchanging pores on the leaf surface are
   open, the greater the supply of carbon dioxide for photosynthesis. But wide-open pores also allow evaporation of water, so the
   plant must balance the benefits of increased carbon dioxide
   against the cost of water loss." [J. A. Miller, "Plant 'Sight' from
   Pores and Pumps," *Science News*, November 30, 1985]

8. "The [Rolling] Stones' songs played at evil; but their lives
   embodied it. Evil is the inability to acknowledge the suffering
   of others. The destruction of life that seems to have followed
   the Stones is a barometer of their indifference. Illegitimate
   children are born and forgotten. Their friends get hooked on
   drugs; some of them die." [John Lahr, "Exiles on Easy Street,"
   The New Republic, December 24, 1984]

9. "A foolish consistency is the hobgoblin of little minds, adored
   by little statesmen and philosophers and divines. With consistency a great soul has simply nothing to do. He may as well
   concern himself with his shadow on the wall. Speak what you

think now in hard words and to-morrow speak what to-morrow thinks in hard words again, though it contradict every thing you said to-day." [Ralph Waldo Emerson, "Self-Reliance"]

10. "I have been requested from several quarters to give my opinion on the supposed discovery of a new Shakespeare poem. . . . It is utterly improbable for the following reasons:

   "° It is quite unlike any poem that Shakespeare ever wrote.

   "° We know quite well from the early poems "A Lover's Complaint" and "Venus and Adonis" what Shakespeare's early style was; and this new poem is utterly unlike it.

   "° Shakespeare was so famous in his own time that people would not have overlooked anything of his. Quite the reverse. They published under his name, to exploit it, poems that are definitely known *not* to be his.

   "The conclusion is clear—impossible that this ordinary poem is his." [A. L. Rowse, Letter to the editor, *New York Times*, December 8, 1985]

11. "It is hard to fault the preoccupation with interest rates. Fundamental investment theory holds that a stock is worth all the cash that it will return to investors in the future, discounted by an interest rate. When interest rates fall, investors put higher values on future corporate earnings and dividends and thus bid up share prices. So, even without the prospect of higher corporate earnings, a fall in interest rates should stimulate the stock market. Besides, lower interest rates mean lower yields on alternative investments." [*Wall Street Journal*, January 27, 1986]

12. "Evolution rewards those individuals who are most successful at passing on their genes to surviving generations. Yet through sexual procreation, which involves mixing her genes with those from a male, a female is diluting her evolutionary endowment by half. . . .

   "'Since most species retain sexual reproduction despite its seeming inefficiency,' Dr. Williams said, 'it follows that it must provide advantages great enough to be worth the enormous cost." [Erik Eckholm, "Is Sex Necessary? Evolutionists Are Perplexed," *New York Times*, March 25, 1986. Copyright © 1986 by The New York Times Company. Reprinted with permission.]

D. For each of the following propositions, a) construct an argument to support it, and b) construct an argument against it. Diagram your arguments, and make them as strong as possible (even if that means using premises you don't actually agree with).

1. The athletes at a college or university should have to meet the same academic standards as other students.
2. The government should pay tuition for anyone who wants a college education.
3. Anyone caught cheating on a final exam should be expelled from school.
4. Public high school officials should not have the right to search student lockers for drugs.
5. Before the age of 21, everyone should have to spend a year of mandatory national service, working in the military or in domestic government programs.

E. Use each of the following propositions as a premise in an argument. You may look for a conclusion that will follow from the proposition directly, or you may combine the proposition with other premises to support some conclusion (the latter approach is recommended). Make your argument as strong as possible, and diagram it as you go. When you are finished, write a paragraph expressing the argument as clearly and persuasively as you can.

1. Adults are responsible for their actions.
2. Men and women have the same basic capacities for productive work in every field.
3. No one is going to live forever.
4. War is the most destructive of human activities.
5. Freedom is worth risking one's life for.

6

Fallacies

In the last chapter, we examined the concept of logical strength: the degree of support that premises confer on a conclusion. In this chapter we're going to continue our study of logical strength by examining a class of arguments known as *fallacies:* arguments so weak that the premises do not support the conclusion at all. In one sense we'll be looking at fallacies throughout this book. As we study each kind of argument, and learn the appropriate rules for assessing logical strength, we will also look at fallacious arguments that violate the rules. But there is one particular class of fallacies we should consider at the outset.

These are arguments that one encounters frequently in everyday discussion and debate. They are sometimes called fallacies of *relevance* because the premises are irrelevant to the truth of the conclusion. Yet these arguments have a certain surface plausibility. To the unwary, the premises *seem* relevant to the conclusion. That is why these fallacies are committed with some frequency. We are going to study them now for two reasons. The first is to help you avoid them in your own thinking, and to identify them when they are used against you in debate. Forewarned is forearmed. The second reason is that understanding why these patterns of argument are fallacious will help us understand the nature of good reasoning. Every new disease that doctors identify tells them something about the nature of health, and the same is true in logic.

The fallacies we're going to examine in this chapter should not be regarded as a complete list. The varieties of bad reasoning are too numerous for that. I have included only the fallacies that you are most likely to encounter in everyday discussion, and that illustrate something about the nature of good reasoning. The first section will cover fallacies that involve subjective thinking. The second section will cover fallacies we may commit when we rely on someone else's authority, or attack his credibility. And the third section deals with fallacies of logical structure. Many of these fallacies were identified and labeled by medieval logicians, and thus have Latin names. In a few cases, the Latin name has become part of our vocabulary. In other cases the English name is more common, and I have put the Latin name in parentheses.

Subjectivist Fallacies

The cardinal virtue in reasoning is objectivity: a commitment to thinking in accordance with the facts and interpreting them logically, without bias or prejudice. The fallacies we'll examine in this section involve the rejection of objectivity in one way or another.

Subjectivism

The first and most straightforward violation of objectivity is the fallacy of subjectivism. This fallacy is committed whenever we hold that something is true merely because we *believe* or *want* it to be true. Thus, if *p* is the proposition in question, subjectivism has the form:

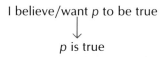

In an argument of this sort, a subjective state—the mere fact that we have a belief or desire—is being used as evidence for the truth of a proposition. We can see what's wrong with this argument by identifying the implicit premise. To make this argument stronger, one would have to accept the premise that whatever I believe or want to be true *is* true. That is, subjectivism implicitly assumes that we are infallible. And of course we aren't. The thoughts and feelings that pass through our minds may or may not correspond to reality. That's why we need a logical method of *discovering* whether they are true; that's why objectivity is a virtue in the first place.

The fact that someone prefaces a statement with the words "I think" or "I feel" does not necessarily imply subjectivism. This is a conventional way of expressing a view, and the person may go on to offer a perfectly objective argument. Nor are statements *about* our thoughts and feelings necessarily subjective. Suppose I am trying to identify an emotion I feel toward a friend; I'm trying to decide whether it is resentment or justifiable anger. My thought process may be either objective or subjective: objective if I am open to the evidence, subjective if I decide that it is justifiable anger merely because I can't bear to think of myself as resentful. In other words, subjectivism is not an issue of what a statement or conclusion is about, but rather an issue of the kind of evidence one uses to support a conclusion. The fallacy is committed only when someone uses the mere fact that he believes or feels something as a reason for thinking it to be true.

It is unlikely that you will ever hear someone commit the fallacy of subjectivism in the pure form diagrammed above. As with most fallacies, the pure, textbook cases are too obviously fallacious for anyone to fall for them. In real life, the fallacies take more subtle and disguised forms. Here are some examples:

"I'll think about that tomorrow." This is Scarlett O'Hara's line from *Gone with the Wind.* It is her way of dealing with unpleasant facts. The point, of course, is that tomorrow never comes: she is simply putting the facts out of mind, on the implicit assumption that they will then cease to exist. Subjectivism is not only a way of *adopting* conclusions on subjective grounds, but also—and probably more often—a way of *evading* conclusions by refusing to believe in them. Some people have perfected the skill of simply not seeing what they don't want to see, and most of us indulge this habit occasionally. If the habit were put into words, it would take the form "I don't want to accept *p,* therefore *p* isn't true." That's subjectivism.

"I was just brought up to believe in *X.*" This statement typically occurs when people encounter challenges to their basic convictions. In a discussion of premarital sex, for example, someone might respond to arguments in its favor by saying "Well, I was just taught to believe it's wrong." The fact that one was brought up to believe something may explain how one came to have that belief, but it doesn't explain why one *ought* to believe it; it does not provide any reason for thinking that the belief is true. It simply reinforces the claim that one has that belief, and is thus a type of subjectivism. This is not to say that you are irrational if you refuse to abandon a belief just because you've heard an argument against it that you can't answer on the spot. Many of our beliefs—especially on fundamental issues of religion, ethics, and politics—are rooted in a lifetime of experience and reflection. We can't always put that experience and reflection into words right away, and we shouldn't throw out a well-rooted belief on the basis of a single counterargument. But we shouldn't ignore the counterargument, either. To dismiss it on the grounds that it's easier and less threatening not to reexamine our convictions is a type of subjectivism.

"That may be true for you, but it isn't true for me." Suppose two people are discussing man's biological origins. Pat argues that our species arose by evolution; Mike, a creationist, says "Well, that may be true for you, but it's not for me." What does Mike mean when he says that something is (or is not) true for him? Perhaps he means simply that he does (or does not) believe it. In that case, the statement means: you may believe in evolution, but I don't. There's no fallacy here, just the recognition that a disagreement exists, without any claim as to which side is right. But then he should say so directly, and not introduce the concept of truth. The point of introducing the concept of truth is usually to give an objective gloss to a belief without having to do the work of actually providing any evidence for it, or to paper over a disagreement by suggesting that both sides are legitimate, even though they contradict each other and cannot both be true. In this case, the concept of something as "true for me" contains an element of subjectivism: it attributes an objective status to a proposition merely because one happens to believe it. At the very least, this concept ought to be a warning flag to keep an eye out for the fallacy.

Appeal to Majority

A newspaper commentary criticizes the Catholic Church for opposing birth-control measures even though "studies show that 90 percent of Catholics no longer consider birth control a sin." [Lawrence Lader, "The Family-Planning Ploy," *New York Times*, Op-ed, December 12, 1985] The author, who approves of birth control, is appealing to majority opinion in support of his belief. This is a fallacy for essentially the same reason that subjectivism is. The argument has the form:

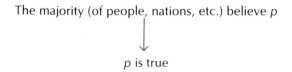

The majority (of people, nations, etc.) believe *p*

p is true

In this case, the subjective state of large numbers of people, not just a single person, is being used as evidence for the truth of a proposition. But the argument is still subjectivistic—and still fallacious. We can see why, once again, by identifying the implicit assumption: namely, that whatever the majority believes to be true *is* true. Majority opinion is obviously *not* infallible. At various times, majorities have believed that the earth is flat, that bathing is unsanitary, that certain women are witches and should be burned.

The fallacy of appealing to the majority is committed whenever someone takes a belief to be true merely because large numbers of people accept it (regardless of whether those people actually constitute a majority). This fallacy probably occurs more often in political debate than in any other area. One version is the argument from tradition—as in "I oppose socialized medicine because it is inconsistent with our tradition of private medical practice." To say that a principle or policy is traditional is merely to say that it was widely accepted by our predecessors, and the mere fact that they accepted it does not prove it correct. Another version of the fallacy might be called the "wave of the future" argument—as in "Every other progressive nation has already adopted a program of government-provided health care; the U.S. likewise should abandon its outmoded system of private medicine." To say that some principle or policy is the wave of the future is merely to say that many people or countries have already accepted it; so an appeal to their preferences in support of that principle or policy is, once again, an appeal to majority. The only difference between these opposing arguments is that they appeal to *different* majorities.

The fact that such an appeal is fallacious doesn't mean we should ignore majority opinion. Objectivity requires a willingness to consider the views of others. If large numbers of people have accepted a principle or policy, it may well be because the principle is true, the policy sound. The possibility is certainly worth exploring. When we explore it, however, we should look for objective evidence; mere popularity doesn't count. In a democracy, moreover, certain political decisions are made by majority vote. That is not fallacious. But even in this context, majorities are not infallible. Majority support for a policy does not prove the policy to be objectively correct. The point to remember is that this fallacy is committed if, but only if, the views of other people are used as evidence that a certain proposition is *true*.

Appeal to Emotion

This fallacy is the attempt to persuade someone of a conclusion by appealing to emotion instead of evidence. A person who commits this fallacy is hoping that his listeners will adopt a belief on the basis of a feeling he has instilled in them: outrage, hostility, fear, pity, guilt, or whatever. In effect, he is hoping that *they* will commit the fallacy of subjectivism. The appeal to emotion may be quite explicit. In the 1964 presidential election, Barry Goldwater's supporters used the slogan, "In your heart you know he's right." More often, the appeal is less direct. It may take the form of rhetorical language that is heavily laden with emotive connotations, as in propaganda and other sorts of incendiary political speech. Indeed, medieval logicians called this fallacy *argumentum ad populum*—appeal to the mob—because one of the clearest examples is the "rabble-rousing" language used by demagogues. The fallacy may also take the form of visual images that have a strong emotional impact. On television, for example, you can find examples of the fallacy not only in advertising but in news and documentary programs that use images to sway the viewer.

Rhetoric and other emotive devices are not fallacious per se. If you have a logical argument to back up a conclusion, there is nothing wrong with stating it in such a way that your audience will endorse it with their feelings as well as their intellects. Good writers and speakers combine logic and rhetoric to produce exactly that effect. Even in advertising, the emotional pitch may be accompanied by a bona fide reason to buy the product. The fallacy occurs only when rhetoric *replaces* logic, only when the intent is to make an audience act on emotion *instead* of rational judgment.

How can we tell when this intent is present? A good test is to translate the argument into neutral language. If the translation leaves a large gap between premises and conclusion, then there is reason to suspect that the emotive language (or visual image, as the case may be) was intended to make a nonrational appeal to the audience. Let's apply this test to some examples.

In a famous speech, Martin Luther King, Jr., said:

> I have a dream that one day this nation will rise up and live out the true meaning of its creed: "We hold these truths to be self-evident—that all men are created equal.". . . I have a dream that one day even the state of Mississippi, a desert state sweltering with the heat of injustice and oppression, will be transformed into an oasis of freedom and justice. I have a dream that my four little children will one day live in a nation where they will not be judged by the color of their skin but by the content of their character. [Quoted from *Let the Trumpet Sound*, by Stephen B. Oates]

This passage certainly makes an appeal to the emotions. But it is not fallacious, because King is also presenting a logical argument. In neutral language, the argument might be stated as follows: "America was founded on the principle that all men are created equal. This implies that people should not be judged by skin color, which is an accident of birth, but rather by what they make of themselves ('the content of their character'). To be consistent with this principle, America should treat black people and white people alike." The emotional devices in King's speech—the repetition of "I have a dream," the description of Mississippi as a "desert state," the reference to his children—do not compete with or replace his argument. On the contrary, they make the meaning of the abstract principles more concrete and vivid, and thus more powerful.

By way of contrast, let's look at an example that does commit the fallacy, from a flyer on nuclear war:

> The chances for a nuclear holocaust increase with every new missile. As I stare at the button, I see our children skinned alive by a flash of fire, San Francisco a mass of twisted steel; I hear the dying groan as their arteries burst. Then, the victors march in: thousands of rats and an army of cockroaches.

The author's conclusion is stated in the first sentence; he believes that increasing the number of missiles we have will increase the chances of nuclear war. This is a controversial position; some people would argue that increasing our missile defenses would *deter* attack, and thus *reduce* the chances of war. So the author wants us to reject the policy of deterrence. What is his argument? If we translate the rest of the passage into neutral language, all it says is that nuclear war would be very bad. So the argument is:

Nuclear war would be very bad
↓
Deterrence is the wrong policy

This is an extremely weak argument; the gap between premise and conclusion is enormous. The fact that nuclear war would be very bad doesn't tell us anything about how to prevent it. But the author covers up the logical gap by his graphic description of San Francisco in the aftermath of a bomb. He is using rhetoric here to induce emotions that will blind us to the weakness of his argument, and thus sway us to his position by nonlogical means.

Appeal to Force (Argumentum ad Baculum)

The eighteenth-century essayist Joseph Addison once wrote (with his tongue in his cheek):

> There is a way of managing an Argument . . . which is made use of by States and Communities, when they draw up a hundred thousand Dispu-

tants on each side, and convince one another by dint of sword. A certain grand Monarch was so sensible of his strength in this way of Reasoning, that he writ upon his great Guns—Ratio Ultima Regum, The Logick of Kings. [*The Spectator*, No. 239, December 4, 1711]

Addison's remark is sarcastic: the use of force is *not* a type of reasoning, but is actually its antithesis. A threat is not an argument, a club (in Latin, "baculum") is not a reason. If I persuade you of something by means of threats, I have not given you a reason for thinking the proposition is true; I have *scared* you into thinking it true, or at least into saying you think so. In this respect, the appeal to force might be regarded as a form of the appeal to emotion.

An appeal to force may well involve direct coercion. When a government engages in censorship, for example, it uses force to prohibit the expression of certain ideas and to compel agreement with other ideas. The point of this control over verbal expression is to influence what people believe. But the fallacy need not involve actual *physical* force or violence. It is committed whenever *any* sort of threat is used; and nonphysical threats are probably more common than physical ones. Parents who threaten to withdraw their support unless a child adopts their religious beliefs, a teacher who threatens a dissenting student with a lower grade, someone who "persuades" a friend by threatening the loss of affection—all of these would be forms of the fallacy. As the examples illustrate, the fallacy is usually committed in the effort to breed conformity in belief, and society has many nonphysical means of intimidating people to accept the conventional views. Dissenters may be held up to ridicule, threatened with moral disapproval ("Only a pig would believe *that*"), told they aren't "with it," and so on. Whenever intimidation of this sort replaces logic in an effort to persuade, it is no less fallacious than the use of actual force.

Practice Quiz

Each statement below commits one of the fallacies discussed in this section: subjectivism, appeal to majority, appeal to emotion, or appeal to force. Identify which fallacy it is.

1. The Golden Rule is a sound moral principle, for it is basic to every system of ethics in every culture.
2. Foreign imports are wrecking our economy and savaging our workers, the backbone of this country. Buy American! Before you put your money on that Honda, think of the guy in Detroit whose kids

may not eat tomorrow. Before you buy those Italian pumps, ask your-self whether a little glamour is worth the job of the shoemaker in Bos-ton who's worked all his life to make an honest living.

3. You can argue all you want that democracy gives us only the illusion of control over the government, but I don't buy it. I was brought up to believe in the democratic system.

4. The most effective way to increase government revenues would be to raise the corporate income tax, since opinion polls show wide-spread support for this approach.

5. Teacher to student: ". . . and finally, in reconsidering your position, you might remember who gives the grades in this course."

6. "Fine. Go ahead and marry him. Why should you care about break-ing your mother's heart? I guess you love him more than me—but why should I care? Who am I to complain? I'm only your mother. I only spent twenty years trying to make a good match for you, a nice boy, and now you run off. . . ."

Credibility

We noticed at the beginning of Chapter 5 that we rely on other people for much of what we know. Most of us lack firsthand knowl-edge of the evidence for the theory of relativity, the DNA model of genes, the link between smoking and lung cancer; we accept these and other scientific ideas because we accept the authority of experts in the various fields. We know about historical events largely through the records and memoirs left by our predecessors. We learn about current events from reading newspaper accounts by journalists. Courts of law rely on eyewitness testimony and expert witnesses. Indeed, we can extend the legal concept of *testimonial evidence* to cover all of these cases.

The value of such evidence depends on the *credibility* of the wit-ness. When we accept a conclusion on the basis of someone's testi-mony, our reasoning can be diagrammed as follows:

$$X \text{ says } p$$
$$\downarrow$$
$$p \text{ is true}$$

If such an argument is to have any logical strength, two assumptions must be true. First, X must know what he's talking about, he must be competent to speak on the subject. If p is a statement in some technical area, then X must have some expertise in that area. If it is a statement about some event, X must be someone who was in a position to know what happened. Secondly, X must be reporting what he knows honestly and objectively, without bias, distortion, or deceit. In other words, X must be someone who *knows* the truth, and who *tells* the truth. Both conditions are essential for credibility. Ideally, we should have a positive reason to think that X is competent and objective. At the very least, we must not have any evidence that X is *in*competent or *non*objective.

In this section, we'll look at two fallacies that involve a misuse of the standards for credibility.

Appeal to Authority (Argumentum ad Verecundiam)

An authority is someone whose word carries special weight, someone who can speak with authority because of expertise in some area of knowledge such as law, science, or medicine. It is perfectly appropriate to rely on the testimony of authorities if the conditions of credibility are satisfied. If they are not satisfied, however, appealing to authority is fallacious.

The first condition is that the alleged authority be competent—an expert on the subject matter in question. It is typically violated when people speak outside their fields of expertise. For example, advertisers often use celebrity endorsements. A basketball star praises his favorite brand of orange juice, a famous actor extols the virtues of a certain photocopier. If the role of the celebrity is merely to add glamour, there's no fallacy involved, because there's no attempt at logical argument. But the advertiser's point is usually to persuade you that the product is a good one because someone you respect says so. That's a fallacy. Skill on the basketball court does not imply a discriminating taste for orange juice, nor does acting ability give one expertise in judging photocopiers. The same fallacy would be committed in a political argument if one cited the opinion of a scientist, or a rock star, or an eminent businessman. When people of talent or expertise speak on matters outside their fields, their opinion carries no more weight than that of any layman. That much ought to be obvious. But there is another, less obvious point to notice about the competence assumption.

It often happens that experts disagree. One psychiatrist says a criminal is insane, another says the criminal is sane. One economist says that a certain change in the tax laws will eliminate jobs, another says the measure will create jobs. Across a wide array of issues—from the safety of nuclear plants, to the causes of inflation, to the historical origins of capitalism—specialists disagree. What do we do in this situation? First, of course, we should make sure that the parties to the dispute are genuine authorities, and not merely self-proclaimed "experts." If they *are* authorities, we have to be cautious. It may be that one group of specialists are objectively right and can prove their case, and their opponents are merely being irrational. But we are not in a position, as laymen, to make that judgment—otherwise we wouldn't have to rely on experts in the first place. As long as an issue remains controversial even among specialists, we simply don't know whether any of them satisfies the competence assumption, and any argument that appeals only to one group of authorities is fallacious. We have to take into account both sides of the dispute, and try to reach some judgment on our own.

The second condition for credibility is that the alleged authority be objective. Since celebrities are paid to appear in advertisements, for example, they have an obvious motive to praise the product regardless of what they really think about it. In general, this condition is violated when an expert has an emotional commitment or vested interest in an issue—even if it lies within his field of expertise. Professionals themselves recognize the dangers here: doctors do not operate on members of their own family; lawyers say that an attorney who represents himself in court has a fool for a client.

It is very difficult, however, to assess objectivity. For example, media coverage of technological risks, such as nuclear plants or chemical accidents, usually relies much more heavily on expert sources in government than on those in industry. The reporters' rationale is that industry experts have a vested interest in downplaying risks posed by the companies that employ them. But critics point out that government experts have a vested interest in exaggerating risks, because that will increase support for government action and thus increase *their* job security.

The problem is that with enough imagination, and enough cynicism, we can find a reason to impugn *anyone's* objectivity. If we go to that extreme, however, then we lose all the advantages of having specialists in different fields; we lose the advantages of cooperation in the pursuit of knowledge. The cognitive division of labor, like any other social arrangement, depends to some extent on mutual trust. So it seems more reasonable to presume an expert innocent until proven guilty—that is, to presume he is objective unless we have good reason to doubt it. In any case, we should be even-handed. On economic issues, for example, government and industry experts should be judged by the same standard, regardless of whether we favor more or less government regulation.

The use of authorities, finally, is appropriate only when the issue in question requires specialized knowledge or skill that the ordinary person does not possess. If the issue is *not* a technical one—if it is a matter of common sense, or a value judgment, or a political view, or an observation about human nature—then the ordinary person is capable of understanding the evidence for it, and we should simply be given the evidence, not asked to rely on someone else's judgment. Why should we settle for secondhand knowledge, when we could have firsthand knowledge? This distinction is especially important to keep in mind when an author uses lots of quotations to back up his argument: he may well be trying to cover a hole in his argument by citing eminent people who happen to agree with him.

Ad Hominem

An *ad hominem* argument rejects or dismisses another person's statement by attacking the person rather than the statement itself. As we will see, there are many different forms of this fallacy. But the goal is always to escape the responsibility of dealing with a statement logically, and the method is always to try to discredit the speaker. An *ad hominem* argument has the form:

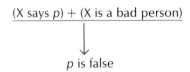

$$\frac{(X \text{ says } p) + (X \text{ is a bad person})}{}$$

$$\downarrow$$

$$p \text{ is false}$$

This is a fallacy because the truth or falsity of a statement, or the strength of an argument for it, has nothing to do with the character, motives, or any other trait of the person who makes the statement or argument.

In a case of testimonial evidence, of course, we do have to consider such traits. If someone cites an authority in defending his position, we should make use of information showing that the alleged authority is incompetent or nonobjective. In a trial where the jury is asked to accept the testimony of witnesses, information about the ability, character, or motives of a witness is likewise relevant. But even in this context, discrediting authorities or witnesses does not provide evidence that what they say is actually false; it merely eliminates any reason for thinking that what they say is true. So we go back to square one: we are left with no evidence one way or the other. Outside this context—that is, when there is no use of testimony—the *ad hominem* argument is fallacious, period. If someone offers an argument for his position, there is no issue of credibility involved. It doesn't matter how rotten or stupid the person is. We have to consider the argument on its own merits.

In its crudest form, the fallacy involves nothing more than insults

—calling one's opponent an idiot, slob, lowlife, airhead, fascist, pinko, nerd, fairy, bleeding heart, wimp, Neanderthal, and so on through the rich vocabulary of abuse our language offers. Unlike the other fallacies, moreover, this one is committed fairly often in its crude form. In personal disputes, disagreement often breeds anger, and angry people hit below the belt. In politics, *ad hominem* arguments are a common technique of propaganda, and a common device of politicians who try to enlist support by finding enemies to attack. But the fallacy also takes more sophisticated forms. Let's look at a few.

Suppose that someone criticizes you for telling a white lie. If your critic is himself a notorious liar, you would probably be tempted to say, "Look who's talking!" This response is certainly understandable—no one enjoys being censured by a moral inferior —but it is fallacious. It's a species of *ad hominem* known as the *tu quoque* ("you're another") argument. The fact that someone else is guilty of an accusation doesn't prove that you are innocent. It may be unseemly for the pot to call the kettle black, but the kettle is black nonetheless.

A related version of the *ad hominem* fallacy occurs when we attack a person's position by claiming that it is inconsistent with his practice or with his other positions. The classic example is the patient who says to his doctor: "How can you tell me I should stop smoking when you still smoke yourself?" The fact that a doctor doesn't take his own advice hardly means that it isn't good advice; a hypocrite may still say something true, or make a valid argument. Here's a more complex example from politics. Many conservatives oppose economic sanctions against South Africa on the grounds that the sanctions would hurt us more than them, and that we could do more good by remaining in South Africa and trying to influence the government from within. Yet conservatives often *support* sanctions against Marxist regimes such as Nicaragua. Liberals tend to take the opposite position in both cases. So whenever sanctions are proposed, liberals and conservatives spend a good deal of time accusing each other of inconsistency. These accusations may well be true, and they may help to clarify the issue. In the end, however, you can't establish your position merely by showing that your opponents are inconsistent. That's their problem. *Your* problem is to find some actual evidence to support your view.

A final version of the *ad hominem* argument is the effort to impugn someone's objectivity by claiming he has a vested interest in the view he defends. Except in the case of someone posing as an authority (as we discussed above), this tactic is usually fallacious, and it is usually done in a sneaky way. Here's an example from a newspaper editorial: "The conservative audience in Dallas, deep in the heart of oil-rich Texas, shouted a predictable 'No' to the question whether the President should 'roll over and play dead as Congress passes more and more legislation to strangle free enterprise.'" The writer obviously opposes the free enterprise views of the president and his conservative audience. But instead of giving a reasoned argument against free enterprise, the writer takes a shortcut: the reference to "oil-rich Texas" plants the idea that their conservatism is merely an expression of economic self-interest, and can therefore be dismissed without further consideration. This tactic is sometimes called "poisoning the well," and it is obviously fallacious. The fact that someone might have a nonrational motive for supporting a position does not mean the position is false, and it certainly does not mean we can decide ahead of time that all his arguments for the position can be dismissed.

In face-to-face disputes, poisoning the well usually takes the form of the statement, "You're just saying that because. . . ." For example: "You're only supporting Julie for class president because she's your friend," or "You're just defending the draft because you know you'd get a medical exemption." Statements of this type are fallacious: if you have given an argument for the draft, or in favor of Julie's candidacy, the soundness of your argument is unaffected by the existence of other motivations you may have for your position. And such statements are insulting. They say, in effect, "I won't even listen to what you have to say because I know ahead of time that you can't be objective; your reasoning is nothing more than a mouthpiece for your emotions and your vested interests." This is a particularly insidious form of the *ad hominem* fallacy, because it tries to undercut your confidence in your ability to think objectively; it breeds self-doubt and timidity. It's true that we do have to be careful not to let our judgment be biased by subjective factors. Otherwise we run the risk of subjectivism. But we should not accept undeserved accusations that we are guilty of this (or any other) logical sin.

Practice Quiz

Each of the statements below commits one of the fallacies discussed in this section: appeal to authority, or *ad hominem* (including *tu quoque* and poisoning the well). Identify which fallacy is committed.

1. I think America should be more careful about the international organizations we join, and the treaties we sign. After all, wasn't it George Washington himself who warned against "foreign entanglements"?

2. Why should Congress consult the joint chiefs of staff about military funding? They are military men, so obviously they will want as much money as they can get.

3. "The poor nations of the world will have to learn to produce their own food if they are to solve the problem of hunger in the long run." "That's a heartless position. You wouldn't say that if you had ever really been hungry."

4. This must be an important event—the *Times* gave it four columns on the front page.

5. TV commentators are always attacking big business for making "obscene profits," but the companies they work for have higher profits than almost any other industry.

Fallacies of Logical Structure

In the previous sections, we examined arguments that are fallacious because they introduce irrelevant considerations into the reasoning process: emotions, threats, personal traits. In this section, we'll examine fallacies that involve errors within the reasoning process itself. The problem in these arguments is not the premises they use, but the relation between the premises and the conclusion.

Begging the Question (Circular Argument)

During the Middle Ages, the scholastic philosophers developed a formal style of debate. The goal, as in modern debate, was to prove one side or the other of a certain question: one contestant would try to prove the proposition *p*, the other would try to prove its opposite. To establish your conclusion, however, you could use only those premises to which your opponent would agree. You had to ask: will you grant me *q*? How about *r*? And so forth. Now, if you were trying to prove *p*, the fastest way would be to get your opponent to grant you *p* itself; then you wouldn't have to do any more work. But for that very reason, of course, you couldn't expect your opponent to do so. In effect, you would be asking (begging) him to grant the very question at issue. So "begging the question" was not permitted.

Nor *should* it be permitted in reasoning. The point of reasoning is to throw light on the truth or falsity of a proposition (the conclusion) by relating it to other propositions (the premises) that we already have some basis for believing to be true. If our reasoning does nothing more than relate *p* to itself, then it hasn't gained us anything. Circular arguments are no more productive than circular definitions. So it is always fallacious to use a proposition as a premise in an argument intended to support that proposition.

The most obvious way to commit the fallacy would be simply to restate the conclusion as a premise, in an argument of the form:

This usually occurs only when the proposition is formulated in two different ways, so that it is not immediately apparent that the person is simply restating his conclusion. For example: "[1] Society has an obligation to support the needy, because [2] people who cannot provide for themselves have a right to the resources of the community." Statement (2) expresses the same proposition as (1): "society" means the same thing as "community," "the needy" are the same class of people as "those who cannot provide for themselves," and the obligation mentioned in (1) is merely another way of expressing the right mentioned in (2). Both statements, therefore, should be given the same number, and the diagram would be:

People typically beg the question in this way when a proposition seems so obvious to them that they aren't sure what further evidence could be given for it; so they keep restating it in the hope that some formulation will strike a chord in the listener and lead him to agree.

A more subtle form of the fallacy occurs when the circle is enlarged to include more than one step: the conclusion p is supported by premise q, which in turn is supported by p (though there could be any number of intervening steps). Suppose I am arguing with an atheist about the existence of a Supreme Being. He asks why I believe that God exists, and I say, "Because the Bible says so." If he then asks why we should take the Bible's word for it, and I answer that the Bible is trustworthy because it is the Word of God, I am arguing in a circle: my premise assumes the existence of God, which was precisely the question at issue. As this example illustrates, circular reasoning of this type often occurs in debates when we try to answer an objection by falling back on the conclusion we are trying to establish.

Another common form of circular reasoning is the question-begging definition. Here's an example:

Hank: "All communist governments are aligned with the Soviet Union in foreign policy."
Alice: "What about Yugoslavia, or China?"
Hank: "But they are not genuinely communist countries."
Alice: "Why not?"
Hank: "Because they aren't aligned with the Soviet Union."

In this argument, Hank has incorporated the conclusion he wants to defend—that all communist countries are aligned with the Soviet Union—into his *definition* of a communist country. He is using this alignment as a criterion for deciding which countries count as "genuinely" communist. Sometimes an argument does turn on a definition, so we can't dismiss what Hank has done as wrong in principle. But it's clear that in this particular case, he is tailoring his definition to suit his conclusion. So it is fair to accuse him of begging the question. (Notice that his definition is not circular *as a definition:* the concept COMMUNISM is not being defined in terms of itself. The circularity here pertains to the *role* of the definition in the argument. A question-begging definition need not be a circular one.)

Yet another species of begging the question is known as the *complex question*. The classic example is the prosecutor who asks the witness, "Have you stopped beating your wife?" If the witness says "Yes," he has admitted that he *was* beating his wife; but if he answers "No," he seems to admit the same thing. The reason for this is obvious. Despite its appearance, the question is not simple but complex. There are really two questions here: has the man ever beaten his wife? and if so, has he stopped? We can't even raise the second question, much less answer it, until we have answered the first one. By not asking the first question, the prosecutor simply assumes that the answer to it is "Yes"—he begs that question. In general, most questions rest on certain assumptions. If we accept those assumptions, we can go ahead and answer the question. But if we reject those assumptions, then we should say so, and refuse to answer the question. Thus the witness in the classic example should say, "Your question is invalid because I never *started* beating my wife."

Post Hoc

The Latin name of this fallacy is short for *post hoc ergo propter hoc:* "after this, therefore because of this." The fallacy has to do with causality, and it has the structure:

A occurred before B

↓

A caused B

Such reasoning is fallacious because many events that precede a given event have nothing to do with it, as in the old joke: "Why are you whistling?" "To keep the elephants away." "But there aren't any elephants around here." "See? It works."

The *post hoc* fallacy is probably the source of many superstitions. Someone, somewhere, had a run of bad luck, and attributed it to breaking a mirror, walking under a ladder, stepping on a crack, or some other previous action. A student does well on an exam, and thereafter always wears the same "lucky" sweater on exam days. More serious examples of the fallacy occur in situations where causal relationships are extremely complex and difficult to identify. Stock market advisers sometimes make predictions on the basis of a few indicators which, in the past, happened to precede a rise or fall in prices. *Post hoc* reasoning can also occur in speculation about the causes of historical events such as the Civil War, the causes of economic phenomena such as the Great Depression, or the causes of sociological trends such as the increasing divorce rate.

It's certainly true that, if we want to know what caused an event or phenomenon B, we have to *start* by identifying the factors that preceded it. But we can't stop there. To show that some particular factor A was the cause, we have to show that there is some actual connection between A and B. We need to find evidence that something more than a temporal relationship exists between them. In Part IV, we will study in detail the types of argument that provide such evidence. For now, we will have to rely on our intuitive judgment. When someone presents an argument that A caused B, ask yourself: Could it be merely a coincidence that A happened just before B? Is A the *kind* of thing that could have an effect on B? Has the person offered any explanation of *how* A affected B?

False Alternative

When we reason about the truth or falsity of a conclusion, we rarely consider the conclusion in a vacuum. We have in mind a range of other possible conclusions. When we think about whether to take a certain action, we weigh it against other options. When we consider a hypothesis to explain why something happened, we test it against other hypotheses. When we take one side on an issue, we are aware of what the other positions are. In short, thinking often involves a choice among alternatives. The fallacy of false alternatives occurs when we fail to consider *all* the relevant possibilities.

If you told me that someone is not rich, I would commit the fallacy if I inferred that the person is poor. Rich and poor are the extreme points on a continuous dimension that contains many degrees of wealth between the extremes. The fallacy also occurs frequently in the context of a complex question. One of the exercises in a previous chapter referred to the following question from a 1979 opinion poll: "Do you think the shortage of oil we hear about is real or are we just being told there are shortages so oil companies can charge higher prices?" [CBS/*New York Times,* March 1979] This question assumes that the only possibilities are (1) that the shortage is real, and (2) that it's a conspiracy by the oil companies. But there are other possibilities as well: (3) the alleged shortage could be a government excuse to cover up the failure of its policies, or (4) it could be an honest mistake, and not a conspiracy on anyone's part. We could treat the poll question as a complex question because it assumes without argument that (3) and (4) are false; or we could consider it a case of false alternative, because it simply ignores them.

The most subtle examples of the fallacy are those in which relevant alternatives are excluded by some implicit, unspoken, and thus invisible assumption. Some political philosophers argue, for example, that as a society becomes more secular, it will tend to drift toward collectivism, because if man does not give meaning to his life through service to God, he can find meaning only in service to the state. But why are these the only possibilities? The argument clearly assumes that the individual gives meaning to his life only through service to something outside himself, something "higher." It excludes the possibility that the individual can give meaning to his *own* life. It may be that the assumption is true; perhaps the latter possibility *should* be excluded. But this is not self-evident: some further argument would be required to justify the assumption. If the argument excludes an alternative without justification, it is fallacious.

The best safeguards against this fallacy are an open mind and a good imagination. No matter how certain we are of our conclusions and our arguments, it is always worthwhile to stop and ask: is there anything I've overlooked? could there be some other explanation for these facts? is there some other perspective one might take? When we can't find the solution to a problem, it is often because we're looking at it from some angle, making some assumption, which excludes an alternative approach that might solve the problem. If we are not satisfied with any of the standard positions on a given issue, it may be because they all make some assumption that should be called in question, thus opening up other possible positions.

Appeal to Ignorance (Argumentum ad Ignorantiam)

Suppose I accused you of cheating on an exam. "Prove it," you say. "Can you prove that you didn't?" I ask—and thereby commit the fallacy of appeal to ignorance. The appeal to ignorance is the argument that a proposition is true because it hasn't been proven false. To put it differently, it is the argument that a proposition is true because the *opposing* proposition hasn't been proven true. If we use the symbol $-p$ to stand for the denial or negation of p, the fallacy has the structure:

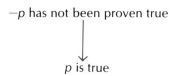

$-p$ has not been proven true

p is true

This is a fallacy because a lack of evidence for $-p$ does not imply that there is evidence for p. All it means is that we do not know that $-p$ is true. I can't prove that a storm is not brewing in the atmosphere of Jupiter, but that would hardly count as evidence that a storm *is* brewing. The absence of evidence usually means that we simply don't know enough to make a judgment. Such ignorance cannot be transmuted into knowledge, any more than brass can be transmuted into gold.

In the preceding examples of the fallacy, the proposition p was a positive claim: that you cheated, that a storm is brewing on Jupiter. But the fallacy can also be committed when p is a negative claim. The absence of evidence that you *did* cheat does not prove that you *didn't;* the absence of evidence that a storm *is* brewing doesn't prove that one *isn't.* In the diagram above, p may be either negative or positive, and $-p$ will have the opposite quality; the structure of the fallacy is the same in either case. Strictly speaking, there is a logical symmetry between positive and negative claims.

In practice, however, the fallacy is normally committed by those who assert the positive. The reason is that we rarely have occasion to make negative claims except in response to positive ones. We rarely have occasion to assert that something is *not* the case until someone has suggested that it *is.* Suppose you and I were having a conversation when I suddenly announced that there is an invisible leprechaun hovering over your left shoulder. You would probably be somewhat skeptical, and you would naturally ask me what reason I had for believing this (we couldn't settle the matter by looking, since I said it was invisible). I'm the one making the assertion here, so I have to provide evidence. Apart from my statement, it would never occur to you to deny that there is an invisible leprechaun over your left shoulder. In the same way, it would not occur to you to deny that you cheated on the test unless someone accused you of it, and then the accuser has the burden of offering evidence.

As a rule, it is the positive claim that puts the ball in play, and the positive claim that carries the initial burden of proof. If someone makes an unsupported statement, therefore, the proper response is not to make an equally unsupported denial. Nor should you accept the burden of disproving the person's statement; if you do, you are cooperating in an implicit appeal to ignorance. (This is a trap that paranoid people often spring on their listeners: they make an arbitrary claim about a conspiracy against them, and then take their claim to be vindicated unless others can disprove it.) The proper response is simply to point out that the claim is unsupported, and ask the person to provide some evidence for it. If evidence *is* forthcoming, then the ball is in your court; if you do not find the evidence convincing, it is your responsibility to explain why.

One application of this rule is the legal principle that a person is innocent until proven guilty. To assert that someone is guilty is to make a positive claim: that he committed a certain act. Innocence, no matter how desirable, is a negative trait: it means the absence of guilt, it means that the person did *not* commit a certain act. A defendant is on trial only because he has been charged with a crime, so those who brought charges have the initial burden of backing them up. But we need to be careful here. The criminal law also requires that guilt be proven beyond a reasonable doubt. If the prosecution fails, the defendant will be acquitted and treated as legally innocent. But does the prosecutor's failure prove that the defendant is innocent in fact? Does it prove that the defendant did not commit the crime? No. We would commit the fallacy of appealing to ignorance if we thought so. In this respect, the legal rule goes beyond the burden of proof principle. It also reflects the ethical principle that it is better to let a guilty person go than to punish an innocent one.

Non Sequitur

A literal translation of *"non sequitur"* would be: "It does not follow." A *non sequitur* argument is one in which the conclusion simply does not follow from the premises; the premises are *irrelevant* to the conclusion (thus another name for the fallacy is "irrelevant conclusion"). Of course, we could say this about any of the fallacies we have studied: it is in the very nature of a fallacy that the conclusion does not follow from the premises. So *non sequitur* is actually a kind of miscellaneous category for fallacious arguments that do not fit the specific patterns of any of the other fallacies. In its crudest form, there is an obvious leap between premise and conclusion, as in the accident reports we used in a previous exercise—"The pedestrian had no idea which direction to go, so I ran over him." Such logical leaps are often the stuff of comedy. But there are also more subtle forms of the fallacy, in which the gap between premise and conclusion may not be so obvious. Let's look at some common patterns.

"X is____; there ought to be a law against it." The blank can be filled with any number of adjectives. If the speaker is a conservative, *x* may be an action which he considers *morally wrong*. If the speaker is a consumer advocate, *x* may be a product he considers *dangerous* or *ineffective*. If the speaker is a doctor, *x* may be something he considers *unhealthy*. In each case, the argument would be a *non sequitur* because the fact that something is undesirable is a separate issue from the political question of what the government should do about it. To bridge the logical gap, we would need an implicit premise of the form "The government should ban anything that is____." This would be a substantive premise, an assumption about the proper role of government, and it would require some defense. We would have to be prepared to answer objections from people who argue that individuals should be free to decide for themselves whether to take immoral actions, use dangerous products, and so on. The same point applies to positive arguments of the form "X would be____; there ought to be a law requiring it." If the speaker is a liberal, *x* may be an act of *charity* or *compassion toward the poor;* if the speaker is an environmentalist, *x* might be something that would *beautify the landscape.* Here again, there is an assumed premise about the proper role of government, and the argument is a *non sequitur* unless that assumption is defended.

Another common type of *non sequitur* is the argument that, because an action had certain consequences, those consequences must have been intended. The most obvious example is the tendency to see conspiracies behind everything. The U.S. government makes a decision that turns out advantageously for the Soviet Union —so there must be Communist secret agents at work. A foreign policy decision would benefit U.S. businesses—therefore the State Department is controlled by giant corporations. These are fallacious arguments because actions normally have some consequences that are not intended—effects that are by-products of the main goals, or are completely unanticipated. To support the claim that a consequence was the product of someone's intention, therefore, we cannot argue merely that the consequence occurred, or that it was to someone's advantage; we also have to provide evidence of the intention itself.

This is especially important when the consequence is a large scale, statistical pattern, which is usually beyond the power of any individual or group to bring about intentionally. In recent years, for example, the percentage of poor families headed by single women has been growing. This "feminization of poverty" is a statistical fact, and is certainly grounds for concern. But to regard it as an act of discrimination against women is to assume that someone intentionally brought it about. Unless we have evidence of that intention, this would be a *non sequitur.*

A third sort of *non sequitur*, sometimes known as the fallacy of *diversion*, consists in changing the issue in the middle of an argument. A prosecutor in a child abuse case might go on and on about the horrors of child abuse—the child's suffering and future psychological problems, statistics showing that the problem is a growing one, and so on—when the real issue is whether the defendant is guilty of the crime. The argument would run:

1) The defendant is guilty of child abuse.
2) Child abuse is an awful crime.
3), 4), . . . , n) statements concerning immediate and long-term effects on children, statistics on the extent of the problem, and other evidence.

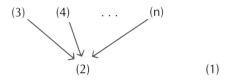

The prosecutor's strategy is obvious. He is diverting attention from (1) to (2), because (2) is much easier to prove. Who could deny that child abuse is awful? At the same time, however, he is hoping that the jury will not notice the diversion, and that the strength of the argument for conclusion (2) will carry over in their minds to (1), even though the defendant's guilt is a completely separate question. As the example illustrates, diversion often works hand in glove with the appeal to emotion: diversion works best when the nonrelevant conclusion arouses powerful emotions. For this reason, a nonrelevant issue is sometimes called a *red herring*—herring turns red when it rots, and a rotten fish has such a powerful smell that dragging it across the ground will throw a dog off the scent.

A special form of diversion is called the *straw man* argument. This fallacy occurs in debate when someone distorts an opponent's position, usually stating it in an oversimplified or extreme form, and then refutes the distorted position, not the real one. Suppose you are a student in my class, and you come to me with the suggestion that I allow more class discussion. I would commit the straw man fallacy if I replied: "I don't want to give the entire class period over to an aimless bull session, because no one would learn anything." This may be an excellent argument against giving the entire class period over to an aimless bull session, but that is not what you suggested. (If you diagram this example, you will see that it fits the pattern of diversion.) Straw man arguments occur most often when issues are complex and emotions run high. Look for them especially in politics, and in quarrels between friends and lovers.

We have now examined eleven common fallacies, along with several subsidiary ones that have been given special names; they are listed and defined in the following box. As indicated at the outset, this is not an exhaustive list of logical errors; it includes only the more common and more significant ones. It should also be emphasized that a given argument may commit more than one of the fallacies. If you encounter such an argument, in the exercises below or in real life, you should try to identify all the fallacies it commits.

Practice Quiz

Each of the following arguments commits one or more fallacies of logical structure; identify the fallacy or fallacies.

1. The federal government should save New York City from default, for New York deserves such aid.
2. The layoffs at Acme Corporation were obviously racist: over sixty percent of the people laid off were black or Puerto Rican.
3. Hard-core pornography is disgusting and offensive to any civilized person, so it cannot be included in the right to free speech.

Fallacies

Note: each definition below gives only the differentia; the genus in each case is FALLACY.

Subjectivism: using the fact that one believes or wants a proposition to be true as evidence of its truth.

Appeal to majority: using the fact that large numbers of people believe a proposition to be true as evidence of its truth.

Appeal to emotion: trying to get someone to accept a proposition on the basis of an emotion one induces.

Appeal to force (argumentum ad baculum): trying to get someone to accept a proposition on the basis of a threat.

Appeal to authority (argumentum ad verecundiam): using testimonial evidence for a proposition when the conditions for credibility are not satisfied, or the use of such evidence is inappropriate.

Ad hominem: using a negative trait of a speaker as evidence that his statement is false or his argument weak.

> *Tu quoque:* trying to refute an accusation by showing that the speaker is guilty of it.

> *Poisoning the well:* trying to refute a statement or argument by showing that the speaker has a nonrational motive for adopting it.

Begging the question (circular argument): trying to support a proposition with an argument in which that proposition is a premise.

> *Complex question:* trying to get someone to accept a proposition by posing a question that presupposes it.

Post hoc: using the fact that one event preceded another as sufficient evidence for the conclusion that the first caused the second.

False alternative: excluding relevant possibilities without justification.

Appeal to ignorance (argumentum ad ignorantiam): using the absence of proof for a proposition as evidence for the truth of the opposing proposition.

Non sequitur: trying to support a proposition on the basis of irrelevant premises.

> *Diversion:* trying to support one proposition by arguing for another proposition.

> > *Straw man:* trying to refute one proposition by arguing against another proposition.

4. Six months after President Hoover took office in 1929, the stock market crashed and the Great Depression began. He is therefore responsible for this tragic episode in our national history.

5. Only short poems can be good, not long ones. Of course, many so-called poems, such as *Paradise Lost,* take up a large number of pages. But if they are any good, they must really be collections of short poems, because a long poem as such cannot be of any great value.

6. Why are you so skeptical about ESP? Can you prove that it doesn't exist?

7. Congressman Jones denies that he's a liberal, so he must be a conservative.

8. As a determinist, I believe that none of our actions results from free choice, and that all of them are determined by the strongest motive acting upon us. To be sure, it sometimes does seem that we choose to act on the weaker of two motives. But if we do that, it only shows that the motive which seemed weaker was really the stronger of the two, since it determined our action.

9. Twenty-five years after graduation, Harvard alumni have average incomes much higher than the average college graduate. A Harvard education must be the road to riches.

10. "I don't see how you can support distribution requirements. Don't you want students to have any choice about their courses?"

11. Opinion poll question: Do you favor more money for welfare programs, or do you feel we should let people starve in the streets?

12. Mary *says* she loves me. I don't know whether to believe her or not, but I guess I do, because I don't think she would lie to someone she loves about something that important.

SUMMARY

A fallacy is an error in reasoning, an argument in which the premises do not in fact support the conclusion. This chapter covered a category of fallacies—sometimes called fallacies of relevance—which occur fairly often in everyday thought and speech.

Subjectivist fallacies involve the attempt to support a conclusion by appealing to nonobjective, nonrational factors: one's desire to believe the conclusion, majority opinion, emotion, force.

Two other fallacies—appeal to authority and *ad hominem*—involve a misuse of the standards of credibility for evaluating testimonial evidence.

The third subcategory includes more subtle fallacies of logical structure, errors involving the relation between premises and conclusion: begging the question, *post hoc*, false alternative, appeal to ignorance, and *non sequitur*.

Exercises

A. Identify the fallacy (or fallacies) committed by each of the following arguments.

1. The Beatles were the best rock group of the 1960s—they sold more records than any other group.
2. "That was a great movie."
   "Why do you think so?"
   "Well, I just loved it."
3. I'm shocked to hear you preaching atheism. Does your father know you believe that?
4. How can you deny that the belief in an afterlife is universal? After all, everyone believes in it.
5. "C'mon, spend the night with me."
   "Why should I?"
   "Why shouldn't you?"
6. Interviewer: "Senator, you voted for the B-1 bomber. Would you explain your reasons, particularly in light of criticisms about the effectiveness of the plane?"

   Senator: "I'd be glad to. America needs a strong defense. We'd all like to live in peace with the other nations of this world, but we deceive ourselves if we think we can do that without being prepared to defend ourselves and our allies, our rights and our interests. It's a dangerous world out there, and I'd be derelict in my duty to the people of this nation if I allowed us to lie down and cry "Uncle."
7. No one can criticize the Freudian theory unless he has been psychoanalyzed, for opposition to the theory is normally caused by unconscious resistance, arising from the Oedipal complex, that distorts one's thinking.
8. My logic teacher says it's a fallacy to appeal to authority, but I noticed in class today that she cited Aristotle in answering an objection we had.
9. Salesman to customer: "I think you'll find that those shoes are the ones you want. Shall I wrap them up, or would you prefer to wear them?"
10. Student to teacher: "How can you give me a C in this course? I've been getting B's from all my other teachers. Maybe your grading standards are too high."

B. For each of the propositions below, make up an argument that commits the fallacy named in brackets. Try not to make the fallacy too blatant; make it as subtle and persuasive-sounding as you can.

1. Mary lied when she said she saw a ghost [false alternative].
2. The U.S. should adopt regulatory policies favoring entrepreneurs [appeal to majority].
3. Megadoses of vitamin C can cure cancer [post hoc].
4. Children should not be spanked [appeal to authority].
5. *Moby Dick* is the greatest novel ever written [non sequitur].
6. U.S. savings bonds are a good investment [appeal to force].
7. Many crimes result from TV violence [appeal to ignorance].
8. Logic is worth studying [begging the question].
9. I'll pass this course [subjectivism].
10. Capitalism exploits the working class [appeal to emotion].

C. Identify any fallacies committed in the following passages.

1. "On the November 21 editorial page, J. J. Boddewyn argues that 'Smoking Ads Don't Get People Hooked.' However, the majority of Americans consider tobacco advertising a major influence in promoting the killer habit.

   "Approximately 57% of the public thinks that cigarette advertising causes youngsters to smoke. Also, 47% thinks that cigarette advertising makes it harder for smokers to give up the habit." [Letter to the editor, *Wall Street Journal*, December 5, 1986]

2. "Sen. Rudman advanced a 'pizza theory' to resolve disputes; budget negotiators were stalled for five hours but reached agreement 20 minutes after Rep. Aspin had pizza delivered." [*Wall Street Journal*, December 13, 1985]

3. "Jews are part of the Soviet people. They are a fine people, intelligent, very valued in the Soviet Union. Therefore, the problem of Jews in the Soviet Union does not exist." [Mikhail Gorbachev, quoted in Geneva, November 1985]

4. "In addition, city, state and Federal governments should become more involved [in day care]. The only industrialized nation that lacks a national policy on child care is the United States." [Tony Schwartz, "Good Day Care—A National Need," *New York Times*, Op-ed, January 3, 1986. Copyright © 1986 by The New York Times Company. Reprinted with permission.]

5. "Edward Maher advocates that the Government 'uphold the prestige and dignity of the United States' at the expense of the lives of the captives in the American Embassy in Teheran. He does not, I take it, have a son or daughter in that embassy." [Letter to the editor, *New York Times*, December 4, 1979]

6. "Voting 'yes' for the new Iranian constitution will satisfy the will and wrath of God Almighty." [Ayatollah Khomeini, quoted on "ABC News," December 2, 1979]

7. "Q. Senator McGee, why do you oppose ending the monopoly of the Postal Service on delivery of first-class mail?

   "A. Because it undermines the basic premise of the U.S. Postal system. George Washington described this system as the unbroken chain that holds the nation together. The central government of every modern country of the world has a monopoly on letter mail." [Interview with Senator Gale McGee, *U.S. News and World Report*, September 13, 1976]

8. "The difficulty . . . is that you do not recognize abortion, the direct killing of an innocent unborn child, as the most violent oppression of the weak our world has ever known. You do not turn in revulsion when that new, living human being—defenseless, unseen and unheard in his mother's womb, but our neighbor—is sucked to smithereens, dismembered by a surgeon's scalpel or burned to death by a saline solution." [Letter to the editor, *New York Times*, October 8, 1980]

9. "After deciding to sell his home in Upland, California, novelist Whitney Stine pounded a 'For Sale' sign into his front yard. But he deliberately waited to do so until 2:22 p.m. one Thursday.

   "The house sold three days later for his asking price—$238,000. And Mr. Stine credits the quick sale to the advice of his astrologer, John Bradford, whom he has consulted for 12 years in the sale of five houses.

   "'He always tells me the exact time to put out the sign according to the phases of the moon, and the houses have always sold within a few months,' Mr. Stine says." [Kathleen A. Hughes, "Thinking of Buying or Selling a House? Ask Your Astrologer," *Wall Street Journal*, October 12, 1986]

10. "While most scientists are still studying the causes for the two successive harsh winters to hit North America, researcher George Stone believes he has found the answer. Stone, who claims to be a geologist and a weather expert, and to have worked secretly with the CIA, says that the abnormally cold weather was probably caused by the Soviet Cosmos satellite which crashed early this year in northern Canada. 'I feel that satellite may well have been controlling our weather all along the East Coast, and probably the other parts of the country,' he told the tabloid *The Star*. 'The satellite that crashed in Canada in January was in just the right position to control our weather all along the East Coast, where the snowstorms hit. . . . I admit I have no hard evidence, but then there is no negative evidence either. . . .'" [*The Sceptical Inquirer*, Fall 1978]

11. ". . . Ronald Reagan has prided himself on appointing the best possible judges to the state of California when he was governor

and to the Federal bench as President. The quality of the judges in both cases proves that he succeeded in that objective." [Attorney General Edwin Meese, quoted in the *New York Times*, August 12, 1986]

12. "But don't wrangle with us so long as you apply, to our intended abolition of bourgeois property, the standard of your bourgeois notions of freedom, culture, law, &c. Your very ideas are but the outgrowth of the conditions of your bourgeois production and bourgeois property. . . ." [Karl Marx and Friedrich Engels, *Communist Manifesto*]

13. "Benedict Cairoli, 51, a curly-haired retail-store department manager, was a big booster of business deductions when he had the use of a company car. 'But I'm not in that category anymore,' he says seriously. "'So I don't think that you should have such a deduction.'" [*Wall Street Journal*, December 12, 1984]

14. "The travel promoted by detente was one of the causes of the Solidarity movement [in Poland]. A group of sociologists who studied 10,000 Solidarity activists at all levels found that about 70 percent had spent at least a month in the West, mainly in Sweden or West Germany." [Lucy Komisar, "Why Dissidents Need Detente," *New York Times*, Op-ed, December 2, 1985]

15. "[New York Mayor Ed Koch] dismisses *I, Koch* with a wave of the hand: 'It is not a good book. It did not sell well.'" [Nicholas Lemann, "Koch as Koch Can," *The New Republic*, January 20, 1986]

16. "'We just don't know what the distribution of quality [in day care centers] is,' says Dr. Alfred Kahn. . . .

"'And about 90 percent of the family day care in this country is underground. It's not licensed, it's not regulated, and you have to assume that a lot of it is very low quality. We have some excellent care, and the research shows that either kids gain or aren't hurt by day care. However, the research hasn't gone into places that aren't licensed and aren't standardized, so I would have to guess that there are a lot of terrible things out there.'" [*New York Times*, September 3, 1984]

17. ". . . the concourse [in Heathrow airport] was temporarily immobilized by a hundred or more Muslim pilgrims, with 'Saracen Tours' on the luggage, who turned to face Mecca and prostrated themselves in prayer. Two cleaners leaning on their brooms . . . viewed this spectacle with disgust.

"'Bloody Pakis,' said one. 'If they *must* say their bloody prayers, why don't they go and do it in the bloody chapel?'

"'No use to them, is it?' said his companion, who seemed a shade less bigotted. 'Need a mosque, don't they?'

"'Oh yerse!' said the first man sarcastically. 'That's all we need in 'Eathrow, a bloody mosque.'

"'I'm not sayin' we ought to 'ave one,' said the second man patiently. 'I'm just sayin' that a Christian chapel wouldn't be no use to 'em. Them bein' in-fi-dels.' . . .

"'I s'pose you think we ought to 'ave a synagogue an' a 'Indoo temple too, an' a totem pole for Red Indians to dance around? . . .'"

[David Lodge, *Small World*]

18. ". . . we do not believe that any [telephone] service efficient, progressive and permanent can be given by companies not making fair profits. No community can afford to be served by unprofitable or bankrupt companies which are bound to give inefficient, unprogressive service." [Theodore M. Vail, *AT&T Annual Report*, 1914]

19. "Soon after the Corporate Accountability Research Group's proposal to federally charter giant corporations was released in report form in January 1976, Wilmington's leading attorneys began a sustained attack on the scholarship of this five-year-long study. The January 25th edition of the DuPont-owned *Wilmington News Journal* quoted Delaware attorneys as labeling our work 'immature . . . uninformed . . . superficial . . . distorted.' 'Much of the more than 400 pages contains heavily biased, badly researched diatribe,' said a related editorial. Two lawyers on the Corporation Law Committee of the Delaware Bar Association published a column in the *Journal* with the breathtaking conclusion that: 'Proponents of federal chartering have not advanced any valid reason to abandon our present system.'

"Obviously, Delaware's corporate bar does not wish to lose the goose that lays all the golden fees." [Ralph Nader, Mark Green, and Joel Seligman, *Taming the Giant Corporation*]

D. We classified the fallacies covered in this chapter into three categories: those that involve subjective thinking, those that misuse standards of credibility, and those that contain errors of logical structure. a) Is this classification mutually exclusive? b) Can you think of another way to classify the same set of fallacies? (You may use more than three species, or fewer.)

E. Diagram each of the following arguments, and assess it for validity. Identify any fallacies you feel it commits.

1. "This Administration has been attacked for going too far in terms of affirmative action, and it's been attacked for not going

far enough. It would be our hope—which would seem to be demonstrated by the criticism [on both sides]—that we have chosen the course that helps to correct the discrimination which was present for many, many years." [Carter administration spokesman, quoted by the *New York Times*, October 3, 1977]

2. "If the task of the painter were to copy for men what they see, the critic could make only a single judgment: either that the copy is right or that it is wrong. . . . No one who has read a page by a good critic . . . can ever again think that this barren choice of yes or no is all that the mind offers." [Jacob Bronowski, *Science and Human Values*]

3. "Don B. Kates, Jr., has not convinced me in his argument ["Against Civil Disarmament," September] in favor of each American having his own handgun. A curious omission in his discussion is the fact that selling firearms is big business. Those against the sale have to battle powerful lobbies in state and federal government, who fight, with their enormous resources, to keep profits intact for their patron, the arms manufacturers." [Letter to the editor, *Harpers Magazine*, November 1978]

4. "Certain chemicals cause cancer in humans and certain chemicals cause cancer in animals. All chemicals known to induce cancer in humans cause cancer in laboratory animals. Thus, reducing exposure to chemicals known or suspected to cause cancer in humans or animals will reduce chemically induced cancer in humans." [J. E. Huff, Letter to the editor, *Barrons*, May 7, 1984]

5. "Thus did Braniff set off on a course of willy-nilly, we-don't-care-where, cost-is-no-object expansion. The firm had accumulated a debt of $288 million in its first 30 years. In the three years following deregulation, it borrowed $451 million to finance the expansion." [John Doherty, "Who Burst the Braniff Bubble?" *Reason*, May 1985]

6. "The fact that a majority of the States, reflecting after all the majority sentiment in those States, have had restrictions on abortions for at least a century seems to me as strong an indication there is that the asserted right to an abortion is not 'so rooted in the traditions and conscience of our people as to be ranked fundamental.'" [*Roe v. Wade*, J. Rehnquist, dissenting]

7. "William Butler, chief counsel for the Environmental Defense Fund, which led the attack on DDT between 1966 and 1972, repeats the argument today: 'You can't prove a negative,' he said when I called him in April. 'You can't say something doesn't exist because there's always a chance that it does exist

but nobody has seen it. Therefore you can't say something doesn't cause cancer because there's always the chance that it does cause cancer but it hasn't showed up yet. . . .'" [William Tucker, "Of Mice and Men," *Harpers Magazine,* August 1978]

7

Advanced Argument Analysis

Now that we have learned the basic technique for analyzing and evaluating arguments, and honed our evaluation skills on fallacious arguments, it is time to add a few refinements. These refinements will give us more flexibility in applying the basic techniques to a wider range of arguments. We need to examine the principles for identifying *assumed* premises in an argument, and the process of *distilling* an argument from passages that are longer than the ones we have worked with so far. We will also develop the diagramming technique further, so that we can analyze *debates* about controversial issues.

Assumed Premises

We have seen that arguments often leave one or more premises implicit; such premises are assumed, but not stated explicitly. This is a very efficient way to present an argument, since it allows one to focus attention on the new or substantive premises, and avoid cluttering up the presentation with obvious and well-known ones. Nevertheless, we must identify the implicit premises in order to understand an argument fully, and to evaluate it. In Chapter 5, we identified implicit premises by asking what assumptions would be necessary to close the gap between the stated premises and the conclusion. This is the basic technique. But there are guidelines to follow in deciding which particular premise best fills the gap.

Identifying the implicit premises of an argument serves one of two goals, and usually both. In some contexts, our primary goal is to understand an argument presented by a specific person—someone we are talking to, or an author whose work we are reading. The goal is to *interpret* someone else's thoughts; we want to know which assumptions the person is actually making. In other cases, the goal is to *analyze* the argument itself. We are not concerned with any particular person; we want to know what assumptions would be necessary to make the argument itself logically strong, regardless of who is presenting it. Thus interpretation and analysis are somewhat different tasks. Fortunately, the guidelines to follow are essentially the same for both.

There are three basic rules for identifying an assumed premise in an argument: (1) the premise should close the gap between the stated premises and the conclusion, (2) the premise should be informative, and (3) the premise should not commit us to more than is necessary. To illustrate these rules, let's examine an extremely simple bit of reasoning. Suppose a friend tells you that a mutual acquaintance named Elizabeth is failing French, and then draws the conclusion that she probably doesn't like the subject. In diagram form:

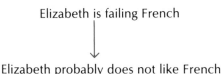

What premise is assumed by this argument?

1) The first rule is to find a premise that will close the gap between the stated premises and the conclusion. Consider the following candidates for the role of assumed premise:

a) French is a hard subject.
b) Elizabeth comes from Scarsdale.
c) Paris is beautiful in the springtime.
d) If Elizabeth were failing French, then she probably would not like French.

Candidates (a)–(c) would not help close the gap in the original argument. If we used one of them, the argument would be a *non sequitur*. But that would be our fault, not the fault of the argument. Insofar as we are analyzing the argument itself, remember, the goal is to find out what assumption is required for the argument to have a reasonable degree of logical strength. And insofar as we are interpreting our friend's train of thought, we should follow what is called the *principle of charity*: we should assume that he is reasoning logically unless there is evidence to the contrary. So once again we should not gratuitously make the argument weak.

By contrast, candidate (d) would make the argument a strong one. Notice that it is a compound proposition with the form *if p, then q*, where *p* is our original premise, and *q* is the conclusion. The resulting argument then has the form:

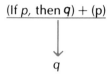

$$(\text{If } p, \text{ then } q) + (p)$$

$$q$$

An argument of this form always eliminates the gap, regardless of what the component propositions *p* and *q* are. It will always be possible, therefore, to satisfy rule (1) by using an assumed premise with an "if . . . then" structure. But there are other rules.

2) The premise should be informative. Premise (d) does not tell us very much. It says there is a connection between (1) and (2), but it doesn't say what that connection is. So it is not very informative. If possible, we should find a proposition that conveys some substantive information—a proposition which, if true, would explain the relationship between the stated premise and the conclusion. If we cannot find such a premise, we'll have to fall back on the strategy of using an "if . . . then" statement. But we should at least try to find something better. Here are some possibilities:

e) No one likes any subject in which he is failing.
f) Elizabeth does not like any subject in which she is failing.
g) Elizabeth does not like most subjects in which she is failing.

Any of these propositions would close the gap between (1) and (2). And any of them would be more informative than (d), because we would be appealing to a general trait involving success in a course and enjoyment of it. So they all satisfy the first two rules. In order to choose among them, we must appeal to our third rule.

3) The premise should not commit us to more than is necessary. Notice that (e) goes much further than (f) or (g), because it says that *all* human beings—not just Elizabeth—possess the trait in question. A statement about an entire class asserts more—is going farther out on a limb—than a statement about one member (and a statement about a broader class asserts more than a statement about a narrower one). In the same way, (f) commits us to more than (g) does, because it says that Elizabeth feels this way about *all* her courses, not just most of them. This is the point at which the third rule comes into play.

We should not read into an argument a premise that commits us to more than necessary, a premise that goes beyond what is necessary to close the gap in the argument. Insofar as we are analyzing an argument in itself, we want to know how far out on a limb we'll have to go in order to accept it. We don't want a premise that will push us farther out on the limb than necessary. And insofar as we are interpreting someone else's ideas, it would not be fair to attribute to him an unnecessarily strong assumption; that would be akin to the straw man fallacy. By this standard, we certainly do not need to make any assumption about human beings in general, so (e) is too strong. And because the conclusion says that Elizabeth *probably* does not like French, it does not express certainty on the point. So we don't even need a premise as strong as (f). We should choose (g) instead. That premise says less than the alternatives, but it says enough to close the gap in the argument.

To apply these three rules to a given argument, you will have to use your judgment, and the decision might not always be as clearcut as in our example. The best approach is to think of several alternative premises, and then use the rules as guidelines for selecting the best candidate. In most cases, there will be a fairly clear winner.

Practice Quiz

Identify the assumed premise in each of the following arguments. Try to think of more than one candidate, and provide a reason for choosing the one you do.

1. Tom is a very successful salesman, so he's probably an outgoing person.
2. There's the bell. Someone must be at the door.
3. The 55 mile/hour speed limit saves lives, as Dr. Robert Jones has recently testified.
4. The traditional wax record, played on top-of-the-line equipment, can reproduce the spatial features of music such as the positions of the instruments in an orchestra. So in that respect it is superior to most compact disk recordings.
5. The government should continue to deregulate the telecommunications industry, because we need an industry that can act quickly and flexibly to exploit the new communication technology.

Distilling an Argument

In order to analyze the structure of an argument, we have to identify its premises and conclusion. We did this in Chapter 5 simply by going through the statement of the argument, numbering the propositions. But this technique works only for short arguments, and only when the argument is presented in a fairly condensed and straightforward way. It works very well for newspaper editorials and letters to the editor. It works for paragraphs in which an author summarizes his argument. But an argument can also be presented over the course of an entire essay, or even an entire book. Such arguments are normally more complex than the ones we have considered so far, and there may be no summary statement. The reader may be left to extract the main argument from a mass of illustrations, historical background, explanatory material, dramatic narratives, digressions, and so on. In these cases, it would be tedious at best to number every statement in the essay or book, since we would have to ignore most of them. And we might still miss a key premise or conclusion, which may be present only as the central point or drift of a passage that does not state it explicitly.

Before we can diagram or evaluate such an argument, therefore, we have to *distill* it from the work as a whole. In effect, we have to write our own summary statement of the argument. (It is often a good idea to do this literally: write out a paragraph summarizing the argument concisely, and then use the paragraph as the basis for diagramming.) This requires that we step back from the text of the argument and ask ourselves some questions. What is the author's basic purpose? What conclusion does he want us to believe? What evidence does he offer for that conclusion? Why does he think this evidence proves his case? As we answer these questions, we can write down the propositions—the premises and the conclusion—as we identify them.

When we restate an argument in our own words, the distinction between explicit and implicit premises becomes blurred. Instead of a clear distinction, we have a continuum, from propositions that the author clearly endorses, to those that are suggested but not stated in so many words, to those that are entirely implicit and unspoken. As a result, it may be very difficult to tell which propositions should be given numbers (as explicit statements), and which should be given letters (as implicit ones). The safest approach in this context is to number all of them, and then to apply to all of them the rules for identifying assumed premises. Because we are putting the argument in our own words, we have to be especially careful about rule (3), not committing an author to more than is necessary for him to make his case.

Let's look at several examples that will illustrate the process of distillation. The first is an argument for population control:

> We know the world is finite. There is only so much pie. We may be able to expand the pie, but at any point in time, the pie *is* finite. How big a

piece each person gets depends in part on how many people there are. At least for the foreseeable future, the fewer of us there are, the more there will be for each. [Johnson C. Montgomery, "The Island of Plenty," *Newsweek*, December 23, 1974]

This is a brief argument, formulated rather clearly. It might seem we could analyze it by the technique of Chapter 5, numbering the propositions as stated, and diagramming the structure. But there is a problem. The core of the argument is presented in the form of a metaphor, and we have to extract its literal meaning.

At one level, the metaphor is easy to interpret. The pie represents a society's material wealth: the sum total of goods and resources. And each person's share of that wealth is a piece of the pie. So we could go through the passage, translating into literal terms, and the result would be:

1) The world is finite.
2) At any point in time, there is a fixed amount of wealth.
3) At any point in time, the fewer people there are, the larger each person's share of the wealth will be.
4) For the foreseeable future, reducing the number of people will increase each person's share of wealth.

(1)

(2)

(3)

(4)

But our analysis is not yet complete. Notice that proposition (3) pertains to a given moment in time, whereas (4) refers to the foreseeable future. This creates a gap in the argument. If we have a fixed amount of wealth being divided up at a certain moment, it's a mathematical certainty that fewer people would mean larger shares for each. But if we are talking about the foreseeable future, we have to consider how wealth is produced. In particular, we have to consider whether reducing the number of people might reduce the total amount of wealth, and conversely whether more people might produce more wealth. If each new person produces as much as he consumes, for example, a ten percent rise in population might bring a ten percent rise in wealth; a ten percent fall in population would bring an equivalent decline in wealth. Either way, each person's share would remain the same.

The metaphor of a pie serves to exclude this possibility. We picture the pie already baked, and of course its size does not depend on the number of people waiting at the table. For a full analysis of the argument, then, we must translate this dimension of the metaphor into literal terms. We must extract from it proposition (5): for the foreseeable future, the amount of wealth does not depend on the number of people. And (5) must be combined with (3) in order to bridge the gap between the present and the foreseeable future:

We have now distilled the author's argument. We have identified the premises implicit in the metaphor, and their logical relationships; and we could go on to assess the strength of the argument in the usual way.

Let's turn now to a second example. This is a longer passage from the British writer G. K. Chesterton, and it will bring out other aspects of distilling an argument.

> It is not fashionable to say much nowadays of the advantages of the small community. . . . There is one advantage, however, in the small state, the city, or the village, which only the wilfully blind can overlook. The man who lives in a small community lives in a much larger world. He knows much more of the fierce varieties and uncompromising divergences of men. The reason is obvious. In a large community we can choose our companions. In a small community our companions are chosen for us. Thus in all extensive and highly civilized societies groups come into existence founded upon what is called sympathy, and shut out the real world more sharply than the gates of a monastery. There is nothing really narrow about the clan; the thing which is really narrow is the clique. The men of the clan live together because they all wear the same tartan or are all descended from the same sacred cow; but in their souls, by the divine luck of things, there will always be more colours than in any tartan. But the men of the clique live together because they

have the same kind of soul, and their narrowness is a narrowness of spiritual coherence and contentment. . . . A big society exists in order to form cliques. A big society is a society for the promotion of narrowness. It is a machinery for the purpose of guarding the solitary and sensitive individual from all experience of the bitter and bracing human compromises. [G. K. Chesterton, *Heretics*]

This is an arresting argument because it is paradoxical. Chesterton is saying, in effect, that life in a small village is more cosmopolitan than life in a large city. And he flaunts the paradox by restating it in a variety of ways. This makes the passage colorful as a piece of writing, but somewhat redundant in logical terms, and we need to boil the argument down to its essence.

As usual, our first step is to identify the conclusion. Chesterton is defending the small community by describing a trait that he considers advantageous, and the passage is an effort to persuade us that small communities do have this trait. The point is put most concisely in the sentences: "The man who lives in a small community lives in a much larger world. He knows much more of the fierce varieties and uncompromising divergences of men." What are these "varieties" and "divergences"? Chesterton does not give us any detailed analysis, but it is clear that he is talking about psychological differences among people—differences in character, opinion, values, personality. If we use the term "personality" to include all these factors, we can formulate his conclusion as:

1) A person who lives in a small community acquires a deeper knowledge of the variety in human personality than does a person who lives in a large community.

The essential argument for this conclusion is presented in the next few sentences. In a large community we can select our companions—the people we interact with. And we tend to choose people who are similar to ourselves, so that our companions are likely to represent a single type of personality. In a small community, on the other hand, we have to interact with the people who happen to be our neighbors. Since we do not choose them, the laws of probability ("the divine luck of things") make it likely that they will represent a wider range of human personalities. We can formulate this argument as follows:

2) A person in a large community can select his companions.
3) People tend to select companions similar to themselves.
4) A person in a large community will be exposed to a single type of personality.
5) A person in a small community cannot select his companions.

6) Unchosen companions are likely to be diverse.
7) **A** person in a small community will be exposed to many types of personality.

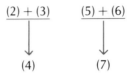

Propositions (4) and (7) will have to be combined additively to support the conclusion, because the conclusion makes a comparison between large and small communities. But notice that those propositions refer to the types of personalities with which we have actual *experience*, whereas the conclusion is a statement about our *knowledge* of human variety. There is a gap here, and it is bridged by an assumption that is implicit in the passage, though very close to the surface. This assumption is: (8) Knowledge of personalities depends on actual experience with them. So the second step of the argument can be diagrammed:

Now that we have distilled the argument, drawing chiefly on the first half of the paragraph, we can see that the rest of the paragraph is repetition and embellishment. Chesterton restates the general argument in terms of the particular case of the clan, which allows him to contrast the clan with the clique, which allows him to talk about the narrowness of a big society. All of this adds color and drama, but it does not add anything substantive to the logical structure of the argument. And once we have the logical structure, we can go on to evaluate the argument, using the method of assessing strength that we learned in Chapter 5.

These two examples illustrate the process of distilling an argument from a text in which it is not laid out for us step by step. The interpretation of such arguments is inherently more difficult, more subject to uncertainty and alternative readings, than was the case for the arguments treated in Chapter 5. But once we have distilled an argument, the basic tools of analysis and evaluation are the same.

Practice Quiz

Distill and diagram the following argument from a Sherlock Holmes story ("The 'Gloria Scott,'" by Arthur Conan Doyle):

"Come now, Mr. Holmes," said he, laughing good-humoredly. "I'm an excellent subject, if you can deduce anything from me."

"I fear there is not very much," I answered; "I might suggest that you have gone about in fear of some personal attack within the last twelvemonth."

The laugh faded from his lips, and he stared at me in great surprise.

"Well, that's true enough," said he, . . . "though I have no idea how you know it."

"You have a very handsome stick," I answered. "By the inscription I observed that you had not had it more than a year. But you have taken some pains to bore the head of it and pour melted lead into the whole so as to make it a formidable weapon. I argued that you would not take such precautions unless you had some danger to fear."

Diagramming Debates

In Chapter 5 we learned how to diagram an argument, or set of arguments, put forward in defense of a conclusion. But how do we diagram a *debate*—a set of opposing arguments for and against a given conclusion? We could just diagram the two arguments separately. It would be useful, however, to include the opposing arguments in a *single* diagram. After all, there's a single issue at stake. If we are trying to decide which position to take, we need to see how the reasons stack up on each side; and to do that we have to bring the arguments on each side into the same picture, to weigh them on a single balance. In a typical case, moreover, the opponents do not merely present arguments on behalf of their own conclusions; they also try to show what is wrong with the opposing arguments. Indeed, there are often many levels in the give-and-take: argument, objection to the argument, reply to the objection, objection to the reply, and so on. The only way to capture this aspect of a debate is, once again, to include both sides in the same diagram.

In order to do this, we need to add a few refinements to the basic diagramming technique. Let's work through the sequence of steps one would typically follow in analyzing a debate.

Step (1): Identify the Conclusions

With a debate, as with a single argument, the first step is to identify the conclusion. We do this by looking for indicator words and by following the logical flow of the argument. With a debate, however, we have two conclusions to identify, one for each side, and we need to make sure that the conclusions speak to the same issue. Otherwise we do not have a genuine debate; the two sides are talking past each other. The test for a genuine debate is whether the conclusions defended by the two sides are *incompatible*—whether they couldn't both be true. If the two conclusions are

Abortion should be made illegal, and
Abortion should not be made illegal

then we have a debate. These propositions are incompatible; they contradict each other; they could not both be true. But if the two sides are arguing for the conclusions

Abortion is wrong, and
Abortion should not be made illegal

we don't have a debate. These propositions are compatible; they could both be true. Whether an action is morally wrong, and whether it should be made illegal, are two different issues.

The clearest case of incompatibility is a disagreement, pro and con, about a single proposition. Person A defends *p*, person B rejects it. For example, person A argues that an oil import tax would benefit the economy, while B denies that it would do so. We can diagram this situation as follows:

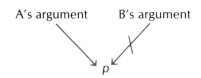

The slash mark on the right-hand arrow means that B's argument is intended as a reason for *rejecting p*, whereas the regular arrow on the left retains its usual meaning: A's argument is intended as a reason for accepting *p*. As we will see, the arrow with the slash mark— let's call it the *negative arrow*—is extremely useful in diagramming debates. Now suppose, to continue with the same example, that person B says an oil import tax would actually *harm* the economy. This illustrates a more complex type of incompatibility. B's position is still incompatible with A's. The net effect of the tax can't be *both*

positive and negative. But now **B** is going further than he did in the first case, because he is now denying that the effect of the tax might be neutral. In the first case, person **A** was making a claim and person **B** was merely denying it; in the second case, **B** is making a definite claim of his own. So we should diagram it:

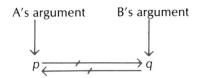

The negative arrows between p and q represent their incompatibility: accepting one would be a reason for rejecting the other.

Step (2): Diagram the Main Arguments on Each Side

Once we have identified the conclusions, we can start to work on the arguments. In most cases, **A** and **B** will each have some main argument to offer in support of their respective conclusions. We can diagram each argument in the standard way, numbering the premises and using arrows and plus signs—except that the last step of **B**'s argument may be a negative arrow pointing at **A**'s conclusion. To distinguish between the premises used by the two sides, we should number them separately: A1, A2, . . . , B1, B2, . . . , for the explicit premises, and Aa, Ab, . . . , Ba, Bb, . . . , for the implicit ones.

In Chapter 5, we diagrammed two arguments, pro and con, about gun control. We could combine these into a single diagram, as follows:

A's argument

A1) Restricting gun ownership will reduce crime
Aa) Reducing crime is desirable
A2) The government should restrict gun ownership

B's argument

B1) People have a right to life
B2) People have a right to self-defense
B3) Restricting gun ownership violates that right

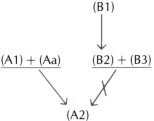

Notice that since B's conclusion—the government should *not* restrict gun ownership—is a denial of A's, we don't need to list it separately in the right-hand column. All the information we need is contained in the negative arrow.

Step (3): Diagram the Counterarguments

In a real debate, the contestants do not merely present their arguments. They also respond to each other's arguments. At this level of a debate, people argue, not directly in support of their own conclusion, but *against* the arguments for the opposing side. To describe this level of a debate, we'll use the term *counterargument*. A counterargument is an objection to another argument. And there are two kinds of objection one can raise. Remember that a good argument has two traits: the premises must be true (the issue of factual strength), and the premises must support the conclusion (the issue of logical strength). To challenge an argument, therefore, we can argue that one or more of its premises are false, or we can argue that the conclusion doesn't follow from the premises, that there's a logical gap in the argument. Let's take an example of each kind of counterargument, and see how to diagram it.

Suppose I argue that a friend of ours, Jerry, is going to have difficulty in his computer science class because he isn't mechanically inclined; he's hopeless with machines. You might reply that Jerry is *not* hopeless with machines. True, you say, he doesn't know anything about cars, but he did build his own stereo system. This is an objection of the first type—you are challenging my premise—and we would diagram it as follows:

A1) Jerry will have difficulty in his computer science class.

A2) Jerry is not mechanically competent.

B1) Jerry built his own stereo system.

Ba) Anyone who can build a stereo system is mechanically competent.

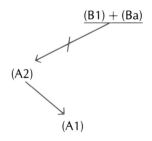

The negative arrow here indicates that your argument is a reason for rejecting my premise.

Counterarguments of the second type, in which we challenge the internal logic of an argument, are a little trickier. Suppose that you accept my premise (A2), but deny that my conclusion follows. It's true that Jerry is hopeless with machines, you say, but it doesn't follow that he'll have trouble with the course, because in computer science you don't do much work with the hardware; the main thing you do is programming, which depends more on logical and mathematical skills. In terms of the diagram, you are saying that my premise (A2) is okay, but I don't have a right to put an arrow from (A2) to (A1). How are we going to diagram that claim? Well, remember that the gap in an argument can be closed by finding an assumed premise. An attack on the internal logic of an argument can therefore be represented as an attack on the premise that would be necessary to close the gap. In this case, I am assuming that success in computer science depends on mechanical skill. If we label this assumption (Aa), then we can diagram your objection as an argument against (Aa), using the same pattern as we did above, when you challenged premise (A2). Thus:

(A1) Jerry will have difficulty in his computer science class.

(A2) Jerry is not mechanically inclined.

(Aa) Success in computer science requires mechanical skill.

(B1) Work in computer science is mostly programming.

(B2) Success in programming does not require mechanical skill.

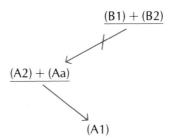

Once again, the negative arrow means that your argument is a reason for rejecting my assumption.

We now have all the elements we need in order to diagram any debate. We can represent the fact that the two sides are defending incompatible conclusions. We can represent the main arguments they offer for their respective conclusions. And we can represent the ways in which they respond to each others' arguments. In most cases, of course, there is more than one round of responses. In the example above, I might challenge your critique of my argument, and you might reply to my challenge, and so on until we both get tired. But in each round, a challenger must either deny a premise in the other's argument, or deny that the conclusion follows. And we now know how to diagram both types of counterargument. So let's look at a final example that will illustrate the whole process.

Applying the Method

One of the least controversial political ideas in this country is the proposition that people have a right to freedom of speech. This right is protected by state constitutions as well as the First Amendment of the U.S. Constitution. It is not always easy to apply the principle of free speech to specific cases, however, and controversial issues often arise. One of them is whether the right to free speech includes the right to distribute pamphlets and other political materials in privately owned shopping malls. The U.S. Supreme Court has ruled that this is an open question as far as the First Amendment is concerned; individual states are free to decide the matter as they choose. Some states have granted their citizens this right, others have not. Let's examine the opposing arguments.

To begin with, we should formulate the issue precisely. The issue is one of *rights:* should people have the legally enforceable right to distribute material in shopping malls? We cannot argue merely that it would be *nice* for mall owners to allow this, or even that it would be *morally* desirable. An opponent of the policy could agree with these claims, and still deny that owners should be forced against their will to allow it. There is a danger here that the two sides will speak to different issues, and thus speak past each other. To ensure that we have a genuine debate, therefore, we should formulate the positive conclusion as follows:

A1) The right of free speech includes the right to distribute political materials in shopping malls, regardless of the owners' permission.

The A-team argues in favor of (A1), the B-team argues against it.

What are the arguments? The main argument in favor of (A1) is that the right of free speech includes the right to speak on political issues in public places, and that shopping malls are public places. We'll label these premises (A2) and (A3). The main argument against (A1) is that malls are privately owned, and the right of free speech does not include the right to use other people's property without their permission—premises (B1) and (B2). The two arguments are represented by the last two lines of the diagram on page 158, and each of them seems logically strong.

Let's go on, then, to ask how the premises might be supported. At first glance, premises (A3) and (B2) seem incompatible, because the terms "public" and "private" are usually considered opposites. So we might expect (A3) and (B2) to be the focus of the debate. But in this context, the terms are not opposites. In (A3), "public" does not mean publicly owned, like the city streets in a downtown shopping district (in which case there would be a contradiction); it means open to the public without special invitation. So there is no incompatibility here. Supporters of (A1) would agree that the malls are privately owned, and opponents would agree that the malls are open to the public without special invitation. So the real debate will be over premises (A2) and (B1).

These are general propositions about what is included in the right of free speech, and they would typically be defended by appealing to the underlying purposes of this freedom. Those on the right-hand side of the debate argue as follows. Freedom of speech means that no one may use force to prevent you from speaking your mind. The purpose of the right is to protect people against *coercion*, primarily in the form of government censorship. It is not a right to have others help you express or communicate your ideas. It is not a right to force me to listen to you, nor is it a right to force your way into my living room and harangue me against my will. Conversely, my refusal to let you use my property to express and communicate your ideas is not coercive. I am not using force to suppress you, I'm merely refusing to help you. We can distill from this argument the premises (B3) and (B4); together they support (B1), as indicated on the diagram.

Those on the left-hand side argue that the basic purpose of free speech is to encourage robust debate, especially on political matters, and to disseminate information so that the public can make informed choices about the issues that confront them. To some extent, it is possible to address people in the privacy of their homes, through the use of radio, TV, newspapers, or the postal system. But these are expensive vehicles to use, and if they were the only ones available, many groups could not afford to communicate their views. Their only hope of reaching an audience is to go where the people are, to make use of places open to the public, where crowds tend to congregate. Thus, to be effective, free speech must include the right of access to such public places. We can distill from this argument premises (A4) and (A5)—(A5) in turn is supported by

A1) The right of free speech includes the right to distribute political material in shopping malls, regardless of the owners' permission. *(Conclusion)*

A2) The right of free speech includes the right to speak on political matters in public places.

A3) Shopping malls are public places.

A4) The purpose of free speech is to encourage debate and the dissemination of information.

A5) This purpose would be frustrated if speakers were not allowed to use public places freely.

A6) It would be too expensive for many speakers to use media for communicating with people in their own homes (TV, radio, mail, newspapers).

Aa) The purpose mentioned in (A4) takes precedence over other rights.

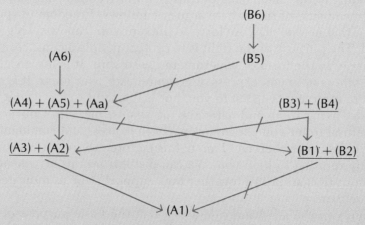

B1) The right of free speech does not include the right to use other peoples' property without their permission.

B2) Shopping malls are privately owned.

B3) The purpose of free speech is to protect people against coercive restraints on their speech.

B4) A private owner's refusal to allow speakers to use his property is not coercive.

B5) Owners deserve the right to decide how their property will be used.

B6) Owners built their malls by their own work, at their own risk.

(A6)—and together they constitute an argument for (A2), as indicated on the diagram.

So far we have treated the opposing arguments in isolation, but obviously the two sides are going to reject each others' reasoning. To begin with, premises (A2) and (B1) are incompatible; hence an argument for one is an argument against the other, and we indicate this on the diagram by the criss-crossing negative arrows. But let's go one step further. Why do opponents of the policy reject the argument put forward in support of (A2)? They might use various counterarguments; here is one of them. It's true that one purpose of free speech is to allow debate and the flow of information. It may also be true that some people could not achieve this purpose without using public spaces. But it doesn't follow that they have a *right* to make use of public places that are privately owned, unless you make the additional assumption that the purpose of encouraging debate takes precedence over property rights. And that assumption is not warranted. People congregate in a shopping mall only because the owner has made it an attractive place for them; that required a financial risk and a lot of hard work. No one has a right to freeload on the owner's achievement; he is entitled to decide how it will be used. This objection can be formulated as proposition (B5), supported by (B6). Since it is directed against the validity of the inference from (A4) and (A5) to (A2), we represent it on the diagram as an attack on the implicit premise of that inference—assumption (Aa).

There is much more to this debate, of course, and it would be a good exercise to take it further on your own. How would the left-hand side respond to the objection we just outlined? And how would they criticize the main argument put forward on the right? And how would the right respond to that criticism? If you pursue these questions, you will soon find yourself exploring some of the deepest questions in political philosophy. But we have taken the argument far enough to illustrate the process of analyzing and diagramming a debate.

Practice Quiz

Diagram the following debate, using the method we have just reviewed.

A: In this year's federal budget, I think Congress should increase the funds it gives to cultural programs: the National Endowment for the Arts, the

Endowment for the Humanities, and so on. The programs are a vital government function, and funds for them have not kept pace with inflation lately.

B: I disagree. In fact, I don't think the government should be subsidizing artists and intellectuals in the first place. Their work involves fundamental beliefs and values. That's fine, but taxpayers shouldn't be forced to support viewpoints they may not share. We don't allow the government to subsidize religion. Why should it be any different for nonreligious issues?

A: But cultural activities are a crucial part of the life of the nation. Man does not live by bread alone, and a society without art, music, scholarship, and the like would be grossly impoverished. These things can't be sustained in the private sector, like material goods, so it is vital for government to support them.

B: Suppose I agree for the sake of argument that cultural activities can't be supported by charging for them in the marketplace. It doesn't follow that government subsidies are the only alternative. They could be funded by voluntary contributions, like religion again, or private colleges.

SUMMARY

This chapter added several refinements to the basic method of analyzing arguments. To identify an implicit premise in an argument, we should find a premise that closes the gap between the stated premises and the conclusion, that is informative, and that does not commit us to more than is necessary. These guidelines should also be followed in distilling an argument from a lengthy presentation, where we must put the author's reasoning into our own words. To diagram a debate, finally, we should make sure the opposing sides are defending incompatible conclusions, and then diagram their respective arguments and counterarguments.

This completes our general study of arguments. So far we have developed a single technique—the use of diagrams—for analyzing the structure of any argument. And we have used a single technique for assessing strength: we estimate the size of the gap between premises and conclusion, usually by finding the assumption that would be necessary to close the gap. These general-purpose techniques will help you deal critically with any argument you encounter. But we also need to recognize that there are different types of argument, different patterns of reasoning. To make further progress—to notice fine points of structure, and to find more precise methods for assessing strength—we need to look at each kind of argument separately. The two basic categories are *deductive* and *inductive* arguments. Parts Three and Four are concerned with the first, Part Five with the second.

Exercises

A. Identify the implicit assumptions in the arguments below.

1. "No man is allowed to be a judge in his own cause, because his interest would certainly bias his judgment." [James Madison, *Federalist Papers*, #10]
2. "Science is knowledge and thus an end in itself." [Irving M. Copi, *Introduction to Logic*, 6th ed.]
3. "You see, we don't believe that *any* of the investment information you can get in financial newsletters, magazines and newspapers will *ever make you rich.* That's because mass publications, by definition, are written for the masses. They've got to be somewhat trite and conventional." [promotional letter, Royal Society of Lichtenstein]
4. "All languages are the product of the same instrument, namely, the human brain. It follows, then, that all languages are essentially the same in their deep structure, regardless of how varied the surface structures might be." [National Council of Teachers of English, *Students' Right to Their Own Language*]
5. "Meanwhile, we might turn our attention to the runaway domestic consumption that sustains South America's drug producers. 'No nation that contributes to [drug] problems should be considered our friend,' says a Senate summary of the argument for the Hawkins amendment. In that sense, America is its own worst enemy." ["Going to the Source," unsigned editorial, *The New Republic*, February 3, 1986]

B. Distill and diagram the arguments in the following passages. Identify any implicit assumptions, and weigh the argument for strength.

1. "If you accept the idea of representative government as the servant of the people, you can make a pretty strong case against any government secrets. After all, if government is nothing more than an agent of the people, how can it justify keeping secrets from the people in whose name it is supposedly acting? If a private attorney did that to a client it might constitute betrayal of trust—perhaps grounds for a malpractice suit." [Alan Bock, "A Free Press Must Expose State Secrets," *Free Press Network*, Fall 1985]
2. "A tree trunk does not grow from the bottom up, as some people think, lifting its branches as it grows. A tree develops vertically only at the top while increasing its girth below to support the weight of its growing crown; the points at which the

branches spring from the trunk stay at the same levels. You can see this fact demonstrated if you drive along a country road where pastures are fenced with barbed wire nailed to trees. The fencing may have been nailed up so long ago that the trunks now envelop the wire, but it is still at the height at which it was originally placed, as you can verify from the height of wires on nearby fence posts." [James Underwood Crockett, *Trees*]

3. "It has been speculated that crotonaldehyde—which is a violent stomach irritant, and as such has been used in the compounding of 'Mickey Finns' when the bartender in a rough bar wishes to cause an obnoxious customer to leave the premises— may be the ingredient that causes some people to break out in hives when they eat strawberries. However, this is not firm speculation, because raspberries also contain crotonaldehyde and some people who cannot eat strawberries can eat raspberries without difficulty." [P. J. Wingate, "EPA Says Watch Out for the Nicotine Truck," *Wall Street Journal*, January 23, 1986]

4. "The insurance industry's flight from day care is based more on vague alarm than on firm actuarial data. Although day-care policies have turned out to cost more to administer than insurers expected, there seems to be little evidence that they have proved particularly risky. James Strickland of Child Inc. in Austin did a computer search of articles in insurance journals from the past five years, which failed to turn up a single one citing child care either as 'high risk' or 'high loss.' Strickland's own survey found that liability claims from child care and preschools were rare, and that when they did occur, the settlements weren't particularly large. Numerous insurance agents and brokers readily agree with him. What's more, although in the last year several insurance companies have settled claims for abuse, so far no jury has made an award for a case of physical or sexual abuse at a day-care center." [Dorothy Wickenden, "Good-Bye Day Care," *The New Republic*, December 9, 1985]

5. "Let me now re-emphasize . . . the extreme looseness of the structure of all objects. . . . [T]here is no perceptible object that does not consist of a mixture of matter and vacuity. In the first place, we find that in caves the rocky roofs exude moisture and drip with trickling drops. Similarly in our own bodies sweat oozes from every surface; hairs grow on the chin and on every limb and member; food is suffused through every vein, building and sustaining the most outlying parts even to the nails. . . . The stone partitions of houses are pervious to voices and to scent and cold and heat of fire, which penetrates also through hard

iron." [Lucretius, *The Nature of the Universe,* translated by Ronald Latham]

6. "Soviet officials continued to weed out books from the American exhibits at the Moscow International Book Fair today. . . .

"Asked at a news conference why the books were being confiscated and how this could be squared with freedom of speech, Boris I. Stukalin, chairman of the State Publishing Committee and of the organizing committee for the fair, said:

"'. . . It is not correct to say that this is a violation of freedom of speech. It is the highest affirmation of freedom of speech, since freedom to propagandize fascism is the kind of freedom that all honest people in our country and in other countries must oppose.

"'Books of that nature do not bring people closer together and do not serve the cause of detente. Instead, they stir up hatred and hostility between people and hamper the process of detente.'" [Anthony Austin, "Moscow, Still Seizing U.S. Books, Hails Freedom of Speech," *New York Times,* September 4, 1979. Copyright © 1979 by The New York Times Company. Reprinted with permission.]

7. "But let us also remember that the SATs [Scholastic Aptitude Tests] do serve a valid purpose. The availability of nationwide, standardized tests has made it possible for selective colleges to recruit students from all over the country, not just from schools they happen to be familiar with. It has facilitated the change in function of places like Yale—where I worked in the admissions office for two years—from the grooming of the socially elite to that of challenging the academically elite." [Letter to the editor, *Wall Street Journal,* October 14, 1986]

C. Diagram each of the following arguments. Then find a counterargument challenging either a premise or the strength of the argument.

1. Antitrust laws promote competition, and thus help maintain the free enterprise system, because they counteract the tendency of large firms to acquire monopoly power and drive smaller firms out of an industry.

2. Thursday night I had some Scotch and soda, and I got drunk. On Friday night, it was brandy and soda, and I got drunk again. Saturday, I had wine and soda—spritzers—and I got drunk a third time. There's a pattern here. Soda is what's causing me to get drunk.

3. People with a strong sense of self-esteem want to be loved for themselves, for their virtues; they are not interested in uncon-

ditional love. The idea of unconditional love, therefore, appeals to anyone who lacks self-esteem.

4. The nation's supply of housing expanded rapidly when the baby-boom generation entered the market as first-time buyers. But the generation behind them, born during the 1960s and 1970s, is much smaller. So the increased supply will eventually face a decreased demand. Prices will fall, therefore, and the construction industry will suffer.

D. In each of the following arguments, a key premise is a definition of the term printed in **boldface**. The definition may be explicit or implicit. Diagram the argument and identify the definitional premise; then evaluate the definition.

1. "In his book *Public Opinion*, published 65 years ago, Walter Lippmann gave what is still the best definition of the subject. '**News**,' he said, 'is what protrudes from the ordinary.' In a basically secure and peaceful nation such as ours, it is the problems, not the virtues, that protrude. Were a newscast merely to worship God, the flag and the status quo, as [Senator Jesse] Helms would like, it would quickly lose its audience and its sponsors to the competition. Thus it is not ideological bias but hard-boiled news judgment governed by the dynamics of free enterprise— to which Mr. Helms and his supporters are committed—that determines what appears on the TV news." [Milton Gwirtzman, "Conservatives Are Not Heard?" *New York Times,* Op-ed, March 15, 1985]

2. "Still talked about is a 1983 commentary in which [WBBM-TV commentator Walter] Jacobson strongly implied—if never quite said—that [Chicago Mayor Harold] Washington was using city painters to redecorate his apartment. (It turned out that the painters were touching up new equipment installed for the Mayor's security.) Washington has denounced Jacobson as 'the bottom of the barrel.' Jacobson concedes that sometimes he may be 'unfair' to the Mayor, adding, 'I'm not only a reporter, I'm a **commentator,** and by definition I'm unfair.'" [J. Anthony Lukas, "Chicago: Bad Press," *Atlantic,* January 1986]

3. "To limit the deduction for charitable contributions to amounts in excess of 2 percent of adjusted gross income, as the Treasury has also proposed, would not violate the Constitution but it would be very bad policy. Again, it taxes **income** that taxpayers do not obtain. Someone who earns $25,000 and gives $500 to charity actually has only $24,500 for himself. For the Government to tax that $500 would be ludicrous." [Frederick B.

Campbell, "Leave Intact Tax, Charity Deductions," *New York Times*, Op-ed, December 14, 1984]

4. "The only proof capable of being given that an object is visible, is that people actually see it. The only proof that a sound is audible, is that people hear it: and so of the other sources of our experience. In like manner, I apprehend, the sole evidence it is possible to produce that anything is **desirable,** is that people do actually desire it." [John Stuart Mill, *Utilitarianism*]

E. Diagram the following debate, and evaluate the arguments on each side. Identify any fallacies committed.

He: You were working as a waitress in a cocktail bar,
When I met you.
I picked you out, I shook you up, and turned you around,
Turned you into someone new.
Now five years later on you've got the world at your feet,
Success has been so easy for you.
But don't forget it's me who put you where you are now,
And I can put you back down, too.
Don't, don't you want me?
You know, I can't believe it when I hear that you won't see me.
Don't, don't you want me?
You know, I don't believe it when you say that you don't need me.
It's much too late to find you think you've changed your mind.
You'd better change it back or we will both be sorry. . . .

She: I was working as a waitress in a cocktail bar—
That much is true.
But even then I knew I'd find a much better place,
Either with or without you.
The five years we have had have been such good times;
I still love you.
But now I think it's time I led my life on my own.
I guess it's just what I must do.

[Human League, "Don't You Want Me?" © 1982 Virgin Music (Publishers) Ltd. & Sound Diagrams. All rights controlled by Virgin Music Inc. and WB Music Corp. Used by permission. All rights reserved.]

F. The debate in the Practice Quiz on page 159 consisted of two rounds: A and B each spoke twice. Add another round. What is the most compelling point A could make next? How might B respond?

G. Diagram the following debate, and evaluate the arguments on each side. Identify any fallacies committed.

"All of which brings us to the air bag, over which a great debate —with [Ralph] Nader inevitably in favor of mandating the device by law—is currently raging. In front-end collisions, all hands agree, air bags probably save lives. Even then, however, they function no better than the seat belts which most U.S. motorists disdain to buckle up. In side and rear crashes, they are useless. Moreover, they constitute a built-in hazard—GM has reported three cases of accidental deployment—cost upwards of $200 and evoke scant interest among potential users. Thus, despite sizable outlays to advertise and promote them, GM, which had tooled up to make 100,000 per year, succeeded in selling barely 6,000. Passive devices (as the things are known) one survey after another suggests, turn motorists off." [Robert Bleiberg, "Editorial Commentary," *Barrons*, August 23, 1976]

". . . again contrary to Mr. Bleiberg, the airbags of equivalent restraint systems are not unproven. Even GM admits they work beautifully in tests and on actual highway crash conditions where they have already saved lives and injuries. They can save 10,000 lives and nearly a million injuries annually. They become visible only in a crash and they cost less than a vinyl roof. They more than save their cost by lower insurance premiums and fewer tax dollars devoted to post crash emergency activities on the highway and in court. Former GM President Ed Cole has them in his car to protect his family. Former GM Vice President John DeLorean, All State Insurance Co. and Forbes Magazine are for a federal automatic restraint standard that would include air bags. Can't you share, Mr. Bleiberg, the compassion of Dr. William Haddon, the former auto safety administrator, who calls air bags one of the great technological life savers of our generation?" [Ralph Nader, Letter to the editor, *Barrons*, November 1, 1976]

H. Write a debate on some controversial issue. Formulate the opposing positions, then think of the main arguments on each side, and diagram them. Then think of the objections each side might raise against the other, and add them to your diagram. Finally, write out the debate as a dialogue between A and B. Some possible issues are listed below.

1. Should children ever be spanked?
2. Which is the best professional football team this season?
3. Is extramarital sex always wrong?
4. Should the government design its agricultural policy to preserve the family farm?
5. Does man have free will?

PART THREE

Classical Deductive Logic

Arguments can be classified under two broad categories: *deduction* and *induction*. Deductive reasoning draws out the implications of knowledge we already possess, whereas inductive reasoning extends our knowledge beyond the information contained in the premises. The distinguishing feature of a deductive argument is that the conclusion is contained implicitly in the premises. If the premises are true, the conclusion will necessarily be true as well.

In classical deductive logic, the unit of reasoning is an argument containing two premises, known as a *syllogism*. Our goal in Part Three is to learn how to analyze and evaluate the different types of syllogism. We're going to take each one apart to see how it works. The different types of syllogism are distinguished chiefly by the propositions they use as premises. Chapters 8 and 9 are concerned with the *categorical* syllogism, which involves the most elementary type of proposition. Chapter 10 is concerned with *hypothetical* and *disjunctive* syllogisms, which involve more complex types of proposition. In Chapter 11 we will learn how to identify deductive arguments as they occur in everyday thought and speech.

8

Categorical Propositions

A **categorical proposition** makes a straightforward, *categorical* assertion. For example:

Whales are mammals.
Mammals breathe by means of lungs.

Categorical propositions are typically expressed by the simple type of sentence we discussed in Chapter 4, containing a subject and predicate, but not conjunctions, noun clauses, or other grammatical devices involved in more complex sentences.

Categorical propositions are used in the first sort of deductive reasoning we're going to study, the categorical syllogism. For example:

1) Whales are mammals.
2) Mammals breathe by means of lungs.
3) Whales breathe by means of lungs.

$$\frac{(1) + (2)}{}$$
$$\downarrow$$
$$(3)$$

The standards of validity for this type of argument depend on the inner logical structure of the categorical propositions that serve as premises and conclusion of the syllogism. In this chapter, we'll examine that structure. We will turn to the syllogism itself in the next chapter.

Standard Form

Components of Categorical Propositions

A categorical proposition can be regarded as an assertion about the relations among classes. This is easy to see in the example above. Both whales and mammals are classes; whales are a species of animal, mammals are the genus to which that species belongs. And the proposition says that the first class is included in the second. Every categorical proposition says that a certain relationship exists between two classes. The parts of the proposition that refer to the classes are called the **terms** of the proposition, and there are two terms: the **subject** and the **predicate,** symbolized by S and P. In our example, the subject is "whales" and the predicate is "mammals."

It isn't always so obvious that we are talking about classes of things. In the proposition "Whales breathe by means of lungs," the phrase "breathe by means of lungs" does not indicate a kind or class of object, but rather a property that some objects have. But any property defines a class of objects which possess that property—in this case, things that breathe by means of lungs. In logic, we would rewrite this proposition as "Whales are things that breathe by means of lungs," in order to make it clear that we are talking about two classes. In the same way, we would rewrite the proposition "Whales are large" as "Whales are large things." In general, we revise each proposition (without changing the meaning) so that it has the form "*S* is *P*" or "*S*'s are *P*'s."

The subject and predicate are not always single words. In fact, that is rarely the case. More often, one or both of the terms is a complex phrase. But phrases can designate classes of things just as well as individual words can. In each of the following examples, the subject and predicate terms are indicated by parentheses.

1) (Computers) are (electronic machines that can be programmed to follow a sequence of instructions).
2) (Soldiers who have won the Congressional Medal of Honor) are (heroes).
3) (Commodities such as corn and wheat) are (economic goods subject to the law of supply and demand).

In (1), the subject is a single word, but the predicate is not. The opposite is true in (2). And in (3) neither term is a single word. But all three have the same basic form: *S*'s are *P*'s.

In addition to the subject and predicate, there is a third component of categorical propositions, indicated by the word "are." This is called the **copula** because it links subject and predicate. In all the examples so far, the copula has been **affirmative.** We said that S is P. But the copula can also be **negative,** as in the propositions:

Whales are not fish.

Copper is not a precious metal.

Businesses with fewer than twenty employees are not required to have a pension plan.

In terms of classes, we can make both the affirmative statement that S is included in P and the negative statement that S is excluded from P. The affirmative or negative character of a proposition is called its **quality.**

The fourth and final component of a categorical proposition is a little less obvious than the others. The subject of "Whales are mammals" is "whales," and it is clear that we are talking about all of them. But sometimes we make statements about only *some* members of a class: some whales prefer cold water, some politicians are crooks, some of Charles Bronson's movies are worth seeing. In ordinary language, we often do not say "all" or "some" explicitly; the context makes it clear which we mean. But the difference is crucial in logic, and we need to make it explicit.

This fourth component of a proposition is called its **quantity.** A proposition with the form "All S are P" is **universal.** A proposition with the form "Some S are P" is **particular.** Notice that both of these are affirmative. The distinction between universal and particular also applies to negative propositions. Thus "Some of the apples are not ripe" is a particular negative proposition. "No freshman is allowed to have a car on campus" is a universal negative proposition. Notice that the word "No" does double duty here: it indicates both the negative quality and the universal quantity of the proposition.

A categorical proposition, then, has four components: 1) a subject term; 2) a predicate term; 3) a copula, which is either affirmative or negative in quality; 4) one or more words indicating quantity, universal or particular. The quality and quantity, taken together, determine the logical **form** of a proposition; the subject and predicate determine its **content.** Thus the two statements "All whales are mammals" and "All snakes are reptiles" have the same logical form—affirmative and universal—although their content is quite different. Since there are two possible qualities, and two possible quantities, there are altogether just four standard logical forms for categorical propositions, no matter how complex their subject and predicate terms may be. These four forms are:

	Affirmative	*Negative*
Universal	A: All S are P	E: No S is P
Particular	I: Some S are P	O: Some S are not P

The letters A, E, I, and O are the traditional labels for the four standard forms. A and I are the first two vowels of the Latin word "affirmo" (I affirm), and stand for the two affirmative propositions. Similarly, E and O, which stand for the two negative propositions, come from "nego" (I deny).

As we will see, the logical rules for a categorical syllogism depend solely on the logical forms of the propositions that serve as its premises and conclusion. It is therefore important to learn to identify the form of a given proposition. Sometimes a statement in ordinary language is already in perfect standard form. For example:

All graduate students are scholars.—A
No self-respecting person is a snob.—E
Some movie stars are good actors.—I
Some movie stars are not good actors.—O

In these cases, all we need to do is look for the words that indicate logical form: "all," "some," "no," "is," "is not." But in most cases we have to rework the sentence a bit in order to put it in standard form.

Translating into Standard Form

If the predicate of a sentence is not a term designating a class of objects, we have to turn it into one. "All whales are large," as we saw, must be rewritten as "All whales are large things." Similarly, "Some blondes have more fun" becomes "Some blondes are people who have more fun"; "No mammal can breathe under water" becomes "No mammal is a thing that can breathe under water"; and so on. The goal is always to arrive at the basic form: All/some S are/ are not P. The copula must always be some form of the verb "to be": "are," "were," "will be" (and their negative forms).

As we go along, I will point out other problems connected with putting statements in standard form, as well as the techniques for dealing with them. This will be especially important in Chapter 11, when we focus on arguments in ordinary language. But let's take care of some of the easier problems now.

Subject-predicate order. In English, the subject normally comes first in a sentence, with the predicate following it. But there are exceptions. In the statement "Tender is the night," for example, "the night" is the subject; that is what the statement is about. Similarly, the subject of the sentence "In the middle of the table were some pears" is "pears." In both of these cases, the order of subject and predicate is simply reversed. But consider another nonstandard statement: "No code has been made that cannot be broken." What is the subject term? "Codes." But which codes? "Codes that cannot be broken." The subject has been split in half, with the predicate ("has been made") coming in between the two halves of the subject. In standard form, this statement would be "No code that cannot be broken is a thing that has been made." In all cases of nonstandard order, you can identify the subject by asking what the statement is about.

Singular terms. Is the proposition "New York is a large city" universal or particular? It isn't either, really, because "New York" does not name a class; it names a particular, individual city. In logic, this sort of statement is called a **singular** proposition. Other examples of singular propositions are "Tom is a good basketball player," "I am not afraid," "The third car in the lot is filthy." The mark of a singular proposition is that the subject term is a name, pronoun, or phrase standing for a single object. For purposes of analysis, these propositions are treated as universal. Thus an affirmative singular statement is an A proposition, and a negative one is an E proposition. The rationale is that a singular term may be thought of as naming a class with one member, and so of course the statement is about all the members of that class. You don't need to do any translating with singular propositions; just remember that they are to be treated as universal.

Nonstandard quantifiers. Words that indicate quantity—such as "all," "some," and "no"—are called *quantifiers.* As we noticed before, statements do not always contain an explicit quantifier, and we need to determine from the context which one to insert. The statement that whales are mammals, for example, is clearly meant as a universal statement. So is the statement "Objects heavier than air must fall when unsupported": if such objects *must* fall, then all of them do. On the other hand, when you stay at a friend's house and he says, "Beer is in the refrigerator," it's a safe bet he means some beer, since the refrigerator has not been built that would hold all the beer that exists.

A special problem arises with statements that have the form "All *S* are not *P*." Despite its appearance, this is not a standard form. It is ambiguous. Consider the statement "All politicians are not crooks." Does this mean that no politicians are crooks (an E proposition), or that some politicians are not crooks (an O proposition)? It could mean either. So when you encounter a statement with that form, you will need to decide from the context whether an E or an O statement is intended, and translate it accordingly.

The English language contains many nonstandard quantifiers in addition to the standard ones. Some are universal—"every," "everything," "nothing," "none"—and can easily be translated as "all" or "no." As for particular quantifiers, remember that "some" means "at least one." "Some" is an extremely unspecific quantifier. It says, in effect: I know that at least one S is/is not P, but I don't know (or I'm not saying) how many are. Certain other nonuniversal quantifiers are much more specific than "some"—for example, "few," "several," "many," "most." But they should all be translated as "some," and the statements containing them should be treated as particular propositions. To be sure, this can change the meaning of the statement; sometimes important information is lost. But the logic of the syllogism recognizes only two degrees of quantity: all, and less than all. Reasoning that depends on the more specific degrees of quantity will be treated in Part Five.

Practice Quiz

Put each of the following statements into standard form (if it isn't already); identify the subject and predicate terms; identify the quality and the quantity; and name its form (A, E, I, or O.)

1. All men are rational.
2. Some baseball players are not golfers.
3. Nobody's perfect.
4. A family that plays together stays together.
5. Some things are better left unsaid.
6. No one who laughs at my teddy bear is a friend of mine.
7. The political party that wins a presidential election can expect to lose congressional seats two years later.
8. Some of the members of the Capitol Rotunda Exercise and Reducing Club have not been pulling their weight.
9. Foolish is the man who seeks fame for its own sake.
10. The window in my study is not open.

The Square of Opposition

If you are given a subject term S and a predicate term P, there are four possible categorical propositions you can form with them: the four standard forms **A**, **E**, **I**, and **O**. It is traditional to arrange these in a square:

> A: All *S* are *P*   E: No *S* is *P*
> I: Some *S* are *P*   O: Some *S* are not *P*

Each proposition is logically related to each of the others, and the whole set of these relationships makes up the **square of opposition.**

Contraries

Let's start with the two universal propositions, **A** and **E**. Consider "All bread is nutritious" and "No bread is nutritious." Obviously, these are opposing statements. They cannot both be true. Even if you don't know what *S* and *P* stand for, you can tell in the abstract that "All *S* are *P*" and "No *S* is *P*" cannot both be true. But notice that they could both be false. If some bread is nutritious and other bread is not—if some *S* are *P* and some *S* are not *P*—then both statements would be false. In general, an **A** proposition and an **E** proposition that have the same subject and predicate terms cannot both be true, but they could both be false. We identify this relationship in logic by calling **A** and **E** *contrary* propositions. We can enter this relationship on our diagram:

A: All *S* are *P* ←——— contraries ———→ E: No *S* is *P*

I: Some *S* are *P*   O: Some *S* are not *P*

Contradictories

Our discussion of contraries suggests another possible relationship: statements that cannot both be true *and* cannot both be false. Does this relationship exist in our square? Yes. Look at **A** and **O**. If you accept the **O** proposition "Some bread is not nutritious," then you cannot also accept the **A**, "All bread is nutritious," and vice versa. They cannot both be true. But they cannot both be false, either. The only way for **A** to be false is for there to be at least one *S* that is not *P*, and in that case **O** is true. (Remember that "some" means "at least one.") Similarly, the only way for **O** to be false is for there to be not even one *S* that is not *P*, and in that case all *S* are *P*—the **A** proposition is true. So **A** and **O** cannot both be true and they cannot both be false. Propositions that have this relationship are called *contradictories*.

It should be easy to see now that E and I are also contradictories. They cannot both be true and they cannot both be false. If it is false that no bread is nutritious, that could only be because at least some bread is nutritious, in which case I is true. On the other hand, if I is false, that means not even one S is P, and thus it would be true to say that no S is P—E would be true. So our diagram now looks like this:

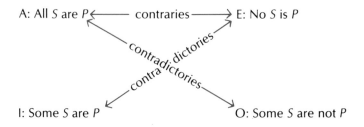

It's important to be clear about the difference between contrary and contradictory propositions. If you want to challenge a universal statement that someone else has made, you do not have to prove the contrary statement; you just have to prove the contradictory. Suppose someone says that all men are male chauvinists, and you object. You don't have to show that *no* man is a male chauvinist, only that *some* men are not. For the same reason, if you're the one claiming that all men are male chauvinists and someone else objects, you can't say, "Oh, you think no man is a male chauvinist?" You would be committing the fallacy of false alternatives, because you would be ignoring the possibility that some men are not chauvinists—a claim that is more limited, but still incompatible with your own assertion.

Subalternates

Let's consider now the relationship between A and I, a vertical relation on the diagram. Both A and I are affirmative propositions; they differ only in quantity. A is the more sweeping statement, because it makes a claim about all S's (that they are P). I is more cautious: when we say that some S are P, we are not committing ourselves to any claim about the whole class of S's. We can see from this that if A is true, I must be true as well. If *all* S's are P, then it is safe to say that *some* S's are P—though we usually wouldn't bother to say it.

What about going in the opposite direction? Here we have to be careful. Normally when a person says "Some S are P," we take him to mean also that some S's are not P. If *all* S were P, we assume he would have said so. Thus, in everyday speech, an I proposition is often taken to imply that the corresponding O proposition is true, and the corresponding A false. But in logic we do not make this assumption. We take the I proposition quite literally as a statement that at least one S is P. That leaves it an open question whether the other S's are P or not. It might turn out that the others are not P (in which case the O proposition would be true). But it also might turn out that all the others *are* P, in which case the A proposition would be true. We don't know. So the truth of the I proposition leaves the truth or falsity of the corresponding A and O propositions *undetermined.*

In logic, the I proposition is called a *subalternate* to the A. This technical term is drawn from the military hierarchy, where "subaltern" means "lower in rank," and this gives us a good analogy. A general can issue orders to a private, but not vice versa; in the same way, the truth of an A proposition implies the truth of the I, but not vice versa. For exactly the same reasons, the O proposition is subalternate to the E. In this case, both propositions are negative, but that doesn't matter; the universal one always implies the particular, but not vice versa.

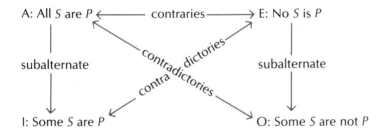

Before we leave the subalternate relation, notice what happens when we consider false statements instead of true ones. Now the tables are turned. If the I proposition is false, then the A must be false as well. If not even one S is P, then it is certainly false that all S are P. In the same way, on the negative side of the square, if not even one S is *not* P, then it is certainly false that no S is P: if O is false, E is false as well. But suppose that A is false. Does that mean I must be false, as well? No. Even if it isn't true that all politicians are honest, it might still be true that some are. Similarly, the falsity of an E proposition leaves the truth or falsity of the O undetermined. It would be false, for example, to say that no natural substances cause cancer, but it is still possible that some do not.

Subcontraries

There is only one relationship we haven't considered yet: the relationship between I and O. Can they both be true? Yes—that happens quite often. Some movie stars are good actors, some are not. Some clothes are made of wool, some are not. But can they both be false? No. Any given object in the class of *S*'s must either be *P* or not be *P*. If it is *P*, that makes the I proposition true. If it is not *P*, that makes the O proposition true. So I and O cannot *both* be false. Notice that this is the mirror image of the relationship between **A** and **E**, which cannot both be true but can both be false. **A** and **E** are contraries, so I and O are called *subcontraries*.

When we add this relationship to our diagram, we have the completed square of opposition:

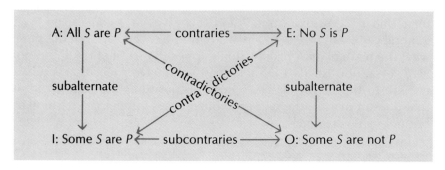

In laying out the square of opposition, I have used fewer examples than usual, and I've explained the logical relationships in a more abstract way as relationships among *S* and *P*. This was deliberate, and the reason can best be conveyed by an analogy. When you learned arithmetic, you learned a set of rules about specific numbers: $1 + 1 = 2$, $3 \times 7 = 21$, $8 - 5 = 3$, and so forth. When you went on to algebra, you had to master the idea of variables (x, y, z), which stand for any number, so that you could learn rules applying to all numbers: $x + x = 2x$, $x + y = y + x$, and so on. A number like 4 is abstract because it can stand for anything that has four units or members. But the variable x represents a higher level of abstraction, because it can stand for any number.

In the same way, a specific proposition is abstract because it contains concepts: "whales," "mammals," etc. As we saw in Chapter 2, these are abstract terms. But *S* and *P* represent a higher level of abstraction, because they are variables: *S* stands for a class of things, any class, just as x in algebra stands for a number, any number. What we are doing now is the algebra of concepts, not the arithmetic. And the relationships in the square of opposition are like the laws of algebra, not like the rules for adding or subtracting specific numbers. Thus, in order to grasp these relationships, you need to be able to think at the higher level of abstraction, in terms of the variables *S* and *P*. The more you practice this, the easier it will be for you to spot logical relationships in concrete examples.

Practice Quiz

Each of the statements below asks you to assume that a given proposition is either true or false. Given that assumption, determine whether the other statements in the square of opposition are true, false, or undetermined.

1. "All *S* are *P*" is true.
2. "No *S* is *P*" is true.
3. "Some *S* are *P*" is true.
4. "Some *S* are not *P*" is true.
5. "All *S* are *P*" is false.
6. "No *S* is *P*" is false.
7. "Some *S* are *P*" is false.
8. "Some *S* are not *P*" is false.

Distribution

An A proposition says that all *S*'s are *P*. It makes a claim about the entire class of *S*'s, each and every one of them. But what about the predicate, *P*? Have we said something about all *P*'s? When we say "All whales are mammals," have we made a claim about the entire class of mammals, each and every one? No. The statement leaves it open whether or not there are any other mammals besides whales —any other species in that genus. We know that there are, but we haven't *said* it. Think of the class of mammals as a large circle. By placing whales inside that circle, we have made a statement about one region of the circle, but we haven't said a thing about the other regions. So far as our statement is concerned, they are unexplored territory.

To mark this distinction, which is crucial in logic, we say that the subject term in "All *S* are *P*" is **distributed,** while the predicate term is **undistributed.** The concept of distribution applies to the terms in all categorical propositions—E, I, and O, as well as A—and we need to learn the rules for telling whether a given term is distributed or undistributed.

The rule for the subject term is easier. The subject term is distributed if the proposition is universal, and undistributed if the proposition is particular. A statement about all *S*'s obviously makes a claim about the whole class. Just as obviously, a statement about some *S*'s does not make such a claim, so *S* in this case is undistributed. Similarly, "No *S* is *P*" says something about the entire class of *S*'s, so the subject is distributed. And "Some *S* are not *P*" does not cover all the *S*'s, so the subject here is undistributed. For the subject term, what matters is *quantity*. Quality is irrelevant.

A different rule applies for the predicate term. As we noticed above, the predicate of an **A** proposition is undistributed because the proposition does not make a claim about all the members of the class *P*. Think of it this way: "All *S* are *P*" says that each member of *S* is identical to some member of *P*. But it does not imply that each member of *P* is identical to some member of *S*. There may be *P*'s that are not *S*. We don't know whether there are or aren't. The same is clearly true for the predicate in an **I** proposition. "Some *S* are *P*" does not make a claim about all the *S*'s *or* about all the *P*'s. So in both affirmative propositions, the predicate term is undistributed.

Now look at the negative propositions, starting with **E**. When we say "No communist country is a democracy," we are drawing a line between communist countries and democracies. We are saying that the first class lies completely outside the second. We are saying that no communist state is identical with any democracy. But this also means we are saying something about each and every member of the class of democracies, because it implies that none of them is identical with any communist state. In general, when we say that no *S* is *P*, we are excluding all the *P*'s from the class of *S*'s just as much as we are excluding all the *S*'s from the class of *P*'s. So in this case *P* is distributed.

The same reasoning applies to the **O** proposition, though it may be a little harder to see. In "Some *S* are not *P*," the subject term is undistributed, as we saw, because we are talking only about some members of *S*, not all of them. But those members are being excluded from the class of *P*'s in the same way that, in the **E** proposition, all the members were being excluded. Suppose the statement is "Some stockbrokers are not very bright." Which stockbrokers? We don't know, but let's suppose there's just one, and let's call him Tom. We are saying that Tom is not identical with anyone in the class of bright people. This implies that no one in the class of bright people is identical with Tom. Here again we are making a claim about the entire class of bright people, so the predicate of our statement is distributed.

For the predicate, then, what matters is *quality*, not quantity. The predicate term is distributed if the proposition is negative (**E** or **O**), and undistributed if the proposition is affirmative (**A** or **I**).

The two rules for distribution are summarized in the box below, with distributed terms printed in boldface:

	Affirmative: predicate undistributed	*Negative:* predicate distributed
Universal: subject distributed	All **S** are P	No **S** is **P**
Particular: subject undistributed	Some S are P	Some S are not **P**

Before we leave the topic of distribution, a word of warning about two common errors. The first is to think that a proposition as a whole can be distributed or undistributed. Unlike quality and quantity, distribution is not a feature of the proposition as a whole. It is a feature of its terms. The second mistake is to treat distribution as a feature that a term has in and of itself. The term "whales," standing by itself and not part of any proposition, is neither distributed nor undistributed. It simply picks out a certain class of animals and stands for all the members of that class. It is only when the term is used as the subject or the predicate of a proposition that it acquires a distribution, for only then is it being used to make a *statement* about all or some members of that class.

Practice Quiz

Put the following propositions in standard form (if they are not already), identify the subject and predicate terms, and mark each term with a D if it is distributed, or a U if it is undistributed.

1. All machines are manufactured objects.
2. No inanimate object is conscious.
3. Some countries are not at peace.
4. Some trees are deciduous.
5. Every day is a new beginning.
6. Some of my best friends are trapeze artists.
7. No one with any manners would clean his teeth at the dinner table.
8. Some cars are lemons.

Immediate Inference

This chapter so far has been about propositions, not arguments. Normally, two or more premises are necessary in order to have an argument for a conclusion, and we'll see how that's done with the categorical syllogism in the next chapter. But there are several inferences that can be made from a single premise. They are called **immediate inferences,** and we have already encountered a few of them. In the square of opposition, for example, the A proposition "All *S* are *P*" is a premise from which we can infer the I, "Some *S* are *P*." But there are three other immediate inferences we haven't looked at yet.

Converse

The first immediate inference is called **conversion,** or taking the **converse.** The converse of a proposition is the result of switching its subject and predicate terms. Thus the converse of the I proposition "Some Englishmen are Scotch drinkers" is "Some Scotch drinkers are Englishmen." Notice that if the first proposition is true, the second must be true as well; the converse follows logically from the original statement. Notice also that the converse is itself an I proposition. Taking the converse of a proposition does not alter its quality or quantity, so the form of the proposition remains the same. Similarly, the converse of "No women have been U.S. presidents" is "No U.S. presidents have been women." Once again, the converse has the same form as the original proposition; they are both E. And once again the converse follows logically. As we saw in the last section, an E proposition says that *S* is excluded from *P*, and that implies that *P* is excluded from *S*.

It is not legitimate, however, to take the converse of an A proposition. The converse of "All pickpockets are criminals" would be "All criminals are pickpockets." As you can see, the converse here does not follow: the first proposition is true, but its converse is false. "All *S* are *P*" does not imply "All *P* are *S*," because saying that *S* is included in *P* does not imply that *P* is included in *S*. The most we can say is that some *P* are *S*, "Some criminals are pickpockets." That much does follow, and it is called taking the converse **by limitation.** Since we can't infer that all *P* are *S*, we limit our claim and infer only that some *P* are *S*.

There is one situation in which "All *S* are *P*" might seem to imply "All *P* are *S*." That is the situation in which *S* and *P* are terms standing for the same class. Consider the definition of "man" we discussed several chapters ago. Both of the following propositions are true: (1) "All men are rational animals," and (2) "All rational animals are men." The fact remains, however, that (2) does not logically follow from (1). If it seems to follow, that is because we know that there are no rational animals other than man. But that information is not contained in (1); it is extra information we happen to have in this case.

Taking the converse of an A proposition (without limiting it) is sometimes called the fallacy of **illicit conversion.** Have you ever heard someone say, when he was being ridiculed for a new or unconventional idea, "Yeah, well they laughed at Columbus, too"? In saying that, he is appealing to the proposition "All brilliant new ideas were ridiculed," which may well be true. But he is implicitly inferring the converse, namely "Any idea that is ridiculed is a brilliant new idea," and that proposition is almost certainly false. In any case, it does not follow. Be careful, then, to avoid illicit conversion. As we will see in the next chapter, it is a common error in syllogistic reasoning.

Finally, let's look at the O proposition. It often happens that an O proposition and its converse are both true. For example: some officers are not gentlemen and some gentlemen are not officers; some teachers are not gifted people and some gifted people are not teachers. Nevertheless, the converse does not logically follow from an O proposition, as we can see from another example: "Some human beings are not Americans" does not imply "Some Americans are not human beings." You can generate other examples like this if you use a genus as the subject term and a species as the predicate term. (Try it with "Some animals are not dogs," "Some legislators are not senators.")

The rules for the converse are summarized in the table below. An "x" indicates that the converse does not follow.

Proposition	*Converse*
A: All S are P	A: All P are S (x)
	I: Some P are S (by limitation)
I: Some S are P	I: Some P are S
E: No S is P	E: No P is S
O: Some S are not P	O: Some P are not S (x)

Notice that the converse follows only when the subject and predicate terms have the same distribution value—either both distributed, as in E, or both undistributed, as in I. If the terms in the original proposition have different distribution values, as in A and O, then the result of taking the converse is to move a term that was undistributed into a position where it is distributed. And this results in a claim that is unwarranted by the original proposition. Thus the predicate in "All *S* are *P*" is undistributed: we are not making a statement about all *P*'s. And that is why we cannot take the converse, "All *P* are *S*," because then *P* would be distributed: we would be making a claim about all *P*'s.

Obverse

The second type of immediate inference—**obversion**—is based on a fact about classes. When we group things together into a class, we are distinguishing them from everything else. For every class, there's an "us" and a "them." So for every class *C*, there is a complementary class composed of everything else, everything not included in *C*. This is called the *complement* of *C*, and it is usually labeled "non-*C*." Thus the complement of "abrasive things" is "nonabrasive things." Consider the proposition "All sandpaper is abrasive." We could say the same thing by saying "No sandpaper is nonabrasive." The second proposition is called the **obverse** of the first. We arrive at the obverse of a proposition by making two changes: we replace the predicate term with its complement, and we change the quality of the proposition (affirmative to negative or negative to affirmative). Thus the obverse of an A proposition, "All *S* are *P*," is always an E proposition, "No *S* is non-*P*." Notice that the subject term remains unchanged, and that the quantity also stays the same. If the predicate term already has the form "non-*P*," we follow the same rule: "non-*P*" is changed to its complement, which is "*P*." Thus the obverse of "All heavy elements are unstable" is "No heavy element is stable."

We can take the obverse of any categorical proposition:

Proposition	*Obverse*
A: All *S* are *P* All sandpaper is abrasive	E: No *S* is non-*P* No sandpaper is nonabrasive
I: Some *S* are *P* Some people are kind	O: Some *S* are not non-*P* Some people are not unkind
E: No *S* is *P* No machine is conscious	A: All *S* are non-*P* All machines are nonconscious
O: Some *S* are not *P* Some chemicals are not toxic	I: Some *S* are non-*P* Some chemicals are nontoxic

In each case, the obverse follows logically. The two changes we make—replacing *P* with non-*P* and switching the quality—cancel each other.

Strictly speaking, the complement of a term refers to everything in the universe not included under the term. A term and its complement divide the entire universe into two mutually exclusive and jointly exhaustive categories. Now consider the terms "mature" and "immature." These do not divide the universe exhaustively. They apply only to things that develop from a young to an adult stage. A six-penny nail is neither mature nor immature. Strictly speaking, therefore, "immature" is not the complement of "mature"; the complement would be "non-mature." The same is true of many words that have the prefixes "im-," "a-," and "un-."

Nevertheless, when we take the obverse of the proposition "All the dogs in Fleabite Kennels are mature," it would be acceptable to use "None of the dogs in Fleabite Kennels are immature." That's because the subject term, "dogs in Fleabite Kennels," restricts the universe of discourse to a genus that *can* be exhaustively divided into mature and immature members. Since we're talking about dogs, we can be sure that if they are all mature, then none are immature. In general, we can use obversion whenever *P* and non-*P* exhaustively divide the class of *S*'s.

We do need to distinguish carefully, however, between terms that are complementary, even in this extended sense, and terms that are opposed in other ways. The obverse of "All logic students are smart," for example, is not "No logic student is stupid." The class of stupid people does not include everyone outside the class of smart people; it leaves out the middle range of average intelligence. "Smart" and "stupid" are opposites, but not complements. The real obverse would be "No logic student is non-smart." You need to be careful about this wherever you are dealing with terms at opposite ends of a spectrum—black and white, tall and short, fat and thin. The fallacy of false alternatives is often committed in such cases. "No one in that family is thin," says Joe. "You mean," says Martha, "everyone in the family is fat?" No. All that Joe said is that everyone in the family is non-thin.

When you take an obverse, finally, be sure to distinguish between the word "not" and the prefix "non-." "Not" is a mark of quality and is part of the form of a proposition. "Non-" is part of the predicate term. With the I proposition, it is easy to forget that we need both: *P* must become non-*P*, and "is" must become "is not." Notice also that the obverse of an O proposition is an I proposition. "Some *S* are non-*P*" is affirmative, even though it sounds negative, because the "non-" is part of the predicate term and does not indicate negative quality.

Contrapositive

The **contrapositive** of a proposition is formed by two steps: switching the subject and predicate terms, as in taking the converse; and replacing both the subject and the predicate terms with their complements. The quality and quantity of the proposition remain as they were. Thus the A proposition

All experts are experienced people,

which has the form "All S are P," becomes the A proposition "All non-P are non-S":

All inexperienced people are non-experts.

It is always legitimate to take the contrapositive of an A proposition. You can see why by thinking once again in terms of classes. An A proposition says that the class of S's is included within the class of P's. If so, then anything outside the class of P's (i.e., all the non-P's) must also be outside the class of S's (i.e., it must be a non-S). Switzerland is in Europe, so if you're not in Europe, you're not in Switzerland. The same reasoning shows why the contrapositive is a useful technique, used quite often in ordinary reasoning. Suppose you wanted to argue that computers are not conscious—that they are not in the class of conscious things. You might try to do this by assuming that all conscious things (S) are living things (P), which means that all nonliving things (including computers) are nonconscious. You just took the contrapositive.

We can see why the contrapositive follows logically from an A proposition by using what we already know about the converse and obverse. If we take the obverse of the A proposition, and then the converse, and then the obverse again, we will arrive at the contrapositive. Thus:

1) All S are P
2) No S is non-P   [the obverse of (1)]
3) No non-P is S   [the converse of (2)]
4) All non-P are non-S   [the obverse of (3)]

Notice that (3) involves taking the converse. We could not take the converse of the A proposition directly, but we can take the converse of (2), which is an E proposition.

Let's use the same procedure to see whether the contrapositive follows for the other propositions:

I	E	O
1) Some *S* are *P*	No *S* is *P*	Some *S* are not *P*
2) Some *S* are not non-*P*	All *S* are non-*P*	Some *S* are non-*P*
3) Some non-*P* are not *S*	All non-*P* are *S*	Some non-*P* are *S*
4) Some non-*P* are non-*S*	No non-*P* is non-*S*	Some non-*P* are not non-*S*

The step from (2) to (3) in each case involves taking the converse, and that step is illegitimate in the case of the I and the E. In the derivation for I, line (2) is an O proposition, and we know that the O proposition does not have a valid converse. In the derivation for E, line (2) is an A proposition, and we know that that also lacks a valid converse. Remember, though, that an A proposition does have a converse by limitation. "All *S* are *P*" does imply "Some *P* are *S*." If we incorporate this into the derivation for E, we can show that it has a contrapositive by limitation:

Contrapositive	*Contrapositive by limitation*
1) No *S* is *P*	No *S* is *P*
2) All *S* are non-*P*	All *S* are non-*P*
3) All non-*P* are *S*	Some non-*P* are *S*
4) No non-*P* is non-*S*	Some non-*P* are not non-*S*

Notice that the contrapositive by limitation of an E proposition is not itself an E but rather an O proposition.

The O proposition is the only one, besides the A, for which the contrapositive follows without limitation. Even so, it is rarely used in ordinary speech. The closest we can come to a natural-sounding example would be something like the following. If we were considering candidates for some job or office, we might say with a sigh,

Some talented candidates are not acceptable.

The contrapositive would be

Some unacceptable people are not untalented.

The A proposition, however, is far and away the most common case in which we use the contrapositive—and there, as we saw, it is quite common.

This completes our review of the three immediate inferences. The table below summarizes the key information about all three. In order to test your understanding, try to reproduce the table without looking at it. List the converse, obverse, and contrapositive for each of the four types of propositions (twelve items in all), and determine whether they follow or not.

Immediate Inferences

	A	E	I	O
Proposition	All S are P	No S is P	Some S are P	Some S are not P
Converse	All P are S (x)	No P is S	Some P are S	Some P are not S (x)
	Some P are S (by limitation)			
Obverse	No S is non-P	All S are non-P	Some S are not non-P	Some S are non-P
Contrapositive	All non-P are non-S	No non-P is non-S (x)	Some non-P are non-S (x)	Some non-P are not non-S
		Some non-P are not non-S (by limitation)		

Practice Quiz

For each proposition below, find the converse, obverse, or contrapositive as indicated in brackets, and determine whether it follows.

1. Some S are P [contrapositive].
2. No S is P [converse].
3. Some S are not P [converse].
4. All S are P [obverse].
5. Some S are not P [contrapositive].
6. No S is P [obverse].
7. Some S are non-P [obverse].
8. Some non-S are P [converse].
9. No non-S is non-P [contrapositive].
10. All non-S are P [converse].
11. Some S are not P [obverse].
12. All S are non-P [contrapositive].

SUMMARY

In this chapter, we have studied the structure of categorical propositions, and some of the logical relations among them. A categorical proposition has a subject and a predicate term, which give it its content. It also has an affirmative or negative quality, and a universal or particular quantity. The quality and quantity together determine the form of the proposition—A, E, I, or O. These four standard forms can be arranged in a square of opposition, which exhibits their logical relationships: contraries, contradictories, subalternates, and subcontraries. The terms in a categorical proposition are either distributed or undistributed. The subject term is distributed if the proposition is universal; the predicate term is distributed if the proposition is negative. Each term also has a complementary term: non-S, non-P. Categorical propositions can serve as premises of immediate inferences: conversion, obversion, and contraposition.

In the next chapter, we'll use what we've learned about these propositions to analyze and evaluate categorical syllogisms.

Exercises

A. The following statements are in standard form. Name the form of the proposition (A, E, I, or O), and determine whether its subject and predicate terms are distributed. Then reformulate them so that they are more concise (see how many words you can eliminate) and less awkward.

1. Some large corporations are not things that paid any income tax last year.
2. No Spanish playwright is a person who has won the Nobel Prize for literature.
3. All planets are things whose motion is governed by the gravitational attraction of the sun.
4. No Friday is a day on which my family ate meat.
5. Some statistics that indicate economic growth are statistics that can be misleading.
6. All persons who chronically tell lies are persons who feel insecure about their ability to succeed on the basis of the truth.
7. Some academic subjects are branches of study that require the use of mathematical techniques.
8. Some proponents of radical economic change are not thinkers who have carefully considered the consequences of their ideas.
9. Some fast-food restaurants are establishments in which you are permitted to have a hamburger prepared "your way."
10. No automobile produced in the U.S. as a standard factory model is a vehicle that can safely be driven at over 200 miles per hour.

B. Translate each of the following statements into standard form, identify the form, and determine whether the subject and predicate terms are distributed. Then find the logically related proposition mentioned in the brackets.

1. All sonnets have fourteen lines [contrary].
2. Some metals rust [converse].
3. Some fish are not carnivores [obverse].
4. No one has run a mile in less than 3:40 [contradictory].
5. Every country with the word "Democratic" in its official name is a communist dictatorship [contrapositive].
6. That man in the corner is drunk [obverse].
7. "Big girls don't cry"—Frankie Vallee [contrary].
8. "War is hell"—General Sherman [contradictory].
9. Someone is knocking at my door [subcontrary].
10. Sugar is sweet [subalternate].
11. So are you [obverse].
12. "Men at work"—highway sign [contradictory].
13. At the edge of the clearing were some deer [subcontrary].
14. Some criminals don't come from poor families [contrapositive].
15. Alice doesn't live here any more [contrary].
16. Real men don't eat quiche [converse].
17. Students who return after midnight are required to sign in [converse by limitation].
18. No law is just that forces a person to act against his judgment [contrapositive].
19. Some proposals put forward for the control of nuclear arms would not affect the levels of submarine-based missiles [contradictory].
20. Nobody knows the trouble I've seen [subalternate].

C. Name the logical relationship that exists between each pair of propositions below. Then state whether the second one follows logically from the first.

1. No man is an island. Some men are not islands.
2. Some water is not fit to drink. Some water is unfit to drink.
3. All sailors are swimmers. All swimmers are sailors.
4. Some cases of cancer are hard to diagnose. Some cases of cancer are not hard to diagnose.
5. Some people are unlucky in love. Some people are not lucky in love.
6. All voluntary actions are actions for which we can be held responsible. All actions for which we cannot be held responsible are involuntary.

7. No one of my acquaintance is in trouble with the law. No one who is in trouble with the law is an acquaintance of mine.
8. All medical expenses are deductible. Some deductible items are medical expenses.
9. No dishonest person is happy. No unhappy person is honest.
10. Some of the union members were not pleased with the new contract. Some people who were pleased with the new contract were not union members.

D. Find a literal translation for each of the following proverbs. Your translation should be a universal categorical proposition (A or E).

1. Every cloud has a silver lining.
2. Birds of a feather flock together.
3. Rome wasn't built in a day.
4. People in glass houses shouldn't throw stones.
5. A penny saved is a penny earned.
6. A rolling stone gathers no moss.
7. Forewarned is forearmed.
8. Uneasy lies the head that wears a crown.
9. Money talks.
10. Faint heart never filled a flush.

E. The passages below contain immediate inferences. Put the premise and conclusion in standard form, and determine whether the conclusion follows.

1. "He said he would acquire no knowledge which did not bear upon his object. Therefore all that knowledge which he possessed was such as would be useful to him." [Arthur Conan Doyle, *A Study in Scarlet*]
2. "The East Coast was hammered by its second snowstorm in a week yesterday. . . . Most intriguing of all was the word out of Washington, D.C., possibly the most snow-fearing town anywhere in the U.S. . . . All 'nonessential federal workers' were allowed to go home. So that means those who lashed themselves to their desks during the 10-inch 'blizzard' are essential. Did anyone make the list?" [*Wall Street Journal*, January 27, 1987]
3. "The chief foundations of all states, new as well as old or composite, are good laws and good arms; and as there cannot be good laws where the state is not well armed, it follows that where they are well armed they have good laws." [Niccolo Machiavelli, *The Prince*]

4. Just as my fingers on these keys
   Make music, so the selfsame sounds
   On my spirit make a music, too.

   Music is feeling, then, not sound;
   And thus it is that what I feel,
   Here in this room, desiring you,

   Thinking of your blue-shadowed silk,
   Is music.

[Wallace Stevens, "Peter Quince at the Clavier." Copyright 1921, renewed 1951 by Wallace Stevens. Reprinted from *The Collected Poems of Wallace Stevens* by permission of Alfred A. Knopf.]

9

Categorical Syllogisms

One of the goals of artificial intelligence is to give computers the ability to make inferences. A newspaper story on a Japanese project gave the following example: "If the computer is informed that a trout is a fish and that fish live in water, then the computer must be able to conclude that trout live in water." [*New York Times*, August 13, 1984]

Let's analyze this inference by the method we learned in Chapter 5. The conclusion is "Trout live in water." There are two premises offered in support: 1) "A trout is a fish," and 2) "Fish live in water." It is clear that these are additive premises; they are not independent, but must be combined in order to support the conclusion. Thus the argument would be diagrammed as follows:

1) A trout is a fish.
2) Fish live in water.
3) Trout live in water.

As you can see by looking at the diagram, the premises provide very strong support for the conclusion. In fact, if the premises are true, then the conclusion must be true as well. We are now in a position to examine the nature of this argument in greater depth, and to understand more fully why the conclusion follows.

The Structure of a Syllogism

Both the premises and the conclusion of this argument are categorical propositions, so we can put them into standard form. There are no explicit quantifiers in any of them, but it is clear that all three are universal and affirmative. All of them are A propositions. The predicate in (2) and (3) will also have to be translated into a term designating a class. The argument can now be formulated as:

1) All trout are fish.
2) All fish are animals that live in water.
3) All trout are animals that live in water.

We don't need the addition sign, because all arguments of this type are additive; all we need is the line between the premises and the conclusion.

Any argument that has two categorical premises, a categorical conclusion, and the same internal structure as this argument is a **categorical syllogism.** Let's look more closely at the structure. There are three propositions. Since every proposition has two terms, there could have been six distinct terms here. But there aren't. There are only three, "trout," "fish," and "animals that live in water"—each term occurring twice. This pattern exists in every categorical syllogism, and each of the three terms has a distinct name.

The term that occurs in the predicate of the conclusion ("animals that live in water") is called the **major term** of the syllogism. This term also occurs in one of the premises (2), which is therefore called the **major premise.** The term that occurs in the subject of the conclusion ("trout") is called the **minor term.** This term occurs as well in the other premise (1), which we therefore label the **minor premise.** That leaves "fish," which is not part of the conclusion, but occurs once in each of the premises. It is called the **middle term,** because it serves to link together the major and minor terms. Schematically, the pattern of repetition is:

Maj	All M are P	All fish are animals that live in water
Min	All S are M	All trout are fish
Con	All S are P	All trout are animals that live in water

"P" stands for the major term, "S" for the minor term, and "M" for the middle term. Notice that we have switched the order of the premises. This makes no logical difference in the argument, but it is a convention that we always put the major premise first. The schematic argument on the left is the *form* of the argument on the right;

the left side represents the structure of the right side, in the same way that "All *S* are *P*" represents the structure of any universal affirmative proposition.

An argument need not have exactly this structure in order to be a categorical syllogism. For one thing, it need not consist solely of A propositions. Suppose that you didn't know whether moose were predators or not, but you did know that horned animals are not predators. Then you might reason as follows:

No *M* is *P*	No horned animal is a predator
All *S* are *M*	All moose are horned animals
No *S* is *P*	No moose is a predator

In this argument, the conclusion and one of the premises are E propositions, but it is still a categorical syllogism, for we can still identify a major, a minor, and a middle term.

The premises and conclusion of a categorical syllogism, in fact, can have any of the standard forms: A, E, I, or O. A categorical syllogism is identified, in part, by reference to this fact. We list the letters that identify the forms of the propositions in the syllogism in the following order: major premise, minor premise, conclusion. This list is called the **mood** of the syllogism. The mood of the argument about trout is **AAA**; the mood of the argument about moose is **EAE**. Syllogisms can vary, then, in respect to their mood.

There is another way in which they can vary. Notice the arrangement of terms in the following argument:

No *P* is *M*	No Marxist advocates private property
All *S* are *M*	All conservatives advocate private property
No *S* is *P*	No conservative is a Marxist

The mood of this argument is also **EAE**. But the terms are arranged differently: the middle term is now the predicate in both premises, whereas in the argument about moose it was the subject of the major premise.

The position of the middle term in the premises is called the **figure** of the syllogism. Since there are two premises, and two possible positions in each premise, there are four figures. They are identified by number, as follows:

	1st		2nd		3rd		4th	
Maj	*M*	*P*	*P*	*M*	*M*	*P*	*P*	*M*
Min	*S*	*M*	*S*	*M*	*M*	*S*	*M*	*S*
Con	*S*	*P*	*S*	*P*	*S*	*P*	*S*	*P*

Within each figure, the premises and the conclusion can have any of the standard forms for categorical propositions. That is, within each figure, a syllogism can have any mood. Conversely, any given mood describes four different syllogisms, one in each figure. To identify a syllogism completely, therefore, we must indicate figure as well as mood. The argument about trout would be labeled AAA-1, the argument about moose is EAE-1, and the argument about private property is EAE-2. In this way mood and figure together uniquely identify the form of any categorical syllogism, just as the letters A, E, I, and O uniquely identify the form of a single categorical proposition.

In each figure, the middle term serves as a link between major and minor terms. But in everyday reasoning, the different figures are typically used to express different kinds of links. The first figure, for example, is a natural way to express a species-genus relationship. Thus we inferred that trout have a certain property (they live in water) because they belong to a genus (fish) that has the property. And we inferred that moose do not have a certain property (they are not predators) because they belong to a genus (horned animals) that lacks the property. In both cases, the minor term *S* was the species, the middle term *M* its genus.

In the second figure, the middle term is the predicate of both premises. It is therefore commonly used when we try to find out the relation between two classes, *S* and *P*, by seeing whether there is some property *M* that one has and the other lacks. In the example above, we inferred that conservatives (*S*) cannot be Marxists (*P*) because one group believes in private property and the other doesn't.

In the third figure, the middle term is the subject of both premises. Thus it can be used to show that there is some overlap between two classes, *S* and *P*, by pointing out that *M*'s are members of both groups. Suppose we were wondering whether any great plays (*S*) had been written in blank verse (*P*). We might think of Shakespeare, and reason thus:

All *M* are *P*	All of Shakespeare's dramas are in blank verse
Some *M* are *S*	Some of Shakespeare's dramas are great plays
Some *S* are *P*	Some great plays are in blank verse.

The form of this argument is AII-3.

The fourth figure is somewhat odd. In structure it is the mirror image of the first figure, and perhaps because the first figure strikes us as a natural way to reason, the fourth seems very unnatural. You will probably not encounter it often in everyday speech. Nevertheless, it can be a valid mode of inference. Suppose you wanted to correct someone's mistaken idea that all felonies are violent crimes (so that crimes against property are always misdemeanors). You might argue: "Some crimes against property are frauds, and frauds are felonies; therefore some felonies are crimes against property." In schematic form:

Some *P* are *M*   Some crimes against property are frauds
All *M* are *S*   All frauds are felonies
Some *S* are *P*   Some felonies are crimes against property

This has the form IAI-4.

Of course, these examples are merely the typical uses of the different figures. In each figure there are also many atypical examples. Moreover, in all the examples we've considered so far, the conclusion followed from the premises, but this is not always the case. The next section will cover rules for evaluating syllogistic arguments.

Practice Quiz

A. For each mood and figure, write out the syllogism it describes. Hint: start with the figure, and lay out the positions of *S, M,* and *P*; then use the mood to fill in the blanks.

  1. AII-1
  2. EIO-3
  3. AEE-2
  4. AAI-4
  5. IEO-2

B. Put each of the following syllogisms in standard form (remember to put the major premise first), and identify mood and figure.

  1. No Greek poet was a genius, because no Greek poet was eccentric, and geniuses are eccentric.
  2. Some bureaucrats are not chosen on the basis of their ability, and all bureaucrats are civil servants. Therefore some civil servants are not chosen on the basis of their ability.
  3. No machine is capable of perpetual motion, because every machine is subject to friction, and nothing that is subject to friction is capable of perpetual motion.
  4. Any good poem is worth reading, but some good poems are difficult. Thus some things worth reading are difficult.
  5. Any ambitious person can learn logic, and anyone reading this book is ambitious. So anyone reading this book can learn logic.

Validity

When we evaluate an argument, as we saw in Chapter 5, we should distinguish between two questions: Are the premises true? And do the premises support the conclusion? The second question pertains to the logical *strength* of the argument, and we measure strength by estimating the logical gap between premises and conclusion. For deductive arguments, we use the term **validity** to designate logical strength, and validity is all or nothing. A valid syllogism has no internal gap whatever: if the premises are true, the conclusion *must* be true; you cannot accept the premises and deny the conclusion without contradicting yourself. An invalid syllogism, on the other hand, is a *non sequitur*: the premises confer no support on the conclusion. In deductive reasoning, then, strength does not come in degrees. But it is still a matter of the relation between the premises and the conclusion, not between the premises and reality. A valid argument can have false premises and/or a false conclusion. And an argument whose premises and conclusion are all true can nevertheless be invalid. The relationship between validity and truth is that a valid syllogism cannot have true premises and a false conclusion.

The validity of a syllogism is determined by its form. If two syllogisms have the same form, they are either both valid or both invalid, even if one has true premises and the other has false ones. Consider, for example, two syllogisms that have the form AAA-1:

All fish are animals	All *M* are *P*	All bananas are animals
All trout are fish	All *S* are *M*	All trout are bananas
All trout are animals	All *S* are *P*	All trout are animals

As you can see, the two arguments have the same form. The only difference is that the middle term has been changed in the right-hand argument from "fish" to "bananas," making the premises of that argument false—indeed, preposterous. The fact remains that if all bananas were animals, and all trout bananas, then all trout would have to be animals. AAA-1 is a valid form of syllogism, and so any syllogism that has this form is valid.

But not all forms are valid. In fact, if you chose a form at random, your chances of picking a valid one would be pretty small. There are three propositions in a syllogism, each of which can have any of four forms (A, E, I, or O). That's $4 \times 4 \times 4 = 64$ possible syllogisms within a given figure. With four figures, we have 256 syllogistic forms. But only 24 of them are valid. So we need a way to distinguish the valid from the invalid forms.

We could use the seat-of-the-pants method, checking to see whether a given argument intuitively seems valid. In some cases, such as AAA-1, this works for most people. And as you become more familiar with syllogisms, your intuitive feel for their validity will get better and better. That's all to the good. But there are some valid syllogisms that will always seem unnatural, and some plausible-sounding arguments that are in fact invalid. So the intuitive method is not enough by itself.

Another method would be to memorize all 24 forms, and then check every argument we encounter to see whether it fits one of them. This method also has its value. Some forms are so common— AAA-1 is again the best example—that it is worth getting to know them individually. But memorizing all the valid forms would be far too cumbersome. We need a general set of rules that can be applied to any syllogism and that will allow us to identify quickly whether it is valid or not.

There is such a set. It consists of four rules, four tests that a syllogism must pass to be valid. Any syllogism that satisfies all four is valid; any syllogism that fails even one of the tests is invalid. Let's go over each rule in turn.

1) In a valid syllogism, the middle term must be distributed in at least one of the premises. As we saw in the last chapter, a term is distributed in a given proposition if the proposition makes a statement about the entire class designated by the term. Thus the rule says that at least one of the premises in a syllogism must make a statement about the entire class designated by the middle term. Otherwise, the middle term will not provide a strong enough link between the other two terms to make the syllogism valid.

Consider the following argument, which has the form AAA-2:

All *P* are *M*	All conservatives believe in private property
<u>All *S* are *M*</u>	<u>All people who defend capitalism believe in private property</u>
All *S* are *P*	All people who defend capitalism are conservatives

If we look at the abstract form on the left, we can see that in each premise, *M* is the predicate of an affirmative proposition. *M* is therefore undistributed in both premises, and the argument violates the rule. If we look at the example on the right, we can see why an argument of this form is invalid. The fact that conservatives believe in private property does not mean that they are the *only* people who do. So the fact that pro-capitalists believe in private property does not necessarily mean that they are conservatives. They may or may not be. The premises locate the two classes, *P* (conservatives) and *S* (pro-capitalists), within the wider class (*M*) of believers in private property. But that doesn't tell us whether *S* is included in *P*, or *P* in *S*, or whether there is any overlap at all. Again, there may or may not be.

A syllogism that violates rule (1) commits the fallacy of the *undistributed middle,* and AAA-2 is the classic example, one that occurs fairly often. The reason that people often take such an argument to be valid is probably that they switch *M* and *P* in the major premise. They hear "All *P* are *M*," but switch it to "All *M* are *P*." They hear "All conservatives believe in private property" but take it to mean "Any one who believes in private property is a conservative"— treating the belief as a defining trait of conservatives. If this transformation were legitimate, it would change the argument from AAA-2 to AAA-1:

AAA-2	*AAA-1*
All *P* are *M*	All *M* are *P*
All *S* are *M*	All *S* are *M*
All *S* are *P*	All *S* are *P*

But this transformation is not legitimate. The major premise on the right is the *converse* of the major premise on the left, and we know that it is invalid to take the converse of an A proposition.

Another situation in which people often commit the fallacy of the undistributed middle is the attribution of guilt by association. Someone might be accused of being a communist, for example, because he supports the same cause as communists, or belongs to the same group. Here are two examples:

All communists support the Sandinistas in Nicaragua
So-and-so supports the Sandinistas
So-and-so is a communist

Some communists belong to the Rosa Luxemburg Cooperative
So-and-so belongs to the Rosa Luxemburg Cooperative
So-and-so is a communist

In both these arguments, the minor premise and the conclusion are singular propositions—but remember that we are treating these as universal. So the form of the first example is AAA-2, and the form of the second is IAA-2. In both cases, the middle term is undistributed and the argument is invalid.

2) If either of the terms in the conclusion is distributed, it must be distributed in the premise in which it occurs. Once again, the rationale for this rule is based on the nature of distribution. If the predicate of the conclusion (the major term) is distributed, then the conclusion is making a statement about all the members of that class. If that term is not distributed in the major premise, then the premise is not making a statement about the entire class. So the conclusion is making a stronger claim than the premise can support; it goes beyond the information given in the premise. The same reasoning applies to the minor term. A syllogism that violates this rule is said to have an *illicit major* or *illicit minor,* depending on which term is at fault.

An illicit minor often occurs in the third figure, because there the minor term occurs in the predicate of the minor premise, and we are less sensitive to distribution in predicates than in subjects. An example would be the following argument:

All *M* are *P*   All vertebrates reproduce sexually
All *M* are *S*   All vertebrates are animals
All *S* are *P*   All animals reproduce sexually

S is distributed in the conclusion, but not in the minor premise. And the fallacy is easy to see. The minor premise says that vertebrates are a species of the genus animals, and it is not valid to assume that what is true of all vertebrates (that they reproduce sexually) must be true of other species in the same genus, such as lower invertebrates. The only conclusion we can draw here is that *some* animals reproduce sexually. That is, we must keep S undistributed in the conclusion.

The classic example of the illicit *major* is the syllogism AEE-1, and it occurs frequently in political debate as a way of attacking one's opponents. Liberals sometimes argue:

All *M* are *P*   All supporters of the nuclear freeze want to preserve peace
No *S* is *M*   No conservatives support the nuclear freeze
No *S* is *P*   No conservatives want to preserve peace

And conservatives sometimes argue:

All *M* are *P*   All supporters of increased defense spending are concerned about defending American freedom
No *S* is *M*   No liberals support increased defense spending
No *S* is *P*   No liberals are concerned about defending American freedom

Both of these arguments boil down to the assertion "If you don't agree with my policies, you don't accept my goals." And of course that isn't true. People can share a goal but disagree about the best means of achieving it.

It is important to remember that rule (2) applies only if a term in the conclusion is distributed. If the term is undistributed in the conclusion, then it doesn't matter whether or not it is distributed in the premise.

3) No valid syllogism can have two negative premises. In syllogistic reasoning, two negatives don't make a positive. They don't make anything. If both premises are negative, they tell us that both the major and the minor term are excluded, wholly or in part, from the middle term. And that won't tell us how the major and minor terms are related to each other. Thus knowing that

No M is P, and
No S is M

will not tell us whether no S is P, or all S are P, or anything else. You can see this for yourself by thinking of different examples for S, M, and P.

4) If either premise of a valid syllogism is negative, the conclusion must be negative; and if the conclusion is negative, one premise must be negative. If a premise is negative, it tells us that one class (either S or P, depending on which premise it is) is excluded from another class (M). From this information, we might be able to infer that S is excluded from P—if the other rules are satisfied. But we could never infer that S is *included* in P. Conversely, if the conclusion is negative, it says that S is excluded from P. The only information that would justify this conclusion is the information that S is excluded from M (which is included in P), or that S is included in M (which is excluded from P). In either of those cases, we have one negative premise.

Violations of rules (3) and (4) occur much less often than violations of (1) and (2). (Perhaps that is why the fallacies do not have their own names.) In most cases, syllogisms that commit either of the fallacies of negation are so obviously invalid that we avoid them instinctively. But there are a few contexts in which syllogisms that violate rules (3) or (4) do seem plausible, and we have to be careful. Here's an example:

No P is M No one who competes for money is an amateur
No S is M No member of the Bush League is an amateur
All S are P All members of the Bush League compete for money

This syllogism violates both rules (3) and (4): it has two negative premises, and an affirmative conclusion. By our rules, it is hopelessly invalid. Yet the conclusion does seem to follow. Why is that?

Well, for one thing, we assume that members of the Bush League are involved in some competitive sport. But that information is not actually given in the minor premise; it is merely suggested by the name "Bush League." We also assume that competing for fun (or whatever) rather than money is the defining trait of an amateur, so that any nonamateur competitor must be competing for money. That, too, is not given or implied by the premises. What makes the argument seem valid, therefore, is that in our minds we substitute for it the following syllogism, which is valid (it is our old friend AAA-1):

All M are P All nonamateur competitors compete for money
All S are M All members of the Bush League are nonamateur
            competitors
All S are P All members of the Bush League compete for
            money

As always, it is important to focus on what the premises actually say, and to be careful not to read into them any background knowledge we happen to possess.

When we apply the rules of negation, finally, we need to remember a point from the last chapter: the use of complementary terms, such as S and non-S. Suppose someone says that Ruth does not make friends easily because she is not communicative, and uncommunicative people do not make friends easily. We might represent this syllogism as follows:

No uncommunicative people make friends easily
Ruth is not communicative
Ruth does not make friends easily

Intuitively, this argument seems valid, and indeed it is. Yet both premises are negative, and so you might conclude that it is invalid. The problem is that the syllogism is not yet in standard form, so we can't apply the rules just yet.

"Communicative" and "uncommunicative" are complementary terms—logically related, to be sure, but still distinct. So the argument has four terms altogether, whereas a syllogism can have only three. Because those two terms are logically related, however, we can change one into the other by using an immediate inference.

What we would do in this case is take the *obverse* of the minor premise, so that we now have the standard form syllogism:

No uncommunicative people make friends easily
Ruth is uncommunicative
Ruth does not make friends easily

We now have just three terms, so the argument is in standard form. And the minor premise is now affirmative, so that the syllogism satisfies all the rules. When you encounter complementary terms, you will have to use the obverse, or occasionally the contrapositive, to change one of them into the other before you can apply the rules.

We now have a complete set of rules for assessing validity. Two of them involve distribution, and two involve negation. A syllogism is valid if, but only if, it satisfies all four rules.

Distribution	1) The middle term must be distributed in at least one premise.
	2) If a term is distributed in the conclusion, it must be distributed in the premise in which it occurs.
Negation	3) The premises cannot both be negative.
	4) If one premise is negative, the conclusion must be negative; and if the conclusion is negative, one premise must be negative.

Practice Quiz

For each of the following syllogisms, put it in standard form, identify its mood and figure, and use the rules to determine whether it is valid or invalid.

1. It's obvious that Tom has something to hide. He pleaded the Fifth Amendment in court last week; people with things to hide always plead the Fifth.
2. Protestant churches do not accept the authority of the Pope. Since the United Church of Christ does not accept the Pope's authority, it must be a Protestant church.
3. Some of the students in this class are freshmen, and of course no freshman will graduate this year. So none of the students in this class will graduate this year.

4. Some things that are well made are not expensive, for paperback books are inexpensive, and some of them are well-made.
5. All journalists are people with low salaries, and some people on low salaries are free-lance writers, so at least some journalists must be free-lancers.
6. Some of the proposals before this committee, I have to conclude, are not inspired. All of the proposals are reasonable, but some inspired ideas are not reasonable.
7. Some flowers that bloom all season flourish in the shade, and thus some shade-loving flowers are not perennials (since no perennial blooms all season).

Venn Diagrams

It is often helpful to think of a term in a proposition as a circle containing the members of the relevant class. There is in fact a systematic way of doing this, and it provides us with another method for determining the validity of categorical syllogisms. This is the method of **Venn diagrams,** invented by the English mathematician John Venn.

To use this method, we need a way to represent each of the different forms of proposition. The simplest case is the I proposition. "Some S are P" says that at least one member of S is also a member of P. We can represent this by putting an x in the intersection of two overlapping circles that represent S and P:

Some S are P

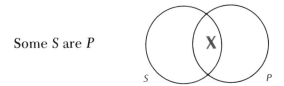

An A proposition contains the same information as the I: "All S are P" implies that some S are. So to diagram an A proposition, we keep the x in the central region. But we also need to indicate universality. We cannot do this by adding more x's in that region, since we don't know how many there are. What we can do is shade out the region of the S circle that lies outside the P circle, to indicate that none of the S's are non-P (notice that this is the obverse of "All S are P"). Thus the A proposition is:

All S are P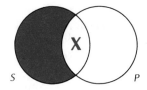

We follow the same procedure for the O and E propositions. "Some S are not *P*" means that the region of S outside *P* contains at least one member, so we put an *x* in that region:

Some S are not P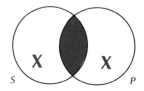

Once again, the universal proposition implies the particular, so we keep the *x* where it is; but we also shade out the intersection to show that none of the S's are located there, that none of the S's are *P*'s. And we put another *x* in the region of P outside S, because "No S is *P*" implies "No *P* is S," and the same diagram should indicate both. Thus:

No S is P
No *P* is S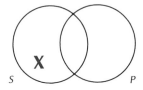

We now have a way to diagram each statement in a syllogism, no matter what logical form it has. To represent a syllogism, however, we do not need three separate diagrams for the premises and conclusion. We can represent the argument as a whole in a single diagram using *three* overlapping circles, one for each term. We always use the following structure:

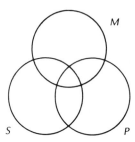

Notice that any two of these circles overlap in the same way as the simpler diagrams we used to represent individual propositions. This means we can diagram any of the propositions in a syllogism by focusing just on the relevant pair of circles, and ignoring the third one.

The technique of Venn diagrams is based on the fact that in a valid syllogism, the conclusion asserts no more than what is already contained, implicitly, in the premises. If the conclusion asserts more than that, it does not follow from the premises, and the syllogism is invalid. The technique is to diagram the premises, and then see whether anything would have to be added in order to diagram what the conclusion asserts. If so, the syllogism is invalid; if not, it is valid.

Let's take an example we've used before:

No *M* is *P*   No horned animal is a carnivore
All *S* are *M*   All moose are horned animals
No *S* is *P*   No moose is a carnivore

The procedure for diagramming this argument is laid out in the box on the next page.

The first step is to diagram the major premise, using just the circles representing *M* (horned animals) and *P* (carnivores). So we shade out the area of overlap between *M* and *P*. We put an *x* in the region of *M* outside *P*. This region is divided by the *S* circle into two areas. The upper area represents *M*'s that are neither *S* nor *P*. The lower area represents *M*'s that are not *P* but are *S*. Since the major premise tells us nothing about *S*, we have no reason for putting our *x* in one area rather than the other, so we put it on the line between them. Finally, we put an *x* in the region of *P* outside *M*, placing it on the line for the same reason as above.

The second step is to diagram the minor premise, using the circles representing *S* and *M*. We shade out the region of *S* outside *M*, and put an *x* in the region of overlap. Once again, this region contains two areas, and the premise gives us no reason for locating the *x* in one rather than the other, so we put it on the line dividing them.

In step (3), we combine into a single diagram the information contained in the separate diagrams for the premises. The two regions shaded out in steps (1) and (2) are both shaded out in (3). And (3) contains all three of the *x*'s from the previous diagrams. The first *x* from diagram (1) remains on the line, because we still don't know where to put it. But the second *x* from diagram (1) has moved off the line, into the region of *P* that is outside both *S* and *M*. That's

Constructing Venn Diagrams

No *M* is *P*   No horned animal is a carnivore
All S are *M*   All moose are horned animals
No *S* is *P*   No moose is a carnivore

1) Major premise: 2) Minor premise:
   No *M* is *P*   All *S* are *M*

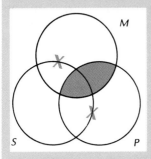   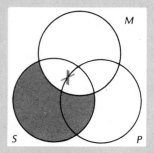

3) The premises combined

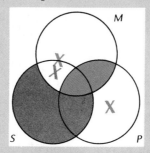

4) Conclusion: No *S* is *P*

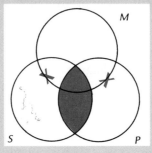

because the shading out we did for the minor premise tells us that the area inside S is empty, so the x must be in the area outside S. For the same reason, the x from the minor premise has moved off its line, into the intersection of S and M that is outside P.

When you make a combined diagram, do all the necessary shading before you enter any x's. If both premises are universal, enter the shading from both premises, then add the x's. If one premise is universal and the other is particular, do the universal one first, even if it is the minor premise.

The combined diagram includes all the information contained in the premises. The final step is to diagram the conclusion separately, and compare it with the premises. For a syllogism to be valid, the combined diagram must include all the information asserted by the conclusion. It may contain more information, but it cannot omit anything. In this example, we can see that the syllogism is valid. The conclusion requires that the region of overlap between S and P be shaded out, and it is shaded out in (3). The conclusion also requires an x somewhere in the region of S outside P, and an x somewhere in the region of P outside S. Diagram (3) does contain x's in those regions. So the Venn diagram gives us the same result we would have obtained by checking the syllogism against the rules.

If a syllogism is invalid, a Venn diagram will reveal that fact in one of two ways. The combined diagram for the premises will either fail to shade out an area excluded by the conclusion, or it will fail to put an x where the conclusion requires one. Let's look at an example of each.

Consider the syllogism AAA-2:

All *P* are *M*
All *S* are *M*
All *S* are *P*

It is invalid because it has an undistributed middle. The Venn diagram reveals the invalidity by failing to shade out the right areas:

Premises combined   Conclusion

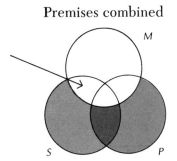 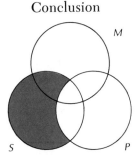

I have left out the *x*'s so that we can focus on the shading. In the combined diagram, the area of *P* outside *M* has been shaded to represent the major premise, and the area of *S* outside *M* has been shaded to represent the minor. But one area in the region of *S* outside *P*—the one indicated by the arrow—has not been shaded. Thus the premises leave open the possibility that some *S* are not *P*; they do not guarantee that all *S* are *P*. That conclusion does not follow, so the syllogism is invalid.

Now let's examine another case of undistributed middle, in which the problem is revealed by the placement of *x*'s:

All P are M
<u>Some S are M</u>
Some S are P

Major   Major plus minor   Conclusion

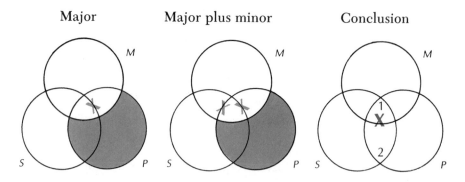

To diagram the major premise, we put an *x* on the line between the two areas in the overlap of *M* and *P*. In the combined diagram, the left-hand *x* represents the minor premise, and it must be placed on the line between the two areas in the overlap of *S* and *M*.

Now look at the diagram for the conclusion. The *x* is on the line in the overlap between *S* and *P*. The conclusion asserts that at least one *S* is *P*. It may also be an *M*, and thus belong in area (1); it may not be an *M*, and thus belong in area (2). We don't know. But there must be at least one member in one of the two areas. Do the premises guarantee this? No. Area (2) has been shaded out; the major premise tells us that this area is empty. That leaves area (1). But the premises don't give us an *x* in that area. The *x*'s are both on the lines bordering it, which means that area (1) could be empty. Thus the conclusion makes a stronger statement than the premises can support, and the syllogism is invalid.

Remember that the premises of a valid syllogism may contain more information than the conclusion, but they cannot contain less. The combined diagram may shade out areas that the conclusion leaves open, but it cannot leave open the areas that the conclusion says are shaded out. In the same way, the combined diagram may locate an *x* inside an area while the conclusion says merely that the area *may* contain one. But if the conclusion requires an *x* inside an area, the premises must put one there; otherwise the syllogism is invalid.

That's all there is to the method of using Venn diagrams. With a little practice, you will probably find that you can do a Venn diagram fairly quickly. You will probably be able to skip the first two steps, and enter the information from the premises directly onto a combined diagram. Some people find Venn diagrams easier to use than the four rules as a method of checking validity. Even if you prefer the rules, the diagrams are a good way to double-check your results.

Practice Quiz

For each mood and figure, write out the syllogism in standard form; then use Venn diagrams to determine whether it is valid.

1. EOI-3
2. EAO-3
3. AEE-4
4. OOO-2
5. IAI-3
6. IAO-1
7. OAO-2
8. AII-4
9. EIO-1
10. AEE-2

Enthymemes

As we saw in Part Two, arguments in real life often have assumed premises. We normally do not make explicit mention of all the premises implicit in an argument, especially if they are obvious or noncontroversial. A categorical syllogism with an unstated premise is called an **enthymeme.** For example, someone infers that Jones would support a gun control law because he's a liberal, leaving out the implicit premise that all liberals support gun control laws. In standard form:

(All liberals support gun control laws.)
<u>Jones is</u> a liberal.
Jones would support a gun control law.

We use parentheses around the major premise to indicate that it was not stated explicitly. We don't use letters to identify implicit premises here, as we did in Part Two, because we aren't using numbers to represent explicit ones.

The term enthymeme is also applied to a syllogism in which the conclusion is left unstated. For example, "Anyone who drives his car across the Police Department lawn is looking for trouble, right? Well, that's what Mitch did last night." The conclusion here (Mitch is looking for trouble) is so obvious that it's rhetorically more powerful to leave it unspoken. But this is a rare case. The more common type of enthymeme has a missing premise.

How do we identify the missing premise? In Part Two, we learned to look for a premise that will increase the logical strength of the argument. In deductive reasoning, validity is the measure of strength, so we look for a premise that will make the syllogism valid. Remember that filling in missing premises serves two goals. One is to understand what another person's actual reasoning is. In this context, we follow the principle of charity; we assume that the other person is reasoning validly unless we have evidence to the contrary. The other goal is to determine what assumptions are required by an argument in and of itself, regardless of what any particular person has in mind; here again the purpose is defeated if we supply a premise that makes the argument invalid.

In some arguments, like the one about Jones, it is obvious what the missing premise is. If you are not sure, however, you can use what you know about the internal structure of syllogisms. The first step is to lay out the conclusion and the one premise that is given. We can tell from the conclusion what the major and minor terms are, and the premise will give us the middle term. So we know what terms are contained in the missing premise: P and M if it is the major premise, S and M if it's the minor. The four rules of validity give us further information. If the middle term is not distributed in the explicit premise, then it must be distributed in the implicit one. If the explicit premise is negative, then the implicit one must be affirmative.

Let's try this on an example from the business pages of the newspaper. "'Who made money in telephones in 1984? Absolutely nobody,' said J. Dennis Burke, the general manager of Cobra Consumer Electronics. 'That tells me that everybody misread the market.'" [*New York Times*, January 12, 1985] The second sentence contains the conclusion: all producers in the telephone industry misread the market. The premise we're given is: no producers in the telephone industry made money in 1984. Notice that the conclusion is positive, while the premise is negative. This looks like a violation of the rule that a syllogism with a negative premise must have a negative conclusion—in which case no missing premise could make the argument valid. But the conclusion can easily be made negative by taking the obverse, so that we have:

(?)
<u>No producer</u> in the telephone industry made money in 1984.
No producer in the telephone industry read the market correctly.

The missing premise must contain the middle term (people who made money in 1984) and the major term (people who read the market correctly). The major term must be distributed in the missing premise, because it is distributed in the conclusion—otherwise we'll have an illicit major. But the middle term need not be distributed, since it is distributed in the minor premise. The missing premise must be affirmative, finally, because a syllogism can't have two negative premises. Putting this all together, we can see that the premise we need is:

(All producers who read the market correctly [would have] made money in 1984)

Most of the syllogisms you will encounter in everyday discourse will be enthymemes. This is not a defect of such discourse; on the contrary, it makes our reasoning more efficient. We state only the new or nonobvious parts of an argument, so that we can focus attention on them.

But it is important to identify missing premises because sometimes they are controversial, dubious, or false. A businessman might argue in favor of a government subsidy program on the grounds that it kept his firm from bankruptcy. If we lay out the argument, we can see that the assumed premise is "Any program that keeps my business from going bankrupt is a good program." It is not obvious, to say the least, that this proposition states a good criterion for public policy. The argument as a whole is less plausible, now that we have made the assumption explicit, than it may have seemed at first. The ability to identify assumed premises, then, is an important skill to develop. Without this skill, we would rarely be able to use the rest of what we have learned about syllogistic reasoning.

Practice Quiz

Find the missing premise (or conclusion) in each of the following enthymemes, put the argument into standard form, and identify its mood and figure. Be sure to complete the syllogism so that it is valid, if that is possible.

1. No creature whose actions are wholly determined by heredity and environment is a moral agent. Thus no animal other than man is a moral agent.
2. Economic arrangements are important because they affect the distribution of power.
3. No one who trades stocks on the basis of proprietary information is an honest businessman. Some investment bankers, therefore, are not honest businessmen.
4. Some Europeans are Moslems, since some Cypriots are.
5. Squares are rectangles, since they have four sides.
6. It isn't true that all politicians are honest, for some have taken bribes.
7. Any food that generates stomach acid is bad for an ulcer patient, and fried foods generate stomach acid.
8. Not one of the union demands deserves any serious consideration, since none of them is compatible with the labor contract that is still in effect.

SUMMARY

This chapter covered the analysis and evaluation of categorical syllogisms. The two premises and the conclusion of a categorical syllogism are categorical propositions, and they contain three terms: the major, the minor, and the middle. We analyze a categorical syllogism by identifying its logical form, consisting of its mood and its figure. The mood identifies the logical form of the component propositions, and the figure identifies the position of the middle term in the premises.

We evaluate a syllogism by testing for validity. A syllogism is valid if the truth of the premises would guarantee the truth of the conclusion. A syllogism is either valid or invalid; there are no degrees in between. Validity depends on the logical form of the argument. We can assess validity by seeing whether the syllogism satisfies four rules, two involving the distribution of terms, and two involving negation. Validity can also be tested by the method of Venn diagrams.

Finally, a categorical syllogism often leaves one of the premises or the conclusion unstated. Such an argument is called an enthymeme, and we analyze it by looking for a premise that will make the argument valid.

Exercises

A. Using the rules of validity and/or Venn diagrams, determine whether the following argument forms are valid.

1. All *M* are *P*
   Some *S* are *M*
   Some *S* are *P*

2. No *M* is *P*
   Some *S* are not *M*
   Some *S* are *P*

3. No *M* is *P*
   Some *M* are not *S*
   Some *S* are *P*

4. Some *P* are *M*
   No *S* is *M*
   Some *S* are not *P*

5. No *P* is *M*
   All *S* are *M*
   No *S* is *P*

6. No *M* is *P*
   All *M* are *S*
   Some *S* are not *P*

7. All *M* are *P*
   Some *S* are not *M*
   Some *S* are not *P*

8. All *P* are *M*
   Some *S* are not *M*
   Some *S* are *P*

9. Some *M* are *P*
   Some *M* are not *S*
   Some *S* are not *P*

10. All *P* are *M*
    Some *M* are *S*
    Some *S* are *P*

11. No *P* is *M*
    All *M* are *S*
    No *S* is *P*

12. Some *M* are *P*
    No *M* is *S*
    Some *S* are not *P*

13. No *P* is *M*
    Some *S* are *M*
    Some *S* are not *P*

14. Some *M* are not *P*
    All *M* are *S*
    Some *S* are not *P*

15. Some *M* are *P*
    All *S* are *M*
    Some *S* are *P*

B. Put each of the following syllogisms in standard form, identify mood and figure, and determine whether it is valid or invalid, using both the rules and Venn diagrams. (Remember to make sure, when you put the argument in standard form, that it has only three terms.)

1. Some democracies are tyrannies, because any state that ignores human rights is tyrannical, and some democracies do just that.
2. Amy must have done all her studying at the last minute, for anyone who crams like that does poorly on the final exam, and Amy certainly did poorly.
3. Amoebas are not plants, because they are capable of locomotion, and no plant has that capacity.
4. Those who supported the Voting Rights bill were opposed to racial discrimination. So conservatives, who did not support the bill, do not oppose discrimination.
5. We should never confuse music and noise: music is an orderly progression of sounds, noise a disorderly one.
6. Some philosophy courses are graded objectively, for while any course in which the grade is based exclusively on essays is graded nonobjectively, some of those courses, at least, are not in philosophy.
7. A person who overreacts to the charge that he is motivated by envy invariably is envious. But people with a strong sense of justice are not motivated by envy, and so they don't overreact that way.
8. No nonprofit corporation sells stock, but some hospital corporations do sell stock, and are therefore for-profit organizations.
9. Some international conflicts arise from honest motives, but no aggressive war arises in that way. Hence some aggressive wars are not international conflicts.

10. Some politicians are dishonest, for politicians by nature depend on reputation for their offices, and some people who depend on reputation are dishonest.
11. All great orchestra conductors are flamboyant, but none of them is careless. Thus some flamboyant people are not careless.

C. Put each of the following statements into standard categorical form, and identify the form. Then find a syllogism that uses the statement as a premise.

1. "No Civil War picture ever made a nickel." [Irving Thalberg to Louis B. Mayer, advising him not to make *Gone With the Wind.* Otto Friedrich, *City of Nets*]
2. "Some books are undeservedly forgotten; none are undeservedly remembered." [W. H. Auden, *Apothegms;* find two syllogisms.]
3. "He that speaks much, is much mistaken." [Benjamin Franklin, *Poor Richard's Almanack*]
4. "Not all who have vices are contemptible." [La Rochefoucauld, *Maxims*]

D. For each mood and figure, write out the syllogism in standard form. Then find an actual example of a syllogism with that form. Try to find terms for S, P, and M that give you a plausible argument.

1. AAA-1.
2. AEE-2.
3. IEO-3.
4. EIO-3.
5. EAE-1.

E. Put each of the propositions below into standard form, and identify the subject and predicate terms. Then use either a genus or a species of the subject as the middle term in a syllogism that supports the proposition.

1. Electrons do not travel faster than the speed of light.
2. Some bonds yield tax-free interest.
3. Trees need water.
4. Some methods of doing research are not ethical.

F. Put each of the following syllogisms in standard form, filling in the missing premise or conclusion if it is an enthymeme; identify mood and figure; and determine whether it is valid or invalid.

1. "First, there is an argument from the universality of physical laws. It runs: All material systems are governed by the laws of physics. All living systems are material. Therefore, all living systems are governed by the laws of physics." [Marjorie Grene, "Reducibility: Another Side Issue?" in *Interpretations of Life and Mind*]

2. "A member of a free democracy is, in a sense, a sovereign. He has no superior." [William Graham Sumner, *What the Social Classes Owe to Each Other*]

3. "I want to believe I'm losing my mind. But I can't believe it. Then I say that people who are crazy can never believe they are, and that means I . . . am." [John D. MacDonald, *The Turquoise Lament*]

4. "He who would rejoice loudly of his victories cannot expect to thrive in the world of men, for he who rejoices over victory does so at the expense of other men." [*Tao Te Ching*]

5. "That man must be tremendously ignorant: he answers every question that is put to him." [Voltaire, *Dictionnaire Philosophique*]

6. ". . . the Constitution suggests that what must be proscribed as cruel [punishment] is (a) a particularly painful way of inflicting death, or (b) a particularly undeserved death; and the death penalty, as such, offends neither of these criteria and cannot therefore be regarded as objectively "cruel." [William F. Buckley, "Capital Punishment," in *Execution Eve and Other Contemporary Ballads*]

7. "Because no man by merit has a right to the grace of God, I, having no merit, am entitled to it." [C. S. Lewis, *The Four Loves*]

8. "Certainly some individuals who suffer organic abnormalities or psychoses that produce rage attacks can properly be diagnosed as insane; they do not, for one thing, revert to normalcy after a violent episode." [Carol Tavris, *Anger*]

9. "There was no wound upon the dead man's person, but the agitated expression upon his face assured me that he had foreseen his fate before it came upon him. Men who die from heart disease, or any sudden natural cause, never by any chance exhibit agitation upon their features." [Arthur Conan Doyle, *A Study in Scarlet*]

10. "My contention is that no good thing harms its owner, a thing which you won't gainsay. But wealth very often does harm its owners . . ." [Boethius, *Consolation of Philosophy*]

11. "Seymour Kety of Harvard, long associated with genetic studies of schizophrenia, is the first to admit that 'things that run in

families are not necessarily genetic—wealth runs in families.'"
[*New York Times*, November 13, 1979]

G. For each of the following propositions, a) create a valid syllogism with the proposition as its conclusion; b) create an invalid syllogism with the proposition as its conclusion; c) create a valid
syllogism with the contradictory proposition as its conclusion; and
d) create an invalid syllogism with the contradictory proposition as
its conclusion.

1. All women should have careers.
2. Some lies are morally permissible.
3. Some courses should not be graded.
4. No dictatorship is truly benevolent.
5. All true art is representational.

H. Using what you know about categorical syllogisms, particularly
the four rules, explain why each of the following statements is true.

1. A valid syllogism in the second figure must have a negative
   conclusion.
2. In a valid syllogism of the first figure, the minor premise must
   be affirmative.
3. In a valid syllogism of the third figure, the conclusion must be
   particular.
4. No valid syllogism has two particular premises.
5. If either premise of a valid syllogism is particular, the conclusion must be particular as well.

10

Disjunctive and Hypothetical Syllogisms

Compare these three propositions:

1) Whales are mammals.
2) Either whales are mammals, or they are very large fish.
3) If whales are mammals, then they cannot breathe under water.

The first is a categorical proposition. The second has the structure *p or q*; it is a **disjunctive** proposition. The third has the structure *if p then q*; it is a **hypothetical** proposition. Both (2) and (3) contain (1) as a component, but neither of them asserts that (1) is true. As we saw in Chapter 4, these are compound statements in which the components are expressed but *not* asserted. What the compound statement asserts is that a certain relationship exists between the components. The disjunctive proposition says that whales belong to one or the other of two wider classes—without saying which one. The hypothetical proposition tells us what the implication would be *if* whales are mammals.

When we use compound propositions in our reasoning, it is the relationship among the components that is important. We don't need to break down the component propositions into subject and predicate terms, or to identify their categorical form. So we won't bother writing out the components. We'll just use single lower-case letters like *p*, *q*, and *r* to stand for the components as whole propositions.

In this chapter, we will examine the types of syllogisms that use disjunctive and hypothetical premises. Even though these are compound propositions, we will see that the corresponding syllogisms are actually simpler to analyze and evaluate than are categorical syllogisms.

Disjunctive Syllogisms

The components of a disjunctive proposition—*p* and *q*—are called **disjuncts.** Such a statement does not actually assert that *p* is true, or that *q* is; but it does say that one or the other of them is true. Thus if we knew independently that one of the disjuncts was *not* true, we could infer that the other must be true. If you know that the meeting will be either in room 305 or in room 306, and you find that it is not in 305, you can infer that it is in 306. This is a **disjunctive syllogism,** and it has the structure:

Either *p* or *q*   Either the meeting is in room 305, or it is in room 306

$\underline{-p}$ $\underline{\text{It is not in room 305}}$

q   It is in room 306

The symbol "-*p*" on the left means "it is not the case that *p*": the hyphen is the mark of negation. Thus *p* and -*p* are contradictory propositions. If *p* were itself a negative proposition, then -*p* would be affirmative: as with numbers, two negatives make a positive here. But we would still call it "-*p*" in order to indicate that it is the denial of *p*.

You can see that the argument above is valid. If the premises are both true, then the conclusion must be true as well. It does not matter which disjunct we deny in the second premise. If we checked the other room first and found it empty, we could have reasoned: Either *p* or *q*, but -*q*, therefore *p*. This too is valid. In fact, it doesn't matter how many disjuncts there are. It is simpler to deal just with two, but this is a game that any number can play. Suppose we have four: we know that either *p* or *q* or *r* or *s*. Then we could reason:

Either *p* or (*q* or *r* or *s*)

$\underline{-p}$

Either *q* or *r* or *s*

   Either *q* or (*r* or *s*)

   $\underline{-q}$

   Either *r* or *s*

      Either *r* or *s*

      $\underline{-r}$

      s

So long as we eliminate all the disjuncts but one, that one must be true—assuming, of course, that the disjunctive premise is true to begin with.

We use the disjunctive syllogism when we know that there is a certain range of possibilities, and we want to find out which one is actual. If we want to know who committed a crime, for example, we might start out with a list of suspects; and then cross them off the list one by one, as we acquired more evidence, until we were left with just one. As Sherlock Holmes said, when you have eliminated the impossible, what is left, however improbable, must be true. Again, in making a personal decision, we might start with a set of alternatives, and then by a process of elimination narrow the set down to one.

It is quite common with the disjunctive syllogism, as with the categorical, to leave one of the premises unstated. If you are looking for a book and decide that it must be at the library because it isn't in your bag, you are using a disjunctive syllogism with an assumed premise:

> (Either my book is in my bag or I left it in the library)
> My book is not in my bag
> I left it in the library

It is usually the disjunctive premise, as in this example, that is left implicit. Indeed, the fallacy of false alternatives is often committed because we rely implicitly on a disjunctive premise that does not identify all the possible alternatives. In the argument above, for example, it might occur to you, once you have identified the implicit assumption, that there are other places you might have left the book.

The disjunctive syllogism proceeds by denying one of the disjuncts. Is it equally valid to argue by *affirming* a disjunct? What happens if we start with a disjunctive proposition, and we know that one of the disjuncts is true? Can we then infer that the other one is false? Is the inference

$$\text{Either } p \text{ or } q$$
$$\underline{p}$$
$$-q$$

valid? The answer depends on how we are using the conjunction "or." We sometimes use it in what is called the *exclusive* sense, to mean "p or q but not both," and sometimes use it in the *inclusive* sense, to mean "p or q or both." An argument that denies a disjunct is valid in either case, but an argument that affirms a disjunct is valid only if "or" is used in the exclusive sense. The problem is that nothing in the logical form of the argument tells us which sense is being used. To make it clear that p and q are exclusive alternatives, people sometimes say *"p* or *else q."* But in most cases we have to decide from the context which sense is intended. For logical purposes, therefore, we assume that "or" is used inclusively; affirming a disjunct is therefore fallacious. In cases where such an argument seems valid intuitively, it is easy to translate the argument into a different form that makes the validity clear.

Suppose someone has just given birth. We know the child is either a boy or a girl. If we find out that it is a girl, can we infer that it is not a boy? Of course we can. But the inference is valid only because we know that male and female are mutually exclusive possibilities. To make the role of this premise explicit, we should recast the argument:

> If it's a girl, it's not a boy
> It is a girl
> ————————
> It is not a boy

This inference is an example of a hypothetical syllogism, which we will examine in the next section. For now, the point to remember is that whenever an argument affirming a disjunct seems valid, it is because information about the context allows us to treat "or" in the exclusive sense. For purposes of logical analysis, it is better to cast the argument into some other form that makes the relevant information explicit.

Practice Quiz

Put each of the following disjunctive syllogisms into standard form, identify the disjuncts, identify any implicit elements, and determine whether the syllogism is valid.

1. Either I'm hearing things, or someone is out in the hall singing "Jingle Bells." I know I'm not hearing things. So there's someone out there singing.
2. I have to get the book here in town, or else in New York next weekend. But I can't get it here; therefore I will have to get it in New York.
3. Either I'm out of money, or I made a mistake in my checkbook. I'm sure I made a mistake, though, so I'm not out of money.
4. Jackson must be a liberal, because he certainly isn't a conservative.
5. According to the union contract, either we have to close the plant on Labor Day, or we have to pay the workers twice the regular wage. But we have too much work to close the plant, so we'll have to pay the workers double-time.

Hypothetical Syllogisms

A hypothetical proposition has the form "If p, then q," where p and q once again are the component propositions. But in this case they are not called disjuncts. The "if" component is called the **antecedent,** and the "then" component is the **consequent.** Thus, in the statement "If it's a girl, then it isn't a boy," the antecedent is "it's a girl," and the consequent is "it isn't a boy." Hypothetical propositions are used pervasively in ordinary speech to identify relationships of dependence among facts, events, and possibilities. The statement "If you leave your bike out in the rain, it will rust" identifies the consequence of a certain action. The statement "If it's four o'clock, then I'm late for class" says that the existence of one fact ("It's four o'clock") implies the existence of another ("I'm late"). In a hypothetical proposition, we are not actually asserting the truth of p or q, but we are saying that the truth of p would be sufficient for the truth of q.

One sort of inference involving such propositions is the **pure hypothetical syllogism,** which has the following form:

$$\begin{array}{l} \text{If } p, \text{ then } q \\ \underline{\text{If } q, \text{ then } r} \\ \text{If } p, \text{ then } r \end{array}$$

Notice that q here plays the same role as the middle term in a categorical syllogism. It is the consequent of the first premise and the antecedent of the second. It serves to link together p and r, which appear together in the conclusion. Any argument of this form is valid.

We often use pure hypothetical syllogisms in describing chains of events in which each event causes the next. For example, if we asked an economist how government deficits are related to inflation, he might say: "If the government runs a deficit, then the Federal Reserve Bank creates more money; if the Bank creates more money, prices will eventually rise; so if the government runs a deficit, prices will eventually rise." We also use these syllogisms in planning strategies, in games or in real life. A chess player, for example, might reason: "If I move my Queen here, he will move his rook there. But if he moves his rook there, I will have to sacrifice a pawn. So if I move my Queen there, I will have to sacrifice a pawn."

Notice that in these examples, both premises are hypothetical, and so is the conclusion. At no point do we assert that p, q, or r is actually the case. Our reasoning is, so to speak, purely hypothetical. But there is another sort of inference that allows us to derive a non-hypothetical conclusion:

If p, then q	If you play with fire, you will get burned
p	You played with fire
q	You got burned

In an argument of this form, the second premise is categorical; it affirms the antecedent of the hypothetical premise. This entitles us to infer the consequent, which is also categorical. Such inferences are called **mixed hypothetical syllogisms.**

Any argument of this form is valid, because it merely unfolds what is implicit in the meaning of the hypothetical premise. That premise says that the truth of p would be sufficient for the truth of q. If we then assume that p is true, we may conclude that q is true as well. We can also work this in the opposite direction. If we assume that q is false, we can infer that p is false—for if p were not false (i.e., if it were true), then q could not have been false either. Thus the following mixed hypothetical syllogism is valid:

If p, then q	If God had wanted us to fly, He would have given us wings
$-q$	He has not given us wings
$-p$	He did not want us to fly

In this case, we denied the consequent, and that allowed us to deny the antecedent. Once again, the conclusion is a categorical proposition.

Thus there are two valid mixed hypothetical syllogisms. The medieval logicians called the first one **modus ponens:** the method of affirming the antecedent. They called the second one **modus tollens:** the method of denying the consequent. Both are valid for the same reason: they spell out the implications of the hypothetical premise.

There is another way to see this. When we studied immediate inferences, we saw that an A categorical proposition has a valid contrapositive: "All S are P" implies "All non-P are non-S." A hypothetical proposition also has a valid contrapositive: "if p, then q" implies "If $-q$, then $-p$." If it rained last night, then the ground would be wet; so if the ground is not wet, then it did not rain. We can use contraposition to transform any *modus tollens* argument into *modus ponens:*

If p, then q ←—— contrapositive ——→ If -q, then -p

-q   -q

-p   -p

Merely by taking the contrapositive of the hypothetical premise, but leaving everything else the same, we have changed the *modus tollens* argument on the left into the *modus ponens* argument on the right.

There are two other possible forms of mixed hypothetical syllogism:

Denying	If p, then q	If my car is out of gas, it will stop running
the	-p	My car is not out of gas
antecedent	-q	It will not stop running

Affirming	If p, then q	If my car is out of gas, it will stop running
the	q	My car stopped running
consequent	p	It is out of gas

Both of these arguments are invalid. In each case, the hypothetical premise says that being out of gas is sufficient to make my car stop running. Both arguments assume, however, that being out of gas is the *only* thing that can do so. That is not true, of course, and it is not implied by the hypothetical premise. Suppose I have a full tank but my battery is dead. That would make the premises of both arguments true, but the conclusion in each case would be false. A valid deductive argument cannot have true premises and a false conclusion.

There are circumstances in which these inferences may *seem* valid. Suppose someone says "If I get a C on the next exam, then I'll pass the course." Someone else who is skeptical of the first person's chances might reason:

> If he gets a C on the exam, he will pass the course
> But he won't get a C
> So he won't pass

This is a case of denying the antecedent, and it is invalid as stated. What makes it seem valid is the background knowledge that if he does not get a C, he will not pass. If we used this premise, then the argument would be valid. But this premise is not contained in or implied by the one that was actually asserted; it is extra information.

We have now covered all the possibilities. There are two valid mixed hypothetical syllogisms, and two invalid ones. We don't need a separate set of rules for testing validity; we just need to remember these forms, which are summarized in the box below:

	Valid		Invalid
Affirming the antecedent	If p, then q p q	Affirming the consequent	If p, then q q p
Denying the consequent	If p, then q $-q$ $-p$	Denying the antecedent	If p, then q $-p$ $-q$

Like the other types of syllogism, a hypothetical syllogism may leave a premise unstated. Suppose you are indoors and cannot see the sky, but you infer that the sun isn't shining because there are no shadows on the ground outside. Your reasoning contains an assumed hypothetical premise:

(If the sun were shining, there would be shadows)
<u>There are</u> no shadows
The sun is not shining

In other cases, both premises are given but the conclusion is left implicit; this is more common with the hypothetical than with other syllogisms. If you can find an example of this, you have grasped the material in this chapter—and I'm sure you *can* find an example.

Practice Quiz

Put each of the following hypothetical syllogisms into standard form, identify antecedent and consequent, identify any implicit elements, and determine whether the syllogism is valid.

1. If he had even mentioned her name, I would have hit him. But he didn't, so I didn't.
2. If God had wanted man to fly, He would not have given us Buicks. But He has given us Buicks; therefore. . . .
3. If a child is deprived of affection as an infant, he will learn not to expect it; and if he learns not to expect it, he won't seek it out later in life. So if a child is deprived of affection early in life, he won't look for it later on.

4. If someone had been snooping around here last night, there would be footprints, right? Well, there are. So someone was snooping around last night.
5. The battery can't be dead—the lights are still working.
6. I don't think you really do want to marry him. If you did, you wouldn't be running around with other men the way you have been.
7. If the Soviet Union completes a missile defense system before we do, they will gain enormous leverage over us in any confrontation. For if they complete a defense first, they will pose a credible threat of a first strike, and if they can pose such a threat, they will gain enormous leverage.
8. Our visual system must have some way of detecting edges. If we did not have such a capacity, we could not perceive objects.

Nonstandard Forms

Once you have a disjunctive or hypothetical syllogism in standard form, it is usually easy to determine whether the syllogism is valid. But in ordinary speech, there are various nonstandard ways of expressing disjunctive and hypothetical propositions, so we need to learn to transform these into the standard forms.

Instead of using the word "either" to express disjunction, for example, we sometimes say "There are two (or more) possibilities," or "There are two alternatives," and then simply list them. Such statements are easy to translate into "either p or q or. . . ." But there is another case that is not so obvious. There's an old saying that goes "You can't have your cake and eat it, too." What does this mean? It means that you either eat the cake, in which case you no longer have it; or else you keep the cake (i.e., you have it) by choosing not to eat it. Similarly, opponents of President Reagan often said during his first term, "There's no way to raise defense spending and cut taxes and avoid deficits; something's got to give."

In these examples, the key word is "and." A proposition of the form "p and q" is called a **conjunctive** proposition, and it is true only if both p and q are true. It is false if either p or q is false. Schematically:

$$1) \ -(p \text{ and } q)$$
$$\text{implies}$$
$$2) \ \text{either } -p \text{ or } -q$$

Both of our examples had the form of (1); they denied that a certain conjunction was true. The statements can be put in standard form as disjunctive propositions that have the form of (2): "Either you don't eat the cake, or you don't have it," and "Either you don't raise defense spending or you don't cut taxes or you don't avoid deficits." Any inferences drawn from such statements can then be formulated as disjunctive syllogisms.

For hypothetical propositions, the range of nonstandard forms is somewhat wider. The first and easiest case occurs when the consequent is stated first, the antecedent second, as in:

1) I'll stay home tomorrow if I still feel sick.

The component proposition "I still feel sick" is the antecedent, even though it comes second, because it is the "if" component. Thus, in standard form: "If I still feel sick, then I will stay home tomorrow." In general "*p* if *q*" should be translated "If *q*, then *p*."

What about a statement with the form "*p* only if *q*," such as:

2) I'll stay home tomorrow only if I'm sick?

Does (2) say the same thing as (1)? Am I saying that if I am sick I will stay home tomorrow? No. I am saying that if I am not sick, then I will not stay home. Being sick is the only thing that would keep me home. Think of (2) as a promise I've made to you. Now suppose I am sick, but I show up anyway. Have I broken my promise? No. But I would break the promise if I stayed home and was not sick. Thus the statement "*p* only if *q*" can be translated in either of two equivalent ways:

$$p \text{ only if } q \qquad \begin{array}{l} 1) \text{ if } -q, \text{ then } -p \\ 2) \text{ if } p, \text{ then } q \end{array}$$

Translation (1) will sound more natural in some contexts, (2) in others. But since they are contrapositives, they are logically equivalent.

When we want to claim that *p* and *q* are mutually sufficient, so that the truth of either implies the truth of the other, it is natural to combine the preceding forms: *p* if and only if *q*. As the word "and" suggests, we are making two statements:

$$p \text{ if } q \longrightarrow \text{if } q, \text{ then } p$$

and   and

$$p \text{ only if } q \longrightarrow \text{if } p, \text{ then } q$$

The analysis on the right makes it clear that in the "if and only if" construction, both *p* and *q* serve as antecedents, and both also serve as consequents. This means that all four possible mixed inferences are valid: both *p* and *q* can be either affirmed or denied, and the appropriate conclusion will follow.

Another nonstandard hypothetical statement has the form "*p* unless *q*." For example, "The plant will die unless you water it." This means the plant will die if you do not water it. "Unless" means "if not." Thus the following three propositions are equivalent:

p unless *q*
p if −*q*
if −*q*, then *p*

Does "*p* unless *q*" also imply "if *q*, then −*p*"? Are we also saying that if you do water it, the plant will not die? No. In some contexts it might be assumed that we are also saying this, but it is not asserted by the original statement. Once again, think of the statement as a promise I have made to you. If you water the plant and it still dies, I haven't broken my promise, strictly speaking; I didn't promise that water alone would keep the plant alive, only that the absence of water would kill it. Consequently, "*p* unless *q*" is exactly equivalent to "if −*q*, then *p*," and should be translated that way.

There are two final cases to consider. 1) "Whenever I get anxious, I start eating more." A proposition of this form, "Whenever *p*, *q*" is about a class of occasions; it states a general rule. It would thus be possible to formulate it as an A categorical proposition: "All occasions on which I feel anxious are occasions on which I eat more." But it is usually more natural to formulate it as a hypothetical: "If I get anxious, then I eat more." Thus "Whenever *p*, *q*" means "if *p*, then *q*."

2) "Without distribution requirements, most students would take too narrow a range of courses." Here we do not have two component propositions: the phrase beginning "without" does not contain a whole statement. Yet it is easy to turn that phrase into a whole statement: "If distribution requirements did not exist, most students would take too narrow a range of courses." In general, "Without *X*, *q*" can be translated "If *X* did not exist, then *q*."

Of course there are other nonstandard ways of expressing disjunctive and hypothetical propositions. Our language is far too rich and subtle for us to capture every possibility in a small set of rules. But the rules we've just learned will allow us to put a great many statements occurring in everyday speech into standard form.

Practice Quiz

Determine whether each of the following statements is disjunctive or hypothetical; then put it into the appropriate standard form.

1. If you miss your first serve in tennis, you get a second try.
2. You lose the point if you miss the second try.
3. Without a cooling mechanism, a car's engine would rapidly overheat.
4. I'll call you unless you call me first.
5. Speak now or forever hold your peace.
6. Whenever bubbles form in the test tube, a gas is being produced by the reaction.
7. A term in the conclusion of a valid categorical syllogism may be distributed only if it is distributed in the premise in which it occurs.
8. You may not take this course unless you have satisfied the prerequisites.
9. I only have two hands: I can't make dinner and take out the trash, too.
10. I'll go out with you tonight if and only if you promise not to bring your parrot.

SUMMARY

Categorical propositions can be combined into compound propositions, two of which are especially important in deductive reasoning: the disjunctive proposition, *p or q;* and the hypothetical proposition, *if p, then q.*

A deductive argument employing a disjunctive proposition as a premise is a disjunctive syllogism. It is valid to deny one disjunct and infer the other. Because we interpret the conjunction "or" in the inclusive sense, however, it is not valid to affirm one disjunct and infer that the other is false.

A hypothetical syllogism may be either pure or mixed. In the pure form, both premises and the conclusion are hypothetical propositions. In a mixed hypothetical syllogism, one premise is hypothetical; the other premise either affirms or denies one of the components, and the conclusion affirms or denies the other. It is valid to affirm the antecedent or deny the consequent, invalid to deny the antecedent or affirm the consequent.

The chapter also reviewed some of the nonstandard forms in which disjunctive and hypothetical propositions can be expressed in ordinary language.

Exercises

A. Determine whether the following argument forms are valid.

1. If p, then q
   q
   p

2. p unless q
   $-p$
   q

3. p or q
   $-q$
   p

4. If p, then q
   $-p$
   $-q$

5. p if q
   $-q$
   $-p$

6. p or q
   q
   p

7. If p, then q
   p
   q

8. p only if q
   p
   q

9. p or q
   p
   $-q$

10. Not (p and q)
    $-p$
    q

11. Whenever p, q
    q
    p

12. p unless q
    q
    $-p$

13. p only if q
    $-p$
    $-q$

14. p if and only if q
    q
    p

B. For each of the following arguments, determine which type of syllogism it is, put it into standard form, and determine whether it is valid.

1. I knew I would be late if I didn't hurry, but I did hurry, so I wasn't late.
2. I'd be willing to take statistics only if I could take it in the morning, when my brain is functioning. But it isn't offered in the morning, so I won't take it.
3. Frank must be jealous of Cindy. He was following her around yesterday with a sour expression, which is exactly what he *would* do if he were jealous.
4. If the time it takes Mercury to rotate around its axis (its period of rotation) is the same as the time it takes to revolve once around the Sun (its period of revolution), it always presents the same side to the Sun. And if it always presents the same side to the Sun, then that's the only side we can see. So if Mercury's

period of rotation equals its period of revolution, we can see only one side.

5. "There's milk in the refrigerator if you want some."
"But I don't want any, Mom."
"Then there isn't any milk there, wise guy."

6. We can either negotiate with the Soviets, or else make ourselves strong enough to resist any attack. But we should certainly make ourselves strong enough to do that, so there's no point in negotiating.

7. Robin wasn't really embarrassed, because the blotch she gets whenever she's embarrassed wasn't there.

8. Current will not flow unless the circuit is unbroken, and this circuit is broken. So the current isn't flowing.

9. If Rome had been cohesive enough in the fourth century to enlist the efforts of all its citizens, it would have repelled the barbarian invaders. But by that time Rome had lost its cohesion, and so it could not resist invasion.

10. I can't go to the movies with you tonight and study for the exam; and I have to study for the exam. So I can't go.

11. You won't be able to master logic unless you are serious about it. But if you have read this far, you must be serious. So if you have read this far, you will be able to master logic.

12. If the errors and distortions in TV news were not the result of political bias, but merely of sloppy reporting, they would be randomly distributed across the political spectrum. But in fact they are all slanted in a single direction.

13. Anarchy would be a fine and beautiful system for society to adopt—if men were angels. Alas, they are not.

C. Creating arguments: follow the instructions for each of the problems below.

1. Find a *modus ponens* syllogism to support this conclusion: the economy will go into recession next year.

2. Find an invalid mixed hypothetical syllogism with this conclusion: Jane does not speak Spanish.

3. Use a pure hypothetical syllogism to explain why pushing down the accelerator makes the car go faster.

4. Find a valid disjunctive syllogism to support this conclusion: honesty is the best policy.

5. Find the most plausible argument you can that commits the fallacy of affirming the consequent.

D. Put each of the following arguments into standard form and determine whether it is valid.

1. "If the Moral Law was one of our instincts, we ought to be able to point to some one impulse inside us which was always what we call good. . . . But [we] cannot. . . . The Moral Law is not any one instinct." [C. S. Lewis, *Mere Christianity*]

2. "'If these charges on Watergate were true, nobody would have to ask me to resign—I wouldn't serve for one month,' Mr. Nixon told Rabbi Baruch Korff on May 13, 1974. 'But I know they are not true, therefore I will stay here and do the job. . . .'" [*New York Times*, September 4, 1986]

3. "Meanwhile, the [1984 election] coverage demolished an old network argument that when a network makes an early projection it is only reporting news. If the argument had merit, the networks would report what the other networks were saying. If an early projection was really news, it would be news on all three networks, and not just on the network that was making it. But on Tuesday night, the networks assiduously ignored each other." [John Corry, *New York Times*, November 8, 1984]

4. "'The White House cannot function properly without a strong and effective chief of staff,' reasoned Mr. [Stuart] Eizenstat, who was a domestic policy adviser to Mr. Carter. 'And if the White House cannot function properly, then the executive branch can't.'" [*New York Times*, January 22, 1982]

5. "At present, then, there is no evidence on the effects of imitation [on language learning] that is very conclusive. This in itself is somewhat surprising in view of the importance that many theorists have attributed to imitation. If it is an important factor in language development, it should be relatively easy to find evidence of its importance. We are forced to conclude that imitation . . . does not contribute importantly to language development." [Donald J. Foss and David T. Hakes, *Psycholinguistics*]

6. ". . . social writer Barbara Ehrenreich is quoted as stating that people are more interested in cars and careers than sex. Either she knows nothing about sex or I know nothing about cars after being in the automobile business for over 30 years." [Letter to the editor, *Wall Street Journal*, October 10, 1985]

7. "[T]he value of the monetary unit should have a real objective regulator. But the value of money has an objective regulator only when it is linked to a real commodity, like gold, itself requiring the cost of human labor to be produced." (Notice that in this case, the conclusion is not explicitly stated; but the intended conclusion is clearly "the value of money should be linked to a real commodity.") [*Harpers Magazine*, August 1980]

8. "'If epidemiological studies gave us any hint at all that insects played a role in spreading AIDS, we'd do more detailed stud-

ies,' [Dr. Jaffe] said. 'But they haven't.'" [*New York Times*, August 27, 1986]

E. Using what you learned in this chapter, answer the following theoretical questions.

1. How many hypothetical propositions are contained in the statement "*p* if and only if *q*"?
2. What would the converse of a hypothetical proposition be? Does the converse follow from the proposition?
3. If we negate a conjunction, we get a disjunctive proposition. What happens if we negate a disjunction?
4. Show that any disjunctive proposition may be reformulated as a hypothetical.
5. Show that any hypothetical proposition may be reformulated as a disjunctive. (*Hint:* a hypothetical says that *p* cannot be true and *q* false.)

11

Syllogisms in Ordinary Reasoning

The three kinds of syllogism we've studied—categorical, disjunctive, and hypothetical—are not the only forms of deductive reasoning, but they are probably the most common. Indeed, it should be clear, after all the examples of the last three chapters, that we use them pervasively in everyday thought and speech. But those examples were carefully chosen to illustrate the logical form of the syllogisms, and we studied each form in isolation. It is time now to leave the laboratory, so to speak, and observe the behavior of these arguments in their natural environment: the context of everyday reasoning. In the first section of this chapter, we'll learn more about how to spot the logical form of a syllogism beneath the verbal dress it is wearing. This is similar to the process of distilling an argument, which we studied in Chapter 7, but here we'll need to incorporate what we've learned about deductive logic. In the second section, we will examine deductive arguments that have more than a single step—extended arguments that involve *chains* of syllogisms.

Distilling Deductive Arguments

Like any other language, English offers an endless variety of ways to express our thoughts. By choosing words carefully, we can capture subtle shades of meaning that do not affect the logic of an argument, but are important in other ways. By varying the grammatical structure of our sentences, we can focus attention on different parts of the same argument. These resources of our language often enable us to convey our reasoning more powerfully—and sometimes more clearly—than if we put it into standard form. But those same resources can make it difficult to evaluate the validity of an argument; they can even be used to disguise poor reasoning. To analyze and evaluate a deductive argument, therefore, we need to put it into standard form.

In order to do this, we need to know what *type* of argument we are dealing with. The syllogisms we encounter in everyday thought and speech do not wear labels identifying themselves as disjunctive, hypothetical, or categorical. But we need to know this in order to know which standard form is appropriate. To distinguish among the types of syllogism, we rely on two basic criteria. We use *linguistic* clues: conjunctions like "if . . . then" and "either . . . or," quantifiers like "all" and "some," and so on. And we look at the *substance* of the argument, its content. What is it about? What kinds of facts does it use as premises? What kind of conclusion is it trying to establish?

Disjunctive Syllogisms

To see how this works, let's begin with the disjunctive syllogism, which is the easiest to spot. The abstract logical form of this syllogism, as we saw, is:

$$\text{Either } p \text{ or } q$$
$$\frac{-p}{q}$$

If the disjunctive premise in such an argument is stated explicitly, it is easy to identify. In the last chapter, we saw that there are just a few nonstandard ways in which to express a disjunctive proposition. If the disjunctive premise is not stated explicitly, there's another linguistic feature to look for. A disjunctive syllogism has a positive conclusion and a negative premise. In a mixed hypothetical syllogism, by contrast, the second premise and the conclusion are either both positive or both negative. So we can look for the pattern "$-p$, therefore q."

In substantive terms, disjunctive reasoning has a characteristic logical flow. It proceeds by listing a set of alternative possibilities, and then eliminating all but one. We saw that this pattern of reasoning is often employed in deliberating about what action to take. We also use it when we try to *explain* something: a person's behavior, a rise in the stock market, the loss of ozone in the atmosphere. Various theories are proposed, and the process of establishing one particular theory usually involves the use of evidence to rule out its rivals. Look for disjunctive syllogisms, therefore, in the context of explanation as well as choice.

Hypothetical and Categorical Syllogisms

Hypothetical and categorical syllogisms come in a greater variety of nonstandard forms, but the same kinds of criteria will help distinguish between them. The hypothetical syllogism is used primarily to deal with relationships of dependence among facts, events, and possibilities. We typically use it in reasoning about cause and effect, or means and ends. The categorical syllogism is used primarily to deal with relationships among classes of things. We typically use it in applying a general rule to a specific instance, and in connection with genus-species hierarchies.

Corresponding to that substantive distinction is a linguistic one: the pattern of repetition in the argument. In a hypothetical syllogism, *propositions* are repeated as units, as wholes: *p, q, −p, −q.* In a categorical syllogism, on the other hand, it is the *terms*—S, P, and M—that are repeated.

Consider the following argument:

> It rains whenever a mass of hot, humid air collides with a high-pressure mass of colder air. Since it has been hot and muggy, and a cold front is moving in from the west, I expect it will rain.

As we saw in the last chapter, the conjunction "whenever" is a sign of an "if-then" proposition. So we might expect this argument to be a hypothetical syllogism. That expectation is confirmed by the pattern of repetition. The component proposition "It rains/will rain" is contained in each sentence. And saying that a hot, humid air mass collides with a mass of colder air describes the same situation as saying that it has been hot and muggy and that a cold front is moving in. So we could put this argument into standard form as a hypothetical syllogism:

> If a mass of hot, humid air collides with a mass of cold air, then it rains.
> A mass of hot, humid air is colliding with a mass of cold air.
> It will rain.

By contrast, consider an argument that you might hear in a courtroom:

> Some of the witnesses who have testified so far on behalf of the accused cannot be considered reliable—not because they are dishonest, but because reliability in a matter as complex as this requires a level of training and experience that some of the witnesses do not possess.

No proposition is repeated in this argument, but there is a repetition of the terms "witnesses" and "reliable (people)."

This argument also contains a second linguistic mark of a categorical syllogism: the explicit use of a quantifier, "some." As we have seen, the quantity of a proposition is an essential element in a categorical syllogism, but does not play any essential role in a hypothetical syllogism. If the components of a hypothetical proposition are categorical, of course, they may contain explicit quantifiers. On the other hand, the quantifier in a categorical proposition may be implicit. So this is not a criterion that works in every case. But a categorical syllogism is more likely to mention and stress the quantity of its premises than is a hypothetical syllogism.

In order to put a categorical syllogism in standard form, it is best to begin our analysis with statements that contain an explicit quantifier. Thus, in our example, the first part of the sentence, which is the conclusion, is the easiest to put into standard form: "Some of the witnesses are not reliable." A quantifier also appears in the last clause, which tells us that some of the witnesses do not possess an adequate level of training and experience. In standard form:

(?)
Some witnesses do not possess an adequate level of training and
  experience
Some witnesses are not reliable

The remaining part of the sentence—"reliability in a matter as complex as this requires an (adequate) level of training and experience"—must be the major premise. This statement contains no quantifier. And it is a statement about attributes—reliability, training, and experience—whereas the minor premise and conclusion are about classes of people. But if attribute A (reliability) depends on attribute B (training and experience), then all people who have A must have B. So the major premise can be formulated:

All reliable people possess an adequate level of training and
  experience.

In the same way, a statement to the effect that attribute A is incompatible with attribute B can be translated as a universal negative proposition: no thing with A is a thing with B.

Nonstandard Quantifiers

You can see the value, then, of beginning the analysis of a categorical syllogism by looking for explicit quantifiers. They focus our attention on classes, and once we know what sort of classes the argument is about, it is much easier to put into standard form any premises that do not seem to deal with classes at all. It's important to remember, in this regard, that English contains many quantifiers in addition to "all," "some," and "no." We looked at a few non-standard quantifiers in Chapter 8, but there are others. Let's look at three.

1) The subject term in English normally comes at the beginning of a sentence, before the verb. But when a sentence begins "There is . . . ," the subject is not "there." The real subject occurs later. "There is soot in the fireplace": the subject is "soot," so in standard form this would be "Some soot is (a thing that is) in the fireplace." The quantity in such sentences is usually particular, as in this example, but not always. The statement "There are no snakes in Ireland" is universal: "No snakes (are things that) exist in Ireland." Once you have identified the subject term in such sentences, the quantity will normally be obvious.

2) There is a set of words indicating quantity pertaining to time: "always," "never," "sometimes," "occasionally," and so on. In some cases, the reference to time is not really essential, and the statement can easily be put into standard form. "Triangles always have three sides" means "all triangles have three sides." "Syllogisms in the fourth figure are never easy" means "no syllogism in the fourth figure is easy."

In other cases, however, the reference to time is essential. Suppose it occurs to you that your friend Sally won't be coming to the party because it's 20 below outside, and she never leaves home when the temperature falls that low. What you are doing here is applying a generalization about Sally's behavior. To put the inference in standard form, we need to state the generalization in terms of classes of times or occasions:

> All times when it's extremely cold are times when Sally does not
> leave home
> <u>Now is</u> a time when it's extremely cold
> Now is a time when Sally won't leave home

This formulation of the major premise is rather awkward and pedantic, but it's necessary in order to convey the logical form of the inference. We would use the same technique for statements like "He is never willing to admit he made a mistake," or "My car sometimes won't start when it's cold." And we can use the same technique for quantifiers relating to place instead of time, quantifiers like "everywhere," "anywhere," "nowhere," "somewhere." For example, the complaint "You can't find a decent meal anywhere in this town" means "No place in this town is a place where you can find a decent meal."

3) We have seen that the word "only" is used in hypothetical propositions of the form "*p* only if *q*." "Only" is also used to indicate quantity in categorical propositions such as:

   i)   Only a fool would believe that story.
   ii) Only people with self-esteem are happy.

These propositions have the form "Only *S* is *P*." This is not the same as saying that all *S* are *P*. Proposition (i) does not mean that all fools believe the story: some may never have heard it. Proposition (ii) does not say that everyone with self-esteem is happy: there may be other factors that are also necessary for happiness. Instead, we must translate such statements in one of two equivalent ways.

In cases like (i), the most natural translation is "All people who believe that story are fools": All *P* are *S*. In cases like (ii), the most natural translation is "No one who lacks self-esteem is happy": No non-*S* is *P*. These two modes of translation are logically equivalent, as we can prove by immediate inferences:

   All *P* are *S*
   No *P* is non-*S* (taking the obverse)
   No non-*S* is *P* (taking the converse)

In distilling a categorical syllogism, however, it's a good idea to use the "All *P* are *S*" translation in all cases, even if it seems less natural. Some other proposition in the argument is likely to contain the term *S*, and this way you won't have to translate *S* into non-*S* or vice versa.

The guidelines for distilling syllogisms we've reviewed in this section do not cover all the problems you will encounter. The resources of our language are too rich and varied for us to list all the possible nonstandard ways of expressing a deductive argument. We've discussed only the major ones. But if you understand these, you should be able to handle the others by common sense.

Practice Quiz

Put each of the following syllogisms into standard form, and determine whether each is valid.

1. Only computers with 320 kilobytes of internal memory can run Lotus's Symphony program, and my computer doesn't have that much memory. So I can't run Symphony.
2. The theory that the Constitution merely reflects the economic interests of the Founding Fathers has been refuted. That leaves the theory that it reflects their intellectual commitment to the principles of natural rights and democratic government.
3. Anyone who can strike a log with an ax in just the right place can split it with one blow. But it takes a good eye to hit the log just right, so only someone with a good eye can split logs in a single blow.
4. Were the Earth's crust a single rigid layer, the continents could not have shifted their positions in relation to each other, but such "continental drift" has clearly occurred.
5. Photosynthesis must occur as far down as 250 meters below the surface of the ocean, for there are algae that live at those depths.

Extended Arguments

In our study of argument structure in Part Two, we saw that arguments often involve more than a single step. Premises combine to support an intermediate conclusion, which is then itself used as a premise to support an ultimate conclusion. Or, moving in the opposite direction, an ultimate conclusion is supported by premises that are themselves supported by further premises. When such an extended argument is deductive, we can use what we know about syllogisms to analyze it in more depth than was possible in Part Two.

Consider the following argument: "A nervous system contains many individual cells, so no one-celled animal, by definition, could have one. But only something with a nervous system could be conscious, so no one-celled animal is conscious." This is certainly a deductive argument, and it has the marks of a categorical syllogism. There's an explicit quantifier, "no," and various terms are repeated: "one-celled animal," "conscious (beings)," and so on. Notice, however, that the argument has two conclusions, both introduced by the word "so." It is clear that the first one (no one-celled animal has a nervous system) is an intermediate conclusion, because a further inference is drawn from it. The ultimate conclusion of the argument is "no one-celled animal is conscious." The argument, then, has more than one step, and must be analyzed accordingly.

We begin, as we did in Part Two, by isolating and numbering the propositions that play a role in the argument. Thus:

(1) A nervous system contains many individual cells, so (2) no one-celled animal, by definition, could have one. But (3) only something with a nervous system could be conscious, so (4) no one-celled animal is conscious.

Before we start looking for syllogisms in an argument like this, it's a good idea to step back and try to get a feel for the flow of the argument as a whole. It seems clear that (1) is a premise used to support (2), and that (2) and (3) together support the ultimate conclusion. So we would diagram this argument as follows:

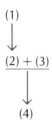

As the diagram reveals, the argument has two steps: from (1) to (2), and from (2) + (3) to (4). So now we need to look at each step individually. It doesn't matter which one we do first, but since the second step has two premises and looks as if it is a syllogism, let's start there. Putting everything in standard form—notice especially the "only" in (3)—we have:

3) All conscious organisms have nervous systems
2) No one-celled animal has a nervous system
4) No one-celled animal is conscious

Let's go back to the first step, from (1) to (2). The apparent subject term in (1) is "nervous systems," but the argument is clearly about classes of organisms that do or do not have them, so we would put (1) in standard form accordingly:

1) All organisms that have nervous systems have many cells
2) No one-celled animal has a nervous system

This is clearly an enthymeme, and the missing premise is: (a) No one-celled animal has many cells. (Since we are using the numbering technique of Part Two, we use letters instead of parentheses to indicate missing premises.)

The argument as a whole then looks like this:

1) All organisms with nervous systems have many cells
a) No one-celled animal has many cells
2) No one-celled animal has a nervous system

3) All conscious organisms have nervous systems
2) <u>No one-celled</u> animal has a nervous system
4) No one-celled animal is conscious

What we have done here is to break up a single chain of reasoning into its component syllogisms, so that we can evaluate each step for validity. There is an analogy here with addition. To add a column of numbers, you add two of them, then add their sum to the third, and that sum to the fourth, and so on. Similarly, in an extended argument, we combine two premises in a single syllogism to derive a conclusion, then combine that conclusion with the next premise to yield a further conclusion, and so on until we reach the ultimate conclusion. Just as we can add a column of numbers of any length, so we can have an argument with any number of steps. And just as we must add each pair of numbers correctly for the final sum to be correct, so each step must be valid if an argument as a whole is to be valid.

But the analogy is not perfect. When you are given a column of numbers, the intermediate sums are never part of the column itself, whereas intermediate conclusions are often given in the statement of an argument. Thus we need to distinguish premises from intermediate conclusions. Moreover, you can add numbers in any order and get the same final sum, but in an argument you have less freedom: to break it down into individual steps, you must put the premises together in the right order.

So analyzing extended arguments is a little more difficult than adding numbers. And there is no single procedure to follow that will work in every case. What we need is a set of procedures from which we can pick and choose, adapting our method to the circumstances of the particular case. In the remainder of this section, therefore, we will look at a variety of specific arguments that illustrate common problems and techniques. As we work through them, it would be a good idea to have paper and pencil handy so that you can keep track of where we are in the analysis.

In the example we just analyzed, the intermediate conclusion was stated explicitly. Let's look at a somewhat more difficult example in which the intermediate conclusions are *not* stated:

> Since (1) values are nothing more than our own evaluations of the facts, (2) they are not objective. (3) Knowledge of the facts is based on empirical evidence, and (4) anything based on such evidence is objective. But (5) evaluating facts is different from knowing them.

The ultimate conclusion here is (2): "No values are objective." Four premises are used to support the conclusion, whereas a single syllogism can have only two premises, so we know that this is an extended argument. Premise (1) is directly related to the conclusion, but the other premises do not appear to support (1). So on our first pass, we would have to represent the argument's structure as:

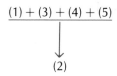

$$\underline{(1) + (3) + (4) + (5)}$$

$$\downarrow$$

$$(2)$$

Let's try working backward from the conclusion. Since (1) contains the minor term ("values"), we will assume that it is the minor premise of a syllogism. What major premise would be needed to complete the syllogism? Using the technique we learned for enthymemes, and labeling the new premise as (a), we have:

a) No evaluation of the facts is objective
1) All values are evaluations of the facts
2) No values are objective

If this were an enthymeme—that is, if (1) were the only premise we were given—then we would treat (a) as an assumed premise, and our job would be done. But since there are other premises in the argument, we should see whether they provide support for (a) as an intermediate conclusion. We are now looking for the following structure:

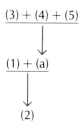

$$\underline{(3) + (4) + (5)}$$

$$\downarrow$$

$$\underline{(1) + (a)}$$

$$\downarrow$$

$$(2)$$

We cannot combine (3), (4), and (5) in a single step. But (3) and (4) look like the premises of a syllogism, so let's see what conclusion we get by putting them together.

4) Anything based on empirical evidence is objective
3) All knowledge is based on empirical evidence
b) All knowledge is objective

(b) is not explicitly stated, so we have to give it a letter, but it follows validly from (3) and (4), which were stated.

We are almost done now. Working down from the top (from premises (3) and (4)), we found that (b) followed as an intermediate conclusion. Working up from the bottom (from the ultimate conclusion), we saw that we would have to get to (a) as an intermediate conclusion. So the question is whether (b), together with the remaining premise (5), will support (a). That is, we now know that the argument has the structure:

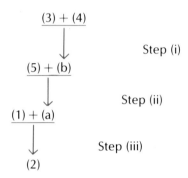

We identified (b) as the intermediate conclusion that follows from (3) and (4), so we know that step (i) is valid. Likewise, we supplied (a) as a premise that would make step (iii) valid. So everything turns on the middle step. Writing it out as a standard form syllogism, we have:

  b) All knowledge of the facts is objective
  5) No evaluation of the facts is knowledge of the facts
  a) No evaluation of the facts is objective

This syllogism is invalid; it has an illicit major. What we needed, in order to reach the ultimate conclusion, was a reason for believing that *only* knowledge of the facts is objective—that all objective states of mind are knowledge of the facts. But this is not implied by (b), nor supported by (3) and (4). So the argument as a whole is invalid.

Hypothetical Syllogisms in Extended Arguments

Extended arguments need not be categorical. Hypothetical syllogisms can also be combined into longer arguments. Suppose that during a shortage of consumer goods, the government issued this statement:

As unpleasant as the current shortage is, it means (1) we are consuming less. And so (2) in the long run our standard of living will rise. For (3) in order to improve our standard of living, we must save, and (4) in order to save we must forgo current consumption.

If this argument sounds fishy to you, that's because it is. Let's see why.

The speaker here is trying to convince us that because we are consuming less at the moment, our standard of living will rise in the long run: (1) is being offered as a reason for (2). The link between them is provided by (3) and (4), both of which are hypothetical propositions about means and ends, and can easily be combined in a pure hypothetical syllogism:

3) If we are to improve our living standards, we must save
4) If we are to save, we must forgo current consumption
a) If we are to improve our living standards, we must forgo current consumption

The question now is whether (a), together with (1), will support the conclusion. The statement that we are consuming less is categorical, and it is just another way of saying what the consequent of (a) says. So these premises together give us a mixed hypothetical syllogism:

a) If we are to improve our living standards, we must forgo current consumption
1) We are forgoing current consumption
2) We will improve our living standards

And since it isn't valid to affirm the consequent, as this step does, the argument as a whole is invalid.

Notice that for this example I did not use a diagram. That's because it would not have been much help. It would have told us that (1) + (3) + (4) support (2), but it would not have told us how to break the argument down into steps. Once we put the two hypo-thetical premises together, on the other hand, the analysis was straightforward. Remember that diagrams are like maps. They are useful for keeping track of where we are in an argument, and in many cases we would be lost without them. But just as you don't always need a map to reach your destination, you won't always need a diagram to see how to reach a conclusion.

Extended Arguments with Elements of Different Types

It is possible to combine hypothetical with categorical elements in an argument—indeed, this is quite common. Consider the following:

(1) Certainty would be possible in human knowledge only if some method of ascertaining the facts were infallible. But (2) all of our methods are subject to the influence of emotion, bias, peer pressure, and other subjective factors. Hence (3) certainty is impossible.

At first glance, the structure of this argument is simple: (1) and (2) together support (3). But the structure is actually a little more complex. Premise (1) is a hypothetical proposition of the form *p only if q*, which we put into standard form as *if p then q*. Since the conclusion is categorical, let's try to formulate it as a mixed hypothetical syllogism:

1) If certainty is possible, then some method is infallible
   ?)
3) Certainty is not possible

Since the conclusion is the negation of the antecedent of (1), it looks as if the argument is an instance of denying the consequent. Thus the second premise must be the negation of "some method is infallible," which would be the E proposition "no method is infallible." And that is not what premise (2) says. But premise (2) can be used in a categorical syllogism to establish the E proposition as an intermediate conclusion. Thus the argument as a whole would be:

a) No method subject to the influence of emotion, etc., is infallible
2) All of our methods are subject to emotion, etc.
b) No method is infallible

1) If certainty is possible, then some method is infallible
b) No method is infallible
3) Certainty is not possible

So the actual structure of the argument consists of one categorical syllogism and one mixed hypothetical syllogism, both valid.

An extended argument may also contain disjunctive syllogisms, along with hypothetical and categorical ones, as in the following example from the Sherlock Holmes novel *A Study in Scarlet.*

And now came the great question as to the reason why. (1) Robbery had not been the object of the murder, for (2) nothing was taken. Was it politics, then, or was it a woman? That was the question which confronted me. I was inclined from the first to the latter supposition. (3) Political assassins are only too glad to do their work and to fly. (4) This murder had, on the contrary, been done most deliberately, and the perpetrator had left his track all over the room, showing that he had been there all the time. (5) It must have been a private wrong, and not a political one, which called for such a methodical revenge.

Holmes arrives at his conclusion—that the motive for the murder was revenge for a private wrong involving a woman—by excluding the other alternatives. Thus the argument has the basic structure of a disjunctive syllogism, with the disjunctive premise partially (but not fully) suggested by the question in the middle of the paragraph:

a) The murderer was either a robber, or a political assassin, or someone seeking private revenge
1) The murderer was not a robber
<u>b) The murderer was not a political assassin</u>
5) The murderer was someone seeking private revenge

Premise (1), which is stated explicitly, rules out the first disjunct. Premise (b), which rules out the second disjunct, is clearly implied by premises (3) and (4). (Remember that a disjunctive proposition can have more than two disjuncts, but then it needs more categorical premises to rule out all but one of the disjuncts.)

The remaining premises are used to justify the exclusion of robbery and political assassination—to support premises (1) and (b). Thus the structure of the argument is:

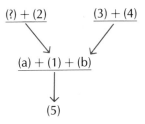

To complete the argument for (1), we need a hypothetical proposition as the missing premise:

c) If the murderer had been a robber, something would have been taken
<u>2) Nothing was taken</u>
1) The murderer was not a robber

And the argument in support of (b) can be formulated most naturally as a categorical syllogism:

3) All political assassins work quickly
<u>4) The murderer did not work quickly</u>
b) The murderer was not a political assassin

You can confirm for yourself that each step of this argument, and thus the argument as a whole, is valid. You can also see the value of analyzing the argument as we have, for in doing so we found that it depends crucially on the disjunctive premise (a). And once we have made that assumption explicit, we can go on to ask whether it is true—whether there really are just three possible motives for murdering someone. Sherlock Holmes may be guilty of the fallacy of false alternative. At the very least, the argument loses some of its plausibility when it is spelled out in full.

Complex Components

When we discussed disjunctive and hypothetical propositions in the last chapter, we assumed that their components, *p* and *q*, were always categorical propositions. That is not the case. The components can themselves be complex. Thus, for example, a proposition might have the form "If *p or q*, then *r*," where the antecedent is a disjunctive proposition. Another possibility of this type can be illustrated, once again, by Sherlock Holmes. In the following passage, Holmes is trying to find out who was with the murdered man on the night of his death; he already knows that the two drank rum together in the victim's cabin.

> You remember that I asked whether whiskey and brandy were in the cabin. You said they were. How many landsmen are there who would drink rum when they could get these other spirits? Yes, I was certain it was a seaman. [Arthur Conan Doyle, "Black Peter"]

The conclusion is that (1) the visitor was a seaman—a sailor. The first two sentences together tell us that (2) whiskey and brandy were available in the cabin. What about the rhetorical question in the third sentence? The most accurate way to formulate Holmes's assumption here would be as a complex hypothetical proposition:

3) If whiskey and brandy were available in the cabin, then if the visitor were a landsman, he would not have had rum.

This proposition has the form: if *p*, then (if *q*, then *r*)—a hypothetical proposition in which the consequent is itself hypothetical. And since premise (2) affirms the antecedent of (3), we can formulate the first step of the argument as a *modus ponens* syllogism:

3) If whiskey and brandy were available in the cabin, then if the visitor were a landsman, he would not have had rum
2) Whiskey and brandy were available
a) If the visitor were a landsman, he would not have had rum

Since Holmes has already established that (4) the visitor *did* drink rum, the consequent of (a) is false, so we can formulate the second step of the argument as another mixed hypothetical syllogism (in this case, *modus tollens*):

a) If the visitor were a landsman, he would not have had rum
4) The visitor had rum
1) The visitor was not a landsman

The conclusion here is the obverse of the conclusion as stated in the passage—on the assumption that landsmen and seamen are complementary classes. If we want to make this assumption explicit, we would have to add a disjunctive premise. But we need not bother with that here.

Distilling an Extended Argument

The examples we have discussed illustrate the basic method for analyzing extended deductive arguments. First, identify the conclusion. Then, label as many of the premises as you can in the passage, and diagram as much of the structure as possible. Sometimes you can identify the whole structure this way. If not, then use what you know about syllogisms to find missing premises and intermediate conclusions, working up from the ultimate conclusion or down from the premises. Remember that the individual steps of the argument need not all be syllogisms of the same type. Finally, evaluate each step for validity.

The examples so far have also been fairly self-contained and easy to follow. In everyday speech and thought, extended arguments are normally embedded in a context of descriptions, examples, rhetorical asides, disclaimers, and other material that is not directly relevant to the argument itself. In order to analyze such arguments, you need to extract them from this context. So as our final illustration, let's look at a more realistic case. The two passages below are from a key chapter in John Kenneth Galbraith's *The Affluent Society*. Together they constitute his central argument for the claim that, in our society, private production is no longer urgent, and that more resources should be transferred to the public sector (government).

> If the individual's wants are to be urgent, they must be original with himself. They cannot be urgent if they must be contrived for him. And above all, they must not be contrived by the process of production by which they are satisfied. For this means that the whole case for the urgency of [private] production, based on the urgency of wants, falls to the ground. One cannot defend production as satisfying wants if that production creates the wants.

The even more difficult link between production and wants is provided by the institutions of modern advertising and salesmanship. These cannot be reconciled with the notion of independently determined desires, for their central function is to create desires—to bring into being wants that previously did not exist.

Let's go through each of these passages in turn, trying to follow the drift of Galbraith's argument. In the first passage, he is criticizing the economists who say that an increase in production is necessary (urgent) because it will satisfy consumer desires. Even though Galbraith doesn't say it in so many words, his conclusion is clearly that increased production is not necessary. And his basic reason is indicated by the first three sentences: an increase in production is necessary only if the desires it will satisfy are "original with" the consumer—that is, only if the consumer has those desires independently, not because they have been "contrived" for him by the producers of the goods.

So far, then, we have a hypothetical premise and a conclusion:

1) If an increase in production is necessary, then the desires it satisfies must be original with the consumer
2) None of the desires it satisfies are original with the consumer
3) An increase in production is not necessary

Galbraith does not actually assert (2) in the first passage, but it is necessary for his argument, and it seems clear that he is gearing up to try to prove it.

Let's turn, then, to the second passage, which introduces his discussion of advertising. Advertising is the key "link between production and wants"; its "central function is to create desires" that did not exist before. Galbraith takes it as obvious that no desire instilled by advertising is "original with" the consumer. And he assumes that any desire which an increase in production *would* satisfy would have to be instilled by advertising. Thus he is giving us a categorical syllogism in support of (2):

4) No desire instilled by advertising is original with the consumer
5) All desires that would be satisfied by increased production must be instilled by advertising
2) No desire that would be satisfied by increased production is original with the consumer

As a result of our analysis, then, we can see that Galbraith's argument is an inference in two steps. The analysis required that we read between the lines, distilling the essential points he was making, to a much greater extent than in previous examples. (And of course I performed part of the "distillation" for you, by isolating those two passages; had you been given the whole chapter to analyze, you would have had to pick them out yourself.) A good deal of interpretation was involved here, which means that you might have come up with a different wording for some of the premises. This will generally be the case with extended arguments in real life. But different formulations will not affect the basic logic of the argument.

This example illustrates the value of identifying the basic logic. Both steps of Galbraith's argument are valid. So the soundness of the argument depends on the truth or falsity of the premises—specifically on (1), (4), and (5). (Statement (2) is an intermediate conclusion.) Knowing that those are the key premises would help you in reading the text, because you would then be on the lookout for the evidence he offers in support of those premises. In addition, Galbraith's argument has been criticized by many other writers, so if you know the basic structure of his argument, you can organize and evaluate the counterarguments by asking which premises they are directed against.

Practice Quiz

Analyze the extended arguments below. Identify the structure of the argument, formulate each step as a syllogism, and determine whether the argument is valid.

1. If Jones was not at the meeting, then all the witnesses have been lying. But some of the witnesses, at least, have been clergymen.
2. Any metal that can oxidize at normal temperatures will rust. But some steel contains chromium, and is therefore rustproof.
3. The killer left fingerprints all over the place, so he couldn't have been a pro. A pro would not have been so sloppy.
4. Lower animals do not have a sense of humor, because humor presupposes a rational faculty, which only man possesses.
5. It isn't true that only conscious beings can manipulate symbols, because some computers can do that, and computers aren't conscious—only living organisms are.

SUMMARY

In order to analyze deductive arguments as they occur in ordinary language, we need to identify the kind of syllogism involved: categorical, hypothetical, or disjunctive. We rely partly on linguistic criteria of various kinds, such as the presence or absence of explicit quantifiers. We also rely on substantive criteria: disjunctive syllogisms typically deal with alternative possibilities, hypothetical syllogisms with relationships of dependence, categorical syllogisms with relationships among classes. Moreover, deductive arguments in everyday thought and speech are normally extended. To analyze and evaluate them, we need to break the arguments down into component steps, identifying assumed premises and intermediate conclusions.

This completes our study of deductive reasoning. Even though the essential feature of deduction is that the conclusion is already contained implicitly in the premises, it should be clear by now that such reasoning is enormously valuable. It is indispensable for clarifying our thoughts, enlarging our understanding of the issues, bringing order to complex material. It is used pervasively in politics, law, ethics, and the sciences, as well as in everyday thinking. It allows us to apply the knowledge embodied in our concepts for classes of things; to draw conclusions about cause and effect, means and ends; to find our way among the alternatives set by a given situation. In the end, however, deductive reasoning is only as good as the premises on which it relies, and those premises ultimately depend, in one way or another, on *inductive* reasoning. We will examine induction in Part Five.

Exercises

A. Put each of the following statements into standard form as a categorical, hypothetical, or disjunctive proposition.

1. Pride goeth before a fall.
2. "Separate educational facilities are inherently unequal." [Chief Justice Warren, Opinion of the Court, *Brown vs. Board of Education*, 1954]
3. "Where there's marriage without love, there will be love without marriage." [Ben Franklin, *Poor Richard's Almanack*]
4. "Curiosity is one of the permanent and certain characteristics of a vigorous mind." [Samuel Johnson, *Rambler*]
5. "Were we faultless, we would not derive such satisfaction from remarking the faults of others." [La Rochefoucauld, *Maxims*]
6. "Not to know what happened before one was born is to remain a child." [Cicero, *De Oratore*]
7. "You can't think and hit at the same time." [Yogi Berra]

8. "The whole of science is nothing more than a refinement of everyday thinking." [Albert Einstein, *Physics and Reality*]

9. "The people never give up their liberties but under some delusion." [Edmund Burke, *Speech at County Meeting of Buckinghamshire*]

B. The syllogisms below are taken from previous exercises. Each is in standard form (or very close to it). Translate it into ordinary language. Use what you have learned in this section to express the argument in a more natural, idiomatic way: reformulate the propositions, leave an obvious premise unstated, but above all make them sound like things people would actually say!

1. Some bureaucrats are not chosen on the basis of ability
   All bureaucrats are civil servants
   Some civil servants are not chosen on the basis of ability

2. All geniuses are eccentric
   No Greek poet was eccentric
   No Greek poet was a genius

3. If the circuit is broken, current will not flow
   The circuit is broken
   The current will not flow

4. Any state that ignores human rights is a tyranny
   Some democracies ignore human rights
   Some democracies are tyrannies

5. If a child is deprived of affection early in life, he will learn not to expect it
   If a child learns not to expect affection, he will not seek it out later in life
   If a child is deprived of affection early in life, he will not seek it out later in life

C. Put each of the following arguments into standard form as a categorical, hypothetical, or disjunctive syllogism, supplying any missing premise or conclusion. Then determine whether it is valid.

1. "The wound upon the dead man was, as I was able to determine with absolute confidence, fired from a revolver at the distance of something over four yards. There was no powder-blackening on the clothes." [Arthur Conan Doyle, "The Reigate Puzzle"]

2. "A clown is someone who stands before a crowd and gestures wildly to get their attention. So is a politician." ["Today's Chuckle"]

3. "Yet despite everything zoologists learned about the duckbills, they never seemed entirely certain as to where to place them in

the table of animal classification. On the whole, the decision was made because of hair and milk. In all the world, only mammals have true hair and only mammals produce true milk. The duckbill and the spiny anteater have hair and produce milk, so they have been classified as mammals." [Isaac Asimov, "What Do You Call A Platypus?" in *National Wildlife Magazine,* March-April 1972]

4. "It is only about the things that do not interest one, that one can give a really unbiassed opinion; and this is no doubt the reason why an unbiassed opinion is always absolutely valueless." [*More Letters of Oscar Wilde,* ed. Rupert Hart-Davis]

5. ". . . if a moving object does possess acceleration, that is, if *a* in formula (1) [F=ma] is not zero, then the force F cannot be zero. Now an object falling to Earth from some height does possess acceleration. Hence some force must be acting." [Morris Kline, *Mathematics in Western Culture*]

6. "Had we but world enough, and time,
This coyness, lady, were no crime. . . .
But at my back I always hear
Time's winged chariot hurrying near; . . ."
[Andrew Marvell, "To His Coy Mistress"]

7. "Defense Minister Moshe Arens of Israel today accused Syria of bombing the United States Marine headquarters in Beirut. . . . 'Nobody else could have done it,' he said in a television interview. . . . 'The reason we know it's the Syrians, first of all, it's got to be a group with that kind of subhuman moral standards, and that's the Syrians.'" [*New York Times,* October 31, 1983]

8. "Saccadic eye movements occur whenever the eyes move without a [moving] target to follow. In reading, of course, there is no moving target to follow; so reading involves saccadic eye movements." [Donald J. Foss and David T. Hakes, *Psycholinguistics*]

9. ". . . as it is impossible for the whole race of mankind to be united in one great society, they must necessarily divide into many." [William Blackstone, *Commentaries on the Laws of England*]

10. "This gain [in entropy] occurs every time heat flows from a higher to a lower temperature, and since nothing interesting or useful happens unless heat does make this descent, all interesting and useful things are accompanied by an irreversible increase in entropy." [Jeremy Campbell, *Grammatical Man*]

11. "A prince should therefore have no other aim or thought, nor take up any other thing for his study, but war and its organiza-

tion and discipline, for that is the only art that is necessary to one who commands." [Niccolo Machiavelli, *The Prince*]

12. "One black leader in Phoenix, the Rev. Warren Stewart Sr., accused [Arizona Governor-elect] Mr. Mecham of 'racist thinking.' He said that at a recent meeting of Mr. Mecham and black leaders, the Governor-elect 'said some of his best friends were black.' Mr. Stewart said this was 'the type of jargon that you hear from whites who are apologetic of being accused of racism and do not want to confront their racist thinking.'" [*New York Times*, December 1, 1986]

13. ". . . if we look at the actual tasks of working science, we shall find that not all prediction is scientific—or horserace tipsters would be scientists—and not all science is predictive, or evolutionary biologists would not be scientists." [Stephen Toulmin, "From Form to Function: Philosophy and History of Science in the 1950s and Now"]

D. Analyze the extended arguments below: identify the structure of the argument, formulate each step as a syllogism, and determine whether the argument is valid.

1. Price controls will not work in controlling inflation. They would work, perhaps, if every law of economics were false, but some of those laws are supported by overwhelming evidence.

2. If the direction of the flow of time, from past to present to future, depends on the expansion of the universe, then time would reverse its direction if the expansion stops and the universe begins contracting—as current evidence from astrophysics suggests it will.

3. Liberals believe in government support for academic research. Since no one who favors liberty can accept interference by the state in the realm of ideas, liberals do not really favor liberty.

4. The law that requires that one have a driver's license in order to drive in this state implies that illiterates cannot drive, since they would obviously fail the test one must pass to get a license.

5. In the early 1770s, the American colonies came to a crisis point: they would obtain full and fair representation in the English Parliament, or else they would seek independence. But they would receive full representation only if the existing Parliament were willing to accept a diminution of its power, and it was not. So the outcome was rebellion.

E. For each of the statements below, (a) find a syllogism to support the statement, (b) find a syllogism to support one of the premises of the syllogism in (a), and (c) write out the complete argument in a short paragraph.

1. Mary will win the election for student body president.
2. Dancing is good exercise.
3. If interest rates decline, stock prices will rise.
4. Cheating is wrong.
5. Nothing ventured, nothing gained.

F. In the passage below, Friedrich Hayek criticizes the views of John Kenneth Galbraith about production and consumer desires. Given our analysis of Galbraith's argument, which premise is Hayek rejecting? Analyze Hayek's argument (you will have to decide for yourself whether it is a single syllogism or an extended argument).

"How complete a non sequitur Professor Galbraith's conclusion represents is seen most clearly if we apply the argument to any product of the arts, be it music, painting, or literature. If the fact that people would not feel the need for something if it were not produced did prove that such products are of small value, all those highest products of human endeavor would be of small value. . . . Surely an individual's want for literature is not original with himself in the sense that he would experience it if literature were not produced." ["The Non Sequitur of the 'Dependence Effect'"]

G. Analyze the arguments below: identify the structure of the argument, formulate each step (there may be one or more) as a syllogism, and determine whether the argument is valid.

1. "Appellant's conduct is not a nuisance unless it is unreasonably noisy for an industrial area. What a reasonable amount of noise will be depends on the character of the neighborhood. Although appellant produces more noise in the area of the industrial park than any other source, it has not been shown that the level of noise it produces is out of keeping with the character of its location. Since it has not been shown that the noise from appellant's operation is out of keeping with its industrial location, it cannot be found to be a nuisance." [Legal brief]
2. "Since happiness consists in peace of mind, and since durable peace of mind depends on the confidence we have in the future, and since that confidence is based on an understanding of the nature of God and the soul, it follows that true happiness requires that understanding." [Gottfried Leibnitz, *Preface to the General Science*]
3. "[Milton] identifies four reasons why [censorship will not

work]. First, the decisions of the censor cannot be trusted unless the censor is infallible and beyond corruption. No mortal possesses such grace; therefore no mortal is qualified to be a censor." [Irving Younger, "What Good Is Freedom of Speech?" *Commentary*, January 1984]

4. Touchstone: . . . Wast ever in court, shepherd?
   Corin: No, truly.
   Touchstone: Then thou art damned. . . .
   Corin: For not being at court? Your reason.
   Touchstone: Why, if thou never wast at court, thou never saw'st good manners; if thou never saw'st good manners, then thy manners must be wicked; and wickedness is sin, and sin is damnation. Thou art in a parlous state, shepherd. [Shakespeare, *As You Like It*]

5. "Anything that changes over time has, by definition, a history —the universe, countries, art and philosophy, and ideas. Science also, ever since its emergence from myths and early philosophies, has experienced a steady historical change and is thus a legitimate subject for the historian." [Ernst Mayr, *The Growth of Biological Thought*]

6. "As Japan and West Germany point out, much of the responsibility for the trade imbalance lies with the United States: if America cut its budget deficit, it wouldn't need sell [sic] as many Treasury securities. If it didn't sell as many Treasury securities, Japanese and German savers would be forced to invest elsewhere. If Japanese and German capital went elsewhere, American consumers would lack the means to finance their foreign spending." [*New York Times* editorial, November 8, 1986]

7. "Q. How many angels can dance upon the head of a pin?
   "A. I think none can. The size mentioned—that of a pin's head —distracts our attention from the real question: Can angels— any angel—dance upon the head of a pin? As I understand it, angels are beautiful creatures, but they have no physical substance. This means that one can't touch an angel with a pinhead or anything else. And if nothing—including pinheads—can touch an angel, angels can't touch anything themselves. Therefore, no angels at all can touch—or dance upon—a pinhead or anything else, no matter how large or small." ["What Would You Ask a Genius?"—Interview with Marilyn Mach Vos Savant, *Parade*, June 22, 1986]

8. "'If we find a gene that increases the risk of alcoholism, manic-depression or whatever,' [Dr. C. Robert Cloninger] says, 'then we'll find what protein the gene codes for. If we then find out

what the protein does, we can understand the basic mechanism of the disease. And if we understand the basic mechanism, then we can develop new treatments.'" [*Wall Street Journal*, February 12, 1986]

9. "The fifth way [of proving that God exists] is taken from the governance of the world. We see that things which lack knowledge, such as natural bodies, act for an end, and this is evident from their acting always, or nearly always, in the same way, so as to obtain the best result. Hence it is plain that they achieve their end, not fortuitously, but designedly. Now whatever lacks knowledge cannot move towards an end, unless it be directed by some being endowed with knowledge and intelligence as the arrow is directed by the archer. Therefore some intelligent being exists by whom all natural things are directed to their end; and this being we call God." [Thomas Aquinas, *Summa Theologica. Note:* The last sentence is included for the sake of completeness, but it raises problems for analysis that we have not yet discussed. For the purposes of this exercise, therefore, assume that Aquinas's conclusion is "some things are directed by a being with knowledge and intelligence."]

10. Robespierre's opponents accused him of having treated his personal enemies as enemies of the state. "I deny the accusation," he answered, "and the proof is that you still live."

11. "But if we prohibit owners from moving their factories and simultaneously provide tariff protection from foreign competition, we will be granting entrenched unions and oligopoly management carte blanche to hike wages and prices way out of line. In short, we will be strongly encouraging these protected industries to become even more uncompetitive than they are now. That, in turn, will generate pressures for more protection." [Charles Schultze, Forum, *Harpers Magazine*, January 1985]

12. "Between these alternatives there is no middle ground. The constitution is either a superior paramount law, unchangeable by ordinary means, or it is on a level with ordinary legislative acts, and, like other acts, is alterable when the legislature shall please to alter it.

"If the former part of the alternative be true, then a legislative act contrary to the constitution is not law: if the latter part be true, then written constitutions are absurd attempts, on the part of the people, to limit a power in its own nature illimitable." [Chief Justice John Marshall, Opinion of the Court, *Marbury v. Madison,* 1803]

13. ". . . every man has a property in his own person. This nobody has any right to but himself. The labour of his body and the work of his hands, we may say, are properly his. Whatsoever, then, he removes out of the state that nature hath provided and left it in, he hath mixed his labour with it, and joined to it something that is his own, and thereby makes it his property. . . . For this labour being the unquestionable property of the labourer, no man but he can have a right to what that is once joined to. . . ." [John Locke, *Second Treatise of Civil Government*]

PART FOUR

Modern Deductive Logic

The forms of inference studied by classical deductive logic represent the simpler and more common sorts of inference we make in everyday thought and speech. The goal of modern deductive logic has been to develop a more comprehensive system that will allow us to analyze and evaluate more complex arguments. The characteristic features of modern theories are their use of symbols to represent the elements of logical form; and their use of a small set of rules to generate and test arguments of any complexity.

The conventional approach, known as symbolic logic, is presented in Chapters 12 and 13. Chapter 12 covers propositional logic, which deals with arguments like those in Chapter 10, in which component propositions serve as the basic units. Chapter 13 covers predicate logic, which deals with arguments that depend on the internal structure of categorical propositions. An alternative to conventional symbolic logic is presented in Chapter 14. This approach, which is known as term logic, and which deals with both propositional and categorical inferences, is an extension of the classical approach discussed in Part Three.

12

Propositional Logic

The principles of deductive reasoning that we have studied so far represent a portion of classical logic, as it was developed by ancient and medieval logicians. We've seen that these principles allow us to analyze and evaluate many of the arguments we encounter every day. But they are incomplete in certain respects.

Consider the following argument:

If p or q, then r	If you visited New York either in May or in October, you saw the city at its best
p	You visited New York in May
r	You saw the city at its best

This is a deductive argument. It's rather simple, and it's obviously valid. But it doesn't fit any of the argument forms we studied in Chapter 10. It looks like an example of affirming the antecedent, but the antecedent is the disjunctive proposition p *or* q, and the second premise affirms p, not the disjunction as a whole. In Chapter 10 we learned to recognize disjunctive and hypothetical arguments in isolation, but we didn't learn how to analyze arguments that *combine* disjunctive and hypothetical elements. These arguments involve more complex relationships among propositions than we are used to, and we need a more elaborate system of rules. Logicians have devised such a system, called **propositional logic.**

The classical analysis of the categorical syllogism, which we studied in Chapter 9, is also incomplete. Consider the argument:

All M are V	All Monet paintings are valuable things
I am OM	I am the owner of a Monet painting
I am OV	I am the owner of a valuable thing

Once again the argument is clearly valid. It looks like a categorical syllogism, but notice that it has five terms, not three. The term "Monet painting" (*M*) is not the same as "owner of a Monet painting" (*OM*), and "valuable thing" (*V*) is not the same as "owner of a valuable thing" (*OV*). The predicate terms in the second premise and the conclusion do not simply repeat the terms in the first premise. These four terms are related in a more complex way, and once again we need a more elaborate system to understand these relationships. To serve this purpose, logicians have devised a system called **predicate logic.**

Propositional and predicate logic are the two main branches of what is known as **symbolic logic.** In earlier chapters, we used symbols such as *p* and *q* for propositions, *S* and *P* for terms. We symbolized the *content* of propositions. But we did not symbolize the logical *forms* of propositions and arguments; we used words like "all," "some," "if . . . then," "or." Modern symbolic logic replaces all these with symbols. In this respect it is like mathematics, which not only uses variables to represent numbers but also uses special symbols for operations like addition or multiplication that we can perform on numbers.

Logicians have introduced the new symbols and rules to serve various purposes. The analysis of complex arguments is only one of these purposes. But it's the one that concerns us, given the focus of this book on thinking skills. In this chapter, we'll study propositional logic, and we'll see that the patterns of inference we learned in Chapter 10 are part of a larger system. The next chapter covers predicate logic. We'll look at the modern way of breaking a proposition down into its component terms; and we will study the rules for assessing the validity of arguments that depend on relationships among terms. Finally, in Chapter 14, we will examine a recently developed alternative to the conventional predicate logic. This new system is closer in many respects to the classical theory of categorical syllogisms, but it gives us the same ability as predicate logic to work with more complex arguments.

Connectives

Propositional logic is the logic of compound statements—statements that are made up of other, simpler propositions. Here are some examples:

1) The Democrats will win *or* the Republicans will win.
2) *If* the Democrats win, *then* my sister will be happy.
3) My sister is happy *and* she's throwing a party.

Each of these statements has two component propositions along with an italicized expression, called a **connective.** The connective tells us how the components are related.

We're already familiar with statements like (1) and (2): (1) is a disjunctive statement, or **disjunction;** (2) is a hypothetical statement, or **conditional,** as it is usually called in symbolic logic. In (3), the connective is "and"; statements of this form are called **conjunctions.** A fourth type of compound statement is the **negation,** as in:

4) My brother is *not* coming to the party.

Here there is only one component statement ("My brother is coming to the party"), but the negation word, "not," is still called a connective because it transforms the component into a more complex proposition.

These are the four basic types of compound statement in propositional logic, and the four connectives have special symbols, indicated in the box below. Let's look a little more closely at each of them.

Type	*Connective*	*Statement form*
Conjunction (and)	•	$p \cdot q$
Negation (not)	$\sim$	$\sim p$
Disjunction (or)	$\vee$	$p \vee q$
Conditional (if–then)	$\supset$	$p \supset q$

A conjunction is a way of asserting two component propositions, called *conjuncts,* in a single statement. For example:

5) The rent is due and I have no money.

For (5) to be true, both conjuncts must be true. And if the conjuncts are both true, the conjunction is true. The conjunction sign • (called the dot) represents this relationship between the truth of the components and the truth of the compound statement as a whole. In ordinary speech and thought, of course, the word "and" may indicate a richer connection. It may suggest a time relation between the components, as in "I went upstairs and went to bed." Or it may suggest a relation of common relevance for some conclusion, as in "A station wagon would be too big and it would be too expensive." In propositional logic, however, we are not concerned with these further connotations. We use the symbol "•" to abstract from them and consider just the truth relationship.

It is useful to formulate this relationship graphically. The form of a conjunction is $p • q$. p and q can be any component statements, and each of them can be either true or false (represented by T and F, as on a True/False test). So we have four possibilities to consider, and we lay them out in a **truth table:**

p	q	$p • q$
T	T	T
F	T	F
T	F	F
F	F	F

The table shows that $p • q$ is true only in the first case, where p and q both have the truth value T. In all other cases, $p • q$ is false.

The truth table may strike you as a complicated way of stating the obvious. But it is valuable because, as we will see, it gives us a systematic way of describing and relating all the connectives. It also allows us to understand several important points about conjunction. For one thing, it helps us to see that other words in English, besides "and," indicate conjunction. Consider the following:

6) I want to go skydiving *but* I have a sprained ankle.
7) *Although* steel rusts, it is often used for underwater construction.
8) Julie worked hard to pass the course; *nevertheless* she failed.

In each case, the italicized word suggests some incongruity between the component propositions, but the sentence still asserts that both components are true. If we did a truth table for each of these conjunctions, we would see that the statement forms—*p but q; although p, q;* and *p, nevertheless q*—are true only in the first line, where both p and q are true. So all these forms are treated as logical conjunctions, and the connective in each case is symbolized by "•."

In addition, the truth table shows the basis for the rules of inference regarding conjunction. We're going to study these rules more systematically later, but let's take a quick look at one example. An argument of the form

$$\frac{p • q}{p}$$

is called **simplification.** It is obviously valid, as we can see very clearly in the truth table:

p	q	$p \bullet q$	
T	T	T	
F	T	F	×
T	F	F	×
F	F	F	×

An argument is valid if there is no possibility that the premises are true and the conclusion false. So we cross off every line except the first one, where $p \bullet q$ is true, and then look to see that the conclusion p is true on that line.

By contrast, consider an inference in the other direction:

$$\frac{p}{p \bullet q}$$

In this case the premise allows us to cross off only two lines in the truth table, leaving two lines on which p is true:

	p	q	$p \bullet q$
	T	T	T
×	F	T	F
	T	F	F
×	F	F	F

The conclusion $p \bullet q$ is false on line 3, where the premise is true. So the inference is invalid.

There's one final point to remember about conjunction. The components in $p \bullet q$ must be separate statements. The word "and" can be misleading in this respect. The statement "Tony and Sue got married" does not mean merely that Tony got married (to someone) and that Sue also got married (to someone). It means that Tony and Sue got married to each other. So the sentence makes a single statement about a pair of people; it is not a pair of statements that can be joined by conjunction, or represented by the truth table for the dot.

Negation

Imagine the tail end of the classic children's quarrel: 'It is." "It isn't." "It is so." "It is not." We don't know from this excerpt what the children are arguing about, but one is asserting something—call it p—that the other is denying. We represent the denial of a proposition by the negation sign ⌐, called the tilde. If p is the statement

"The temperature is rising," then $\smile p$ could be expressed in any of the following ways:

9a) It's not the case that the temperature is rising.
9b) It's false that the temperature is rising.
9c) The temperature is not rising.

Since p and $\smile p$ are contradictory propositions, they cannot both be true, and they cannot both be false. It can't be raining *and* not raining—not at the same time and same place. But it must be *either* raining *or* not raining. The truth table for negation therefore has just two lines:

p	$\smile p$
T	F
F	T

If p is true, then $\smile p$ is false, and vice versa.

Since a negation sign reverses truth value, two negation signs cancel out. For example, the statements

10a) It's not the case that Larry will not come, and
10b) Larry will come

are equivalent. In other words, a double negation has the same truth value as the original proposition. Negation is an on/off switch; flip it twice and you're back where you started.

Practice Quiz

For each of the following statements, identify the component propositions and the connective. Then put the statement in symbolic form, using the letters indicated in parentheses, and construct a truth table for it.

1. Mickey heard the story, and he is angry (*M, A*.)
2. It's not the case that time is on my side (*T*).
3. The campers were tired, but they were happy (*T, H*).
4. The junk–bond market is thinly traded, and may soon collapse (*J, C*).
5. The Cucumber County seed–spitting contest is not a world–class event (*C*).
6. Winning is not everything (*W*).
7. A disjunction has two components, while a negation has only one (*D, N*).
8. Color film is good for outdoor shots, but black–and–white is best for portraits (*C, B*).

9. He is an excellent cook, although he hates food (C, F).
10. It's not the case that winning is not everything (W).

Disjunction

Instead of asserting that *p* and *q* are both true, as in a conjunctive statement, we can assert that either *p* or *q* is true. This is a disjunction. The components *p* and *q* are called the disjuncts, and the connective "or" is represented by ∨—the vee or wedge sign. As with conjunction and negation, the truth value of *p* ∨ *q* is determined by the truth values of its components. If *p* and *q* are both false, then *p* ∨ *q* is false. If only one of them is true (it doesn't matter which one), then the disjunction is true. What about the case in which both components are true? The word "or" sometimes has an *exclusive* sense: we're saying that either *p* or *q* is the case, but not both, as in "either I'll be at home or I'll be at work." But "or" can also have an *inclusive* sense, which allows the possibility that *p* and *q* are both true. Observing the pallor on a friend's face, you might say "Either she's very tired or she's sick." Of course you are not denying the possibility that she is both sick and tired. It is this inclusive sense that we use in logic. The truth table for disjunction, therefore, is as follows:

p	*q*	*p* ∨ *q*
T	T	T
F	T	T
T	F	T
F	F	F

In Chapter 10 we studied the disjunctive syllogism, which has the form:

$$p \lor q$$
$$\underline{\smile p}$$
$$q$$

The truth table shows why this inference is valid:

$p \lor q$
$\underline{\smile p}$
q

	p	*q*	*p* ∨ *q*
×	T	T	T
	F	T	T
×	T	F	T
×	F	F	F

The first premise asserts that $p \lor q$ is true, so it's saying that the last line of the table can be ruled out as a possibility. The second premise, in denying that p is true, rules out the first and third lines. So the two premises together leave open only one possibility—line 2 —and on that line q is true.

Another disjunctive inference (called **addition**) has the form:

$$\frac{p}{p \lor q}$$

In asserting the truth of p, the premise rules out lines 2 and 4 of the truth table, leaving only the first and the third lines as possibilities. On both lines $p \lor q$ is true, so the inference is valid. What this means is that given a proposition p, we can infer any other statement in which p is a disjunct. For example, the inference

Napoleon was French
Napoleon was French $\lor$ Napoleon was Italian

is valid by this rule. If we know that the premise is true, there may be no reason to infer the conclusion, which is a weaker statement. But the conclusion does follow.

Conditional

A conditional statement has the form *if p then q*. p is called the antecedent and q the consequent. The connection between them, the if-then relationship, is represented by the symbol $\supset$, called the horseshoe. A statement involving this connective says that if the antecedent is true, the consequent is true as well. In propositional logic, such a statement is defined by the following truth table:

p	q	$p \supset q$
T	T	T
F	T	T
T	F	F
F	F	T

To understand the rationale for this truth table, let's look at an example.

Consider the statement

11) If I study hard, I'll pass the exam,

where the antecedent is "I study hard" and the consequent is "I'll pass the exam." Now let's ask: which combinations of truth values for the antecedent and consequent are consistent with the truth of the conditional statement as a whole? Suppose first that I do study hard and I do pass the exam: p and q are both true, as in the first line of the truth table. That's certainly consistent with the truth of the conditional. Likewise if I *don't* study hard and I *don't* pass—the last line of the table. What about the second line? Suppose I don't study hard but I still pass. Would that prove the conditional statement false? No: the statement doesn't say that studying hard is the *only* way to pass; perhaps the exam was easy, or perhaps I already knew the material well. But if I do study hard and I don't pass—the situation represented by the third line—then we'd have to conclude that the conditional is false. In propositional logic, therefore, $p \supset q$ is defined as false in line 3, where p is true and q false, and as true in the other lines.

This example involved a relationship between a means (studying) and an end (passing the exam). Conditional statements are also used to describe various other relationships, such as cause and effect (if the jet stream shifts to the north, there will be drought in the Midwest), policy and consequence (if the city imposes rent control, there will be a housing shortage), or moves in a game (if I expose my king, my opponent will attack). But just as we use the letters p and q to abstract from the particular content of individual propositions, we use the symbol $\supset$ to abstract from the particular nature of the relationship between them. We do this in order to study the general patterns of inference that are possible with any conditional.

An example is the inference known as affirming the antecedent, or *modus ponens*, which has the form indicated in the left below:

modus ponens		p	q	$p \supset q$
$p \supset q$		T	T	T
p		X F	T	T
q		X T	F	F
		X F	F	T

The conditional premise asserts that the third line of the truth table is not the case. The second premise asserts that p is true, ruling out the second and fourth lines. That leaves only the first line, in which the conclusion q is true.

A conditional statement in English need not take the form *if p then q*. Each of the following statements is also a conditional:

12a) I will go camping this weekend if I finish my work.
12b) I will go camping this weekend only if I finish my work.
12c) We will go camping this weekend unless it rains.

Each of these statements can be translated systematically into an if-then structure, and symbolized, according to the following rules:

$$p \text{ if } q = \text{ if } q \text{ then } p = q \supset p$$
$$p \text{ only if } q = \text{ if } p \text{ then } q = p \supset q$$
$$p \text{ unless } q = \text{ if } \smallsmile q \text{ then } p = \smallsmile q \supset p$$

Thus (12a) says that if I finish my work, then I will go camping. (12b) makes the different statement that if I go camping I have finished my work. And (12c) says that if it does not rain, then I will go camping. (The translation rules were described in more detail in Chapter 10, pages 229–30. If they are not clear to you, you should go back and review that material.)

Practice Quiz

Identify the components and the connective in each of the following statements. Then put the statement into symbolic form, using the letters indicated, and construct a truth table for it.

1. If these shoes go on sale, I'll buy two pairs (S,B).
2. If the cat's away, the mice will play (C,M).
3. I can pay the rent, or I can buy groceries (R,G).
4. He'll go away if you ignore him (G,I).
5. She's either a lunatic or a genius (L,G).
6. If average temperatures on the Earth rise by five degrees, the polar ice caps will start melting (T,P).
7. You will succeed only if you work hard (S,W).
8. Either the guest of honor wore brown, or he fell in the mud on the way to the party (B,M).
9. I'll stand by what I said unless you prove I'm wrong (S,P).
10. I'll go swimming only if I can wear my water wings (S,W).

Truth Functions

We have described each of the connectives in terms of a truth table. Compound statements involving these connectives are therefore *truth-functional*. That is, the truth or falsity of the compound statement is a function solely of the truth values of its components, and does *not* depend on any other connection between the components. We need to appreciate the implications of this way of defining the connectives, including some of the problems it poses.

We saw that a statement of the form $p \bullet q$ is true as long as p and q

are both true, even if those component statements have no other relationship. In real life we would be puzzled if someone said something like:

13) Apples are red and the United Nations was formed in 1945.

The word "and" carries at least the suggestion that the elements it joins have some relevance to each other, however remote. But if we treat this compound statement truth-functionally, then the truth of the components is all that matters.

This is not much of a problem with conjunction. The statement above is odd, but if someone pressed us we would acknowledge that it is true. An "and" statement is nothing more than the sum of its parts, and both parts in this case are true. But a disjunctive statement in ordinary language is not merely the sum of its parts. The truth-functional interpretation is less natural here. And it is less natural still when we turn to conditionals.

When we assert a statement of the form *p or q*, it's normally because *p* is related to *q* in some way that makes them the only alternatives in a given situation. We also assume that *p* and *q* are both genuine possibilities. But the truth-functional connective ∨ is not bound by these constraints. We can take any true statement, and combine it with any other statement whatever to form a true disjunction. Thus

14) Napoleon was French ∨ caffeine is addictive

is true even though the components are not related in any way that makes them alternatives to each other. And

15) The Earth is round ∨ $2 + 2 = 5$

is true even though the second disjunct is impossible. These statements would seem more than odd if we encountered them outside a logic text; we might well hesitate to call them true.

We would be even more hesitant about comparable examples of conditional statements. As we noted, the connective ⊃ is a way of abstracting from the particular nature of the connection—causal, logical, means-end, etc.—between *p* and *q*. As a truth-functional connective, however, it does not require the existence of *any* connection. Let's look at the truth table again:

	p	*q*	*p* ⊃ *q*
1.	T	T	T
2.	F	T	T
3.	T	F	F
4.	F	F	T

The table shows that $p \supset q$ is true in both cases where p is false: lines 2 and 4. Thus a conditional with a false antecedent is true even if there is no connection between antecedent and consequent, as in:

16) If grass is red, then humans can breathe under water.

The table also shows that $p \supset q$ is true in both cases where q is *true*. So a conditional with a true consequent is true, again regardless of any connection, as in:

17) If water runs uphill, then grass is green.

Thus a conditional statement is really a disjunction. All it says is that either the antecedent is false or the consequent is true. That is, $p \supset q$ and $\smallsmile p \vee q$ are equivalent.

It certainly goes against the grain of common sense to say that statements like (16) and (17) are true. The conditional form strongly suggests that antecedent and consequent are connected in some way, even if it does not specify how. And some conditionals clearly do assert the existence of such a connection. For example:

16a) If grass *were* red, then humans *could* breathe under water.

Because of the words "were" and "could," this statement asserts a nonexistent connection between the color of grass and our respiratory capacities, and it is therefore false.

So you can see there's a problem with interpreting compound statements, especially conditionals, in a truth-functional way. The problem is quite complex, and touches on a number of basic issues concerning logic and language. Those who have explored these issues have not come to an agreement about a solution. We can't go into all this in an introductory text, but you do have a right to know the assumptions on which we're going to proceed.

The if-then structure in language is used to make various types of statements, all of which are truth-functional in one respect: if the antecedent is true and the consequent false, then the conditional must be false. This is the situation described in line three of the truth table. In my view, however, it is rarely if ever the case that a conditional is *true* merely because its antecedent is false or consequent true—the situation described in the other lines. The truth of a conditional is *consistent* with those combinations of truth values, but most conditionals say something more than that, something not captured by the truth table.

As it happens, this "something more" is not relevant for most inferences. We saw, for example, that the validity of *modus ponens* depends solely on the third line of the truth table. So we will make the simplifying assumption that the conditional is true in the other three lines. This assumption allows us to use truth tables as a systematic and powerful device for argument analysis. In the vast majority of cases it is a reliable test for the validity of propositional inferences. When a conditional statement serves as the conclusion of an argument, however, we need to be careful. The "something more" that it asserts may not be warranted by the premises. An example would be the following:

1) Grass is not red $\sim p$
2) Therefore, grass is not red or humans can
   breathe under water $\sim p \vee q$
3) Therefore, if grass were red, humans could
   breathe under water $p \supset q$

In the symbolic inference on the right, (2) follows from (1) by the principle of addition, which we discussed earlier, and (3) follows from (2) by the equivalence between the two statement forms. So the inference is valid by the rules of propositional logic. The argument on the left, however, is not valid—the premise is true and the conclusion false. So we would go astray if we analyzed the argument as an instance of the symbolic form.

With this caveat in mind, let's go on now to develop the implications of what we've learned about the connectives.

Practice Quiz

Put each of the following statements in symbolic form, using appropriate letters to stand for component statements.

1. Roses are red and violets are blue.
2. If you're in a jam, I'm your man.
3. Either we pay the fine now, or we pay a larger fine later.
4. Art is long but life is short.
5. I am not a crook.
6. I'm ready if you are.
7. Although the beach was beautiful, the water was shark-infested.
8. A bank will lend you money only if you're able to repay it.
9. The French Revolution was either an act of liberation or an act of destruction.
10. Starting the charcoal with napalm is not a good idea.
11. Either Spitball Harry gets his act together, or we're going to lose this game.
12. You and I can be friends unless you take advantage of me.
13. If Morley won the lottery, he is being unusually quiet about it.

14. Gainor is a brilliant scholar of ancient languages, though she is so absentminded she needs business cards to remember her own name.
15. I will definitely come to your party, unless something better comes along.

Statement Forms

So far we have dealt with compound statements containing a single connective and two components (or just one in the case of negation). We can also put together much more complex statements, involving any number of connectives and components. To do so, however, we need some rules of punctuation in order to avoid ambiguities.

Consider the two statements:

1) Either I'll go home and watch TV or I'll think about the election.
2) I'll go home and I'll either watch TV or think about the election.

These statements involve the same component propositions: I'll go home, I'll watch TV, I'll think about the election. We can abbreviate them with the letters H, T, and E. And both have the same connectives: one conjunction and one disjunction. But they don't say the same thing. (2) implies that H is true (i.e., that I will go home), while (1) does not imply this. To mark the difference, we would use parentheses:

$$1) \ (H \bullet T) \vee E$$
$$2) \ H \bullet (T \vee E)$$

The parentheses in (1) indicate that disjunction is the *main* connective, but that one disjunct $(H \bullet T)$ is itself a conjunction. The parentheses in (2) indicate that the main connective is conjunction, but that one conjunct $(T \vee E)$ is itself a disjunction.

The basic rule is to use parentheses so that the connectives $\bullet$, $\vee$, and $\supset$ join two components, where one or both components may themselves be compound statements marked off by parentheses. If a statement involves connectives of different types, as in (1) and (2), it's crucial to decide which connective is the main one. But what if all the connectives are of the same type? If we have a string of components all linked by conjunction, as in

3) I'm going home and I'm going to bed and I'm going to sleep until Wednesday,

it doesn't matter how we group them. The statements $(H \bullet B) \bullet S$ and $H \bullet (B \bullet S)$ are equivalent. The same is true for disjunction: $(p \vee q) \vee r$ is equivalent to $p \vee (q \vee r)$. But it isn't true for conditionals. The statements

4) If I had a million dollars, then if I were $M \supset (H \supset C)$
   happy I'd have nothing to complain about
                    and
5) If it's true that if I had a million dollars $(M \supset H) \supset C$
   I'd be happy, then I have nothing to com-
   plain about

are not equivalent. (For many of us, (4) is true and (5) false.)

A second major rule has to do with negation. A negation sign in front of a component statement is a denial of that component only, while a negation sign in front of a compound statement marked off by parentheses is a denial of the compound statement as a whole. Thus the statement "Either Leslie is not sad or she's a good actress" would be symbolized: $\sim\!S \vee G$. The formula $\sim\!(S \vee G)$ would represent the very different statement that Leslie is neither sad nor a good actress. So when you are translating from English into symbolic notation, you'll need to decide whether the verbal indicators of negation ("not," "isn't," "neither . . . nor," etc.) apply to individual component propositions or to compound ones.

Let's see how these rules apply to a more complex sample:

6) If Gorbachev succeeds in restructuring the Soviet economy (G), and either cuts military expenditures (C) or attracts new foreign investment (A), then the Soviet economy will improve (S) unless some natural disaster strikes (D).

The statement has the overall form of a conditional. The comma clearly separates the sentence into an "if" component and a "then" component, so the main connective will be a horseshoe. But both the antecedent and the consequent are themselves compound statements. The antecedent is "G and either C or A." The placement of the word "either" makes it clear how this should be punctuated: $G \bullet (C \vee A)$. The consequent is "S unless D." As we have seen, *p unless q* is to be translated *if not q then p*. So the consequent is itself a conditional, and would be symbolized: $\sim\!D \supset S$. So the statement as a whole is:

$$[G \bullet (C \vee A)] \supset (\sim\!D \supset S).$$

Notice that we use square brackets around the antecedent because we used parentheses around one of its components. This is a convenience to help us keep our groupings clear.

You may have noticed that we use capital letters, as well as the lowercase letters p and q, to represent statements. The capital letters are abbreviations for actual statements, so that we don't have to keep writing them out. We use lowercase letters, by contrast, when we want to talk about statements in general, so that we can identify the logical forms that compound statements can take.

To see the importance of this distinction, consider statement (6) again. What is its logical form? One answer would be:

6a) $[p \cdot (q \vee r)] \supset (\sim s \supset t)$.

This answer is certainly correct: (6a) captures the full logical structure of (6), including all of its connectives, and any statement with the same structure would have the same logical properties, no matter what component statements played the roles of p, q, r, s, and t. But it would also be true to say that (6) has the logical form:

6b) $p \supset q$.

This does not give the full logical structure of (6), but we have captured its basic structure as a conditional statement, with $\supset$ as the main connective.

(6b) helps us to realize that (6) has the logical properties common to all conditionals, regardless of the fact that its antecedent and consequent are themselves compound. Thus, if we want to know whether the argument

$$[G \cdot (C \vee A)] \supset (\sim D \supset S)$$
$$\underline{G \cdot (C \vee A)}$$
$$\sim D \supset S$$

is valid, it would help to notice that the first premise has the form $p \supset q$. It then becomes obvious that this is an example of *modus ponens*, which we already know is a valid argument form. The internal structure of the antecedent and consequent play no role in the argument.

As we proceed through this chapter, we're going to learn how to analyze arguments involving rather complex propositions. Our tools of analysis, however, will be some fairly simple rules, like *modus ponens*. So it's important that you learn to spot these simple patterns even when they are embedded within a more complex structure. The way to do that is to keep in mind the difference between actual statements and statement forms.

Finally, we can use what we've learned about punctuation and logical form to introduce a new connective. Suppose I say that I will teach a certain class if and only if ten or more students enroll. I am asserting a conjunction of two conditional statements, one of them indicated by the "if," the other by the "only if":

7a) If ten or more students enroll, I teach the
    class ("if") $E \supset T$

7b) If I teach the class, ten or more students
    enroll ("only if") $T \supset E$

In propositional logic we use a special symbol, $\equiv$, for the *if and only if* relationship between components. As the example makes clear, a statement of the form $p \equiv q$, which is called a **biconditional**, is equivalent to the conjunction:

$$(p \supset q) \cdot (q \supset p).$$

The truth table for biconditionals is:

p	q	$p \equiv q$
T	T	T
F	T	F
T	F	F
F	F	T

The truth table makes sense if you think about the meaning of the connective. $p \equiv q$ has to be false on the third line because $p \supset q$ is one element in the biconditional, and $p \supset q$ is false on that line. In the same way, the biconditional must be false on line 2 because the other element, $q \supset p$, is false there. But on lines 1 and 4, both conditionals are true. As a result, a biconditional statement is true if p and q have the same truth value, false if they have different truth values.

The biconditional is thus a truth–functional connective, and is subject to the same caveat that applies to the other connectives. The symbol $\equiv$ stands for a relationship among truth values; it does not imply any further connection between the components. The statement

8) Squirrels eat nuts $\equiv$ London has a subway

is true because both components are true. And

9) Harold Robbins wrote *Hamlet* $\equiv$ Triangles have four sides

is true because both components are false. The lack of any connection in either case is irrelevant.

Practice Quiz

Put each of the following statements into symbolic notation, using appropriate letters to abbreviate the components.

1. You can't hide your lying eyes, and your smile is a thin disguise.
2. I'll tell it to a priest or I'll tell it to a bottle, but I won't go to see a psychiatrist.
3. We may lose and we may win, but we will never be here again.
4. It's my party and I'll cry if I want to.
5. Either we'll move and buy a house, or we'll stay and keep renting.
6. I'll scratch your back if and only if you'll scratch mine.
7. If you convinced me and I convinced you, then there would still be two points of view.
8. The woods are lovely, dark and deep.
   But I have promises to keep.
9. If you don't feel guilty about lying, then either you have a good reason for lying or you have no conscience.
10. If nominated I will not run, and if elected I will not serve.
11. If deuterium did change to helium, then fusion did take place, and we have discovered a new source of energy.
12. He's either a knave or a fool, but he isn't both a knave and a fool.
13. It isn't true that he quit his job, but if he did I'd be the first to know.
14. It's not the case that if men were angels, government would not be necessary.
15. If an object is dropped, it will fall unless some other force counteracts gravity.
16. The fowls of the air sow not, neither do they reap, nor gather into barns; yet your heavenly Father feedeth them.
17. If you stand I will stand with you, and if you fall I will trip over you.
18. If you violate the law you will go to jail, unless you are very rich or a politician.
19. This liquid is water if and only if it will freeze if we chill it to 32 degrees Fahrenheit and will boil if we heat it to 212 degrees Fahrenheit.
20. If ticket offices are open or ticket vending machines are available, and you buy your ticket on the train, you will be charged an additional $1.00, but you will not be charged the additional dollar if the local station is not open.

Validity

Now that we understand how to put statements into symbolic notation, it's time to look at *arguments*. In this section, we will learn how to use truth tables to determine whether an argument is valid. In later sections, we'll see how to establish that a conclusion follows from a set of premises by constructing a proof.

A valid argument is one in which the truth of the premises guarantees the truth of the conclusion. The premises need not actually be true. What matters for validity is the *relation* between premises and conclusion. In a valid argument, the relation is such that *if* the premises are true, the conclusion must be true as well. And we have seen that the truth or falsity of a compound statement involving one of the connectives is determined by the truth or falsity of its components, according to a truth table. This means we can also use truth tables to assess the validity of arguments involving compound statements. We've already seen how this works in a kind of intuitive way. Not let's lay it out more systematically.

Consider the inference form *modus tollens*:

$$p \supset q$$
$$\frac{\smallfrown q}{\smallfrown p}$$

To show that it is valid, we construct a truth table with columns for the components at the left, then columns for the premises, and then, at the right, a column for the conclusion:

p	q	$p \supset q$	$\smallfrown q$	$\smallfrown p$
T	T	T	F	F
F	T	T	F	T
T	F	F	T	F
F	F	T	T	T

The assignment of truth values to the components p and q determines the truth value of each premise and of the conclusion; all three propositions in the argument have truth values dependent on the same component propositions. The test for validity is whether the conclusion can be false while the premises are both true. So we look first at the column for the conclusion. $\smallfrown p$ is false in two cases: the first and third lines. But in the first line, the premise $\smallfrown q$ is false, and in the third line the premise $p \supset q$ is false. So there is no case in which the conclusion is false and both premises true. Alternatively, we could start with the premises. There is only one case—the fourth line—in which they are both true, and in that case the conclusion is true as well.

Now consider an invalid argument that affirms the consequent:

$$C \supset D$$
$$\frac{D}{C}$$

Once again we construct a truth table:

C	D	C ⊃ D	D	C
T	T	T	T	T
F	T	T	T	F
T	F	F	F	T
F	F	T	F	F

As before, we start with the components on the left, then the premises in order, and finally the conclusion on the right. Since the second premise and the conclusion are the components themselves, these columns simply repeat the ones on the left. Once you get used to this method, you can simplify things by skipping the repetition. In any case, we can see why the argument is invalid. In the second line, both premises are true and the conclusion is false.

In the arguments above, the statements involved at most one connective, so it was obvious how to assign truth values to them in the truth table for the argument. But what about more complex statements, with more than one connective? Suppose we had an argument with the conditional premise $A \supset (A \cdot B)$. As with any compound statement, its truth value depends on the values of its components, A and $A \cdot B$. Since $A \cdot B$ is itself compound, its truth value depends on the value of its components, A and B. So we start with these basic components, then compute $A \cdot B$, and then the conditional statement as a whole. In general, we work from the inside out, doing the main connective last.

We can represent this procedure in either of two ways, illustrated below:

A	B	A • B	A ⊃ (A • B)	A	B	A ⊃ (A • B)	
T	T	T	T	T	T	T	T
F	T	F	T	F	T	T	F
T	F	F	F	T	F	F	F
F	F	F	T	F	F	T	F

The only difference is that the method on the right involves a slight shortcut. Instead of writing out both $A \cdot B$ and $A \supset (A \cdot B)$ separately, we have put two columns under the conditional, one for the conjunctive component and one for the conditional as a whole. This method is more efficient, as long as you remember that the truth value of the statement as a whole is given by the column under the *main* connective, the one that stands outside the parentheses. If you use the method on the left, you need to remember that $A \cdot B$ is not itself a premise, so you should disregard it when you check to see whether the conclusion can be false while the premises are true.

The truth table test for validity will work with arguments of any complexity. Let's try the argument:

$$A \supset B$$
$$\frac{C \supset B}{A \supset C}$$

We have three components here (A, B, and C), so to represent all the possibilities, we need a truth table with $2 \times 2 \times 2 = 8$ lines:

	A	B	C	$A \supset B$	$C \supset B$	$A \supset C$
1.	T	T	T	T	T	T
2.	F	T	T	T	T	T
3.	T	F	T	F	F	T
4.	F	F	T	T	F	T
5.	T	T	F	T	T	F
6.	F	T	F	T	T	T
7.	T	F	F	F	T	F
8.	F	F	F	T	T	T

The conclusion is false on lines 5 and 7, but in line 5 both of the premises are true. So the argument is not valid.

It's rather cumbersome to work with an eight-line truth table, and for every additional component proposition, we double the number of lines we need. So the problem gets worse exponentially: for an argument with n components, we need a table with 2^n lines. Fortunately, there's a shorter and more efficient way to use the truth table test of validity. We want to know whether the conclusion can be false while the premises are true. So we need only consider those lines in a truth table where the conclusion *is* false. If we can find those lines without writing out the entire truth table, we can save a great deal of effort.

The procedure is to write out premises and the conclusion in order, from left to right. Then we find the assignments of truth values to the components, if any, that will make the conclusion false. Let's do this for an argument form (called **constructive dilemma**) that has four components:

$$(p \supset q) \bullet (r \supset s)$$
$$\frac{p \vee r}{q \vee s}$$

There is only one condition in which the conclusion is false: q and s must both be false. The short version of the truth table that incorporates this information looks like this:

$$(p \supset q) \bullet (r \supset s) \qquad p \vee r \qquad q \vee s$$
$$ F \qquad\qquad F \qquad\qquad F\ F\ F$$

Since we have assigned the value F to *q* and to *s* in the conclusion, we have to give them the same value where they occur in the premises, in order to be consistent. We haven't specified the truth values of *p* and r yet, so we don't know whether the premises could be true when *q* and *s* are both false. The procedure at this point is to see whether we can find truth values for *p* and *r* that will make both premises true. If we can, the argument is invalid; if we can't, it's valid.

In the first premise, the main connective is a conjunction, so we must try to make both conjuncts true. Each conjunct is a conditional whose consequent is false. The two conditionals will be true, therefore, only if both antecedents—*p* and *r*—are false. So there is only one assignment of truth values that makes the conclusion false and the first premise true:

$$(p \supset q) \bullet (r \supset s) \qquad p \vee r \qquad q \vee s$$
$$F\ T\ F\ T\ F\ T\ \ F \qquad\qquad\qquad F\ F\ F$$

And now we can see that if *p* and *r* are both false, the disjunctive premise *p* ∨ *r* must be false. What we have shown is that if the conclusion is false, there is no consistent assignment of truth values that makes both premises true. The argument form is therefore valid.

The short method worked out very easily with this argument because there was only one pair of truth values for *q* and *s* that made the conclusion false. This will not always be the case. In the argument

$$A \vee C$$
$$C \supset D$$
$$D \bullet B$$
$$\overline{A \bullet B}$$

the conclusion is a conjunction, which can be false in three different ways. So we have three lines to consider:

	$A \vee C$	$C \supset D$	$D \bullet B$	$A \bullet B$
1.	T		F	T F F
2.	F		T	F F T
3.	F		F	F F F

We can see right away that there is no way to make the conjunctive premise $D \bullet B$ true in the first and third lines, where B is false. But we can make that premise true in the second line, by assigning D the value True. And if C is true, then the other two premises are true as well:

$$
\begin{array}{ccccc}
 & A \vee C & C \supset D & D \bullet B & A \bullet B \\
2. & \text{F T T} & \text{T T T} & \text{T T T} & \text{F F T}
\end{array}
$$

Since we have this one case in which the premises are true and the conclusion false, the argument is invalid. Even though we had to consider three different cases, the short method was easier and faster than constructing the entire truth table for this argument.

The use of truth tables, in either the full or the abbreviated form, allows us to determine the validity of any propositional argument: it tells us whether the premises can be true while the conclusion is false. As we have noted, however, we're working on the assumption that the truth of a compound statement is determined by the truth values of its components, regardless of any other connection that may or may not exist among them. As we saw at the end of the first section, this truth-functional standard of validity may not always agree with our ordinary judgments, which do take account of those connections.

Practice Quiz

Test each of the following arguments for validity by means of truth tables, Use the short form of the test for arguments with three or more components.

1. $A \supset B$
   $\underline{\sim A}$
   $\sim B$

2. $C \supset D$
   $\overline{C \supset (C \bullet D)}$

3. $E \supset F$
   $F \supset G$
   $\overline{E \supset G}$

4. $H \supset I$
   $I \supset H$
   $\overline{(H \bullet I) \vee (\sim H \bullet \sim I)}$

5. $J \bullet K$
   $\underline{L \vee K}$
   $\sim L$

6. $M \vee (N \bullet O)$
   $\underline{\sim N}$
   $\sim M$

7. $A \supset (B \supset C)$
   $\underline{A \bullet C}$
   B

8. $(D \bullet E) \vee (E \bullet F)$
   $\underline{E \supset \sim D}$
   F

9. $(G \lor H) \supset (I \bullet J)$
   $\frac{\smile H \bullet I}{G \lor \smile J}$

10. $(K \supset L) \bullet (M \supset N)$
    $\frac{\smile L \lor \smile N}{\smile K \lor \smile M}$

Proof

For arguments that involve complex statements, or more than a few premises, even the short version of the truth table method can be cumbersome. It is often easier and more natural to look for a proof by which the conclusion can be derived from the premises. Proof in logic is like proof in geometry. It is a series of small steps, each of which is itself a valid inference. If we can get from premises to conclusion by valid steps, then the argument as a whole is valid. Constructing a proof often takes some ingenuity, so the fact that you haven't found a proof in a given case does not establish that the argument is invalid. Perhaps you haven't looked hard enough. Unlike the truth table method, therefore, the method of proof won't establish that an argument is invalid. If an argument *is* valid, however, a proof will often reveal the connection between premises and conclusion more clearly than the truth table method does.

In principle, we could use *any* valid inference form to take an individual step in a proof. But it would be impossible to remember all the valid forms, even the simpler ones. It is better to work with a small set that is easily memorized. The nine inference forms described below are commonly used in propositional logic as building blocks from which proofs can be constructed. They can all be proven valid by the truth table method, and you are already familiar with most of them.

The first three rules involve basic operations with disjunction and conjunction:

Simplification (Simp)   **Conjunction (Conj)**   **Addition (Add)**

$\dfrac{p \bullet q}{p}$ or $\dfrac{p \bullet q}{q}$ $\begin{array}{c} p \\ q \\ \hline p \bullet q \end{array}$ $\dfrac{p}{p \lor q}$ or $\dfrac{q}{p \lor q}$

Simplification is often useful when we have a conjunction and can see that one conjunct is not relevant to the conclusion. Conjunction allows us to put together two statements into a single conjunctive statement. Addition allows us to introduce a new statement by adding it, in the form of a disjunction, to a statement we already have. We discussed these inference forms when we reviewed the connectives, and each form is easily proven valid by truth tables.

A second group consists of the hypothetical and disjunctive syllogisms that we studied in Chapter 10:

Disjunctive Syllogism (DS)

$$p \vee q \qquad p \vee q$$
$$\underline{\smallsmile p} \quad \text{or} \quad \underline{\smallsmile q}$$
$$q \qquad\qquad p$$

Hypothetical Syllogism (HS)

$$p \supset q$$
$$\underline{q \supset r}$$
$$p \supset r$$

Modus Ponens (MP)

$$p \supset q$$
$$\underline{p}$$
$$q$$

Modus Tollens (MT)

$$p \supset q$$
$$\underline{\smallsmile q}$$
$$\smallsmile p$$

Once again, we have seen by the truth table method why each of these is valid (you did the hypothetical syllogism in the last Practice Quiz).

The last two inference forms are called **dilemmas.** Argument by dilemma is a common tactic in debates, and we sometimes use inferences of this form in thinking about alternative courses of action. Here's an example:

> If I go to bed early, I'll be unprepared for the test; but if I stay up late studying, I'll be too tired to do well. But those are my choices: either I go to bed early or I stay up late studying. So either I'll be unprepared for the test or I'll be too tired to do well.

If we put this into symbolic notation, we can see that it involves a combination of conditional and disjunctive elements:

$$(E \supset U) \bullet (L \supset T)$$
$$\underline{E \vee L}$$
$$U \vee T$$

The first premise asserts a pair of conditional statements; the second premise says that at least one of the two antecedents is true; and the conclusion is that at least one of the two consequents is true.

Another type of dilemma argues that one of the two consequents is false, therefore one of the two antecedents is false:

> If conservatives are right, welfare breeds dependency; while if liberals are right, it is merely a temporary transition to self-supporting work. But either welfare does *not* breed dependency, or it is *not* merely a temporary transition. So either the conservatives or the liberals are not right.

$$(C \supset D) \bullet (L \supset T)$$
$$\underline{\smallsmile D \vee \smallsmile T}$$
$$\smallsmile C \vee \smallsmile L$$

These two types of argument are called constructive and destructive dilemma, respectively. Generalizing from the examples, the inference forms are:

Constructive Dilemma (CD)   **Destructive Dilemma (DD)**

Constructive Dilemma (CD)	Destructive Dilemma (DD)
$(p \supset q) \bullet (r \supset s)$	$(p \supset q) \bullet (r \supset s)$
$\underline{p \vee r}$	$\underline{\sim q \vee \sim s}$
$q \vee s$	$\sim p \vee \sim r$

You may have noticed that constructive dilemma is an inference we tested by the short truth table method in the last section. And destructive dilemma was one of the inferences you tested in the last Practice Quiz.

Each of the inference rules identifies a form of valid inference, using the letters p, q, etc., for the component propositions. We must remember that these components may themselves be compound statements. For example, the inference

$$\frac{(A \supset B) \bullet [D \vee (\sim E \bullet F)]}{D \vee (\sim E \bullet F)}$$

is an instance of simplification. The internal complexity of each conjunct in the premise is irrelevant; the argument fits the pattern $p \bullet q$, therefore q.

Practice Quiz

Each of the arguments below is an instance of one of the basic inference forms. Identify the form in each case.

1. $A \vee \sim B$
   $\underline{\sim \sim B}$
   A

2. $(D \vee E) \supset F$
   $\underline{D \vee E}$
   F

3. $(G \supset H) \bullet (I \supset J)$
   $\underline{G \vee I}$
   $H \vee J$

4. $\underline{(K \bullet L) \bullet M}$
   M

5. $A \supset (B \bullet C)$
   $\underline{(B \bullet C) \supset (D \vee E)}$
   $A \supset (D \vee E)$

6. $(F \supset G)$
   $\overline{(F \supset G) \vee H}$

7. $I \vee J$
   $K \vee L$
   $\overline{(I \vee J) \bullet (K \vee L)}$

8. $(A \supset B) \bullet (C \supset D)$
   $\underline{\sim B \vee \sim D}$
   $\sim A \vee \sim C$

To see how these inference rules are used in constructing a proof, let's start with the very simple argument at the beginning of this chapter:

> If you visited New York either in May or in October, you saw the city at its best. You did visit New York in May, so you saw the city at its best.

$$(M \vee O) \supset B$$
$$\underline{M}$$
$$B$$

We observed that this is not an instance of *modus ponens*, because the antecedent of the first premise is a disjunction, and the second premise affirms only one disjunct. But we can infer $M \vee O$ from M by means of addition, and then we can use $M \vee O$ in a *modus ponens* inference.

To keep track of what we're doing in a proof, it helps to use a special notation. A proof is a sequence of steps, so we number each step, starting with the premises and ending with the conclusion. In a separate column to the right, we make a note of our justification for each step:

1. $(M \vee O) \supset B$ Premise
2. M / B Premise/Conclusion
3. $M \vee O$ 2, Add
4. B 1,3 MP

The first two lines state the premises, and after the second premise we make a note of the conclusion, so that we know where we're headed. The slash mark indicates that this is merely a note to ourselves, and that we can't use B in the proof itself (that would be circular). Line 3 is our first inference from the premises; the justification to the right tells us that the statement $M \vee O$ was derived from line 2 by means of addition. Similarly, the justification in line four says that B was derived from lines 1 and 3 by means of *modus ponens*. Each line in a proof, therefore, is either a premise or a statement that follows from statements on preceding lines in accordance with one of the nine basic inference forms.

It's important to remember that an inference rule applies only to whole lines in a proof; it can't be applied to part of a line. An error of this kind occurs in the following proof:

1. $(A \bullet B) \supset C$ Premise
2. $\neg C / \neg A$ Premise/Conclusion
3. $A \supset C$ 1 Simp [error]
4. $\neg A$ 2,3 MT

We cannot apply the rule of simplification to the conjunction in line 1, because $A \cdot B$ is not itself stated as a premise; it is only the antecedent of a conditional statement. To see why this is invalid, consider an actual instance of this argument:

> If I got the breaks, and had the talent, I'd be a Hollywood star. But I'm not a star, so obviously I haven't had the breaks.

I'm admitting at the outset that becoming a Hollywood star depends on two factors: talent and luck. In blaming my lack of stardom on luck, however, I am conveniently forgetting the talent factor. This is illicit simplification.

We should also remember to apply the rules one at a time, and not try to combine two or more inferences into a single step. Suppose we're given the premises: $A \supset B$, $B \supset C$, and $C \supset D$. It's obvious that we can infer $A \supset D$, but we can't do it in one step:

1. $A \supset B$	Premise
2. $B \supset C$	Premise
3. $C \supset D / A \supset D$	Premise/Conclusion
4. $A \supset D$	1, 2, 3, HS [error]

The proof requires two steps:

4. $A \supset C$	1, 2 HS
5. $A \supset D$	3, 4 HS

This rule may seem a little fussy now, but as you begin to work with more complex proofs, it will help you avoid careless errors.

The process of constructing a proof is not mechanical. You have to think about what steps, in what order, will get you to the conclusion. But there are two broad strategies to follow: working forward from the premises, and backward from the conclusion. If one premise is a conditional statement, and another premise affirms the antecedent (or denies the consequent), try drawing the appropriate conclusion by *modus ponens* (or *modus tollens*), and see if that gets you any closer to the conclusion. The premises might also suggest a hypothetical or disjunctive syllogism. On the other hand, the nature of the conclusion may give you an idea about how to proceed. If it's a conjunction, you might see whether you can establish each conjunct separately. If it's a disjunction, you might see whether you can prove one disjunct, and then use addition.

Let's apply these strategies to one last example:

1. $A \supset B$
2. $C \cdot {\sim}B$
3. $(C \lor D) \supset E$
4. $\underline{E \supset F}$
   ${\sim}A \cdot F$

We might notice first that the conclusion is a conjunction, which suggests that we try to establish $\sim A$ and F separately. Premises 3 and 4 may be combined in a hypothetical syllogism, to give us the intermediate conclusion $(C \vee D) \supset F$. So if we can derive $C \vee D$, we can get F. And premise 2 asserts C as part of a conjunction, so we can use simplification, then addition. We can also derive $\sim B$ by simplification, and that can be combined with premise 1 to get $\sim A$ by *modus tollens*. So now we can lay out the proof:

1.	$A \supset B$	Premise
2.	$C \cdot \sim B$	Premise
3.	$(C \vee D) \supset E$	Premise
4.	$E \supset F / \sim A \cdot F$	Premise/Conclusion
5.	$(C \vee D) \supset F$	3,4 HS
6.	C	2, Simp
7.	$C \vee D$	6, Add
8.	F	5,7 MP
9.	$\sim B$	2, Simp
10.	$\sim A$	1,9 MT
11.	$\sim A \cdot F$	8,10 Conj

Practice Quiz

Show that each of the following arguments is valid by constructing a proof.

1. $A \vee B$
$A \supset C$
$\underline{\sim C}$
B

2. $D \supset E$
$F \supset G$
$\underline{D \vee F}$
$E \vee G$

3. $H \supset I$
$J \supset K$
$H \vee J$
$\underline{\sim K}$
I

4. $(A \vee B) \supset [C \cdot (D \supset E)]$
$\underline{A}$
$D \supset E$

5. $(F \cdot G) \vee H$
$H \supset I$
$\underline{\sim (F \cdot G)}$
$I \vee G$

6. $(J \supset K) \supset (L \cdot M)$
$(N \vee O) \supset (J \supset K)$
$\underline{O}$
L

7. $A \vee B$
$C \supset D$
$\underline{\sim A \cdot \sim D}$
$B \cdot \sim C$

8. $(E \supset F) \cdot (\sim F \vee \sim G)$
$H \supset I$
$\underline{I \supset G}$
$\sim E \vee \sim H$

Equivalence

When we talked about punctuation several sections ago, I pointed out that the statement forms $(p \bullet q) \bullet r$ and $p \bullet (q \bullet r)$ are equivalent: it doesn't matter how we group the conjuncts. The concept of equivalence here is truth-functional. The two statements have the same truth value on every line of the corresponding truth table. We can express the same fact by saying that the biconditional statement $[(p \bullet q) \bullet r] \equiv [p \bullet (q \bullet r)]$ is true no matter what truth values p, q, and r have:

p	q	r	$(p \bullet q) \bullet r$		$p \bullet (q \bullet r)$		$[(p \bullet q) \bullet r] \equiv [p \bullet (q \bullet r)]$
T	T	T	T	T	T	T	T
F	T	T	F	F	F	T	T
T	F	T	F	F	F	F	T
F	F	T	F	F	F	F	T
T	T	F	T	F	F	F	T
F	T	F	F	F	F	F	T
T	F	F	F	F	F	F	T
F	F	F	F	F	F	F	T

The importance of this point for our purposes is that equivalent statements can be substituted for each other in a proof. Consider the argument:

$$(A \bullet B) \bullet C$$
$$\underline{(B \bullet C) \supset D}$$
$$D$$

To show that this is valid, we need to replace the first premise with $A \bullet (B \bullet C)$. Then we can derive $B \bullet C$ by simplification, and D by *modus ponens*. The substitution does not affect the validity of the argument, but it does make a *proof* of validity much easier:

1. $(A \bullet B) \bullet C$ Premise
2. $(B \bullet C) \supset D / D$ Premise/Conclusion
3. $A \bullet (B \bullet C)$ 1 [?]
4. $B \bullet C$ 3 Simp
5. D 2,4 MP

How shall we describe our justification for step 3? We could adopt a general rule allowing any statement to be replaced by any other statement equivalent to it. But there are many such equivalences, too many to remember. So once again, as with inference forms, it is customary to work with a limited set. In each case, the equivalent statement forms always have the same truth value, and we assert that fact by expressing the equivalence in the form of a biconditional. (As we go through them, you might want to prove the equivalence by constructing a truth table like the one on the preceding page.)

Let's start with an obvious equivalence known as **tautology.** When Robert Frost says he has "miles to go before I sleep, and miles to go before I sleep," the repetition is merely for dramatic effect. The conjunction of a statement with itself, $p \cdot p$, says nothing more or less than p. The same is true for the disjunction of a statement with itself: $p \vee p$. (Imagine a child being offered the following "choice" by a parent: you can clean your room, or you can clean your room.) So the rule is:

$$\textbf{Tautology (Taut): } p \equiv (p \cdot p)$$
$$\equiv (p \vee p)$$

The second equivalence is one we've seen before:

$$\textbf{Double Negation (DN): } p \equiv {\sim}{\sim}p$$

As we noted, negation is an on-off switch, so the two signs on the right cancel out. You'll need to use DN more often than you might think. If you had the two premises ${\sim}A \vee B$ and A, for example, it would be natural to infer B by disjunctive syllogism. Strictly speaking, however, you can't use that inference form until you have transformed A into ${\sim}{\sim}A$:

	$p \vee q$	1. ${\sim}A \vee B$	Premise
disjunctive		2. A	Premise
syllogism	${\sim}p$	3. ${\sim}{\sim}A$	2, DN
	q	4. B	1,3 DS

The conjunctive equivalence we talked about at the beginning of this section is called "association," and it's one of several that you will probably recognize from mathematics:

$$\textbf{Commutation (Com): } (p \cdot q) \equiv (q \cdot p)$$
$$(p \vee q) \equiv (q \vee p)$$

$$\textbf{Association (Assoc): } [p \cdot (q \cdot r)] \equiv [(p \cdot q) \cdot r]$$
$$[p \vee (q \vee r)] \equiv [(p \vee q) \vee r]$$

The commutation rules say that the order of disjuncts or conjuncts makes no difference, and the association rules say that the grouping doesn't matter either.

Another kind of equivalence you may recall from mathematics is:

Distribution (Dist): $[p \bullet (q \vee r)] \equiv [(p \bullet q) \vee (p \bullet r)]$
$[p \vee (q \bullet r)] \equiv [(p \vee q) \bullet (p \vee r)]$

These rules are a little trickier, because they involve both kinds of connectives, but they should be obvious when you think them through. We can illustrate the first distributive rule with an earlier example. The statement

1a) I'll go home and either watch TV or $H \bullet (T \vee E)$
think about the election

is clearly equivalent to

1b) I'll go home and watch TV or I'll go $(H \bullet T) \vee (H \bullet E)$
home and think about the election

Another very important pair of equivalences are named after the nineteenth-century logician Augustus De Morgan:

De Morgan's Law (DM): $\smile(p \bullet q) \equiv (\smallfrown p \vee \smallfrown q)$
$\smile(p \vee q) \equiv (\smallfrown p \bullet \smallfrown q)$

We noticed the first of these equivalences in Chapter 10: the statement "You can't have your cake and eat it too," or $\smile (H \bullet E)$, means either you don't have your cake or you don't eat it: $\smallfrown H \vee \smallfrown E$. The second equivalence is equally obvious. A statement of the form $\smallfrown (p \vee q)$ would normally be expressed in English by "neither . . . nor," as in

2a) Cheating is neither honest nor smart.

This is equivalent to

2b) Cheating is not honest and cheating is not smart.

De Morgan's law is useful because it allows us to get rid of a negated compound statement, which is usually hard to work with in a proof.

Practice Quiz

Each of the following statements is an instance of one of the equivalence rules we've examined so far. Identify the rule.

1. $A \lor B \equiv B \lor A$
2. $C \lor (D \bullet E) \equiv (C \lor D) \bullet (C \lor E)$
3. $\backsim (F \bullet G) \equiv \backsim F \lor \backsim G$
4. $H \lor I \equiv \backsim \backsim (H \lor I)$
5. $J \lor (K \lor L) \equiv (J \lor K) \lor L$
6. $(M \supset N) \bullet O \equiv O \bullet (M \supset N)$
7. $A \bullet B \equiv (A \bullet B) \lor (A \bullet B)$
8. $\backsim C \bullet \backsim (D \lor E) \equiv \backsim [C \lor (D \lor E)]$

The preceding equivalence rules dealt with conjunction, disjunction, and negation. Another group of rules we're going to use pertains to conditionals and biconditionals. The first is

Contrapositive (Contra): $(p \supset q) \equiv (\backsim q \supset \backsim p)$

We dealt with contrapositives in Chapter 10, and you may recall our example:

3a) If it rained last night, the ground would be wet, and
3b) If the ground is not wet, it did not rain last night.

These statements are obviously equivalent.

Another rule was mentioned in connection with the truth-functional character of the conditional. We noticed that a conditional statement is disjunctive; it asserts that either the antecedent is false or the consequent true: $\backsim p \lor q$. An example of this equivalence in ordinary language would be:

4a) If I stay for dinner, I'll have to listen to my uncle doing his Ed Sullivan impression; and
4b) Either I don't stay for dinner, or I'll have to listen to my uncle doing his Ed Sullivan impression.

Notice what happens now when we apply De Morgan's law and double negation to the disjunction above:

$$\backsim p \lor q$$
$$\backsim p \lor \backsim \backsim q \qquad \text{DN}$$
$$\backsim (p \bullet \backsim q) \qquad \text{DM}$$

The conclusion reflects the fact that a conditional cannot be true if its antecedent is true and its consequent false. The equivalence rule therefore has two forms:

$$\textbf{Implication (Imp)} \quad (p \supset q) \equiv (\sim p \vee q)$$
$$\equiv \sim (p \bullet \sim q)$$

The rule is so named because "implication" (or "material implication") is another name for the conditional.

Next we have two rules telling us how to translate a biconditional:

$$\textbf{Biconditional (Bicon):} \ (p \equiv q) \equiv [(p \supset q) \bullet (q \supset p)]$$
$$\equiv [(p \bullet q) \vee (\sim p \bullet \sim q)]$$

The first rule follows from the way we introduced the connective "≡." The second rule follows from the fact that a biconditional is true only if both components have the same truth values. These rules are essential when we encounter a biconditional statement in a proof, because (as you may have noticed) none of the basic inference forms include biconditional statements.

Our final rule is

$$\textbf{Exportation (Exp):} \ [(p \bullet q) \supset r] \equiv [p \supset (q \supset r)]$$

This looks a little strange, but it makes sense when you think about it. In the last section, we examined an argument with the premise

5a) If I got the breaks, and had the talent,
   I'd be a Hollywood star $(B \bullet T) \supset S$

The same statement in a different form would be

5b) If I got the breaks, then if I had the
   talent I'd be a Hollywood star $B \supset (T \supset S)$

In this way, exportation allows us to substitute a conditional for a conjunction sign and vice versa—useful techniques in many proofs.

Practice Quiz

Each of the following statements is an instance of one of the equivalence rules for conditionals or biconditionals. Identify the rule.

1. $(\backsim A \vee B) \equiv (A \supset B)$
2. $(C \equiv D) \equiv [(C \bullet D) \vee (\backsim C \bullet \backsim D)]$
3. $(E \supset F) \equiv (\backsim F \supset \backsim E)$
4. $[\backsim G \supset (H \supset I)] \equiv [(\backsim G \bullet H) \supset I]$
5. $(J \supset \backsim K) \equiv \backsim (J \bullet \backsim \backsim K)$
6. $[(L \bullet M) \supset (N \vee O)] \equiv [\backsim (N \vee O) \supset \backsim (L \bullet M)]$
7. $[(\backsim A \supset \backsim B) \bullet (\backsim B \supset \backsim A)] \equiv (\backsim A \equiv \backsim B)$
8. $[(C \bullet D) \supset E] \equiv \backsim [(C \bullet D) \bullet \backsim E]$

When we use the equivalence rules in a proof, we write a new line to substitute one equivalent statement for another, and we give our justification off to the right. For example:

1.	$A \supset (B \supset C)$	Premise
2.	$\backsim C \,/\, \backsim A \vee \backsim B$	Premise/Conclusion
3.	$(A \bullet B) \supset C$	1, Exp
4.	$\backsim (A \bullet B)$	2,3 MT
5.	$\backsim A \vee \backsim B$	4 DM

In step 3 we transformed the first premise by exportation into a single conditional with C as its consequent, so that we could use it with the second premise in a *modus tollens* inference. Then we used De Morgan's law to reach the conclusion.

The equivalence rules, in other words, are used in essentially the same way as an inference rule. But they do have one distinctive property. We saw in the last section that inference rules can be applied only to whole lines in a proof, not to components within a line. But we *can* apply the equivalence rules to components, as in the following example:

1.	$(C \supset D) \vee E$	Premise
2.	$C \,/\, D \vee E$	Premise/Conclusion
3.	$(\backsim C \vee D) \vee E$	1, Imp
4.	$\backsim C \vee (D \vee E)$	3, Assoc
5.	$\backsim \backsim C$	2, DN
6.	$D \vee E$	4,5 HS

In line 3, we applied the implication rule to the first disjunct in premise (1), substituting $\backsim C \vee D$ for $C \supset D$. Since these are equivalent, they must have the same truth value. So the substitution cannot affect the truth values of the compound statements in which they serve as components, and thus cannot affect the validity of the argument as a whole.

Practice Quiz

Construct a proof to show that each of the arguments below is valid.

1. $(B \cdot C) \vee \sim A$
    $B \supset D$
    $\overline{A \supset D}$

2. $(E \vee F) \supset G$
    $H \supset E$
    $\sim H \supset F$
    $\overline{G}$

3. $(I \vee J) \supset K$
    $(L \vee M) \supset \sim K$
    M
    $\overline{\sim J}$

4. $A \vee (B \supset C)$
    $\sim C$
    $\overline{B \supset A}$

5. $(D \cdot E) \vee (F \cdot G)$
    $(D \supset H) \cdot (F \supset I)$
    $\overline{H \vee I}$

6. $(J \supset K) \supset (J \supset L)$
    $J \cdot \sim L$
    $\overline{\sim K}$

7. $(A \supset B) \cdot (A \supset C)$
    $(B \cdot C) \supset (D \cdot E)$
    $\sim D$
    $\overline{\sim A}$

8. $(F \cdot G) \supset H$
    F
    $(I \supset \sim H) \cdot (F \supset G)$
    $\overline{G \equiv H}$

Conditional and Indirect Proof

In this section we're going to learn two additional techniques that can be used in proofs. Given the rules we're using, these techniques are necessary in order to construct proofs for certain valid arguments. And even where they are not necessary, they can make life easier by reducing the number and complexity of the steps we need to derive a conclusion.

The first technique is called **conditional proof,** and we can see the rationale for it if we examine the following argument:

$$A \supset (B \supset C)$$
$$B$$
$$\overline{A \supset C}$$

It should be intuitively clear that this argument is valid. The first premise doesn't tell us whether A is true, but suppose it is. On that supposition, $B \supset C$ would follow. From $B \supset C$, together with the second premise (B), we could derive C. If A is true, therefore, C must be true as well—and that's exactly what the conclusion says. The method of conditional proof is a way of capturing this process of thought. The method is used to prove a conditional statement. We start by assuming the antecedent p, then we use that assumption (along with the premises we're given) to derive the consequent q, and this justifies the conclusion that $p \supset q$.

To keep track of what we're doing, it helps to use a special notation. A conditional proof for the argument above would be formulated as follows:

1.	$A \supset (B \supset C)$	Premise
2.	$B \, / \, A \supset C$	Premise/Conclusion
3.	A	Assumption
4.	$B \supset C$	1,3 MP
5.	C	2,4 MP
6.	$A \supset C$	3–5 CP

The indented lines (3–5) are the conditional part of the proof. This is the part where we are assuming that A is true and showing that C follows. But the premises don't tell us that A is true. So we can't end the proof on line 5. We have borrowed A, and now we have to pay it back. We do that on line 6. At this point in the proof, we're no longer assuming that A is true. We're merely saying that *if* A is true, C is true as well. This conclusion is justified by the fact that C follows from A, along with the other premises. We make a note of this fact in the column to the right, which says that line 6 is justified by the conditional proof (CP) in lines 3–5. Nothing in the logic of conditional proof, by the way, requires that we indent those lines. Indentation is just a handy visual way to keep track of our debts.

To see the value of this technique, compare the conditional proof above with the kind of proof we would need if we used only the basic inference forms and equivalence rules:

1.	$A \supset (B \supset C)$	Premise
2.	$B \, / \, A \supset C$	Premise/Conclusion
3.	$\sim A \lor (B \supset C)$	1 Imp
4.	$\sim A \lor (\sim B \lor C)$	3 Imp
5.	$(\sim A \lor \sim B) \lor C$	4 Assoc
6.	$(\sim B \lor \sim A) \lor C$	5 Com
7.	$\sim B \lor (\sim A \lor C)$	6 Assoc
8.	$\sim\sim B$	2 DN
9.	$\sim A \lor C$	7,8 DS
10.	$A \supset C$	9 Imp

You can see that the conditional proof is much simpler. It saves us all the trouble of translating the first premise into a disjunction and rearranging all the terms.

A conditional proof can be used only to prove a conditional statement. But that conditional statement need not be the conclusion of the argument as a whole. We can use the method at any point in an argument to derive a conditional that will help us get to the ultimate conclusion. When we do this, however, we have to obey an important restriction. Once we discharge the assumption and get back to the main proof, we can no longer use any line that was part of the conditional proof. Those lines depend on an assumption that we're no longer making.

We can also use one conditional proof inside another, so long as we are careful to pay back all our loans. Here is an example:

$$
\begin{array}{lll}
1. & (D \bullet E) \supset [F \supset (G \bullet H)] & \text{Premise} \\
2. & D \supset E \,/\, D \supset (F \supset H) & \text{Premise/Conclusion} \\
\quad 3. & D & \text{Assumption} \\
\quad 4. & E & \text{2,3 MP} \\
\quad 5. & D \bullet E & \text{3,4 Conj} \\
\quad 6. & F \supset (G \bullet H) & \text{1,5 MP} \\
\qquad 7. & F & \text{Assumption} \\
\qquad 8. & G \bullet H & \text{6,7 MP} \\
\qquad 9. & H & \text{8 Simp} \\
\quad 10. & F \supset H & \text{7–9 CP} \\
11. & D \supset (F \supset H) & \text{3–10 CP}
\end{array}
$$

Lines 7–9 are a secondary conditional proof within the primary conditional proof (lines 3–10). Notice that we had to close the secondary proof on line 10 in order to get back to the primary one—and then of course we had to close that one on line 11.

The second additional technique we're going to consider is called proof by **reductio ad absurdum** (RA). The Latin phrase means a reduction to absurdity or contradiction; the technique is to show that if we accept the premises of an argument, but deny the conclusion, we contradict ourselves. This is a good way to establish that the argument is valid, and it's the easiest method of proof for arguments like the following:

$$
\begin{array}{l}
(A \lor B) \supset (C \bullet D) \\
\underline{\smile(D \bullet A)} \\
\smile A
\end{array}
$$

To see that this is valid, let's deny the conclusion. That is, let's assume that A is true. If it is, then the antecedent of the first premise is also true (by addition). So we can infer the consequent: C and D are both true. But if D is true, and A is true, then the second premise is false. So the premises taken together are not consistent with the truth of A; they entail the conclusion $\smile A$.

The *reductio ad absurdum* technique is to take the negation of the conclusion, add it as an assumption (just as in conditional proof), and then from the premises and that assumption derive a contradiction—a statement of the form $p \bullet \smallsmile p$. For the argument above, the RA proof would look like this:

$$
\begin{array}{llll}
 & 1. & (A \lor B) \supset (C \bullet D) & \text{Premise} \\
 & 2. & \smallsmile(D \bullet A) \:/\: \smallsmile A & \text{Premise/conclusion} \\
 & 3. & \smallsmile\smallsmile A & \text{Assumption} \\
 & 4. & A & \text{3 DN} \\
 & 5. & A \lor B & \text{4 Add} \\
 & 6. & C \bullet D & \text{1,5 MP} \\
 & 7. & D & \text{6 Simp} \\
 & 8. & \smallsmile D \lor \smallsmile A & \text{2 DM} \\
 & 9. & \smallsmile D & \text{3,8 DS} \\
 & 10. & D \bullet \smallsmile D & \text{7,9 Conj} \\
 & 11. & \smallsmile A & \text{3–10 RA} \\
\end{array}
$$

We indent the *reductio* part of the argument, as we do in conditional proof, since our reasoning there is based on an assumption. Then on line 11 we state the conclusion we're entitled to draw from the *reductio* segment as a whole.

This completes our study of propositional logic, the logic of inferences involving the truth-functional connectives. Any such argument that is valid can be proven valid by the methods we covered in the last three sections. As we noted, however, our failure to find a proof for a given argument does *not* establish that the argument is invalid. Invalidity can be established only by the truth table tests.

Practice Quiz

Construct proofs for the following arguments. Use conditional proof for (1) and (2), *reductio* for (3). For the others, you'll have to decide which is the better method.

1. $A \supset (B \lor C)$
   $\dfrac{\smallsmile C}{A \supset B}$

2. $D \supset (E \supset F)$
   $\dfrac{D \supset (F \supset G)}{D \supset (E \supset G)}$

3. $(H \supset I) \supset J$
   $\dfrac{(H \bullet \smallsmile I) \supset J}{J}$

4. $K \supset (L \equiv M)$
   $\dfrac{\smallsmile L}{\smallsmile K \lor \smallsmile M}$

5. $\smallsmile(A \bullet B) \lor (C \supset D)$
   $A \lor \smallsmile C$
   $\dfrac{C}{B \supset D}$

6. $(E \supset F) \bullet (G \supset H)$
   $\dfrac{E \lor (I \supset G)}{I \supset (F \lor H)}$

7. (J ⊃ K) ⊃ (L • M)
   K ⊃ N
   L ⊃ ⌐N
   ⎯⎯⎯⎯
   ⌐K

8. (A ∨ B) ⊃ C
   ⌐A ⊃ (D • E)
   ⎯⎯⎯⎯⎯⎯
   C ∨ D

SUMMARY

Propositional logic is the logic of compound statements. We defined five basic types of compound statement, involving five different connectives: $p • q$ (conjunction), $⌐p$ (negation), $p ∨ q$ (disjunction), $p ⊃ q$ (conditional), and $p ≡ q$ (biconditional). From these basic forms, together with rules of punctuation, we can construct more complex compound statements. The truth value of each compound statement is a function of the truth values of its components, in accordance with the truth table for the connectives involved.

We can also use truth tables to test the validity of inferences. Both the premises and the conclusion of a propositional argument are truth functions of the component statements. We can therefore construct an entire truth table (or, in a shorter version, look for a particular assignment of truth values) to see whether it is possible for the conclusion to be false while the premises are true.

Alternatively, we can try to construct a proof: a derivation of the conclusion from the premises. An individual step in such a derivation may be justified by one of the ten basic inference forms, or by one of the ten rules of equivalence. We may also use the techniques of conditional proof and *reductio ad absurdum*.

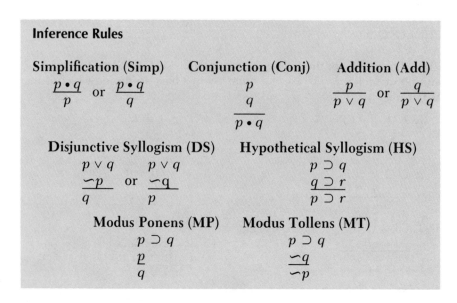

Inference Rules

Simplification (Simp)

$$\frac{p • q}{p} \text{ or } \frac{p • q}{q}$$

Conjunction (Conj)

$$\frac{\begin{matrix} p \\ q \end{matrix}}{p • q}$$

Addition (Add)

$$\frac{p}{p ∨ q} \text{ or } \frac{q}{p ∨ q}$$

Disjunctive Syllogism (DS)

$$\frac{\begin{matrix} p ∨ q \\ ⌐p \end{matrix}}{q} \text{ or } \frac{\begin{matrix} p ∨ q \\ ⌐q \end{matrix}}{p}$$

Hypothetical Syllogism (HS)

$$\frac{\begin{matrix} p ⊃ q \\ q ⊃ r \end{matrix}}{p ⊃ r}$$

Modus Ponens (MP)

$$\frac{\begin{matrix} p ⊃ q \\ p \end{matrix}}{q}$$

Modus Tollens (MT)

$$\frac{\begin{matrix} p ⊃ q \\ ⌐q \end{matrix}}{⌐p}$$

Constructive Dilemma (CD)

$$(p \supset q) \cdot (r \supset s)$$
$$\underline{p \vee r}$$
$$q \vee s$$

Destructive Dilemma (DD)

$$(p \supset q) \cdot (r \supset s)$$
$$\underline{\sim q \vee \sim s}$$
$$\sim p \vee \sim r$$

Equivalence Rules

Tautology (Taut): $p \equiv (p \cdot p)$
$$\equiv (p \vee p)$$
Double Negation (DN): $p \equiv \sim \sim p$
Commutation (Com): $(p \cdot q) \equiv (q \cdot p)$
$$(p \vee q) \equiv (q \vee p)$$
Association (Assoc): $[p \cdot (q \cdot r)] \equiv [(p \cdot q) \cdot r]$
$$[p \vee (q \vee r)] \equiv [(p \vee q) \vee r]$$
Distribution (Dist): $[p \cdot (q \vee r)] \equiv [(p \cdot q) \vee (p \cdot r)]$
$$[p \vee (q \cdot r)] \equiv [(p \vee q) \cdot (p \vee r)]$$
De Morgan's law (DM): $\sim(p \cdot q) \equiv (\sim p \vee \sim q)$
$$\sim(p \vee q) \equiv (\sim p \cdot \sim q)$$
Contrapositive (Contra): $(p \supset q) \equiv (\sim q \supset \sim p)$
Implication (Imp): $(p \supset q) \equiv (\sim p \vee q)$
$$\equiv \sim(p \cdot \sim q)$$
Biconditional (Bicon): $(p \equiv q) \equiv [(p \supset q) \cdot (q \supset p)]$
$$\equiv [(p \cdot q) \vee (\sim p \cdot \sim q)]$$
Exportation (Exp): $[(p \cdot q) \supset r] \equiv [p \supset (q \supset r)]$

Exercises

A. Find statements in English that have the following logical forms.

1. $(p \vee q) \cdot r$
2. $p \supset (q \vee \sim r)$
3. $(p \cdot q) \vee (r \cdot s)$
4. $(p \cdot \sim q) \supset r$
5. $(p \vee q) \cdot (r \vee s)$
6. $p \supset (q \supset r)$
7. $\sim p \supset (q \vee r)$
8. $p \supset \sim(q \cdot r)$
9. $\sim(p \cdot q) \supset (r \supset s)$
10. $[p \supset \sim(q \vee r)] \cdot s$

B. Each of the following statements is taken from a legal document. Translate the statement into symbolic notation.

1. *Publishing contract*: If the Author shall not have delivered the final manuscript by the date stipulated, and if within six months

of written notice from the Publisher to the Author said delivery shall not have been made or a new delivery date mutually agreed to, the Publisher may terminate this agreement and recover any advances made to the Author hereunder.

2. *U.S. Constitution (I,7)*: If any bill shall not be returned by the president within ten days, the same shall be a law . . . unless the Congress [has adjourned], in which case it shall not be a law.

3. *Credit card agreement*: If we find that we made a mistake on your bill, you will not have to pay any finance charges related to any questioned amount. If we didn't make a mistake, you may have to pay finance charges, and you will have to make up any missed payments on the questioned amount. In either case, we will send you a statement of the amount you owe and the date that it is due. [Treat this as a single conjunctive statement.]

4. New York State Penal Code: A person is guilty of murder in the first degree when [i.e., if and only if]:
    1. With intent to cause the death of another person, he causes the death of such person; and
    (a) Either:
        (i) the victim was a police officer . . . who was killed in the course of performing his official duties, and the defendant knew or reasonably should have known that the victim was a police officer; or
        (ii) the victim was an employee of a correctional institution . . . who was killed in the course of performing his official duties, and the defendant knew or reasonably should have known that the victim was an employee of a correctional institution; or
        (iii) at the time of the commission of the crime, the defendant was confined in a state correctional institution . . . upon a sentence for the term of his natural life . . . , or at the time of the commission of the crime, the defendant had escaped from such confinement . . . ; and
    (b) The defendant was more than eighteen years old at the time of the commission of the crime.

5. *California Penal Code Project*: A person's belief that his conduct does not constitute a crime is a defense only if it is reasonable and,
    (a) if the person's mistaken belief is due to his ignorance of the law defining the crime, he exercised all the care which . . . a law-abiding and prudent person would exercise to ascertain the law; or
    (b) if the person's mistaken belief is due to his misconception

of the meaning or application of the law defining the crime to his conduct,

(i)he acts in reasonable reliance upon an official statement of the law . . . ; or

(ii)he otherwise diligently pursues all means available to ascertain the meaning and application of the crime to his conduct.

C. Use truth tables to test each of the following arguments for validity.

1. $A \equiv B$
   $(A \cdot C) \supset D$
   $B \lor E$
   $\overline{D \lor E}$

2. $(F \cdot G) \supset [H \supset (I \cdot J)]$
   $G \supset H$
   $F \supset \neg J$
   $\overline{\neg F \lor \neg G}$

3. $[(K \lor L) \cdot M] \supset N$
   $(L \cdot M) \supset O$
   $\overline{\neg O \supset K}$

4. $(A \cdot B) \equiv (C \cdot D)$
   $\neg B \lor \neg D$
   $\overline{\neg A \cdot \neg C}$

5. $E \supset (F \cdot G)$
   $H \supset (I \lor J)$
   $F \supset (\neg I \cdot \neg J)$
   $\overline{\neg (E \cdot H)}$

6. $(K \supset L) \supset (M \supset N)$
   $\overline{(K \supset M) \supset (L \supset N)}$

7. $A \supset [B \supset (C \supset D]$
   $(C \supset D) \supset E$
   $F \lor A$
   $\overline{F \lor (B \supset E)}$

8. $(G \supset H) \cdot [(I \lor J) \supset K]$
   $(G \cdot I) \lor (G \cdot J)$
   $\overline{H \cdot K}$

9. $[A \lor (B \cdot C)] \supset D$
   $\neg (D \cdot E)$
   $A \supset E$
   $\overline{B \cdot C}$

10. $\{F \cdot [(G \lor H) \supset (I \cdot J)]\} \supset (F \lor G)$
    $F \cdot I$
    $G \supset \neg L$
    $\overline{\neg K \supset (H \lor \neg J)}$

D. Each of the following is an instance of one of the basic inference forms. Identify the form.

1. $(A \equiv B) \cdot [C \supset (D \cdot \neg E)]$
   $\overline{A \equiv B}$

2. $[(F \supset G) \lor H] \lor (G \cdot I)$
   $\neg [(F \supset G) \lor H]$
   $\overline{G \cdot I}$

3. $[J \lor (K \cdot L)]$
   $\overline{[J \lor (K \cdot L)] \lor J \supset L}$

4. $[(A \cdot B) \supset C] \cdot [(C \vee D) \supset B]$
   $\underline{[(A \cdot B) \vee (C \vee D)]}$
   $C \vee B$

5. $\smallfrown(E \cdot F) \supset [(E \supset G) \cdot (F \supset H)]$
   $\underline{\smallfrown(E \cdot F)}$
   $(E \supset G) \cdot (F \supset H)$

6. $\smallfrown I \supset [J \cdot (K \vee L)]$
   $\underline{J \supset (K \vee I)}$
   $\{\smallfrown I \supset [J \cdot (K \vee L)]\} \cdot [J \supset (K \vee L)]$

7. $(M \cdot N) \supset [(M \vee O) \cdot (N \vee O)]$
   $\underline{\smallfrown[(M \vee O) \cdot (N \vee O)]}$
   $\smallfrown(M \cdot N)$

8. $(A \vee B) \supset \smallfrown(C \vee D)$
   $\underline{\smallfrown(C \vee D) \supset (A \vee E)}$
   $(A \vee B) \supset (A \vee E)$

9. $[(F \vee G) \supset (G \vee H)] \cdot [(H \cdot I) \supset J]$
   $\underline{\smallfrown(G \supset H) \vee \smallfrown J}$
   $\smallfrown(F \vee G) \vee \smallfrown(H \cdot I)$

10. $(K \cdot L) \supset [M \cdot (N \vee O)]$
    $\underline{(K \cdot L) \supset (M \supset O)}$
    $\{(K \cdot L) \supset [M \cdot (N \vee O)]\} \cdot \{(K \cdot L) \supset [M \supset O)]\}$

11. $(A \cdot B) \vee [(A \cdot C) \supset (B \cdot C)]$
    $\underline{\smallfrown[(A \cdot C) \supset (B \cdot C)}$
    $A \cdot B$

12. $\underline{[(D \cdot E) \vee (D \cdot F)] \cdot [(E \cdot F) \vee (E \cdot D)]}$
    $(E \cdot F) \vee (E \cdot D)$

13. $[G \supset (H \cdot I)] \supset [J \cdot (I \supset K)]$
    $\underline{[J \cdot (I \supset K) \supset [(K \cdot G) \supset I]}$
    $[G \supset (H \cdot I)] \supset [(K \cdot G) \supset I]$

14. $\{(L \vee M) \supset [N \supset (O \supset M)]\} \cdot [(L \cdot N) \supset \smallfrown O]$
    $\underline{(L \vee M) \vee (L \cdot N)}$
    $[N \supset (O \supset M)] \vee \smallfrown O$

15. $[(A \vee B) \cdot (C \vee D)] \supset \{\smallfrown A \supset [D \cdot (E \vee C]\}$
    $\underline{\smallfrown\{\smallfrown A \supset [D \cdot (E \vee C)]\}}$
    $\smallfrown[(A \vee B) \cdot (C \vee D)]$

E. Each of the inferences below can be justified by one of the rules of equivalence. (The rule may have been applied to the whole premise or only to a component of the premise.) Name the rule.

1. $\dfrac{(A \bullet B) \vee C}{\backsim\backsim[(A \bullet B) \vee C]}$

2. $\dfrac{[(D \vee E) \vee F] \supset G}{[D \vee (E \vee F)] \supset G}$

3. $\dfrac{\backsim\{(H \supset I) \vee [J \bullet (K \vee L)]\}}{\backsim(H \supset I) \bullet \backsim[J \bullet (K \vee L)]}$

4. $\dfrac{[(A \vee B) \supset C] \supset (D \vee E)}{\backsim[(A \vee B) \supset C] \vee (D \vee E)}$

5. $\dfrac{[(F \bullet G) \bullet H] \supset (I \bullet J)}{\backsim(I \bullet J) \supset \backsim[(F \bullet G) \bullet H]}$

6. $\dfrac{(K \vee L) \bullet [M \supset (N \bullet O)]}{[M \supset (N \bullet O)] \bullet (K \vee L)}$

7. $\dfrac{(A \vee B) \supset (C \supset D)}{[(A \vee B) \supset (C \supset D)] \vee [(A \vee B) \supset (C \supset D)]}$

8. $\dfrac{[(E \vee F) \bullet G] \supset [(H \bullet I) \supset (I \supset J)]}{[(E \vee F) \bullet G] \supset [\backsim(H \bullet I) \vee (I \supset J)]}$

9. $\dfrac{(K \bullet L) \vee [(M \supset N) \bullet O]}{[(K \bullet L) \vee (M \supset N)] \bullet [(K \bullet L) \vee O]}$

10. $\dfrac{[(A \vee B) \supset C] \equiv (C \vee D)}{\{[(A \vee B) \supset C] \supset (C \vee D)\} \bullet \{(C \vee D) \supset [(A \vee B) \supset C]\}}$

11. $\dfrac{[(E \bullet F) \bullet G] \supset [(E \vee H) \bullet (E \vee I)]}{(E \bullet F) \supset \{G \supset [(E \vee H) \bullet (E \vee I)]\}}$

12. $\dfrac{\{(J \supset K) \supset [L \equiv (M \vee N)]\} \supset [J \supset (N \vee K)]}{\{(J \supset K) \supset [(L \vee L) \equiv (M \vee N)]\} \supset [J \supset (N \vee K)]}$

13. $\dfrac{[(A \bullet B) \vee C] \bullet [(A \vee C) \bullet (C \vee D)]}{[(A \bullet B) \vee C] \bullet [(C \vee A) \bullet (C \vee D)]}$

14. $\dfrac{[(E \bullet F) \vee (G \bullet H)] \bullet [(E \bullet F) \vee (I \supset J)]}{(E \bullet F \vee [(G \bullet H) \bullet (I \supset J)]}$

15. $\dfrac{\backsim\{[(K \vee L) \supset M] \bullet (N \vee O)\} \bullet [(L \bullet M) \supset N]}{\{\backsim[(K \vee L) \supset M] \vee \backsim(N \vee O)\} \bullet [(L \bullet M) \supset N]}$

F. Translate each of the arguments below into symbolic notation, and test it for validity by the truth table method. If it is valid, construct a proof.

1. Gravity is solely an attractive force. If so, then if the universe is not expanding, it is contracting due to gravitational attraction. But if the universe were contracting, the average density of

matter in space would be increasing, and it isn't. So the universe is expanding.

2. If the boss snaps at you if you make a mistake, he's irritable. So if he's irritable, and you make a mistake, he'll snap at you.

3. Smith is guilty of burglary if and only if he took the goods from Jones's residence and she did not consent to their removal. Smith did take the goods, but Jones consented. So Smith is not guilty of burglary.

4. Either human beings as a species evolved in Africa and later dispersed in migration to various other regions, or their precursors migrated at an earlier time and modern humans evolved independently in various regions. If the precursors of humans migrated at an earlier time, then it should not be the case—and it is—that we find their remains only in Africa. Therefore humans evolved in Africa.

5. It's a sure bet that the antacid division of the Hi-5 corporation is going to be sold. Hi-5 stock is going to decline unless the company improves its profits or the economy as a whole improves. The company will not improve its profits unless it sells the antacid division. On the other hand, if Hi-5 stock declines, the company will be taken over and its antacid division will be sold.

6. Bosnia has threatened to attack our commercial vessels in the shipping lanes off its shores. If we take preventive action, and the threat is not real, we will be denounced for aggression. If the threat is real and we do not take preventive action, the attack will succeed; and if it succeeds, lives will be lost and further attacks will be encouraged in the future. None of these consequences is acceptable. We shall not be denounced for aggression, and we shall neither lose lives nor encourage future attacks. Therefore we will take preventive action if and only if the threat is real.

7. If I take his pawn with my knight, he will either take my knight or move his bishop to the space my knight is now guarding. If he takes my knight, I'll lose a valuable piece, but his queen will be exposed. If he moves his bishop to that space, *my* queen will be exposed. But if I don't take his pawn with my knight, my queen will be exposed anyway. I'm either going to take his pawn or not take it. So either his queen or mine will be exposed.

8. If the traditional religious view is correct, God is both omnipotent and perfectly benevolent. If God is omnipotent, He is capable of preventing evil, and if He is perfectly benevolent, he would want to prevent evil. But if God wanted to prevent evil, and was capable of doing so, then there would be no evil, and there is. So the traditional religious view is not correct.

G. Show that each of the following arguments is valid by constructing a proof.

1. $A \supset (B \cdot C)$
$\frown(A \supset D)$
$\overline{B}$

2. $(E \lor F) \supset G$
$\frown H \supset F$
$\frown G$
$\overline{H \cdot \frown E}$

3. $A \supset (B \supset C)$
$(\frown D \lor E) \supset (F \lor G)$
$\frown(D \supset E) \supset (B \cdot \frown C)$
$\overline{A \supset (F \supset G)}$

4. $(H \cdot I) \supset J$
$(I \supset J) \supset (K \lor L)$
$\overline{\frown L \supset (H \supset K)}$

5. $A \cdot (B \supset C)$
$(B \cdot \frown A) \lor (B \cdot D)$
$\overline{C \cdot D}$

6. $(\frown E \cdot F) \supset G$
$(H \cdot J) \supset (E \lor J)$
$\frown E \cdot (F \lor \frown J)$
$\overline{H \supset (J \supset G)}$

7. $[(A \cdot B) \lor C] \supset [D \supset (E \cdot F)]$
$B \cdot \frown(A \supset E)$
$\overline{D \supset F}$

8. $(G \cdot H) \lor [(I \lor J) \cdot (K \supset L)]$
$(J \supset M) \cdot \frown I$
$G \equiv N$
$\overline{M \lor N}$

9. $(A \supset B) \cdot \frown(C \supset D)$
$\frown A \supset D$
$[(A \cdot C) \lor B] \supset E$
$B \supset (F \equiv G)$
$\overline{G \supset E}$

10. $(H \equiv J) \lor (H \equiv K)$
$J \supset (L \cdot M)$
$K \supset (N \cdot M)$
H
$\overline{M}$

11. $A \equiv B$
$[(C \supset D) \bullet \sim D] \vee [A \bullet \sim(C \bullet \sim D)]$
$\dfrac{(B \vee E) \supset F}{C \supset F}$

12. $[(G \bullet H) \supset (I \vee J)] \supset \sim G$
$\dfrac{(K \vee G) \supset (I \bullet L)}{\sim G}$

13. $[(A \vee B) \bullet C] \supset [(A \vee D) \bullet (A \vee E)]$
$\dfrac{C \bullet \sim A}{B \supset (D \bullet E)}$

14. $(F \bullet G) \supset [H \supset (I \bullet J)$
$G \supset \sim J$
$\dfrac{F \supset H}{\sim F \vee \sim G}$

15. $\sim(A \bullet B) \supset [C \supset (D \supset E)]$
$[(A \bullet B) \vee F] \supset (G \bullet H)$
$[(C \bullet D) \supset E] \supset I$
$\dfrac{J \supset (G \supset \sim H)}{J \supset I}$

16. $\dfrac{[K \supset (L \supset K)] \supset (\sim M \supset M)}{M}$

17. $(A \vee B) \supset [\sim(C \bullet D) \supset E]$
$B \bullet C$
$E \supset (F \vee G)$
$\dfrac{(B \supset \sim F) \bullet (C \supset \sim G)}{D}$

18. $H \equiv \{ I \bullet [(J \bullet K) \vee (L \bullet M)] \}$
$\dfrac{[I \bullet (K \vee L)] \supset N}{H \supset N}$

19. $(A \bullet \sim B) \supset (C \bullet D)$
$E \bullet \sim F$
$(G \bullet E) \supset \sim(A \equiv B)$
$\dfrac{(B \bullet \sim A) \supset F}{G \supset C}$

20. $H \supset \{ I \bullet [(J \bullet K) \supset (L \bullet M)] \}$
$\dfrac{K \supset \sim(I \bullet L)}{J \supset \sim(H \bullet K)}$

13

Predicate Logic

Propositional logic allows us to analyze arguments that depend on logical relationships among compound propositions. The units of analysis are component propositions—p, q, r, etc.—along with the truth-functional connectives. But some arguments require a finer-grained analysis. An obvious example is the categorical syllogism:

> No herbivore eats meat
> <u>All horses</u> are herbivores
> No horse eats meat

Neither the premises nor the conclusion of this argument are compound, so the representation of the argument in propositional logic would be:

$$p$$
$$q$$
$$r,$$

which gives no clue that the argument is valid. To understand its validity, we need to break the propositions down into their elements, and this is the function of **predicate logic.**

Like the classical logic of categorical syllogisms, which we studied in Chapter 9, predicate logic breaks a proposition down into a subject and a predicate. But it does so in a different way from classical logic. In the first two sections of this chapter, we'll go over the symbolic notation that is used to represent the inner structure of propositions. Then we'll go on to learn a few new rules of inference, and see how to use them (along with the propositional rules from the last chapter) in constructing proofs.

Quantifiers

Singular Statements

Consider the statements:

1) London is a city.
2) Our galaxy is immense.
3) Jane got married last Saturday.

Each of these is a *singular* proposition; it makes a statement about a single thing. This is true even in (2): our galaxy contains a great many things, but the statement treats it as a single unit. In each case, the subject—"London," "our galaxy," and "Jane"—is a name for the particular thing that the statement is about. And in each case, the rest of the statement is the predicate, whose function is to say something about what is named.

The predicate may indicate a category of things to which the object belongs, as in (1). It may indicate an attribute of the object, as in (2), or an action, as in (3). It is important to note that the predicate includes the copula ("is" in the first two examples) as well as the predicate term. Modern predicate logic does not separate these elements, as classical logic did. One consequence is that we don't need to translate a statement like (3) into a form that contains "is": "Jane is a person who got married last Saturday." The statement as given is already in standard form; the predicate is "got married last Saturday."

To represent the statements symbolically, we need two symbols, one for the subject, one for the predicate. It is conventional to use capital letters for the predicate, lower case letters for the subject, with the predicate letter given first. Thus the statements above would be symbolized:

1) *Cl*
2) *Ig*
3) *Mj*

This will probably seem foreign to you at first, since it reverses the order of English grammar. It may help to think of the symbolic formula as saying that the predicate is true of the subject: *C* is true of *l*, *I* is true of *g*, *M* is true of *j*. Notice too that the letters we used were suggested by the actual examples. When we are not working with an actual example, it is customary to use *a, b, c, . . .* as subjects, and *P, Q, R, . . .* as predicates.

Singular statements can be combined into compound statements by means of the usual connectives, and everything we learned about the logic of connectives applies to such statements. Here are some examples:

4) Tom is not married: ⁻*Mt*
5) If London is a city, then it has a mayor: *Cl* ⊃ *Ml*
6) Our galaxy is immense, and so is Freddie's ego: *Ig* • *Ie*
7) If the moon is out tonight and the sea is calm, I'll go for a sail or a walk on the beach: (*Om* • *Cs*) ⊃ (*Si* ∨ *Wi*)

Notice that the component singular statements may share the same subject or the same predicate.

Practice Quiz

Put each of the following statements into symbolic notation.

1. Tobias is bored.
2. President Reagan was popular.
3. The solar system is billions of years old.
4. My car is a Volkswagon and his car is a Rolls.
5. Monaco is either a big city or a small nation.
6. If Dean Witter speaks, I listen.
7. I'm confused and you are not helping.
8. If we win, we'll either go dancing or go to a movie.

General Statements

But suppose we want to make a general statement about a class of things rather than an individual object. Suppose we want to say that all cities have mayors. We can't take the predicate *C* ("is a city") and make it the subject: *MC*. The literal translation of this would be "is a city has a mayor," which doesn't make any sense. Instead, predicate logic uses a device called the **bound variable**. Let's see how it works.

In statement (5) above, the consequent is "it has a mayor." We know that the pronoun "it" stands for London because London is named in the antecedent. That's why we symbolized the consequent as *Ml*. But suppose the consequent were a free-standing statement, without any antecedent. In that case we would know that "it" stands for something, but we wouldn't know what; it could stand for anything. In logic, we would represent such an "it" by the letter *x*, and the statement "it is a mayor" would be symbolized *Mx*. The letter *x* functions as a variable. In the mathematical equation $x + x = 2x$, *x* stands for *any* number, without specifying *which* number; in the logical formula Mx, x can stand for any individual thing without specifying which thing.

The formula Mx—"it has a mayor"—is not a complete statement. Because it doesn't tell us what x stands for, it doesn't make an assertion that is true or false. To complete it, we need to connect x with individual things in the world. We could do this by replacing x with an individual name: London, Paris, Rome, etc. But then we would have a singular statement again, and what we want is a way to make general statements. We can accomplish this by introducing a **quantifier**, which tells us whether Mx is being asserted of all x (everything in the world) or of some x (at least one thing in the world).

In the first case, we use a **universal** quantifier, symbolized by an x in parentheses at the front of the statement: $(x)Mx$. Any of the following would be a literal translation of this formula:

> For any x, x has a mayor
> Take anything whatever: it has a mayor
> "It has a mayor" is true of everything

All of these are fancy ways of saying that everything has a mayor. Of course this statement is quite false. You and I and the Liberty Bell are all individual things in the world, and none of us has a mayor. At most we can say that some things (namely, cities) have mayors. To make this statement, we use the **existential** quantifier, symbolized by a backwards E and placed, once again, at the front of the statement: $(\exists x)Mx$. Any of the following would be a literal translation:

> For some x, x has a mayor
> There exists something such that it has a mayor
> "It has a mayor" is true of at least one thing

All of these are equivalent to the statement, in ordinary English, that something has a mayor.

The use of a quantifier, then, completes a statement containing a variable. An expression of the form Px is called an **open sentence,** and its variable is said to be *free.* When we preface it with a quantifier, the quantifier *binds* the variable by telling us how to interpret it, and the result is a **closed sentence** or statement. You may have noticed that the universal and existential quantifiers are analogous to the quantifiers "all" and "some" in classical logic. In particular, $(\exists x)$ and "some" both mean "at least one." But there's an important difference. In classical logic, the quantifier modifies the subject term; it tells us whether we are talking about all or some S. In predicate logic, however, the quantifier modifies the variable, which ranges over everything that exists; the quantifier tells us whether we are talking about all or some of the things in the universe.

And this brings us back to our question: how do we symbolize a statement of the form "All S are P," such as "All cities have mayors"? This statement does not say that everything is a city, nor that everything has a mayor. But it does say that *if* something is a city, then it has a mayor. This is the key to the symbolic translation. A statement of this form is treated as a conditional statement, with the same variable used as the subject in both antecedent and consequent: $(x)(Cx \supset Mx)$. This formula employs both the bound variable of predicate logic and a connective from propositional logic. A literal translation would be: for any x, if x is a city, then it has a mayor. What about a statement of the form "Some S is P," such as "Some tests are difficult"? This tells us that there is at least one thing in the world that is both a test and difficult. So in this case we would use the existential quantifier and conjunction: $(\exists x)(Tx \cdot Dx)$.

The general rule, then, is that universal statements are treated as conditionals, particular statements as conjunctions. The four traditional standard forms of categorical statement would be translated as follows:

A: All S are P $\qquad$ $(x) (Sx \supset Px)$
E: No S is P $\qquad$ $(x) (Sx \supset {\sim}Px)$
I: Some S are P $\qquad$ $(\exists x) (Sx \cdot Px)$
O: Some S are not P $\qquad$ $(\exists x) (Sx \cdot {\sim}Px)$

Notice that the subject term becomes a predicate in the symbolic translation. In predicate logic, the only things that can be subjects are names and variables. The result is that what looks like a simple statement in English becomes a compound statement involving a connective, with a single variable occurring twice.

The two components in which the variable occurs are both placed within parentheses immediately after the quantifier. This is to indicate that the quantifier applies to the entire statement, and binds the variable in both occurrences. If we did not use parentheses—$(x)Sx \supset Px$ or $(\exists x)Sx \cdot Px$—the quantifier would apply only to the component immediately following it, and the second component in each case would remain an open sentence with a free variable. To have a closed sentence, or statement, we must use parentheses to bring every variable within the *scope* of a quantifier.

Notice finally that a particular statement is translated as a conjunction, while a universal statement is translated as a conditional. That is, they differ in the *connective* as well as the quantifier that is used. Why can't we use the same connective? Well, let's try it. Suppose we use conjunction for the universal statement. "Every accountant understands arithmetic" would be $(x)(Ax \cdot Ux)$. This won't work because the English statement is true, but the symbolic statement, which says that everything in the universe is both an accountant and understands arithmetic, is obviously false. The other possibility is to treat the particular statement as a conditional. "Some cheese is introverted" would then be $(\exists x)(Cx \supset Ix)$. Once again the translation fails, this time because the English statement is false and the symbolic one true. The symbolic statement says: there is at least one thing of which it is true to say "if it's a cheese then it's introverted." And there are many things of which this statement is true (you, Mussolini, the Grand Canyon) because the antecedent is false. Because the quantifiers range over everything in the universe, therefore, we must use different connectives for the two types of statement.

We can use the apparatus of variables, predicates, and quantifiers to make statements of any complexity. We are not limited to two terms, as in classical logic. We can have more than two predicates, linked by more than one connective. Here are some examples:

1) All banks that are chartered by the federal government can borrow from the Federal Reserve System: $(x)[(Bx \cdot Cx) \supset Fx]$, where Bx means x is a bank, Cx means x is chartered by the federal government, and Fx means x can borrow from the Federal Reserve System.

2) Butter and eggs are rich in cholesterol: $(x)[(Bx \vee Ex) \supset Cx]$. Notice that we have to translate "and" as disjunction rather than conjunction. The same substance cannot be both butter and egg; the point is that if it falls into either category, then it is rich in cholesterol.

3) Some plants will grow only if they are fertilized: $(\exists x)[Px \cdot (Gx \supset Fx)]$. Notice that even though this involves a conditional element, the main connective is conjunction. We're saying of something that it has two properties: it's a plant and if it grows then it has been fertilized.

Practice Quiz

Put each of the following statements into symbolic notation.

1. All skyscrapers are buildings.
2. Some buildings are skyscrapers.
3. No person is omniscient.
4. Some people are not sensible.
5. Some knights wore armor.
6. A convertible debenture is a bond.
7. Some ketones are used as solvents.

8. No fallacious argument is sound.
9. Some great books are not remembered or not appreciated.
10. Every great book is appreciated if it is remembered.

Existential Import

The symbolic translations of the standard categorical propositions raise an important issue. In our earlier treatment of such propositions, we assumed that the subject term S stood for some category of things in reality. We assumed that the category had some members; the only question was whether we were speaking about all or some of them. In predicate logic, the particular statements, symbolized by the existential quantifier, carry the same implication. Because these statements involve conjunction, they can't be true unless there exists at least one S. These statements therefore have what logicians call **existential import.** But the universal propositions lack existential import. Because they are conditionals, they do not actually assert the existence of any Ss; all they say is that *if* anything is S, it is also P (or is not P, in the case of the E statement). This lack of existential import has a surprising consequence. Suppose that a certain term S is *vacuous*—that is, there are no Ss, so that Sx is not true of anything. Then any universal statement about Ss is true by default. Any statement of the form $(x)(Sx \supset \ldots)$ is true, regardless of the consequent, because the antecedent is not true of anything.

Is it proper to treat universal statements as lacking existential import? Something can be said on both sides of this question. If I told you that all nematodes are worms, you would have a right to feel cheated if I went on to say that the statement is true because there aren't any nematodes. In a discussion of mythology, on the other hand, there would be no problem if you said that a phoenix is a bird, even though no such creature actually exists. Again, the statement "Everyone convicted of treason last year was executed" seems to imply that some people were in fact convicted of treason last year. But the warning "No trespassing! All violators will be prosecuted" does not seem to imply the existence of any actual violators; indeed, the purpose of the warning is to prevent there from being any.

Like the question we raised in the last chapter about the truth-functional interpretation of conditional statements, this question about existential import is controversial, and it raises a number of deep issues about logic and language that we can't go into here. Suffice it to say that modern predicate logic is built around the assumption that universal statements are to be treated as conditionals, and thus lack existential import. The resulting translations will seem unnatural for statements like "Everyone convicted of treason last year was executed." To capture the existential import of this proposition in English, we must conjoin the universally quantified statement $(x)(Cx \supset Ex)$ with the existentially quantified statement $(\exists x)Cx$, which says that someone was convicted.

The assumption that universal statements lack existential import also affects the logical relationships among categorical propositions. In Chapter 8, we used the square of opposition to represent these relationships:

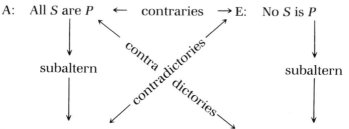

A: All S are P   ⟵   contraries   → E: No S is P

subaltern   subaltern

contra dictories

contra dictories

I: Some S are P ⟵ subcontraries → O: Some S are not P

Now let's put each proposition into symbolic form:

A: $(x)\,(Sx \supset Px)$ E: $(x)\,(Sx \supset \mathord{\sim} Px)$

I: $(\exists x)\,(Sx \cdot Px)$ O: $(\exists x)\,(Sx \cdot \mathord{\sim} Px)$

Because the A statement lacks existential import, the subaltern relation no longer holds. If there are no Ss, A is true and I is false. The same point applies to E and O. What about the relation between A and E? In Chapter 9 we said these are contraries because, while they might both be false, they could not both be true. But that was based on the assumption that A and E are always statements about a class of actual Ss. If S is a vacuous term, however, then both $(x)(Sx \supset Px)$ and $(x)(Sx \supset \mathord{\sim} Px)$ are true because the antecedent of each conditional (Sx) is false of every object. Similarly, I and O are no longer subcontraries because they could both be false —if, once again, there are no Ss.

The one thing that survives from the traditional square of opposition is the fact that A and O are contradictory, and so are E and I. In each case, the two statements cannot both be true, and they cannot both be false. If there exists a single thing that is both S and not P, the O statement is true and the A statement false. But if nothing is both S and not P, then the O statement is false, and the A statement is true—even if the absence of things that are S and not P is due to the fact that there aren't any Ss at all. The same reasoning applies to

E and I. So A is true if and only if O is false, and E is true if and only if I is false.

The symbolic square of opposition, then, looks like this:

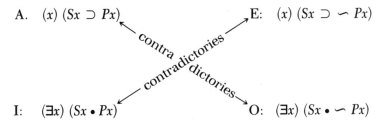

A. $(x) (Sx \supset Px)$
E: $(x) (Sx \supset \sim Px)$

contradictories

contradictories

I: $(\exists x) (Sx \cdot Px)$
O: $(\exists x) (Sx \cdot \sim Px)$

Practice Quiz

Put each of the following statements into symbolic notation. Then determine whether it has existential import.

1. Everything's groovy.
2. Something smells.
3. Some galaxies do not have a spiral shape.
4. Every cloud has a silver lining.
5. Some pitchers are good hitters.
6. No freshman can take this course.
7. Only freshmen can take this course. [Careful: "only" is a quantifier here, not a connective; see page 241.]
8. Some cars are turbocharged.
9. Any car that is turbocharged is fun to drive.
10. All trees are either evergreen or deciduous.
11. Dobermans and German shepherds are loyal and fierce.
12. Some near-sighted people cannot wear soft lenses.
13. Some people who can't swim enjoy sailing.
14. No flower will grow if it doesn't get water.
15. Only seniors who have completed the requirements for the major are eligible for this course.

Relations and Multiple Quantification

The apparatus of variables and quantifiers takes some getting used to. But it has the virtue of giving us a flexible way to put complex statements into standard logical form. In the last section, we saw how predicates can be related by connectives within the scope of a single quantifier. In this section, we'll see how the apparatus handles two additional types of complexity, both involving the use of more than one quantifier.

Combining Quantified Statements

The statements we have dealt with so far had propositional connectives occurring within the scope of the quantifier. But connectives may also occur outside its scope. For example:

1) There are no ghosts: $\sim (\exists x)Gx$.

The negation sign precedes the quantifier, so that the symbolic expression is to be read: it's not the case that there exists a ghost. This is a different statement from

1a) $(\exists x) \sim Gx$,

which says merely that something is not a ghost, and doesn't deny that something (else) might be a ghost.

Now consider the statement:

2) If everything is physical, there are no ghosts.

This is a conditional statement; the antecedent is "everything is physical," and the consequent is "there are no ghosts." Because each component is separately quantified, we'll use separate variables and quantifiers. And the horseshoe symbol that joins these statements, like the negation sign, will fall outside the scope of either quantifier:

2) $(x)Px \supset \sim (\exists y)Gy$

In short, quantified statements, like any other kind, can be put together by means of connectives into compound statements, and this often provides us with the most natural translation of a sentence in English. Here's a more complex example:

3) Either all the gears are broken, or a cylinder is missing

$$(x)(Gx \supset Bx) \vee (\exists y)(Cy \bullet My)$$

In this case we have connectives both inside and outside the scope of the quantifiers.

In the examples above, we used different variables to indicate that the components of the compound statement are separately quantified. This isn't really necessary. The parenthesis after Bx in (3) tells us that that is where the scope of the universal quantifier ends. Its scope does not overlap with that of the existential quantifier governing the second disjunct. So by the time we get to the missing cylinder, we're free to use x again to refer to it; there would be no ambiguity about which quantifier governed the variable. Later in the section, however, we will deal with quantifiers that *do* overlap in scope. In that case it will be necessary to use different variables, so we might as well adopt this practice from the outset.

It is usually obvious which connectives to use in symbolizing a statement. In order to tell whether they belong inside or outside the scope of the quantifiers, we need to think carefully about what the statement means. Let's look at a few more examples where the placement of the connective makes a difference. Consider the statement:

4) Everything has a location in space and time.

Using S for "has a location in space" and T for "has a location in time," we could translate this in either of two ways:

4a) $(x)(Sx \cdot Tx)$, or
4b) $(x)Sx \cdot (y)Ty$

(4a) says that for each thing, it has a location in space and a location in time. (4b) says that for each thing, it has a location in space, and for each thing, it has a location in time. These are clearly equivalent. But now consider a different statement:

5) Everything is either mental or physical.

Once again we might think of two possible translations:

5a) $(x)(Mx \lor Px)$, or
5b) $(x)Mx \lor (y)Py$

These are *not* equivalent. (5a) says of each thing that it is either mental or physical, and thus allows that the universe might contain two different kinds of thing. But (5b) says that the universe is monolithic: either everything is mental or everything is physical.

Thus with a universal quantifier, it doesn't matter where we put a sign of conjunction, but it does matter where we put a sign of disjunction. The opposite is true for the existential quantifier:

6a) Something is hot and cold $(\exists x)(Hx \cdot Cx)$
6b) Something is hot and something is cold $(\exists x)Hx \cdot (\exists y)Cy$
6c) Something is hot or cold $(\exists x)(Hx \lor Cx)$
6d) Something is hot or something is cold $(\exists x)Hx \lor (\exists y)Cy$

Can you see why (6c) and (6d) are equivalent, but (6a) and (6b) are not?

Practice Quiz

Put each of the following statements into symbolic notation. Decide whether each connective falls inside or outside the scope of the relevant quantifiers. If it makes no difference, do it both ways.

1. A building collapsed.
2. Someone got hurt, and no one helped.
3. If everyone cheated, no grades would be meaningful.
4. Some laws are not enforced.
5. Not every law is enforced.
6. Someone is either whistling or playing a radio.
7. Every physical object has a size and a mass.
8. Every corporation is either making money or losing money.

Relations

In addition to talking about things and their properties, we can talk about the *relationships* among things, and to represent such statements symbolically, we often need more than one quantifier. To see how this works, let's start, as before, with singular statements about relationships. Here are some examples:

7) Brazil is larger than Uruguay.
8 Jane was married to Dan last Saturday.
9) Ed Koch is mayor of New York.

Each of these asserts that two things are related in a certain way. Grammatically, the statements have a subject-predicate structure, and in each case the second thing named (Uruguay, Dan, and New York) is part of the predicate. And we could follow the grammar when we translate into symbolic notation. In (7), for example, the predicate would be "is larger than Uruguay," and we would translate the statement as: *Lb*.

But we can also break things down in a different way. We could treat Uruguay as a *subject*, alongside Brazil. The predicate would then be "is larger than," and we would interpret the statement as saying that this relational predicate is true of Brazil and Uruguay as a pair. To symbolize the statement, on this approach, we need a predicate letter and *two* subject letters: *Lbu*. In the same way, "Jane" and "Dan" are the subjects of (8), and the predicate is "was married to last Saturday": *Mjd*. In (9), "Ed Koch" and "New York" are subjects of the relational predicate "is mayor of": *Mkn*. Notice that we have to be careful about the order in which we list the subject letters. This doesn't matter much in (8) because getting married is a symmetrical relationship: Jane and Dan were married to each other. But that's a special case. If we reversed the letters in (7), we'd have the false statement that Uruguay is larger than Brazil; if we reversed the letters in (9), we'd be saying that New York is mayor of Ed Koch, which doesn't even make sense.

Once we allow that a statement can have more than one subject, there's no reason to stop at two. Many statements assert that some relationship exists among three or more items. In symbolic form, we use a relational predicate and as many subject letters as we need. Consider the statement:

10) Lorna sold the Brooklyn Bridge to June.

Here we have a relationship among three things: two people and a bridge. It would be a little awkward to put the predicate in a phrase, as we have been doing. It's easier to think of it as a sentence structure, with slots in the places where the subjects go:

_____ sold _____ to _____.

If we let S stand for this structure, we can symbolize statement (10) by adding letters for the subjects, in the proper order: $Slbj$. Since the structure has three slots for subjects, S is called a three-place predicate. "Is mayor of" is a two-place predicate, and "is white" is a one-place predicate; moving in the other direction, we can have n-place predicates, where n is any number.

All of our relational statements thus far have been *singular* statements. Even though they are statements about more than one thing, they say something about particular items that are named as individuals. In the last section, we saw that we can form general statements by replacing names with variables. We can do the same for statements involving relations. Suppose we know that Ed Koch is mayor of *something*, but we don't know what. Instead of using the letter n, for New York, we'd use the variable x, along with the existential quantifier:

11) Ed Koch is mayor of something: $(\exists x)Mkx$.

Here are some other examples of quantified relational statements. Look them over carefully to make sure you understand the rationale behind each symbolic translation.

12) Everything that exists is a product of the Big Bang: $(x)Pxb$
13) Something caused the explosion: $(\exists x)Cxe$
14) No South American country is larger than Brazil: $(x)(Sx \supset \sim Lxb$

15) Something is rotten in the state of Denmark: $(\exists x)(Sxd \bullet Rx)$ [where S means "is in the state of"]
16) Lorna sold something to June: $(\exists x)Slxj$
17) I gave my dog a bone: $(\exists x)(Bx \bullet Gixd)$ [where B means "is a bone" and G means "_____ gave _____ to _____."]

Practice Quiz

Put each of the following statements into symbolic notation.

1. The Mets lost to the Cubs.
2. I ran into Alison at Disneyland.
3. Adam ate an apple.
4. A snake spoke to Eve.
5. All roads lead to Rome.
6. Some people are not fans of Bruce Springsteen.
7. Some actions of the government are capricious.
8. If someone enters the premises, an alarm will go off.

Overlapping Quantifiers

The relational statements we've examined so far have a variable in one of the subject positions, bound by a single quantifier. But we can also have variables in more than one position, each bound by a separate quantifier, as long as we observe a few simple rules. Suppose we wanted to symbolize the general statement that everything has a cause. We would use the same two-place predicate we used above in (13): _____ causes _____. But now we will need variables in both slots. For any given event like the explosion, we're saying that something caused it: $(\exists x)Cxe$. But we're saying much more than this. We're saying that this is true of *everything*, not just the explosion. So instead of putting e in the second slot, we use a second variable y, and then bind that variable with a second quantifier:

18) For everything that exists, there's something that causes it: $(y)(\exists x)Cxy$

We had to use a second variable here to refer to that which is caused, because we are already using x to refer to that which causes. If we used the same variable in both roles—Cxx—we'd be talking about things that cause themselves, and that was not our intent.

Because we have a second variable, we need a second quantifier to bind it, and the order of variables is important. A literal translation of $(y)(\exists x)Cxy$ would be: for every y, there is an x such that x causes y. This statement allows the possibility that things do not all have the same cause; each y may be caused by a different x. But the statement $(\exists x)(y)Cxy$ *does* imply a single cause for everything; it says that there exists an x that causes all y. The order of quantifiers is important here because one is universal and the other particular; you should always be careful, in cases of this kind, to put the quantifiers in the order that captures the meaning of the statement. If we have a statement with two or more quantifiers of the *same* kind, however, then order does not matter. At some point in your studies you may have had the insight that everything is related to everything; this could be symbolized either as $(x)(y)Rxy$ or as $(y)(x)Rxy$. Likewise, the statement that something bumped into something could be symbolized either as $(\exists x)(\exists y)Bxy$ or as $(\exists y)(\exists x)Bxy$.

Relational predicates and multiple quantification are devices that make predicate logic a very flexible and powerful instrument for analyzing statements. But learning to use these devices properly takes practice. We've been working so far with rather simple statements. To get a better feel for the system, it will help to work through some examples that are more complex.

Let's start with the statement:

19) Everyone is afraid of something.

This looks like the statement about causality, but we can't analyze it in quite the same way. The parallel translation would be $(x)(\exists y)Axy$. But this says that every thing—rocks, trees, and hurricanes as well as people—is afraid of something, and we're talking only about people. The most natural way to add this information would be as follows: $(x)(Px \supset (\exists y)Axy)$. This says it's true of every x that if x is a person, then there is a y such that x is afraid of it. The scope of the universal quantifier is the entire statement, so it binds x in both occurrences, whereas the scope of the existential quantifier is limited to Axy. That's okay, because Axy is the only occurrence of y. All that matters is that every occurrence of a given variable fall within the scope of the corresponding quantifier.

To illustrate another important point, let's go back to an earlier example:

8) Jane was married to Dan last Saturday.

We treated this as a statement with a two-place predicate: "_____ was married to _____ last Saturday." But we could also treat the time, last Saturday, as a subject filling a slot in a three-place predi-

cate: "_____ was married to _____, _____." It would be necessary to do this if we were dealing with the statement that Jane and
Dan got married at some point in time; the translation would be
$(\exists x)(Tx \cdot Mjdx)$, where Tx says that x is a time. Similarly, we would
translate the statement that they were married somewhere as
$(\exists x)(Px \cdot Mjdx)$, where Px says that x is a place. Bound variables for
times and places are used to translate words like "at some time,"
"once," "always," "somewhere," "everywhere." (Be careful,
though. As we noted in Chapter 11, these expressions are sometimes used merely as alternative ways of making ordinary universal
or particular statements, as in "triangles always have three sides.")

Before we can translate a statement, we need to know how many
different things we are referring to, and which predicates are being
asserted of them, in which combinations. With complex statements,
this is not always obvious, and it helps to proceed in stages. Consider the statement:

20) Any undergraduate who excels in a subject knows more about
it than some graduate students in that subject.

It is immediately clear that this is about undergraduates who excel,
and that it's about all of them. So let's let x stand for them, and
rewrite the sentence in a kind of pidgin English-symbolic form:

$(x)[(x$ is an undergraduate $\bullet x$ excels in a subject) $\supset$ (x knows more
about it than some graduate student in that subject)]

Because this is a universal statement, it is formulated as a
conditional.

For the second conjunct in the antecedent, which refers to "a
subject," we'll need another variable y, and y is also referred to in
the consequent ("it" and "that subject"). So now we have:

$(x)(y)[(x$ is an undergraduate $\bullet y$ is a subject $\bullet x$ excels in y) $\supset$ (x
knows more about y than some graduate students in y)]

Now we can add a third variable for graduate students:

$(x)(y)[(x$ is an undergraduate $\bullet y$ is a subject $\bullet x$ excels in y) $\supset$
$(\exists z)(z$ is a graduate student $\bullet x$ knows more about y than z
does)]

We have now quantified everything that needs quantifying, and
used connectives to define the propositional structure of the statement. In doing so, we have isolated the predicate elements, and the
only remaining task is to introduce symbols for them:

$$(x)(y) \{[(Ux \cdot Sy) \cdot Exy] \supset (\exists z)(Gz \cdot Kxyz)]\}$$

Let's pause here for some practice at translation. In the next section, we'll turn to the nature of proof in predicate logic.

Practice Quiz

Put each of the following statements into symbolic notation. If you need to use the same letter for different predicates, use primes: *P, P', P''*, etc.

1. The mailman is afraid of my dog.
2. Memphis is south of St. Louis and north of New Orleans.
3. Memphis is between St. Louis and New Orleans.
4. I have a dream.
5. Peggy married some guy from Duluth.
6. Mary had a little lamb.
7. If there were no evil, there would be no good.
8. Something I ate did not agree with me.
9. Every senior is older than every freshman.
10. Some freshman is older than any senior.
11. There are no resorts in Greenland.
12. No student may cheat at any time.
13. Something there is that does not love a wall.
14. If whales are mammals, then not all mammals live on land.
15. Everyone is someone's fool.
16. Not a sound was heard by anyone.
17. Anyone who buys a used car from Marty is either a fool or has money to burn.
18. No one can please everyone all of the time.

Proof

In predicate as in propositional logic, we use proofs to establish that a conclusion follows validly from a set of premises. And proof in predicate logic has the same structure: we proceed step by step from the premises, in accordance with equivalence rules and rules of inference, until we reach the conclusion. In order to work with quantifiers, we're going to need several new rules. But first let's see what we can do with the rules we already have.

Predicate logic deals with two sorts of statements: singular and general. Singular statements contain only names and predicates; general statements contain variables and quantifiers as well. The rules of propositional logic, along with the techniques of conditional and *reductio* proof, can be applied in a straightforward way to singular statements, as in the following example:

1. $Pa \supset (Qa \supset Rab)$ Premise
2. $\smile Rab / \smile Pa \vee \smile Qa$ Premise/Conclusion
3. $(Pa \bullet Qa) \supset Rab$ 1 Exp
4. $\smile (Pa \bullet Qa)$ 2,3 MT
5. $\smile Pa \vee \smile Qa$ 4 DM

Indeed, if we didn't have to worry about general statements, the propositional rules are all we'd need.

The propositional rules are also sufficient for some arguments involving general statements. An example would be the argument that if everything is physical, then the soul is not immortal; everything is physical; therefore the soul is not immortal:

1. $(x)Px \supset (y)(Sy \supset \smile Iy)$ Premise
2. $(x)Px / (y)(Sy \supset \smile Iy)$ Premise/Conclusion
3. $(y)(Sy \supset \smile Iy)$ 1,2 MP

The whole argument is nothing more than a simple *modus ponens*; we don't need to look at the internal structure of the quantified statements.

Most arguments in predicate logic, however, require some additional rules. The system of proof we're going to adopt uses one additional equivalence rule, and four new rules of inference.

Equivalence Rule

The statement that nothing is infinite in size might be symbolized in either of two ways:

i) $(x) \smile Ix$, or
ii) $\smile (\exists x)Ix$.

(i) says that for all x, x is not infinite, while (ii) says it is *not* the case that some x *is* infinite in size. These are clearly equivalent. If everything lacks a certain property, then not a single thing possesses it. In the same way, if not everything possesses the property, then at least one thing lacks it: $\smile (x)Px$ is equivalent to $(\exists x) \smile Px$. When the negation sign passes across the quantifier, therefore, it is like a current that changes the quantifier into its opposite. And if there's already a negation sign in the place where the first sign is moving, the two signs cancel out: $\smile (x) \smile Px$ is equivalent to $(\exists x)Px$.

Since this principle is true in virtue of the nature of quantifiers and negation, it is not restricted to statements with a single predicate. It is true no matter how complex the expression governed by the quantifier may be. For example,

$$\sim (x)[Sx \supset (Px \vee Qx)] \equiv (\exists x) \sim [Sx \supset (Px \vee Qx)].$$

To state these equivalences in their general form, therefore, we will use the notation $(\ldots x \ldots)$ to represent any expression involving x that is bound by a quantifier. We have four such equivalences altogether:

$$\sim (x)(\ldots x \ldots) \equiv (\exists x) \sim (\ldots x \ldots)$$
$$(x) \sim (\ldots x \ldots) \quad\equiv \sim (\exists x) (\ldots x \ldots)$$
$$\sim (x) \sim (\ldots x \ldots) \equiv (\exists x)(\ldots x \ldots)$$
$$(x)(\ldots x \ldots) \equiv \sim (\exists x) \sim (\ldots x \ldots)$$

The **quantifier-negation** (QN) rule allows us to make substitutions in accordance with these equivalences. A statement of the form $\sim (x)(\ldots x \ldots)$, for example, can be replaced by $(\exists x) \sim (\ldots x \ldots)$. Like an equivalence rule in propositional logic, QN can be applied either to a whole statement or to a part.

If we have more than one quantifier, we can still apply QN, but we have to do it in stages. Thus the statement $\sim (x)(\exists y)Rxy$ would be transformed first into $(\exists x) \sim (\exists y)Rxy$, and then into $(\exists x)(y) \sim Rxy$. Or suppose we want to say that not every student owns a computer. The following statements are all equivalent:

i) $\sim(x)(\exists y)[(Sx \bullet Cy) \bullet Oxy]$
ii) $(\exists x) \sim (\exists y)[(Sx \bullet Cy) \bullet Oxy]$
iii) $(\exists x)(y) \sim [(Sx \bullet Cy) \bullet Oxy]$

The literal translation of (i) is: it's not the case that for all x, there's a y such that x is a student, y is a computer, and x owns y. What are the literal translations of (ii) and (iii)?

Practice Quiz

Which of the following pairs of statements are equivalent by QN?

1. $(x)(Px \supset Qx), \sim (\exists x) \sim (Px \supset Qx)$
2. $(x) \sim (Px \bullet Qx), \sim (\exists x) (Px \bullet Qx)$
3. $(\exists x) \sim [Px \bullet (Qx \vee Rx)], \sim (\exists x)[Px \bullet (Qx \vee Rx)]$
4. $\sim (x) \sim [Px \supset (Qx \bullet Rx)], (\exists x) [Px \supset (Qx \bullet Rx)]$
5. $(x)(y) \sim [(Px \bullet Qx) \bullet Rxy], \sim (\exists x)(\exists y)[(Px \bullet Qx) \bullet Rxy]$
6. $(x) \sim (\exists y) [Px \bullet Qx) \supset Rx], (\exists x)(y) \sim [(Px \bullet Qx) \supset Rx]$
7. $(\exists y) \sim (x)[Px \supset (Qy \vee Rxy)], \sim (y)(x)[Px \supset (Qy \vee Rxy)]$
8. $\sim (x)(\exists y)(z)[Px \vee Qz) \supset (Ry \supset Sxyz)],$
    $(\exists x)(\exists y)(\exists z) \sim [(Px \vee Qz) \supset (Ry \supset Sxyz)]$

Inference Rules

The need for some additional rules of *inference* will be clear if we
consider the classic syllogism:

All humans are mortal $(x)(Hx \supset Mx)$
Socrates is human $\underline{Hs}$
Socrates is mortal Ms

This argument looks like *modus ponens*, but it isn't. The first premise is not a conditional statement, because the conditional sign
occurs within the parentheses, within the scope of the quantifier.
And the predicates H and M are ascribed to the variable x rather
than to s. In order to treat the argument as a case of *modus ponens*,
we must first get rid of the quantifier and variable, and transform
the first premise into the conditional statement $Hs \supset Ms$. Then we
would have a simple *modus ponens* proof.

This is the basic strategy of proof in predicate logic. We transform quantified statements into singular statements, and then use
the rules of propositional logic. If the conclusion we're trying to
prove is itself a singular statement, we can stop at this point. If the
conclusion is quantified, then we must have some way of transforming singular statements back into quantified ones. So we need additional rules for *instantiation* and *generalization*. Instantiation rules
allow us to replace variables with names, thereby transforming
quantified statements into statements about particular instances.
Generalization rules allow us to move in the opposite direction,
replacing names with variables and adding quantifiers to bind the
variables. There are two rules of each type, one for each quantifier.

Let's start with the rule of **universal instantiation** (UI). In the
argument above, the statement $(x)(Hx \supset Mx)$ says that the expression $Hx \supset Mx$ is true of any x. So it is true of you and me, and Gan-
dhi, and Shakespeare, and everyone else. For that matter it is true
of the Hudson Bay or your mailbox, though in these cases it is true
only because the antecedent is false. In short, we can replace the x
with the name of anything whatever, and the resulting singular
statement follows from the universal statement. Thus $Hs \supset Ms$ follows from $(x)(Hx \supset Mx)$ by the rule of universal instantiation, and
we would establish the validity of the argument above by the following proof:

1. $(x)(Hx \supset Mx)$ Premise
2. $Hs \;/\; Ms$ Premise/Conclusion
3. $Hs \supset Ms$ 1, UI
4. Ms 2, 3, MP

In this case we instantiated the universal premise with the name *s*, because the argument is concerned with Socrates. In other arguments, as we'll see, neither the premises nor the conclusion mention any particular individual. If we need to use UI in such a case, we pick a letter (by convention, from the beginning of the alphabet) to stand for some arbitrary individual. Thus the general form of universal instantiation can be represented as follows:

$$\frac{(x)(\ldots x \ldots)}{\ldots a \ldots}$$

where the dots stand for any formula inside the scope of the quantifier. All of the following would be examples:

1. $\dfrac{(x)Px}{Pa}$ 　 2. $\dfrac{(x)(Px \lor Qx)}{Pa \lor Qa}$ 　 3. $\dfrac{(x)(\sim Px \bullet Qa)}{\sim Pb \bullet Qa}$ 　 or 　 $\dfrac{(x)(\sim Px \bullet Qa)}{\sim Pa \bullet Qa}$

Notice that in (2), the variable occurred twice in the universal statement, as the subject of both predicates. So it had to be replaced by *a* in both occurrences. If we instantiated only the first occurrence of *x*, we would have *Pa* ∨ *Qx*, and this has a free variable, which is not permitted. In general, the same name must replace the variable everywhere it occurs. In (3), the name *a* is already present in the universal statement, so when we instantiate we might want to use another letter to replace *x*. But we don't have to. Since the statement is about all *x*, it makes a claim about *a*; the second version is therefore valid.

Universal instantiation can also be used for statements with more than one variable. The following are examples:

4. $\dfrac{(x)(y)(Px \supset Qy)}{(y)(Pa \supset Qy)}$ 　 5. $\dfrac{(x)(\exists y)Pxy}{(\exists y)Pay}$ 　 6. $\dfrac{(x)[Px \supset (\exists y)(Qy \bullet Rxy)]}{Pa \supset (\exists y)(Qy \bullet Ray)}$

As before, we need to make sure that we replace the variable with the same name wherever it occurs in the statement; notice in particular how this works in the relational statements (5) and (6). We must also observe a second restriction: UI is permissible only if the entire statement falls within the scope of the quantifier we instantiate. One implication is that UI can be used only on the quantifier that begins the statement—the outermost quantifier. In (4), for example, we couldn't instantiate *y* because its quantifier is embedded within the scope of (*x*). Once we've instantiated *x*, then (*y*) becomes the outermost quantifier, and we can go on to instantiate *y*. But we can't start there.

Here are some examples of inferences that violate the restriction:

7. $\dfrac{(x)Px \supset Qa}{Pa \supset Qa}$ 8. $\dfrac{\sim (x)(Px \supset Qx)}{\sim (Pa \supset Qa)}$ 9. $\dfrac{(x)Px \supset (\exists y)Qy}{Pa \supset (\exists y)Qy}$

In (7) and (9), the quantifier begins the statement, but doesn't cover all of it. In (8), the quantifier does not begin the statement: the negation sign precedes it, and is thus outside its scope. (To do anything with (8), we would first have to use the quantifier-negation rule to move the negation sign inside the scope of the quantifier. But in that case the universal quantifier would become an existential quantifier, requiring the use of a different instantiation rule.) The problem in all these cases is that the conclusion doesn't follow from the premise. Thus the premise in (9) says that if everything is *P*, then something is *Q*. For example: if everyone gets in the elevator, some of the cables will break. It doesn't follow that if Alan gets in the elevator, some of the cables will break.

The rule of **existential generalization** (EG) allows us to move in the opposite direction, from a singular to a quantified statement. Such an inference has the form:

$$\dfrac{\ldots a \ldots}{(\exists x)(\ldots a \ldots)}$$

If we know that object *a* has property *P*, we can certainly infer that *something* has this property. If we know that Tom is both an actor and a waiter, we can infer that some actors are waiters (remembering that "some" means "at least one"). If we know that everyone loves Mary, we can infer there is someone whom everyone loves. These inferences would be represented as follows:

$$\dfrac{Pa}{(\exists x)Px} \qquad \dfrac{At \cdot Wt}{(\exists x)\,(Ax \cdot Wx)} \qquad \dfrac{(x)(Px \supset Lxm)}{(\exists y)(x)(Px \supset Lxy)}$$

In existential generalization, then, we replace a name with a variable, and add an existential quantifier. When we do so, we must be sure to place the quantifier at the beginning of the statement, so that the entire statement falls within its scope. But we do not have to replace every occurrence of the name with the variable. Suppose Julie loves herself: *Ljj*. We might generalize that someone loves herself: $(\exists x)Lxx$. But we could also infer that someone loves Julie and that Julie loves someone: $(\exists x)Lxj$ and $(\exists x)Ljx$.

Let's see how our two rules, UI and EG, work together in a proof. Consider the argument:

$$\dfrac{\begin{array}{l}(x)[Px \supset (Qx \vee Rx)]\\ Sa \cdot Pa\end{array}}{(\exists x)[Sx \cdot (Qx \vee Rx)]}$$

Since the second premise is a singular statement about *a*, we will need to instantiate the universal premise using the same name. We will then have two singular statements, to which we can apply the rules of propositional logic. Our goal is to get the statement *Sa* • (*Qa* ∨ *Ra*), from which the conclusion will follow by generalization. The proof looks like this:

1.	(*x*)[*Px* ⊃ (*Qx* ∨ *Rx*)]	Premise
2.	*Sa* • *Pa* / (∃*x*)[*Sx* • (*Qx* ∨ *Rx*)]	Premise/Conclusion
3.	*Pa* ⊃ (*Qa* ∨ *Ra*)	1 UI
4.	*Pa*	2 Simp
5.	*Qa* ∨ *Ra*	3,4 MP
6.	*Sa*	2 Simp
7.	*Sa* • (*Qa* ∨ *Ra*)	5,6 Conj
8.	(∃*x*)[*Sx* • (*Qx* ∨ *Rx*)]	7, EG

The two rules we have just learned are natural ones, in the sense that each expresses something essential about the quantifier involved. A universal statement says something about everything, so we may naturally instantiate it with the name of any particular. An existential statement says that something is true of at least one thing, so we can naturally support the claim by inferring it from a particular example. The next two rules are less natural, and the inferences they permit are valid only if we observe certain special restrictions. (Of course, these rules are also subject to the general restrictions we've discussed: names and variables must be interchanged consistently, and the quantifier must cover the entire statement.)

Existential instantiation (EI) is the reverse of existential generalization. It has the form:

$$\frac{(\exists x)(\ldots x \ldots)}{\ldots a \ldots}$$

This does not appear to be a valid inference. The premise tells us that *something* in the world fits a certain description, but if *a* is the name of a specific individual with which we are already familiar, we cannot infer that *a* fits the description. Suppose we know, for example, that some actors are waiters: (∃*x*)(*Ax* • *Wx*). Does this imply that Margaret Thatcher is both an actor and a waiter? Obviously not. Nevertheless, it is valid to reason as follows: At least one thing in the world is both an actor and a waiter. Let's call that thing *a*. We can now assert that *Aa* • *Wa*. Existential instantiation is valid if we replace the variable with a name that is introduced solely for the purpose of standing for that thing, whatever (or whoever) it may be, which makes the premise true. This means that when we use EI in a proof, the name we use must be one that has not been used previously in the proof, and that does not occur in the conclusion.

To see the importance of this restriction, consider the following argument, in which *Pxy* means that *x* is a parent of *y*:

1. $(\exists y)(\exists x)Pxy$ / $(\exists x)Pxx$ Premise/Conclusion
2. $(\exists x)Pxa$ 1 EI
3. *Paa*   2 EI [error]
4. $(\exists x)Pxx$ 3 EG

The premise says that someone has a parent, which is true. The conclusion says that someone is his own parent, which is false. The argument is clearly invalid, and the problem in the proof occurs in step 3. We can't use *a* to instantiate *x*, because *a* has already been used to instantiate *y*. Line 2 says that someone is *a*'s parent; this does not imply that *a* is his own parent. To instantiate *x*, we need a fresh name.

This restriction does not apply to universal instantiation. So if we need to instantiate both a universal and an existential statement in a proof, it's best to instantiate the existential statement first. An example would be the argument we encountered at the beginning of the last chapter: I am the owner of a Monet painting; any Monet painting is valuable; therefore I own something valuable. The proof would be:

1. $(\exists x)(Mx \bullet Oix)$ Premise
2. $(x)(Mx \supset Vx)$ / $(\exists x)(Vx \bullet Oix)$ Premise/Conclusion
3. *Ma* • *Oia*   1 EI
4. *Ma* $\supset$ *Va*   2 UI
5. *Ma*   3 Simp
6. *Va*   4,5 MP
7. *Oia*   3 Simp
8. *Va* • *Oia*   6,7 Conj
9. $(\exists x)(Vx \bullet Oix)$ 8 EG

To obtain line 8, we had to use the same name to instantiate both premises (since *Va* comes from the second premise, and *Oia* from the first). If we had tried to instantiate the second premise before the first—i.e., if we had tried to obtain line 4 before line 3—we would have been blocked by our restriction. The name *a* could not have been used for the existential instantiation, because it would already have been used. So we had to proceed in the opposite order.

Practice Quiz

Each of the following inferences is an attempt to apply one of the three inferences rules we've discussed (UI, EG, and EI). Identify the rule, and determine whether it has been properly applied.

1. $\underline{(\exists x)(Px \bullet Qx)}$
   $Pa \bullet Qa$

2. $\underline{Pa \lor Qa}$
   $(\exists x)(Px \lor Qx)$

3. $\underline{(x)(Px \bullet Qx) \supset (y)Ry}$
   $(Pa \bullet Qa) \supset Ra$

4. $\underline{Pa \supset (Qb \bullet Rab)}$
   $(\exists x)[Px \supset (Qb \bullet Rxb)]$

5. $\underline{(\exists x)Pxx \supset (y)(Qy \supset Ry)}$
   $Paa \supset (y)(Qy \supset Ry)$

6. $\underline{(x)[Px \supset (Qx \lor Rx)]}$
   $Pa \supset (Qa \lor Ra)$

7. $\underline{(x)(\exists y)[Px \bullet Qy) \supset (Rxy \bullet Syx)]}$
   $(\exists y)[(Pa \bullet Qy) \supset (Ray \bullet Sya)]$

8. $\underline{(\exists x)[(Px \bullet Qx) \supset Ra]}$
   $(Pa \bullet Qa) \supset Ra$

9. $\underline{(x)[Px \supset (Qa \bullet Rxa)]}$
   $(x)[Px \supset (\exists y)(Qy \bullet Rxy)]$

10. $\underline{(\exists x) \mathbin{\backsim} (y)[(Px \bullet Qy) \supset Rxy]}$
    $\mathbin{\backsim} (y)[(Px \bullet Qa) \supset Ray]$

The fourth rule of inference we need is **universal generalization** (UG), which has the form:

$$\frac{\ .\ .\ .a\ .\ .\ .}{(x)(\ .\ .\ .x\ .\ .\ .)}$$

We typically use this rule when the conclusion of an argument is a universal statement, as in the syllogism: All alcoholic beverages are intoxicating; May wine is an alcoholic beverage; therefore. . . . The proof would be:

1. $(x)(Ax \supset Ix)$	Premise
2. $(x)(Mx \supset Ax) / (x)(Mx \supset Ix)$	Premise/Conclusion
3. $Aa \supset Ia$	1 UI
4. $Ma \supset Aa$	2 UI
5. $Ma \supset Ia$	3,4 HS
6. $(x)(Mx \supset Ix)$	5 UG

We had to instantiate both premises in order to connect them by a hypothetical syllogism, and then we had to generalize to get our conclusion.

Our procedure here was legitimate because *a* was introduced as a representative instance of May wine, so that anything we proved about it would hold for any other instance. Our procedure was analogous to that of a mathematician who proves a theorem about a triangle drawn on the blackboard, and then assumes that the theorem is true of all triangles because the proof didn't depend on anything distinctive about the particular example he used. But this means that universal generalization is valid *only* if the name stands for a representative instance. Before we generalize from . . . *a* . . . to (*x*) (. . . *a* . . .), we must review the earlier lines of the proof to make sure that . . . *a* . . . does not involve or rest upon any claim about *a* as a distinctive, non-representative example. We can do this by observing certain restrictions on UG. To understand the rationale for these restrictions, let's look at sorts of fallacies we want to avoid.

It is clear, to begin with, that we cannot use UG on a name that occurs in the premises. The premise that Kenya is a member of the United Nations, for example, does not allow us to infer that every country, or every thing in the world, is a U.N. member. Similarly, we cannot generalize on a name that was introduced by existential instantiation. Otherwise we could infer that everything is wet from the premise that something is wet:

1. $(\exists x)Wx$ / $(x)Wx$ Premise/Conclusion
2. Wa 1 EI
3. $(x)Wx$ 2 UG

In this proof, *a* is not a representative example of things in the world because the premise doesn't tell us that everything is wet, only that some things are, and *a* has been specially designated as one of them.

If the name on which we generalize cannot come from the premises or existential instantiation, it may seem that it must come from universal instantiation. That was the case above, in the argument about May wine. But it is not the only possibility. The techniques of conditional and *reductio* proof can be used in predicate logic, and a name may be introduced in the assumption of such a proof. An example would be the argument that since leopards are carnivorous mammals, and all mammals are vertebrates, leopards are vertebrates:

1. $(x)[Lx \supset (Cx \cdot Mx)]$ Premise
2. $(x)(Mx \supset Vx)$ / $(x)(Lx \supset Vx)$ Premise/Conclusion
3. La Assumption
4. $La \supset (Ca \cdot Ma)$ 1 UI
5. $Ca \cdot Ma$ 3,4 MP

6. *Ma*	5 Simp
7. *Ma* ⊃ *Va*	2 UI
8. *Va*	6,7 MP
9. *La* ⊃ *Va*	3–8 CP
10. (*x*)(*Lx* ⊃ *Vx*)	9 UG

The name *a* was introduced in line 3 as a representative instance of a leopard, so it is valid to generalize on it in line 10.

If a name is contained in the assumption of a conditional or *reductio* proof, however, we must be careful not to use universal generalization until we have discharged the assumption and returned to the main flow of the proof. If we fail to observe this restriction, we commit a fallacy, as the following proof illustrates:

1. (*x*)(*Lx* ⊃ *Mx*) / (*x*)(*Lx* ⊃ (*y*)*My*)	Premise/Conclusion
2. *La*	Assumption
3. *La* ⊃ *Ma*	1 UI
4. *Ma*	2,3 MP
5. (*y*)*My*	4 UG [error]
6. *La* ⊃ (*y*)*My*	2–5 CP
7. (*x*)(*Lx* ⊃ (*y*)*My*)	6 UG

The premise says that all leopards are mammals, which is true. The curious-looking conclusion says that if anything is a leopard, then everything is a mammal, which is certainly false. The problem lies in step 5, where we generalized on *a* within the scope of the conditional proof. This is *not* to say that we can never use UG inside a conditional segment; it's just that we can't do it if the name occurs in the initial assumption.

A final sort of fallacy can occur when an argument has more than one variable being instantiated. A typical case involves relations. The premise that everyone loves someone (or other) does not imply that there is someone (a particular individual) whom everyone loves. But consider the following "proof" (where *Px* means "*x* is a person" and *Lxy* means "*x* loves *y*"):

1. (*x*)(*Px* ⊃ (∃*y*)*Lxy*) / (∃*y*)(*x*)(*Px* ⊃ *Lxy*)	Premise/Conclusion
2. *Pa* ⊃ (∃*y*)*Lay*	1 UI
3. *Pa*	Assumption
4. (∃*y*)*Lay*	2,3 MP
5. *Lab*	4 EI
6. *Pa* ⊃ *Lab*	3–5 CP
7. (*x*)(*Px* ⊃ *Lxb*)	6 UG [error]
8. (∃*y*)(*x*)(*Px* ⊃ *Lxy*)	7 EG

Step 2 says that *a* is a person and *a* loves someone. Step 5 says: let's use the name *b* for the person *a* loves. This doesn't mean that *everyone* loves *b*—but that's exactly the fallacious conclusion that step 7 draws. The problem here is that *b* was introduced on a line where *a* was already present, so we can't generalize on *a* until we get rid of *b*.

We can now state the restrictions on universal generalization. An inference of the form

$$\frac{\dots a \dots}{(x)(\dots x \dots)}$$

is valid if, but only if:

1. *a* was introduced by UI or in the assumption of a conditional or *reductio* proof (not in a premise or by EI);
2. the inference does not occur within a conditional or *reductio* proof whose assumption contains *a*; and
3. The statement . . . *a* . . . does not contain any other name introduced by EI on a line containing *a*.

The full set of new rules for predicate logic is summarized in a box at the end of the section. To get a feel for their use in longer proofs, let's look at two examples that illustrate the strategies to follow. As we work through each of them, it might help to have paper and pencil handy so that you can keep track of where we are.

Here's the first example:

1. $(x)\{Px \supset (y)[Qy \bullet Ry) \supset Sxy]\}$ Premise
2. $(x)(y)(Txy \supset Qy)$ Premise
3. $(x)(\exists y)Txy \,/\, (x)[Px \supset (\exists y)(Ry \supset Sxy)]$ Premise/Conclusion

We can see that we're going to have to instantiate all the variables in order to relate the premises. In the case of *x*, that won't be a problem, since it is bound in each premise by a universal quantifier, and there are no special restrictions on universal instantiation. In the third premise, however, *y* is bound by an existential quantifier. So when we reach the point of instantiating *y*, we should use EI on that statement before using UI on the other two. We might as well start with premise 3:

4. $(\exists y)Tay$ 3 UI
5. Tab 4 EI
6. $(y)(Tay \supset Qy)$ 2 UI
7. $Tab \supset Qb$ 6 UI
8. $Pa \supset (y)[(Qy \bullet Ry) \supset Say]$ 1 UI

Now we cannot instantiate y in line 8 because it does not occur at the beginning of the statement. To detach the consequent from Pa, we can use conditional proof with Pa as the assumption. This is a reasonable strategy to follow because the conclusion has the internal structure of a conditional, with Px as the antecedent.

9.	Pa	Assumption
10.	$(y)[(Qy \cdot Ry) \supset Say]$	8,9 MP
11.	$(Qb \cdot Rb) \supset Sab$	10 UI

From this point, the proof is straightforward:

12.	$Qb \supset (Rb \supset Sab)$	11 Exp
13.	Qb	5,7 MP
14.	$Rb \supset Sab$	12,13 MP
15.	$(\exists y)(Ry \supset Say)$	14 EG
16.	$Pa \supset (\exists y)(Ry \supset Say)$	9–15 CP
17.	$(x)[Px \supset (\exists y)(Ry \supset Sxy)]$	16 UG

Let's check, finally, to make sure that we used UG properly. First, was a introduced in a premise or by EI? No—it was introduced by UP in line 4. Did we use UG inside a conditional segment? No. So we don't have to worry about the second restriction. Did line 16 contain any other name introduced by EI? No—we got rid of b, which was introduced by EI, in line 15. Notice that our use of EG to get rid of b occurred inside a conditional segment. That's okay, because there are no special restrictions on EG. Could we have used UG in line 15? We didn't need to, given the conclusion, but could we have? The fact that line 15 is inside a conditional segment would not have prevented us, since b was not contained in the conditional assumption. But b *was* introduced by EI, so UG would not have been permitted.

Our second example illustrates the use of *reductio* proof and the quantifier-negation rules:

1.	$(\exists x)Pax \supset Qa$	Premise
2.	$(x)(\exists y)[(Rx \supset Pxy) \cdot$	
	$(\neg Rx \supset Pxy)] / (\exists x)Qx$	Premise/Conclusion

We can't do anything with 1, because the quantifier does not cover the whole statement. So let's instantiate both variables in 2, using a for x so that we can eventually connect the two premises:

3.	$(\exists y)[(Ra \supset Pay) \cdot (\neg Ra \supset Pay)]$	2 UI
4.	$(Ra \supset Pab) \cdot (\neg Ra \supset Pab)$	3 EI

At this point we can see that Pab has to be true. If it weren't, we could infer both Ra and $\smile Ra$ by *modus tollens,* and we would have a contradiction. This suggests that we use a *reductio* proof to derive that contradiction:

$$
\begin{array}{lll}
5. & \smile(\exists x)Qx & \text{Assumption} \\
6. & (x) \smile Qx & \text{5 QN} \\
7. & \smile Qa & \text{6 UI} \\
8. & \smile(\exists x)Pax & \text{1,7 MT} \\
9. & (x) \smile Pax & \text{8 QN} \\
10. & \smile Pab & \text{9 UI}
\end{array}
$$

Notice that we had to use QN twice to move a negation sign inside the scope of the quantifier. And in each case we ended up with a universal quantifier, which we could instantiate to suit our purposes. Now we can easily go on to derive the contradiction:

$$
\begin{array}{lll}
11. & Ra \supset Pab & \text{4 Simp} \\
12. & \smile Ra & \text{10,11 MT} \\
13. & \smile Ra \supset Pab & \text{4 Simp} \\
14. & \smile \smile Ra & \text{10,13 MT} \\
15. & Ra & \text{14 DN} \\
16. & Ra \bullet \smile Ra & \text{12,15 Conj} \\
17. & (\exists x)Qx & \text{5–16 RA}
\end{array}
$$

We have now completed our survey of predicate logic. The previous chapter and this one form a natural unit. Together they illustrate the basic concepts and some of the techniques of proof employed by modern symbolic logic. In the next chapter, we'll look at a recently developed alternative that is closer in many respects to the classical logic of the syllogism.

Practice Quiz

Construct a proof for each of the following arguments.

1. $(x)(Px \supset Qx)$
   $(\exists x)Px \bullet Rx)$
   $\overline{(\exists x)(Rx \bullet Qx)}$

2. $(x)(Px \supset \smile Qx)$
   $(x)(Rx \supset Qx)$
   $\overline{(x)(Rx \supset \smile Px)}$

3. $(x)(Px \supset \smile Qx)$
   $(\exists x)(Rx \bullet Px)$
   $\overline{(\exists x)(Rx \bullet \smile Qx)}$

4. $(\exists x)(y)Pxy$
   $\overline{(y)(\exists x)Pxy}$

5. $(x)[(Px \vee Qx) \supset Rx]$
   $(\exists x)(Px \bullet Sx)$
   $\overline{(\exists x)Rx}$

6. $(x)(Rx \supset Sx)$
   $(x)(Px \supset Qx)$
   $(\exists x)(PX \vee Rx)$
   $\overline{(\exists x)(Sx \vee Qx)}$

7. $(x)(y)[(Px \cdot Qy) \supset Rxy]$
   $(x)(\exists y)(Sxy \supset Px)$
   $\overline{(x)(\exists y)[Sxy \supset (Qy \supset Rxy)]}$

8. $\sim (\exists x)[Px \cdot (Sx \cdot Tx)]$
   $(x)[(Sx \lor Qx) \cdot (Tx \lor Rx)]$
   $\overline{(x)[Px \supset (Qx \lor Rx)]}$

SUMMARY

Predicate logic analyzes proposition in terms of names, predicates, variables, and quantifiers. A singular statement consists of a predicate attached to a name, or a truth-functional compound of such elementary units. A general statement consists of a predicate attached to a variable (or a truth-functional compound of such elementary units), with the variable bound by a universal or existential quantifier. The terms of traditional categorical statements are treated as predicates. Universal statements (A or E) are treated as conditionals bound by a universal quantifier; particular statements (I or O) are treated as conjunctions bound by an existential quantifier.

Quantified statements may be combined by truth-functional connectives. The predicates of such statements may also be relational. Relational statements typically involve more than one variable, and thus require more than one quantifier. The order of the quantifier can make a difference to the meaning of the statement.

We can show that an argument stated in predicate notation is valid by constructing a proof. In addition to the rules of propositional logic, a proof in predicate logic makes use of one additional equivalence rule (the quantifier-negation rule), and four additional rules of inference (the instantiation and generalization rules).

Rules for the Use of Quantifiers

Quantifier-negation (QN): A negation sign may be moved across a quantifier in accordance with the following equivalences:

$$(x) \sim (\ldots x \ldots) \equiv \sim (\exists x)(\ldots x \ldots)$$
$$\sim (x) (\ldots x \ldots) \equiv (\exists x) \sim (\ldots x \ldots)$$
$$\sim (x) \sim (\ldots x \ldots) \equiv (\exists x)(\ldots x \ldots)$$
$$(x)(\ldots x \ldots) \equiv \sim (\exists x) \sim (\ldots x \ldots)$$

Instantiation and Generalization Rules
General restrictions:

1) The same variable must replace all occurrences of the same name (for universal but not existential generalization), and vice versa (for both types of instantiation).

2) The quantifier that is added (in the case of generalization) or dropped (in the case of instantiation) must include the entire line within its scope.

Universal instantiation (UI): $\dfrac{(x)(\,\ldots x \ldots)}{\ldots a \ldots}$

Existential generalization (EG): $\dfrac{\ldots a \ldots}{(\exists x)(\,\ldots x \ldots)}$

Existential instantiation (EI): $\dfrac{(\exists x)(\,\ldots x \ldots)}{\ldots a \ldots}$

Restriction: *a* must not have occurred previously in the proof, or in the conclusion.

Universal generalization (UG): $\dfrac{\ldots a \ldots}{(x)(\,\ldots x \ldots)}$

Restrictions:

1. *a* was introduced by UI or in the assumption of a conditional or *reductio* proof (not in a premise or by EI);
2. the inference does not occur within a conditional or *reductio* proof whose assumption contains *a*; and
3. the statement . . . *a* . . . does not contain any other name introduced by EI on a line containing *a*.

Exercises

A. Translate each of the following statements into symbolic notation, using appropriate letters as predicates and names.

1. Sticks and stones may break my bones.
2. Nothing is black or white; there are only shades of gray.
3. If there were no black and white, there would be no gray.
4. Every little breeze seems to whisper "Louise."
5. No poem is as beautiful as a tree.
6. Any object in motion continues in motion unless some force acts on it.
7. It isn't true that an authorized biography of a celebrity is always less revealing than an unauthorized biography.
8. "God helps them that help themselves" (Benjamin Franklin).
9. People who live in glass houses should not throw stones.
10. For everyone who steals and gets away with it, there are some who steal and get caught.

11. "We shall defend every village, every town and every city" (Winston Churchill).
12. "I would not join any club willing to have me as a member" (Groucho Marx).
13. A government is democratic if and only if all its adult citizens are eligible to vote.
14. A nation that protects all of its citizens against failure will prevent some of its citizens from succeeding.
15. "There never was a good war or a bad peace" (Benjamin Franklin).
16. "Everyone complains of his memory, and no one complains of his judgment" (La Rochefoucauld).
17. Two people are cousins if and only if they are children of siblings.
18. Every mother is someone's daughter, but not every daughter is someone's mother.
19. "No person except a natural born citizen, or a citizen of the United States, at the time of the adoption of this constitution, shall be eligible to the office of president; neither shall any person be eligible to that office, who shall not have attained the age of 35 years, and been 14 years a resident within the United States" (U.S. Constitution).
20. "You may fool all of the people some of the time; you can even fool some of the people all the time; but you can't fool all the people all the time" (Abraham Lincoln).

B. Each of the following arguments can be justified by one of the inference or equivalence rules of propositional logic. Name the rule.

1. $Pa \lor (Qa \cdot Rab)$
   $\overline{(Pa \lor Qa) \cdot (Pa \lor Rab)}$

2. $(x)(Px \supset Qx) \supset (\exists y)Ry$
   $\underline{\smallsmile (\exists y)Ry}$
   $\smallsmile (x)(Px \supset Qx)$

3. $[Pa \cdot (Rab \lor Sab)] \supset Qb$
   $\overline{Pa \supset [(Rab \lor Sab) \supset Qb]}$

4. $(x)(Px \cdot Qx) \lor (\exists y) \smallsmile (Py \lor Qy)$
   $\underline{\smallsmile (\exists y) \smallsmile (Py \lor Qy)}$
   $(x)(Px \cdot Qx)$

5. $(Pa \cdot Qb) \supset Rab$
   $\underline{(Sa \supset Pa) \cdot (Sa \supset Qb)}$
   $[(Sa \supset Pa) \cdot (Sa \supset Qb)] \cdot [(Pa \cdot Qb) \supset Rab]$

6. $(\exists x)Px \supset (y)[(Qy \supset (Ry \lor Sy)]$
   $\underline{(y)[(Qy \supset (Ry \lor Sy)] \supset (z) \backsim Tz}$
   $(\exists x)Px \supset (z) \backsim Tz$

7. $\underline{(\exists x)(Px \cdot Qx) \supset (y)(Py \supset Qy)}$
   $\backsim (\exists x)(Px \cdot Qx) \lor (y)(Py \supset Qy)$

8. $\underline{(x)(\exists y)[(Px \cdot Qy) \supset Rxy] \cdot (x)(Sx \supset (\exists y)Txy)}$
   $(x)(Sx \supset (\exists y)Txy)$

9. $\underline{(\exists x)(Px \cdot Qx) \lor [(\exists y)(Ry \cdot Qy) \lor (Pa \cdot Ra)]}$
   $[(\exists x)(Px \cdot Qx) \lor (\exists y)(Ry \cdot Qy)] \lor (Pa \cdot Ra)$

10. $[Pa \supset (Qa \cdot Rab)] \cdot [Pb \supset (Qb \cdot Rba)]$
    $\underline{\backsim (Qa \cdot Rab) \lor \backsim (Qb \cdot Rba)}$
    $\backsim Pa \lor \backsim Pb$

C. In each of the following "proofs," one line involves an error in the use of a rule of predicate logic. Identify the error.

1. 1. $(x)(\exists y)(Px \equiv \backsim Py) / (Pa \equiv \backsim Pa)$ Premise/Conclusion
    2. $(\exists y)(Pa \equiv \backsim Py)$ 1, UI
    3. $Pa \equiv \backsim Pa$ 2, EI

2. 1. $(x)Px \supset (y)Qy / (x)(Px \supset Qx)$ Premise/Conclusion
    2. Pa Assumption
    3. $(x)Px$ 2 UI
    4. $(x)Qx$ 1,3 MP
    5. Qa 4 UI
    6. $Pa \supset Qa$ 2–5 CP
    7. $(x)(Px \supset Qx)$ 6 UG

3. 1. $(x)(Px \supset Qx) \supset (y)Ry$ Premise
    2. $(\exists x) \backsim Rx / (\exists x)(Px \cdot \backsim Qx)$ Premise/Conclusion
    3. $\backsim Ra$ 2 EI
    4. $(Pa \supset Qa) \supset Ra$ 1 UI
    5. $\backsim (Pa \supset Qa)$ 3,4 MT
    6. $\backsim \backsim (Pa \cdot \backsim Qa)$ 5 Imp
    7. $Pa \cdot \backsim Qa$ 6 DN
    8. $(\exists x)(Pa \cdot \backsim Qa)$ 7 EG

4. 1. $(x)(Px \lor Qx) \supset (\exists y)Ry$ Premise
    2. $(\exists x) \backsim Rx / (\exists x)(\backsim Px \cdot \backsim Qx)$ Premise/Conclusion
    3. $\backsim (\exists x)Rx$ 2, QN
    4. $\backsim (x)(Px \lor Qx)$ 1,3 MT
    5. $(\exists x) \backsim (Px \lor Qx)$ 4 QN
    6. $\backsim (Pa \lor Qa)$ 5 EI
    7. $\backsim Pa \cdot \backsim Qa$ 6 DM
    8. $(\exists x)(\backsim Px \cdot \backsim Qx)$ 7 EG

5. 1. $(x)[Px \supset (\exists y)(Qy \cdot Rxy)]$ Premise
    2. $(x)(Qx \supset Sx) / (\exists y)(x)[Px \supset (Sy \cdot Rxy)]$ Premise/Conclusion

3. $Pa \supset (\exists y)(Qy \bullet Ray)$ 1 UI
  4. Pa Assumption
  5. $(\exists y)(Qy \bullet Ray)$ 3,4 MP
  6. $Qb \bullet Rab$ 5 EI
  7. Qb 6 Simp
  8. $Qb \supset Sb$ 2 UI
  9. Sb 7,8 MP
  10. Rab 6 Simp
  11. $Sb \bullet Rab$ 9,10 Conj
12. $Pa \supset (Sb \bullet Rab)$ 4–11 CP
13. $(x)[Px \supset (Sb \bullet Rxb)]$ 12, UG
14. $(\exists y)(x)[Px \supset (Sy \bullet Rxy)]$ 13 EG

6.   1. $(x)[Px \supset (Qx \vee Rx)]$ Premise
  2. $(\exists x)(Sx \bullet \smallsmile Qx)$ Premise
  3. $(x)[Rx \supset (Px \bullet Sx)] \, / \, (x)(Px \supset Sx)$ Premise/Conclusion
  4. $Sa \bullet \smallsmile Qa$ 2 EI
  5. $Pa \supset (Qa \vee Ra)$ 1 UI
  6. $Ra \supset (Pa \bullet Sa)$ 3 UI
   7. Pa Assumption
   8. $Qa \vee Ra$ 5,7 MP
   9. $\smallsmile Qa$ 4 Simp
  10. Ra 8,9 DS
  11. $Pa \bullet Sa$ 6,10 MP
  12. Sa 11 Simp
13. $Pa \supset Sa$ 7–12 CP
14. $(x)(Px \supset Sx)$ 13 UG

D. Show that each of the following arguments is valid by constructing a proof.

1. $(x)[Px \supset (Qx \vee Rx)]$
$\underline{(\exists x)(Px \bullet \smallsmile Rx)}$
$(\exists x)Qx$

2. $(\exists x)(y)[Px \bullet (Qy \bullet Rxy)]$
$\underline{(x)(Px \supset Qx)}$
$(\exists x)Rxx$

3. $\underline{(\exists x)Px \supset (y)Qy}$
$(y)(\exists x)(Px \supset Qy)$

4. $(x)(Px \supset Qx)$
$\smallsmile (\exists x)(Qx \bullet Sx)$
$\underline{(x)(Rx \supset Sx)}$
$(x)(Px \supset \smallsmile Rx)$

5. $\underline{(x)[(Px \vee Qx) \supset Rx]}$
$(x)Px \supset (x)Rx$

6. $(x)(Px \equiv Qx)$
   $(x)(Px \supset (\exists y)Rxy)$
   $\underline{(\exists x)Qx}$
   $(\exists x)(\exists y)Rxy$

7. $(x)[(Qx \cdot Rx) \supset Px]$
   $(x)[(Qx \cdot Sx) \supset Tx]$
   $\underline{(\exists x)[Qx \cdot (Rx \lor Sx)]}$
   $(\exists x)(Px \lor Tx)$

8. $(x)[(Px \lor Qx) \supset (\exists y)Sy]$
   $\underline{(\exists x)[Px \cdot (y)(Sy \supset Rxy)]}$
   $(\exists x)(\exists y)Rxy$

9. $(x)(Px \lor (\exists y)Rxy)$
   $(x)(Qx \supset \smallfrown Px)$
   $\underline{(x)(y)(Rxy \supset Sy)}$
   $(\exists x)Qx \supset (\exists x)Sx$

10. $(\exists x)[Qx \cdot (Rx \lor Sx)]$
    $(x)[(Qx \cdot Sx) \supset Tx]$
    $\underline{(x) \smallfrown (Px \lor Tx)}$
    $(\exists x)[(Qx \cdot Rx) \cdot \smallfrown Px]$

11. $(x)(Px \supset Qx) \supset (\exists y)(Ry \cdot Sy)$
    $\underline{(x) \smallfrown Sx}$
    $(\exists x)(Px \cdot \smallfrown Qx)$

12. $(x)(Pxa \supset Rx)$
    $(\exists x)(Qx \cdot Pxb)$
    $\underline{(x)(Qx \supset \lor \smallfrown Rx)}$
    $\smallfrown (x)(Pxb \supset (Pxa)$

13. $(x)(Px \lor Qx)$
    $(x)(\exists y)(Rxy \supset \smallfrown Px)$
    $\underline{(x)(y)(Qx \supset Sxy)}$
    $(x)(\exists y)(Rxy \supset Sxy)$

14. $(\exists x)\{Px \cdot (y)(z)[(Qy \cdot Rz) \supset Sxyz]\}$
    $\underline{(x) (Px \supset Rx)}$
    $(y)(\exists x)(Qy \supset Sxyx)$

15. $(x)[Px \supset (Qa \cdot Rxa)]$
    $\underline{(\exists x)(Qx \lor Sx) \supset (y)(z)(Ryz \supset Tyz)}$
    $(x)(\exists y)(Px \supset Txy)$

16. $(x) \{Px \supset (y)[(Qy \cdot Ry) \supset \lor Sxy]\}$
    $(x)(y)(Txy \supset Sxy)$
    $\underline{(x)(y)Txy}$
    $(x)[Px \supset \smallfrown (\exists y)(Qy \cdot Ry)]$

17. $(\exists x)(Px \cdot Qx) \supset (y)(Ry \supset Sy)$
    $\underline{(\exists x)(Px \cdot Rx)}$
    $(\exists x)(Qx \supset Sx)$

18. $(\exists x)(Px \cdot \backsim Qx) \supset Ra$
    $(\exists x)Rx \supset (y)(Py \supset Qy)$
    $\overline{(x)(Px \supset Qx)}$

19. $(x)\{Px \supset (y)[(Qy \cdot Rxy) \supset (\exists z)(Sz \cdot Txyz)]\}$
    $(x)(\exists y)(Sx \equiv \backsim Sy)$
    $\overline{(\exists x)(\exists y)[Px \cdot (Qy \cdot Rxy)] \supset \backsim (z)Sz}$

20. $(x)[Px \supset (\exists y)(z)(Qy \cdot Rxyz)]$
    $(x)(Qx \supset Sx)$
    $(x)(y)(z)(Rxyz \supset Txz)$
    $\overline{(\exists x)(\exists y)(z)[Px \supset (Sy \cdot Txz)]}$

E. Translate each of the following arguments into symbolic notation, and construct a proof.

1. Anyone who buys a used car from Marty is either a fool or has money to burn. Jamie bought a used car from Marty, and he doesn't have money to burn. So there's at least one fool in the world.

2. The aerospace plane will have a speed of Mach 4, and will therefore have to use hydrogen fuel. That's because any plane moving at Mach 4 must use a fuel that ignites in air moving at that speed, and only hydrogen will ignite in air moving at Mach 4.

3. Anyone who passes an advanced philosophy course has a logical mind, and anyone with a logical mind can master any field of law. Gabrielle passed metaphysics, which is an advanced philosophy course, so she can master torts, which is a field of law.

4. According to Soviet law, any worker employed by a state-owned enterprise must cooperate with the KGB. Since anyone who works is employed by some state-owned enterprise, all workers must cooperate with the KGB.

5. One is a member of a club only if the club is willing to have him and if he joins the club. But I wouldn't join any club willing to have me, so I am not a member of any club.

6. All physical things have a finite duration. If everything is physical, then the soul is physical; and the soul, if it has a finite duration, is not immortal. So if everything is physical, the soul is not immortal.

7. Every decision is an event, and every event is caused by something. A cause is either an event or an agent. So every decision is caused either by an event or by an agent.

8. For any number there is a number larger than it. Therefore there is no number larger than every other (assuming it is true of all numbers that if one is larger than another, the second is not larger than the first).

14

Term Logic

The classical logic of categorical syllogisms that we studied in Part III was originated by the ancient Greek philosopher Aristotle. Though it was modified and developed further by later logicians, it remained essentially unchanged until the nineteenth century, when it was rapidly eclipsed by the kind of symbolic logic we studied in the last two chapters. As I indicated at the beginning of Chapter 12, this change occurred because classical logic was inadequate in two major respects: it could not deal with inferences involving relationships among things, and it had only a rudimentary apparatus for propositional inferences involving connectives such as "and," "or," and "if . . . then."

As we have seen in the last two chapters, conventional symbolic logic offers a powerful way of solving both problems. But it pays a price for this power, by departing in various ways from our ordinary understanding of the statements it symbolizes. Consider the standard categorical proposition "All S are P." S is the grammatical subject of this proposition. But the symbolic translation is $(x) (Sx \supset Px)$, in which S is a predicate whose subject is the variable x. This variable is bound, moreover, by a universal quantifier, which ranges over everything in the universe. So the symbolic translation treats the proposition as a statement about everything, even though it appears to say something only about Ss and Ps.

In addition, because Sx and Px are distinct propositions, they must be joined by a propositional connective. Even though categorical statements are the simple grammatical units from which a compound statement is built, therefore, conventional symbolic logic treats them as a special kind of compound statement. That's why we had to study propositional logic before predicate logic. Finally, we've seen that the truth-functional interpretation of the propositional connectives raises a number of problems, but this controversial view about the meaning of the connectives is built into the rules governing their use in inference.

In all these ways, the classical approach seems closer to the way we understand categorical propositions in ordinary thought and language. It retains the subject-predicate structure in which S and P are terms (hence the name "term logic") rather than disguised propositions. It employs quantifiers ("all," "some") that range over the referents of its terms, not over everything in the universe. It does not use propositional connectives to analyze the internal structure of categorical statements, nor does it require the truth-functional interpretation of these connectives.

There seems to be a tradeoff, therefore, between the greater naturalness of the classical approach and the greater logical power of modern symbolic logic. In recent years, however, a contemporary philosopher, Fred Sommers, has developed the classical term logic so that it has a comparable degree of logical power. Sommers's logic is fully symbolic; he uses the plus and minus signs of arithmetic to represent the logical form of categorical propositions. But he retains the classical view that S and P are terms within the subject-predicate structure of such propositions. He goes on to show how relations can be represented within this structure. And reversing the conventional order, he shows how the logic of the propositional connectives can be built up from the logic of categorical inferences.

It will therefore be worth our while to examine his system as a possible alternative to the conventional approach. In the first section, we'll learn Sommers's method of representing the logical form of categorical propositions with plus and minus signs. Then we'll see how this allows a simple test for the validity of categorical syllogisms. In later sections, we'll extend the system to handle more complex statements and arguments.

Terms and Connectives

The logic of a deductive argument is governed by the logical form of the statements involved. So our first task is to abstract the logical form of a categorical statement from its content. As we saw in Chapter 8, the content is provided by the subject and predicate terms, which we symbolize with the letters S and P. To isolate the formal elements, we need to identify the various things we can do with a given pair of terms to make different statements.

Since we're going to represent the elements of form by plus and minus signs, let's pause for a moment to recall how these signs are used in arithmetic. Their most common use is to represent addition and subtraction. In this context, they are connectives that operate on two numbers to produce a sum or difference: $7 + 3 = 10$, $7 - 3 = 4$. Because they operate on a pair of numbers, we call them *binary* connectives. But we can also use them as *unary* connectives, operating on a single number, to indicate whether it is positive or negative: $(+7)$, (-7). The minus sign is also unary in $-(7 + 3)$; the parentheses indicate that we first add 7 and 3 and then negate the single number that is their sum.

We use the same sign, in other words, for two different jobs. This ambiguity is in fact a great asset, because it simplifies our calculations and gives us a lot of flexibility. If we have a unary minus sign, for example, we don't need subtraction as a binary connective. Instead of subtracting a (positive) number, we can add a negative number: $7 - 3 = 7 + (-3)$.

Now let's get back to logic. Just as we can talk about positive or negative numbers, we can talk about a term T or its complement non-T: mortal/immortal, citizen/noncitizen, finite/infinite (to review the relation between a term and its complement, see pages 184–86). To represent this distinction, we use plus and minus signs as unary connectives:

$$S \text{ is } P = (+S) \text{ is } (+P)$$
$$S \text{ is non-}P = (+S) \text{ is } (-P)$$
$$\text{Non-}S \text{ is } P = (-S) \text{ is } (+P)$$
$$\text{Non-}S \text{ is non-}P = (-S) \text{ is } (-P)$$

As in arithmetic, we normally omit the plus signs; we take a term as positive unless it is prefixed by a minus sign. Unlike negation in propositional logic, the minus sign operates on a term rather than on a proposition. But it performs the same function: it changes the term into its opposite, and the law of double negation holds: $(--P) = (+P) = P$. So from now on we'll refer to $(-T)$ as the *negation* of T rather than its complement.

In the classical approach, two other elements determine logical form. Every categorical proposition has a positive or negative *quality*, determined by the copula ("is," "is not"); and it has a particular or universal *quantity*, determined by a quantifier ("some," "all"). Sommers observed that these too can be represented by plus or minus signs. To see how this works, let's start with the I proposition "Some S is P." When we make this assertion, we are joining S and P in a positive way. We're saying that the terms have referents in common. It's natural to represent this link between the terms by plus signs:

$$\text{Some } S \text{ is } P = +S + P.$$
$$\text{Some fabrics are washable} = +F + W$$
$$\text{A baby is crying} = +B + C$$
$$\text{Some idiot is double-parked} = +I + D$$

The two plus signs represents a binary connective, $+ \underline{\quad} + \underline{\quad}$, that operates on a pair of terms to produce a statement, just as the plus sign of addition is a binary connective for numbers. In effect, the first sign stands for "some" and the second one for "is."

Now consider the O proposition "Some S is not P." We could represent this in either of two equivalent ways:

$$\text{i) } +S + (-P) = \text{Some } S \text{ is non-}P$$
$$\text{ii) } +S - P \quad = \text{Some } S \text{ isn't } P.$$

In (i), we have used the same binary connective as above, but we have added a unary minus sign to negate P. In (ii), we kept the terms positive, but used a new binary connective, $+ \underline{\quad} - \underline{\quad}$, to represent "Some . . . isn't. . . ." This new connective is to the old one as subtraction is to addition. And just as we could get along in arithmetic without subtraction, we don't really need the new connective; we could always express an O proposition in the form of (i). But our language gives us the freedom to express the proposition either way, so it's convenient to have the same freedom in our logical notation.

So far we have used unary and binary signs to represent three dimensions of logical form. We apply unary signs to subject and predicate terms in order to indicate whether we're talking about S or non-S, P or non-P. That's two dimensions. And we've represented positive or negative quality by the second sign in our binary connectives: $+ \underline{\quad} + \underline{\quad}$ and $+ \underline{\quad} - \underline{\quad}$. But what about the fourth dimension, quantity? Well, the first sign in each connective means "some," which suggests that we can use a minus sign for universal quantity: "all" or "every." This may seem strange; universality does not seem to be a negative feature. But in fact it makes sense. To see why, we need to consider one last dimension of logical form.

In representing the I and O propositions, we've made the obvious assumption that each proposition— $+ S + P$ or $+ S - P$—is being affirmed or said to be true. To make this explicit, we might use a unary plus sign that applies to the entire proposition: $+(+ S + P)$ and $+(+ S - P)$. The plus sign means "It is the case that," or "Yes:" or "It's true that." And now we may remember that each universal proposition contradicts one of the particular ones. The E proposition "No victory is cheap" denies that some victory is cheap. And the A proposition "All athletes are in good shape" says it is not the case that some athletes aren't in good shape. So both universal statements can be represented as denials, using a unary minus sign that means "It is not the case that," or "Not:" or "It's not true that."

A: Not: some S isn't P   E: Not: some S is P
$\quad -(+ S - P)$ $\quad -(+ S + P)$

I: Yes: Some S is P   O: Yes: Some S isn't P
$\quad +(+ S + P)$ $\quad +(+ S - P)$

The E proposition contradicts the I; it denies that some S is P. Similarly, the A proposition contradicts the O; it denies that some S isn't P.

The plus and minus signs outside the parentheses represent affirmation or denial. They are unary connectives, like the signs that apply to an individual term, because they apply to the statement inside the parentheses as a single unit. We can omit the plus sign for affirmation, just as we normally omit the plus in (+P). We can't omit the minus sign for denial without changing the meaning of our statement. But we can get rid of it by adding it algebraically into the expression within the parentheses. Since it governs the whole expression, it changes each sign into its opposite:

A. Not: some S isn't $P = -(+ S - P) = - S + P =$ Every S is P
E. Not: some S is P $\quad = -(+ S + P) = - S - P =$ Every S isn't P
$\quad$ No S is P

In effect, we now have two new binary connectives: $-\underline{\quad} + \underline{\quad}$ and $-\underline{\quad} - \underline{\quad}$. In each case the first minus sign represents universal quantity, while the second sign indicates quality. In the E proposition, the connective $-\underline{\quad} - \underline{\quad}$ is best captured by the English formula "Every S isn't P," because the latter has a negative copula. The traditional expression "No S is P" is really an abbreviation of "Not: Some S is P." But since "No S is P" *is* the traditional way to express the E proposition, we will use it to translate $-\underline{\quad} - \underline{\quad}$.

Altogether, then, we have five dimensions of logical form. On each dimension there are two opposing values (affirmation/denial, universal/particular, etc.), and we represent them all by plus or minus signs. They can be arrayed schematically as follows:

1		2	3	4	5	
$\pm$	(	$\pm$	$(\pm S)$	$\pm$	$(\pm P)$	)
Yes:		some	S	is	P	
Not:		all	non-S	isn't	non-P	

This is the fully explicit representation of logical form. It looks a bit forbidding, but we normally don't need to make everything explicit. From here on, we're going to adopt certain conventions that will simplify matters.

To begin with, we will omit unary plus signs. That's the common practice in arithmetic, and we'll follow the same convention here. The unary signs are those in columns 1, 3, and 5. So if we're dealing with terms rather than their negations, we won't bother with the plus signs in columns 3 and 5. And if we're affirming a proposition, we won't bother with the initial plus sign. Moreover, as we've seen, a minus sign in column 1 can be dropped by changing a denial into an affirmation. We do that by driving the minus sign into the expression within the parentheses, reversing the signs in columns 2 and 4. That's because contradictory propositions have opposite quantity and quality. It is always possible, therefore, to get rid of the sign in column 1. When we have done so, we have a statement in *affirmative standard form*. The statement will consist of one of the four binary connectives,

$$
\begin{array}{llll}
\text{I:} & + \underline{\quad} + \underline{\quad} & (\text{Some } \underline{\quad} \text{ is } \underline{\quad}) \\
\text{O:} & + \underline{\quad} - \underline{\quad} & (\text{Some } \underline{\quad} \text{ isn't } \underline{\quad}) \\
\text{A:} & - \underline{\quad} + \underline{\quad} & (\text{Every } \underline{\quad} \text{ is } \underline{\quad}) \\
\text{E:} & - \underline{\quad} - \underline{\quad} & (\text{No } \underline{\quad} \text{ is } \underline{\quad}),
\end{array}
$$

with the blanks filled by terms or their negations.

There's a simple procedure to follow, then, in translating statements from ordinary language into logical notation. First identify the terms, and notice whether one or both terms are negated; enter each term or its negation into the appropriate position. Then find the quantity and quality. If the statement is affirmative, this will be straightforward. If it's negative, you will need to reverse the signs for quality and quantity. Until you get the hang of it, you may want to start with a fully explicit translation, including the initial minus sign for negation, and then make the reversals.

Here's an example:

1) It isn't true that all nonreflex actions are voluntary.

The subject term is "reflex actions," and it is negated. We represent it by $(-R)$. The predicate term is "voluntary (actions)": V. Next we notice that (1) is a denial, so we'll start by using an initial minus sign. What is being denied is the claim that all $(-R)$ are V, which is universal and positive in quality. So the translation would be:

1a) $-(- (-R) + V)$—Not all nonreflex actions are voluntary.

Now we'll get rid of the initial minus sign:

1b) $+(-R) - V$—Some nonreflex actions aren't voluntary.

(1a) looks pretty messy, with three minus signs preceding the term R. We combined the first two into a plus sign that means "some." But we cannot combine the third one, which indicates non-R, with either of the first two. To see why, consider the following pair of statements:

2) All noncitizens are aliens $-(-C) + A$
3) Some citizens are aliens $+ C + A.$

These are algebraically equal, since the two minus signs in (2) add up to the plus in (3). But (2) and (3) are obviously not equivalent. So when a subject term is negated, we must leave it that way. We'll talk about the reason for this in the next section.

There's one final point we need to discuss here. In addition to universal and particular statements, we can make singular statements in which the subject term designates an individual rather than a class of things. For example:

4) Socrates is mortal.
5) Benedict Arnold was not a hero.
6) The AT&T building is ugly.

In classical logic, such statements were regarded as having universal quantity, on the ground that the name can be thought of as representing a class with a single member, so that we're making a statement about the entire class. But we can just as easily regard them as particular. We might interpret (4), for example, as saying that someone named Socrates is mortal. If a class has only one member, there's really no difference between "some" and "all." That's why we don't use a quantifier in ordinary language when we speak of individuals. For logical purposes, therefore, we will treat singular propositions as having "wild" quantity, represented by an asterisk:

4) $* S + M$
5) $* A - H$
6) $* A + U$

The asterisk indicates that the subject term is a name of an individual, and that the statement has the logical properties of both a particular and a universal proposition.

Practice Quiz

Put each of the following statements into algebraic notation, using appropriate letters to represent the terms.

1. Every machine is an artifact.
2. Some countries are not at peace.
3. Some trees are deciduous.
4. Bette Davis has brown eyes.
5. No perishable item is taxable.
6. Every road was impassable.
7. Not a creature was stirring.
8. Princess Di is not uncouth.
9. The cat next door is a killer.
10. Some of the term papers are inadequate.
11. Some retired people aren't unhappy.
12. It's not the case that every rock star is rich.
13. No inanimate object is conscious.
14. Not all that glitters is gold.
15. It isn't true that no conductor is nonmetallic.

Equivalence and Syllogisms

In Chapter 8 we studied the various relations in the square of opposition, as well as certain relationships—converse, obverse, and contrapositive—that hold among pairs of equivalent propositions. In Chapter 9 we learned four rules for telling whether a categorical syllogism is valid. Now that we have developed our notation for categorical propositions, we can replace all of that with two simple rules, one for equivalence and one for validity.

Equivalence

In order to state the rule of equivalence, we need to make explicit a concept that is implicit in our notation. We use a minus sign for a universal statement because it is a denial of a particular statement. A particular statement asserts the *existence* of something—an S that is P, an S that is non-P. A universal statement asserts the *nonexistence* of something. "No S is P" asserts the nonexistence of Ss that are P. "All S are P" asserts the nonexistence of Ss that are non-P. This feature of a statement is called its **valence**. Particular statements have positive valence, because they assert existence; universal statements have negative valence, because they assert nonexistence.

If we deny a given statement, then we reverse its valence. Denying a particular proposition is equivalent to affirming a universal one, and vice versa. Thus, in the fully explicit representation of logical form,

$$\begin{array}{ccccc} 1 & 2 & 3 & 4 & 5 \\ \pm\,(& \pm\,(& \pm S) & \pm\,(& \pm P)), \end{array}$$

valence is a function of the first two signs. If they are the same (both positive or both negative), then the statement has positive valence. If they are different, the valence is negative. Normally, however, we won't use the fully explicit form; we'll use the affirmative standard form. In that case, valence is the same as quantity, and can be determined simply by looking at the quantity sign.

With the concept of valence in hand, we can now state our rule:

Principle of Equivalence (PEQ): Two categorical statements are equivalent if and only if:

   i) They have the same valence; and
   ii) They are algebraically equal.

The first part of this test is easy to apply; we have just seen how to determine the valence of a statement. Part (ii) exploits the fact that we've used plus and minus signs to represent different aspects of logical form. It tells us to add up the signs governing the terms in each proposition. The subject term is governed by the sign for term negation (if the term is being negated) as well as the sign for quantity. The predicate term is governed by its term negation sign as well as the sign for quality. And if we have an initial sign for affirmation or denial, it governs both terms. When we add up the signs governing each term, we follow the same rule as in algebra. A series of plus signs, or an even number of minus signs, add up to a plus; an odd number of minus signs add up to a minus.

Let's apply the test to some examples. The following propositions are contrapositives, so we know they're equivalent:

1) All graduates are competent people
2) All incompetent people are nongraduates

In both cases we're affirming a universal proposition; the only difference is that the terms have been switched and replaced by their negations. So the statements would be translated as:

1) $-G + C$
2) $-(-C) + (-G)$

(1) and (2) are both universal, so they have the same valence. And they are algebraically equal. It's easy to see that G is negative in both cases. C is positive in (1), and positive again in (2) because the two minus signs preceding it add up to a plus.

What about the following pair?

3) Some nonadults are thumbsuckers: $+ (-A) + T$
4) All adults are thumbsuckers: $- A + T$

These pass the equality test; A is negative in both propositions, and T is positive. But they differ in valence—(3) is particular and (4) is universal—so they're not equivalent. This is why, when we simplify a statement in logical notation, we cannot add the sign for quantity to the sign for subject term negation; in doing so we might alter the valence and produce a nonequivalent statement. It's important to stress, however, that when we apply PEQ, it is the *valence* criterion that handles this problem. The *equality* test is not concerned with this issue; it tells us to add pluses and minuses wherever they occur.

Consider now the statements:

5) Every non-sale item is returnable: $-(-S) + R$
6) Not a (single) returnable thing is a sale item: $-(+R + S)$

(5) and (6) are both negative in valence (notice that (6) is a denial of a particular statement), but they aren't equal: R and S are positive in (5), but negative in (6). So they are not equivalent.

As a final example, let's consider the nonstandard quantifier "only," as in "Only members are welcome." As we saw in Chapter 11, statements of this form can be translated in either of two ways:

7a) All who are welcome are members: $-W + M$
7b) No nonmember is welcome: $-(-M) - W$

Since these have the same valence, and are algebraically equal, they are equivalent.

Practice Quiz

Put each pair of statements into algebraic notation; then determine whether they are equivalent.

1. All bachelors are unmarried. No married man is a bachelor.
2. Some politicians are dishonest. Some honest people are not politicians.

3. No punk haircuts are acceptable. All punk haircuts are unacceptable.
4. Some valid arguments have untrue premises. Some arguments with true premises are invalid.
5. All sonnets have 14 lines. Not all sonnets fail to have 14 lines.
6. Every challenge is an opportunity. Not a single opportunity is unchallenging.
7. It isn't true that no human is perfect. Some perfect thing is not non-human.
8. Not a word was spoken. All words were unspoken.
9. No state that is not well-armed has good laws. Every state that is well-armed has good laws.
10. Some municipalities with less than 100,000 in population are cities. Not all cities are municipalities with 100,000 or more in population.

Validity

Let us turn now to the rule for syllogisms. The classical syllogism consists of three statements, which contain altogether three terms, each term occurring twice in different statements. The middle term is the one that occurs in both premises but not the conclusion. For example:

$$
\begin{array}{ll}
\text{Every felony is a crime} & -F + C \\
\underline{\text{Every embezzlement is a felony}} & \underline{-E + F} \\
\text{Every embezzlement is a crime} & -E + C
\end{array}
$$

Notice that if we add up the premises in the algebraic notation, we get the conclusion; the positive and negative occurrences of F cancel out and we are left with $-E + C$. This provides us with one condition for syllogistic validity: the sum of the premises must be equal to the conclusion.

As in the principle of equivalence, however, equality is not enough; we also need a condition pertaining to quantity. Consider the argument:

$$
\begin{array}{ll}
\text{Some bananas are ripe} & +B + R \\
\underline{\text{Some apples are not ripe}} & \underline{+A - R} \\
\text{Some apples are bananas} & +A + B
\end{array}
$$

The middle term R cancels out, and the sum of the premises equals the conclusion, but the syllogism is obviously invalid. The problem is that both premises are particular, and nothing follows from two particular statements. Strictly speaking, the problem here is one of valence, not quantity per se. We might have expressed the second premise in the argument as a denial:

Some bananas are ripe $+ B + R$
Not all apples are ripe $-(- A + R)$
Some apples are bananas $+ A + B$

It is the positive valence of the two premises that makes this argument invalid.

But when we work with syllogisms, it is a good idea to put the premises and the conclusion in affirmative standard form. This will make life much easier, especially when we get to more complex syllogistic arguments. And for statements in affirmative standard form, valence is the same as quantity. So we will state the rule of validity in terms of quantity rather than valence:

Rule of Syllogistic Validity (SV): A syllogistic argument in affirmative standard form is valid if and only if:

i) It contains only universal statements, or else just one particular premise and a particular conclusion; and
ii) The premises are equal to the conclusion.

In addition to its simplicity, this rule has two other advantages over the set of rules for validity that we learned in Chapter 9. First, it does not require that we get rid of negated terms before we apply the rule. The plus and minus signs take care of that. Consider the argument:

No uncommunicative people make friends easily $-(-C) - M$
Some introverts are not communicative $+ I - C$
Some introverts do not make friends easily $+ I - M$

Part (i) of SV is satisfied because the syllogism has just one particular premise and a particular conclusion. And C has a positive occurrence in the first premise, since the two minus signs add up to a plus, and it therefore cancels the negative occurrence in the second premise.

The second advantage is that the rule is not restricted to classical syllogisms consisting of three statements and three terms. It applies to arguments with *any* number of premises, so long as their terms recur in the syllogistic pattern. Here's an example with three premises:

Only evidence that is admissible in court is reliable $-(-A) - R$
No hearsay evidence is admissible in court $- H - A$
All gossip is hearsay evidence $- G + H$
All gossip is unreliable $- G + (-R)$

It's easy to determine that all the premises are universal, and that the premises add up to the conclusion. Instead of one middle term we have two (*A* and *H*), and they both cancel out.

When a syllogistic argument contains singular statements, we have to remember that such statements have wild quantity. The argument is valid if we can assign quantities to them in such a way as to satisfy the syllogistic rule. For example:

$$
\begin{array}{ll}
\text{All humans are mortal} & -H+M \\
\underline{\text{Socrates is human}} & \underline{*\ S+H} \\
\text{Socrates is mortal} & *\ S+M
\end{array}
$$

In this case we could give the two singular statements either quantity; the rules are satisfied as long as they have the same quantity. But consider a different argument:

$$
\begin{array}{ll}
\text{Senator Moynihan is an intellectual} & *\ M+I \\
\underline{\text{Senator Moynihan is a politician}} & \underline{*\ M+P} \\
\text{Some politicians are intellectuals} & +\ P+I
\end{array}
$$

Here the individual name serves as the middle term, so we must assign opposite quantity to the two premises in order to make the middle term cancel out.

Let us consider, finally, an argument that is similar in structure to the last one:

$$
\begin{array}{ll}
\text{All pineapples are sweet} & -P+S \\
\underline{\text{All pineapples are nutritious}} & \underline{-P+N} \\
\text{Some sweet things are nutritious} & +S+N
\end{array}
$$

This argument seems valid. But it violates both parts of our test: it has a particular conclusion without a particular premise, and *P* is negative in both premises, so it doesn't cancel out. Notice what happens, however, when we add the obvious premise that some pineapples are pineapples:

$$
\begin{array}{l}
+P+P \\
-P+S \\
\underline{-P+N} \\
+S+N
\end{array}
$$

Now we have an argument that satisfies the test. Why did the addition of an obvious premise make such a difference?

The answer has to do with existential import. We saw in the last chapter that modern predicate logic interprets universal statements as conditionals. "All pineapples are sweet" would be translated as "If anything is a pineapple, then it is sweet," which is true even if there are no pineapples. Modern term logic takes the same view, though for a different reason. We have said that universal statements have negative valence because they assert the nonexistence of something. When we say that all pineapples are sweet, we are denying the existence of unsweet pineapples; we are barring the doors of the pineapple class against unsweet things. In doing so we take it for granted that the class has some members. But it is not the job of the universal statement to say so; logically speaking, that's the job of a particular statement. So to get this job done, in the argument above, we had to add a particular premise.

With the principles of equivalence and syllogistic validity, we can deal with all the arguments covered by classical logic. These arguments involve categorical statements with simple terms that can be represented by a single letter. In the remainder of the chapter, we'll see how modern term logic deals with more complex statements and arguments.

Practice Quiz

Formulate each of the following arguments in algebraic notation, and test for validity.

1. All outfielders are fast runners, and any fast runner can steal base. So every outfielder can steal base.
2. Some actions that are legal are unjust, but no morally permissible action is unjust. So some legal actions are not permissible.
3. Dr. Martin is a professor, and she is also a good writer. So some professors are good writers.
4. Since no banker is irresponsible, every banker is punctual; for all responsible people are punctual.
5. Not all rock stars are rich, but some rock stars own BMWs. Therefore some non-rich people own BMWs.
6. Some research methods are not ethical. But all research methods are motivated by the desire for knowledge, and nothing inspired by that motive is contemptible. Thus some unethical things are not contemptible.
7. Some of the winners were gracious, and no ungracious person was invited to the party. Therefore some Republicans were winners, because everyone invited to the party was a Republican.
8. Ideas are not physical things. But some ideas are patented, and anything patented is privately owned. So it isn't true that only physical things are privately owned.

Relational Terms

In term logic, every statement has a *dyadic* structure: it consists of a subject and a predicate term, linked by a binary connective. So far we have been dealing with simple terms. But a term may also be complex, having its own internal dyadic structure. This is the key to Sommers's analysis of statements about the relationships among things.

Consider the statement:

1) A hailstorm ruined some of the crops.

This tells us about the relationship between a hailstorm and the crops. Its basic structure would be represented as $+H+X$, where X stands for the complex term "ruined some of the crops." Within the basic structure of (1), this is a predicate term. But it has its own internal dyadic structure, in which "crops" is a subject with its own quantifier ("some") and "ruined" is an internal predicate. To understand the inferences we make about relationships, we normally need to represent this internal structure.

Notation

The notation we've developed so far gives us a natural way to do this. Using C for crops, R for "ruined," and the usual sign for "some," we formulate (1) as follows:

1a) $+H+(R+C)$

The parentheses indicate that R and C combine to form a single predicate term, which is then linked to the subject in the usual way. Inside the parentheses, we have put the internal predicate R first and the internal subject C second, following the order of the English statement. But we could have put C first:

1b) $+H+(+C+R)$

This would be read as saying "A hailstorm is what some crops were ruined by," which says the same thing as (1) but in a more awkward way. Notice that in (1b) we used the normal $+\underline{\quad}+\underline{\quad}$ connective inside the predicate. In (1a), by contrast, we only needed a single $+$ to represent the same connection between C and R. Similarly, the statement

2) A hailstorm ruined all of the crops

would be represented in either of two ways:

2a) $+ H + (R - C)$, or
2b) $+ H + (- C + R)$

From here on, we will normally follow the English order, putting the internal predicate first and using a single plus or minus sign. But occasionally we'll need the other pattern.

There's another device we need in order to represent relational statements clearly. Suppose we expressed (1) in a passive form: "Some crops were ruined by a hailstorm." If we put this into our notation by following the order of the English sentence, as we did above, we would have:

1a) $+ C + (R + H)$

And now we have a problem. Nothing in the notation tells us to read R in a passive way, as meaning "were ruined by," rather than in an active way, as meaning "ruined." But we aren't saying that some crops ruined a hailstorm. We avoid this problem by using subscripts on the term letters. R gets two subscripts—R_{12}—to indicate that it stands for a relationship in which something (1) ruins something else (2). Now we put the subscript 1 on H, to indicate that the hailstorm is what did the ruining, and the subscript 2 on C, to indicate that the crops are what got ruined. This eliminates any ambiguity:

1) A hailstorm ruined some crops: $+ H_1 + (R_{12} + C_2)$
1a) Some crops were ruined by a hailstorm: $+ C_2 + (R_{12} + H_1)$
1b) Some crops ruined a hailstorm: $+ C_1 + (R_{12} + H_2)$

The subscripts tell us that (1) and (1a) are equivalent, and that (1) and (1b) are not.

A relational term can appear in the subject as well as the predicate. Consider the statement:

4) Every owner of a car is required to have an insurance policy.

The subject term is "owner of a car," and we would represent it as $(O_{12} + C_2)$. The statement is about a certain class of people, indicated by the subscript 1 in O_{12}, but they are referred to only as car owners, so there is no term letter with the single subscript 1. This class of people bears a certain relationship to insurance policies: they are required to have one. So the predicate term is $(R_{13} + I_3)$. We're still talking about the same people here, so we use the subscript 1 again, but we use the new subscript 3 for the insurance policies they must have. The statement as a whole is therefore:

4) $- (O_{12} + C_2) + (R_{13} + I_3)$

When we introduced the signs for quantity, we noticed that singular statements have wild quantity, represented by an asterisk that means plus *and* minus. We need to keep this in mind when we translate relational terms that refer to individuals as individuals. For example:

5) Someone assassinated President McKinley: $+ P_1 + (A_{12} * M_2)$
   [I.e., some person was an assassin of McKinley]
6) Some of my critics are airheads: $+ (C_{12} * M_2) + A_1$ [I.e., some who are critics of me are airheads]
7) Whatever Lola wants, Lola gets: $- (W_{12} * L_1) + (G_{12} * L_1)$
   [I.e.,everything wanted by Lola is gotten by Lola]

It is also possible for one relational term to be embedded within another. Consider the statement

8) Some deer ate everything I planted.

In the predicate we will need the relation letter A_{12} for the relation between the deer and what they ate. But what they ate is not described directly. It's described in terms of another relation—the fact that I planted it. So the translation would have to be

8) $+ D_1 + (A_{12} - (P_{32} * I_3)_2)$.

The subscripts here keep track of the players: the deer (1) are what did the eating, I (3) am the one who did the planting, and what got planted (2) is what got eaten. Notice that we put the subscript 2 on the embedded term as a whole: $(P_{32} * I_3)_2$. This is to indicate that the things described by this relational term are the object of the relation A_{12}.

As in modern predicate logic, finally, we are not limited to relations among just two items. The following examples involve three place relations:

9) Latvia is between Estonia $* L_1 + (B_{123} * E_2 * L'_3)$
   and Lithuania
10) Some student has done every $+ S_1 + (D_{123} - E_2 * B_3)$
   exercise in this book

We would follow the same pattern for relations among four or more items.

Practice Quiz

Put each of the following relational statements into logical notation.

1. Some children hate all vegetables.
2. Rabbits are afraid of dogs.
3. Larry hired a lawyer.
4. Those who fail a course will be on probation.
5. Marjorie borrowed some money from Sam.
6. Some lobbyist knows every congressman.
7. Some sailors have a girl in every port.
8. A thief stole everything I own.
9. Some who win an Oscar don't deserve one.
10. Lena married someone who didn't love her.

Equivalence

We have seen that simple categorical statements can be transformed in various ways. The Principle of Equivalence (PEQ) served as an overall test for such transformations. By telling us whether two statements are equivalent, it automatically weeded out the legitimate transformations that preserve equivalence from the illegitimate ones that do not. For statements with relational terms, however, there is no comparable principle that will give us a single, decisive test. Instead, we're going to use four rules of equivalence that specify particular kinds of legitimate transformation.

The first rule applies wherever we have a $+$ ____ $+$ ____ connective, and it says that the two terms may be switched:

Commutation (Com): $+ X + Y = + Y + X$

According to this principle, an I proposition and its converse are equivalent. A nonrelational example would be the pair:

9a) Some snakes are poisonous
9b) Some poisonous (things) are snakes

The same rule applies to I propositions with relational terms. Thus

10a) A farmer went to a market: $+ F_1 + (W_{12} + M_2)$

is equivalent to

10b) Someone who went to a market was a farmer: $+ (W_{12} + M_2) + F_1$

The second rule is called association. It allows us to switch the order among three or more component terms, as follows:

Association (Assoc): $+ X + (+ Y + Z) = (+ X + Y) + Z$

When we apply this rule to relational statements, Y is the term that designates the relation, X and Z designate the things related. At the beginning of this section, we observed that the statements

11a) A hailstorm ruined some crops $+ H_1 + (R_{12} + C_2)$, and
11b) Some crops were ruined by a hailstorm $+ C_2 + (R_{12} + H_1)$

are equivalent. We can now prove this equivalence by using commutation and association to drive (11b) from (11a):

$$+ H_1 + (R_{12} + C_2)$$
$$+ (+ H_1 + R_{12}) + C_2 \quad \text{Assoc}$$
$$+ C_2 + (+ H_1 + R_{12}) \quad \text{Com}$$

In the second line, we moved R_{12} from the predicate to the subject by association. Then we switched the subject and predicate terms by commutation. In the third line, the predicate term $(+ H_1 + R_{12})$ is simply an alternative way of expressing $(R_{12} + H_1)$, as we saw at the beginning of this section.

Commutation and association apply only to statements with plus-plus connectives. Two other rules will help us deal with statements involving negation. Both of these rules permit transformations that we're familiar with from our study of simple categorical statements.

External Negation (EN): $- (\pm X \pm Y) = \mp X \mp Y$
Internal Negation (IN): $\pm X - (\pm Y) = \pm X + (\mp Y)$

External Negation is the rule we follow in transforming a denial into affirmative standard form. We drive the initial minus sign into the dyad inside the parentheses, changing each sign of the binary connective into its opposite. We can also move in the opposite direction, changing an affirmative statement into a denial, and once again changing both signs of the connective. We could use this rule, along with commutation, to show that an E proposition and its converse are equivalent:

$$- S - P$$
$$- (+ S + P) \quad \text{EN}$$
$$- (+ P + S) \quad \text{Com}$$
$$- P - S \quad \text{EN}$$

Internal negation allows the operation known as obversion: it allows us to change the quality of a statement if we simultaneously change the predicate term into its negation. By this rule, for example, the following are equivalent:

12a) Some facts aren't known: $+F-K$
12b) Some facts are unknown: $+F+(-K)$

Let's see how these rules apply to relational statements. Suppose we made the surprising discovery that

13) Some scholar doesn't own any books.

This has the same basic logical form as the statement that some scholar doesn't drive. It is an O proposition, and might be represented initially as $+S-(X)$, where X is a temporary place holder for the relational term. The word "any" suggests that "books'" has universal quantity, but this can't be right. The statement that some scholar doesn't own every book would hardly be surprising. What we're denying is that the scholar owns even a single book. Thus X stands for the relational term $(O_{12}+B_2)$—"owner of a book"—and the statement as a whole is:

13) $+S_1-(O_{12}+B_2).$

Now let's use IN to transform (13) into an I proposition with a negated predicate term:

13a) $+S_1+(-(O_{12}+B_2)).$

The minus sign is a unary connective, indicating term negation. But since we have a relational term with a dyadic structure, we can use EN to drive that sign into the dyad, reversing the signs for each term:

$$-\ (O_{12}\qquad +\qquad B_2)\ =\ +(\ (-O_{12})\qquad -\qquad B_2)$$
Not: an owner of some book $=$ a nonowner of every book

So the statement as a whole becomes:

13b) $+S_1+((-O_{12})-B_2).$

This is clearly equivalent to (13). To say that someone is not an owner of a (single) book is to say that he is a non-owner of every book.

When we use the negation rules with relational terms, there's one error we must be especially careful to avoid. We've seen that statements of the forms

$$- (-S) + P, \text{ and}$$
$$+ S + P$$

are not equivalent. We're not allowed to add a unary minus sign for subject term negation to a minus sign for universal quantity. The same is true inside a relational term, even though in this case the subject normally comes second, after the relation letter. Thus the statements

14a) A student aced every test: $+ S_1 + (A_{12} - T_2)$, and
14b) A student aced some nontest: $+ S_1 + (A_{12} + (-T)_2)$,

are not equivalent. Since T is a subject term in the relational dyad, the IN rule does not apply.

The four rules we have just learned cover all the ways in which relational statements may be transformed while preserving equivalence. In the next section, we'll learn the basic *inference* rule that applies to such statements.

Practice Quiz

Put each pair of statements into algebraic notation. Then show that they are equivalent by using the rules to derive the second from the first.

1. Some Greeks are shipping magnates. Some shipping magnates are Greek.
2. It's not the case that every tree is deciduous. Some trees are not deciduous.
3. A baseball player wrote a book. Someone who wrote a book was a baseball player.
4. Some errors are honest. It's not the case that every error is dishonest.
5. Some accountant made an error. An error was made by some accountant.
6. Some beliefs are not supported by any evidence. Some beliefs are unsupported by all evidence.
7. No man is an island. No island is a man.
8. Some people who do not own any property are rich. Some rich people do not own any property.
9. Some athletes excel in every sport. It isn't true that every athlete fails to excel in some sport.
10. Every runner cleared every hurdle. Every hurdle was cleared by every runner.

Dictum de Omni

The Principle of Syllogistic Validity gives us a decisive test for the validity of any argument that fits the syllogistic pattern. But it won't work for inferences involving relational terms, or the compound terms we're going to study in the next section. As in propositional and predicate logic, we need to learn how to construct *proofs* in which we derive the conclusion from the premises by a series of valid steps. And as you might expect from the notation, proof in term logic is modeled on algebra.

In solving an algebraic problem, we typically start with certain information expressed as equations. For example:

i) $4x - y = x + 9$
ii) $y = 2x$

To find the value of x and y, we perform two kinds of operations. The first is the operation of transforming a single equation into a form that is more useful, closer to the answer. Thus we might subtract x from each side of (i), so that we have the simpler equation: $3x - y = 9$. This is like an immediate inference in logic: it is the transformation of a single premise into something equivalent. The second operation is to combine the information from two premises. Since (ii) tells us that $y = 2x$, we can replace y by $2x$ in our simplified version of (i): $3x - 2x = 9$. And now we can simplify this equation once again to conclude that $x = 9$.

Algebra gives us various rules for transforming one equation into another that is equivalent. We can subtract the same quantity from each side of the equation, as above, or add the same quantity, or take the square root; there are many other, more complex transformations of this kind. When we combine information from different equations, however, we always do it in accordance with a single rule: we replace an expression E in one equation with another expression E' when a second equation tells us that $E = E'$. This rule allowing the substitution of identical quantities is the essence of mediate (two-premise) inference in algebra. So the basic strategy for solving problems is to transform each equation until we can see how to substitute identities. Term logic follows the same pattern. There is one basic principle for mediate inference, and the strategy is to use equivalence rules to get each premise into a form to which the principle applies.

The basic principle of inference is called the **Dictum de Omni** (**DDO**), a Latin phrase that means "rule concerning the all." It says that whatever is true of all X is true of whatever is X. The validity of this rule is obvious in the basic syllogism:

$$\begin{array}{ll}
\text{Every } M \text{ is } P & -M + P \\
\underline{\text{Some/every } S \text{ is } M} & \underline{\pm\, S + M} \\
\text{Some/every } S \text{ is } P & \pm\, S + P
\end{array}$$

The first premise says that *P* is true of every *M*. Since some or all *S* are *M*, we may conclude that some or all *S* are *P*. Every valid syllogism can be put into this form, and thus proven valid by DDO, if we use immediate inferences to transform the premises and/or the conclusion.

Suppose we are given the premises:

$$\begin{array}{ll}
\text{Every } P \text{ is } M & = -P + M, \text{ and} \\
\text{Some } S \text{ is not } M & = +S - M.
\end{array}$$

We cannot apply DDO to these premises in their present form, because neither of them is a statement about all *M*. But the first premise could be transformed by contraposition into a statement about all non-*M*: $-(-M) + (-P)$. And it's easy to formulate the second premise in terms of non-*M* rather than *M*: $+S + (-M)$. Now we have an argument that fits the pattern above:

$$\begin{array}{l}
-(-M) + (-P) \\
\underline{+S + (-M)} \\
+S + (-P)
\end{array}$$

In order to use DDO with more complex inferences in algebraic notation, Sommers has formulated the rule in a more general way. The rule requires a pair of premises with a common term *M*. In one of the premises, *M* must have a positive occurrence; in the other it must occur with universal quantity. The premise with the positive occurrence of *M* is the *host* premise; it is analogous to the equation $3x - y = 9$ in our algebraic example above. The premise in which *M* occurs with universal quantity is the *donor* premise, because it contributes part of its content to the host premise. It tells us what *M* will be replaced by, and is thus analogous to the equation $y = 2x$.

Consider our first example again:

$$\begin{array}{ll}
\text{Donor premise:} & -M + P \\
\text{Host premise:} & +S + M
\end{array}$$

The boxed area in the donor premise is what it's going to contribute: $+P$. And we're going to insert it into the box around *M* in the host premise. In other words, DDO is a matter of transferring the contents of the first box into the second. The result of this operation is $+S + (+P)$. Notice that in this conclusion, we keep the plus sign that preceded M in the host premise, but the minus sign preceding M in the donor premise drops out of the picture.

Once we have the boxes drawn correctly, transferring contents is easy. The trick is to get the boxes right. The first step is to identify which premise has the positive occurrence of the middle term; that will be the host premise. The premise with a universal occurrence of M is the donor premise. If you mix these up, you will be inserting the wrong thing in the wrong place. It will be like trying to park the garage in the car. The second step is to draw a box around M in the host premise, leaving the plus sign outside, and to draw a box around everything *except* M in the donor premise, but leave the minus sign outside. Now you can transfer contents.

DDO does not require that the donor premise be positive in quality. It might be of the form "Every S isn't P" (i.e., "No S is P"):

$$
\begin{array}{ll}
\text{Donor premise:} & -M-P \\
\text{Host premise:} & -S+M \\
\text{Conclusion:} & -S+(-P)
\end{array}
$$

In this case what we insert into the host box is $-P$, because that's what is being attributed to all M in the donor premise.

What happens when M is the subject term of the host premise?

$$
\begin{array}{lll}
\text{Donor premise:} & -M+P & -M-P \\
\text{Host premise:} & +M+S & +M-S \\
\text{Conclusion:} & +(+P)+S & +(-P)-S
\end{array}
$$

In both cases, the conclusion has the same form as the host premise except for the contents of the box. You can make sure that both syllogisms are valid by checking to see that they satisfy the Rule of Syllogistic Validity (SV).

The Dictum De Omni is the basic principle of syllogistic reasoning; it's the principle that justifies the SV rule. For standard syllogisms of the kind we've been dealing with, SV is usually the easiest way to establish validity. But SV does not work for nonstandard inferences, including relational ones. In these cases, we must go back to basics, and use the *Dictum*.

Let's see how this works with an argument we've encountered before:

> Every Monet painting is a valuable thing
> I am the owner of a Monet painting
> I am the owner of a valuable thing

The second premise, like the conclusion, is a relational statement, and the term "Monet painting" occurs inside the relational term. In algebraic notation, this premise is: $* I_1 + (O_{12} + M_2)$. The term M occurs here in a positive context; it has particular quantity. And the other premise is a universal statement about Ms. So we can apply the *Dictum*:

$$\begin{aligned} \text{Donor premise:} &\quad -M + V \\ \text{Host premise:} &\quad * I_1 + (O_{12} + M_2) \\ \text{Conclusion:} &\quad * I_1 + (O_{12} + V_2) \end{aligned}$$

The conclusion retains everything from the host premise preceding M, including O as well as the subject term I. Notice that we didn't use subscripts in the donor premise, because it does not involve any relational term. But it wouldn't hurt to add the subscript 2 to both M and V, if that makes things clearer.

The middle term in the host premise must have a positive occurrence, but it need not be preceded by a plus sign. It may be governed by two minus signs that cancel out. For example:

$$\begin{aligned} \text{Every misspelled word is an error:} &\quad -M + E \\ \text{No proofreader catches every mispelled word:} &\quad -P_1 - (C_{12} - M_2) \\ \text{No proofreader catches every error:} &\quad -P_1 - (C_{12} - E_2) \end{aligned}$$

In the second premise, M occurs in a positive context, even though we're talking about every misspelled word, because the predicate has negative quality. We can confirm this by driving the negation sign into the predicate term, reversing the quantity of M. We would then have the statement "Every proofreader fails to catch some misspelled word," and the inference would be:

$$\begin{aligned} \text{Donor premise:} &\quad -M + E \\ \text{Host premise:} &\quad -P_1 + ((-C_{12}) + M_2) \\ \text{Conclusion:} &\quad -P_1 + ((-C_{12}) + E_2) \end{aligned}$$

In both of the preceding examples, the relational term occurred in the host premise. But the donor premise may also be relational, as long as the middle term has universal quantity. For example:

$$\begin{aligned} \text{Every action occurs at some place:} &\quad -A_1 + (O_{12} + P_2) \\ \text{Every thought is an action:} &\quad -T + A \\ \text{Every thought occurs at some place:} &\quad -T_1 + (O_{12} + P_2) \end{aligned}$$

Here we must be careful to remember that even though the second premise is the shorter of the two, it is the host premise because it includes the positive occurrence of A. If we keep that in mind, the application of DDO is easy.

It's a little harder when the middle term in the donor premise occurs *inside* a relational term, rather than in the subject position. Consider the following premises:

All contractors hate all architects: $-C_1 + (H_{12} - A_2)$
Joseph is married to an architect: $* J_3 + (M_{32} + A_2)$

We can apply DDO to these premises because A occurs in the first with universal quantity, and it is positive in the second. But we must be careful in transferring the contents of the box from the donor to the host premise. What we get is the conclusion

$$* J_3 + (M_{32} + (-C_1 + H_{12})_2)$$

The inserted term—$(-C_1 + H_{12})$—stands for that which every contractor hates. It is not in standard form for a relational term because the relation letter comes second. In this form the conclusion would be read: Joseph married someone whom every contractor hates. But we can reverse the order inside the parentheses, so that H and C are in the standard order for a relational dyad:

$$* J_3 + (M_{32} + (H_{12} - C_1)_2)$$

Joseph married someone hated by every contractor

In the donor premise, we must box the entire premise except the middle term and the sign for universal quantity that precedes it. With relations among three or more items, this may require a "split" box, as in the following example:

A teacher gave every student a book: $+T_1 + (G_{123} - S_2 + B_3)$
Antoine is a student: $* A + S$

The contents of both boxes in the donor premise must be put into the box around S in the host premise. The result is

$$* A_2 + (T_1 + G_{123} + B_3) = * A_2 + (G_{123} + B_3 + T_1)$$

Antoine was given a book by a teacher

The *Dictum de Omni* is the basic rule of proof in term logic. It may be formulated as the inference form

$$\begin{array}{l} D\,(-M) \\ \underline{H\,(M)} \\ H\,(D), \end{array}$$

where D stands for the contents of the box in the donor premise, and H for the expression outside the box in the host premise. The rule always operates on two premises, so in longer arguments we have to take two premises at a time. We'll work with some longer arguments in the final section of the chapter. But first we need to learn how to formulate compound terms in algebraic notation.

Practice Quiz

Apply DDO to each pair of statements. First determine which is the host premise and which the donor, then use DDO to draw a conclusion.

1. $-A + B$
   $-C + A$
2. $+A_1 + (R_{12} + B_2)$
   $-B + C$
3. $+A_1 + (R_{12} + B_2)$
   $-A + C$
4. $-B - D$
   $+A_1 + (R_{123} + B_2 + C_3)$
5. $-(R_{12} + A_1) + B_2$
   $-B_2 + (S_{23} + C_3)$

6. $-A_1 + (R_{12} - B_2)$
   $+A - C$
7. $-A + B$
   $+(R_{12} + A_2) + C_1$
8. $-A_1 - (R_{12} - B_2)$
   $-B + C$
9. $+A_1 + (R_{12} - B_2)$
   $+C + B$
10. $-A + B$
    $-(R_{12} - A_2) + C_1$

Compound Terms

It's a sad truth that

1) Some people are both knaves and fools.

This is a categorical statement, and the predicate term is "both knaves and fools." We could treat this as a single unanalyzed term, representing it by a single letter. Yet it clearly has an internal logical structure; it is composed of the simple terms "knave" and "fool." And we need to represent this structure so that we can explain an inference like:

> Some people are both knaves and fools
> <u>Every</u> knave is dishonest
> Some people are both dishonest and fools,

which is clearly valid. What we need is a way of representing such *compound* terms algebraically.

Conjunction

The structure "both . . . and . . ." is a binary connective that indicates a conjunction of terms, and is therefore naturally transcribed as $+ \ldots + \ldots$. In other words, we can use the same connective for "both . . . and . . . " that we used for "some . . . is . . . ." In the latter case, the connective operates on a pair of terms to produce a statement. In the former case it operates on a pair of terms to produce a compound term. To distinguish between these cases, we'll use angle brackets for the compound term.

Thus the statement above would be translated:

$$1) \quad + \; P + < \; + \; K + F >$$
$$\text{Some are both and}$$

The position of each plus sign, together with the brackets, tells us how to read it. And given this notation, the inference above is a straightforward instance of DDO:

$$\begin{aligned} \text{Donor premise: } &- K + (-D) \\ \text{Host premise: } &+ P + <+ K + F> \\ \hline \text{Conclusion: } &+ P + <+ (-D) + F> \end{aligned}$$

The word "both" is often left out when a conjunctive term is expressed in English. Sometimes the word "and" is not used either. This is the normal case with adjectives: "a red house" means "both red and a house." We can also express a conjunctive term with a relative clause. Consider the statement:

2) Conrad is a writer who is underrated.

The relative clause "who is underrated" modifies "a writer" to make up a single conjunctive term. In our notation, therefore, (2) *would be:* $* \, C + <+ W + U>$. A conjunctive term may also serve as the subject of a statement, as in the following examples:

3) A mighty oak has fallen: $+ <+ M + O> + F$
4) All employees except guards will leave: $- <+ E + (-G)> + L$

Notice that in (4) we have translated "all employees except guards" as "all who are both employees and nonguards."

A compound term may also occur as the object of a relation, as in:

5) Mary had a little lamb: $* \, M_1 + (H_{12} + <+ L + L'>_2)$

We put the subscript 2 outside the angle brackets to indicate that what Mary had was something both little and a lamb. The reverse situation is also possible. A relational term may occur *inside* a conjunction:

6) A woman I know was elected: $+ <+ W_2 + (K_{12} * M_1)> + E_2$

In other words: someone who is both a woman and known by me was elected.

The use of plus signs to represent the conjunction of terms suggests that they might also be used to represent the conjunction of *propositions*. This is indeed the case. We would translate *p and q* as $+ p + q$, using *p* and *q* in the customary way to stand for propositions whose internal structure we don't need to represent. If we do want to represent their internal structure, we would use square brackets around each component proposition:

7) Some books are worth reading, and some are not

$$+ [\quad + \; B + W] + [\quad + \; B - W]$$
$$\text{both some are} \quad \text{and some aren't}$$

Once again the position of each sign, together with the brackets, tells us how to read it.

The use of the same connective to perform different functions is justified by the fact that these functions share certain important logical properties. For one thing, the connective is *commutative*: $+ x + y = + y + x$, regardless of whether *x* and *y* stand for terms in a categorical proposition, terms in a compound term, or propositions in a conjunctive proposition. Thus:

$$\text{Some } S \text{ is } P = \text{Some } P \text{ is } S$$
$$+ S + P = + P + S$$
$$\text{Some } S \text{ is } P \text{ and } Q = \text{Some } S \text{ is } Q \text{ and } P$$
$$+ S + <+ P + Q> = + S + <+ Q + P>$$
$$p \text{ and } q = q \text{ and } p$$
$$+ p + q = + q + p$$

The plus-plus connective also obeys the *associative* law: $+ x + (+ y + z) = + (+ x + y) + z$, again regardless of what *x*, *y*, and *z* stand for. In Chapter 12 we used this as an equivalence rule for propositional inference:

$$p \text{ and } (q \text{ and } r) = (p \text{ and } q) \text{ and } r$$
$$+ p + (+ q + r) = + (+ p + q) + r$$

And earlier in this chapter we saw how this law applies to relational statements. The law has no application to simple categorical statements, because they involve only two terms. But it does apply to categorical statements with compound terms:

Some people are both knaves = Some people who are knaves
          and fools   are fools
$$+ P + <+ K + F> = + <+ P + K> + F$$

Practice Quiz

Put each of the following statements into logical notation, using angle or square brackets as necessary.

1. Some experiments are quick and dirty.
2. Some split-level houses are expensive.
3. Jack is nimble but I am quick.
4. Tina ran into a late-model Ford.
5. Every utopian idea is a snare and a delusion.
6. He is a charming prince, and she is an uncharming princess.
7. A tall blond man was injured.
8. The children lit a bonfire and toasted some marshmallows.
9. All of the campers were tired but happy.
10. Every hero of a Gothic novel is tall, dark, and handsome.

Other Connectives

When we learned the notation for simple categorical statements, we started with the $+\underline{\quad}+\underline{\quad}$ connective for "Some S is P," and then modified it to derive binary connectives for other types of statement. In the same way, starting with $+\underline{\quad}+\underline{\quad}$ to mean "both p and q," and using unary minus signs in various ways, we can derive connectives for other types of *compound* statement. For example, the statement *p and not q* could be presented in either of two equivalent ways:

$$+ p + (-q), \text{ or}$$
$$+ p - q$$

The second formulation gives us a new binary connective that means "both . . . and not . . . ." For example: there is smoke and there is not a fire. And now we may recall that this is precisely what is *denied* by the conditional statement "if there is smoke, then there is a fire." In other words, a conditional statement may be represented as follows:

$$\text{not both } p \text{ and not } q = \text{if } p \text{ then } q$$
$$-(+ p - q) = - p + q$$

(Notice that the symbolic equation is justified by the rule of External Negation.)

The new binary connective, $-\underline{\quad}+\underline{\quad}$, is the same one we used for categorical propositions of the form "All S are P." This reflects the fact, which we have noted on several occasions, that the same statement in English may often be formulated as asserting

either an A categorical or a conditional proposition. These propositions share certain important logical properties that are captured by
the common algebraic notation. For example, both have valid
contrapositives:

$$-S + P = - (-P) + (-S)$$
$$-p + q = - (-q) + (-p)$$

The second line would read: *if p then q* is equivalent to *if not-q then
not-p.*

Another similarity is that both the A categorical and the conditional statement have negative valence, indicated by the initial
minus sign. In a conditional statement, that minus sign means "if"
rather than "every." But it is still a sign of negative valence. A conditional statement denies the existence of a state of affairs in which
p and $-q$ are both true, just as the universal statement denies the
existence of an S that is non$-P$.

What about a disjunctive statement: *p or q?* We want to derive
this from the preceding connectives, and we might do it in one of
two ways. To say that either p or q is true, first of all, is to deny that
$-p$ and $-q$ are both true. So we might represent it as a denial of a
conjunction:

i) $-(+(-p) + (-q)) = - (-p) - (-q)$

Or we might recall that *p or q* is equivalent to *if $-p$ then q*, and so
represent it as a conditional:

ii) $- (-p) + q = - (-p) - (-q)$

It is clear from the right-hand sides of these equations that we get
the same result on either approach.

To bring out the meaning of each minus sign, we read this
expression as: if not-p, then not not-q. That is, the $-$ ____ $-$ ____
connective, which we used for E categorical propositions, means
"if . . . then not . . . ." By itself, this connective does *not* represent
the disjunction of the terms filling the slots. To represent the disjunction of p and q, we must put $(-p)$ and $(-q)$ into the slots. Notice
that in (ii), the two minus signs preceding q add up to a plus sign, by
the rule of Internal Negation. But we cannot add together the minus
signs preceding p. That would give us $+ p + q$, implying that *p or q*
is equivalent to *p and q*—and of course it isn't. We are subject here
to the same restriction we imposed on categorical statements:

Every non-S is $P = - (-S) + P$, and
Some S is $P = + S + P$

are not equivalent because they differ in valence. In the same way, a disjunctive statement has negative valence, and we can't alter that fact by adding the two initial negative signs.

Now that we understand what each minus sign means in a disjunctive statement, we can make life easier by dropping the parentheses. We can treat $--p --q$ as a single binary connective that means *either p or q*. Even so, disjunction is more awkward to work with in the algebraic notation of term logic than it is in the notation of modern propositional logic. We have four minus signs to keep track of, instead of a single symbol ($\vee$). This is the price we pay for a notation that is otherwise quite simple, and that allows a uniform representation of categorical and compound statements.

We have seen, then, that in addition to $+ \_\_\_ + \_\_\_$, the derived connectives

$$+ \_\_\_ - \_\_\_ ,$$
$$- \_\_\_ + \_\_\_ , \text{ and}$$
$$- \_\_\_ - \_\_\_$$

can be used to represent the standard forms of compound propositions. Like $+ \_\_\_ + \_\_\_$, they can also be used to represent compound *terms*. The following statements illustrate this use:

8) Some occupations are dangerous and not well-paid
   $+ O + <+ D - W>$
9) All trees are either deciduous or evergreen
   $- T + <-(-D) - (-E)>$
10) Babies are cranky if hungry
    $- B + <- H + C>$
    [A literal reading would be: all babies are, if hungry, then cranky.]
11) Some policies are neither honorable nor safe
    $+ P - <- (-H) - (-S)>$
    ["Neither" means "not either," so we interpret the predicate of this statement as denying a disjunction.]
12) I'll give Josephine either a blender or a toaster
    $* I_1 + (G_{123} * J_2 + <-(-B) - (-T)>_3)$
    [The disjunctive term gets the subscript 3 because it refers to what I'm giving Josephine.]
13) If a supporting beam cracks, the roof will fall
    $-[+<+ S + B> + C] + [*R + F]$
    [A compound term is embedded within a compound statement. Notice that "the roof" refers to a specific roof, so the consequent is a singular statement.]
14) I have a plan that is brilliant if it works
    $* I_1 + (H_{12} + <+ P + <- W + B>>_2)$

[One compound term is embedded within another. What I have is described in terms of two features: it's a plan (*P*) and it's brilliant if it works (<– *W* + *B*>).]

Practice Quiz

Put each of the following statements into logical notation, using angle and square brackets as necessary.

1. Some paved roads are slippery when wet. [Interpret "when" as "if."]
2. Any income tax is either progressive or nonprogressive.
3. Some art is symbolic but not representational.
4. Any qualified candidate may join if nominated.
5. Every charged particle is either positive or negative.
6. Any gas expands if heated.
7. Some Westerns are trashy, but not all Westerns are trashy.
8. Anyone who gets angry if criticized is defensive.
9. If a pipe is leaking, we will call a plumber.
10. Anyone who murders someone is either vicious or insane.

Equivalence

In order to establish equivalence among statements with compound components, we're going to need three new rules of equivalence. But let's start by seeing how the rules we've already learned apply to compound statements.

The first is one we've been taking for granted all along:

$$\textbf{Double Negation } (DN): \; -- X = X$$

The two minus signs here must both be unary. They may be term negation signs, where X is a simple, relational, or compound term. Or they may be signs of denial, where X is a complete statement. Thus:

$$+ S + (--P) = + S + P$$
$$+ S + (--<- P + Q>) = + S + <- P + Q>$$
$$-- [- S - P] = - S - P$$

We will also make use of the rules introduced for dealing with relational statements:

$\textbf{Commutation (Com): } + X + Y = + Y + X$
$\textbf{Association (Assoc): } + X + (+ Y + Z) = + (+ X + Y) + Z$
$\textbf{External Negation (EN): } - (\pm X \pm Y) = \mp X \mp Y.$
$\textbf{Internal Negation (IN): } \pm X - (\pm Y) = \pm X + (\mp Y)$

Because these rules hold in virtue of the connectives involved, they may be applied regardless of whether those connectives have a categorical or a compound meaning. As we've seen, for example, Commutation holds for "both . . . and . . . " as well as "some . . . is . . . " In the same way, External Negation covers both of the following equivalences:

15a) It's not the case that some innocent $- (+ <+ I + B> + K$
      bystanders were killed
15b) No innocent bystanders were killed $- <+ I + B> - K$
16a) It's not the case that there's smoke $- (+ s - f)$
      and there's not fire
16b) If there's smoke then there's fire $- s + f$

For all these rules, moreover, X, Y, and Z may be terms (simple, relational, or compound) in a categorical proposition, terms in a compound term, or propositional components of a compound proposition.

We may use these rules to establish the equivalence of pairs of statements. Consider the following pair, from an earlier example:

11a) Some policies are neither $+ P - <- (-H) - (-S)>$
      honorable nor safe
11b) Some policies are both $+ P + <+ (-H) + (-S)>$
      dishonorable and unsafe

We would first apply Internal Negation to (11a), and the result would be

$$+ P + (- <- (-H) - (-S)>),$$

where the first minus sign negates the compound term. But since that term has a dyadic structure, we may apply External Negation, changing the $- \_\_\_\_ - \_\_\_\_$ connective inside the angle brackets into $+ \_\_\_\_ + \_\_\_\_$. The result is (11b).

A somewhat more difficult example is the pair:

10a) Babies are cranky if hungry $- B + <- H + C>$
10b) Hungry babies are cranky $- <+ H + B> + C$

We would prove these equivalent as follows:

$$
\begin{array}{ll}
-B + <- H + C> & \\
- (+ B - <- H + C>) & \text{EN} \\
- (+ B + (- <- H + C>)) & \text{IN} \\
- (+ B + <+ H - C>) & \text{EN} \\
- (+ B + <+ H + (-C)>) & \text{IN}
\end{array}
$$

$$- (+ <+ B + H> + (-C) \quad \text{Assoc}$$
$$- <+ B + H> - (-C) \quad \text{EN}$$
$$- <+ H + B> - (-C) \quad \text{Com}$$
$$- <+ H + B> + C \quad \text{IN}$$

Notice that we could not use Association to rearrange the terms until we had used Internal and External Negation to produce the structure $+ \underline{\quad} + <+ \underline{\quad} + \underline{\quad}>$.

Let us turn now to the new rules we need for compound statements. The first, **Tautology (Taut)**, says that the conjunction of a proposition with itself, or its disjunction with itself, says nothing more or less than the proposition:

i) $p = + p + p$, and
ii) $p = - (-p) - (-p)$.

(i) and (ii) are the version of this rule that we learned in Chapter 12, as a rule for propositions. But Tautology also applies to terms. Wherever a term S occurs in a statement, we may replace it with its conjunction or disjunction with itself:

iii) $\ldots S \ldots = \ldots <+ S + S> \ldots$, and
iv) $\ldots S \ldots = \ldots <- (-S) - (-S)> \ldots$.

Once again the substitution gives us equivalent statements.

Another new rule is

Contraposition (Contra): $- X + Y = - (-Y) + (-X)$

As we saw earlier in this section, this law applies to A categorical and to conditional statements. In the former case, we must remember that the terms X and Y may be relational or compound. When we negate such terms, we can take the further step of driving in the term negation sign by the rule of External Negation. The following derivation illustrates the process:

$$- <+S + P>_1 + (R_{12} + Q_2)$$
$$- (- (R_{12} + Q_2)) + (- <+ S + P>_1) \quad \text{Contra}$$
$$- ((-R_{12}) - Q_2) + <- S - P>_1 \quad \text{EN}$$

The final rule is called **Predicate Distribution** (*PD*). If I say that all tigers are mammals and carnivores, I'm saying that all tigers are mammals and that all tigers are carnivores. In other words:

i) $- S + <+ P + Q> = + [- S + P] + [- S + Q]$

These statements are equivalent because we're talking about *all* S. What happens if we try this with a particular statement?

17a) Some metals are hard and soft.
17b) Some metals are hard and some metals are soft.

These are obviously not equivalent, since (17a) is false and (17b) true. But they would be equivalent if we replaced "and" with "or," and this gives us another rule of predicate distribution:

ii) $+ S + <- (-P) - (-Q)> = -- [+S + P] -- [+ S + Q]$
    some S are P or Q   =   either some S are P or some S
                                          are Q

Like the other rules we've learned, Predicate Distribution is true by virtue of the connectives involved: $- \ldots + \ldots$ in (i), and $+ \ldots +$ $\ldots$ in (ii). So the rule also holds when these connectives operate on propositions rather than terms:

iii) $- p + (+ q + r)$ $= + (-p + q) + (- p + r)$
     if p then q and r $=$ if p then q and if p then r
iv) $+ p + <- (-q) - (-r)> = -- (+ p + q) -- (+ p + r)$
     p and either q or r $=$ either p and q, or p and r

This completes our discussion of compound terms and statements. We now have at our disposal the tools for symbolizing a wide array of things that we can express in ordinary language. Any statement consists of two terms linked by one of the four basic connectives. Each term may be negated or unnegated. If a term involves a relation, we put it in parentheses, with a relation letter and a separate letter for the object of the relation, using subscripts on all terms. If a term is compound, we put it in angle brackets with an internal connective joining the component terms. And if the statement as a whole is compound, we put each component statement inside square brackets. For both compound terms and compound statements, the brackets tell us how to read the connectives we're using. The rules of equivalence, finally, are stated in terms of the connectives involved, regardless of whether the connectives have a categorical or a propositional (compound) reading. Thus in Sommers's system, unlike conventional symbolic systems, categorical and propositional reasoning are treated as parallel branches of the same basic logic.

Practice Quiz

Show that each pair of statements below is equivalent by deriving the second from the first, using the rules we've studied.

1. $+ S + <- Q + R>, + <+S + S> + <- Q + R>$
2. $+ p + (-(-q) - (-r)), -- (+ p + q) -- (+ p + r)$
3. $- S_1 + (R_{12} - <+ P + Q>_2), - S_1 + (R_{12} - <+ Q + P>_2)$
4. $- (-p) - (-q), - (-q) - (-p)$
5. $- [+ S + P] + [+ Q + R], - [- Q - R] + [- S - P]$
6. $+ p - q, - (- p - (-q))$
7. $+ (- p + q) + r, + (-p + q) + (- (-r) - (-r))$
8. $+ <+ S - P> + R, + <+ S + R> - P$
9. $+ <+ S + P> + <+ Q + R>, + <+ S + Q> + <+ P + R>$
10. $+ S + <- P - Q>, -- [+ S - P] -- [+ S - Q]$

Proof

To derive a conclusion from a set of premises, as we've seen, there are two basic kinds of step we can take: transforming one statement into another that is equivalent, and combining two premises by means of the *Dictum de Omni*. In the last section we assembled all the equivalence rules we'll need. Now we need to add one more inference rule as an auxiliary to DDO.

The rule is **Simplification (Simp)**, and it includes the inference form we called by that name in propositional logic:

$$\frac{+ p + q}{p} \qquad \frac{+ p + q}{q}$$

In term logic, however, Simp also allows the following inferences:

$$\frac{+ <+ S + P> \pm Q}{+ S \pm Q} \qquad \frac{+ <+ S + P> \pm Q}{+ P \pm Q} \qquad \frac{+ <+ S + P> \pm Q}{+ S + P}$$

For example, from the premise:

1) Some people who are smokers are happy

we may infer any of the following:

1a) Some people are happy
1b) Some smokers are happy
1c) Some people are smokers

Notice that the premise must be particular in quantity (that is, it must be an I or O proposition), and that the conjunctive term must be in the subject position.

Simplification is a rule that operates on a single premise; DDO remains the only rule for combining two premises. We can afford to rely on it so heavily because it is extremely versatile. We can apply it wherever we have a term with a positive occurrence in one statement and a universal occurrence in another. We've seen how this allows us to "reach inside" relational terms, in inferences such as:

$$-P+T$$
$$+S_1 + (R_{123} + P_2 - Q_3)$$
$$\overline{+S_1 + (R_{123} + T_2 - Q_3).}$$

We can also reach inside compound terms. Consider an argument we dealt with in Chapter 13: Since all leopards are carnivorous mammals, and all mammals are vertibrates, leopards are vertebrates. In symbolic notation:

$$-L + <+C + M>$$
$$\underline{-M+V}$$
$$-L+V$$

M has a positive occurrence in the first premise, and occurs with universal quantity in the second. We can therefore apply DDO to derive:

$$-L + <+C + V>$$

We can go on to derive the conclusion in two steps, with the justification noted to the right:

$$+[-L+C] + [-L+V] \quad \text{PD}$$
$$-L+V \qquad\qquad\quad \text{Simp}$$

In the chapters on propositional and predicate logic, we treated disjunctive syllogism, hypothetical syllogism, and *modus ponens* as separate inference forms. All of these are covered by DDO if we make a slight alteration in our formulation of the rule. So far we have used it with categorical statements, where the donor premise usually had the form $-M+$ _____ . In a compound statement of the form $-p+$ _____ , the minus sign means "if" rather than "all." But it still indicates negative valence, and it allows us to cancel a positive occurrence of p. For compound statements, therefore, DDO may be applied if some component proposition has a positive occurrence in one premise and a *conditional* occurrence in another. So each of the following is an instance of DDO:

Hypothetical syllogism	*Modus ponens*	Disjunctive syllogism
$-p + q$	$-p + q$	$-(-p) - (-q)$
$\underline{-r + p}$	$\underline{+p}$	$\underline{+(-p)}$
$-r + q$	$+q$	$+(-(-q)$

It should be clear why the rule covers the hypothetical syllogism. In the case of *modus ponens*, the host premise consists of nothing but p itself, which is replaced. The only framework surrounding p is the normally implicit plus sign preceding it, and that is the framework into which we insert $+q$. In the disjunctive syllogism, the "middle term" is $(-p)$, and as in *modus ponens* the plus sign is the only thing left out of the box in the host premise. The two minus signs preceding q in the conclusion are unary, so they cancel out by Double Negation.

In this way, the notation and rules of term logic allow us to construct proofs for purely propositional arguments. We're going to concentrate on arguments with categorical elements. Nevertheless, the propositional application of **DDO** is useful for certain inferences in which the internal structure of the propositions is specified. Suppose we had the two premises:

$$+ S + <- (-P) - (-Q)> \text{ and}$$
$$- S - P$$

The first premise is equivalent by **PD** to:

$$-- [+ S + P] -- [+ S + Q]$$

The second minus sign indicates denial, so it can be driven into the expression within brackets by **EN**, and the third and fourth minus signs add up to a plus by **IN**. So now we have:

$$- [- S - P] + [+S + Q]$$
$$\underline{+ [- S - P]}$$
$$+ [+ S + Q], \text{ or simply } + S + Q$$

The propositional use of **DDO** can therefore help us derive a categorical conclusion.

Since disjunctive terms are hard to work with, it's usually a good idea to get rid of them if possible. **PD** offers us one way to do that, as in the argument above. Another method is to change a disjunction into a conjunction by using **EN** to drive in a negation sign. Here's an example:

Everything that is either S or P is Q	$-<-(-S) - (-P)> + Q$
$\underline{\text{Some } R \text{ is } S}$	$\underline{+ R + S}$
Some R is Q	$+ R + Q$

The disjunctive term in the first premise can be negated if we take the contrapositive, and then drive in the negation sign:

$$- (-Q) + (-<-(-S) - (P)>) \quad \text{Contra}$$
$$- (-Q) + <+ (-S) + (-P)> \quad \text{EN}$$

Now we can expand this statement by PD, and then simplify to get rid of *P*:

$$+ [- (-Q) + (-S)] + [- (-Q) + (-P)] \quad \text{PD}$$
$$- (-Q) + (-S) \quad \text{Simp}$$
$$- S + Q \quad \text{Contra, DN}$$

We now have something that can be combined with the second premise by DDO to produce the conclusion.

To construct a proof in term logic, we will use the same format we used for propositional and predicate logic. We list the premises, with the conclusion stated after the last premise, and separated by a slash mark. Then we list each derived statement, stating the lines from which we derived it and the rule we used, until we reach the conclusion. The proof for the argument just above would be:

1. $- <- (-S) - (-P)> + Q$ Premise
2. $+ R + S / + R + Q$ Premise/Conclusion
3. $- (-Q) + (- <- (-S) - (-P)>)$ 1 Contra
4. $- (-Q) + <+ (-S) + (-P)>$ 3 EN
5. $+ [- (-Q) + (-S)] + [- (-Q) + (-P)]$ 4 PD
6. $- (-Q) + (-S)$ 5 Simp
7. $- (- (-S)) + (- (-Q))$ 6 Contra
8. $- S + Q$ 7 DN
9. $+ R + Q$ 2,8, DDO

Proofs in term logic are normally shorter than comparable proofs in conventional symbolic logic. But the price we pay is that each step is harder to take; it covers more logical distance. So in addition to listing the steps, we will often need a "scratch" area off to the side where we do some calculations, just as in solving an algebraic problem. This will be particularly useful when we are applying DDO to complex statements.

Suppose we want to analyze the argument:

An alumnus gave a present to every freshman.
Some freshman was a religion major.
Everyone given a present by an alumnus was elated.
Therefore, some religion major was elated.

In logical notation, the premises and conclusion are:

1. $+A_1 + (G_{123} + P_2 - F_3)$
2. $+F + R$
3. $- (G_{123} + P_2 + A_1) + E_3 \,/ + R + E$

The first thing to notice is that we have a positive occurrence of F in (2), and a universal occurrence in (1), so **DDO** can be applied. But it's hard to apply it in our heads and write down the result immediately as line 4. So let's do it off to the side:

$$\frac{\begin{array}{l} + A_1 + (G_{123} + P_2 - F_3) \\ + F + R \end{array}}{+ (A_1 + G_{123} + P_2) + R_3}$$

Once we put the subject term in standard form for a relational term, we can use Commutation to switch the terms:

4. $+(G_{123} + P_2 + A_1) + R_3$ 1,2 DDO
5. $+ R_3 + (G_{123} + P_2 + A_1)$ 4 Com

(5) can now be combined with (3). Working once again in our scratch area, we apply **DDO**:

$$\frac{\begin{array}{l} - (G_{123} + P_2 + A_1) + E_3 \\ + R_3 + (G_{123} + P_2 + A_1) \end{array}}{+ R + E}$$

The result here is the conclusion we wanted, so we would enter it as line (6), noting that it follows from (3) and (5) by **DDO**.

So far we have used direct proofs: we proceeded from premises to conclusion in a straight line. In many cases, however, it is easier to use the indirect mode of proof know as *reductio ad absurdum*. As we saw in Chapter 12, a *reductio* proof begins by assuming the denial of the conclusion, and then showing that this assumption, together with the premises, leads to a contradiction. This is a good way to prove an argument valid, because it shows that you can't accept the premises and deny the conclusion without contradicting yourself. In term logic, a contradiction is any statement of the form $+ x - x$, where x can be either a proposition or a term. Thus the following are all contradictions:

$+ p - p$: both p and not p

$+ [-S + P] - [-S + P]$: every S is P and not every S is P

$+ S - S$: some S is not S

$+ <+ S - P> - <+ S - P>$: some S and not P isn't an S and not P

$+ (R_{12} + S_2) - (R_{12} + S_2)$: something R'ed by some S isn't R'ed by some S

To see how *reductio* works, consider the classic argument:

Every circle is a figure $-C + F$
Anyone who draws a circle $-(D_{12} + C_2) + (D_{12} + F_2)$
   draws a figure

The use of *reductio* is suggested here by the fact that the conclusion has a relational term not mentioned in the premises. So let's deny the conclusion:

$$+ (D_{12} + C_2) - (D_{12} + F_2)$$

The premise tells us that every circle is a figure, so DDO allows us to replace C_2 with F_2, and we have a contradiction:

$$+ (D_{12} + F_2) - (D_{12} + F_2).$$

Since DDO is our primary inference rule, the basic strategy in devising a proof is to look for possible applications of the rule. If we can't find a term that has a positive occurrence in one premise and a universal occurrence in another, we should look for ways to transform the premises to create these conditions. Sometimes denying the conclusion, and using *reductio*, will give us what we need. Here's an example:

Anyone arriving from a country suspected of terrorism was questioned by a guard
A traveler who arrived from a Middle-Eastern country was not questioned by any guard
Therefore, some Middle-Eastern country is not a country suspected of terrorism

The premises and conclusion would be formulated as follows:

1. $- (A_{12} + <+ C + S>_2) + (Q_{13} + G_3)$
2. $+ <+ T_1 + (A_{12} + <+ M + C>_2)> - (Q_{13} + G_3)$ /
    $+ <+ M + C> - <+ C + S>$

Notice that each premise contains a term referring to an arrival from somewhere $(A_{12} + <X>_2)$. This term is universal in the first premise and positive in the second. So we can apply DDO if we can make the X components the same. We can do just that by denying the conclusion and combining it with (2) in a preliminary use of DDO:

$- <+ M + C> + <+ C + S>$
$+ <+ T_1 + (A_{12} + <+ M + C>_2)> - (Q_{13} + G_3)$
$+ <+ T_1 + (A_{12} + <+ C + S>_2)> - (Q_{13} + G_3)$

So now we add two more lines to our proof:

3. $- <+ M + C> + <+ C + S>$ Assumption
4. $+ <+ T_1 + (A_{12} + <+ C + S>_2)> - (Q_{13} + G_3)$ 2,3 DDO

And now we may combine (4) with (*1*):

$$- (A_{12} + <+ C + S>_2) + (Q_{13} + G_3)$$
$$+ <+ T_1 + (A_{12} + <+ C + S>_2)> - (Q_{13} + G_3)$$
$$+ <+ T_1 + (Q_{13} + G_3)> - (Q_{13} + G_3)$$

Once we enter this result, the rest of the proof is easy:

5. $+ <+ T_1 + (Q_{13} + G_3)> - (Q_{13} + G_3)$ 4,1 DDO
6. $+ (Q_{13} + G_3) - (Q_{13} + G_3)$ 5 Simp
7. $+ <+ C + M> - <+ C + S>$ 3–6 RA

Lines 3–6 are indented to indicate that they are the *reductio* portion of the proof. Since (6) is a contradiction, we're entitled to enter our conclusion as line (7).

This completes our study of Sommers's version of term logic. We've seen that the plus/minus notation for logical form provides a simple algebraic test for the validity of standard syllogisms. By extending this notation to cover relational and compound terms, and introducing a small set of rules, we can construct proofs for more complex arguments that classical logic could not previously handle. It's not surprising that the proofs look rather complex. But they will become much easier with practice. And you will see that by relying on DDO, we have simply extended the basic technique of deductive reasoning we learned for simple syllogisms.

Practice Quiz

Construct a proof for each of the following arguments.

1. $+ S_1 - (R_{12} - Q_2)$
   $- Q + T$
   $+ S_1 - (R_{12} - T_2)$

2. $- S + <+ P + Q>$
   $+ R + <+ T + S>$
   $+ T + P$

3. $- S + <+ R + T>$
   $- R + P$
   $- T + Q$
   $- S + <+ P + Q>$

4. $\dfrac{\begin{aligned}&-[-P+Q]+[+R+S]\\&-R-S\end{aligned}}{+P-Q}$

5. $\dfrac{\begin{aligned}&-<+S+P>+Q\\&-S-Q\end{aligned}}{-S-P}$

6. $\dfrac{\begin{aligned}&+S+<-(-P)-(-Q)>\\&-P+M\\&-S-M\end{aligned}}{+S+Q}$

7. $\dfrac{\begin{aligned}&+S_1+<+Q_1+(R_{12}-T_2)>\\&+T+P\end{aligned}}{+Q_1+(R_{12}+P_2)}$

8. $\dfrac{\begin{aligned}&+S_1+(R_{123}-<+Q+P>_2+T_3)\\&-X+<+Q+P>\end{aligned}}{-X_2+(R_{123}+S_1+T_3)}$

SUMMARY

In modern term logic, as in classical logic, a categorical statement consists of two terms, either positive or negative, together with a quantifier and a positive or negative copula. We represent these elements of logical form by plus and minus signs. A universal statement, or the denial of a particular statement, has negative valence; a particular statement, or the denial of a universal statement, has positive valence. Two statements are equivalent if they are covalent and algebraically equal.

Statements about relations have a subject-predicate structure, but the relational term has an internal dyadic structure, consisting of the relation itself and one or more internal subjects; all component terms are marked by subscripts to indicate their role in the relationship. The four basic term connectives can also be used as propositional connectives. We use angle brackets to symbolize compound terms, square brackets to symbolize compound statements.

For simple categorical statements and syllogisms, we rely on a single Principle of Equivalence and a single Rule of Syllogistic Validity. For statements and inferences involving relational or compound components, we rely instead on eight rules of equivalence and two inference rules. The *Dictum de Omni* is the primary inference rule.

Rules

Principle of Equivalence *(PEQ)*: Two categorical statements are equivalent if:
  i) They have the same valence; and
 ii) They are algebraically equal.

Rule of Syllogistic Validity (SV): A syllogistic argument in affirmative standard form is valid if and only if:
  i) It contains only universal statements, or else just one particular premise and one particular conclusion; and
 ii) The premises are equal to the conclusion.

These two principles apply only to categorical statements with simple terms, and to arguments composed of such statements. The rules that cover all cases, both simple and complex, are as follows:

Equivalence Rules

Double Negation (DN): $-- X = X$
Commutation (Com): $+ X + Y = + Y + X$
Association (Assoc): $+ X + (+ Y + Z) = + (+ X + Y) + Z$
External Negation (EN): $- (\pm X \pm Y) = \mp X \mp Y.$
Internal Negation (IN): $\pm X - (\pm Y) = \pm X + (\mp Y)$
Tautology (Taut): $X = + X + X$
$$X = - (-X) - (-X)$$
Contraposition (Contra): $- X + Y = - (-Y) + (-X)$
Predicate Distribution (PD):

$$- X + <+ Y + Z> \qquad = + [- X + Y] + [- X + Z].$$
$$+ X + <- (-Y) - (-Z)> = --[+ X + Y] --[+ X + Z]$$

Inference Rules

Dictum de Omni (DDO): $D (-M)$
$$\frac{H (M)}{H (D)}$$
Simplification (Simp): $\dfrac{+ p + q}{p}$ $\qquad \dfrac{+ p + q}{q}$

$$\dfrac{+ <+ S + P> \pm Q}{+ S \pm Q} \quad \dfrac{+ <+ S + P> \pm Q}{+ P \pm Q} \quad \dfrac{+ <+ S + P> \pm Q}{+ S + P}$$

Exercises

A. Use **PEQ** to determine whether the statements in each pair are equivalent.

1. $- S + P, + (-P) - (-S)$
2. $+ S + (-P), - (- S + P)$
3. $- S + P, - S - (- P)$
4. $- (- S) + P, + S + P$
5. $+ (- S) - P, + (- P) - S$
6. $- S - (-P), + P - S$
7. $+ S - (-P), - (- S - P)$
8. $+ S + P, - (- P + (-S))$
9. $- (- S - (-P)), + (-P) - S$
10. $+ (-S) + (-P), - (- (-P) - (-S))$

B. The following exercises are adapted from the work of Lewis Carroll, who was an eminent logician as well as the author of *Alice in Wonderland*. The goal is to determine what conclusion follows from each set of premises. Each premise should be treated as a categorical statement with simple terms, even if it involves some relation. Symbolize the premises, and then cancel out middle terms to find the conclusion that is consistent with **SV**.

1. No new potatoes have been boiled
   Every potato in this dish is fit to eat
   No unboiled potatoes are fit to eat
2. No duck is willing to waltz
   No officer is unwilling to waltz
   All my poultry are ducks
3. Every sane person can do logic
   No insane person is fit to serve on a jury
   None of your sons can do logic
4. No terriers wander among the signs of the zodiac
   Nothing that does not wander among the signs of the zodiac is a comet
   Only terriers have curly tails
5. Things sold in the street are of no great value
   Nothing but rubbish can be had for a song
   Eggs of the Great Auk are greatly valuable
   Only what is sold in the street is rubbish
6. I despise anything that cannot be used as a bridge
   Everything that is worth writing an ode to would be a welcome gift to me

No rainbow will bear the weight of a wheelbarrow
Whatever can be used as a bridge will bear the weight of a wheelbarrow
I would not welcome as a gift any thing that I despise

7. Everyone except my footman has a certain amount of common sense
No one who lives on barley-sugar can be anything but a mere baby
None but a hop-scotch player knows what real happiness is
No mere baby has a grain of common sense
No engine driver ever plays hopscotch
No footman of mine is ignorant of what true happiness is

8. No shark ever doubts that it is well fitted out
A fish that cannot dance a minuet is contemptible
Any fish that doesn't doubt it is well fitted out has three rows of teeth
Only sharks are unkind to children
No heavy fish can dance a minuet
No fish with three rows of teeth is contemptible

9. All the policemen on this beat sup with our cook
No man with long hair can fail to be a poet
Amos Judd has never been in prison
Our cook's cousins all love cold mutton
None but policemen on this beat are poets
Only her cousins ever sup with our cook
Men with short hair have all been in prison

10. The only animals in this house are cats
Every animal that loves to gaze at the moon is suitable for a pet
Animals that I detest are animals that I avoid
Only animals that prowl at night are carnivorous
No cat fails to catch mice
Only the animals in this house ever take to me
Kangaroos are not suitable for pets
None but carnivores kill mice
I detest animals that do not take to me
Animals that prowl at night always love to gaze at the moon

C. Put each of the following statements into algebraic notation. Then use the equivalence rules to find three equivalent statements.

1. Every gourmet loves some dish.
2. Some gourmet loves every dish.
3. No gourmet loves every dish.
4. Some activist sent every congressman a letter.
5. Every activist sent some congressman a letter.

6. Someone I know completed a marathon.
7. Everyone I know completed a marathon.
8. No halfback scored a touchdown in every quarter.
9. A friend of a judge wrote a book about a murder.
10. Everyone who likes me likes everyone I like.

D. In each pair of statements below, the second is a conclusion that follows by DDO from the first statement together with another premise. Find that other premise.

1. $+ S + M \,/+ S - P$
2. $+ M - S \,/+ P - S$
3. $- M + P \,/- S + P$
4. $- S_1 + (R_{12} + M_2) \,/- S_1 + (R_{12} + P_2)$
5. $- M_1 + (R_{12} - P_2) \,/+ S_1 + (R_{12} - P_2)$
6. $+ M + P \,/- S_1 + (R_{12} + P_2)$
7. $- S_1 - (R_{12} - M_2) \,/- S_1 - (R_{12} - P_2)$
8. $- M + P \,/+ S_1 - (R_{12} - P_2)$
9. $+ (R_{12} + M_2) - (P_{13} + Q_3) \,/+ (R_{12} + S_2) - (P_{13} + Q_3)$
10. $+ S_1 + (R_{123} + M_2 - Q_3) \,/+ S_1 + (R_{123} + (T_{14} + U_4)_2 - Q_3)$

E. Translate each of the following symbolic statements into English, using the brackets and parentheses to give each connective its proper meaning. For example, $- <- (-S) - (-P)_1 + (R_{12} + Q_2)$ would be read "Anything that is either S or P is R to some Q." For extra credit, think of an actual English sentence that fits the pattern. For example, "Anything that is either too big or too small will be sold at a discount."

1. $+ S_1 + (R_{12} + P_2)$
2. $- S + <+ P + Q>$
3. $- [+ S + P] + [- Q - R]$
4. $+ (R_{12} - S_2) + P_1$
5. $- <+ S + P> + <- (-Q) - (-R)>$
6. $- [-S + <+ P + Q>] + [-S - R]$
7. $- <+ S_1 + (R_{12} + P_2> + (-Q)_1$
8. $+ S + <+ <- P + Q> + <- R + T>>$
9. $- (R_{123} + S_2 + <+ P + Q>_3) + (T_{14} + X_4)$
10. $-- [* S_1 + (R_{12} - P_2)] -- [* S + <+ Q + R>]$

F. Construct a proof for each of the following arguments.

1. $- P + Q$
   $- (+ Q + S)$
   $- R + S$
   $\overline{- P - R}$

2. $- S + <- (-P) - (-Q)>$
   $+ R + S$
   $\underline{- R - P}$
   $+ R + Q$

3. $- S + <- (-P) - (-Q)>$
   $- P + R$
   $\underline{- Q + T}$
   $- <+ (-R) + (-T)> - S$

4. $- <+ S + P>_1 + (R_{12} + <+ Q + T>_2)$
   $- T + X$
   $\underline{- Y + <+ S + P>}$
   $- Y_1 + (R_{12} + <+ Q + X>_2)$

5. $- <+ S + P>_1 + (R_{12} - Q_2)$
   $\underline{+ T + Q}$
   $+ (R_{12} - <+ S + P>_1) + T_2$

6. $- <+ S + (-Q)> + R$
   $\underline{- <+ S + P> - Q}$
   $- <+ S + P> + R$

7. $- <+ S_1 + (R_{12} + Q_2)> + P_1$
   $\underline{- S_1 + (R_{12} + Q_2)}$
   $- S + P$

8. $- (R_{123} + S_2 - P_3) - Q_1$
   $\underline{- P + <+ U + V>}$
   $- Q_1 - (R_{123} + S_2 - <+ U + V>_3)$

9. $- (P_{12} + S_2) + R$
   $+ Q_1 + (P_{13} + T_3)$
   $\underline{- Q - R}$
   $+ (P_{13} + T_3) - (P_{12} + S_2)$

10. $- (R_{12} - S_2) + (P_{13} + <+ Q + T>_3)$
    $- Y_4 + (X_{34} - Q_3)$
    $\underline{+ U_1 + (R_{12} - S_2)}$
    $+ U_1 + (P_{13} + <+ (X_{34} - Y_4) + T>_3)$

11. $+ (R_{12} + S_2) + P_1$
    $\underline{- Q_3 + (T_{32} - S_2)}$
    $+ (R_{12} + P_1) + (T_{32} - Q_3)$

12. $- <+ S_1 + (R_{12} - P_2)> + Q_1$
    $- V - Q$
    $\underline{+ V_1 + <+ S_1 + (R_{12} - T_2)>}$
    $+ P - T$

13. $- (R_{12} + Q_2) + P_1$
   $\quad - P_1 + (S_{13} - T_3)$
   $\quad * A_1 + (R_{12} + X_2)$
   $\quad - X + Q$
   $\quad \underline{+ Y + T}$
   $\quad * A_1 + (S_{13} + Y_3)$

14. $- S + <+ P + Q>$
   $\quad \underline{- R + <+ T + V>}$
   $\quad - [- P + R] + [- S + V]$

15. $- P + T$
   $\quad - - [+ S + P] - - [+ S_1 + (R_{12} + Q_2)]$
   $\quad \underline{- (R_{12} + Q_2) - (U_{13} - V_3)}$
   $\quad + S + <- (-T) - (U_{13} - V_3)>$

G. Formulate each of the following arguments in algebraic notation. Then construct a proof to show that it is valid.

1. If not all actions are determined, then people need some standard of choice, and any standard is a moral code. Since some
   actions are not determined, every person does need a moral
   code.
2. A is larger than B, and B is larger than C. Since anything larger
   than B is larger than anything B is larger than, A is larger than
   C.
3. Anyone who aids a criminal is immoral, and every dictatorial
   government is a criminal. No moral person, therefore, would
   aid a dictatorial government.
4. Socrates was put to death for some of the things he believed.
   Socrates was a philosopher, and everything he believed is being
   taught today at some American universities. So a philosopher
   was put to death for things being taught today at some American universities.
5. Some bills have been attacked by every commentator, and anyone who votes for something attacked by every commentator is
   either brave or stupid. Senator Smooth has voted for every
   bill, and he is not brave, so he's stupid.
6. All personnel except guards left the building. No executive
   personnel are guards. Since everyone who left the building was
   safe, all executive personnel were safe.
7. Anyone who finished a marathon is in excellent condition, and
   anyone in excellent condition can climb a mountain. Tom finished the "Do Run Run" race, which is a local marathon. So he
   can certainly climb Old Baldy, a mountain in Tennessee.

8. People who drink too much are either aggressive or withdrawn. Anyone who's aggressive is dangerous, and anyone who's withdrawn is boring. I don't like dangerous or boring people, so I don't like those who drink too much.

9. No journalist who pays a source is professional. Some journalists employed by the *Daily Metropolis*, which is a major newspaper, have paid whistle blowers, who are sources. Some major newspapers, therefore, employ unprofessional journalists.

10. Nothing that injures no one is a violation of any right. But no one is injured by a derogatory remark, and some remarks of this kind are banned by some states. Not everything banned by a state, therefore, is a violation of a right.

PART FIVE

Inductive Logic

Induction is the second broad category of human reasoning, and it differs from deduction in several fundamental ways. In an inductive argument, the conclusion goes beyond the information contained in the premises. As a result, the concept of deductive validity does not apply to such arguments, and we must use the broader concept of logical strength that we developed in Part Two. The standards of evaluation we are going to study are guidelines for assessing the degree of support that the premises of an inductive argument confer on the conclusion. The strength of an inductive argument, moreover, depends on the wider context in which the argument occurs.

The basic mode of inductive reasoning consists of drawing a universal conclusion about a class of things from premises about certain members of that class. We will study this process of *generalizing* in Chapter 15, with particular attention to generalizations about causality. In Chapter 16 we will study arguments based on *analogies*. Chapter 17 covers *statistical* inferences. In Chapter 18, finally, we'll look at the reasoning involved in giving *explanations*.

15

Inductive Generalizations

We use deductive reasoning whenever we act on the basis of general knowledge. We acquire that knowledge in various ways, but primarily by generalizing from our experience—a form of **inductive** reasoning. This process is captured by the old saying "Once burned, twice shy." A child who burns himself on a stove does not treat this as an isolated experience; he draws a general conclusion that will guide his future transactions with hot stoves. In the same way, all of us rely on countless generalizations we have drawn from experience: an egg will break if it's dropped; steel is stronger than wood; we can't breathe underwater; shy people tend to be nervous at parties. Imagine trying to live your life without the benefit of such knowledge, treating each experience as a completely new encounter with the world, with no expectations about how things will behave or what the consequences of your actions will be.

Generalizing

In logical terms, we can see the importance of generalizing by going back to what we learned about deductive arguments. Each of the following propositions was a premise in a syllogism from previous chapters:

1) All of Shakespeare's plays are in blank verse.
2) No horned animal is a predator.
3) All geniuses are eccentric.
4) Uncommunicative people do not make friends easily.
5) Bill never admits he's wrong.
6) If a mass of hot, humid air collides with a high-pressure mass of cooler air, then it rains.

Each of these is a *general* proposition. It says something about an entire class—Shakespeare's plays, horned animals, and so on. The first five are universal categorical statements, A or E; (6) is a hypo-thetical proposition that states a general rule about the weather. When we were studying syllogisms, we took these premises for granted; we wanted to see what conclusions could be drawn from them. But now let's ask how we could support the premises themselves.

Each of them could be treated as the conclusion of a further syl-logism. For example, (2) might be supported by the argument:

No herbivore is a predator.
<u>All horned</u> animals are herbivores.
No horned animal is a predator.

This is a perfectly good argument, but it doesn't really solve the problem, because now we have two new general premises that will need some support. In the same way, proposition (6) might be deduced from a more general theory about the properties of air masses, but then we would have to ask what evidence we have for that theory. The implication is that we cannot support a general proposition merely by deducing it from other general propositions. At *some* point in our reasoning, we have to look at the actual instances of the general propositions. We have to examine Shake-speare's plays, the different species of horned animals, the geniuses we know or have read about, and then draw the general conclusion from the particular cases.

But there are dangers here. We often generalize too quickly, on the basis of insufficient evidence, committing the fallacy known as **hasty generalization.** A single bad experience while traveling can prejudice our view of an entire city or country. Most of us have stereotypes about ethnic groups, professions, or people from differ-ent regions of the country, based on our exposure to a few individ-uals. Even a judgment about the character or personality of a particular individual is a generalization drawn from our observation of that individual on specific occasions; here, too, we often jump to conclusions. And we sometimes jump to conclusions about our-selves: someone makes a mistake, fails a test, has a problem in a relationship, and overgeneralizes to the conclusion that he's no good. In short, generalizing is not an infallible process, and we need some guidelines to avoid errors.

To understand the nature of hasty generalization, and the need for guidelines, let's look more closely at what we're doing when we generalize. The conclusion of such an inference is typically a universal categorical proposition: *All S are P* or *No S is P.* Sometimes it is hypothetical, as in (6). But a hypothetical proposition stating a general rule can be translated into categorical form ("All occasions on which a mass of hot, humid air . . ."), and the categorical form makes the universal character of the proposition more explicit. When we generalize, then, we are drawing a conclusion about an entire class of S's, and the conclusion is that they all share some property (or relationship, or way of acting) that makes them members of the class P. How can we establish whether such a claim is true or false?

The basic method is to examine individual members of the class of S's. If an individual S is P, it is called a **positive instance,** and it **confirms** the generalization; if it is not P, it is a **negative instance** or counterexample, and it **disconfirms** the generalization. But there's an asymmetry here, which we can see by recalling the square of opposition:

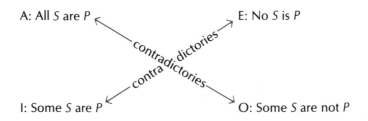

Suppose we find a negative instance. This would be enough to show that the O proposition is true (remember that "some" means "at least one"). And if the O proposition is true, the A proposition is false, since they are contradictories. So a single counterexample is enough to prove a generalization false. But can a single positive instance prove the generalization true? No. It would show that the I proposition is true, but we cannot infer the A from the I. Even if we know that some S's are P, we haven't excluded the possibility that other S's are not P. That is the very thing we overlook when we engage in hasty generalization. The fact that some professors are absent-minded does not imply that all of them are. A symmetrical problem arises for the E proposition (can you see why?). The problem is: how can we support a universal proposition merely by looking at examples?

If S stands for a small, delimited class of things, we can solve this problem by examining each member of the class individually to see whether it is P. In proposition (1) above, for example, the class is Shakespeare's plays—the 37 plays he wrote during his life. It would be feasible to examine each of them and determine whether it is in blank verse. In fact, this is the *only* way to tell whether the proposition is true, because there's no particular reason why Shakespeare *had* to write all his plays in that medium. This is called the method of induction by *complete enumeration*, and it is appropriate when we are dealing with small classes—an author's complete works, the members of a family, the clothes in your closet—where we know something about each member individually.

But most of the generalizations we employ in everyday reasoning do not involve classes of that type. They are about much larger classes that are open-ended in the sense that there is no limit on the number of members they may have. To claim that all geniuses are eccentric, for example, is to make a statement about the entire class of geniuses—*all* of them, past, present, and future, the obscure ones as well as the famous. Obviously, we cannot examine each member of this class individually. Even in proposition (5), which concerns a single individual, we are still concerned with the open-ended class of occasions on which Bill is wrong. We cannot know anything about the future occasions, and even if we know Bill extremely well, we almost certainly don't know about all the past occasions. With the exception of (1), all the propositions on our list are of this type, and we cannot establish their truth or falsity by the method of complete enumeration.

So we have to rely on an incomplete survey of the class, a *sample* taken from the class as a whole. And our generalization rests on the assumption that the sample is representative of the whole class. This raises two questions. First, what justifies the assumption? How could any sample tell us something about an entire class? And second, how do we tell whether a given sample *is* representative? What criteria can we use to determine whether a sample will give us a well-supported generalization rather than a hasty one?

The first is a philosophical question, a complex and very difficult one. Philosophers do not agree about the answer; all I can do here is indicate the approach I would take. *S* and *P* stand for classes of things that possess common traits: properties, relationships, or ways of acting. It seems to be a basic fact about the world that there are inherent connections among different traits, so that anything possessing one will also possess the other. Members of the same biological species are alike in their basic survival needs, their method of reproduction, and many other properties. In general, systems of classification usually pick out classes of objects that share more than a single trait—especially when we classify in accordance with an essential principle. We find the same kind of connection in cause-and-effect relationships. Copper conducts electricity because of its atomic structure, and any substance with the same structure will also conduct electricity. Of course, an object may possess traits that are *not* connected. A given person might have red hair and a short temper, but despite popular mythology there is no known connection between these properties, and thus no reason to expect that all redheads have short tempers. The problem, then, is to find a way of telling whether two given traits *are* connected.

Which brings us to the second question: under what conditions can we generalize from a sample? Under what conditions does the fact that some *S* are *P* support the conclusion that all *S* are *P*? The answer implied by the previous paragraph is that we can generalize when the sample gives us evidence of a *connection* between *S* and *P*. But how do we tell whether we have evidence of a connection? Three rules will help us decide. These rules are standards for assessing the strength of the inference from sample to generalization, and are analogous to the rules for determining whether a syllogism is valid. But remember that generalizing is a species of induction, in which—unlike deduction—strength is a matter of degree. So instead of the clear-cut distinction between valid and invalid arguments that we found in studying syllogisms, we are now going to have to work with a continuum from weaker to stronger. The rules should be regarded as guidelines to help us locate a given generalization along that continuum.

Three Rules of Generalizing

1) *The sample should be sufficiently numerous and various.* A single instance is usually not enough to support a generalization. In the absence of other knowledge, the fact that a single *S* is *P* won't tell us whether *S* and *P* are connected; so generalizing that all *S* are *P* would be hasty. We need to look at a number of *S*'s; if all of them are *P*, then we have better evidence of a connection. That much should be obvious. But it's equally important to test a *variety* of *S*'s. If you were buying a car, and wanted to know whether the Dodge Omni is any good, you might ask people who own Omnis whether they are satisfied. Suppose that all of them have had problems with the car. Does that indicate that Omnis are no good? It depends. If the people all bought cars of the same model year, from the same dealer, with the same package of options, then the problems might be due to one of these other common factors. Your conclusion that Omnis are poor cars would be stronger if you varied these factors, checking cars of different years, with different options, bought from different dealers.

How much variety is enough? The general rule is that a sample of
S's should vary in every property (other than being S) that *might* be
responsible for their being P. Consider the generalization that shy
people are nervous at parties. In your sample of shy people, you
would certainly want to vary such personality factors as intelligence
and degree of interest in people, because these might well affect
their nervousness at parties. You would also want your sample to
vary in background: are shy people with lots of social experience as
nervous at parties as shy people with little social experience? On
the other hand, factors such as blood type, political views, or favorite movie do not seem even potentially relevant to the generalization, and there would be no need to vary them.

As the example indicates, deciding whether a given property
might be relevant is a judgment call, and depends on what other
knowledge we have—a point we'll come back to in discussing rule
(3). It also depends on how broad a conclusion we are drawing. A
given car, for example, can be classified under concepts of increasing abstractness: OMNI, CHRYSLER CARS, AMERICAN CARS. A
generalization about Chrysler cars requires a larger sample than a
generalization about Omnis, and a generalization about American
cars needs an even larger sample. In general, the more abstract the
subject term of your conclusion, the more numerous and varied
your sample should be.

2) *We should look for disconfirming as well as confirming
instances of a generalization.* That is, we should actively look for
counterexamples: S's that are not P, Omni owners who are satisfied
with the car, shy people who are not nervous at parties. If we have
looked hard for negative instances and haven't found any, we can be
more confident of a generalization than we can if we haven't looked
at all.

This rule is important for two reasons, one logical, the other psychological. The logical reason pertains to a key difference between
inductive and deductive inference. A deductive argument is self-
contained: the premises either do or do not support the conclusion,
regardless of what other knowledge we might have. An inductive
argument, on the other hand, is *not* self-contained. The premises in
this case are propositions stating information about the sample, and
the degree to which these premises support the conclusion depends
on whether we have any *other* information about disconfirming
instances. So it's important to look for such information. The psychological reason pertains to the nature of memory. In everyday
contexts we must find evidence for or against a generalization by
searching our memories for positive and negative instances. In most

cases, it would be impossible to remember every single experience that might be relevant. Do you remember, for example, every single egg you have ever dropped or seen dropped? So there is a second level of sampling here. Our experience is a sample from the whole class of eggs that have ever been dropped, and we remember only a sample of our own experience. The psychological point is that what we remember tends to be influenced by what we are looking for. If we search only for positive cases, those are probably the only ones we're going to find. To avoid this bias, we need to look for counterexamples as well.

How do we look for negative instances? There's no general rule; it depends on each particular case. But one technique is worth mentioning. When we look for instances to test a generalization that all S are P, we are looking for individual referents of the concept S. The easiest referents to recall are the prototypical ones, the central, clear-cut cases. But we should also look for referents close to the borderline of the concept, because many generalizations are true only of the prototypical cases, not of atypical S's. If you are wondering whether all birds can fly, don't think just of obvious examples like robins and crows; think also of penguins and ostriches. If you are wondering whether all democracies protect individual rights, don't look just at modern cases like England and the United States; think also of ancient Athens.

3) *We should consider whether a link between S and P is plausible in light of other knowledge we possess.* To see the point of this rule, consider two contrasting cases. If chemists discovered a new metal, they would determine its melting point in a laboratory, and a single test would be sufficient to support the generalization that all instances of the metal would melt at that temperature. On the other hand, the generalization that all swans are white was confirmed by countless instances over a long period of time, yet it was always regarded as somewhat shaky, and eventually black swans were indeed discovered in Australia. Rule (3) explains the difference between these cases. Our theoretical knowledge about physical substances tells us that the melting point of a metal is fixed by its atomic structure, which defines that type of metal. So we can assume ahead of time that all samples of the metal will have the same melting point, whatever it might be, and a single test is enough to identify that point. By contrast, biological theory gives us no reason for thinking that all swans must have the same color, so even a great many positive instances will not make the generalization certain.

Let's look at another, more controversial example. Some people

hold that women, as a group, are not as good as men at mathematical and technical subjects; others deny this. There is a large body of
experimental research on the question, most of it involving tests
given to large numbers of men and women, and on some tests men
do score slightly higher. But the issue is not likely to be settled
solely on experimental grounds, because people interpret the
results in light of their views about the bases of cognitive abilities.
Those who hold that the abilities have a genetic basis find it plausible that there might be some innate differences between males and
females, and tend to take the test scores as evidence of such a difference. Others believe that cognitive abilities are the result of individual training. From this point of view, the experimental evidence
will never be enough to show an inherent difference between men
and women; it will always seem more plausible to attribute differences in test scores to nongenetic factors, such as the way boys and
girls are raised and educated. In other words, we cannot treat the
inductive evidence about certain mathematical abilities in isolation.
We must also look at the more general issue of the sources of cognitive abilities as such. At some point, of course, we will have to settle
the issue inductively, but the inductive evidence on the narrower
question may not be decisive.

These three rules for generalizing, taken together, illustrate a
point already mentioned: the open-ended character of induction.
Unlike a deductive argument, an inductive one is not self-contained. Its strength is affected by the context of other knowledge we
possess. The truth of the premises does not guarantee the truth of
the conclusion, and the degree of support the premises provide for
the conclusion depends on factors not contained in the argument
itself. It is always possible to strengthen an inductive argument further by finding additional positive instances, especially if they
increase the variety of the sample (rule (1)). The strength of the
argument is dependent on our diligence in looking for disconfirming evidence (rule (2)). Its strength also depends on the initial plausibility of the generalization, which is determined by our theories
and basic assumptions (rule (3)). This is not a defect of induction.
But it does mean that inductive reasoning puts a special premium on
integration, on looking beyond the argument itself to see how it fits
with the rest of our knowledge.

The three rules we have just examined are applicable to generalizations of any kind. Appropriately enough, they are *general* rules.
But there are different kinds of generalizations, and for each kind
we can formulate more specific rules. In the next section of this
chapter, we will study the rules for identifying *causal* relationships.
In Chapter 14, we will look at *statistical* generalizations.

Practice Quiz

Evaluate each of the following generalizations inductively, drawing on your own experience. If you feel you don't know enough to tell whether it is true or false, identify the kind of evidence you would need in order to decide. In each case, indicate how each of the rules would guide your reasoning.

1. The food at restaurant X [pick one you know] is lousy.
2. Italians are hot-tempered.
3. Dogs always go around in circles when they lie down.
4. Price controls produce shortages.
5. Without antitrust laws, industries would be dominated by monopolies.

Causality

Generalizing is an effort to identify connections among traits. But the term *connection* is pretty vague. What sort of relationship are we talking about? In most cases, we are talking about **causality**. Causality may take the form of a relationship among events: collisions between air masses produce rain, a lighted match will set paper on fire, the loss of a loved one causes depression. Or it may be a connection between the properties of an object and the way it acts: uncommunicative people don't make friends easily, a car's design affects its performance, a charged particle will attract or repel other charged particles. Or it may involve a causal link among properties themselves: steel is hard because of its structure, human beings possess language because they possess reason. In one way or another, many generalizations have to do with causality, and we need to study this relationship more closely.

If you've ever skidded on an icy road, you can imagine what a world without causality would be like. That sudden loss of control, when turning the wheel or pumping the brakes has no effect on the car—imagine the same thing on a wider scale, imagine losing control over *everything*. We can see by contrast how central causality is to our sense of the world. We expect events to follow regular patterns: touching a hot stove leads to pain, pumping the brakes makes the car slow down, studying improves our grasp of a subject. We expect objects to act within limits set by their natures: human beings cannot fly by flapping their arms, rocks don't engage in reasoning, dictators do not welcome opposition. And even if there is no direct causal relation between two traits that seem connected, they may both be effects of a deeper cause. When you have a cold, a sore throat and sneezing tend to go together. Neither causes the other; they are both symptoms of the virus at work in your system.

As these examples illustrate, the term *causality* covers a very broad range. Different types of causality can be found in different regions of nature and human life, and the various branches of science have developed specialized techniques for studying causality in their own areas. But we are going to look at a general-purpose technique that will help us identify and analyze causal relationships of any type. The basis of this technique is a distinction between necessary and sufficient conditions.

A is a **necessary** condition for *B* when *B* cannot exist or occur without *A*. *A* is a **sufficient** condition for *B* when *A* is enough to guarantee that *B* exists or occurs. To see the difference, let's take a simple example: You drop an egg and it breaks. The effect—condition *B*—is the breaking of the egg. What factors are responsible for making this happen? What factors play the role of *A?* The obvious factor is (1) that you dropped the egg. We would ordinarily think of this as *the* cause, because it is the event that led directly to the effect. But there are other factors involved as well: (2) the hardness of the floor, (3) the fragility of the eggshell, and (4) the fact that the egg is heavier than air. Without (2) and (3), the egg would not have broken when it fell, and without (4) it would not have fallen in the first place. Thus (2), (3), and (4) are all necessary conditions for the effect. What is the sufficient condition? All by itself, (1) is not sufficient—because it would not have produced the effect in the absence of the other conditions. So the sufficient condition is the *combination* of all four factors.

Notice that one condition can be necessary for another condition without being sufficient. The fragility of the eggshell is necessary for it to break, but not sufficient—otherwise the egg would break even without being dropped. On the other hand, a condition can be sufficient without being necessary. Together with the other factors, (1) is a sufficient condition for the effect, but there are other ways in which the eggshell could have broken: it could have been hit with a hammer, the chick inside could have hatched, and so on.

Notice also that (2), (3), and (4) are standing conditions. They are properties of the egg and its environment that endure over time; they were present all along. The act of dropping the egg, by contrast, was a stimulus or *triggering event* that occurred at a specific moment and made the egg break a moment later. In everyday speech, when we speak of *the* cause of an effect, we usually mean the triggering event. But not always. When a bridge with a structural flaw collapses during a high wind, the wind is the triggering event, but we would probably say that the flaw was the cause of the collapse. Why? Because we expect a bridge to be able to withstand winds, and most of them do. It is the flaw that distinguishes this bridge from those that do not fall in high winds. In this way, our notion of *the* cause of an event is governed partly by expectations based on our general knowledge; it is affected by what strikes us as the salient or distinctive feature of a situation. Logically, however, we would analyze this case in exactly the same way as we analyzed the breaking egg.

To see the value of such analysis, consider a political example. In the mid-1980s, media reports were filled with arguments over what caused the federal budget deficit. Some people said it was the tax cuts of 1981; others said it was the continuing high levels of spending enacted by Congress. This whole debate could be clarified by thinking in terms of necessary and sufficient conditions. Since the deficit is merely the difference between revenue and expenditures, both conditions—tax cuts and spending—were necessary. Neither was sufficient by itself; they were sufficient only in combination. When someone claimed that the tax cuts (or spending levels) were the "real" cause of the deficit, he was really saying: "both factors are responsible, but I want to retain the spending levels (or tax cuts), so I'll blame the other factor." It would have been clearer to have put it that way.

So far we have been talking about the cause of an *event,* but we can also talk about the cause of a *property.* The fragility of the eggshell, for example, was a standing condition that was partly responsible for its breaking. In that respect we are treating fragility as a cause. But when we ask *why* eggshells are fragile, we are considering the property of fragility as an effect of deeper causes: the shape and composition of the shell. Many of our generalizations involve causal connections of this type. When we conclude that all *S* are *P,* it is generally because we are convinced there is something in the nature of *S*'s that makes them *P:* something in the nature of steel makes it stronger than wood, something in Bill's personality makes him unwilling to admit he's wrong, something in the design of a car makes it unreliable. One of the main goals of science is to find the necessary and sufficient conditions for the properties of physical substances, social institutions, individual personalities.

In short, we study causal relationships by trying to identify the factors that are necessary and/or sufficient for the effect we want to explain. This is what's wrong with the *post hoc* fallacy, the assumption that because *A* preceded *B, A* must have caused *B.* The fact that *A* came first is certainly relevant, but all by itself it gives us no reason to think that *A* was either necessary or sufficient for *B.*

What sort of evidence, then, *can* we use? The nineteenth-century philosopher John Stuart Mill formulated several methods for establishing evidence of a causal connection. They are known as the methods of *agreement, difference, concomitant variations,* and *residues*. Despite their formidable names, Mill's methods are used in everyday, common-sense reasoning about causality; they are also used by scientists in designing experiments.

Agreement and Difference

Suppose you were trying to figure out why you liked certain courses you've taken. You would probably start by looking for something those courses had in common. Did they all have the same subject matter? Was there something about the class discussions? Did they have teachers with the same style, approach, or ability? Suppose the common factor turned out to be lively class discussions. To test the conclusion that this was the source of your enjoyment, the next step would be to look at courses that did *not* have such discussions, and see whether you *didn't* enjoy them.

This example illustrates two fundamental techniques for identifying the cause of a given effect. 1) We look for a common factor that is present in all the cases in which the effect occurs. When doctors are confronted with a new disease, they typically try to see whether the people who have the disease all ate the same food or were similar in some other way. A detective trying to solve a series of murders might ask whether the victims had something in common. Historians trying to explain the rise of totalitarianism in Nazi Germany, the Soviet Union, and elsewhere look for similarities among these countries in culture, politics, historical background, etc. Mill called this technique the **method of agreement:** we look for some respect in which the different cases agree.

2) To test whether a given factor plays a causal role, we take away that factor, holding everything else constant, and see whether the effect still occurs. If your car makes a funny noise when you accelerate, take your foot off the pedal and see whether the noise goes away. If a baby is crying and you think he might be hungry, see whether the crying stops when you feed him. Scientists use the same technique when they do controlled experiments. In testing the efficacy of a new medicine, for example, they would use two carefully matched groups of people. One group would get the drug, the other would get a placebo; the *only* difference between the groups would be the presence or absence of the drug, and any dif-

ference in results could then be attributed to that factor. Mill called this the **method of difference.**

To understand these techniques, and to identify their use in different contexts, it helps to represent them schematically. The method of agreement has the following structure:

$$\text{Case 1:} \quad a, b, c \longrightarrow E$$

$$\text{Case 2:} \quad a, d, f \longrightarrow E$$

$$\underline{\text{Case 3:} \quad a, g, h \longrightarrow E}$$

Therefore, a is responsible for E.

E stands for the effect. Each row represents a case or situation in which the effect occurs, and is treated as a separate premise of the argument. For example, each row might stand for an individual course, and E would be your response to it. The lower-case letters represent the various factors present in the different situations. There will not always be exactly three cases, or exactly three factors. And it won't always happen that the factors other than a appear only once; b, c, and the others might be present in more than one case. What is crucial to the method of agreement is that only one factor is present in *all* the cases. The conclusion says that the factor present in all cases is responsible for the effect. Notice that this conclusion is a generalization. We are saying that a will cause E in all cases, not just those we have examined, so we are generalizing from a sample to a universal proposition. Indeed, the method of agreement is simply the first rule for generalizing, as applied to the study of causality: we identify a link between a and E by varying the other factors.

The method of difference has the structure:

$$\text{Case 1:} \quad a, b, c \longrightarrow E$$

$$\underline{\text{Case 2:} \quad - b, c \longrightarrow\!\!\!\!/ \; E}$$

Therefore, a is responsible for E.

The arrow with a slash mark in the second row indicates that E does not occur in this case. Once again, there may be any number of factors in each case, but this time there *is* a reason for including just the two cases. The conclusion is a generalization, as before, but we are not generalizing from a sample of positive instances. We are contrasting a single positive instance with a case that is identical except for the absence of one factor, in order to isolate the causal role of that factor. It is crucial, therefore, that all the factors other than *a* be reproduced in case 2.

The methods of agreement and difference are typically combined, both in everyday reasoning and in science. Mill called this combination the *joint method* of agreement and difference, and we can represent its structure as follows:

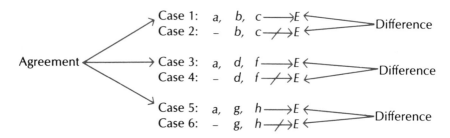

We have simply taken the method of agreement, as diagrammed above, and contrasted each positive instance with a case that is identical except for the absence of *a*. Not every use of the joint method would be this thorough. We might use the method of difference with only one of the positive instances, or only a few, especially if we have a large number of positive instances. But even a single contrasting case strengthens considerably the evidence provided by the method of agreement.

Let's look at an example of the joint method in action. In the effort to find the causes of AIDS, medical researchers found that the disease inhibits certain white blood cells called granulocytes. Why does this happen? According to a newspaper account, "Whatever inhibits the granulocytes appears to be in blood serum, the liquid part of blood, not the granulocytes themselves. 'If we take granulocytes from these patients and put them with normal donor serum, we can correct the defect,' Dr. Cairo said. 'But if we put healthy granulocytes in sick serum, they start acting sick.'" [*New York Times*, September 7, 1985] The effect here is the inhibition of the granulocytes, and we have two factors: the granulocyte cells, and the blood serum. In AIDS patients (case 1, below), both the cells and the serum are diseased. The quote from Dr. Cairo explains how he varied the factors in two other cases to identify the cause:

Case 1: sick cells, sick serum ⟶ inhibition of cells

Case 2: sick cells, healthy serum ⟶̸ inhibition of cells

Case 3: healthy cells, sick serum ⟶ inhibition of cells

Therefore, the cause of the inhibition is in the serum.

Cases 1 and 2 together constitute the method of difference: when sick cells are put in healthy serum, they are no longer inhibited. Cases 1 and 3 together constitute the method of agreement: when the serum is diseased, the granulocytes will be inhibited, regardless of whether they are themselves diseased or healthy.

To see why it is so valuable to combine the methods of agreement and difference, remember the distinction we drew between necessary and sufficient conditions. The method of agreement, by itself, provides evidence that *a* is *sufficient* for E. Since the effect can occur in the absence of any other factor, none of the other factors is necessary, so we have reason to think that *a* is sufficient. But we have less reason to think that *a* is *necessary*, since there may be more than one way to bring about the effect. In the case of your course preferences, you might like some courses because of class discussion, and others because the subject is especially interesting. To tell whether *a* is necessary, we need to see whether the effect can occur in its absence—and that is what the method of difference tells us. This method provides good evidence that *a* is necessary. If used by itself, however, it does not support very well the conclusion that *a* is sufficient. Why not? Because the two cases

$$1: \quad a, b, c \longrightarrow E$$
$$2: \quad - b, c \longrightarrow\!\!\!\!/\!\!\!\!\longrightarrow E$$

leave open the possibility that *b* and *c* are necessary for the effect. (In our example of the egg breaking, *b* might be the fragility of the eggshell, and *c* the hardness of the floor.) Thus the methods of agreement and difference have complementary strengths. If we are trying to show that *a* is necessary and sufficient for E, we need to use the methods in combination.

Agreement and difference are also used in a negative way, to show that a given factor is *not* responsible for an effect. Suppose someone claimed that America's economic wealth was the result of its abundant natural resources. A counterargument would be that some countries with abundant resources, such as the Soviet Union, are *not* wealthy, and that some countries without many resources, such as Luxembourg, *are* wealthy. The first part of this argument is a negative use of the method of agreement. It says that the alleged cause is present in cases where we do not find the effect; hence that factor is not sufficient. The second part of the argument is a negative use of the method of difference. It says that we can take away the alleged cause, and still have the effect; hence that factor is not necessary. In general, a negative use of agreement has the structure:

$$\text{Case 1:} \quad a, b, c \longrightarrow E$$

$$\text{Case 2:} \quad a, d, f \longrightarrow E$$

$$\underline{\text{Case 3:} \quad a, g, h \not\longrightarrow E}$$

Therefore, *a* is not sufficient for *E*.

And a negative use of difference has the structure:

$$\text{Case 1:} \quad a, b, c \longrightarrow E$$

$$\underline{\text{Case 2:} \quad - \, b, c \dashrightarrow E}$$

Therefore, *a* is not necessary for *E*.

Notice that, to the left of the arrows in both cases, we have the same arrangement of factors as in the corresponding positive arguments. The difference lies solely in the arrows—in whether the effect does or does not occur.

The methods of agreement and difference can provide very strong evidence of a causal connection. If we know all the factors involved, if we have varied all of them in accordance with the methods, and if *a* is the only factor in whose presence the effect always occurs and in whose absence it does not occur—then the evidence may be decisive. But these are very big *ifs*. Sometimes there is more than one factor common to all the cases—and sometimes there isn't *any* single common factor. It often happens that we cannot vary all the factors exhaustively. And we are rarely if ever in a position to be sure that we know what all the factors are. Let's look at some of the more common problems in this regard.

Choosing the factors. We have been assuming so far that there is a definite number of antecedent factors, and a small number at that —perhaps three or four. Strictly speaking, however, there is always an indefinitely large number of factors that exist just prior to the effect; and in paying attention only to a few of them we are making a selection. Scientists studying a chemical reaction, for example, will attend to the chemicals involved and the temperature at which the reaction occurs. They will ignore such factors as what they had for breakfast that morning or the price of gold on the London market. So before we can use Mill's methods, we have to choose which factors to study. This choice involves *plausibility* judgments: Is it plausible that a given factor could be related to the effect? Do we need to vary it, or can it safely be ignored? Plausibility judgments in turn are guided by the knowledge we already possess. In the above example, chemical theory gives ample reason for ignoring the price of gold. But we need to remember that these judgments are fallible.

At one point in time, for instance, no one realized that air pressure might affect the temperature at which water boils, so no one thought to do the experiment at different altitudes above sea level.

Levels of causality. Causal relationships exist at many different levels in the world, from the interactions of subatomic particles, to the biological activity of a single cell, to the behavior of an individual person, to the policies of an entire nation. The problem this poses is that we may look to the wrong level in selecting the factors to study.

For example, there is a long-standing debate about the causes of schizophrenia. If the causes are physiological, then we should study the chemistry of the brain; if they are psychological, then we should study such factors as childhood traumas or family influences. To take another example, historians trying to explain the rise of Nazism disagree about what *kind* of explanation to look for: economic conditions, cultural trends, or some other type of factor. In such cases, the ideal procedure would be to vary factors at all the levels in a comprehensive fashion. But this is extremely difficult to do, and often impossible; scientists typically choose some particular level to study, on the assumption that the causes will be found there. So we need to be aware of the issue, and we should try to identify those assumptions whenever possible.

Conceptualization. When we notice that a particular effect occurs in a certain situation, we know that the cause is something in that situation. Before we can use Mill's methods, we have to break the situation down into individual factors. Nature won't do this for us. The factors don't come already divided, packaged, and labeled as *a*, *b*, *c*, etc. We have to analyze the circumstances and isolate the factors ourselves. This is essentially a problem of classification; we try to organize the situation in terms of concepts we possess. But we have seen that there is usually more than one way to classify the same set of things, and this can affect our use of inductive methods. An obvious example is the borderline case. A sociologist studying the effects of economic status on the divorce rate will have to draw a line somewhere between the lower and middle classes. Within limits, that line can be drawn at many different places, so that a family might be treated as lower class in one study, middle class in another. This will obviously affect the results of the studies.

Let's look at a more radical case. Suppose you found that the courses you enjoy don't seem to have anything in common. They don't all have good discussions, the teachers don't give the same sorts of lectures, and so on. It may be that you need to rethink your analysis of the factors. Perhaps the real cause is something that cuts across the factors you've been looking at. Suppose the real source of your enjoyment is that, regardless of how the class is organized in terms of lectures and discussions, the teacher makes the learning process a kind of game. If so, you won't discover that fact until you step back from your original way of analyzing the situation and try to classify factors in a different way. We should also notice that the issue of conceptualization applies to the *effect* as well as to the *factors*. In biology and psychology, for example, there is a vast literature on the causes of aggression. But some people argue that aggression per se is too broad a category to study effectively; the different species of aggression should be studied separately because they may have different causes.

Direction of causality. When the methods of agreement and difference reveal a causal relation between *a* and *E*, we have been assuming that it is clear which is the cause, which the effect. But this is not always so clear. Night follows day with perfect regularity, but day does not cause night; they are joint effects of an underlying cause, the rotation of the earth. It might even turn out that *E* is the cause and *a* the effect. To use our old example one more time, suppose that the courses you enjoyed *did* all have lively class discussions. The liveliness of the discussions might be a consequence, rather than a cause, of the fact that you (and the other students) are enjoying the course. So we cannot use the methods of induction mechanically. We have to interpret the results. There is evidence that criminals have an abnormally high rate of unemployment. Does this mean that unemployment drives people to crime? Or do criminal tendencies lead certain people to avoid regular work? Or are crime and unemployment joint effects of some underlying cause? To answer these questions, we would have to make judgment about plausibility, appeal to broader theories of human nature, and perhaps look for additional inductive evidence.

The problems we have just examined do not discredit induction. We can deal with them by using Mill's methods carefully. But the problems show that we have to be careful if we want to avoid hasty judgments. And they are interesting in a theoretical sense because they reveal once again the contextual nature of induction, the fact that inductive reasoning is affected by the context of other knowledge we possess.

Practice Quiz

Analyze each of the inductive arguments below. First identify the conclusion: is it positive or negative? which factor is being said to be (or not to be) the cause of which effect? Then identify the method used to support the conclusion: agreement, difference, or the joint method. Use the standard schema to represent the cases. Finally, look for problems in the use of the methods.

1. ScourClean Cleansing Powder cleans best! We'll scrub half of this dirty sink with a leading cleanser, the other half with ScourClean. Look at the difference!

2. In the last five years, there have been two great rises in stock prices. The bull market of 1982–83 occurred in the depths of a recession, when unemployment was high and business slack. The bull market of 1985–86 occurred late in a business expansion, when unemployment was lower and business still booming. But in both cases interest rates declined dramatically. So interest rates clearly affect stock prices.

3. "I wonder why this restaurant is so hot."
   "They must have turned up the heat."
   "But I've been here at four in the afternoon, and it isn't hot; and they wouldn't turn down the heat in the afternoon."
   "Then maybe the people make the difference. It's crowded now, but there's no one here at four."

4. Self-esteem appears to be at least a necessary condition for happiness. All the happy people I've known, whatever their other differences in personality and goals, seem to have basic self-esteem, whereas people who don't have that trait never seem to be happy.

5. If product safety regulations discouraged the introduction of new products, then innovation in the widget industry should have declined after the Widget Control Act was passed. But innovation continued at the same pace.

Concomitant Variations and Residues

So far we have been talking about causes and effects in *qualitative* terms. An effect either occurs or does not occur, a factor is either present or absent. But both sides of this equation can vary *quantitatively* as well. You may enjoy different courses in different degrees, the unemployment rate goes up and down, the current in a wire may vary continuously. Two additional methods of induction are especially useful in such cases. Mill called them the methods of *concomitant variations* and *residues.*

Despite its daunting name, **concomitant variations** is a method you have almost certainly used at one time or another. If your car makes a funny noise when you accelerate, you might take your foot off the pedal and see whether the noise goes away. As we saw, that would be the method of difference. But you might also vary the pressure on the pedal, and see whether the noise varies accordingly in intensity. That would be the method of concomitant variations. If quantitative changes in the effect are associated with quantitative changes in a given factor—that is, if they vary concomitantly—then we have reason to believe there is a causal connection between them.

We can represent the method of concomitant variations schematically as follows:

$$\text{Case 1:} \quad a-, \quad b, \quad c \longrightarrow E-$$

$$\text{Case 2:} \quad a, \quad\ \ b, \quad c \longrightarrow E$$

$$\text{Case 3:} \quad a+, \quad b, \quad c \longrightarrow E+$$

Therefore, a is causally connected with E.

As in the method of agreement, there may not be exactly three cases or three factors. As in the method of difference, however, it is important to hold the factors other than a constant, so that we can attribute the variation in E to the variation in a. Notice that I have drawn the diagram to indicate a *positive* correlation: a and E vary in the same direction, up or down. This would represent the relation between a car's speed and the pressure on the accelerator. But the correlation could also be *negative,* as in the relation between the car's speed and pressure on the *brake* pedal. Can you see how the plus and minus signs in the diagram would be changed to represent this?

The method of concomitant variations is subject to several limitations. It does not show that a is a sufficient condition for E. Since b and c are present in all three cases, one or both of them may be necessary for the effect. In our example, the car must have some gas in the tank in order to accelerate at all. Nor does the method show that a is a necessary condition. Perhaps E would occur in some degree even without a: a car on a downhill slope will gain some speed without any pressure on the accelerator. What we *can* conclude is that, given the presence of the other factors, variations in a are sufficient for variations in E. So we do have evidence that there is some causal relationship. But the relation may not be direct. Between the accelerator pedal and the movement of the car is a causal chain with many intervening links. And it is not always clear what the direction of causality is. The fact that a and E vary concomitantly does not, in itself, tell us which causes which.

Against these limitations, the method of concomitant variations has two great advantages. The first is that it can be used in cases where we cannot eliminate a factor altogether, and thus cannot apply the method of difference. For example (to use one of Mill's own illustrations), how do we know that the moon causes tides in the ocean? Obviously, we cannot remove the moon and see whether the tides cease. But we *can* correlate the cycle of high and low tides with changes in the moon's position. Or suppose we wanted to establish the effect of oxygen intake on an athlete's performance. It would be out of the question to cut off the oxygen altogether, but within limits we could vary the rate of intake.

The second advantage relates more directly to the quantitative nature of causal relationships. If you take sugar in your coffee, you know that sugar makes it sweeter, but you also know roughly how much sugar will produce what degree of sweetness. An architect knows how large a beam must be to carry a given amount of weight. A doctor knows how much of a certain drug to prescribe for a patient with a certain condition. A central aim of science, finally, is to identify quantitative relationships among phenomena. Many scientific laws are expressed algebraically in the form $y = f(x)$, to indicate that one variable is a function of another: y varies in accordance with x. For example, the pressure, temperature, and volume of a gas are related by the formula $V = cT/P$ (where c is a constant).

In short, it is one thing to know that certain factors are causally related; it is another thing to know the specific way they are related quantitatively. The method of concomitant variations is especially important in the latter case. We gain our rough, everyday understanding of quantitative relationships through the experience of observing how variations in one thing cause variations in another. How else would you know how much sugar to use? In technical and scientific knowledge, there is more to it than that. Laws relating one variable to another are usually integrated mathematically within larger theories; they are not established solely by induction. Once a law has been formulated, however, concomitant variations is the most direct way to test it. And when a law contains a constant, as in the example above, concomitant variations is typically used to discover the value of the constant.

The last of Mill's methods, the **method of residues,** also requires that we be able to quantify the effect. In outline, the reasoning runs as follows. E occurs in the presence of certain factors: a, b, and c. We know from prior knowledge that c is responsible for part of the effect, and b for another part, so the remainder (the "residue") must be caused by a. This reasoning is quite different in structure from that of the other methods—so different, in fact, that I am not going to represent it schematically as I did with the others. It uses only a single case, and it relies on prior knowledge about the effects of factors b and c. Instead of using several cases to bring out the role of *a*, we infer the role of *a* in a single case by subtracting the known effects of the other factors.

We use the method of residues quite often. A simple example occurs when a veterinarian weighs a dog by stepping on the scale with the dog in her arms; if her own weight is 130 pounds, and the scale reads 150, then the dog must weigh 20 pounds. Here's another, more subtle example. Suppose you agree to meet a friend at a certain time. You are five minutes late, and he flies into a furious rage. You might think: he's overreacting, there must be something else bothering him. Your implicit reasoning is: the fact that I was late would make him a little angry, but not *this* angry, so the feeling must be partly due to something else. In this example, anger is the effect, your lateness is factor *b*, and the "something else" is factor *a*. In science, the classic example of the method is the discovery of radium by Marie and Pierre Curie. Working with pitcheblende—one of the ores in which uranium is found—they noticed that its radioactivity was higher than could be explained by the uranium in it. They concluded that the ore must contain some other radioactive substance, later identified as the new element radium.

Notice that we have used the method of residues in two different ways. In the first example, the residual effect (the extra 20 pounds on the scale reading) was attributed to a specific factor: the weight of the dog. In the other examples, the residual effect (the friend's overreaction, the unexplained portion of the pitcheblende's radioactivity) was *not* attributed to any specific factor, but merely to "something else," to some unknown, indefinite factor. This second use of the method is probably the more common, and is certainly the safer of the two, because we are not going as far out on a limb. If an effect occurs in some amount that is different from what we would have expected, it's a safe bet that *some* cause is at work over and above the ones we already know about. It is riskier to claim that that cause is some particular factor, because then we are assuming that we have identified every single factor in the situation, and that we know about the contribution made by every factor but one. In some cases, this assumption is justified. The veterinarian is certainly justified in thinking that the only thing which could affect the scale reading, other than her own weight, is the weight of the dog she is holding. But we have also seen that we are rarely in a position to be sure that we have identified all the factors.

This problem is involved in the controversy over the use of statistical evidence in proving racial or sexual discrimination. At one time, the average earnings of women were reported to be only 59 percent those of men. One factor accounting for the difference is that married women often stop working in order to raise children, so that over a lifetime they accumulate less working experience than men, and less experienced workers tend to be paid less. But when this and other factors are accounted for, some part of the earnings difference remains—about 13 percent by some estimates. Since this gap cannot be explained by other factors, some people argue that it must be the result of discrimination against women. Other people argue that we do not know all the factors affecting a person's earnings, and that some of the known factors (e.g., luck, personality) can't be measured well enough to be included in the statistical data. Therefore, they claim, it is hasty to attribute the remaining gap to discrimination in particular. Whatever your position on this controversy, it is clear that the method of residues should be used with caution, and that wherever possible we should back it up by using the other methods as well.

Practice Quiz

Analyze each of the inductive arguments below. First identify the conclusion: which factor is being said to be the cause of which effect? Then determine whether the method used to support the conclusion is concomitant variations or residues. Finally, look for problems in the use of the methods.

1. The inkspots I get when I type must be partly due to the carriage of the typewriter, because even after I cleaned the keys, I still got some spots, though not as many.
2. Scientific data show that the death rate from lung cancer increases with the amount that people smoke. For those who smoke up to a pack a day, the rate is six times that for nonsmokers; for those smoking over a pack a day, the rate is about twelve times higher. Smoking is clearly a cause of lung cancer.
3. The ability to perceive objects in depth is due partly to the fact that we have two eyes. Each eye receives a slightly different image from the object, and the disparity produces a sense of depth. But there must be other factors involved. If you shut one eye, you won't be able to perceive depth quite as well, but you will still have some depth perception.

SUMMARY

Generalization is a form of inductive inference in which we conclude that something is universally true of a class on the basis of evidence regarding a sample. To avoid the fallacy of hasty generalization, we should use a sample that is sufficiently numerous and various; we should look for disconfirming instances; and we should consider whether the conclusion is plausible in light of other knowledge.

Causal generalizations are claims that a certain type of factor is necessary and/or sufficient for a certain type of effect. Causal connections can be established by Mill's methods of agreement, difference, concomitant variations, and residues. Mill's methods can also be used negatively to argue against a causal claim. To evaluate an argument that employs one or more of these methods, we should consider whether all the relevant factors have been varied appropriately.

Exercises

A. Evaluate each of the following generalizations. See whether you can find a variety of confirming instances; look for disconfirming instances; and consider whether the generalization is plausible.

1. Women are only interested in clothes.
2. Men are only interested in one thing.
3. Absence makes the heart grow fonder.
4. People who own their homes take better care of them than do people who rent.
5. Heros in tragic drama always have a fatal flaw.
6. Haste makes waste.
7. An insight always seems obvious in retrospect.
8. Work expands to fill the allotted time.

B. Support each of the following statements about cause and effect by using the method indicated in brackets. Diagram the argument schematically (except for the method of residues).

1. Oxygen is a necessary condition for combustion [difference].
2. Sunlight causes newsprint to turn yellow [agreement].
3. Other things being equal, falling interest rates lead to an increase in home purchases [concomitant variations].
4. Moisture will condense on a surface that is colder that the surrounding air [joint].
5. Some of the anxiety people feel at the dentist is caused by the sight and sound of the drill, rather than the pain itself [residues].

C. For each of the following statements, decide whether you think it is true a) by finding a *deductive* argument for or against it; and b) by evaluating the *inductive* evidence for it.

1. Familiarity breeds contempt.
2. Any stable society has a large middle class.
3. People who fear confrontation are eager to forgive those who wrong them.
4. All narrative literature (plays, novels, epic poems) involves conflict.

D. Each of the following passages presents evidence for or against a causal connection. Identify the effect (*E*), the alleged cause (*a*), and decide whether the author is supporting or rejecting the claim that *a* causes *E*. Then identify the method being used.

1. "Rooftop sightings in the Clinton section of Manhattan on a recent morning: one plastic great horned owl at 402 West 46th Street, no pigeons; one plastic great horned owl at 503 West 47th Street, no pigeons; two plastic great horned owls, not courting, at 461 West 47th Street, no pigeons.
    "'The owls work,' said Sarah Weinberg, whose brownstone on West 46th Street bore no trace of pigeons. 'A month ago we could not stand outside the door because of all this gook falling from the sky.'" [*New York Times*, October 29, 1986]
2. "The American auto companies currently point, with some justice, to the price advantage that the dollar's high exchange rate gives to the Japanese. But Japanese sales here were rising rapidly in the 1970s when the dollar was low." [*Washington Post National Weekly Edition*, November 4, 1983]
3. "In fact, speech seems to be rewarding to the infant in a way that other sounds are not. Newborns will learn to suck on an artificial nipple hooked to a switch that turns on a brief portion of recorded speech or vocal music, but they will not suck as readily in order to hear instrumental music or other rhythmical sound." [Peter A. and Jill G. de Villiers, *Early Language*]
4. "New York critics are often credited, or criticized, for wielding so much life and death power. One wonders, then, in this odd day and age, how a musical like 'Marilyn,' which was soundly panned by 14 print and broadcast critics, has managed to survive so long—it is nearing the end of its first week of performances—while 'Brothers,' the drama which starred Carroll O'Connor and which was panned but not as soundly, never survived past its opening night." [*Poughkeepsie Journal*, December 12, 1983]

5. "The fact that the maximum life span for humans has not increased suggests that there may be built-in aging factors. . . . Leonard Hayflick of Children's Hospital Medical Center in Oakland, California, has grown cell cultures of normal human body cells taken from people of different ages. Cells from a human embryo double about fifty times before they die. Cells taken from a middle-aged human divide only about twenty times before they die.

"This control on cell aging could be in the DNA of the nucleus or in the cell body outside the nucleus. Hayflick exchanged nuclei from human embryo and adult cells and found that the primary control is in the nucleus. Whether the cell bodies were from the embryo or the adult, if the nucleus was from an adult the cell only divided about twenty times. If the nucleus was from the embryo, the cell divided about fifty times." [Robert Ornstein and Richard F. Thompson, *The Amazing Brain*]

6. "'The wealth effect is a big reason consumer spending has remained healthy,' says [Robert] Giordano. He notes that in 1984 consumer spending rose 3.4 percent while incomes jumped a big 8 percent. Last year, consumer spending rose again by about 3 percent and incomes by 4.5 percent.

"'The point,' explains Giordano, 'is that we had the same growth in consumer spending last year with half the growth in income. That means the rise in stock and bond prices is helping considerably to buoy consumption by increasing wealth and putting people in a spending mood.'" [*U.S. News & World Report*, April 28, 1986]

7. "In winter, snowshoe hares forage on green alder, among other plants, but only that part of the stem between branches of the alder. They reject such more nutritious parts as the flower buds and the pollen-bearing catkins of the plants.

"Taking samples of the three different parts of the alders—internodal stems, catkins and flower buds—and analyzing them chemically, the scientists found that while the buds and the catkins contained more nutrients, they also contained more of a phenol, pinosylvin methyl ether, which apparently acted as a repellent to the hares.

"To test the theory, in laboratory tests the scientists offered the hares commercial oatmeal, known to be one of their preferred foods, which had been impregnated with the same amount of the phenol compound found in the alder buds and catkins. They found that the captive hares avoided the oatmeal, demonstrating the deterrent properties of the phenol substance." [*New York Times*, November 26, 1983]

8. ". . . decoration is not given to hide horrible things: but to decorate things already adorable. A mother does not give her child a blue bow because he is so ugly without it. A lover does not give a girl a necklace to hide her neck." [G. K. Chesterton, *Orthodoxy*]

9. "Ingesting large amounts of aspartame, the ubiquitous artificial sweetener . . . , may sour the disposition of some severely depressed individuals . . .

"A 54-year-old woman living at home but taking antidepressant medication to quell recurrent bouts of depression suddenly experienced a grand mal seizure. Thereafter, her behavior changed radically and included symptoms of mania—insomnia, euphoric mood, disconnected speech and hyperactivity. . . . The symptoms persisted for three weeks until the woman's family insisted she be hospitalized. Two days after admission and the initiation of lithium therapy, physicians learned that it had long been her custom to consume large amounts of iced tea with sugar. Several weeks before the seizure and behavior changes, she had switched to iced tea with aspartame. Thinking this was more than coincidence, the physicians took her off lithium and advised her to abstain from aspartame. Within four days her symptoms eased and she was discharged. Her antidepressant use was reinstated two months later. Over the next 13 months she functioned well and continues to drink copious amounts of iced tea laced with sugar. [*Science News*, April 19, 1986]

10. "Mr. Snider also claimed that terrorist acts aimed at the U.S. grew in number because the U.S. was held partly responsible for the 1982 massacre of Palestinians in the Sabra and Chatilla refugee camps. Mr. Snider failed to consider that more bloody massacres have taken place in the same camps by the Syrian-supported Shiites, yet no terrorism has been directed at Syria by the Palestinian groups. . . ." [Letter to the editor, *New York Times*, July 14, 1986]

11. "The very first point to note is that the freedom at issue (as indeed the very name 'Free Will Problem' indicates) pertains primarily not to overt acts but to inner acts. . . . We do not consider the acts of a robot to be morally responsible acts; nor do we consider the acts of man to be so save in so far as they are distinguishable from those of a robot by reflecting an inner life of choice. Similarly, from the other side, if we are satisfied . . .

that a person has definitely elected to follow a course which he believes to be wrong, but has been prevented by external circumstances from translating his inner choice into an overt act, we still regard him as morally blameworthy." [C. A. Campbell, "Has the Self Free Will?"]

12. "In his initial experiments, Becquerel chose to work with flourescent uranium material. He placed this in the sunlight over a photographic plate that had been carefully wrapped to protect it from direct radiation of the sun. When the plate was developed, he found the image of the material on the plate. Becquerel incorrectly reported that penetrating rays, presumably X-rays, could be induced by sunlight, and emitted as part of flourescence. However, the weather turned bad and Becquerel had to postpone further studies. While the sun stayed behind the clouds, Becquerel kept the mineral and the wrapped photographic plate in a desk drawer. On March 1, 1896, he decided to develop the plate not expecting to find any images. He was surprised to find very intense silhouettes. Becquerel concluded correctly this time that the mineral was producing a spontaneous radiation and referred to this phenomenon as radioactivity." [Brown and LeMay, *Chemistry, The Central Science*]

13. "As far as causing mental states is concerned, the crucial step is the one that goes on inside the head, not the external or peripheral stimulus. And the argument for this is simple. If the events outside the central nervous system occurred, but nothing happened in the brain, there would be no mental events. But if the right things happened in the brain, the mental events would occur even if there was no outside stimulus. (And that, by the way, is the principle on which surgical anaesthesia works: the outside stimulus is prevented from having the relevant effects on the central nervous system.)" [John Searle, *Minds, Brains and Science*]

16

Argument by Analogy

We talked about analogies, including metaphors and similes, in Chapter 4. We saw that they are often used to express shades of meaning that would be difficult to capture in literal terms, and they make our language more colorful and forceful. Analogies that are used in this way are called *explanatory* or *descriptive*. To convey the Christian idea of God, for example, I might say He is like a father who cares for his children, punishes them for disobedience, etc. This analogy is descriptive: I am not saying that this conception of God is correct, or even that God exists; I am merely describing what it is that Christians believe. But analogies can also be used to *argue* for a conclusion. In this chapter, we will learn how to analyze and evaluate such arguments.

Analogy and Similarity

To convince you that learning to reason well takes a lot of practice, I might argue as follows: The art of reasoning is a skill, like knowing how to play tennis. And you can't learn to play tennis just by reading a book; no matter how much you know about the theory of the game, you can't acquire the skill without actually playing; so you need to practice. In this argument, I am using an analogy as a premise in an argument; I am trying to prove a conclusion. In the same way, one might argue for socialism by comparing society to a family: since a family shares its wealth among all its members, society should do the same. You can distinguish an argumentative from an explanatory analogy by the same techniques we learned in Chapter 5 for identifying arguments of any kind: look for indicator words like "therefore," ask whether the speaker is trying to convince you of some conclusion, etc.

Arguments by analogy are inductive, for reasons we will see in a moment. They occur very often in everyday conversation and debate. They are frequently used in political discussions, as in the argument about socialism. We also use analogy when we argue on the basis of historical comparisons; an example would be the argument that the Soviet Union is like Nazi Germany, and thus détente is like the policy of appeasing Hitler during the 1930s. Many of our expectations about people are based on analogy: John reminds us of Walter so we expect John to act in a similar way. What is the logical structure of these arguments? And what standards should we use to evaluate them?

As a first step in analysis, we can represent the structure of an argument by analogy as follows:

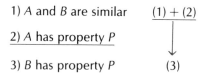

1) *A* and *B* are similar

2) *A* has property *P*

3) *B* has property *P*

$(1) + (2)$

(3)

A and *B* are the two things being compared: the family and society, skill in tennis and the art of reasoning, Nazi Germany and the Soviet Union. The conclusion is that *B* has a certain property: society should be arranged so that members share wealth; the art of reasoning must be acquired by practice; the Soviet Union is an aggressor that should not be appeased. And the argument is that *B* has this property because it is similar to *A*, which has the property. So far, so good. But notice that the relationship between *A* and *B* is not like any of the logical relations we have studied so far. *A* is not a wider class that includes *B*, as in a categorical syllogism. Nor is *A* an instance or subclass of *B*, as in an inductive generalization. Tennis is not a species of logic, nor is logic a species of tennis. So how can a premise about one yield a conclusion about the other?

The answer obviously lies in premise (1): *A* and *B* are *similar*. The similarity may not be stated explicitly, but it is a crucial assumption. If there is no similarity between a family and a society, then the fact that families share their wealth has no bearing on society; that argument would be a complete *non sequitur*. But similarity per se is not enough, because with a little ingenuity we can find *some* similarity between any two things, and thus we could prove *anything* this way. I could prove that you should take your bicycle to the dentist for a regular checkup, because the gear sprockets are shaped like teeth.

That's ridiculous. So we need to look more carefully at the role of similarity.

If two things are similar, they must be similar in some particular respect—in shape, color, function, or whatever. To put it differently, two things are similar because they share some property. So the first task is to identify the respect in which *A* and *B* are similar, to identify the property they have in common. There may be more than one such property, but there must be at least one. In the argument about tennis and logic, the property was stated explicitly: they are both *skills*. The argument about family and society did *not* state how they were similar, but the point might be that families and societies are both social groups, or that in both cases the members have shared interests.

We'll use the letter *S* to stand for the property that *A* and *B* have in common, the property that makes them similar. We can reformulate the first premise in an argument by analogy as follows:

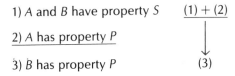

We can now go on to ask the next—and crucial—question. What is the relationship between *S* and *P*? If there is no connection between these two properties, then the conclusion does not follow. That's the problem with the argument about bicycles. The property that gear sprockets and human teeth have in common is *shape*, but it is not because of their shape that human teeth require dental care. Indeed, two things may have many properties in common—*S1, S2, S3, . . .* —but unless there is some link between one or more of these *S*'s and the further property *P*, the analogy just won't work.

So the strength of the argument depends on the likelihood of a connection between the properties involved, and our goal in evaluating an argument by analogy is to estimate this likelihood. As we'll see in the next section, we can do this by using what we've already learned about inductive arguments.

Practice Quiz

Each of the paragraphs below contains an analogy. a) Decide whether the analogy is used for explanation or for argument. b) If it is used for argument, identify *A* and *B* (the two things being compared), and *P* (the property attributed to *B* in the conclusion).

1. Murray's mind is a cave: deep, dark, and full of bats.
2. Our planet is like a ship sailing on the vast ocean of space; hence the nations of the Earth, like the members of a ship's crew, can survive only if they learn to live together.
3. The layers in a crystal are spaced at regular intervals, like the floors of a building, and connected by chemical bonds that are like girders; so a substance with a crystalline structure is solid and rigid.
4. Writing is a medium of communication, as air is a medium of vision; and good writing is as crisp and clear as the autumn air in Vermont.
5. A person with high blood pressure is like a boiler with too much steam; eventually, something's got to give.

Analysis and Evaluation

Once we have identified the property that *A* and *B* are supposed to have in common—the property we're labeling *S*—we can put an argument by analogy into a standard format. This format includes an inductive step and a deductive step, and it allows us to evaluate the argument by using what we have already learned about induction and deduction. To see how this works, let's continue with the analogy between tennis and reasoning.

The common property here is that both are skills, and the relevance of this property is that skills must be learned by practice. Tennis is a particular instance in which a skill requires practice, and it serves as inductive evidence for a generalization about *all* skills; this generalization is then applied deductively to the case of reasoning. We can thus diagram the argument:

1) Tennis is a skill
2) Tennis must be learned by practice
3) All skills must be learned by practice
4) Reasoning is a skill
5) Reasoning must be learned by practice

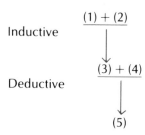

The first step in the argument is the inductive one, supporting the generalization that all skills require practice. This generalization serves as the first (or major) premise in the second step, which is deductive; it is a categorical syllogism. The major premise expresses the link between skills and practice, and without this premise we have no basis for the conclusion. The second (or minor) premise says that reasoning is a skill—it states the property that makes reasoning similar to tennis.

Let's try this technique on another example. People who oppose government regulation of business sometimes argue that business-men, like journalists, have to use their minds and follow their own judgment in their work; therefore, like journalists, they should not be regulated. This is an argument by analogy: businessmen are being compared to journalists. The conclusion is that businessmen should not be regulated, and the argument tells us explicitly what the professions have in common. So we can analyze the argument as follows (using a format that separates clearly the inductive and deductive steps):

1) Journalists have to rely on their own judgment in their work   +   2) Journalists should not be regulated

↓

3) No one who has to rely on his own judgment in his work should be regulated
4) All businessmen have to rely on their own judgment in their work
5) No businessmen should be regulated

You can see that this argument fits the general pattern; the only dif-ference is that the conclusion is negative, so the major premise of the syllogism is negative as well. But it is still a generalization drawn from the particular case of journalists.

Any argument by analogy can be analyzed in this way, once we have identified the common property, *S*, that makes *A* and *B* similar. So an argument by analogy has the form:

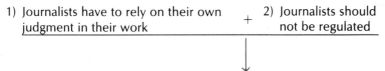

A is S   +   A is/is not P

↓

All/No S is P
B is S

B is/is not P

To *analyze* an argument by analogy, the main task is to find the common property *S* that functions as a middle term in the deductive step. To *evaluate* the argument, the main task is to evaluate the inductive step. You can see from the general form that the deductive step will always be valid (the syllogisms will be either AAA-1 or EAE-1, both of which are valid). But the generalization that all or no *S* is *P* may or may not be based on solid inductive evidence. Let's look a little more closely at each of these tasks.

Finding the Middle Term

In some cases, it will be easy to identify the middle term, especially if the argument explicitly mentions what *A* and *B* have in common. This was true in both of the arguments above. In many cases, however, the common property will not be mentioned explicitly, there may be more than one common property, and it may not be so clear which ones are relevant to the conclusion. When we use historical analogies, as in the argument that détente is like appeasement, we are comparing two very complex situations that have many similarities (and many differences). When we try to decide how we feel about another person, we often compare that person to others we've known in the past, and our decision usually turns on more than one personality or character trait. And in the law, the use of precedents is a kind of analogical reasoning: a lawyer will argue that the present case is like one that was decided in the past, and will try to find as many similarities as possible.

The problem in such cases is not merely that *A* and *B* have more than one property in common. There is often a deeper problem as well: we may have an intuitive sense that *A* and *B* are similar without being sure exactly how to break that similarity down into distinct properties. Two pieces of music may sound quite similar to you, leading you to infer that they are from the same historical period; but if you don't know much about musical theory, you may be unable to say specifically what they have in common. Indeed, we tend to use arguments by analogy precisely when two things are similar in ways that are hard to analyze. Nevertheless, we must break the similarity down before we can evaluate the argument, so we'll have to do the best we can.

A useful technique here is to construct a table of similarities and differences. In outline, the table would look like this:

	A	B
	S1	S1
Similarities	S2	S2
	S3	S3
Differences	D1	D1
	D2	D2
	P	P

The two columns represent the properties of A and B. Since the conclusion of the argument is the claim that B is P, we put P at the bottom, and draw a line above it in the B column to indicate that it is supposed to follow from information available in the rest of the table. S1, S2, S3, etc.—there could be any number—are similarities between A and B, properties that they share and that are candidates for the role of middle term. To decide which of them is the middle term, we ask which of them seem connected to P. If they are all relevant, then the middle term will be a combination: S1 + S2 + S3. . . . Usually, however, we can throw some of the similarities out as irrelevant to the analogy. It's a good idea to include any differences (D1, D2, . . .) as well, because we'll have to consider these when we evaluate the inductive element in the argument.

Suppose someone argues that personal computers will expand individual freedom to acquire and use information—in the same way that, earlier in the century, the automobile expanded individual mobility. This argument assumes that cars and PCs are similar, but doesn't say *how* they are similar. So let's try to find the common properties. Both cars and personal computers are products of sophisticated technology. In both cases the technology is packaged in a form that allows the average person to use it for his own purposes without being an expert. Both products are cheap enough for someone of ordinary means to purchase. The automobile freed people from dependence on trains, an earlier and highly centralized form of mechanized transportation; in the same way, the PC frees people from dependence on mainframe computers, an earlier and highly centralized form of information processing. In addition to these similarities, of course, there are differences. There's the basic difference in function: transportation vs. computing. They also differ in size and the form of power they use. If you had written all this down in a table as the different points occurred to you, the result might look like this:

Automobile	*Personal computer*
Sophisticated technology	Sophisticated technology
Doesn't require expertise	Doesn't require expertise
Affordable by individual	Affordable by individual
Replaced centralized technology	Replaced centralized technology
Transportation	Information/communication
Uses gasoline	Uses electricity
Expanded individual freedom	/ Will expand individual freedom

We have broken down the similarity between cars and PCs into four properties they share. We can now ask which property is linked to the question of individual freedom. That is, which property should be the middle term in our analysis of the argument? Let's go down the list. The fact that both use sophisticated technology does not in itself seem relevant, since the same could be said of many things—from nuclear power plants to the space shuttle—that do not have the same effect for the individual, at least not in any direct way. By contrast, both the price of the machines and the fact that they don't require expertise do seem essential, since they imply that the average person can own and operate them. Finally, the historical point that both products replaced earlier, centralized forms of the technology does not seem crucial. It's interesting, but the argument would not be any weaker without this point. So we have located a plausible middle term for the argument, and we can now formulate the generalization: any technological product that individuals can afford and can use without being experts expands their freedom. In our analysis of the original argument, this statement would be the conclusion of the inductive step and the major premise of the deductive step.

Evaluation

Once we have selected the most plausible middle term, and analyzed the argument accordingly, we need to evaluate the inductive step. Does the example of the automobile provide good evidence for the statement we just formulated? In general, is the premise "All/No *S* is *P*" supported by the example of *A*? Notice that the argument gives us only a single instance to support these generalizations. This limitation is inherent in the nature of an argument by analogy. We are supporting a claim about *B* on the basis of its similarity to *A*, so *A* is the only instance available to support the generalization. And we have seen that a single instance usually does not provide very much evidence for a general proposition. In this respect, an argument by analogy is a kind of logical shortcut, and it is a relatively weak mode of argument. Nevertheless, such arguments vary a great deal among themselves in their degree of strength, and we can assess their strength by applying our rules for evaluating generalizations.

The first rule is to consider the number and variety of the positive instances. In the case of an analogy, where we have only a single instance, the key question to ask is whether increasing the number or variety would affect the argument. In the analogy between reasoning and tennis, for example, tennis is a physical skill, but the generalization is about *all* skills: physical, mental, social, etc. So we need to consider whether or not examples from the other categories would confirm the generalization. Are the differences, say, between physical and mental skills relevant to the question of whether they must be acquired by practice? (This is a crucial question for us because the art of reasoning is a mental skill.) In this case, I would say that the differences are not relevant, so the argument is a fairly strong one. But this will not always be the case. That's why it is important to include differences as well as similarities when you construct a table.

The second rule is to look for disconfirming instances. Suppose someone argued that war is like arm wrestling, so victory usually goes to the strongest. The point of similarity between war and arm wrestling is that both are contests. So we would analyze the argument as follows:

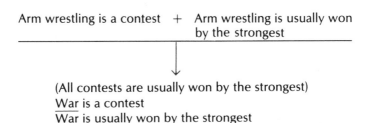

Arm wrestling is a contest   +   Arm wrestling is usually won
                                   by the strongest

(All contests are usually won by the strongest)
War is a contest
War is usually won by the strongest

It is obvious that the major premise in the syllogism is not very well supported by the inductive evidence. Arm wrestling is a particular type of contest that happens to depend largely on strength, but other types of contest depend on other traits. Chess matches are usually won by the player with better strategy, basketball games by the side with better speed, precision, and teamwork. Both chess and basketball are negative instances that disconfirm the generalization. So you might reply to the original argument by saying "Yes, but war is also like a chess game, so victory will go to the best strategy," or "Yes, but war is also like basketball, so the side with the most speed, precision, and teamwork will win." These are called *counter-analogies*, and they are one of the most effective ways of rebutting an argument by analogy.

The third rule is to consider the initial plausibility of a generalization, the plausibility that there could be a connection between subject and predicate—in this case, between *S* and *P*. Given everything we know about skills, for example, it is quite plausible to think they are acquired by practice; on the other hand, it is quite clear that the shape of our teeth has little if anything to do with their need for dental care.

An interesting case that lies between these two extremes is the analogy between the mind and a computer. Some people hold that the brain is like the hardware of a computer, and the mind is like the software, the programs that run on the machine. They use this analogy to derive various conclusions about the nature of the mind and the way it should be studied. The basis of the analogy is the fact that both computers and minds process information, and the computer is used to support the generalization that any information-processing device must have a hardware and a software component. But critics of this view find the analogy, and the generalization, completely implausible because the idea of a program doesn't make sense to them unless there is a programmer—which there isn't in the case of the mind. Whichever side you take in this dispute, the point is that people generally take sides on the basis of their general views about the nature of minds, brains, and programs.

The use of analogies in arguments, then, does not represent a fundamentally new mode of reasoning. It involves a combination of inductive and deductive elements that we can evaluate by rules we've already learned. The trick is to isolate those elements, which are normally implicit in the argument, not explicit. The technique described in this section can be summarized in four steps:

1) Identify the two things being compared (*A* and *B*) and the property attributed to *B* in the conclusion (*P*).
2) Identify the property (*S*) that is supposed to make *A* and *B* similar. If this is not stated explicitly, construct a similarity table and choose the most plausible candidate.
3) Analyze the argument into its inductive and deductive elements. The deductive step will be a syllogism with the major premise "All/No *S* is *P*."
4) Evaluate that premise as a generalization, looking for counter-analogies.

Practice Quiz

Analyze and evaluate each of the following analogical arguments:

1. Jim is an intellectual, like Fred, and Fred doesn't like sports. So Jim probably doesn't like them either.
2. A photon of light is like a billiard ball in having a definite velocity, position, and mass. A photon is therefore a particle.
3. A photon of light is like an air vibration in having a definite frequency and wavelength. Light is therefore a wave phenomenon.
4. Psychotherapies that promise instant happiness are comparable to "get rich quick" schemes in the economic realm, and therefore cannot be expected to work.

5. Efforts by the major European powers to achieve arms control, at the turn of the century and again in the 1920s and 1930s, were not successful. So arms control negotiations between the U.S. and the Soviet Union today are not likely to succeed either.

SUMMARY

Analogies can be used to argue for a conclusion as well as to describe or explain. When it is used in an argument, an analogy purports to show that *B* has the property *P* because *A* has that property and because *B* is similar to *A*. To analyze such an argument, we must identify the respect in which *A* and *B* are similar—the property *S* that they share. To evaluate the argument, we must use inductive methods to determine whether there is a link between *S* and *P*.

Exercises

A. Find an argument by analogy to support each of the following conclusions. Even if you don't agree with the conclusion, try to find the most plausible analogy.

1. Friend to potential car buyer: "That Firebird is going to cost more to insure."
2. Doctors should be allowed to advertise their services and prices.
3. The U.S. should not support the Contras in Nicaragua.
4. Clint Eastwood will probably seek higher office.
5. Children should not be overprotected against the vicissitudes of life.

B. Each of the passages below contains an analogy. a) Decide whether the analogy is being used in an argument. b) If so, analyze and evaluate it.

1. "Dr. John F. Beary III, director of the Georgetown University Medical Group, . . . argues that [physical] exams should be given to people under age 40 every other year and to those over 40 annually. "People take their car in for servicing every few months without complaint," he says. "Why shouldn't they take similar care of their bodies?" [*U.S. News & World Report*, August 11, 1986]
2. "The total absence of civil defense preparations . . . [is] among

the most dangerous characteristics of our present defense efforts. . . . [A] 'socially responsible' physician claims that saving lives through civil defense encourages war. Did the British encourage Hitler's attack by adopting civil defense measures that reduced the number of blitz victims by hundreds of thousands? . . . Do seat belts encourage reckless driving? Does owning a smoke alarm and fire extinguisher make people careless with fire?" [Edward Teller, "Civil Defense Is Crucial," *New York Times,* Op-ed, January 3, 1984]

3. "Vigorous writing is concise. A sentence should contain no unnecessary words, a paragraph no unnecessary sentences, for the same reason that a drawing should have no unnecessary lines and a machine no unnecessary parts." [William B. Strunk, Jr., and E. B. White, *The Elements of Style*]

4. "The mode of taxation is, in fact, quite as important as the amount. As a small burden badly placed may distress a horse that could carry with ease a much larger one properly adjusted, so a people may be impoverished and their power of producing wealth destroyed by taxation, which, if levied another way, could be borne with ease." [Henry George, *Progress and Poverty*]

5. Life's but a walking shadow, a poor player,
That struts and frets his hour upon the stage,
And then is heard no more. It is a tale
Told by an idiot, full of sound and fury,
Signifying nothing.
[William Shakespeare, *Macbeth*]

6. "What, after all, is the difference between shipping arms to Khomeini's Iran in 1986 and shipping arms to Hitler's Germany in 1939? Germany was of long-run strategic importance to America; the triumph of Ayatollah Khomeini's fundamentalism is likely to be as destructive to the Middle East as Hitler's Nazism would have been to Europe." [Karen Elliott House, "This Iran Policy Makes Carter's Look Good," *Wall Street Journal,* November 13, 1986]

7. "If 'good' and 'better' are terms deriving their sole meaning from the ideology of each people, then of course ideologies themselves cannot be better or worse than one another. Unless the measuring rod is independent of the things measured, we can do no measuring." [C. S. Lewis, *Christian Reflections*]

8. "As former Salvadoran Ambassador to the United States, I am shocked by the unsubstantiated and simplistic allegations which continue to flow from Robert E. White, former U.S. Ambassador to El Salvador.

"Mr. White wonders 'why the revolutionaries fight so much better than Government troops.' That is like noting that criminals in the United States do much better than the police. Of course guerrillas and criminals 'do better': they choose their victims and targets at will—and no army or police force in the world can be everywhere at once to anticipate and defeat every guerrilla attack or crime." [Roberto Quinonez-Meza, Letter to the editor, *New York Times*, December 20, 1983]

9. "Insurance companies say the high cost of insuring people with pre-existing medical conditions would sharply increase premiums for other policy holders. 'An analogy would be selling fire insurance on a burning building,' says James Dorsch, an attorney for the Health Insurance Association of America. . . ." [*Wall Street Journal*, August 12, 1986]

10. "Taxation of earnings from labor is on a par with forced labor. Some persons find this claim obviously true: taking the earnings of n hours labor is like taking n hours from the person; it is like forcing the person to work n hours for another's purpose." [Robert Nozick, *Anarchy, State, and Utopia*] (You may assume from the character of the analogy that Nozick's conclusion is: taxation of earnings from labor is *wrong*.)

11. "Absence diminishes small loves and increases great ones, as the wind blows out the candle and blows up the bonfire." [La Rochefoucauld, *Maxims*]

12. "We can follow the path taken by physics and biology by turning directly to the relation between behavior and the environment and neglecting supposed mediating states of mind. Physics did not advance by looking more closely at the jubilance of a falling body, or biology by looking at the nature of vital spirits, and we do not need to try to discover what personalities, states of mind, feelings, traits of character, plans, purposes, intentions, or the other perquisites of autonomous man really are in order to get on with a scientific analysis of behavior." [B. F. Skinner, *Beyond Freedom and Dignity*]

C. The arguments below are classic arguments by analogy, widely used to support widely accepted views. For each one, find a counter-analogy.

1. In defense of equality of opportunity: life is a race; victory should go to the swiftest, but the runners should start at the same place.

2. Anger is like steam under pressure, so you shouldn't keep it bottled up.

3. Society is like a family, and the more productive members should provide for the needs of the less productive.
4. Human knowledge is like a building, and it must therefore rest on foundations.

D. Perhaps the most famous argument by analogy is the "argument from design," used to defend the belief in the existence of God. The passages below are from a work by the eighteenth-century philosopher David Hume. The first one is a statement of the argument itself; the second is a counter-analogy to the argument. Using what you have learned in this section, decide which side of this debate is more persuasive.

1. "Look round the world: Contemplate the whole and every part of it: You will find it to be nothing but one great machine, subdivided into an infinite number of lesser machines, which again admit of subdivisions to a degree beyond what human senses and faculties can trace and explain. All these various machines, and even their most minute parts, are adjusted to each other with an accuracy which ravishes into admiration all men who have ever contemplated them. The curious adapting of means to ends, throughout all nature, resembles exactly, though it much exceeds, the productions of human contrivance—of human design, thought, wisdom, and intelligence. Since therefore the effects resemble each other, we are led to infer, by all the rules of analogy, that the causes also resemble, and that the Author of Nature is somewhat similar to the mind of man, though possessed of much larger faculties, proportioned to the grandeur of the work which he has executed."

2. "Now, if we survey the universe, so far as it falls under our knowledge, it bears a great resemblance to an animal or organized body, and seems actuated with a like principle of life and motion. A continual circulation of matter in it produces no disorder; a continual waste in every part is incessantly repaired; the closest sympathy is perceived throughout the entire system; and each part or member, in performing its proper offices, operates both to its own preservation and to that of the whole. The world, therefore, I infer, is an animal; and the Deity is the *soul* of the world, actuating it, and actuated by it."

   [David Hume, *Dialogues Concerning Natural Religion*]

17

Statistical Reasoning

Consider the following statements:

1) About 7 million new jobs have been created in the U.S. in the past decade.
2) The U.S. homicide rate in 1982 was 9.6 per hundred thousand residents.
3) 36 percent of the students at Tiptop College are majoring in the humanities.
4) The median sales price of existing homes is $84,400.
5) Other things being equal, someone who smokes is ten times more likely to get lung cancer than someone who does not.

Each of these statements is a **statistical** proposition. It attributes a quantitative, numerical property to some class of things: students, jobs, new homes, smokers, etc. We have not encountered this sort of proposition in our study of reasoning so far. Logic deals primarily with qualitative reasoning, while mathematics deals with quantitative. And a full treatment of statistical reasoning would require a separate book going over the relevant mathematical techniques. But the subject is too important to ignore.

Logic and Statistics

For one thing, statistical arguments are often used in connection with the kinds of topics we have been dealing with: political issues, personal decisions, generalizations about human nature. It is not unusual for a given conclusion to be supported by statistical as well as nonstatistical arguments. A proposed change in the tax laws, for example, might be supported by the claim that it will spur the economy as well as by the claim that it would be fairer. The first argument would involve statistical data, the second would not. The daily paper and the nightly news offer plenty of other examples. So you need to know how to evaluate *both* kinds of argument in order to weigh all the evidence for the conclusion.

For another thing, statistical evidence is indispensable for conclusions about causality in complex systems—such as the health of a human body or a trend in the economy—where no single factor by itself is either necessary or sufficient. In this respect, some understanding of statistics is necessary to complete our study of Mill's methods.

It's important at the outset to avoid two opposite mistakes about statistics. One mistake is a misplaced worship of numbers. Statements involving numbers have a hard, clean, precise air about them; they give the impression of objectivity and expertise. For that reason, political advocates seem to feel that no argument is complete without a statistic to back it up. But we should remember that a statistic is no better than the reasoning process by which it was derived. When the reasoning is fallacious, or arbitrary, or flawed in some other way, the statistic may bear no relation to reality. If someone complains that Americans represent only 8 percent of the world's population, but have 23 percent of the world's fun, you would be right to wonder how the second statistic was arrived at. Or if someone defends a change in the tax code on the ground that it will create 34,578 new jobs, we should be skeptical. It's extremely doubtful whether anyone could predict, with that kind of precision, the effects of legislation on something as complex as an economy. Indeed, the first and fundamental rule for evaluating a statistical claim is to step back and ask whether the phenomenon can be counted or measured at all (how could anyone measure the amount of fun in the world?), and if so, with what kind of accuracy.

The opposite mistake is to mistrust statistics entirely, an attitude expressed in the statement that "you can prove anything with statistics." This is not true. It *is* true that you can often create the *appearance* of proof by manipulating statistical information, just as fallacious reasoning can give the appearance of a strong argument. But the proper response is to learn how to identify and avoid the fallacies, not to throw the baby out with the bath water. In this chapter, we are going to cover some of the more common fallacies involving statistics. To spot them when they occur, it's a good idea to adopt a healthy skepticism about statistics in general. But you should balance that skepticism with an awareness of the value statistics can have. We rely on them in our daily lives when we make decisions about our health or our jobs, about where to live and where not to, about where to travel and how to get there. Statistical information is often relevant to political arguments. And statisticians have given us some amazingly powerful instruments for discovering patterns in nature and in human affairs that are not visible to the naked eye.

In Chapter 3, we saw that a definition takes a mass of information about the referents of a concept and reduces it to a single statement. In the same way, a statistic takes a mass of quantitative information about a group of objects and reduces it to a single number (or set of numbers). In the next section, we're going to look at three basic kinds of statistical information: totals and ratios, frequencies and frequency distributions, and averages. Virtually all the statistics you will encounter in everyday discussion and in the media fall into one of these basic categories, or involve some combination of them. Our goal is to understand how the numbers are derived, what they stand for, and the dangers to watch out for when we use these numbers in arguments.

Before we look at the different kinds of statistical information, however, a few general points are in order. Statistics deal with *classes* of things, and for the sake of continuity with previous chapters we will use the letter S to stand for a class (and T, U, etc., if there is more than one class). Statistics also deal with the *properties* that members of a class possess, especially the measurable properties. In this respect, we need to recall a point from our study of classification. As we saw in Chapter 2, the genus-species relation applies to properties as well as to classes of objects. Color, for example, is a generic quality in relation to specific colors such as red or green. In statistics, a generic quality is called a *variable,* and the specific qualities are called *values* of that variable. So red and green are values of the variable *color;* A, B, AB, and O are values of the variable *bloodtype;* Republican and Democrat are values of the variable *political party affiliation.*

The concept of a variable is a key link between logic and mathematics. To see why, consider two variables that we might use to classify people:

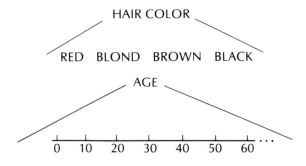

The diagram on the left is our familiar classification scheme, with the generic quality or variable above, and the specific qualities or values below. The same is true of the diagram on the right. The only difference is that hair color is a *qualitative* variable: its values differ from one another qualitatively, and could have been listed in any order, whereas age is a *quantitative* variable: a specific age can be measured by number of years, and thus the values are arranged in a specific order along the numerical scale. But in either case, the variable could serve as a principle of classification, and we would group together people who have the same value. Statistics make use of both kinds of variable, but as we will see, certain kinds of statistics apply only to quantitative variables.

Using Statistics in Argument

Let's turn now to the various types of statistical information, and the questions to consider when we use this information in reasoning.

Totals and Ratios

The simplest operation in arithmetic is addition, and the simplest statistic, which we'll call a **total,** is the result of adding up a set of units. Examples would include:

1) Total population of the U.S.
2) Total number of new jobs created in the past decade
3) Total number of movies that Fred Astaire and Ginger Rogers made together
4) Total number of traffic fatalities in 1982
5) Total calories consumed in meals at the Twenty-One Club during 1956
6) Total money spent in political campaigns in the 1984 elections

In examples (1)–(4), the total is the number of members in some class—residents of the U.S., new jobs, etc.—and we can find the total simply by counting. In examples (5) and (6), we are also concerned with classes—meals at the Twenty-One Club, political campaigns in 1984—but we are not given the number of members. We are given the sum of their values on some variable: calories and expenditures, respectively.

Totals are probably the kind of statistic we encounter most often in the media. But a simple total by itself is usually not very illuminating. In 1984, about $1.8 billion was spent in political campaigns for office at all levels of government. Is that a lot of money? Is it too much? Too little? It's hard to answer these questions in a vacuum; we need some standard of comparison. It would help to know, for example, how much was spent in previous election years. So we could look up those numbers, and put all the information in a table:

Year	Campaign expenditures (in 1984 dollars)
1972	$1.0 billion
1976	$947 million
1980	$1.5 billion
1984	$1.8 billion

Such a table allows us to compare equivalent totals, and thus identify any trend that may exist, such as the visible trend toward higher expenditures. We are usually more interested in the trend than in the actual numbers.

To be meaningful, however, the comparison must involve *equivalent* totals. That is why I included only years in which, like 1984, there were presidential elections. Since more money is spent in presidential campaigns than in any other kind, it would not be valid to compare 1984 with a nonpresidential year, such as 1982. For the same reason, we should use the same unit of measurement when we compare total values of a variable. That is why I adjusted the figures in the table for inflation, which changes the value of the dollar as a unit of expenditure.

Instead of comparing campaign expenditures in different years, we might want to compare expenditures in different *countries.* This would require a great many adjustments to avoid comparing apples and oranges, since even democratic countries differ widely in the way they organize their electoral systems. We won't go into all that. But one adjustment we would certainly have to make is an adjustment for the *size* of each country. There wouldn't be much point, for example, in comparing total campaign expenditures in the U.S. and England, because the U.S. has so many more voters. What we need to know is the relationship between two totals: total dollars spent and total number of voters. We want the **ratio:** dollars spent per voter. Many statistics are reported as ratios rather than as simple totals—that is, in *relative* rather than *absolute* terms.

When you compare ratios, it is just as important to make sure you're comparing equivalent things as it is when you compare totals. Suppose you wanted to know whether homicide is more prevalent here than in other countries. In 1982, there were 22,358 homicides reported in the U.S. (an absolute number), or 9.6 per

100,000 residents (a relative number). The relative number is clearly the one to use. But when you look up the homicide rates in other countries, you would need to ask whether they define the concept HOMICIDE the same way our legal system does—is manslaughter included? what about self-defense, or suicide?

Before you draw any conclusions from a ratio, it is important to think carefully about what the ratio means. Suppose you wanted to know which is the safer form of travel, commercial airlines or automobiles. You might compare their fatality rates. But which rate—deaths per *vehicle* mile, or deaths per *passenger* mile? Planes carry many more passengers than cars, so more people are likely to die in a single plane crash than in a single auto accident. For the same reason, though, a safe flight logs many more passenger miles than does a safe auto trip of the same distance. To compare overall safety, therefore, we should use fatalities per passenger mile.

Frequency and Distribution

A **frequency** statement says how many things in a class S have the property P; it tells us the frequency with which P occurs in that class. An *absolute frequency* statement gives the actual number of S's that are P—for example, 2149 students at Tiptop College are humanities majors. A *relative frequency* statement gives the *proportion* of S's that are P—for example, 36 percent of the students at Tiptop College are humanities majors. As you can see, an absolute frequency is a special sort of total, and a relative frequency is a special sort of ratio.

But frequencies are worth considering as a separate class of statistics in their own right. Some of the most commonly reported statistics are frequencies, such as the unemployment rate (percent of the workforce that is unemployed), the illiteracy rate (percent of adults who can't read), the poverty rate (percent of the populace living below the poverty line), or a baseball player's batting "average" (which is not an average at all, but the proportion of times at bat on which he gets a hit). In addition, frequencies raise special problems of classification and definition, and they play a special role in estimating probabilities. Let's look at each of these points more closely.

A frequency statement divides the S's into two subclasses, those that are P and those that are not P: humanities majors vs. nonhumanities majors, employed people vs. unemployed people, and so on. But we can also do a more thorough classification, dividing the S's into those that are P, Q, R, etc., indicating the proportion that fall into each subclass. The result is called a frequency **distribution.** From a logical standpoint, a distribution is simply a classification with numbers attached, and could be represented by our standard diagram. For example, the distribution of students by major might look like this:

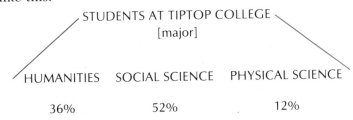

STUDENTS AT TIPTOP COLLEGE
[major]

HUMANITIES   SOCIAL SCIENCE   PHYSICAL SCIENCE

36%   52%   12%

It is more common, however, to see this information expressed by either a bar graph or a pie chart:

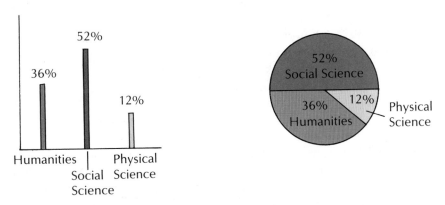

You have probably seen charts of this kind used to represent distributions such as the market share of each company in an industry, the ethnic or racial makeup of a country's population, or the proportion of government spending for military, Social Security, welfare, and other categories.

Because a distribution involves classification, the rules of classification apply. To have a meaningful distribution, we should use a single principle or a consistent set of principles—that is, a single variable or set of variables. The variable could be a qualitative one such as a student's major, or it could be a quantitative one such as age, IQ, income, height, or corporate revenues. The subgroups into which the S's are distributed are defined by specific values of the variable. With a quantitative variable, we would usually pick certain intervals on the scale—such as ages 0–5, 5–10, 11–15, etc. In any case, the subgroups should be mutually exclusive, so that we don't count individual things twice. If they are not mutually exclusive, the frequencies will add up to more than 100 percent. And the subgroups should be jointly exhaustive, so that all the S's can be assigned to one species (value) or another. If they are not jointly exhaustive, the frequencies will add up to less than 100 percent.

Statements about frequencies and distributions also require that we define our terms carefully. If we are going to measure the proportion of S's that are P, or the distribution of S's into subgroups P, Q, and R, we need definitions of all these groups. And unlike a definition used in ordinary reasoning, a definition used for statistical purposes can't have fuzzy borderlines; it must give us a clear criterion for deciding whether to include or exclude any given thing. This usually involves an element of stipulation, and different researchers will make different decisions. One implication is that you cannot always compare statistics compiled by different researchers, even when they deal with the same subject. For example, the Federal Bureau of Labor Statistics estimates the unemployment rate in two different ways. The figure most often reported is based on a survey of households, asking individuals whether they are presently employed. But the Bureau also does a separate survey of business payrolls. Among other differences, the household survey counts people on strike as employed, while the payroll survey counts them as unemployed; so the two numbers are not comparable.

Another implication is that when you see a frequency statement or distribution in the media, it's important to ask what definitions were used before you draw any conclusions or use the statistics in an argument. For example, a headline in a supermarket tabloid reads: "One in five people is as nutty as a fruitcake, says doc." [*Weekly World News,* November 20, 1984] Even allowing for the rhetorical excesses of headline writers, the news that 20 percent of the populace is mentally ill would be fairly alarming. But the story reveals that the researchers defined mental illness to include alcoholism, anxiety, and depression as well as severe psychosis. Perhaps it is reasonable to define mental illness that broadly, but if so, we can hardly draw the conclusion that all these people are "nutty as a fruitcake."

Here's another example. From time to time, the newspapers report estimates on the number of people who are illiterate. These estimates vary enormously, because different definitions of illiteracy are used. One Census Bureau study assumed that anyone with five or more years of schooling was literate; by that standard only .5 percent of people over 14 were illiterate. A later study used a reading and word-use test; anyone who answered 20 out of 26 questions correctly was considered literate. By that standard, 13 percent of adults were illiterate. If the researchers had chosen 21 as a passing score instead of 20, the number of illiterates would have been higher; if they had chosen 19, the number would have been lower. Other studies used different definitions altogether, and produced altogether different numbers. So before you could draw any conclusions about whether literacy is widespread in this country, you would need to decide what a reasonable definition of illiteracy would be. You cannot accept any particular number at face value, without being able to defend the definition that produced it.

Let's consider a final and very important role of frequency information. A relative frequency is often expressed as a **probability.** For example, cancer accounts for about a quarter of all deaths in the U.S., a fact that is sometimes expressed by saying that an individual has one chance in four of dying from cancer. Conversely, if we want to know the probability of something, we would make use of frequency information. To estimate the probability that a new Volvo will last 100,000 miles, we would see what proportion of Volvos last that long. To find the chance of rain today, a weather forecaster uses information about the number of times it has rained on past occasions when conditions were the same as today. If an insurance company wants to know the likelihood that a 35-year-old woman will die during the term of her twenty-year life insurance policy, it consults a mortality table that says what proportion of 35-year-old women die before they reach 55. In general, we estimate the probability of something from its frequency in the class it belongs to, which in this context is called a *reference* group.

But we know that an object or event can be classified in more than one way. It belongs to many different classes. How do we decide which one to use? Suppose we want to know the probability that a certain student will graduate from college. What is the appropriate reference group? The whole population of college students? That's awfully broad; it doesn't take account of factors that affect this particular student's chances of graduating. So perhaps we should consider the frequency of graduation in a narrower class of students. But which one? Students at that particular college? Students with the same SAT scores? the same family, ethnic, or religious backgrounds? the same personality traits? the same degree of intelligence and ambition? You can see that if we tried to find a reference group that takes account of *every* factor that might be relevant, we might very well end up with a group containing only one member—the student himself. And then there would be no frequency to measure.

In practice, this problem can be solved by two considerations. The first is that we usually have limited information about an individual. If all we know is that a student is attending Tiptop College, then we have no choice but to estimate the student's chance of graduating from the frequency of graduation at that school. The second is that we do not have statistical information on all the factors that might be relevant. Ambition cannot be measured very well, for example, so there are no data on the frequency of graduation among people with a particular value of this variable. The implication is that numerical estimates of probability are relative to the information we happen to have. You should keep this relativity in mind, especially when you are trying to weigh your own prospects for the future, because those prospects depend on things that only you can know about yourself. Three-quarters of all new businesses fail in the first five years—but perhaps you have more drive, or a better product, than other entrepreneurs. Half of all marriages end in divorce—but perhaps you and your intended have a better relationship than other couples.

Averages

We are all familiar with averages: grade point averages, average prices of new homes, average SAT scores for this year's freshman class, average yards gained by the Chicago Bears on third-down plays. An **average** gives us information about some class of things, S; what it tells us is the central value of S's on some quantitative variable. It is an especially useful way of reducing a mass of quantitative information to a single number.

There are two different kinds of average: the arithmetic *mean*, and the *median*. (Actually, there are others, but they are seldom used.) To find the arithmetic mean, you add up the values of each S and then divide by the number of S's. Thus, if a class of five students had the following scores on a test,

Joan	97
Nelson	89
Harry	85
Leslie	82
Tom	80

the class average would be

$$\frac{97 + 89 + 85 + 82 + 80}{5} = \frac{433}{5} = 86.6.$$

The median score is the one that lies in the middle of all the scores, so that an equal number of scores are higher and lower. In our example, the median score would be Harry's—85. (If there had been a sixth member of the class who scored below Tom, then the median would have been halfway between Harry's and Leslie's score—with an even number of values, the median lies halfway between the two values closest to the middle.)

Notice that the mean and the median are not the same. That's because there was one extreme value—Joan's score—and the mean is sensitive to extreme values in a way the median is not. If Joan had received a 90, the mean would be different, the median would be the same. Even with a much larger group, an extreme value can pull the mean in its direction, just as a child at the end of a seesaw can balance an adult sitting near the middle. As this is being written, for example, the median price of a new home is $92,300, whereas the mean price is $116,000, reflecting the upward pull of a few extremely expensive homes.

This doesn't imply that there is anything wrong or misleading about the mean. On the contrary, it represents the "center of gravity" in a set of values, and that is often precisely the information we want. Indeed, when someone refers to an average without further specification, it's safe to assume he's referring to the mean. Nevertheless, the mean can be misleading, especially if there are extreme values only in one direction. For example, family income can't get any lower than $0, but the upper end of the scale is effectively unlimited. So the figure you'll see in the newspaper most often is the median family income, not the mean.

Sometimes it isn't clear whether the mean or the median is the better measure, and an argument may hang in the balance. For example, doctors carry malpractice insurance; if someone sues them for malpractice, and wins, the insurance pays the award. Manufacturers carry similar insurance against product liability suits. In recent years, the cost of such insurance has gone through the roof, and people have argued about the causes. Some hold the courts responsible, citing the increase in the average (mean) amount of damages awarded by juries against doctors and manufacturers. Others reject this explanation on the ground that the mean is misleading. It is pulled upward, they argue, by a few "million-dollar" verdicts, whereas the median award is still quite small. Which number do you think better represents the situation (given that our goal is to understand the rise in insurance premiums)?

An average can be expressed in relative as well as absolute terms. We can express the average value of one group as a ratio of the average value of another group. This is a useful way to compare different classes of things on some variable. We can compare average earnings among ethnic groups, average fuel consumption among models of cars, etc. But the technique can be abused. Here's an example from an interview with an authority on women's economic status:

> Q. How do U.S. women compare with those in other countries?
> A. The big surprise is that American women are less well-off. They earn on average 64 percent of the male wage. In Sweden, Italy and Australia, women earn about 80 percent; in France and Germany, 78 and 73 percent. [Interview with Sylvia Ann Hewlett, *U.S. News & World Report*, May 12, 1986]

The conclusion here is that American women are less well-off than women in those other countries. The average wages of women in the various countries is certainly a relevant piece of evidence. But we need to know the absolute figures, and what we are given are relative ones: the ratio of female to male wages in each country. If males in the U.S. earn much more than males in the other countries, then women in the U.S. may still be better off than women elsewhere; the argument is a *non sequitur*.

Let's pull together what we've learned by comparing the different kinds of statistics.

Total:	the total number of things in a class S or the sum of their values on a variable.
Ratio:	the number or sum of S's per unit of some other class T.
Frequency:	the number or proportion of S's that have some property P.
Distribution:	the proportion of S's that have each of the values (P, Q, R, etc.) on some variable, qualitative or quantitative.
Average:	the central value (either the mean or the median) of the S's on some quantitative variable.

If you understand the differences among these numbers, and the dangers to watch out for in using each type of information, you should be able to understand most of the statistics you encounter in everyday contexts, and to use them intelligently in arguing for conclusions. The fundamental point to remember is that the numbers depend on the process by which they were derived, and are informative only to the extent that the process is logical.

Practice Quiz

Identify the type of statistical information contained in each of the statements below. Then determine whether or not the statement supports the conclusion that follows it in brackets.

1. The population of the U.S. is 237.1 million. [The U.S. is a large country.]
2. In 1982, there were 10.6 marriages per 1,000 people in the U.S. [At this rate, everyone in the country will be married in 47.17 years: 1,000 people divided by $10.6 \times 2 = 47.17$.]
3. For first marriages, the median age of the male was 24.1. [Grooms are getting older.]
4. In 1985, about half the (legal) immigrants to this country were Asians. [Asians make up a growing part of the population.]
5. 83.1% of the U.S. population is white, 11.7% black, 1.4% Asian, and 3.5% are American Indians or other races. [There are no Hispanic people in the U.S.]
6. Foreign-born residents constitute 7% of the population in the U.S., 11% in France, 16% in Canada, and 20% in Australia. [The U.S. has fewer immigrants, in relative terms, than these other countries.]
7. Population density in the U.S. is about 65 people per square mile. [It's crowded here.]
8. In the decade 1901–1910, 8.8 million people immigrated to this country, or about 15 for every thousand residents; in the decade 1971–1980, 4.2 million people immigrated to this country, or about 3 for every thousand residents. [The rate of immigration has slowed down recently.]
9. The number of illegal aliens apprehended at the border has tripled in the last decade. [The rate of illegal immigration has increased recently.]
10. In the mid-1970s, the average native citizen received $2279 in social services (welfare, public education, Social Security); immigrants who had resided here less than five years received $1404. [Immigrants are less of a drain on public resources than natives.]

Statistical Generalization

As we saw in the last section, a statistic gives us numerical information about some class of things. In statistics, that class is called a *population* (regardless of whether or not it's a class of people). The different types of statistics—totals, frequencies, averages,—tell us about certain quantitative properties of the class. And we know from our study of the basic nature of induction that there are two ways to support a statement about a class. We can examine each and every member—the method of complete enumeration—or we can study a sample of the class and then generalize our findings to the class as a whole. Statisticians use both methods. Many statistics on health, such as the frequency of various diseases, or the proportion of people who die from various causes, reflect a complete tabulation of data from local public health officials around the country. And the Census Bureau issues a number of statistics based on surveys of the entire population. On the other hand, opinion polls, Nielson TV ratings, the unemployment rate, and many other statistics are based on samples.

Samples can be used to estimate a ratio, a frequency, a frequency distribution, or an average value in a population. The unemployment rate (the *frequency* of unemployment in the workforce) is based on a monthly survey of about 100,000 people. An opinion poll tries to discover the *distribution* of voter preferences for rival candidates by interviewing a random sample of voters. *Average* values for physical and psychological variables—blood pressure, pulse rate, IQ, and the like—are inferred from samples; obviously we can't survey the entire human race. These *statistical generalizations* have much in common with the universal generalizations that we studied earlier (e.g., all S are P). In both cases, we infer that what is true of a sample is true of the entire population. And in both cases, the inference is valid only to the extent that the sample is *representative* of the population. But there are important differences in the way we try to ensure that the sample *is* representative.

For a universal generalization, as we have seen, we want a sample that reflects the qualitative diversity in the class of S's. We should actively seek out instances that vary in every respect (other than being S) that might be relevant to P. We should also look actively for negative instances, because even a single S that is not P would refute the generalization. But this approach would not make sense for a statistical generalization. Suppose we want to know the proportion of S's that are P—a question of frequency (similar arguments would apply to distributions and averages). There is no point in looking for negative instances. Presumably we already know that some S's are not P; the question is not whether such instances exist, but rather how frequent they are. For the same reason, the *qualitative* variety of the sample is not necessarily relevant. We are interested in a *quantitative* property of the population: the proportion of S's that are P. What we need is a method of choosing our sample so that the proportion of P's in the sample will reflect the proportion of P's in the population.

The method statisticians have devised is the use of *random* samples, and the reason is as follows. If we choose our sample randomly, then every member of the population has an equal chance of being included in the sample. Suppose that in the population at large, 17 percent are *P*. This would mean that every time we choose an *S* to be included in the sample, we have a 17 percent chance of getting one that is *P*. So in the long run, we would expect to get a *P* about 17 percent of the time—if our sample is large enough, it should reflect the proportion of *P*'s in the population. Thus, instead of actively designing our sample by looking for certain kinds of instances, as we do for a universal generalization, we sit back and let a random process select the sample blindly.

The use of random samples has certain implications that we should be aware of. First, there is always a specific margin of error attached to the conclusion we draw about the population. Suppose you're in charge of quality control for a grain silo. You take a random sample of the grain and find that 3.2 percent is spoiled. Should you infer that *exactly* 3.2 percent of grain in the silo is spoiled? No. Your conclusion should be that spoilage in the silo is in the neighborhood of 3.2 percent. A sample is an instrument for measuring a quantity, and like other measuring instruments it has a specific margin of error. Second, the margin of error depends on the size of the sample. The larger the sample, the smaller the margin of error, and vice versa. For instance, when the Gallup poll reports the preferences of the electorate in a presidential election, it uses a sample of about 2000 voters, and the margin of error is about 2 percent. So if 56 percent in the sample favor candidate A, we can infer that somewhere between 54 and 58 percent of the voters favor candidate A. If the sample had included only 100 people, the margin of error would have been larger—around 10 percent.

Finally, we should be aware that even when we take the margin of error into account, we are still only dealing with probabilities. Because the sample was randomly chosen, there is some chance, however small, that it radically misrepresents the population. In our example above, suppose that in fact only one percent of the electorate favors candidate A. That's a tiny minority, but it's still about a million voters, and it is possible that 1120 of them were included in the sample (1120/2000 = 56 percent). In generalizing from a sample, therefore, we have to be satisfied with some degree of probability. Most people who use statistics settle for 95 percent. The 2 percent margin of error in the Gallup poll, for example, actually means that there's a 95 percent probability that the proportion of the voters favoring candidate A is within two percentage points of the reported figure.

There are precise mathematical techniques for computing a margin of error, given the size of the sample and the degree of probability we want. We'll leave all that to the experts. The techniques are not controversial, at least not for the types of statistics we are likely to encounter, and we can assume that if a statistic comes from a reputable source, the computations were done correctly. It is important to emphasize, however, that the margin of error refers only to the statistical relationship between the sample and the population. It does not include errors that arise in choosing and testing the sample itself. In particular, the techniques for calculating the margin of error assume that the sample was randomly chosen. This assumption is rarely true in the strict sense. A true random sample would be one chosen randomly from a complete list of the population. For a population the size of the American electorate, however, it is rarely possible to find a complete list, and it is usually too expensive to choose and test a completely random sample. So researchers typically use methods that they think will approximate randomness, but the approximation is never perfect, and there is plenty of room for biases to creep in. Let's look at some examples.

You want to know the average test score of the students in a class you're taking, so you ask the first ten students who arrive at class one day—but that sample may overrepresent the more conscientious students, who may tend to score higher. An opinion poll uses a questionnaire distributed in airports—but people who travel by air are not a random cross-section of the populace, and besides, people who fill out and return questionnaires are not a random cross-section of those who receive them. A study of criminals relies on a sample of prison inmates—but criminals who are caught, convicted, and imprisoned may not be representative of criminals as a whole. All these samples are *biased* in one way or another, and therefore won't tell us what we want to know about the relevant populations. Problems can also arise in testing the sample, once it is chosen. A telephone interview, for example, would be a poor way to estimate the proportion of parents who abuse their children: even if the sample was randomly chosen, you could hardly count on abusers to tell you the truth.

Subtle biases can occur even in studies done by professionals. The chart below summarizes the results of three opinion polls on the same subject: each one purports to represent the distribution of opinion on military spending. As you can see, the results are quite different. In (1), 9 percent of the respondents favored increasing the defense budget; in (2), 54 percent approved of President Reagan's proposal to increase military spending; and in (3), 22 percent favored an increase in military and defense spending. These polls were conducted within two months of each other, in the relatively uneventful winter of 1984–85, so it is unlikely that public opinion changed that much between one poll and the next. What accounts for the difference?

---

1. Harris and Associates survey, December 27, 1984–January 2, 1985

    Question: In general, do you favor increasing or decreasing the present defense budget, or keeping it the same as it is now?
    Favor increasing: 9%
    Favor keeping as is: 52%
    Favor decreasing: 39%

2. *Los Angeles Times* survey, January 19–24, 1985

    Question: Generally speaking, do you approve or disapprove of President Reagan's proposals to increase military spending?

    Approve: 54%
    Disapprove   46%

3. CBS News/*New York Times* survey, November 8–14, 1984

    Question: Are you in favor of increasing government spending on military and defense programs, reducing it, or keeping it about the same? (Note: Based on responses of those 75% who said they voted in 1984 elections.)

    Favor increasing: 22%
    Favor keeping as is: 52%
    Favor decreasing: 26%

Source: All polls adapted from *Public Opinion*, February/March 1985.

One factor might be a difference in the questions. Polls (1) and (3) asked for an opinion about the military budget itself, whereas (2) asked for approval or disapproval of President Reagan's proposal. The issue was the same, but the reference to the president, and the information that he wanted more military spending, may have swayed some people. The question in (1) and (3), moreover, gave respondents three choices, the most popular of which was to keep spending the same. In (2), however, the respondent had only two choices; there was no middle ground. Suppose you had no particular opinion on the subject, and didn't know much about military spending. If you had been asked the question in (1) or (3), you might have figured that the safest answer was the one in the middle.

If you had been asked question (2), you might have figured that the president probably knows what he's doing. Another factor might be a difference in the samples. In (1) and (2), the samples were drawn from the populace at large; in (3) the sample was drawn from those who voted in the 1984 election. These are obviously different groups. Not everyone votes, and the distribution of opinion among voters may not be the same as that among the people as a whole.

An opinion poll is an especially complicated case of generalizing from a sample, because opinions are such intangible and slippery things. It's likely that some respondents make up their minds on the spot, under the influence of subtle factors like the exact wording of the question or the structure of the alternatives they're given. But opinion polls are also the kind of statistical generalization we encounter most often in the media, and they illustrate very well the kinds of biases to watch for.

Despite the problems that can arise in generalizing from a sample, this method can be a reliable way of supporting statistical claims about a population. In particular, it can be as reliable as the method of complete enumeration. Suppose you wanted to know the distribution of land use in the U.S.: the proportion of land used for agriculture, industry, etc. You could study the records in all the relevant local, state, and federal government offices. Or you could take aerial photographs of the entire country. Either way, you would have a complete enumeration. But the process would be extremely expensive and time-consuming; you would have to reconcile the different definitions of "agriculture," "urban area," etc., used in different localities; and by the time you finished, the information you gathered first might no longer be accurate. So land-use experts usually rely on samples.

Another example is the crime rate: the number of burglaries (or other crimes) per thousand people. The FBI computes this figure by complete enumeration; it tabulates all the burglaries reported to all the police departments in the country. The National Crime Survey, on the other hand, uses a sample; it interviews about 60,000 households to see how many were victims of burglary in the previous six months. The NCS runs the risks associated with any use of samples. But the FBI figures have their own flaw: many burglaries are not reported to the police (a fact we know from the survey of victims). So the two approaches must be used to supplement each other.

As you can see, investigating the statistical properties of large populations in the real world takes a blend of common sense and specialized technique. If you need to use statistics in your studies or your work, you will need a separate course of training in the proper methods. This section is intended for the layman—the consumer of statistical information, not the producer. As laymen, we must rely to some extent on the authority of experts. But as in any other case of relying on authorities, we can—and should—use our own common sense to evaluate their credibility.

Practice Quiz

Identify potential biases and other problems in each of the following generalizations.

1. A conservative organization reports that 71% of the populace is opposed to national health insurance, based on a questionnaire sent to its mailing list.
2. A Soviet pollster finds that 94% of Russians approve of the way Mikhail Gorbachev is handling his job as General Secretary of the Communist Party.
3. To find the average salary of doctors, a reporter interviews a random sample of doctors attending a convention of the American Medical Association.
4. To find the average weight of cookie eaters, researchers gather data on people waiting in line at Mrs. Fields stores.
5. A poll is conducted by telephone to find the percentage of men who cannot swim.

Statistical Evidence of Causality

We have seen that a statistic gives us numerical information about a class such as the total number of its members, or their average values on a variable. Statistics can also tell us about **correlations** among these numerical properties. A correlation can take many forms, depending on the type of statistic involved. For example, *average* income correlates with the amount of education people have. The *frequency* of lung cancer is higher among smokers than among nonsmokers. *Total* government revenues from the capital gains tax have increased as the tax rate has gone down. What these examples have in common, what makes them examples of correlations, is a systematic, nonrandom relationship between two variables: income and education, smoking and lung cancer, revenues and tax rates.

Correlation and Causality

Correlations are important because they can give us evidence of causality. Medical researchers use statistical evidence to trace the causes of health and disease—the link between smoking and cancer is the best known example, but there are many others. Economists look for correlations that will explain inflation, unemployment, productivity, etc. In these and other cases, the use of correlations is required by the nature of the subject. In a complex system like the human body or the economy, a given effect is often the result of a great many factors—none of which by itself is either necessary or sufficient. Smoking, for example, is not a necessary condition for lung cancer: some nonsmokers get the disease. Nor is it sufficient: some smokers don't. But smoking *is* a partial or *contributing* factor, something that increases the likelihood of lung cancer, something that weighs in the balance—and can tip the balance if the right combination of other factors is also present.

To identify a contributing factor, we have to look at a large number of cases. For example, a drop in interest rates tends to cause an increase in purchases of homes. That's because individuals take the cost of a mortgage into account in deciding whether to buy. Of course, some people are going to buy a home no matter what, and others are simply not in the market. But for some individuals, a drop in mortgage costs will tip the balance. An economist, however, has no way of knowing who those particular individuals are; he can only examine the class of home buyers as a whole, and see whether the class gets bigger when interest rates fall. In general, a contributing factor usually can't be identified by looking at individual cases, but it will reveal itself in the existence of a correlation among variables in the relevant class.

The existence of a correlation, however, does not prove causality —not by itself. A correlation may occur by chance, or it may reflect a causal relationship quite different from the one it suggests. For example:

1) In 17 of the last 19 years, the stock market has gone up when a team from the NFC won the Super Bowl, and down when the AFC team won.
2) Before the introduction of polio vaccine, investigators found a strong correlation between soft drink sales and new polio cases reported.
3) In certain areas of Europe, there is a correlation between births and the number of stork nests.
4) Arizona has the highest death rate in the country from bronchitis, emphysema, asthma, and other lung diseases.

It should not be surprising that some correlations, like (1), occur by chance. Think of all the variables you could measure—from the average number of Oakland A's home runs during double-headers, to the fertility rate of zebras in Tanzania. If you look long enough, you're bound to find some bizarre correlations. In other cases, variables are correlated because both reflect a third factor. Before the vaccine was developed, polio epidemics tended to occur in the summer, when soft drink sales were also high. Storks do not in fact bring babies, but they do tend to nest in buildings, and the number of buildings increases with population. Arizona's death rate from lung disease, finally, does not mean that clean air kills; it means that many people with these diseases move there to prolong their lives.

Thus inferring that A causes B merely because A and B are correlated is analogous to the *post hoc* fallacy. If one event causes another, the first must precede the second, but the converse doesn't hold; the fact that A came first doesn't imply that it caused B. To establish causality, as we saw, we must use Mill's methods to show that there is a connection between A and B. In the same way, a contributing factor should give rise to a correlation among variables, but not every correlation reveals a causal relation. We need a method for separating the statistical wheat from the chaff.

In the four examples above, you could rely on common sense to avoid drawing the wrong conclusion. But many other cases are less obvious. Does lowering a tax rate cause an increase in tax revenues? How much of a person's intelligence is due to heredity? Does caffeine cause bladder cancer? Is a murderer more likely to get the death penalty for killing a white person than for killing a black person? There is correlational evidence on all these questions, but it is not immediately obvious how to interpret the evidence, and these issues are extremely controversial. What rules should we follow?

Evaluating Correlations

The rules for evaluating statistical evidence of causality rest on the same basic principle as Mill's methods, just as drawing a statistical generalization from a sample is governed by the same basic principle as universal generalizations. But there are also some important differences. Let's start by looking at an idealized case in the abstract. Then we'll look at some of the problems and issues that come up in practice.

Suppose we want to know whether some variable E is causally affected by another variable a. The ideal test would be an experiment in which we can control a and watch for corresponding changes in E; in this context, a would be called the *independent* variable, and *E* the *dependent* variable. One way to design the experiment could be diagrammed as follows:

Group 1: $a, b, c, \ldots$
Group 2: $- b, c, \ldots$

We have two groups that are identical except that one (the *experimental* group) has the property we're testing, while the other (the *control* group) does not. You can see that this is the same basic pattern as Mill's method of differences. Alternatively, if *a* is a quantitative variable, we could give different experimental groups different levels of *a*, using the same pattern as Mill's method of concomitant variation:

Group 1: $a_1, b, c, \ldots$
Group 2: $a_2, b, c, \ldots$
Group 3: $a_3, b, c, \ldots$

Notice, however, that we are comparing two or more *groups* of people instead of comparing two or more *individuals,* as we did when we studied Mill's methods earlier. We have to use groups when *a* is only a contributing factor, for the reason explained above. And we will also have to make an adjustment in the way we measure the dependent variable, the effect. The question is not whether the effect occurs, or in what degree, in a particular case; we are not comparing particular cases directly. We are comparing groups. So the question is whether *a* makes a *statistical* difference in the effect. If *E* is a qualitative variable, we would typically measure a frequency—for example, the frequency of tumors in mice fed a diet high in saccharine. If *E* is a quantitative variable such as SAT scores, we would typically look at average values for experimental and control groups.

But those are fairly minor adjustments to make in our use of Mill's methods. The major adjustment has to do with the other variables—*b, c,* etc. As we have seen, it's essential to the methods of difference and concomitant variations that we hold these factors constant. That is what allows us to infer that *a* is responsible for any differences in *E*. When we use statistical evidence, we have to meet this requirement in a somewhat different way. Suppose you want to know whether a certain cram course can raise people's SAT scores. You would have an experimental group take the course, and a control group not take it, holding all other factors constant. But how are you going to do that? Individual students differ on an enormous number of variables that might affect their SAT scores: IQ, verbal ability, memory, ability to concentrate, ambition, response to stress, test-taking savvy, and so on. It would be extraordinarily difficult to find two individuals who are identical with regard to all these variables. Finding two *groups* whose members are all identical is out of the question. Fortunately, that isn't necessary. Since we are dealing with groups, what matters is that they have the same *distribution* on those variables—the same proportions on each part of the IQ scale, the same distribution by verbal ability, memory, and the other variables. In that case, the experimental and control groups will be *statistically* identical except for the variable we are testing (taking the course vs. not taking it), and a statistical difference in the effect can then be attributed to that variable.

Setting things up this way is easier said than done. It takes a great deal of scientific knowledge and skill to make sure that the groups are statistically similar on these variables. In some cases, researchers try to match the groups by deliberately pairing off individuals. But this is quite difficult, especially if there are more than a few variables to keep track of. And with really complex phenomena, we simply don't know what all the relevant variables are. So it is more common to use random procedures for selecting the two groups, and the rationale is the same as in the case of generalizing from a sample. Suppose that in our pool of volunteers for the SAT experiment, 10 percent have IQs in the 140+ range. If we assign volunteers to groups by a random process, then every time we select someone for either group, there's a 10 percent chance we'll select someone in the 140+ range. So if the groups are large enough, there's a good chance that each one will have about 10 percent in that range. And the same would be true for values on the other variables.

Suppose, then, that we have assigned our volunteers to their groups by a random process; our experimental group has taken the cram course, and their average SAT score is higher than the average for our control group. Does this prove that the course affected the scores? It depends. Remember that we are using a random process, so we have to apply what we learned in the last section about random sampling. First, we would not expect the averages to be *exactly* the same even if the cram course had no effect whatever. The difference in averages must be of a certain size before we have evidence of causality. Second, the size of that difference depends on the size of our groups, just as the margin of error in an opinion poll depends on the size of the sample. As we increase the size of our experimental and control groups, it becomes more likely that traits such as intelligence will be distributed evenly between them, so it becomes less likely that a large difference in average scores could occur merely by chance. In general, the larger the group, the smaller the correlation has to be to count as causally significant. But third, and finally, we are still only dealing with probabilities. Even with a large sample, there is some chance, however tiny, that our random process assigned all the geniuses to the experimental group. So if the difference in average scores is x points, then to be precise we should state our result as follows: there is only a y percent probability that an x point difference could occur by chance, given the size of our groups. Most researchers consider a result *statistically significant* if y is less than 5 percent.

There are mathematical techniques for determining whether a correlation is statistically significant. Once again, as with generalizing from a sample, we'll leave these calculations to the experts. But once again, it's important to emphasize the limitations of these techniques. Just as the margin of error in a poll does not take account of errors in choosing the sample, a correlation that is statistically significant may not be significant in the usual sense of being important. With a large enough sample, it is possible to identify factors that play a very small causal role in contributing to an effect. This is true, for example, of many substances that have been found to "cause" cancer in laboratory animals. Or suppose a researcher found a statistically significant difference in traffic fatality rates between states with different drinking ages. That wouldn't settle the question of whether the drinking age should be raised. Perhaps the difference was minor, and it would be more effective to impose stiffer penalties on drunk driving.

In the previous section, moreover, we saw that the techniques for computing a margin of error rest on the assumption that the sample was randomly selected—an assumption that is rarely true in the strict sense. An analogous point can be made about correlations. A statistically significant correlation is evidence of causality on the assumption that we have taken into account all the other variables that might affect our result. The idealized experiment I described above is an attempt to meet that standard. In practice, however, problems invariably arise that call the assumption into question. Let's look at a few of them.

Observational Studies

The largest problem, from a logical standpoint, is that experiments are not always possible. Suppose we want to know whether there's a significant difference in the way men and women react to stress. We can't randomly assign our volunteers to the two groups, male and female—nature has already made that decision. For a true experiment, the experimenter must be able to control the independent variable. But many variables can't be controlled: meteorologists can't control the properties of storm systems, economists can't manipulate the economy to see what causes depressions, geologists can't decide when to have an earthquake. There are other variables that can't be manipulated for ethical reasons. You can't ask someone to smoke for twenty years for the sake of cancer research. You can't abuse an experimental group of children to see whether abuse breeds violent behavior. In all these cases, we are limited to *observational* studies. We have to observe the variables as they occur naturally, outside our control, and try to find the relevant correlations.

In the right circumstances, an observational study *can* provide evidence of causality. But it has two major drawbacks in relation to an experiment. First, it does not involve random assignment to experimental and control groups. So there's a danger that any correlation we find between two variables may be due to some third variable which is not evenly distributed among the groups. For example, it is plausible to think that a person who was abused as a child is more likely than other people to have certain problems later in life: to abuse his or her own children, engage in criminal activity, etc. And there is correlational evidence to support this hypothesis. But is the abuse actually the cause of these later problems? Parents who abuse their children are not a random sample from the population. They tend to have other traits in common: they tend to be emotionally distant and neglectful of their children, for example, and subject to economic stresses such as unemployment or poverty. Perhaps it is these traits, rather than the physical abuse per se, that contribute to the child's later problems. We can't tell from the correlation itself. In the language of statistics, the correlation we observe between two variables may be *confounded* by some other variable.

Second, an experiment allows us to control one variable and look for changes in another. If we find them, there is no question which is the cause, which the effect. But this question does arise in observational studies. Cities have higher crime rates than rural areas. Is that because urban life breeds criminals, or because criminals migrate to cities to find victims? People with higher levels of education have higher average incomes. Does that mean you can boost your income by getting a college degree? Perhaps. Or perhaps the correlation is a by-product of an underlying factor—people with more intelligence or ambition may tend to do better both in school and in the job market, but for different reasons.

As a general rule, therefore, it is more difficult to draw causal conclusions from an observational study than from an experiment.

But this is merely a general rule. For one thing, experiments are not immune from problems of confounding variables. Suppose you want to study the effects of political advertising on voter preferences. So you show an ad for candidate A to your experimental group, and find that the proportion who say they'd vote for candidate A goes up. That may indicate that the ad had a real effect. Or it may simply mean that your subjects figured out what you were up to, and were simply telling you what they knew you wanted to hear.

Careful researchers can structure experiments to avoid these problems. But an observational study can also take steps to screen out confounding variables. For example, the death rate from lung cancer is about ten times higher for smokers than for nonsmokers. That fact alone would not prove that smoking plays a causal role. The age distribution among smokers and nonsmokers may not be the same. Or perhaps the class of smokers includes a higher proportion who live in cities and are exposed to more air pollution. But cancer researchers control for such factors by comparing people of the same age, who live in the same area, and so on for many other variables—and the death rate for smokers is still higher. Among the class of smokers, moreover, the death rate varies concomitantly with the number of cigarettes a person smokes per day, the number of years he has smoked, and the degree of inhalation. And among ex-smokers, the death rate goes down in correlation with the number of years since a person quit. When you put all this together, there is little doubt that a causal relationship does exist.

The issues we have considered so far pertain to what is sometimes called the *internal* validity of a study or experiment. They pertain to the conclusions we can draw about cause and effect in regard to the class of things actually observed or included in an experiment. But of course we normally want to generalize from that class to a wider population. We want to know whether smoking causes cancer for people in general, not just for those who happened to be included in a particular study. And this raises questions of *external* validity, questions you should ask when a researcher claims that his findings apply to a population as a whole.

External Validity

A great deal of psychological research is conducted at colleges and universities, using undergraduate students as subjects. If an experiment is done properly and finds a significant correlation, we can infer that the independent variable was causally affecting the dependent variable—for the particular subjects involved. But how far can we generalize the result? To all people of college age? Perhaps—if we assume that the differences between those who go to college and those who don't are irrelevant to the outcome. Can we generalize to people of all ages? Perhaps—if we assume that age makes no difference. These assumptions may or may not be reasonable in a given case. The point to remember is that they are not supported by the experiment itself.

For the same reason, you should be careful about arguments in economics or other social sciences that draw causal conclusions from statistics regarding a single locality or period of time. These statistics may or may not be representative of a wider class, and generalizing from them may or may not be valid. When the federal government imposed the 55 miles-per-hour speed limit in 1974, the traffic fatality rate dropped 15 percent, and many people concluded that the lower highway speeds were responsible. Perhaps they were. But the fatality rate had been dropping before 1974, even though highway speeds had been increasing. And in the decade since then, speeds have increased as more people ignore the limit, yet the rate has continued to fall. As a result, there is now a great deal of controversy about whether "55 saves lives."

A similar dispute arose over the claim that the artificial sweetener saccharine causes bladder cancer. In experiments with rats, researchers found a significant difference between experimental and control groups in the number of tumors that developed. There does not appear to be any reason for doubting that saccharin was causally responsible. But can this result be generalized to human beings? Skeptics raised two objections. First, the experimental group was fed extremely high doses of saccharine—the equivalent of a human being drinking 1000 cans of diet soda per day. Perhaps the high dosage was the key factor; perhaps there is a threshold below which saccharine would not have caused bladder cancer in these rats. Second, a substance that causes cancer in one species may not do so in another; we may not be able to generalize from rats to other mammals, including humans. These questions are hotly debated among cancer researchers. It may turn out that the generalization is indeed valid. The point, once again, is that it rests on assumptions that are not supported by the experiment itself.

To evaluate external validity, finally, we should remember the special importance of definitions in statistical reasoning. To establish a correlation between two variables, we must define the variables in such a way that they can be counted or measured. In some cases this is fairly easy. Cancer researchers do not face any major difficulty in defining the category of people who smoke. Economists don't need specialized definitions of male and female to study sex differences in income. But there are a great many interesting variables which, for one reason or another, *can't* be counted or measured so easily. By their very nature, psychological traits such as intelligence, values, attitudes, or feelings cannot be observed directly. Nor is statistical information readily available for many economic and sociological categories—such as illegal aliens, entrepreneurs, fundamentalists.

To test a hypothesis involving one of these variables, therefore, a researcher must find some other variable to stand in for it and serve as a measuring rod. Suppose you wanted to see whether some classroom exercise had any effect on racial prejudice in college students. The dependent variable you are interested in is *prejudice*. But you can't observe what's going on in a student's mind directly, so for the purposes of the experiment you would have to measure prejudice indirectly—say, by the student's willingness to contribute to a civil rights organization. And here's where the problem of external validity arises. Suppose you found a strong correlation between the classroom exercise and the willingness to contribute, a correlation strong enough to convince you that a causal relationship is involved. Does that prove the exercise affects prejudice? Only if we assume that the willingness to contribute is a good barometer of prejudice—an assumption that may or may not be true. In addition to prejudice, the willingness to contribute to a particular organization may reflect a person's level of generosity, his awareness of political issues, his agreement with the specific political goals of the organization, or simply his desire for popularity. And it may be that the exercise affected one of these other variables, not prejudice per se. In general, then, when someone claims to have established a causal relationship, and one or more of the variables involved strike you as things that can't be measured or counted directly, make sure to ask what variables were actually being correlated in the study or experiment, and consider whether those stand-in variables really do reflect the variable they purport to measure.

This completes our discussion of statistical evidence of causality. Once again, we have approached this as consumers of information, not producers. If you are going to conduct experiments or observational studies yourself, you will need more training in the subject matter and relevant statistical techniques. As laymen, we must rely to some extent on the authority of those who have that expertise. But once again, we should be intelligent consumers, using the considerations we've discussed here, along with our common sense, to ask critical questions about the research results we encounter in the media and elsewhere.

Practice Quiz

The paragraph below is a fictional report of research purporting to prove a causal relationship. Using what you've learned in this section, evaluate the causal inference.

Scientists at Flywheel Polytechnic have established that backseat driving can be hazardous to your health. Prior to this research, which was funded by the U.S. Department of Transportation, there had been speculation that nagging advice from passengers on how to drive might cause stress for some exasperated drivers and increase the likelihood of accidents. The Flywheel team, reasoning that spouses and other family members are the commonest source of such advice, compared traffic near DisneyWorld, at the height of the vacation season, with commuter traffic outside New York City, consisting largely of drivers alone in their cars. Average speeds were the same in the two cases, as were driving conditions, but the accident rate in vacation traffic was 34.5 percent higher, a difference found to be statistically significant.

SUMMARY

Statistics give us numerical information about a class or population of things; the information normally concerns their values on one or more variables. A total is the number of things in a class S or the sum of their values on a variable; a ratio is a total stated in relationship to another class T. A frequency is the number or proportion of S's that have some property P; a distribution is the proportion of S's that have each of the values $(P, Q, R, \ldots)$ on some variable. Frequencies and distributions are often used to estimate probability. An average is the central value of S's on a quantitative variable; it may be either a mean or a median value.

A statistical statement about a population can be supported either by complete enumeration or by generalization from a sample. A randomly chosen sample allows us to conclude that the relevant value of the population falls within a certain margin of error, with a certain degree of probability. Perfectly random samples are rarely used, however, and the techniques used to approximate randomness may introduce biases.

Statistical correlations among variables provide an important source of evidence for causal connections. A correlation per se, however, is not proof of causality; we must control for other variables according to the pattern of Mill's methods of difference or concomitant variations. This may be done through an experiment in which subjects are randomly assigned to control and experimental groups, or through an observational study. In either case, we should watch for problems of internal validity: Are there any confounding variables? Is it clear which variable is cause and which is effect? And we should watch for problems of external validity: is it reasonable to generalize from the sample actually studied to a larger population? Are the variables actually measured good stand-ins for the variables of interest?

Exercises

A. For each pair of statements, determine whether the statements are compatible or contradictory.

1. a) The number of people employed in the U.S. economy increased 1.1% last month, to 109.7 million. b) The unemployment rate increased to 7.1% last month, from 7.0% the previous month.
2. a) The human brain contains about 10 billion nerve cells. b) The human brain contains about 100 billion nerve cells.
3. a) Accidental Petroleum's profits this year were up 91% over last year. b) Accidental Petroleum's profits this year were 4% of revenues.
4. a) In eight courses this year, Chris's grade distribution was four As, two Bs, and one C. b) Chris's grade point average this year was 2.2.
5. a) 50% of individuals with incomes of $50,000 or more have Individual Retirement Accounts, while only 25% of individuals earning less than $50,000 have IRAs. b) 90% of IRA contributions are made by people earning less than $50,000 per year.

B. Each question below is followed by references to various statistics. Which statistic would be most helpful in answering the question?

1. Does the U.S. or the U.S.S.R. spend more on its military?
   a) Total expenditures by each country
   b) Total expenditures as a percentage of GNP
   c) Average expenditures over the past five years
2. Has it become more expensive in the last ten years to purchase a house?
   a) The median price of houses on the market, now vs. then
   b) The mean price of houses on the market, now vs. then

c) The median prices, adjusted for inflation

d) The median price as a multiple of the median family's income, now vs. then

3. Is private education cheaper than public education? (Choose one figure from each column.)

Private schools	*Public schools*
Average tuition	Average expenditure per pupil
Median tuition	Average fee charged to pupils from
Median tuition at	outside the district
nonreligious schools	

4. Has divorce become more common in the last ten years?
   a) Total number of divorces, now vs. then
   b) The ratio of divorces to marriages, now vs. then
   c) The divorce rate (per unit of population), now vs. then

5. Has my investment in the Random Walk Fund given me a satisfactory return over the past year?
   a) Dollar amount of increase in value of investment
   b) Amount of increase as percent of amount invested
   c) Percent of increase as compared to interest rate
   d) Percent of increase as compared to increase in Standard and Poor's stock index

C. Analyze and evaluate each of the following arguments. In your analysis, use the diagramming technique of Chapter 3. In your evaluation, pay special attention to the use of statistics.

1. "Alzheimer's Disease is the fourth leading cause of death in America today! Officials estimate the number of victims to be *at least* two million.

   "Yet there's *absolutely nothing* we can do to *treat it, much less cure it!* We don't even know what causes it!

   "And the federal government seems to have other priorities!

   "For the coming year, they've committed only about $25 in research funds for each Alzheimer's victim. . . .

   ". . . *but over $10,000 for each victim of AIDS!*

   "I have no intention of downplaying the seriousness of AIDS, but how can they *justify* those numbers?!" [Fundraising letter from Alzheimer's Disease Research]

2. "According to the National Safety Council, farming is the nation's most dangerous job. . . . In 1983 farming clocked in at 55 job-related deaths per 100,000 workers, or five times the rate for all major industries combined." [Jeffrey L. Pasley,

"The Idiocy of Rural Life," *The New Republic,* December 8, 1986]

3. "In the total winter season from August 25, 1595, through February 28, 1596, . . . the company [the Lord Admiral's Men] gave one hundred and fifty performances of thirty different plays. Eighty-seven performances, or 58 per cent of the total, were of the fourteen new plays produced that season. Five performances, 3.3 per cent, were of one play, *The Jew of Malta,* revived that season. Forty-six performances, or 30.7 per cent, were given of the eight plays from the previous season which were less than a year old. . . . Only twelve performances, 8 per cent, were of the seven plays which were more than a year old. This distribution, which is similar for all the seasons covered by Henslowe's records, emphasizes how dependent the company was on the continuous addition of new plays to its stock in order to maintain itself in London." [Bernard Beckerman, *Shakespeare at the Globe*]

4. "U.S. business wastes $2.6 billion annually on unnecessary photocopies, says a study for Accountemps, a New York-based temporary personnel service. Of the estimated 350 billion photocopies made this year, one-third will end up in the trash." [*Wall Street Journal*, August 28, 1986]

5. "The American Automobile Association reports that since the trucking industry was deregulated in 1980, price wars have forced some truckers to skimp on maintenance, making accidents more likely. . . .

"The statistics dramatize the AAA's concerns. In 1975, heavy trucks accounted for 3,483 highway fatalities in the United States. In 1984, the figure had risen to 4,908.

"The trucking industry claims that trucks are involved in more accidents simply because there are more trucks driving more miles than ever before. But in fact, trucks account for more than their share of fatalities. According to a recent study of accidents on the New York State Thruway, for example, heavy trucks were involved in an average of 2.8 fatalities for every 100 million miles traveled. The rate for passenger cars was less than half of that figure—1.3 per 100 million miles." [Editorial, *Poughkeepsie Journal*, February 21, 1986]

6. "The Soviets have chosen to spend their limited resources on missiles, heavy industry and space technology rather than on disposable medical equipment, modern drugs and costly life-saving devices. Excellence in medical care is simply not a high priority in the Soviet system. The best estimates available indicate that the Soviets allocated 9.8% of the gross national prod-

uct to medical care in 1955, but only 7.5% in 1977. The trend is clear." [Kenneth M. Prager, "Soviet Health Care's Critical Condition," *Wall Street Journal,* January 29, 1987]

7. "University biotechnology researchers whose work is supported by private industry do not, as has been feared, abandon their faculty duties to chase after commercial success, according to a survey published in the June 13 *Science.* On the contrary, researchers with industry ties publish more journal articles, participate in more professional associations and teach as many hours as those with no industry support.

   "Specifically, the survey reports that biotechnology researchers with industry ties publish an average of 14.6 journal articles in a three-year period, compared with about 11.3 for those without industry support; they are involved in an average of 1.4 professional and university activities, compared with 1.1 for their colleagues; and they spend about 22.2 hours per week teaching class or supervising students in the laboratory, compared with 20.3 hours per week for professors not supported by industry." [*Science News,* June 14, 1986]

8. "Yes, there are many low-income elderly who need their Social Security checks to survive. Yes, there are affluent yuppies here and there. But let's talk about these generations as a group. Who is poor? Overwhelmingly, the young are poor. When federal benefits payments are factored in, the poverty rate for children is around 20 percent. Compare that with the poverty rate for senior citizens, which is just three percent. And who has spendable discretionary income (the amount after paying food, housing, taxes, medical expenses, and all other necessities)? Among households with money to spend, senior citizens have more per capita—$4,118—than any other age group. Young people aged 25 to 34 have $1,918, less than half as much, in per capita discretionary income." [James Dale Davidson, "Social Security Rip-Off," *The New Republic,* November 11, 1985]

D. Each of the passages below either draws a causal conclusion from a correlation, or denies that such a conclusion can be drawn. Identify the causal conclusion and the correlation; then evaluate the author's reasoning. Some of the passages are from media reports on scientific research. If you cannot tell from the report whether the research results support a causal claim, identify the questions you would need to ask the researchers.

1. "BAT 1,000, a program by First Georgia Bank, paid $100 to Gwinnett County public school students with combined scores

of 1,000 or more on their Scholastic Aptitude Tests during the past school year. Result: 804 students got checks and average SAT scores in the county rose 12 points." [*Wall Street Journal*, July 17, 1986]

2. "In a study comparing the families of children who caused trouble at school by fighting, temper tantrums, stealing, vandalism and the like with families of children who did not have such problems, Dr. [Gerald] Patterson's research found that the parents of disruptive children were three times more likely to display irritability to their children than were the parents of the other children. He said he has found that when parents learn to use more constructive approaches, their children misbehave less." [*New York Times*, July 23, 1986]

3. "Support for the 55 mph speed limit is strongly influenced by how fast people drive, according to a recent NBC News-*Wall Street Journal* poll. People who say they drive no faster than 60 mph in good weather express overwhelming support for the speed limit. But most people who drive faster than 60 mph— 18 percent of those surveyed—oppose the law."

Poll results:

Q. Do you favor or oppose keeping the 55 miles per hour speed limit?

	Favor	*Opposed*	*Undecided*
Those who drive 55 mph or slower	87%	11%	2%
Those who drive 56–60 mph	70%	29%	1%
Those who drive 61 mph or faster	34%	64%	2%

[*Washington Post National Weekly Edition*, June 9, 1986]

4. "Modern men concerned about aging might track down a University of Oklahoma study. It discusses, in a sober and statistical way, the 'life-enhancing properties of a younger wife.'

"Researchers Laurel Klinger-Vartabedian, Dorothy Foster and Lauren Wispe discovered that younger wives appear to be a basis for a longer lifespan in men aged 50–79. The death rate for older men married to women one to 24 years younger was 13% lower than average for their age group. Men with older wives seemed to have a death rate 20% higher than average." [*Wall Street Journal*, January 22, 1985]

5. "A long-awaited major study . . . found that two relatively new forms of psychotherapy, cognitive behavior therapy and interpersonal psychotherapy, achieved results comparable to a standard antidepressant drug, imipramine, in reducing the symptoms of depression and improving the functioning of patients. All three therapies completely eliminated serious

symptoms in 50 to 60 percent of the patients treated for 16 weeks. . . .

"The study, organized by the National Institute of Mental Health, was conducted at the University of Pittsburgh, George Washington University and the University of Oklahoma. It enrolled some 250 patients who were either moderately or severely depressed according to standard psychiatric definitions and evaluations. . . .

"The patients, of whom 239 underwent treatment, were divided at random into three groups: the first and second groups were treated with one of the two brief psychotherapies, designed to last 16 weeks, while the third group was given the drug. Another control group of patients got harmless pills plus weekly supportive consultations with a psychiatrist.

"The scientists said that while 50 to 60 percent of the patients who received either the psychotherapeutic treatments or the drug reached "full recovery" with no serious symptoms, fewer than 30 percent of those given the placebo reached full recovery." [*New York Times*, May 14, 1986]

6. ". . . while a bachelor's degree is less special, it is still one of the surest tickets to a better living. A recent report by the Census Bureau found that in 1983 the median income of male college graduates age 25 to 34 was $21,988, or 39% higher than the $15,789 median for high-school graduates." [*U.S. News & World Report*, November 25, 1986]

7. "Critical legislative efforts are being sabotaged by special interest campaign money. We're in danger of losing representative government.

"Just look at what's happening:

"The National Rifle Association's PAC [political action committee] spent $1.1 million from 1981 through 1985 on current Members of the House. The House in 1986 approved the McClure-Volkmer bill, a measure which *weakens* federal gun control laws. A Common Cause study found that 80% of the 248 Members voting with the NRA on a key vote had received NRA financial support—an average of *$4,081 each*. On the other hand, 80% of the 176 Members who voted against the NRA received *no* NRA funds." [Common Cause fund-raising letter]

8. "James McKay, a graduate student working with Dr. [David C.] McClelland at Harvard, has found that selfless love, a caring for others without worrying about benefits for oneself, is related to good health.

"Selfless love, according to Mr. McKay's research, is

reflected not just by thoughts of doing things for others without consideration for a personal benefit, but also by such things as a sense of humor and a lack of cynicism.

"In a series of studies, Mr. McKay found that those men and women whose fantasies showed a tendency toward selfless love also reported having fewer infectious diseases than did others in the study. Moreover, an assay of their T-cells, a specialized form of disease-fighting lymphocyte in the blood, showed a pattern reflecting resistance to viruses.

"These results support those from an earlier study by Dr. McClelland, in which immune function was assessed in people before and after they watched a film about Mother Teresa and her work with the poor of Calcutta in India.

"In most people who watched the film, there was a significant, though temporary, rise in a measure of defense against upper respiratory infections.

"And when people were asked to spend an hour recalling times they had loved or been loved, the immune measure stayed at the higher levels the entire time.

"'Dwelling on love seems to strengthen this aspect of immune function,' Dr. McClelland said." [*New York Times*, July 22, 1986]

E. The statistical claims below pertain to the issue of gun control. They were taken from published sources, and from statements issued by groups representing various positions. Using whichever statistics you think are relevant, construct a debate pro and con on the question: Should the government prohibit the manufacture, sale, and private ownership of cheap handguns ("Saturday Night Specials")? You may construct the debate in the form of a dialogue, or as a diagram of the type described in Chapter 7.

1. There are about 120 million privately owned firearms in the U.S. (an estimate with a margin of error of at least 20 million in either direction). About one-third of them (30–40 million) are handguns. About half the households in the country possess a firearm of some kind. [James D. Wright, Peter H. Rossi, Kathleen Daly, *Under the Gun: Weapons, Crime, and Violence in America* (New York: Aldine Publishing Co., 1983)]

2. Murders by handgun in selected countries, 1980: Japan, 77; Great Britain, 8; Sweden, 18; Switzerland, 24; Canada, 8; Israel, 23; Australia, 4; United States, 11,552. All countries except U.S. have national handgun control laws. [Brochure, Handgun Control, Inc.]

3. A study by the coroner in King County, Washington, found that of 743 deaths by firearms in the county over a six-year period, 398 (53.6%) occurred in the home where the firearm was kept. Of those 398 deaths, 9 (2.3%) involved self-defense or justifiable homicide; 12 (3%) were accidents; 41 (10.3%) were criminal homicide; and 333 (83.7%) were suicides. [Arthur L. Kellerman and Donald T. Reay, "Protection or Peril: An Analysis of Firearm-Related Deaths in the Home," *New England Journal of Medicine*, June 12, 1986]

4. In 90% of all domestic homicides, according to a Kansas City study, police had previously been called to the home to stop beatings. In 50% of the cases, police had been called 5 or more times. [Carol Ruth Silver and Don B. Kates, "Gun Control and the Subway Class," *Wall Street Journal*, January 10, 1985]

5. A 1978 survey commissioned by the National Rifle Association and conducted by Decision-Making Information, Inc. found that 15% of the people interviewed said they or a member of their household had used a gun in self-defense (not including military or police work); of that 15%, 56% said the gun was not fired, and 86% said that no one was killed or injured. [Wright, Rossi, and Daly, *Under the Gun*]

6. The District of Columbia Firearms Control Act, which banned ownership of handguns by most private citizens, took effect in 1976. The city had 174 cases of handgun homicide in 1974, two years before the new law; and 112 in 1978, two years afterwards. [Edward D. Jones III, "The District of Columbia's 'Firearms Control Regulations Act of 1975,'" *Annals of the American Academy of Political and Social Science*, 455 (1981)]

7. Handgun homicides in Baltimore, which does not have such a law, fell from 193 to 104 over the same period. [Ibid.]

18

Explanation

Compare these two statements:

1) Joan will be successful because she is bright and ambitious.
2) Joan is sad because her cat just died.

Both of these statements make a claim about Joan, and both of them offer a reason, indicated by the word "because." But there's a difference: (1) is an argument, and (2) is an explanation. In (1), my claim that Joan will be successful is a conclusion I'm trying to convince you to accept on the basis of the premise that she is bright and ambitious. In (2), I'm not trying to convince you that Joan is sad. We can both see that she's sad—I'm taking that fact for granted. Instead, I am trying to *explain* that fact by pointing out that her cat died.

Explanation and Argument

The theoretical relationship between arguments and explanations is complex and controversial. But it seems clear that there is at least a difference in emphasis. The primary goal of an argument is to show *that* some proposition is true, while the primary goal of an explanation is to show *why* it is true. In an argument, we reason forward from the premises to the conclusion; in an explanation we reason backwards from a fact to the cause or reason for that fact. Why does ice float in water? How do salmon find their way back to the streams they were spawned in? Why did the Industrial Revolution occur when it did? Why do human beings so often make war on each other? In all these cases, we know that a certain proposition is true:

ice floats, salmon find their way, etc. This proposition is the **explanandum** (plural: explananda)—a Latin word meaning "that which is to be explained." What we want to know is the cause or the reason for the explanandum. We're looking for a *hypothesis* that will make the explanandum intelligible to us by explaining why it is true. Ordinarily, the word "hypothesis" suggests something tentative, an idea that hasn't been proven yet. But we're going to use the term in a broader sense, to mean any explanatory idea, no matter how well confirmed. In this sense, for example, Newton's law of gravitation is a hypothesis when it is used to explain the motion of physical objects.

Any explanation involves a hypothesis and an explanandum, just as any argument involves premises and a conclusion. When a doctor diagnoses a disease, the patient's symptoms are the explananda, and the diagnosis is the hypothesis. In a criminal trial, the prosecution tries to show that the guilt of the defendant is the only hypothesis that would explain all the evidence, and the defense tries to create doubt in the minds of the jury by arguing that some other hypothesis is possible. If you are given the assignment of interpreting a poem, the explanandum is the poem itself—the words, the rhythms, the images. Your assignment is to find a hypothesis about what the poet was trying to convey. The theories of philosophers and religious thinkers can often be regarded as hypotheses to explain fundamental features of the world and human experience. And of course a central goal of science is to find hypotheses that will explain observable phenomena.

In order for an explanation to serve its purpose, there must be some logical relation between hypothesis and explanandum—just as there must be a logical relation between premise and conclusion in an argument. Indeed, despite the difference between argument and explanation, there is also a fundamental similarity. Let's go back to our original example:

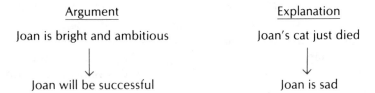

In the argument on the left, we take the premise as a given, and use it to establish the conclusion. In the explanation on the right, the explanandum is the given, and we trying to establish the hypothesis. Nevertheless, the arrow means the same thing in both cases. The hypothesis is related to the explanandum in such a way that if the hypothesis is true, the explanandum is likely to be true as well. Of course, we already know it's true; we know that Joan is sad. But the point is that her sadness is just what we would expect if her cat died. Had we learned about her cat before we saw her, we might have predicted that she would be sad, just as we predict her success from the premise about her character traits. An explanation, then, has the same inner logical structure as an argument, and we can analyze that structure with the same diagramming techniques we learned in Chapter 5 for analyzing arguments. Let's review these techniques briefly, and see how they apply to explanations.

Diagramming Explanations

It is rarely, if ever, possible for a single proposition to serve as a complete and adequate explanation of anything. In history, literature, the sciences, or any other discipline, an explanation can involve a highly complex set of propositions. Even in the example above, there is more than one. The death of Joan's cat is the only part of the hypothesis mentioned explicitly. But we're also assuming that Joan was attached to her cat; otherwise its death would not have meant anything to her. So the explanation includes two points that are combined additively:

1) Joan's cat died.
a) Joan was attached to her cat.
2) Joan is sad.

An explanation, like an argument, can also have a *nonadditive* structure, which we would diagram with convergent arrows. Suppose a detective trying to solve a murder suspects the victim's son. The detective has to find a motive to explain why the son would do it, and as with many human actions, there may be more than one motive. Perhaps father and son had just had a violent argument, and the son also stood to inherit a lot of money. Then the hypothesis would be diagrammed:

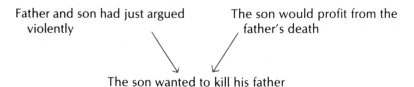

The convergent arrows indicate that the two parts of the hypothesis function independently. Even if one turned out to be false, the other could still (partly) explain the son's motive.

We have also seen that an argument can have more than one step; in fact, most of them do. The same is true of explanations. We explain something by appealing to a hypothesis, and then we can go on to ask why that hypothesis is true, and come up with another hypothesis to explain the first one. As we do so, we increase the *depth* of our explanation, and the deeper the explanation, the more fully we understand the original explanandum. In the early 1600s, for example, the German astronomer Johannes Kepler explained the observed positions of the planets on the hypothesis that they follow elliptical orbits around the sun, obeying certain laws which he formulated mathematically. Later in the century, Isaac Newton showed that this hypothesis is itself explained by his law of gravitational attraction. Schematically, then, we have an explanation in two steps:

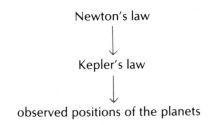

Finally, a single premise in an argument can support more than one conclusion, a situation we diagram with divergent arrows:

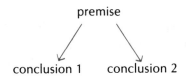

We never made much use of this point in our discussion of arguments. In an argument, we are usually concerned with one conclusion at a time. In the case of explanation, however, this structure is extremely important. One mark of a good explanation is that it unifies a range of phenomena: a single hypothesis explains a number of different explananda. A good explanation, in other words, has *breadth* as well as depth. Indeed, these two virtues are related. As we push deeper in the effort to explain something, we typically come up with hypotheses that explain a wider and wider range of things. Thus Newton's theory did more than explain the motions of the planets. It also explained the laws Galileo discovered concerning the motion of falling objects and projectiles. That is, Newton gave a unified explanation for the motion of terrestrial as well as heavenly bodies. Schematically:

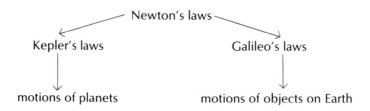

Evaluating Explanations

Explanations and arguments, then, have the same internal structure. The difference between them lies in their goals: an argument tries to show that something is true, an explanation tries to show why it is true. What about the standards of *evaluation?* Once again, there are similarities as well as differences. To evaluate an argument, we have to ask two questions: Do the premises support the conclusion? And are the premises true? In the same way, there are two basic questions to ask about an explanation.

First, is it *adequate*—would the hypothesis, if true, provide a genuine explanation of the explanandum? Does it provide a possible cause or reason, or in some way fit the explanandum into a wider context that makes it intelligible? In a broad sense, adequacy is to explanation what logical strength is to argument. It pertains to the internal relation between the hypothesis and the explanandum. Indeed, it includes strength as one component. A good explanation is one in which the explanandum follows from the hypothesis: the relation between them is such that if the hypothesis is true, the explanandum had to be true as well—or at least was highly likely. But strength is not the only component. To serve the purposes of explanation, as we'll see, an explanation must satisfy other criteria as well.

The second question is whether the hypothesis is *true.* False premises don't prove anything, and false hypotheses don't explain anything. To tell whether a hypothesis is true or false, we would normally use a method that is inductive in the broad sense, but different from the forms of inductive reasoning we've studied so far.

To evaluate explanations, therefore, we need to use what we've already learned about logical relationships, but we also need some additional standards that pertain specifically to explanation. In the next section, we'll look at standards for evaluating adequacy—the relation between hypothesis and explanandum. In the final section, we'll consider methods for determining the truth of hypotheses.

Practice Quiz

For each statement, decide whether it is an argument or an explanation. If it is an explanation, identify the explanandum and the hypothesis, and diagram the relation between them.

1. The stock market went up yesterday because the Federal Reserve lowered interest rates.
2. The stock market will probably rise over the next six months, because the economy is expanding.
3. The electrical system in a house should be grounded, in order to avoid shocks.
4. The nervous system evolved because animals, which are capable of locomotion, needed a fast and flexible means of guiding their motion.
5. In her classic work *The Life and Death of Great American Cities,* Jane Jacobs posed the question: why are some urban areas so much safer and more vibrant than others? Her answer was that the safest areas in a city tend to be those characterized by a mixture of uses—stores, apartments, businesses, restaurants. Such a mixture guarantees that people will be on the streets at all hours, and that in turn is the best deterrent against crime. The presence of people also gives these areas a vibrant feel, attracting new stores and residents.

Adequacy

A hypothesis can be true without providing an adequate explanation. Suppose you notice water dripping from your ceiling, and someone ventures the hypothesis that water runs downhill. This would not be very satisfying to you. The statement is true enough, but it doesn't explain what the water is doing up there. In this section, we'll assume that the hypotheses we discuss are all true. The question is: How do we decide whether they are adequate? Every branch of knowledge has its own specific guidelines for evaluating the adequacy of explanations in that area, but there are also some general standards that apply across the board. 1) The inference from hypothesis to explanandum should have a high degree of logical strength. 2) The explanation should be *complete:* it should explain all significant aspects of the explanandum. And 3) the explanation should be *informative:* the hypothesis should state the fundamental cause or reason for the explanandum. Let's go over each of these in turn.

Strength

Explanations and arguments have different goals, but they have the same logical structure, and the explanandum should follow from the hypothesis in the same way that a conclusion should follow from the premises. A good explanation will show us that the explanandum is not mysterious, but is something we might have expected all along, something we might have predicted or inferred from the facts mentioned in the hypothesis if we had known about them.

The best way to measure strength, in this context, is the general-purpose method we learned in Chapter 5. We try to estimate the size of the gap between hypothesis and explanandum, the amount of "free play" or slippage between them. And we do this by finding the implicit assumption that would be necessary to close the gap. We explained Joan's sadness by the hypothesis that her cat died, and that she'd been attached to it. The implicit assumption is that people who are attached to their pets grieve at their loss. Doubtless there are exceptions to this generalization—it's conceivable that someone would react to loss in a different way. So there is a certain gap here, but it's a small one, and the explanation seems fairly adequate. By contrast, suppose someone said he failed a course because the classroom is on the fifth floor, and he's afraid of heights. There's a sizable gap here between hypothesis and explanandum: to connect fear of heights with performance in a course, we'd have to tell an elaborate and fairly implausible story. So this explanation is much weaker.

Let's examine a more realistic example. President Reagan has not been very successful at eliminating subsidy programs like the Small Business Administration. In his 1987 budget, he proposed to eliminate 45 such programs; Congress kept 43 of them alive. Given Reagan's popularity, and his determination to cut spending, why has he failed in this area? A common explanation runs as follows. The benefits of the programs go to a small class of people, who each have a large stake in the programs and therefore lobby actively to keep them. But the costs are dispersed among all the taxpayers, who have less at stake individually: a $1 billion program would cost about $10 per taxpayer. So they have little incentive to lobby against the subsidies. The political pressures on Congress therefore tend to favor the programs. We could diagram the explanation as follows:

1) Those who benefit have a lot at stake individually.
2) Those who benefit lobby actively to retain the programs.
3) Those who pay do not have a lot at stake individually.
4) Those who pay do not lobby actively against the programs.
5) The political pressures on Congress favor the programs.
6) Congress will not eliminate the programs.

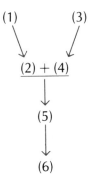

This is certainly a plausible explanation. But let's take a closer look, starting at the bottom and checking the strength of each step. The explanandum is that Congress will not eliminate the programs. Does this follow from proposition (5)—that the political pressures favor the programs? The implicit assumption is that the actions of Congress reflect the sum of pressures acting on it. This doesn't seem like a very large gap. We're not assuming that individual legislators *never* vote independently, on the basis of their own judgment and conscience. We're only assuming that a majority, on most issues, will act in response to pressure. What about the previous step, from (2) and (4) to (5)? Notice that (2) and (4) tell us about the *economic* interests at stake in these programs. This implies something about the *political* pressures on Congress only if we assume that lobbying based on economic interest is the only—or at least the primary—source of political pressure. This is a more substantial assumption to make, and creates a larger gap in the explanation. One might argue that in some areas, such as civil rights or sanctions against South Africa, Congress acts under tremendous political pressure that is rooted in *moral* rather than economic interests. Perhaps economic interests determine political pressure only by default, in cases where no one raises a moral issue. If so, we would have to amend the explanation to include the point that the press and the voters do not view the question of subsidies in moral terms.

In any case, you can see that checking for strength is an important element in evaluating an explanation. It helps us identify hidden assumptions that should be made explicit and examined carefully.

Completeness

While we're on the subject of money and politics, you may recall from the chapter on statistical evidence that the total money spent in political campaigns has been rising faster than the inflation rate. One common explanation is that campaigning has become more expensive. Candidates have to spend huge sums on TV advertising, media consultants, computerized voter lists, and other "high-tech" political tools. A common criticism of this hypothesis is that it explains only part of the phenomenon. It explains why candidates need to raise larger sums of money from contributors, but it doesn't explain why the contributions are forthcoming. People don't part with their money without good reason. So another element in the explanation may be that as government has grown in size and importance, people are willing to invest more money to influence the political process.

This theory may or may not be true, but it illustrates an important point. An explanandum is normally complex. Whether it is a single event, a long-term trend, a fact of nature, or whatever, it will have a number of different aspects that a complete explanation must account for. In the example above, the explanandum had two major components: the increase in politicians' *demand* for campaign funds, and the increase in the *supply* of funds. In a criminal trial, the prosecution has to show that the defendant had the opportunity, the motive, and the inclination for the crime. To explain a biological trait like warm-bloodedness, we would want to know what function it serves in the animal's survival, how it arose in the course of evolution, and how it works in biochemical terms. An historical account of an event like the Civil War should explain not only why it occurred, but why it occurred at that particular time and not five years sooner or later.

In applying the rule of completeness, however, there are several qualifications to consider. First, we can't demand that a hypothesis account for absolutely everything; some points are trivial or irrelevant. The prosecution normally would not have to explain why the burglar used a red Ford instead of some other model as a getaway car. Second, we can't fault a theory for failing to explain something it never set out to explain. Darwin's theory of natural selection, for example, explains how a trait that is favorable to survival and reproduction becomes prevalent in a population. It is not intended to explain how the trait arose in the first place; for that we must turn to genetics and the biochemistry of DNA.

In other words, the rule of completeness is not that a *single* hypothesis must account for *every* aspect of the explanandum. The rule is that a *complete* explanation, which may include several hypotheses of different types, must account for every *significant* aspect. To evaluate an explanation in this respect, we should formulate each significant aspect as a separate proposition. When we draw up a diagram, we can then see whether each proposition follows from some element of the explanation as a whole. If not, then we should recognize that fact and not attribute to the hypothesis more explanatory power than it actually has.

Informativeness

The French playwright Jean Baptiste Moliere gave the classic example of a useless explanation. In one of his plays, Moliere makes fun of a doctor who explains that opium puts people to sleep because of its dormitive power. "Dormitive" means "sleep-inducing," so the explanation is: opium induces sleep because it induces sleep. We would commit the same fallacy if we explained that salt dissolves because it is soluble, or that we're angry at someone's behavior because what he did was infuriating. These are *circular* explanations: they simply rename and restate the explanandum. Circular explanations are useless for the same reason that circular definitions or arguments are useless. They don't get us anywhere; they are *uninformative.*

An explanation should be informative. Its purpose, after all, is to make the explanandum intelligible, to enlarge our understanding of it. At a minimum, this means it should not be circular. Beyond that, however, this rule becomes harder to apply because there are different patterns of explanation that are informative in different ways. In the physical sciences, we explain things in terms of the underlying properties of objects—mass, electrical charge, atomic structure —and the sum of the external forces acting on them. In this context, the more informative explanation is the one that takes us deeper into the inner structure of matter and energy. Biologists explain the traits of living organisms partly in terms of underlying mechanisms (the biochemical processes involved), and partly in terms of the function they serve in helping the organism survive and reproduce. We explain a human action in terms of its purpose: What was the person's goal? Why did he believe this action would achieve the goal? In history, we explain an event in terms of the prior events that led up to it, within the context of the cultural, political, economic, and other conditions of the society at that time.

We could go on adding to this list—there are many different patterns of explanation. It would take a separate book to describe them all, and to review the different standards they give us for telling how informative an explanation is. But there is a common element in these standards. An explanation should get to the bottom of things. No matter what pattern we employ, an explanation is informative to the extent that it identifies the *fundamental* cause or reason for the explanandum. Newton's theory was more informative than Kepler's or Galileo's, and represented an advance in human knowledge, because it went deeper; it identified the laws underlying the phenomena that Kepler and Galileo discovered. Darwin's theory of natural selection was a profound insight, and another major advance in knowledge, because it described a basic mechanism by which organisms come to have traits that promote their survival and reproductive success. We understand a person best when we can trace his actions to fundamental goals and beliefs—the ones that are central to his character, personality, and outlook on the world. In general, the rule that an explanation should be informative is analogous to the rule that a classification or definition should employ essential attributes. In both cases we are looking for fundamentality.

This is an open-ended standard. We can hardly fault Kepler or Galileo for failing to discover Newton's law, or Newton for failing to anticipate the discoveries of Albert Einstein. The fact that later theories are more informative does not imply that earlier ones are totally uninformative. But it *is* uninformative, and thus inadequate, to try to explain the *more* fundamental phenomenon by the *less* fundamental. The cause explains the effect, the essential attribute explains the superficial one, the end explains the means. In every case, an explanation that inverts the proper order is uninformative. Suppose we tried to interpret Shakespeare's *Julius Caesar* along the following lines:

> The main character is Cassius, and the basic theme of the play is that you can't trust thin people. "Let me have men about me that are fat," says Caesar. "Yond Cassius has a lean and hungry look, He thinks too much; such men are dangerous." Everything else in the play—the murder of Caesar, Marc Antony's speech, the campaign against Brutus and his suicide—are all subplots designed to emphasize just how dangerous thin people can be.

This is a ridiculous reading of the play. Cassius is not the main character, his figure is not his essential trait, and Caesar's remark does not express the central theme. These are all tangential elements in the play that would themselves have to be explained in terms of something more basic.

It is not always obvious which of two things is the more fundamental, and there are many controversies on this score. In the early part of the nineteenth century, biologists debated whether structure or function was primary in evolution. One school said that structure changes first, leading a species to adopt a new way of functioning to take advantage of the new structure. Their opponents (who eventually won) said that a change in function comes first, creating evolutionary pressure for new structures that better serve that function. In the social sciences, some theorists hold that economic factors underlie and explain the political institutions of a society and its intellectual-cultural life—its dominant ideology, artistic values, religious beliefs, etc. Others take the opposite view, that ideas are the fundamental factor: a society's basic values and view of the world determine the kind of political and economic institutions it will have. Debates like these indicate how difficult it can be to apply the principle of fundamentality. But they also indicate how important the principle is.

Combining the Standards

An adequate explanation should be strong, complete, and informative. To see how these standards relate to each other, let's look at one final example, a famous hypothesis whose adequacy has been questioned on all three counts. In *The Protestant Ethic and the Spirit of Capitalism*, the German sociologist Max Weber proposed that the rise of capitalism was largely the result of the Protestant Reformation in general, and the doctrines of John Calvin and the Puritans in particular. Weber noted that Calvin regarded productive work as a religious virtue: one's trade or profession is a "calling," a way of serving God, and worldly success is a sign of heavenly grace. The Protestant emphasis on asceticism, moreover, discouraged consumption and thereby encouraged thrift; this is turn allowed for the savings and investment that are essential to a capitalist economy.

Some historians have argued that Weber's theory is *incomplete*. It may explain the rise of capitalism in the Protestant countries of Northern Europe and North America. And the demand for religious freedom that arose out of the Protestant Reformation may have furthered the principle of individual rights, including property rights and economic freedom, that was necessary for the full development of capitalism. But many of the early centers of commerce, such as Venice or Lisbon, were in Catholic countries, and many of the leading merchants and financiers were Catholic or Jewish. So the thesis cannot account for everything.

A different objection to Weber's theory is raised by Marxists. Weber was trying to explain an economic development in terms of religious ideas. But this, they argue, inverts the true relationship. Ideas are consequences, not causes, of underlying economic forces. The Protestant ethic in particular was a by-product of class interest, a rationalization offered by the rising capitalists to sanctify their quest for control over material production. Thus Weber was trying to explain the fundamental phenomenon by something that was less fundamental. His explanation is *uninformative*, and ultimately circular, because to explain the Protestant ethic itself we would be led back to the very economic trends he was trying to explain.

A third criticism is that, while Weber was right to look for the historical roots of capitalism in the realm of ideas, he picked the wrong ideas. Capitalism required a secular philosophy, emphasizing happiness and prosperity in this life, the pursuit of self-interest, and the virtue of rationality. These ideas were on the rise throughout the Renaissance and the Enlightenment, but they were opposed by the early Protestant thinkers, who were other-worldly in outlook, viewed egoism as a sin, and emphasized revelation and mysticism over reason. Indeed, they went further in each respect than the Catholic Church, which they criticized for being too secular. The explanandum, then, simply doesn't follow from the hypothesis: the explanation is *weak*. Anyone observing the Reformation, and unaware of the other forces at work, would have expected a movement away from capitalism.

Of course, this description of Weber's thesis, and the objections to it, is vastly oversimplified. But it serves to illustrate the differences among the standards of adequacy, and the way they are applied in practice.

Practice Quiz

Each of the explanations below can be faulted as inadequate. Identify the standard (or standards) that it violates.

1. Why did the chicken cross the road? To get to the other side.
2. In Western societies, people customarily wear wedding bands on the fourth finger of the left hand. That's probably because the Romans believed a vein ran from the fourth finger directly to the heart.
3. Why was George Washington admired so much, with a kind of reverence and awe, in an age filled with other great men? It was largely his height: he towered over most other men.

4. If the quality of education has declined, and it certainly has, the main reason is that teachers no longer enjoy the public respect and esteem once accorded their profession, and are thus too demoralized to do a good job.

The Truth of Hypotheses

The adequacy of an explanation does not guarantee that the hypothesis is true. A theory may be strong, complete, informative —and false. Innocent people have been convicted in cases where their guilt would have explained all the evidence. Scientists have often seen a beautiful theory murdered by the facts. How is this possible? There's a simple logical reason. The adequacy of an explanation tells us that if the hypothesis is true, the explanandum has to be true as well. It tells us, in other words, that we may accept the hypothetical proposition: if *H*, then *E*. And we know that *E* is true. But to infer from these two propositions that *H* is true would be to affirm the consequent—and that's a fallacy. There might well be some alternative hypothesis *H'* that would explain *E* with equal adequacy.

This point cannot be emphasized too strongly. Affirming the consequent in the manner just described is the most common error in reasoning about explanations. We all want things to make sense, and it's all too easy to accept the first plausible explanation we find. We hear that a medical student is going to specialize in brain surgery, and we assume it must be for the money, without considering any other possible motive. The economy falls into a recession, and we blame the president's policies without considering other factors that might have played a role. We adopt a religion or a philosophy because it offers *an* explanation of human nature and experience, without asking whether it offers the *only* explanation. You can see the same thing happening in the spread of a rumor. A couple breaks up, a friend makes a guess about the reason, and by the time the gossip is repeated once or twice, speculation has become "fact."

To combat this tendency, it is crucial to consider alternatives before we accept a given hypothesis. Courts of law use the adversary system, despite its many faults, partly to ensure that the jury will hear an alternative to the prosecution's account of the crime. The canons of scientific research require that a theory not be accepted until it has proven its superiority to rival theories. In everyday life, when someone asks rhetorically, "What other explanation could there be?," the question should serve as a red flag: there almost always is some other explanation worth considering.

Testing Hypotheses

Assuming, then, that we have several hypotheses on the table, how do we decide which one is true? In some cases, we can use the methods we're already familiar with. If you think the drip in your ceiling might be caused by rain coming in through a hole in the roof, you can check this out by observation: you can look for the hole. Or suppose you want to know why the lilac bush in your garden develops mildew around midsummer. If you consult a gardening book, you will find that this happens to all lilacs. And this generalization can be confirmed by using Mill's methods.

But we can't always test a hypothesis by the standard methods of observation and induction. When you want to explain why someone is acting a certain way, you can't manipulate the person's mind to see which factors caused the behavior. A detective can't go back in time to see who committed the crime. Scientists did not establish the atomic theory by generalizing from a sample—they didn't discover first that chairs are made of atoms, then that tables are, and carrots, and so on until there were enough instances to support the claim that all physical objects are so constituted. When we are trying to explain a unique individual event, or when the possible causes involve things we can't observe directly, the methods of induction we have learned so far will not do the job by themselves.

Instead, we use an indirect approach. If the hypothesis is adequate to begin with, then the explanandum follows from it. The indirect method is to ask what *other* consequences would follow. Having first reasoned backwards from explanandum to hypothesis, we now reason forwards, drawing further conclusions from the hypothesis, and checking to see whether the conclusions are true. The process could be diagrammed schematically as follows:

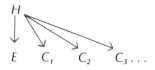

If we find that $C_1, C_2, C_3 \ldots$, are not true, we reject the hypothesis. But if they *are* true, they confirm it, and become explananda that are themselves explained by the hypothesis.

This method of testing hypotheses should not be news; you have almost certainly used it yourself. The toaster isn't working—is the problem in the toaster itself, or in the wall outlet? If the latter were the case, then the toaster should work if you plug it into a different outlet. So you try that and find that it does work, confirming the hypothesis. A friend hasn't shown up for a dinner date—did he have to work late at the office? But then he would have called, and he hasn't, so it must be something else. To a large extent, the confirmation of a scientific theory is simply a more elaborate and more refined application of the same method. Newton's theory, for example, was put to an important test when Edmund Halley used the theory to predict the next appearance of the comet named for him. Though the theory already had a good deal of evidence going for it, it gained further confirmation when the comet appeared on schedule.

If one or more of the consequences we derive from a hypothesis turn out to be *false*, then the hypothesis itself can be rejected, in accordance with the hypothetical syllogism:

$$\text{If H, then } C$$
$$\frac{-C}{-H}$$

You can see that this inference is valid even if a single consequence turns out to be false. On the positive side, however, the fact that a single consequence turns out to be *true* does not prove the hypothesis true. The inference:

$$\text{If } H \text{, then } C$$
$$\frac{C}{H}$$

affirms the consequent, and is thus fallacious. For confirmation, what counts is the number of consequences we test and their relation to the various alternative hypotheses we've considered.

To see why, let's return to our point of departure. If an explanation is adequate, the truth of the hypothesis implies the truth of the explanandum. The truth of the explanandum is not surprising. We already knew it was true; that's what led us to devise the hypothesis in the first place. The further consequences we derive, however, are things we did *not* already know to be true. When we follow out the implications of the hypothesis, we are led to conclusions that might not even have occurred to us otherwise. As we test more and more implications, and they keep turning out to be true, it becomes increasingly unlikely that this could happen unless the hypothesis were true.

We assume from the outset, moreover, that there *is* some explanation, that some hypothesis will account for the explanandum. The question is: which one? At the outset, there may be many alternatives, but as we test more and more consequences, we narrow down the possibilities, ideally to the point where only one hypothesis is consistent with all the evidence. Indeed, we should actively look for cases in which rival hypotheses have different implications: H implies C_x, H' implies $-C_x$. Testing to see whether C_x is true or false will then rule out one of the hypotheses.

Notice that this is an inductive process. The consequences may follow deductively from the hypothesis, as may the explanandum. But the evidence for the truth of the hypothesis is inductive. The strength of the evidence is a matter of degree: it can always be increased by testing additional consequences. And when we accept a hypothesis because we have eliminated alternative explanations, our reasoning rests on the presupposition that we have considered all the relevant alternatives—just as Mill's methods rest on the presupposition that we have varied all the relevant factors. As we learn more, new alternatives may occur to us. Thus establishing a hypothesis is an open-ended process that depends on the context of our knowledge at a given time, and we must allow for the possibility that an explanation will have to be modified—or in extreme cases rejected—as we acquire new knowledge.

Plausibility

Finally, as in the other forms of inductive reasoning, testing a hypothesis requires that we make various judgments of plausibility along the way. To see why, we have to add a few complications to our picture of confirmation. For one thing, we could not hope to test every conceivable hypothesis. We have to exercise our judgment in deciding which ones are plausible enough to be worth testing, just as we have to decide, in using Mill's methods, which factors should be varied and which ones can be ignored. If we wanted to understand why a usually thrifty person suddenly splurged on a cruise in the Bahamas, there would be various hypotheses to consider, depending on what we know about the person's character and circumstances. But there are countless other hypotheses we would ignore: that cosmic rays had altered his consciousness, that he is a Communist agent living a double life, etc.

A further complication is that we can usually derive a consequence from a hypothesis only in conjunction with some additional, *auxiliary assumptions.* We need to modify our standard diagram to include this point:

$$\frac{H + A1 + A2 + \ldots}{}$$
$$\downarrow$$
$$C$$

Suppose we perform the test and find that *C* is false. This will not necessarily refute the hypothesis. It may be that one of the auxiliary assumptions was false instead. In other words, when a hypothesis fails a test, the logical structure diagrammed above allows us to save the hypothesis by blaming an auxiliary assumption. Whether it is reasonable to do so depends on a judgment of plausibility.

For example, the law of gravity implies that if I release a ball in midair, it will fall. But this consequence follows only on the auxiliary assumption that no other force is acting on the ball to counteract gravity. Suppose I release the ball and it remains motionless, floating in midair. I am certainly not going to abandon the law of gravity; it is much more reasonable to reject the auxiliary assumption, and assume that some other force is at work. On the other hand, people sometimes cling to a theory in the face of overwhelming evidence against it by inventing reasons to reject auxiliary assumptions rather than the theory itself. If there were any doubt that the Earth is not flat, for example, one might think the pictures taken from space would have clinched the matter. But the pictures are decisive only on the assumption that they were indeed taken from space, and some Flat Earthers argued that it was all an elaborate hoax.

What standards should we use in deciding what's plausible? The decision is not always as obvious or clear-cut as in the examples above. How do we decide whether a hypothesis is plausible enough to be considered and tested? If a hypothesis fails a test, how do we decide whether it is more reasonable to reject the hypothesis or one of the auxiliary assumptions? As in other areas of inductive logic, these judgments depend partly on one's knowledge and experience in the specific field. But there are also two general standards that apply across the board. Other things being equal, one hypothesis is more plausible than another if it is more *consistent* with the rest of our knowledge, and if it is *simpler*. Let's look at these standards in more detail.

Consistency. Consider two theories that might both be said to assert the existence of a "sixth sense": 1) certain animals such as migratory birds can perceive the Earth's magnetic field; and 2) certain human beings are capable of extrasensory perception (ESP). The first is a routine scientific hypothesis; most scientists would regard it as a plausible explanation for the ability of migratory birds to navigate as well as they do. By contrast, the ESP hypothesis has much less initial plausibility, and would have to meet a much higher standard of evidence than the first one before it would be taken seriously. Why?

One reason is that the idea of a magnetic sense is entirely consistent with everything we know about sense perception. Perception involves a physical organ, containing receptor cells that respond to various forms of energy (light waves, sound waves, etc.), and are capable of detecting various features of the environment (colors, sounds, etc.) with some reliability. A magnetic sense would fit this pattern; we need only accept the possibility of a new type of receptor that responds to a known form of energy. But ESP, as its name implies, is extrasensory. It does not involve identifiable sense organs or receptors. It is not alleged to be a response to any known form of energy. And it does not produce reliable knowledge of the environment: at best, the experiments show that certain people score slightly above chance in various guessing games. So ESP is not consistent with the rest of our knowledge about perception. To accept it as a viable hypothesis, we would have to abandon some fundamental principles derived from the study of vision, hearing, touch, taste, and smell.

We should remember that when we introduce a hypothesis to explain something, we are not operating in a vacuum. We have a vast context of background knowledge—beliefs, principles, and theories for which we have accumulated a great deal of evidence. A new hypothesis therefore starts out with a certain degree of initial plausibility that depends on how consistent it is, how well it fits, with that background knowledge. A hypothesis that conflicts with established principles and theories must meet a higher standard of evidence than a hypothesis that does not conflict. Accepting the first sort of hypothesis, after all, means giving up beliefs for which we have good evidence, so the new evidence must be strong enough and extensive enough to outweigh the old. This does not mean we should be traditionalists and reject every radically new idea just because it conflicts with the established wisdom. It does mean we should know what we're doing, and be prepared to back it up.

In science, revolutions can occur when scientists discover phenomena that can't be explained by prevailing theories. But a new theory must do more than explain these anomalies; it must also explain the phenomena that the old theory explained, and it must give some coherent account of the evidence for the older view. The theory that the Earth is round had to explain why it looks flat. Einstein's theory of relativity had to explain why Newton's laws describe the behavior of physical objects as well as they do. As these examples suggest, the standard of consistency applies with special force in the physical sciences, where we have a vast edifice of highly integrated and well-confirmed theories. It applies with somewhat less force in the social sciences, which are younger and less highly developed, and with less force still in the humanities. In these branches of knowledge, established views do not have the same degree of evidence as in the physical sciences, and new ideas therefore do not have as large an obstacle to overcome. But they must still take account of whatever genuine evidence there is for the older views.

The rule of consistency is especially important in evaluating claims on the fringes of science: claims about ESP and other alleged psychic powers, UFOs, astrology, the Bermuda Triangle, alien astronauts who visited Earth during ancient times, etc. All of these purport to explain "the unexplained," to solve mysteries that established scientific theories cannot account for. And, as we saw in the case of ESP, the explanations conflict with, and would require us to abandon, principles or theories for which we have a great deal of evidence. Before we accept any such explanation, we should recognize that it is not, as the proponents normally claim, the only possible one. Invariably there are alternative hypotheses that might explain the phenomenon and be more consistent with our background knowledge.

One alternative hypothesis is simply that the explanandum isn't true, the event never occurred, there is nothing to explain. The witnesses who claim to have seen UFOs may have misidentified what they saw; the ancient texts that describe miraculous events may be mistaken; the subjects who seem to have powers of telepathy may instead be using the techniques of magicians and con artists. A second alternative hypothesis applies to amazing coincidences: the man who has a sudden feeling of dread, and calls home to find his wife has had a terrible accident; the person who dreams of winning the lottery, and does so the next day. These are often taken as signs of higher powers at work, but they may be just coincidences. The laws of probability make it very likely that among all the premonitions, dreams, and sudden dreads that we experience, most of which come to nothing and are quickly forgotten, a few will turn out to be accurate. These alternative hypotheses may turn out to be false. But because they are fully consistent with our background knowledge, they must be considered and tested before we can accept any explanation that is not consistent.

Simplicity. Suppose someone on trial for burglary tries to explain away the evidence as follows:

Prosecutor: Three witnesses said they saw you in the neighborhood the day before the crime. You don't live near there. Weren't you casing the joint?

Defendant: No, I was just taking a walk.

Prosecutor: Why were you loitering around the victim's building and staring at the fire escape?

Defendant: Well, it's an old building, and the fire escape has some ornamental features that are interesting from an architectural point of view. I'm very interested in architecture.

Prosecutor: Where were you on the night of the crime?

Defendant: In Clancey's Bar.

Prosecutor: Why doesn't anyone remember seeing you there that night?

Defendant: I guess they were all drunk.

Prosecutor: Why were the stolen goods found in your car?

Defendant: The thief must have put them there.

A jury listening to this exchange has two hypotheses to consider. The prosecutor would explain all the evidence with a single claim: the defendant committed the crime. The defendant's explanation, by contrast, involves a string of unrelated claims. It's conceivable, of course, that they are all true. The truth is not always simple. But the jury would be justified in considering the defendant's story less plausible than the prosecutor's, and in need of more evidence to back it up.

This example illustrates the principle of simplicity or parsimony. The rule is that, other things being equal, one hypothesis is more plausible than another if it involves a fewer number of new assumptions. We've seen that an explanation rarely involves a single proposition. A full explanation usually requires a complex hypothesis, involving a number of separate propositions. If these separate propositions are new, and cannot be derived from knowledge we already possess, then the fewer the better. The reason is appropriately simple. Just as an adequate explanation must account for every significant aspect of the explanandum, the evidence for the truth of a hypothesis must cover each positive claim it makes. The fewer the claims, the less evidence will be required. Conversely, the farther out on a limb we go, the stronger the limb must be. This is not to say that the rule is always easy to apply. It can happen that theory A is simpler in one respect, theory B in another. But if one hypothesis is obviously simpler, it is more plausible.

The standard of simplicity is particularly important in deciding what to do when we test a hypothesis and get a negative result. If the hypothesis has survived a series of tests, and provides a single coherent explanation for a number of consequences that have been derived from it, it may be simpler to assume that failure on some further test is due to an auxiliary assumption. On the other hand, if we keep getting negative results, and can save the hypothesis only by a series of unrelated, ad hoc attempts to blame the auxiliary assumptions, the balance tips against the hypothesis.

The standard of simplicity can also be used in evaluating conspiracy theories. Conspiracies certainly do occur, and sometimes we have direct evidence for them, as when one of the conspirators confesses. But the evidence is often indirect, and in such cases the standard cuts both ways. On the one hand, the hypothesis that a conspiracy is at work may provide a single, unified explanation for a series of events that would otherwise have to be given separate explanations. As the villain in an Ian Fleming novel says, after he has encountered James Bond for the third time, "Mr. Bond, they have a saying in Chicago: 'Once is happenstance. Twice is coincidence. The third time it's enemy action.'"

But conspiracy theories do not always simplify. The notion that the U.S. economy and political system are governed by a secret cabal of international bankers, for example, gives only the illusion of simplicity. In fact, it raises more questions than it answers. How did this group gain so much power? Why this particular group, and not some other one? To control a nation of 250 million, these bankers must give marching orders to hundreds of thousands of political and business leaders. How do they manage to keep all these people in line? How do they manage to keep their own role a secret? To answer these questions, the conspiracy theory would have to be spun out into an elaborate web of arbitrary claims.

It's time to pull together what we've learned in this section. The basic method for testing a hypothesis (when more direct methods are not applicable) is to derive consequences from it, and then see whether the consequences are true. This is the essence of the experimental method in science, but it can be used wherever a hypothesis has a definite set of implications. When we apply this test, we should interpret the results in accordance with two basic rules. 1) If we find that one or more consequences are false, we should reject the hypothesis—unless it would be simpler and more consistent with other knowledge to reject an auxiliary assumption instead. 2) If we find that a number of consequences are true, the hypothesis is confirmed—unless an alternative hypothesis is equally consistent with the same evidence, and is at least as simple and consistent. As in other types of induction, testing a hypothesis requires that we exercise our judgment, and allow for the possibility that reasonable people may disagree. That goes with the territory. But the method and the standards outlined above will help organize the process of inquiry, and direct our attention to the relevant issues.

Practice Quiz

The following article reports a set of experiments showing that stress increases the level of cholesterol in the blood. The experiments also test a hypothesis that seems to account for that explanandum. Identify the hypothesis. Then identify the consequences used to test it, expressing them as hypothetical propositions: if H, then C_1; if H, then C_2; etc.

"For more than a decade scientists have known that the body can manufacture morphine-like natural opiates, known as endorphins. Often released in times of stress, these chemicals can temporarily dull one's sensitivity to pain. But George K. W. Yim and his colleagues at Purdue University in West Lafayette, Indiana, appear to have discovered another function—one that seems to chemically link stress and heart disease.

"In research involving mice and rats, they have found signs that some as-yet-unidentified endorphin plays an essential role in the buildup of cholesterol in the blood serum of individuals under stress. . . .

"In one test, the researchers subjected rats over a five-day period to the stress of randomly scheduled restraint in small cages for two to four hours. Compared with unrestrained rats fed the same moderately high-cholesterol diet, the stressed animals developed a near doubling in blood cholesterol levels. There was also at least a doubling of low-density lipoproteins (LDLs) in the blood of these animals and a drop by one-third in high-density lipoproteins (HDLs). Since LDLs are associated with bringing cholesterol into the blood and tissues, and HDLs with removing cholesterol, these are ominous changes, says Henry Bryant, formerly with the Purdue team. . . .

"Rats that were identically stressed after receiving naltrexone—a drug that blocks the effect of endorphins on the brain—developed no cholesterol increase and no change in lipoprotein levels. This ability of naltrexone to prevent the cholesterol-related effects of stress points to the hidden activity of some endorphin, Bryant says.

"Further support for an endorphin role was provided in other studies, he says, when morphine drug implants—replacing restraint as a "stress"—yielded virtually identical serum changes in the animals. This externally derived opiate apparently substituted for the body's own in the mediation of serum changes, he says. Like the endorphin effects, morphine's role was blocked by naltrexone." [*Science News*, August 30, 1986. Reprinted with permission from *Science News*, the weekly newsmagazine of science, copyright 1986 by Science Service, Inc.]

SUMMARY

The goal of an explanation is to show why something is true, to state the cause or reason for the explanandum, or otherwise fit it into a wider context that makes it intelligible. Though an explanation differs from an argument in its primary goal, the logical relation between hypothesis and explanandum is the same as that between premises and conclusion, and we can use the same diagramming techniques to analyze explanations.

To evaluate a proposed explanation, we consider two basic issues: its adequacy and the truth of the hypothesis. An adequate explanation is logically strong (the explanandum follows from the hypothesis), complete (the hypothesis explains all significant aspects of the explanandum), and informative (the hypothesis gives a fundamental cause or reason for the explanandum).

To ascertain the truth of a hypothesis, we should consider alternative hypotheses that would also provide adequate explanations. We decide among rival hypotheses by deriving further consequences from them, and then checking to see whether those consequences are true. To decide which hypotheses to consider, and to decide whether to save a hypothesis in the face of a negative test by rejecting an auxiliary assumption, we rely on the standards of consistency and simplicity.

Exercises

A. Identify the explanandum and the hypothesis in each of the following explanatory passages, and diagram the explanation.

1. "Here we can glimpse the mechanism of Mendelian inheritance: A zygote [fertilized egg] obtains exactly half its genes from its male parent because it receives exactly half its chromosomes from the male parent and the chromosomes bear the genes." [Philip Kitcher, *Abusing Science: The Case Against Creationism*]

2. "Israeli officials say they believe that the easing of Israel's diplomatic isolation is a result of the decline in the power of the Arab oil-producing countries, now that the price of oil has slipped, as well as to the more moderate image that [Prime Minister] Mr. [Shimon] Peres has projected for Israel in the world." ["Cameroonians Greet Israelis in Exuberant Hebrew," *New York Times*, August 26, 1986]

3. "Q. What causes blisters to form on the skin?

   "A. Blisters are usually caused by friction or burns. In friction, the upper layers (epidermis) of the skin move back and forth over the lower layers (dermis), until a small cleft is produced between the layers of skin. Fluid collects in the cleft. When the skin is burned, serum from damaged blood vessels collects between the epidermis and the dermis." [Q & A, science section, *New York Times*, March 3, 1987]

4. Metal workers had known for centuries that three distinct metals could be produced from iron ore. Wrought iron is soft but tough: it can be hammered into shape. Cast iron is hard and brittle; it takes a sharp edge but breaks if struck. The third metal was steel, which has intermediate properties. It is harder than wrought iron but tougher than cast iron. In the late eighteenth century, it was discovered that these differences are due to the amount of carbon mixed with the iron: wrought iron has 0–.15%, steel .15–1.5%, cast iron 1.5% or more.

5. "Many free-swimming animals, mammals, birds, amphibians and fishes, are silvery-white below in order to be invisible to enemies swimming in the depths. Seen from below, the shining white belly blends perfectly with the reflecting surface film of the water." [Konrad Z. Lorenz, "The Taming of the Shrew," in *King Solomon's Ring*]

6. "When a can of mixed nuts . . . is shaken, why does the largest nut end up at the surface, even if it is much denser than the others? That is what researchers at Carnegie-Mellon University in Pittsburgh set out to discover with computerized Monte Carlo simulations of a shaken can containing large and small balls.

   ". . . Anthony Rosato and his co-workers conclude that the size difference among balls makes it more likely that a small, rather than a large, ball will fill a void that may open during the shaking process; for a large ball to move down in the can, several small balls must simultaneously move out of the way, whereas it only takes the movement of one large ball to create a void that several small balls can fall into." [*Science News*, March 28, 1987]

7. "At the Western Economic Association's meeting this summer in San Francisco, Allen Sanai, the chief economist at Shearson Lehman Brothers, commented that '10 years ago, the weak sectors would have resulted in a recession.'

   "So how does the overall prosperity, albeit with lackluster growth, continue? . . .

   "Primarily, the answer may lie in the rapid shift to a service economy. Even as manufacturing employment continues to shrink, service-sector jobs keep increasing—jobs traditionally relatively safe from business cycles and layoffs." [Henry F. Myers, "The Outlook," *Wall Street Journal*, September 22, 1986]

B. Evaluate each of the following explanations for adequacy.

1. "It isn't clear why doo-wop and other forms of early rock 'n' roll are making a comeback now. Robert Palmer, the respected popular-music critic for the *New York Times,* points to the nation's demographics. 'The people in decision-making positions nowadays are the people who grew up with rock 'n' roll.'" [*Wall Street Journal,* April 28, 1987]

2. "Before printing, there had been no elaborate system of censorship and control over scribes. There did not have to be. The scribes were scattered, working on single manuscripts in monasteries. Moreover, single manuscripts rarely caused a general scandal or major controversy. There was little motive for central control, and control would have been impractical." [Ithiel de Sola Pool, *Technologies of Freedom*]

3. "If the umpire can't determine which came first, the ball or the foot, then the batter will be ruled safe. The notion that a tie goes to a runner is a valid one, and here's why: according to baseball rules, the object of any play is for the defense to put out the batter or the runners on base, and if the defense fails to carry out this obligation, then it follows that the batter or runners must advance safely. When the ball and the batter's foot arrived in a dead heat in this example, the fielding team's responsibility to put out the batter was not met; all the fielder did was get the ball to the base at the same time as the runner, not before him. Therefore, the batter must be ruled safe at first on the grounds that he was not out at first." [Ray Corio, "Question Box," *New York Times,* September 1, 1986]

C. The passages below are lead paragraphs from newspaper stories. In addition to the facts it reports, each one offers a hypothesis to explain those facts. Identify the hypothesis, and think of an alternative.

1. "In a move that both supporters and opponents see as one designed to strengthen Prime Minister Margaret Thatcher's hand in a re-election campaign, the Government announced a 2 percent cut today in the income tax rate." [*New York Times,* March 18, 1987]

2. "Reagan ordered the expulsion from the U.S. of 25 Soviet officials. In an apparent effort to look tough in the face of the Kremlin's espionage charges against U.S. News & World Report correspondent Nicholas Daniloff, the president stiffened an earlier demand that Moscow reduce the size of its U.N. mission. He named 25 Soviet officials that would have to leave

the country by October 1, rather than leave the choice of personnel to the Soviet Union." [*Wall Street Journal*, September 18, 1986]

3. "Signalling that organized labor has regained some of its once formidable influence on Capitol Hill, the House of Representatives tonight approved a package of proposals that broaden the rights of unions in the construction industry." [*New York Times*, June 18, 1987]

D. Find an explanation for each of the following facts. Make sure your explanation is adequate, and indicate how you would tell whether the hypothesis is true.

1. The subject I had the most trouble with in school was_____ [fill in the blank].
2. When you drop a piece of bread with jam on it, it usually lands jam-side down.
3. In elections held during a president's sixth year in office, the president's party usually loses seats in Congress.
4. When we spend a lot of time looking forward to something, and expect to enjoy it, we're often disappointed.
5. The number of people working at home instead of an office or factory has been rising, both in absolute terms and as a percentage of the workforce. Some are self-employed, running their own businesses; others are employees of companies, doing such work as sewing garments or word-processing.

E. The headlines below are from the September 16, 1986, edition of the *Sun*. Relying mainly on the standard of consistency, rank them in order of initial plausibility. Does the claim conflict with established principles and theories? If so, to what extent? How radical a change would we have to make in established principles and theories to accept each story as true?

1. Baby Born on Roller Coaster.
2. Snake Tattoo Crawls Up Man's Arm and Chokes Him.
3. Pregnancy Makes Women Able to Predict Future.
4. Amazing Vitamin Keeps Skin Wrinkle-Free.
5. Friendly Bigfoot Saves Dying Girl.
6. Woman Adopts Own Child But Doesn't Know It.
7. Woman Describes How . . . Sparks from UFO Nearly Blinded Me.
8. Bat Attacks Couple Watching Dracula on TV.
9. Glenn Ford Travels through Time to See His Past Lives.
10. Gadget Ends Back Pain Forever.

F. In the essay "Paranoia," Hendrik Hertzberg and David McClelland describe a man named Zero and quote the monologue below as an example of a paranoid conspiracy theory. What is Zero's central hypothesis? What actual facts is the hypothesis supposed to explain? Is the explanation adequate? What further consequences might be used to test the hypothesis? If the theory failed the test, how do you suppose Zero would interpret the result?

"This isn't something I usually run down. People don't want to hear about it. They figure that if this is true then what's the use. Even if somebody brave like the *National Enquirer* ran it down, which I suppose is impossible, nobody could handle it.

"Here's the deal. There's this thing, you know, that would like us all to be very nice polite robots. First, they planned to build androids to replace us. It would either be when you're sleeping or at work or in jail. I used to think that this was unbelievable, but I got busted once, and they really dug on beating me up. I'm sure they get off on offing people, too. You've heard about how every couple of hundred years there's a bunch of people who disappear? Well, they're being offed by GM and getting recycled into new cars. There's a computer under Rochester, Michigan. It completely ran the Vietnam war. That's right, and what's happening now is that the computers of GM have figured out a master scheme to turn us into androids via the food we eat. And McDonald's is the front for the whole thing, and the president of GM is actually Ronald McDonald, who's a front in a scheme to rip off our minds and souls. They're planting electrodes and embalming fluid and synthetic God-knows-what in our food. Did you know that the most widely used preservative in white bread is embalming fluid? We're being turned into robots without a hand being laid on us! Maybe those satellites up there are programmed to control us, and it's some kind of world-wide monitoring system. And with all this shit inside us from eating Quarter Pounders that undoubtedly strangle up our minds, who even thinks about all of this?

"I worked for Pontiac Motors for a while before I went into the Army, and I used to think that maybe the assembly line was once used to turn out robots. Anyway, there was this food company there that filled all the vending machines and ran the plant cafeterias. It was called Prophet Food. Can you dig that? I mean, it's like saying, '. . . we're going to turn you into androids,' you know? Oh man, I ate one of their hamburgers by mistake once. I got sick and couldn't think straight for a few days. Anyway, every day the workers came in like perfect robots and made the cars that were probably melted down years later and made into bombs or something. Hardly anybody picks up on it—you just had a Big Mac or some other kind of poison and you're driving around trying to relate to the cops. Who's going to be able to think about Pontiac Motors? I mean, you gotta get up tomorrow and be there at 6:28 anyway. So pick up a six-pack and forget about it. It's the whole system. It's its own preservative. And it doesn't matter where you work, man, 'cause it's all GM. Generous Motors. What else is there to say? No one believes it. No one dares even think about it. But it's not their fault. We're all just calcium proprionate on this bus." [*Harpers Magazine,* June 1974]

G. In a Virginia criminal case from 1882, Oliver Hatchett was accused of murdering Moses Young. The trial court found Hatchett guilty. The passage below is from the opinion of the Appeals Court, which overturned the conviction on the ground that Hatchett's guilt had not been proved beyond a reasonable doubt. Treating the proposition that Hatchett is guilty as a hypothesis to explain Young's death, and using what you've learned in this chapter, decide whether you would side with the trial or the appeals court.

Opinion of the Court. Lewis, J., delivered the opinion of the Court. The plaintiff in error was indicted in the county court of Brunswick county for the murder of Moses Young, by administering to the said Young strychnine poison in whisky. . . . The facts proved, as certified in the record, are substantially these: That on the night of the 17th day of December, 1880, Moses Young died at his house in Brunswick county, and under such circumstances as created suspicions that he had been poisoned. He was an old man, 65 years of age, and was subject to the colic, and a short time previous to his death had been hurt in his side by a cart. In the afternoon of that day the father of Oliver Hatchett, the prisoner, gave him a small bottle of whisky, with instructions to take it to Moses Young; at the same time telling him not to drink it himself. The deceased lived about three miles from the prisoner's father, to whose house the prisoner at once proceeded. It seems that he was not acquainted with the deceased; or, if so, very slightly, and that he succeeded in finding the house only by inquiry of one of the neighbors. Soon after his arrival at the house of the deceased, he took supper with him, and a few minutes thereafter requested the deceased to go with him into the yard, and point out the path to him—it then being dark. After getting into the yard, the prisoner produced the bottle and invited the deceased to drink—telling him that it was a little whisky his father had sent him. The deceased drank and returned the bottle to the prisoner, who at once started on his return home. The deceased then returned into the house. In a short while thereafter he complained of a pain in his side, began to grow worse, and told his wife that the man (meaning the prisoner) had tricked him in a drink of whisky. He then got up, but fell immediately to the floor. Osborne and Charlotte Northington, two near neighbors, were then called in by his wife; and these three, whom the record describes as ignorant negroes, were the only persons present with the deceased until his death, which occurred about three hours after he drank of the whisky from the bottle handed him by the prisoner. They described his symptoms as follows: The old man had the jerks, complained of great pain, and every now and then would draw up his arms and legs and complained of being cramped; that he put his finger in his mouth to make him vomit, and his teeth clinched on it so that one of his teeth was pulled out in getting out his finger. They also testified that his dying declaration was that the man had killed him in a drink of whisky. From the symptoms as thus described, two physicians, who were examined as witnesses in the case, testified that as far as they could judge from the statements of the ignorant witnesses, they would suppose that Moses Young died from strychnine poison. No post-mortem examination of the deceased body was made or attempted; nor was any analysis made of the contents of the bottle, which was returned about one-third full by the prisoner to his father, and was afterwards found.

After the arrest of the prisoner, and while under guard, he stated to the guard in charge of him that he would not be punished about the matter; that he intended to tell all about it; that his father, Littleton Hatchett, gave him that mess and told him he would give him something, to carry it and give it to Moses Young, and that it would fix him. He further stated that he went to Moses Young's house, called him out and gave him a drink, and returned the bottle and put it where his father had directed him to put it. The next day he made a statement on oath before the coroner's jury, and when asked by the foreman whether he was prepared, upon reflection, to say that what he had stated on the previous day was not true, he answered: "I am prepared to say that a part of what I said yesterday was true." He then made a statement in which he said that he carried the whisky to the deceased by direction of his father, who told him not to drink of it; that he went to the house of the deceased and gave him a drink, and returned the bottle as directed by his father. But he did not state that his father told him that the whisky would "fix" the deceased, or that he (the prisoner) knew that it contained poison or other dangerous thing.

It was also proved that Henry Carroll, who was jointly indicted with the prisoner, gave to Sallie Young, wife of the deceased, about three weeks before his death, something in a bottle which he said was strychnine, and which he told her to put in the coffee or food of the deceased; and that Osborne and Charlotte Northington knew of the fact, but did not communicate it to the deceased. It was also proved that Henry Carroll was the paramour of Sallie Young, which fact was also known to Osborne and Charlotte Northington.

Such are the facts upon which the plaintiff in error was convicted and sentenced to death. Now, under the allegations in the indictment, it was incumbent upon the prosecution, to entitle the Commonwealth to a verdict, to establish clearly and beyond a reasonable doubt these three essential propositions: (1) That the deceased came to his death by poison. (2) That the poison was administered by the prisoner. (3) That he administered it knowingly and feloniously. These propositions, we think, are not established by the evidence in this case.

In the first place, there is no sufficient proof that the deceased died from the effects of poison at all. From the symptoms, as described by ignorant witnesses, one of whom at least was a party to the conspiracy to poison the deceased, and who had been supplied with the means to do so (a fact known to the others), the most that the medical men who were examined in the case could say was that they *supposed* he died from strychnine poison. Strange to say, there was no post-mortem examination of the body of the deceased, nor was there any analysis made of the contents of the bottle from which he drank at the invitation of the prisoner, and which was returned by the latter to his father and afterwards found—all of which, presumably, might easily have been done, and in a case of so serious and striking a character as this ought to have been done. . . . Great strictness should be observed, and the clearest proof of the crime required, to safely warrant the conviction of the accused and the infliction of capital punishment. Such proof is wanting in this case to establish the death of the deceased by the means alleged in the indictment.

Equally insufficient are the facts proved to satisfactorily show that if in fact the deceased died from the effects of poison, it was administered by the prisoner; and if administered by him, that it was done knowingly and feloniously. It is not shown that if the whisky he conveyed to the deceased contained poison, he knew or had reason to know the fact. It is almost incredible that a rational being, in the absence of provocation of any sort, or the influence of some strong and controlling motive, would deliberately take the life of an unoffending fellow man. Yet in this case no provocation or motive whatever on the part of either the prisoner or his father, from whom he received the whisky of which the deceased drank, to murder the deceased, is shown by the evidence. It is true that the facts proved are sufficient to raise grave suspicions against the prisoner; but they fall far short of establishing his guilt clearly and satisfactorily, as required by the humane rules of the law, to warrant his conviction of the crime charged against him. On the other hand, the facts proved show that the wife of the deceased, three weeks before his death, had been supplied by her paramour with strychnine to administer to her husband; and there is nothing in the case to exclude the hypothesis that the death of the deceased may not have been occasioned by the felonious act of his own unfaithful wife. It was not proven that the prisoner at any time procured, or had in his possession, poison of any kind; nor was the attempt made to connect him with, or to show knowledge on his part of, the poison which was delivered by Henry Carroll to Sallie Young, to be administered to her husband.

In short, the facts proved are wholly insufficient to warrant the conviction of the plaintiff in error for the crime for which he has been sentenced to be hanged: and the judgment of the circuit court must, therefore, be reversed, the verdict of the jury set aside, and a new trial awarded him. [From John Henry Wigmore, *The Principles of Judicial Proof*]

Glossary

Addition: a rule of inference in symbolic logic; see endpapers.

Ad hominem: the fallacy of using a negative trait of a speaker as evidence that the speaker's statement is false or the argument weak.

Adequacy: the degree to which a hypothesis, if true, would explain a given explanandum.

Affirmative proposition: a categorical proposition asserting that all or some members of the class designated by the subject term are included in the class designated by the predicate term.

Affirming the antecedent *(modus ponens):* a deductive argument concluding that the consequent of a hypothetical proposition is true because the antecedent is true.

Antecedent: the component in a hypothetical proposition whose truth is asserted to be sufficient for the truth of the other component. In standard form, the proposition p in "if p then q."

Appeal to authority *(argumentum ad verecundiam):* the fallacy of using testimonial evidence for a proposition when the conditions for credibility are not satisfied, or the use of such evidence is inappropriate.

Appeal to emotion: the fallacy of trying to get someone to accept a proposition on the basis of an emotion one induces.

Appeal to force *(argumentum ad baculum):* the fallacy of trying to get someone to accept a proposition on the basis of a threat.

Appeal to ignorance *(argumentum ad ignorantiam):* the fallacy of using the absence of proof for a proposition as evidence for the truth of the opposing proposition.

Appeal to majority: the fallacy of using the fact that large numbers of people believe a proposition to be true as evidence of its truth.

Argument: a unit of reasoning in which one or more propositions (the premises) purport to provide evidence for the truth of another proposition (the conclusion).

Association: a rule of equivalence in symbolic and term logic; see endpapers.

Average: a statistic specifying the central value of the items in a given class on a given variable.

Begging the question (circular argument): the fallacy of trying to support a proposition with an argument in which that proposition is a premise.

Biconditional: 1) a compound proposition asserting that one component proposition is true if and only if the other component is true. 2) A rule of inference in symbolic logic; see endpapers.

Categorical proposition: a proposition containing a subject and a predicate term, and asserting that some or all of the referents of the subject term are included in or excluded from the class designated by the predicate term.

Categorical syllogism: a deductive argument containing two categorical premises, a categorical conclusion, and three terms, each term occurring in two propositions.

Classify: to group things into species and genuses according to their similarities and differences.

Commutation: a rule of inference in symbolic and term logic; see endpapers.

Complement: a term designating the class of all things excluded by another term.

Complex question: the fallacy of trying to get someone to accept a proposition by posing a question that presupposes it. A subcategory of **begging the question.**

Conclusion: the proposition whose truth an argument seeks to establish.

Conditional: see **Hypothetical proposition.**

Conditional proof: a method of proving that a conditional proposition follows from a set of premises; one assumes the antecedent and then derives the consequent from the antecedent together with the premises.

Conjunction: 1) a compound proposition asserting that two or more component propositions (the conjuncts) are all true. 2) A rule of inference in symbolic logic; see endpapers.

Connective: a logical structure that creates a compound proposition from component propositions. In term logic, a connective may also operate on terms.

Consequent: the component in a hypothetical proposition for the truth of which the truth of the other component is asserted to be sufficient. In standard form, the proposition q in "if p then q."

Constructive dilemma: a rule of inference in symbolic logic; see endpapers.

Contradictories: a pair of propositions which, in virtue of their logical form, could neither both be true nor both be false. A and O are contradictories in the square of opposition, as are E and I.

Contrapositive: 1) the proposition which results from replacing the subject term in a categorical proposition with the complement of the predicate, and the predicate with the complement of the subject; or which results from replacing the antecedent of a hypothetical proposition with the negation of the consequent and the consequent with the negation of the antecedent. 2) A rule of equivalence in symbolic and term logic; see endpapers.

Contraries: a pair of propositions which, in virtue of their logical form, could not both be true but could both be false. A and E in the square of opposition are contraries.

Converse: the proposition which results from switching the subject and predicate terms in a categorical proposition.

Copula: the verb of being ("is," "are," "was," etc.) that links subject and predicate terms in a categorical proposition.

Definition: a statement that identifies the referents of a concept by specifying the genus they belong to and their essential distinguishing characteristics.

De Morgan's Law: rules of equivalence in symbolic logic; see endpapers.

Denying the consequent *(modus tollens):* a deductive argument concluding that the antecedent of a hypothetical proposition is false because the consequent is false.

Destructive dilemma: a rule of inference in symbolic logic; see endpapers.

Dictum de Omni: a rule of inference in term logic; see endpapers.

Differentia: the part of a definition that distinguishes the referents of a concept from other species of the same genus.

Disjunct: a proposition that is a component of a disjunctive proposition.

Disjunction: a compound proposition containing two or more component propositions (the disjuncts), and asserting that at least one of them is true.

Disjunctive syllogism: a deductive argument with a disjunctive premise, other premises denying all but one of the disjuncts, and a conclusion affirming the remaining disjunct. DS is an inference rule in symbolic logic; see endpapers.

Distribution: 1) a property of a term in a categorical proposition; the term is distributed if and only if the proposition makes an assertion about all members of the class designated by the term. 2) A rule of equivalence in symbolic logic; see endpapers.

Diversion: the fallacy of trying to support one proposition by arguing for another proposition. A subcategory of **non sequitur.**

Double negation: a rule of equivalence in symbolic and term logic; see endpapers.

Existential generalization: a rule of inference in predicate logic; see endpapers.

Existential instantiation: a rule of inference in predicate logic; see endpapers.

Explanandum: a proposition for whose truth an explanation seeks to provide a cause or reason.

Exportation: a rule of equivalence in symbolic logic; see endpapers.

External negation: a rule of equivalence in term logic; see endpapers.

False alternative: the fallacy of excluding relevant possibilities without justification.

Figure: an identifying feature of a categorical syllogism, determined by the position of the middle term in the two premises.

Frequency: a statistic specifying the number or proportion of items in a class that have a given property.

Frequency distribution: a statistic specifying the proportion of items in a class that have each of the values on some variable.

Generalize: to infer that all members of a class have a trait from the premise that some members have it.

Genus: a class of things regarded as having various subcategories (its species).

Hypothesis: the proposition or propositions in an explanation that purport to show why another proposition (the explanandum) is true.

Hypothetical proposition: a compound proposition containing two component propositions (the antecedent and the consequent), and asserting that the truth of one component would be sufficient for the truth of the other.

Hypothetical syllogism: a rule of inference in symbolic logic; see endpapers.

Implication: a rule of equivalence in symbolic logic; see endpapers.

Internal negation: a rule of equivalence in term logic; see endpapers.

Logical strength: in an argument, the degree to which the truth of the premises would make it likely that the conclusion is true.

Major premise: the premise of a categorical syllogism that contains the major term.

Major term: the term that occurs in the predicate in the conclusion of a categorical syllogism as well as in one of the premises.

Method of agreement: a method of identifying a cause of an effect by isolating a factor common to a variety of cases in which the effect occurs.

Method of concomitant variations: a method of identifying a cause of an effect by isolating a factor whose variations are correlated with variations in the effect, all other factors remaining constant.

Method of difference: a method of identifying a cause of an effect by isolating a factor in whose presence the effect occurs and in whose absence the effect does not occur, all other factors remaining constant.

Method of residues: a method of identifying a cause of an effect by isolating that portion of the effect not explained by known causal relationships.

Middle term: the term in a categorical syllogism that occurs once in each of the premises.

Minor premise: the premise in a categorical syllogism that contains the minor term.

Minor term: the term in a categorical syllogism that occurs in the subject of the conclusion as well as in one of the premises.

Modus ponens: a rule of inference in symbolic logic; see endpapers. See also **Affirming the antecedent.**

Modus tollens: a rule of inference in symbolic logic; see endpapers. See also **Denying the consequent.**

Mood: an identifying feature of a categorical syllogism, determined by the logical forms of its premises and conclusion.

Negative instance: an item that belongs to a given class and does not possess the trait attributed to the class by a given generalization.

Negative proposition: a categorical proposition asserting that all or some members of the class designated by the subject term are excluded from the class designated by the predicate term.

Non sequitur: the fallacy of trying to support a proposition on the basis of irrelevant premises.

Obverse: the proposition that results from changing the quality of a categorical proposition and replacing the predicate term with its complement.

Particular proposition: a categorical proposition that makes an assertion about at least one but not all members of the class designated by its subject term.

Poisoning the well: the fallacy of trying to refute a statement or argument by showing that the speaker has a nonrational motive for adopting it. A subcategory of **ad hominem.**

Positive instance: an item that belongs to a given class and possesses the trait attributed to the class by a given generalization.

Post hoc: the fallacy of using the fact that one event preceded another as sufficient evidence for the conclusion that the first caused the second.

Predicate distribution: a rule of equivalence in term logic; see endpapers.

Premises: those propositions in an argument that purport to provide evidence for another proposition (the conclusion).

Pure hypothetical syllogism: a deductive argument with the logical form "if p then q; if q then r; therefore if p then r."

Quality: the affirmative or negative character of a categorical proposition.

Quantifier: the element in a statement's logical form that indicates "all" or "some." In classical (term) logic, a quantifier specifies whether the statement is about all or some of a subject term. In symbolic logic, a quantifier indicates whether a variable may represent all or some of the things in the world.

Quantifier-negation rule: a rule of equivalence in predicate logic; see endpapers.

Quantity: the particular or universal character of a categorical proposition.

Ratio: a statistic specifying the number of items in a class, or the sum of their values on a variable, per unit of some other class. A ratio is a **total** expressed in relative terms.

Reductio ad Absurdum (Reductio): a method of proving that a proposition follows from a set of premises by deriving a contradiction from the denial of the proposition together with the premises.

Scope: the portion of a statement in symbolic notation that is governed by a quantifier.

Simplification: a rule of inference in symbolic and term logic; see endpapers.

Singular proposition: a categorical proposition whose subject term designates a specific thing rather than a class.

Species: a class of things regarded as a subcategory of a wider class (a genus).

Straw man: the fallacy of trying to refute one proposition by arguing against another proposition. A subcategory of **non sequitur.**

Strength: See **Logical strength.**

Subalterns: the particular categorical propositions (I or O) considered in relation to the universal propositions of the same quality; the particular follows from the universal but not vice versa.

Subcontraries: a pair of propositions which, in virtue of their logical form, could both be true but could not both be false. I and O are subcontraries in the square of opposition.

Subjectivism: the fallacy of using the fact that one believes or wants a proposition to be true as evidence of its truth.

Tautology: a rule of equivalence in symbolic and term logic; see endpapers.

Total: a statistic specifying the number of items in a class or the sum of their values on a variable.

Truth table: a diagram displaying the truth or falsity of a compound proposition as a function of the truth or falsity of its components.

Tu quoque: the fallacy of trying to refute an accusation by showing that the speaker is guilty of it. A subcategory of **ad hominem.**

Universal generalization: a rule of inference in predicate logic; see endpapers.

Universal instantiation: a rule of inference in predicate logic; see endpapers.

Universal proposition: a categorical proposition that makes an assertion about all members of the class designated by its subject term. A and E are universal propositions.

Valence: in term logic, a property of a proposition in virtue of which it asserts existence (positive valence) or nonexistence (negative valence).

Validity: a property of a deductive argument; an argument is valid if and only if it would be impossible, in virtue of the logical form of the argument, for the premises to be true and the conclusion false.

Value: a trait regarded as a specific degree of a generic attribute (a variable).

Variable: in symbolic logic, a symbol that stands for an unnamed individual thing; in statistics, a trait regarded as a generic attribute that can exist in different degrees (values).

Answers to Practice Quizzes

![bar]

Chapter 2

Page 16

A.

Genus	Species	Other species
1. ANIMAL	MAN	CAT, DOG, MOUSE, ETC.
2. GARMENT	COAT	SHIRT, DRESS, ETC.
3. VEHICLE	CAR	TRUCK, BUS, ETC.
4. EMOTION	ANGER	FEAR, LOVE, ETC.
5. MATERIAL SUBSTANCE	SOLID	LIQUID, GAS

B.
1. Elton John, singer, performer, human
2. steer, cattle, mammal, animal, organism
3. square, rectangle, quadrilateral, figure
4. steel, alloy, metal, mineral
5. Exxon, multinational company, corporation, institution

Pages 22–23

1. Not mutually exclusive (hardback first editions); not a consistent principle.
2. Mutually exclusive, jointly exhaustive. Record size is not as essential as musical content (jazz, classical, rock, etc.), but a music store might find it necessary to sort by size for storage and display.
3. Not mutually exclusive (junk bread) or jointly exhaustive (dairy products); not a consistent principle.
4. Not mutually exclusive (foreign pornographic) or jointly exhaustive (horror, drama). Not a consistent principle.
5. Mutually exclusive, jointly exhaustive. Height is not essential in general, but might be essential for basketball coach or model agency.

6. Not mutually exclusive (individual aquatic); no consistent principle.
7. Not mutually exclusive (clerical jobs in a service industry); no consistent principle.
8. May not be mutually exclusive if people change their preferences. Not essential in general, but might be essential for sellers of party favors.

Pages 25–26

A.

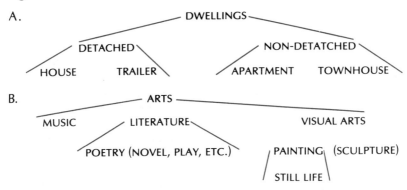

B.

C. Parliamentary governments are a type of democratic governments, and should be classified under the latter. The three branches are not types but components of democratic governments.

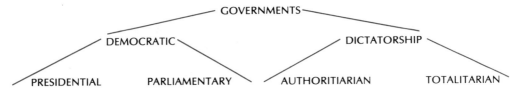

Chapter 3

Page 39

Genus is contained in first parentheses, differentia in second.
1. A pleat is (a fold) (in the fabric of a skirt). Too narrow: shirts and trousers can have pleats.
2. A salad is (a food dish) (containing lettuce). Too narrow: potato salad. Too broad: tacos can have lettuce.
3. An antidote is (a substance) (that counteracts snakebite). Too narrow: antidotes for other toxins.
4. A pen is (a writing implement) (that can be clipped to a pocket). Too narrow: not all pens have clips. Too broad: pencils can have clips.
5. To nod is (to move one's head) (forward and down, indicating assent). Too narrow: nodding off to sleep.

Page 43

1. A necklace is (a jewel) (worn on a pendant around the neck). Too narrow (rule 2): not all necklaces have jewels.
2. A squirrel is (a rat) (in a fur coat). Metaphorical (rule 6).
3. Liberty is (a political condition) (in which people are free). Circular (rule 4): "freedom" and "liberty" are synonymous.
4. An orphan is (a person) (who does not have a living parent). Too broad (rule 2): a sixty-year-old whose parents have died is not an orphan.
5. Garbage is what's left when you finish eating. No genus (rule 1). Too broad (rule 2): silverware.
6. A conservative is (a person) (who opposes legalized abortion). Too broad (rule 2): some liberals oppose it. Too narrow (rule 2): some conservatives don't oppose it. Nonessential (rule 3): stand on abortion is a consequence of underlying political values and beliefs. Negative (rule 5): doesn't say what conservatives stand *for*.
7. A drunk is (a person) (who is not sober). Negative (rule 5). May be circular (rule 4) if "sober" means "not drunk."
8. Education is when someone learns something. No genus (rule 1). Too narrow (rule 2): being educated is not the only way to learn things.
9. A conspiracy is (a collusion) (in machination). Obscure (rule 6).
10. Eloquence is (the ability) (to arouse emotions by means of words). Too broad (rule 2): insults.

Page 51

A newspaper is a periodical published on unbound paper, containing information on current events of interest to the general public.
Flattery is praise that is excessive and insincere.
An apartment is a rented dwelling unit in a multi-unit building.

Chapter 4

Pages 63–64

1. Same
2. Different
3. Basically the same, but (b) is a metaphorical statement that may express a more severe intellectual limitation than does (a).
4. Same
5. Different
6. Almost the same, since differences are chiefly in connotation, but "slob" in (b) implies sloppiness, which (a) does not imply.
7. Same
8. Same
9. Same
10. Different
11. Different
12. Different

Pages 70–71

"A" means "asserted," "e" means "expressed but not asserted."

1. John made a mistake (a)
   John acknowledged that he had made a mistake (a)
2. I would like a Jaguar XJ-S for Christmas (a)
   I have not been good this year (a)
   I would like a Jaguar XJ-S for Christmas, but I haven't been good this
      year (a)
3. If Deborah takes the new job, she will make more money (a)
   Deborah takes the new job (e)
   Deborah will make more money (e)
4. I met a man who had only one shoe (a)
5. I met George McGovern (a)
   George McGovern ran for president in 1972 (a)
6. All objects are made of atoms (e)
   Democritus believed that all objects are made of atoms (a)
   Democritus was a Greek philosopher (a)
7. Many insects communicate by means of chemical substances (a)
   The chemical substances by which insects communicate are known as
      pheromones (a)
8. Miss Devon is the district attorney (a)
   Miss Devon did not have enough evidence to convict the thief (a)
   The thief was guilty (a)
   Miss Devon knew he was guilty (a)
   Although Miss Devon did not have enough evidence to convict the
      thief, she knew he was guilty (a)
9. A harsh editorial appeared in the student newspaper (a)
   The president said that students should be seen but not heard (a)
   Students should be seen (e)
   Students should not be heard (e)
   Students should be seen but students should not be heard (e)
   After a harsh editorial appeared in the student newspaper, the college
      president said that students should be seen but not heard (a)
10. Man is a living organism (a)
    Man is mortal (a)
    Man is mortal because he is a living organism (a)
    Man is rational (a)
    Man is aware of his mortality (a)
    Man is aware of his mortality because he is rational (a)

Chapter 5

Pages 84–85

1. Argument. Premises: cable television can provide the viewer with more
   channels than broadcast television; cable television delivers a higher

quality picture. Conclusion: the number of cable subscribers will probably continue to grow.

2. Not an argument

3. Argument. Premises: the first cable companies increased the TV stations' audiences; the first cable companies increased the TV stations' advertising revenues. Conclusion: broadcasters welcomed the growth of the new industry.

4. Not an argument.

5. Not an argument.

6. Argument. Premise: it is rarely economical for two companies to lay cables in the same area and compete directly. Conclusions: cable television is a natural monopoly; cable television should be regulated by the government.

7. Argument. Premises: cable TV competes with broadcast TV, satellite TV, and other media; cable TV is a medium of communication; cable TV is protected by the First Amendment. Conclusion: cable TV should not be regulated by the government.

Pages 93–94

1. 1) Annette comes from a wealthy family
   2) Last week Annette bought a diamond choker for her ocelot

2. 1) It would not be a good idea to take the American Revolution course this term
   2) The American Revolution course conflicts with a course I need for my major
   3) My schedule would have more balance if I took a science course

3. 1) Key West is the southernmost city in the continental United States
   2) Key West is located at the tip of the Florida peninsula
   3) Key West enjoys year-round warm weather
   4) Key West is vulnerable to Caribbean hurricanes

4. 1) Tax reform is politically possible only if tax rates are reduced before loopholes are closed
   2) Until rates are reduced, loopholes are valuable to interest groups
   3) Many interest groups are powerful enough to block reform

5. 1) An encyclopedia is a valuable possession for a family to have
   2) An encyclopedia is well worth the money
   3) An encyclopedia is a quick reference tool for adults
   4) An encyclopedia provides children with a form of learning that complements what they get in school
   5) In school, children have to follow a structured program
   6) An encyclopedia lets children go from topic to topic following their own curiosity

$$\frac{(5) + (6)}{\downarrow}$$
$$\frac{(3) + (4)}{}$$
$$(1) \quad (2)$$

Pages 102–3

1. 1) Richard and Lisa are in love
   2) They have that dreamy look
   3) I just saw them talking together

(2)   (3)

(1)

This is a very weak argument. Two people who are not in love can talk and have a dreamy look because they are tired or day-dreaming.

2. 1) Without this welfare program, some poor people would have no means of support
   2) We should not eliminate the program
   3) The government has an absolute duty to provide everyone with at least the bare essentials of life

$$\frac{(1) \quad + \quad (3)}{\downarrow}$$
$$(2)$$

This is a very strong argument. If the government has the duty described in (3), and eliminating the program would violate the duty, then (2) follows logically.

3. 1) A welfare program is a type of expropriation
   2) A welfare program takes money from one person and gives it to another
   3) The function of government is to protect individual rights
   4) Individual rights include property rights
   5) The government should not engage in welfare

(2)

↓

(1) + (3) + (4)

↓

(5)

The first step is very strong, since expropriation means taking something away from people. There is more of a gap in the second step; the conclusion follows only on the implicit premise that property rights are violated by government expropriation. This is a substantive and controversial assumption. So the argument as a whole has only a moderate degree of strength.

4. 1) The Soviet Union wants to advance its interests in southern Africa
   2) The media have been agitating about apartheid in South Africa
   3) The Soviet Union wants to prevent the S.D.I.
   4) The media have run lots of hostile stories about S.D.I.
   5) The media are dupes of the Soviets

$$\underbrace{(1) + (2)}\searrow \quad \overbrace{(3) + (4)}\swarrow$$
$$(5)$$

This argument is very weak. The conclusion is a generalization, and it would take more than two examples to support it. In the case of each example, moreover, the premises support the conclusion only on the implicit premise that the media have no other possible reason for their position than subservience to the Soviet Union—a highly dubious assumption.

5. 1) 18-year-olds can vote
   2) 18-year-old males must register for the draft
   3) 18-year-olds are considered old enough to have these responsibilities
   4) 18-year-olds are old enough to decide whether to drink alcohol
   5) The drinking age should not be raised to 21

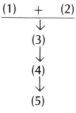

$$\underline{(1) \quad + \quad (2)}$$
$$\downarrow$$
$$(3)$$
$$\downarrow$$
$$(4)$$
$$\downarrow$$
$$(5)$$

The weak link in this argument is the step from (3) to (4). There is a sizable gap here that would have to be filled with two assumptions: a) that deciding about alcohol does not require a higher level of responsibility than voting or registering for the draft; and b) that 18-year-olds are responsible enough to vote and register (notice that (3) says only that they are *considered* to be responsible, not that they actually are). Both implicit premises would require support.

Chapter 6

Pages 116–17

1. Appeal to majority
2. Appeal to emotion

3. Subjectivism
4. Appeal to majority
5. Appeal to force
6. Appeal to emotion

Pages 122–23

1. Appeal to authority
2. *Ad hominem*—poisoning the well
3. *Ad hominem*
4. Appeal to authority
5. *Ad hominem*—tu quoque

Pages 133–34

1. Begging the question
2. *Non sequitur*
3. *Non sequitur*
4. *Post hoc*
5. Begging the question
6. Appeal to ignorance
7. False alternative
8. Begging the question
9. *Post hoc*
10. *Non sequitur*—straw man
11. False alternative
12. Begging the question

Chapter 7

Page 145

1. Most successful salesmen are outgoing people
2. The bell rings only when someone is at the door
3. a) Dr. Robert Jones is an expert on highway safety
   b) Dr. Robert Jones was objective in his testimony
4. a) It is desirable for a recording to reproduce the spatial features of music
   b) Most compact disk recordings do not reproduce the spatial features of music
5. If the telecommunications industry is deregulated, it will be able to act quickly and flexibly to exploit the new telecommunication technology.

Page 151

1) Within the past year you have been in fear of some personal attack
2) You have a stick
3) The stick is inscribed with a date of a year ago
4) You have not had the stick more than a year
5) You have filled the stick with lead
6) You have made the stick a formidable weapon

7) You would not have made the stick a formidable weapon unless you feared some danger

$$
\begin{array}{cc}
(5) & (3) \\
\downarrow & \downarrow \\
\end{array}
$$
$$
\underline{(2) + (6) + (7) + (4)}
$$
$$
\downarrow
$$
$$
(1)
$$

Pages 159–60

A1) The government should increase funds for cultural activities
A2) Support for cultural activities is a vital government function
A3) The funds have not kept pace with inflation
A4) Cultural activities are crucial to the life of the nation
A5) Cultural activities cannot be sustained in the market
Aa) Government subsidies are the only alternative to the market

B1) The government should not fund cultural activities
B2) Cultural activities involve fundamental values and beliefs
B3) Taxpayers should not be forced to support values and beliefs they do not share
B4) Cultural activities are similar to religion
B5) Taxpayers cannot be forced to subsidize religion
B6) Cultural activities can be funded by voluntary contributions
B7) Religion and private colleges are supported by voluntary contributions

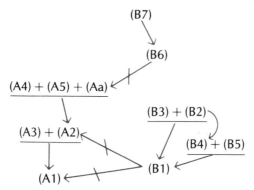

Chapter 8

Page 174

1. All [men] are [rational beings]. Universal affirmative; A
2. Some [baseball players] are not [golfers]. Particular negative; O
3. No [person] is [a perfect being]. Universal negative; E
4. All [families that play together] are [families that stay together]. Universal affirmative; A
5. Some [things] are [things better left unsaid]. Particular affirmative; I

6. No [one who laughs at my teddy bear] is [a friend of mine]. Universal negative; E
7. All [political parties that win presidential elections] are [parties that can expect to lose congressional seats two years later]. Universal affirmative; A
8. Some [members of the Capitol Rotunda Exercise and Reducing Club] are not [members who have been pulling their own weight]. Particular negative; O
9. All [men who seek fame for its sake] are [foolish people]. Universal affirmative; A
10. [The window in my study] is not [a thing that is open]. Singular negative; E

Page 179

1. E false, I true, O false
2. A false, I false, O true
3. E false, A undetermined, O undetermined
4. A false, E undetermined, I undetermined
5. O true, E undetermined, I undetermined
6. I true, A undetermined, O undetermined
7. E true, A false, O true
8. A true, E false, I true

Page 181

1. All [machines—D] are [manufactured objects—U]
2. No [inanimate object—D] is [a conscious thing—D]
3. Some [countries—U] are not [countries at peace—D]
4. Some [trees—U] are [deciduous plants—U]
5. All [days—D] are [new beginnings—U]
6. Some of [my best friends—U] are [trapeze artists—U]
7. No [one with any manners—D] is [a person who would clean his teeth at the dinner table—D]
8. Some [cars—U] are [lemons—U]

Page 188

1. Some non-P are non-S. Does not follow
2. No P are S. Follows
3. Some P are not S. Does not follow
4. No S is non-P. Follows
5. Some non-P are not non-S. Follows
6. All S are non-P. Follows
7. Some S are not P. Follows
8. Some P are non-S. Follows
9. No P is S. Does not follow
10. All P are non-S. Does not follow
11. Some S are non-P. Follows
12. All P are non-S. Follows

Chapter 9

Pages 197–98

A. 1. All M are P
   Some S are M
   Some S are P
  2. No M is P
   Some M are S
   Some S are not P
  3. All P are M
   No S are M
   No S are P
  4. All P are M
   All M are S
   Some S are P
  5. Some P are M
   No S is M
   Some S are not P

B. 1. All geniuses are eccentric
   No Greek poet was eccentric
   No Greek poet was a genius   [AEE–2]
  2. Some bureaucrats are not chosen on the basis of their ability
   All bureaucrats are civil servants
   Some civil servants are not chosen on the basis of their ability   [OAO–3]
  3. Nothing that is subject to friction is capable of perpetual motion
   All machines are subject to friction
   No machine is capable of perpetual motion   [EAE–1]
  4. Some good poems are difficult
   All good poems are worth reading
   Some things worth reading are difficult   [IAI–3]
  5. All ambitious people can learn logic
   All people reading this book are ambitious
   All people reading this book can learn logic   [AAA–1]

Pages 204–5

1. All people with things to hide plead the Fifth
   Tom pleaded the Fifth
   Tom has something to hide
   AAA–2. Invalid: undistributed middle
2. No Protestant church accepts the authority of the Pope
   The United Church of Christ does not accept the authority of the Pope
   The United Church of Christ is a Protestant church
   EEA–2. Invalid: two negative premises, affirmative conclusion
3. No freshman will graduate this year
   Some students in this class are freshman

No student in this class will graduate this year
EIE–1. Invalid: illicit minor
4. No paperback book is expensive
Some paperback books are well-made
Some well-made things are not expensive
EIO–3. Valid
5. Some people on low salaries are free-lancers
All journalists are people on low salaries
Some journalists are free-lancers
IAI–1. Invalid: undistributed middle
6. Some inspired ideas are not reasonable
All of the proposals are reasonable
Some of the proposals are not inspired
OAO–2. Invalid: illicit major
7. No perennial blooms all season
Some flowers that bloom all season flourish in the shade
Some flowers that flourish in the shade are not perennials
EIO–4. Valid

Page 211

Syllogism	*Combined diagram*	*Conclusion*

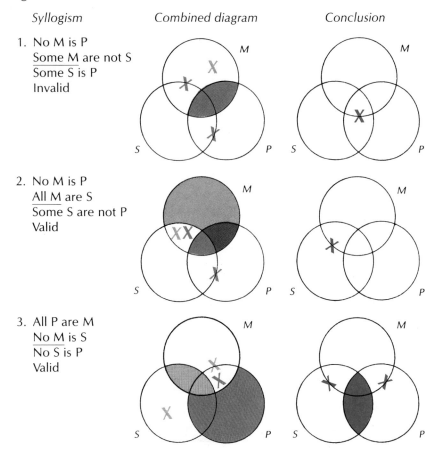

1. No M is P
   Some M are not S
   Some S is P
   Invalid

2. No M is P
   All M are S
   Some S are not P
   Valid

3. All P are M
   No M is S
   No S is P
   Valid

Syllogism	Combined diagram	Conclusion

4. Some P are not M
   Some S are not M
   Some S are not P
   Invalid

5. Some M are P
   All M are S
   Some S are P
   Valid

6. Some M are P
   All S are M
   Some S are not P
   Invalid

7. Some P are not M
   All S are M
   Some S are not P
   Invalid

8. All P are M
   Some M are S
   Some S are P
   Invalid

Syllogism	Combined diagram	Conclusion

9. No M is P
   Some S are M
   Some S are not P
   Valid

10. All P are M
    No S is M
    No S is P
    Valid

Page 214

1. No creature whose actions are wholly determined by heredity and environment is a moral agent
   (All animals other than man are creatures whose actions are determined by heredity and environment)
   No animal other than man is a moral agent   [EAE–1]
2. (All things that affect the distribution of power are important)
   All economic arrangements affect the distribution of power
   All economic arrangements are important   [AAA–1]
3. No one who trades stocks on the basis of proprietary information is an honest businessman
   (Some investment bankers trade stocks on the basis of proprietary information)
   Some investment bankers are not honest businessmen   [EIO–1]
4. Some Cypriots are Moslems
   (All Cypriots are Europeans)
   Some Europeans are Moslems   [IAI–3]
5. (All figures with four sides are rectangles)
   All squares are figures with four sides
   All squares are rectangles   [AAA–1]
6. (No one who takes bribes is honest)
   Some politicians have taken bribes
   Some politicians are not honest   [EIO–1]
7. All foods that generate stomach acid are bad for ulcer patients
   All fried foods generate stomach acid
   (All fried foods are bad for ulcer patients)   [AAA–1]

8. (All demands deserving serious consideration are demands compatible
    with the labor contract that is still in effect)
    <u>No union</u> demand is compatible with the labor contract that is still in
    effect
    No union demand deserves any serious consideration   [AEE–2]
Note: wherever the missing premise is an I or E proposition, it would also be
acceptable to use the converse; this will change the figure of the syllogism,
but not its validity.

Chapter 10

Page 223

1. Either [I'm hearing things] or [someone is out in the hall singing "Jingle
   Bells"]
   <u>I'm not</u> hearing things
   Someone is out in the hall singing "Jingle Bells"
   Valid
2. Either [I will get the book here in town] or [I will get the book in New
   York next weekend]
   <u>I will</u> not get the book here in town
   I will get the book in New York next weekend
   Valid
3. Either [I'm out of money] or [I made a mistake in my checkbook]
   <u>I made</u> a mistake in my checkbook
   I am not out of money
   Invalid
4. (Either [Jackson is a liberal] or [Jackson is a conservative])
   <u>Jackson is</u> not a conservative
   Jackson is a liberal
   Valid
5. Either [we will close the plant on Labor Day] or [we will pay the workers
   twice the regular wage]
   <u>We will</u> not close the plant on Labor Day
   We will pay the workers twice the regular wage
   Valid

Pages 227–28

1. If [he had mentioned her name], then [I would have hit him]
   <u>He did</u> not mention her name
   I did not hit him
   Denying the antecedent; invalid
2. If [God had wanted man to fly], then [He would not have given us
   Buicks]

He has given us Buicks
(He does not want us to fly)
Denying the consequent *(modus tollens)*; valid

3. If [a child is deprived of affection as an infant], then [he will learn not to expect it]
   If [a child learns not to expect affection], then [he won't seek it out later in life]
   If [a child is deprived of affection as an infant], then [he won't seek it out later in life]
   Pure hypothetical syllogism; valid

4. If [someone had been snooping around here last night], then [there would be footprints]
   There are footprints
   Someone was snooping around here last night
   Affirming the consequent; invalid

5. (If [the battery were dead], then [the lights would still be working])
   The lights are not working
   The battery is not dead
   Denying the consequent *(modus tollens)*; valid

                          OR

   (If [the lights are still working], then [the battery is not dead])
   The lights are still working
   The battery is not dead
   Affirming the antecedent *(modus ponens)*; valid

6. If [you wanted to marry him], then [you would not be running around with other men]
   You are running around with other men
   You do not want to marry him
   Denying the consequent *(modus tollens)*; valid

7. If [the Soviet Union completes a missile defense system before we do], then [they will pose a credible threat of a first strike]
   If [the Soviet Union poses a credible threat of a first strike], then [they will gain enormous leverage over us in any confrontation]
   If [the Soviet Union completes a missile defense system before we do], then [they will gain enormous leverage over us in any confrontation]
   Pure hypothetical syllogism; valid

8. If [our visual system did not have some way of detecting edges], then [we could not perceive objects]
   (We can perceive objects)
   Our visual system has some way of detecting edges
   Denying the consequent *(modus tollens)*; valid

Page 231

1. Hypothetical: If you miss your first serve in tennis, then you get a second try
2. Hypothetical: If you miss your second try, then you lose the point

3. Hypothetical: If a car did not have a cooling system, then its engine would rapidly overheat
4. Hypothetical: If you do not call me first, then I'll call you
5. Disjunctive: Either speak now or forever hold your peace
6. Hypothetical: If bubbles form in the test tube, then a gas is being produced by the reaction
7. Hypothetical: If a term in the conclusion of a valid categorical syllogism is distributed, then the term is distributed in the premise in which it occurs
8. Hypothetical: If you have not satisfied the prerequisites, then you may not take this course
9. Disjunctive: Either I will not make dinner or I will not take out the trash
10. Hypothetical: If I go out with you tonight, then you promise not to bring your parrot AND If you promise not to bring your parrot, then I will go out with you tonight.

Chapter 11

Pages 241–42

1. All computers that can run Lotus's Symphony program have 320 kilobytes of memory
   <u>My computer</u> does not have 320 kilobytes of memory
   My computer cannot run Lotus's Symphony program
   Valid
2. (Either the Constitution merely reflects the economic interests of the Founding Fathers, or it reflects their intellectual commitment to the principles of natural rights and democratic government)
   <u>The Constitution</u> does not merely reflect the economic interests of the Founding Fathers
   The Constitution reflects the commitment of the Founding Fathers to the principles of natural rights and democratic government
   Valid
3. All people who can strike a log in just the right place are people with a good eye
   <u>All people</u> who can strike a log with an ax in just the right place are people who can split a log with one blow
   All people who can split a log with one blow are people with a good eye
   Invalid: illicit minor
4. If the Earth's crust were a single rigid layer, then continental drift could not have occurred
   <u>Continental drift</u> has occurred
   (The Earth's crust is not a single rigid layer)
   Valid
5. Some algae exist at 250 meters below the surface of the ocean
   (<u>All algae</u> are plants employing photosynthesis)

Some plants employing photosynthesis exist at 250 meters below the
   surface of the ocean
Valid

Page 253

1. a) No clergyman is a liar
   1) Some of the witnesses are clergymen
   b) Some of the witnesses are not liars

   2) If Jones was not at the meeting, then all the witnesses are liars
   b) Some of the witnesses are not liars
   c) Jones was at the meeting
Valid

2. 1) All metals that oxidize at normal temperatures are metals that rust
   a) No metal containing chromium is a metal that oxidizes at normal
       temperatures
   b) No metal containing chromium is a metal that rusts

   b) No metal containing chromium is a metal that rusts
   2) Some steel is metal containing chromium
   3) Some steel is not metal that rusts
Invalid: first step is illicit major

3. a) All criminals who leave fingerprints all over the place are sloppy
   1) The killer left fingerprints all over the place
   b) The killer was sloppy

   2) If the killer had been a pro, he would not have been sloppy
   b) The killer was sloppy
   3) The killer was not a pro
Valid

4. 1) All beings that possess a rational faculty are human beings
   2) All beings that possess a sense of humor are beings that possess a
       rational faculty
   a) All beings that possess a sense of humor are human beings

   a) All beings that possess a sense of humor are human beings
   b) No lower animal is a human being
   3) No lower animal is a being that possesses a sense of humor
Valid

5. 1) All conscious beings are living organisms
   a) No computer is a living organism
   2) No computer is a conscious being

   2) No computer is a conscious being
   3) Some computers can manipulate symbols
   4) Some things that can manipulate symbols are not conscious beings
Valid

Chapter 12

Pages 270–71
1. $M \cdot A$
2. $\smallsmile T$
3. $T \cdot H$
4. $J \cdot C$
5. $\smallsmile C$
6. $\smallsmile W$
7. $D \cdot N$
8. $C \cdot B$
9. $C \cdot F$
10. $\smallsmile(\smallsmile W)$

Page 274
1. $S \supset B$
2. $C \supset M$
3. $R \vee G$
4. $I \supset G$
5. $L \vee G$
6. $T \supset P$
7. $S \supset W$
8. $B \vee M$
9. $\smallsmile P \supset S$
10. $S \supset W$

Pages 277–78
1. $R \cdot V$
2. $J \supset M$
3. $N \vee L$
4. $A \cdot L$
5. $\smallsmile C$
6. $Y \supset I$
7. $B \cdot W$
8. $L \supset R$
9. $L \vee D$
10. $\smallsmile S$
11. $S \vee L$
12. $\smallsmile A \supset F$
13. $W \supset Q$
14. $B \cdot A$
15. $\smallsmile B \supset C$

Page 282
1. $\smallsmile H \cdot S$

2. $(P \lor B) \bullet \smallfrown P'$
3. $(L \bullet W) \bullet \smallfrown H$
4. $P \bullet (W \supset C)$
5. $(M \bullet B) \lor (S \bullet R)$
6. $I \equiv Y$
7. $(Y \bullet I) \supset T$
8. $(L \bullet D \bullet D') \bullet P$
9. $\smallfrown G \supset (R \lor C)$
10. $(N \supset \smallfrown R) \bullet (E \supset \smallfrown S)$
11. $D \supset (F \bullet S)$
12. $(F \lor K) \bullet \smallfrown (F \bullet K)$
13. $\smallfrown Q \bullet (Q \supset K)$
14. $\smallfrown (A \supset \smallfrown G)$
15. $D \supset (\smallfrown C \supset F)$
16. $\smallfrown S \bullet \smallfrown (R \lor G) \bullet F$
17. $(Y \supset I) \bullet (F \supset T)$
18. $V \supset [\smallfrown (R \lor P) \supset J]$
19. $W \equiv [(C \supset F) \bullet (H \supset B)]$
20. $\{[(O \lor M) \bullet T] \supset C\} \bullet (\smallfrown L \supset \smallfrown C)$

Pages 287–88

1. Invalid
2. Valid
3. Valid
4. Valid
5. Invalid
6. Invalid
7. Invalid
8. Valid
9. Invalid
10. Valid

Page 290

1. DS
2. MP
3. CD
4. Simp
5. HS
6. Add
7. Conj
8. DD

Page 293

1. 1. $A \lor B$
   2. $A \supset C$
   3. $\smallfrown C / B$

      4. $\backsim A$ 2,3 MT
      5. B 1, 4 DS
  2. 1. $D \supset E$
      2. $F \supset G$
      3. $D \vee F / E \vee G$
      4. $(D \supset E) \bullet (F \supset G)$ 1,2 Conj
      5. $E \vee F$ 3,4 CD
  3. 1. $H \supset I$
      2. $J \supset K$
      3. $H \vee J$
      4. $\backsim K / I$
      5. $\backsim J$ 2,4 MT
      6. H 3,5 DS
      7. I 1,6 MP
  4. 1. $(A \vee B) \supset [C \bullet (D \supset E]$
      2. $A / D \supset E$
      3. $A \vee B$ 1 Add
      4. $C \bullet (D \supset E)$ 1,3 MP
      5. $D \supset E$ 4 Simp
  5. 1. $(F \bullet G) \vee H$
      2. $H \supset I$
      3. $\backsim (F \bullet G) / I \vee G$
      4. H 1,3 DS
      5. I 2,4 MP
      6. $I \vee G$ 5 Add
  6. 1. $(J \supset K) \supset (L \bullet M)$
      2. $(N \vee O) \supset (J \supset K)$
      3. O / L
      4. $(N \vee O) \supset (L \bullet M)$ 1,2 HS
      5. $N \vee O$ 3, Add
      6. $L \bullet M$ 4,5 MP
      7. L 6 Simp
  7. 1. $A \vee B$
      2. $C \supset D$
      3. $\backsim A \bullet \backsim D / B \bullet \backsim C$
      4. $\backsim A$ 3 Simp
      5. B 1,4 DS
      6. $\backsim D$ 3 Simp
      7. $\backsim C$ 2,6 MT
      8. $B \bullet \backsim C$ 5,7 Conj
8. 1. $(E \supset F) \bullet (\backsim F \vee \backsim G)$
      2. $H \supset I$
      3. $I \supset G / \backsim E \vee \backsim H$
      4. $H \supset G$ 2,3 HS
      5. $E \supset F$ 1 Simp
      6. $(E \supset F) \bullet (H \supset G)$ 4,5 Conj
      7. $\backsim F \vee \backsim G$ 1 Simp
      8. $\backsim E \vee \backsim H$ 6,7 DD

Page 297

1. Com
2. Dist
3. DM
4. DN
5. Assoc
6. Com
7. Taut
8. DM

Pages 298–99

1. Imp
2. Bicon
3. Contra
4. Exp
5. Imp
6. Contra
7. Bicon
8. Imp

Page 300

1. 1. $(B \bullet C) \lor \mathord{\sim} A$
   2. $B \supset D \ / \ A \supset D$
   3. $\mathord{\sim} A \lor (B \bullet C)$ 1 Com
   4. $(\mathord{\sim} A \lor B) \bullet (\mathord{\sim} A \lor C)$ 3 Dist
   5. $\mathord{\sim} A \lor B$ 4 Simp
   6. $A \supset B$ 5 Imp
   7. $A \supset D$ 2,6 HS

2. 1. $(E \lor F) \supset G$
   2. $H \supset E$
   3. $\mathord{\sim} H \supset F \ / \ G$
   4. $\mathord{\sim} E \supset \mathord{\sim} H$ 2 Contra
   5. $\mathord{\sim} E \supset F$ 3 HS
   6. $\mathord{\sim}\mathord{\sim} E \lor F$ 5 Imp
   7. $E \lor F$ 6 DN
   8. G 1,7 MP

3. 1. $(I \lor J) \supset K$
   2. $(L \lor M) \supset \mathord{\sim} K$
   3. $M \ / \ \mathord{\sim} J$
   4. $L \lor M$ 3 Add
   5. $\mathord{\sim} K$ 2,4 MP
   6. $\mathord{\sim}(I \lor J)$ 1,5 MT
   7. $\mathord{\sim} I \bullet \mathord{\sim} J$ 6 DM
   8. $\mathord{\sim} J$ 7 Simp

4. 1. $A \lor (B \supset C)$
   2. $\mathord{\sim} C \ / \ B \supset A$

3. $A \lor (\neg B \lor C)$ 1 Imp
4. $(A \lor \neg B) \lor C$ 3 Assoc
5. $A \lor \neg B$ 2,4 DS
6. $\neg B \lor A$ 5 Com
7. $B \supset A$ 6 Imp

5. 1. $(D \bullet E) \lor (F \bullet G)$
  2. $(D \supset H) \bullet (F \supset I) \,/\, H \lor I$
  3. $[(D \bullet E) \lor F] \bullet [(D \bullet E) \lor G]$ 1 Dist
  4. $(D \bullet E) \lor F$ 3 Simp
  5. $F \lor (D \bullet E)$ 4 Com
  6. $(F \lor D) \bullet (F \lor E)$ 5 Dist
  7. $F \lor D$ 6 Simp
  8. $D \lor F$ 7 Com
  9. $H \lor I$ 2,8 CD

6. 1. $(J \supset K) \supset (J \supset L)$
  2. $J \bullet \neg L \,/\, \neg K$
  3. $\neg\neg(J \bullet \neg L)$ 2 DN
  4. $\neg(J \supset L)$ 3 Imp
  5. $\neg(J \supset K)$ 1,4 MT
  6. $\neg(\neg J \lor K)$ 5 Imp
  7. $\neg\neg J \bullet \neg K$ 6 DM
  8. $\neg K$ 7 Simp

7. 1. $(A \supset B) \bullet (A \supset C)$
  2. $(B \bullet C) \supset (D \bullet E)$
  3. $\neg D \,/\, \neg A$
  4. $\neg D \lor \neg E$ 3 Add
  5. $\neg(D \bullet E)$ 4 DM
  6. $\neg(B \bullet C)$ 2,5 MT
  7. $\neg B \lor \neg C$ 6 DM
  8. $\neg A \lor \neg A$ 1,7 DD
  9. $\neg A$ 8 Taut

8. 1. $(F \bullet G) \supset H$
  2. F
  3. $(I \supset \neg H) \bullet (F \supset G) \,/\, G \equiv H$
  4. $F \supset (G \supset H)$ 1 Exp
  5. $G \supset H$ 2,4 MP
  6. $I \lor F$ 2 Add
  7. $\neg H \lor G$ 3,6 CD
  8. $H \supset G$ 7 Imp
  9. $(G \supset H) \bullet (H \supset G)$ 5,8 Conj
  10. $G \equiv H$ 9 Bicon

Pages 303–4

1. 1. $A \supset (B \lor C)$
  2. $\neg C \,/\, A \supset B$
  3. A Assump
  4. $B \lor C$ 1,3 MP

      5. *B*   2,4 DS
    6. *A* ⊃ *B*   3–5 CP

2. 1. *D* ⊃ (*E* ⊃ *F*)
   2. *D* ⊃ (*F* ⊃ *G*) / *D* ⊃ (*E* ⊃ *G*)
        3. *D*   Assump
        4. *E* ⊃ *F*   1,3 MP
        5. *F* ⊃ *G*   2,3 MP
        6. *E* ⊃ *G*   4,5 HS
   7. *D* ⊃ (*E* ⊃ *G*)   3–6 CP

3. 1. (*H* ⊃ *I*) ⊃ *J*
   2. (*H* • ⌐ *I*) ⊃ *J* / *J*
        3. ⌐*J*   Assump
        4. ⌐(*H* ⊃ *I*)   1,3 MT
        5. ⌐(*H* • ⌐ *I*)   2,3 MT
        6. *H* ⊃ *I*   5 Imp
        7. (*H* ⊃ *I*) • ⌐ (*H* ⊃ *I*)   4,6 Conj
   8. *J*   3–7 RA

4. 1. *K* ⊃ (*L* ≡ *M*)
   2. ⌐*L* / ⌐*K* ∨ ⌐*M*
        3. *K*   Assump
        4. *L* ≡ *M*   1,3 MP
        5. (*L* ⊃ *M*) • (*M* ⊃ *L*)   4 Bicon
        6. *M* ⊃ *L*   5 Simp
        7. ⌐*M*   2,6 MT
   8. *K* ⊃ ⌐*M*   3–7 CP
   9. ⌐*K* ∨ ⌐*M*   8 Imp

5. 1. ⌐(*A* • *B*) ∨ (*C* ⊃ *D*)
   2. *A* ∨ ⌐*C*
   3. *C* / *B* ⊃ *D*
   4. ⌐⌐*C*   3 DN
   5. *A*   2,4 DS
        6. *B*   Assump
        7. *A* • *B*   5,6 Conj
        8. ⌐⌐(*A* • *B*)   7 DN
        9. *C* ⊃ *D*   1,8 DS
       10. *D*   3,9 MP
  11. *B* ⊃ *D*   6–10 CP

6. 1. (*E* ⊃ *F*) • (*G* ⊃ *H*)
   2. *E* ∨ (*I* ⊃ *G*) / *I* ⊃ (*F* ∨ *H*)
   3. *E* ∨ (⌐*I* ∨ *G*)   2 Imp
   4. (⌐*I* ∨ *G*) ∨ *E*   3 Com
   5. ⌐*I* ∨ (*G* ∨ *E*)   4 Assoc
   6. *I* ⊃ (*G* ∨ *E*)   5 Imp
        7. *I*   Assump
        8. *G* ∨ *E*   6,7 MP
        9. *E* ∨ *G*   8 Com
       10. *F* ∨ *H*   1,9 CD
  11. *I* ⊃ (*F* ∨ *H*)   7–10 CP

7. 1. $(J \supset K) \supset (L \bullet M)$
   2. $K \supset N$
   3. $L \supset \neg N \ / \ \neg K$

4.	K	Assump
5.	N	2,4 MP
6.	$\neg\neg N$	5 DN
7.	$\neg L$	3,6 MT
8.	$\neg L \vee \neg M$	7 Add
9.	$\neg(L \bullet M)$	8 DM
10.	$\neg(J \supset K)$	1,9 MT
11.	$\neg J \vee K$	4 Add
12.	$J \supset K$	11 Imp
13.	$(J \supset K) \bullet \neg (J \supset K)$	10,12 Conj
14.	$\neg K$	4–13 RA

8. 1. $(A \vee B) \supset C$
   2. $\neg A \supset (D \bullet E) \ / \ C \vee D$

3.	$\neg C$	Assump
4.	$\neg (A \vee B)$	1,3 MT
5.	$\neg A \bullet \neg B$	4 DM
6.	$\neg A$	5 Simp
7.	$D \bullet E$	2,6 MP
8.	D	7 Simp
9.	$\neg C \supset D$	3–8 CP
10.	$\neg\neg C \vee D$	9 Imp
11.	$C \vee D$	10 DN

Chapter 13

Page 315

1. Bt
2. Pr
3. Bs
4. $Vm \bullet Rh$
5. $Cm \vee Nm$
6. $Sw \supset Li$
7. $Ci \bullet \neg Hy$
8. $Ww \supset (Dw \vee Mw)$

Pages 318–19

1. $(x)(Sx \supset Bx)$
2. $(\exists x)(Sx \bullet Bx)$
3. $(x)(Px \supset \neg Ox)$
4. $(\exists x)(Px \bullet \neg Sx)$
5. $(\exists x)(Kx \bullet Ax)$
6. $(x)(Cx \supset Bx)$

7. $(\exists x)(Kx \bullet Sx)$
8. $(x)(Fx \supset {\sim}Sx)$
9. $(\exists x)[Gx \bullet ({\sim}Rx \vee {\sim}Ax)]$
10. $(x)[Gx \supset (Rx \supset Ax)]$

Page 321

1. $(x)Gx$
2. $(\exists x)Sx$
3. $(\exists x)(Gx \bullet {\sim}Sx)$
4. $(x)(Cx \supset Sx)$
5. $(\exists x)(Px \bullet Gx)$
6. $(x)(Fx \supset {\sim}Tx)$
7. $(x)(Tx \supset Fx)$
8. $(\exists x)(Cx \bullet Tx)$
9. $(x)[(Cx \bullet Tx) \supset Fx]$
10. $(x)[Tx \supset (Ex \vee Dx)]$
11. $(x)[(Dx \vee Sx) \supset (Lx \bullet Fx)]$
12. $(\exists x)[(Nx \bullet Px) \bullet {\sim}Wx]$
13. $(x)[(Px \bullet {\sim}Sx) \bullet Ex]$
14. $(x)[Fx \supset ({\sim}Wx \supset {\sim}Gx)]$
15. $(x)[Ex \supset (Sx \bullet Cx)]$

Note: Statements 2–3, 5, 8, 12–13 have existential import; the others lack it.

Page 324

1. $(\exists x)(Bx \bullet Cx)$
2. $(\exists x)(Px \bullet Gx) \bullet (y)(Py \supset {\sim}Hy)$
3. $(x)(Px \supset Cx) \supset (y)(Gy \supset {\sim}My)$
4. $(\exists x)(Lx \bullet {\sim}Ex)$
5. ${\sim}(x)(Lx \supset Ex)$
6. $(\exists x)[Px \bullet (Wx \vee Rx)]$ or $(\exists x)(Px \bullet Wx) \vee (\exists x)(Px \bullet Rx)$
7. $(x)[Px \supset (Sx \bullet Mx)]$ or $(x)(Px \supset Sx) \bullet (y)(Py \supset My)$
8. $(x)[Cx \supset (Mx \vee Lx)]$

Page 326

1. Lmc
2. $Riad$
3. $(\exists x)(Ax \bullet A'ax)$
4. $(\exists x)(Sx \bullet S'xe)$
5. $(x)(Rx \supset Lxr)$
6. $(\exists x)(Px \bullet {\sim}Fxs)$
7. $(\exists x)(Axq \bullet Cx)$
8. $(\exists x)(Px \bullet Exp) \supset (\exists y)(Ay \bullet Gy)$

Page 329

1. Amd
2. $Sms \bullet Nmn$

3. *Bmsn*
4. $(\exists x)(Dx \bullet Hix)$
5. $(\exists x)(Fxd \bullet Mpx)$
6. $(\exists x)(Lx \bullet Hmx)$
7. $\smallsmile(\exists x)Ex \supset \smallsmile(\exists x)Gx$
8. $(\exists x)(Aix \bullet \smallsmile A'xi)$
9. $(x)(y)[(Sx \bullet Fy) \supset Oxy]$
10. $(\exists x)[Fx \bullet (y)(Sy \supset Oxy)]$
11. $\smallsmile(\exists x)(Rx \bullet Ixq)$ or $(x)(Rx \supset \smallsmile Ixq)$
12. $(x)(y)[(Sx \bullet Ty) \supset \smallsmile Cxy)$
13. $(\exists x)(y)(Wy \supset \smallsmile Lxy)$
14. $(x)(Wx \supset Mx) \supset \smallsmile(y)(My \supset Ly)$
15. $(x)[Px \supset (\exists y)(Fxy)]$
16. $\smallsmile(\exists x)(\exists y)[(Sx \bullet Py) \bullet Hxy]$
17. $(x)(y)\{[(Px \bullet Uy) \bullet Bxym] \supset (Fx \vee Mx)\}$
18. $(x)\{Px \supset \smallsmile(y)(z)[(Py \bullet Tz) \supset P'xyz]\}$

Page 331

1, 2, 4, 5 and 7 are equivalent by QN.
3, 6, and 8 are not.

Page 337

1. E1.   Valid
2. EG.   Valid
3. U1   Invalid
4. EG   Valid
5. E1   Invalid
6. U1   Valid
7. U1   Valid
8. E1   Invalid

Pages 342–43

1. 1. $(x)(Px \supset Qx)$
    2. $(\exists x)(Px \bullet Rx)$ / $(\exists x)(Rx \bullet Qx)$
    3. $Pa \bullet Ra$ 2   EI
    4. Pa 3   Simp
    5. $Pa \supset Qa$ 1   UI
    6. Qa 4,5 MP
    7. Ra 3   Simp
    8. $Ra \bullet Qa$ 6,7 Conj
    9. $(\exists x)(Rx \bullet Qx)$ 8   EG
2. 1. $(x)(Px \supset \smallsmile Qx)$
    2. $(x)(Rx \supset Qx)$ / $(x)(Rx \supset \smallsmile Px)$
    3. $Ra \supset Qa$ 2   UI
    4. $Pa \supset \smallsmile Qa$ 1   UI
    5. $\smallsmile\smallsmile Qa \supset \smallsmile Pa$ 4   Contra

6. $Qa \supset \smallsmile Pa$ 5   DN
7. $Ra \supset \smallsmile Pa$ 3,6 HS
8. $(x)(Rx \supset \smallsmile Px)$ 7   UG

3. 1. $(x)(Px \supset \smallsmile Qx)$
    2. $(\exists x)(Rx \cdot Px)$ / $(\exists x)(Rx \cdot \smallsmile Qx)$
    3. $Ra \cdot Pa$ 2   EI
    4. Pa 3   Simp
    5. $Pa \supset \smallsmile Qa$ 1   UI
    6. $\smallsmile Qa$ 4,5 MP
    7. Ra 3   Simp
    8. $Ra \cdot \smallsmile Qa$ 6,7 Conj
    9. $(\exists x)(Rx \cdot \smallsmile Qx)$ 8   EG

4. 1. $(\exists x)(y)Pxy$ / $(y)(\exists x)(Pxy)$
    2. $(y)Pay$ 1   EI
    3. Pab 2   UI
    4. $(\exists x)Pxb$ 3   EG
    5. $(y)(\exists x)Pxy$ 4   UG

5. 1. $(x)[(Px \vee Qx) \supset Rx]$
    2. $(\exists x)(Px \cdot Sx)$ / $(\exists x)Rx$
    3. $Pa \cdot Sa$ 2   EI
    4. Pa 3   Simp
    5. $Pa \vee Qa$ 4   Add
    6. $(Pa \vee Qa) \supset Ra$ 1   UI
    7. Ra 5,6 MP
    8. $(\exists x)Rx$ 7   EG

6. 1. $(x)(Rx \supset Sx)$
    2. $(x)(Px \supset Qx)$
    3. $(\exists x)(Px \vee Rx)$ / $(\exists x)(Sx \vee Qx)$
    4. $Pa \vee Ra$ 3   EI
    5. $Pa \supset Qa$ 2   UI
    6. $Ra \supset Sa$ 1   UI
    7. $(Pa \supset Qa) \cdot (Ra \supset Sa)$ 5,6 Conj
    8. $Qa \vee Sa$ 4,7 CD
    9. $(\exists x)(Qx \vee Sx)$ 8   EG

7. 1. $(x)(y)[(Px \cdot Qy) \supset Rxy]$
    2. $(x)(\exists y)(Sxy \supset Px)$ / $(x)(\exists y)[Sxy \supset (Qy \supset Rxy)]$
    3. $(\exists y)(Say \supset Pa)$ 2   UI
    4. $Sab \supset Pa$ 3   EI
    5. $(y)[(Pa \cdot Qy) \supset Ray]$ 1   UI
    6. $(Pa \cdot Qb) \supset Rab$ 5   UI
    7. $Pa \supset (Qb \supset Rab)$ 6   Exp
    8. $Sab \supset (Qb \supset Rab)$ 4,7 HS
    9. $(\exists y)[Say \supset (Qy \supset Ray)]$ 8 EG
    10. $(x)(\exists y)[Sxy \supset (Qy \supset Rxy)]$ 9 UG

8. 1. $\smallsmile(\exists x)[Px \cdot (Sx \cdot Tx)]$
    2. $(x)[(Sx \vee Qx) \cdot (Tx \vee Rx)]$ / $(x)[Px \supset (Qx \vee Rx)]$
    3. $(x)\smallsmile[Px \cdot (Sx \cdot Tx)]$ 1   QN
    4. $\smallsmile[Pa \cdot (Sa \cdot Ta)]$ 3   UI

5. ⌐[Pa • ⌐⌐(Sa • Ta)]	4	DN
6. Pa ⊃ ⌐(Sa • Ta)	5	Imp
7. Pa	Assump	
8. ⌐(Sa • Ta)	6,7	MP
9. ⌐Sa ∨ ⌐Ta	8	DM
10. (Sa ∨ Qa) • (Ta ∨ Ra)	2	UI
11. (⌐⌐Sa ∨ Qa) • (⌐⌐Ta ∨ Ra)	10	DN
12. (⌐Sa ⊃ Qa) • (⌐Ta ⊃ Ra)	11	Imp
13. Qa ∨ Ra	9,12	CD
14. Pa ⊃ (Qa ∨ Ra)	7–13	CP
15. (x)[Px ⊃ (Qx ∨ Rx)]	14	UG

Chapter 14

Page 357

1. − M + A
2. + C − P
3. + T + D
4. * D + B
5. − P − T
6. −R + (−P)
7. − (+ C + S)
8. * D − (−C)
9. * C + K
10. + T + (−A)
11. + R − (−H)
12. − (− S + R)
13. − (−A) − C
14. − (− G + G′)
15. − (− C − (−M))

Pages 359–60

1. − B + (−M), − M − B,   Equivalent
2. + P + (−H), + H − P,   Not equivalent
3. − P − A, − P + (−A),   Equivalent
4. + V + (−T), + T + (−V),   Not equivalent
5. − S + L, − (−S + (−L)),   Not equivalent
6. − C + O, − (+ O + (−C)),   Not equivalent
7. − (− H − P), + P − (−H),   Equivalent
8. − (+ W + S), − W + (−S),   Equivalent
9. − (−W) − G, − W + G,   Not equivalent
10. + M + C, − (− C + (−M)),   Equivalent

Page 363

1. $- O + F$
   $\underline{- F + S}$
   $- O + S$ Valid

2. $+ L + (-J)$
   $\underline{- M - (-J)}$
   $+ L - M$ Valid

3. $* M + P$
   $\underline{* M + W}$
   $+ P + W$ Valid

4. $- B - (-R)$
   $\underline{- R + P}$
   $- B + P$ Valid

5. $- (- S + R)$
   $\underline{+ S + O}$
   $+ (-R) + O$ Invalid

6. $+ R - E$
   $- R + M$
   $\underline{-M - C}$
   $+ (-E) - C$ Valid

7. $+ W + G$
   $- (-G) - I$
   $\underline{- I + R}$
   $+ R + W$ Invalid

8. $- I - T$
   $+ I + P$
   $\underline{- P + O}$
   $- (- O + T)$ Valid

Page 367

1. $+ C_1 + (H_{12} - V_2)$
2. $- R_1 + (A_{12} - D_2)$
3. $* L_1 + (H_{12} + L'_2)$
4. $- (F_{12} + C_2) + P_1$
5. $* M_1 + (B_{123} + M'_2 * S_3)$
6. $+ L_1 + (K_{12} - C_2)$
7. $+ S_1 + (H_{123} + G_2 - P_3)$
8. $+ T_1 + (S_{12} - (O_{32} * I_3)_2)$
9. $+ (W_{12} + O_2) - (D_{12} + O_2)$
10. $* L_1 + (M_{12} + ((-L'_{21}) * L_1)_2)$

Page 370

1. $+ G + S$
   $+ S + G$ Com

2. $- (- T + D)$
   $+ T - D$ EN

3. $+ B_1 + (W_{12} + B'_2)$
   $+ (W_{12} + B'_2) + B_1$ Com
4. $+ E + H$
   $- (- E - H)$ EN
   $- (- E + (-H))$ IN
5. $+ A_1 + (M_{12} + E_2)$
   $(+ A_1 + M_{12}) + E_2$ Assoc
   $+ E_2 + (M_{12} + A_1)$ Com
6. $+ B_1 - (S_{12} + E_2)$
   $+ B_1 + (- (S_{12} + E_2)$ IN
   $+ B_1 + ((-S_{12}) - E_2)$ EN
7. $- M - I$
   $- (+ M + I)$ EN
   $- (+ I + M)$ Com
   $- I - M$ EN
8. $+ ((-O_{12}) - P_2) + R_1$
   $+ R_1 + ((-O_{12}) - P_2)$ Com
   $+ R_1 + (- (O_{12}) + P_2)$ EN
   $+ R_1 - (O_{12} + P_2)$ IN
9. $+ A_1 + (E_{12} - S_2)$
   $- (- A_1 - (E_{12} - S_2))$ EN
   $- (- A_1 + (- (E_{12} - S_2)))$ IN
   $- (- A_1 + ((-E_{12}) + S_2))$ EN
10. $- R_1 + (C_{12} - H_2)$
    $- (+ R_1 - (C_{12} - H_2))$ EN
    $- (+ R_1 + (- (C_{12} - H_2)))$ IN
    $- (+ R_1 + ((-C_{12}) + H_2))$ EN
    $- (+ R_1 + (-C_{12})) + H_2)$ Assoc
    $- (+ H_2 + ((-C_{12}) + R_1))$ Com
    $- H_2 - ((-C_{12}) + R_1)$ EN
    $- H_2 + (- ((-C_{12}) + R_1))$ IN
    $- H_2 + (C_{12} - R_2)$ EN

Page 376

1. $- C + B$
2. $+ A_1 + (R_{12} + C_2)$
3. $+ C_1 + (R_{12} + B_2)$
4. $+ A_1 + (R_{123} + (-D_2) + C_3)$
5. $- (R_{12} + A_1) + (S_{23} + C_3)$
6. $+ (R_{12} - B_2) - C_1$
7. $+ (R_{12} + B_2) + C_1$
8. $- A_1 - (R_{12} - C_2)$
9. $+ C_2 + (R_{12} + A_1)$
10. $- (R_{12} - B_2) + C_1$

Page 379

1. $+ E + <+ Q + D>$

2. $+ <+ S + H> + E$
3. $+ [* J + N] + [* I + Q]$
4. $* T_1 + (R_{12} + <+ L + F>_2)$
5. $- U + <+ S + D>$
6. $+ [* H + <+ C + P>] + [* S + <+ (-C) + P'>]$
7. $+ <+ T + B + M> + I$
8. $* C_1 + <+ (L_{12} + B_2) + (T_{13} + M_3)>$
9. $- C + <+ T + H>$
10. $- (H_{12} + G_2) + <+ T + D + H>_1$

Page 382

1. $+ <+ P + R> + <- W + S>$
2. $- I + <- (-P) - (-(-P))>$
3. $+ A + <+ S - R>$
4. $- < + Q + C> + <- N + J>$
5. $- <+ C + P> + <- (-P) - (-N)>$
6. $- G + <- H + E>$
7. $+ [+ W + T] - [- W + T]$
8. $- <- C + A> + D$
9. $- [+ P + L] + [* W_1 + (C_{12} + P'_2)]$
10. $- (M_{12} + P_2) - <- (-V) - (-I)>_1$

Page 386

1. $+ S + <-Q + R>$
   $+ <+ S + S> + <-Q + R>$ Taut
2. $+ p + (- (-q) - (-r))$
   $-- (+ p + q) -- (+ p + r)$ PD
3. $- S_1 + (R_{12} - <+ P + Q>_2)$
   $- S_1 + (R_{12} - <+ Q + P>_2)$ Com
4. $- (-p) - (-q)$
   $- (+ (-p) + (-q))$ EN
   $- (+ (-q) + (-p))$ Com
   $- (-q) - (-p)$ EN
5. $- [+ S + P] + [+ Q + R]$
   $- (- [+ Q + R]) + (- [+ S + P])$ Contra
   $- [- Q - R] + [- S - P]$ EN
6. $+ p - q$
   $- (- p + q)$ EN
   $- (- p - (-q))$ IN
7. $+ (- p + q) + r$
   $+ (- p + q) + (+ r + r)$ Taut
8. $+ <+ S - P> + R$
   $+ <+ S + (-P)> + R$ IN
   $+ R + <+ S + (-R)>$ Com
   $+ <+ R + S> + (-R)$ Assoc
   $+ <+ S + R> + (-R)$ Com
   $+ <+ S + R> - R$ IN

9. $+ <+ S + P> + <+ Q + R>$
 $+ <+ <+ S + P> + Q> + R$ Assoc
 $+ <+ Q + <+ S + P>> + R$ Com
 $+ <+ <+ Q + S> + P> + R$ Assoc
 $+ <+ Q + S> + <+ P + R>$ Assoc
 $+ <+ S + Q> + <+ P + R>$ Com
10. $+ S + <- P - Q>$
 $+ S + <- (- -P) - (- -Q)>$ DN
 $- - [+ S + (-P)] - - [+ S + (-Q)]$ PD
 $- - [+ S - P)] - - [+ S - Q]$ IN

Pages 392–93

1. 1. $+ S_1 - (R_{12} - Q_2)$
    2. $- Q + T / + S_1 - (R_{12} - T_2)$
    3. $+ S_1 - (R_{12} - T_2)$ 1,2 DDO
2. 1. $- S + <+ P + Q>$
    2. $+ R + <+ T + S> / + T + P$
    3. $+ <+ R + T> + S$ 2 Assoc
    4. $+ T + S$ 3 Simp
    5. $+ T + <+ P + Q>$ 1,4 DDO
    6. $+ <+ T + P> + Q$ 5 Assoc
    7. $+ T + P$ 6 Simp
3. 1. $- S + <+ R + T>$
    2. $- R + P$
    3. $- T + Q / - S + <+ P + Q>$
    4. $- S + <+ P + T>$ 1,2 DDO
    5. $- S + <+ P + Q>$ 3,4 DDO
4. 1. $- [- P + Q] + [+ R + S]$
    2. $- R - S / + P - Q$
    3. $- (- [+ R + S]) + (- [- P + Q])$ 1 Contra
    4. $- [- R - S] + [+ P - Q]$ 3 EN
    5. $+ P - Q$ 2,4 DDO
5. 1. $- <+ S + P> + Q$
    2. $- S - Q / - S - P$
    3. $- (+ S + Q)$ 2 EN
    4. $- (+ Q + S)$ 3 Com
    5. $- Q - S$ 4 EN
    6. $- <+ S + P> + (-S)$ 1,5 DDO
    7. $- (+ <+ S + P> - (-S)$ 6 EN
    8. $- (+ <+ S + P> + S))$ 7 IN
    9. $- (+ S + <+ S + P>)$ 8 Com
    10. $- (+ <+ S + S> + P)$ 9 Assoc
    11. $- <+ S + S> - P$ 10 EN
    12. $- S - P^{\cdot}$ 11 Taut
6. 1. $+ S + <- (-P) - (-Q)>$
    2. $- P + M$
    3. $- S - M / + S + Q$

4. $--[+S+P]--[+S+Q]$ 1 PD
5. $-[-S-P]-(-[+S+Q])$ 4 EN
6. $-[-S-M]-(-[+S+Q])$ 2,5 DDO
7. $-[-S-M]+[+S+Q]$ 6 IN
8. $+S+Q$ 3,7 DDO

7. 1. $+S_1+<+Q_1+(R_{12}-T_2)>$
2. $+T+P/+Q_1+(R_{12}+P_2)$
3. $+<+S+Q>_1+(R_{12}-T_2)$ 1 Assoc
4. $+Q_1+(R_{12}-T_2)$ 3 Simp
5. $+(Q_1+R_{12})+P_2$ 2,4 DDO
6. $+Q_1+(R_{12}+P_2)$ 5 Assoc

8. 1. $+S_1+(R_{123}-<+Q+P>_2+T_3)$
2. $-X+<+Q+P>/-X_2+(R_{123}+S_1+T_3)$
3. $-X_2+(R_{123}+S_1+T_3)$ 1,2 DDO

Chapter 15

Page 411

1. This could be true or false, depending on the restaurant. Rule 1: Consider the quality of the different dishes served; the quality of the food at different times of day and different days of the week, and the quality when the restaurant is crowded as well as when it is not. Rule 2: Visit the restaurant under the most favorable circumstances; ask people who patronize the restaurant regularly. Rule 3: Consider what is the most likely explanation for the quality of the food.

2. This is clearly false as a universal generalization. Rule 1: Consider Italians from different parts of the country, rural as well as urban; Italians working in different jobs and professions; and so on. Rule 2: Consider whether you know any even-tempered Italians; look for Italians in jobs requiring an even temper. Rule 3: Is it plausible that nationality determines temperament?

3. To my knowledge, this is false. Rule 1: Consider different breeds; observe their behavior indoors as well as outdoors. Rule 2: Ask dog owners whether they have seen their dog not lying down in this manner. Rule 3: Is there any evolutionary reason why dogs might have this behavior?

4. Many economists believe this to be true, though it is somewhat controversial. Rule 1: Examine the effects of price controls in different countries, in different industries, in wartime as well as in peace. Rule 2: Consult works of economic history to look for disconfirming instances. Rule 3: Is there a reason to think price controls will produce this effect? If the price of a good is controlled, what effect is this likely to have on suppliers of the good? On buyers of the good?

5. This is also controversial. Rule 1: Consider different types of market economy that lack antitrust laws, including laissez-faire systems as well

as those with various government controls. Rule 2: Consult works of economic history to look for disconfirming instances. Rule 3: In the absence of antitrust laws, are there inherent tendencies toward increasing concentration? Or are there competitive forces that tend to limit concentration?

Pages 420–21

1. Case 1: ScourClean, dirty sink → clean
   Case 2: Leading cleanser, dirty sink ↛ clean
   Method of difference
2. 1982–83: interest rates drop, high unemployment,
   recession → stocks rise
   1985–86: interest rates drop, low unemployment,
   expansion → stocks rise
   Method of agreement
3. Now: crowded, heat on → hot
   4 pm: not crowded, heat on ↛ hot
   Method of difference to show that the number of people affects the temperature; negative use of agreement to show that heating level is not the cause.
4. Case 1: self-esteem, . . . → happiness
   Case 2: no self-esteem, . . . ↛ happiness
   Method of difference. The argument refers to variations in personality and goals, with self-esteem or its lack as a constant factor, which means the method of agreement is also being used. But since the personality traits and goals are not mentioned, the argument is incomplete, and we can't diagram it.
5. Case 1: no product safety regulations, widget industry → innovation
   Case 2: product safety regulations, widget industry → innovation
   Negative use of method of difference

Page 425

1. Cause: carriage. Effect: inkspots. Method of residues.
2. Case 1: 0 packs/day → x rate of lung cancer
   Case 2: 0–1 pack/day → 6x rate of lung cancer
   Case 3: 1+ packs/day → 12x rate of lung cancer
   Method of concomitant variations
3. Cause: other factors. Effect: depth perception. Method of residues

Chapter 16

Pages 433–34

1. Not an argument
2. *A:* ship, *B:* Earth, *P:* necessity of living together

3. *A:* building, *B:* crystal, *P:* solidity and rigidity
4. Not an argument
5. *A:* steam boiler, *B:* person with high blood pressure, *P:* inevitability of breakdown

Pages 440–41

1. Deductive element: No intellectual likes sports; Jim is an intellectual; therefore Jim doesn't like sports. The major premise is supported inductively by the example of Fred. Extremely weak. Athletic and intellectual interests are not incompatible, and many intellectuals like sports.
2. Deductive element: All things with a definite velocity, position, and mass are particles; photons have a definite velocity, position, and mass; therefore photons are particles. The major premise is supported inductively by the example of billiard balls. The analogy seems strong since velocity, position, and mass are essential properties of macroscopic particles. But any analogy between macroscopic and microscopic phenomena is dangerous, as the next example indicates by providing a counter-analogy.
3. Deductive element: All things with a definite frequency and wavelength are wave phenomena; photons have a definite frequency and wavelength; therefore photons are wave phenomena. The major premise is supported by the example of air vibrations. The evaluation of this argument is the same as for (2).
4. Deductive element: Nothing that promises rewards without effort can be expected to work; psychotherapies that promise instant happiness are promising rewards without effort; therefore psychotherapies that promise instant happiness cannot be expected to work. The major premise is supported by the example of "get rich quick" schemes. Since the middle term was not given in the statement of the argument, I supplied one (things that promise rewards without effort); you may have a plausible alternative. The major premise is a generalization covering psychological as well as economic endeavors, and it should be tested against a wider range of examples. But it seems fairly plausible.
5. Deductive element: No effort by rival nations to limit arms will succeed; current arms control negotiations between the U.S. and the Soviet Union are efforts by rival nations to limit arms; therefore current arms negotiations between the U.S. and the Soviet will not succeed. The major premise is supported by the example of efforts in Europe during the 1920s and 1930s. Since the middle term was not given in the statement of the argument, I supplied one (efforts by rival nations to limit arms); you may have a plausible alternative. A key difference between the two cases is that the U.S. and the Soviet Union are ideologically opposed, whereas the European powers earlier in the century were not, at least not in the same way. Whether this weakens the argument depends on the role of ideology in a country's policies.

Chapter 17

Page 457

1. Total. Premise does not support the conclusion, since it tells us nothing about the size of the U.S. in relation to other countries.
2. Ratio. Premise does not support conclusion, since it treats the population as static, ignoring births, deaths, immigration, divorces.
3. Average (median). Premise does not support conclusion, since it doesn't give us the previous median age.
4. Frequency. Premise does not support conclusion. We would need to know what percentage of the existing population is Asian (information given in #5), and what percentage of the population comes from legal immigration as opposed to illegal immigration and native births.
5. Frequency distribution. Premise does not support conclusion. Distribution is by race, whereas "Hispanic" is a classification by nationality; Hispanic people may be white or black.
6. Frequencies. Premise supports conclusion.
7. Ratio. Premise does not support conclusion, since it gives no standard for measuring crowdedness.
8. Totals (8.8/4.2 million) and ratios (15/3 per thousand residents). Premise supports conclusion.
9. Ratio: three apprehensions now for every one ten years ago. Premise supports conclusion, but only weakly. The number of apprehensions could go up if the same people are getting caught more often, without any increase in the number trying, or the number succeeding.
10. Averages (means). Premise supports conclusion moderately. We would also need to know whether immigrants are a relatively greater drain on public resources other than social services, such as the police.

Page 463

1. The mailing list overrepresents conservatives, who are more likely than those of other persuasions to oppose national health insurance.
2. Soviet pollsters presumably work for or are controlled by the state, and thus may not report their results objectively. And respondents may not express their real views to a stranger, since they can be punished for opposition.
3. AMA members may not be a random sample of doctors, and those who can afford to attend a convention may overrepresent the wealthier doctors, biasing the average upwards.
4. Patrons of Mrs. Fields are disproportionately young and urban, and may therefore be leaner than the average cookie eater.
5. Men may not be willing to admit over the phone that they can't swim.

Page 473

Problems of internal validity: This is an observational study, subject to various possibly confounding factors. Vacationers may be more impatient to get to their destination than are those commuting to work. And despite what the report says, it is unlikely that driving conditions were exactly the same in all respects, including the number of police on the road, the number of lanes, the width of shoulders, the outside temperature, etc.

Problems of external validity: Neither New York City commuters nor Disney-World patrons are likely to be representative samples of drivers in general. And the presence or absence of family members is not a good variable to use for estimating the presence or absence of back-seat driving. The presence of the family may distract the driver in other ways: children playing, marital squabbles, etc.

Chapter 18

Page 487

1. Explanation
   1) The stock market went up yesterday
   2) The Federal Reserve Board lowered interest rates

$$(2) \\ \downarrow \\ (1)$$

2. Argument
3. Argument
4. Explanation
   1) The nervous system evolved
   2) Animals are capable of locomotion
   3) Control of locomotion requires a fast and flexible system

$$\frac{(2) + (3)}{} \\ \downarrow \\ (1)$$

5. Explanation
   1) Some urban areas are safer than others
   2) Some urban areas are more vibrant than others
   3) Some urban areas have a mixture of uses
   4) In an area with a mixture of uses, people will be on the streets at all hours
   5) The presence of people on the streets is a deterrent against crime
   6) The presence of people gives an area a vibrant feel

$$\frac{(3) + (4) + (5)}{\downarrow}$$
$$(1)$$

$$\frac{(3) + (4) + (6)}{\downarrow}$$
$$(2)$$

Pages 494–95

1. Extremely uninformative. The hypothesis tells us that the chicken had some motive for crossing the road, but doesn't tell us what it was.
2. Incomplete. The hypothesis explains why the band is worn on the fourth finger, but not why it is worn on the left hand.
3. Logically weak. There were other tall men who were not admired as Washington was.
4. This is at least vulnerable to the charge of being uninformative on the grounds of circularity. Why have teachers lost public respect? A plausible hypothesis would be that they are not doing a good job.

Page 504

The structure of the explanation is:
   1) Stress increases the level of circulating endorphins
   2) Some endorphin raises the level of LDLs and lowers the level of HDLs
   3) Raising the level of LDLs and lowering the level of HDLs will raise the cholesterol level
   4) Some endorphin raises the level of cholesterol
   5) Stress increases the level of cholesterol

Proposition (5) is the explanandum, and the third paragraph describes the experiment that establishes it as a fact to be explained. Propositions (1) and (3) are background knowledge. Proposition (4) is the key hypothesis, and (2) is the more specific hypothesis to explain why stress has this effect.

The last two paragraphs describe experiments that test consequences derived from the hypothesis. i) If endorphins affect lipoprotein and cholesterol levels, then these levels should not be affected in rats injected with an endorphin blocker. ii) If endorphins attributable to stress affect levels of lipoproteins and cholesterol, endorphins injected into the brain (morphine) should have the same effect.

Index